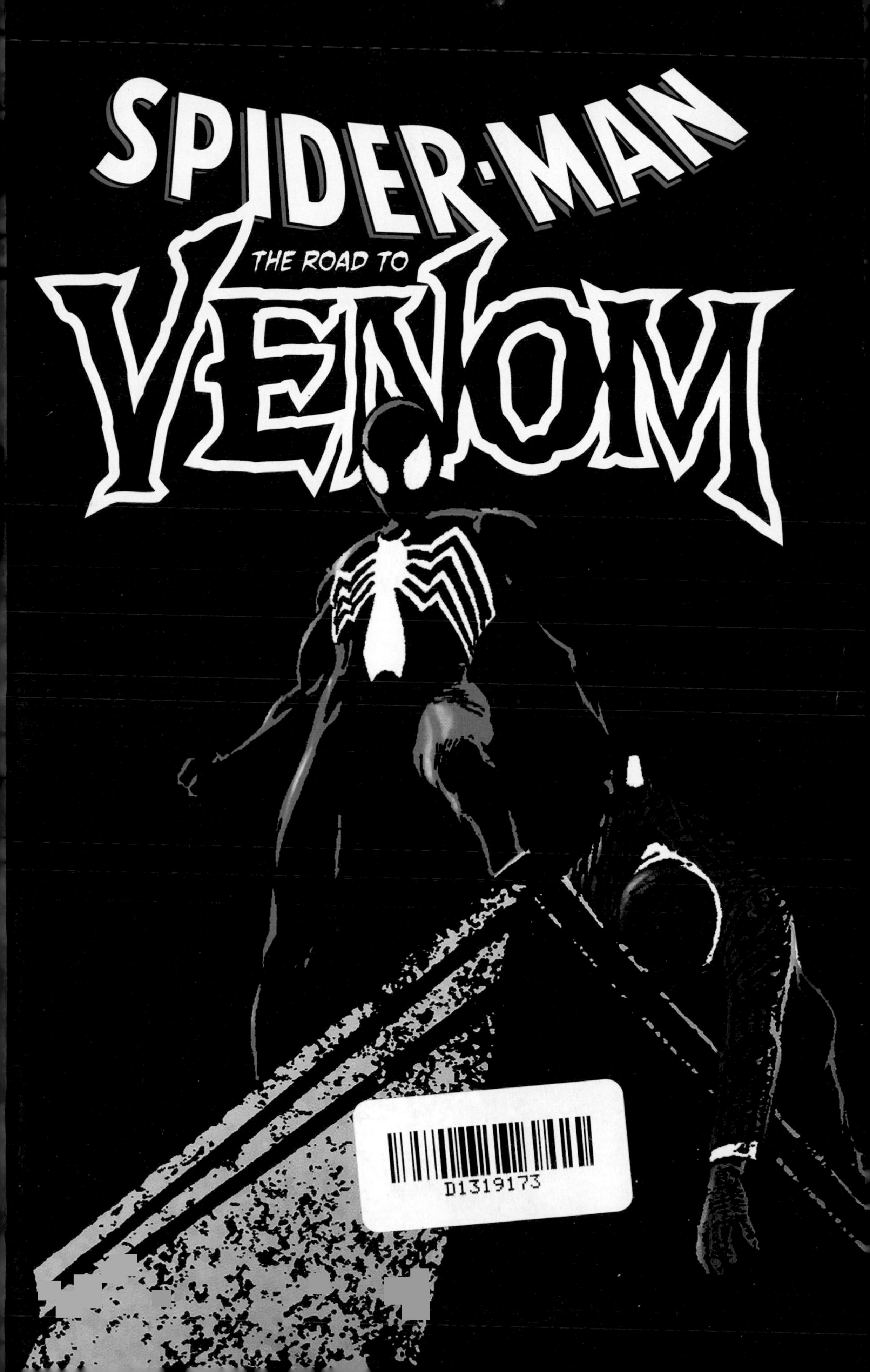
SPIDER-MAN
THE ROAD TO
VENOM

COLLECTION EDITOR: **Jennifer Grünwald**

ASSISTANT MANAGING EDITOR: **Maia Loy**

ASSISTANT MANAGING EDITOR: **Lisa Montalbano**

ASSOCIATE MANAGER, DIGITAL ASSETS: **Joe Hochstein**

EDITOR, SPECIAL PROJECTS: **Mark D. Beazley**

VP PRODUCTION & SPECIAL PROJECTS: **Jeff Youngquist**

RESEARCH & LAYOUT: **Jeph York**

PRODUCTION: **Jerron Quality Color,**
ColorTek & Ryan Devall

BOOK DESIGNER: **Adam Del Re**

SVP PRINT, SALES & MARKETING: **David Gabriel**

EDITOR IN CHIEF: **C.B. Cebulski**

SPIDER-MAN: THE ROAD TO VENOM. Contains material originally published in magazine form as VENOM: SEED OF DARKNESS (1997) -1; AMAZING SPIDER-MAN (1963) #258; WEB OF SPIDER-MAN (1985) #1; PETER PARKER, THE SPECTACULAR SPIDER-MAN (1976) #107-110 and #134-136; and VENOM: DARK ORIGIN (2008) #1-5. First printing 2020. ISBN 978-1-302-92696-0. Published by MARVEL WORLDWIDE, INC., a subsidiary of MARVEL ENTERTAINMENT, LLC. OFFICE OF PUBLICATION: 1290 Avenue of the Americas, New York, NY 10104. © 2020 MARVEL No similarity between any of the names, characters, persons, and/or institutions in this magazine with those of any living or dead person or institution is intended, and any such similarity which may exist is purely coincidental. **Printed in the U.S.A.** KEVIN FEIGE, Chief Creative Officer; DAN BUCKLEY, President, Marvel Entertainment; JOHN NEE, Publisher; JOE QUESADA, EVP & Creative Director; TOM BREVOORT, SVP of Publishing; DAVID BOGART, Associate Publisher & SVP of Talent Affairs; Publishing & Partnership; DAVID GABRIEL, VP of Print & Digital Publishing; JEFF YOUNGQUIST, VP of Production & Special Projects; DAN CARR, Executive Director of Publishing Technology; ALEX MORALES, Director of Publishing Operations; DAN EDINGTON, Managing Editor; SUSAN CRESPI, Production Manager; STAN LEE, Chairman Emeritus. For information regarding advertising in Marvel Comics or on Marvel.com, please contact Vit DeBellis, Custom Solutions & Integrated Advertising Manager, at vdebellis@marvel.com. For Marvel subscription inquiries, please call 888-511-5480. **Manufactured between 8/7/2020 and 9/8/2020 by LSC COMMUNICATIONS INC., KENDALLVILLE, IN, USA.**

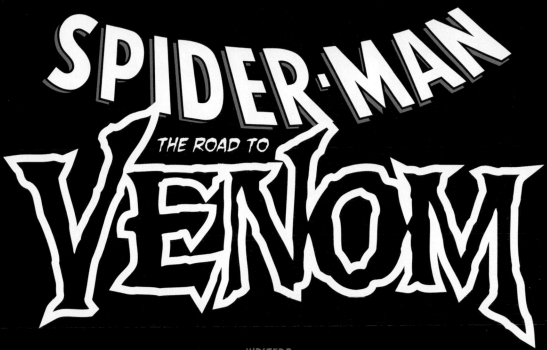

SPIDER-MAN
THE ROAD TO
VENOM

WRITERS:
Len Kaminski, Tom DeFalco,
Louise Simonson, Peter David & Zeb Wells

PENCILERS:
James Fry, Ron Frenz, Greg LaRocque,
Rich Buckler, Sal Buscema & Angel Medina

INKERS:
Chris Ivy, Josef Rubinstein, Jim Mooney, Brett Breeding,
Vince Colletta, Sal Buscema & Scott Hanna with
Kyle Baker, Pat Redding, Derek Fridolfs & co.

COLORISTS:
Tom Smith, Bob Sharen, George Roussos, Nel Yomtov,
Janet Jackson & Avalon's Matt Milla with Ian Hannin

LETTERERS:
Jim Novak, Joe Rosen, Janice Chiang, Phil Felix, Rick Parker & VC's Joe Caramagna

ASSISTANT EDITORS:
Glenn Greenberg, Bob DeNatale, Keith Williams, Adam Blaustein & Glenn Herdling

EDITORS:
Tom Brevoort, Danny Fingeroth, Jim Owsley, Jim Salicrup & Alejandro Arbona

SUPERVISING EDITOR:
Warren Simons

FRONT COVER ART:
Ron Frenz, Josef Rubinstein & Thomas Mason

BACK COVER ART:
Angel Medina, Scott Hanna & Avalon's Matt Milla

Spider-Man CREATED BY Stan Lee & Steve Ditko

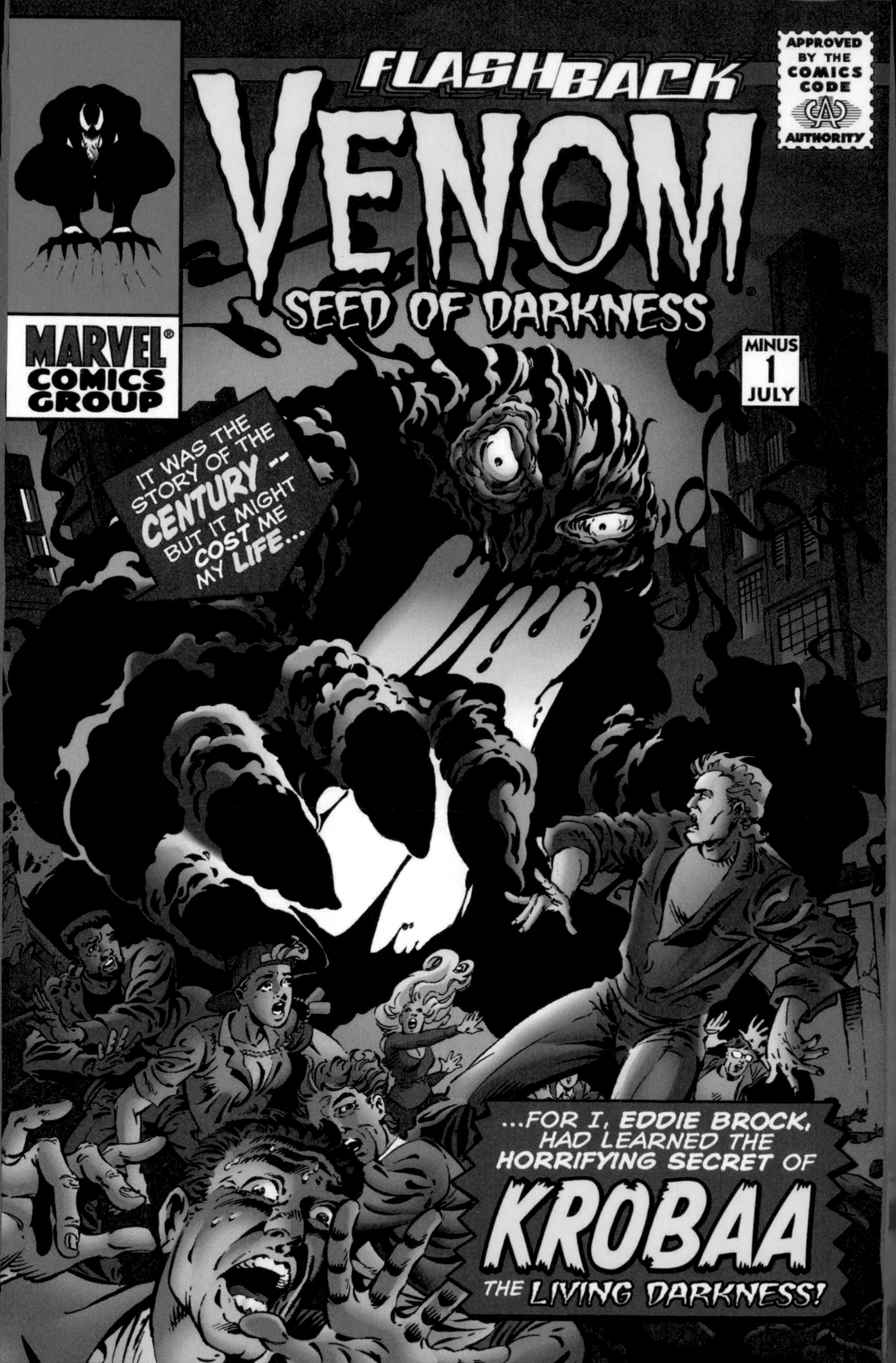
FLASHBACK
VENOM
SEED OF DARKNESS
APPROVED BY THE COMICS CODE AUTHORITY
MARVEL COMICS GROUP
MINUS 1 JULY
IT WAS THE STORY OF THE CENTURY -- BUT IT MIGHT COST ME MY LIFE...
...FOR I, EDDIE BROCK, HAD LEARNED THE HORRIFYING SECRET OF
KROBAA
THE LIVING DARKNESS!

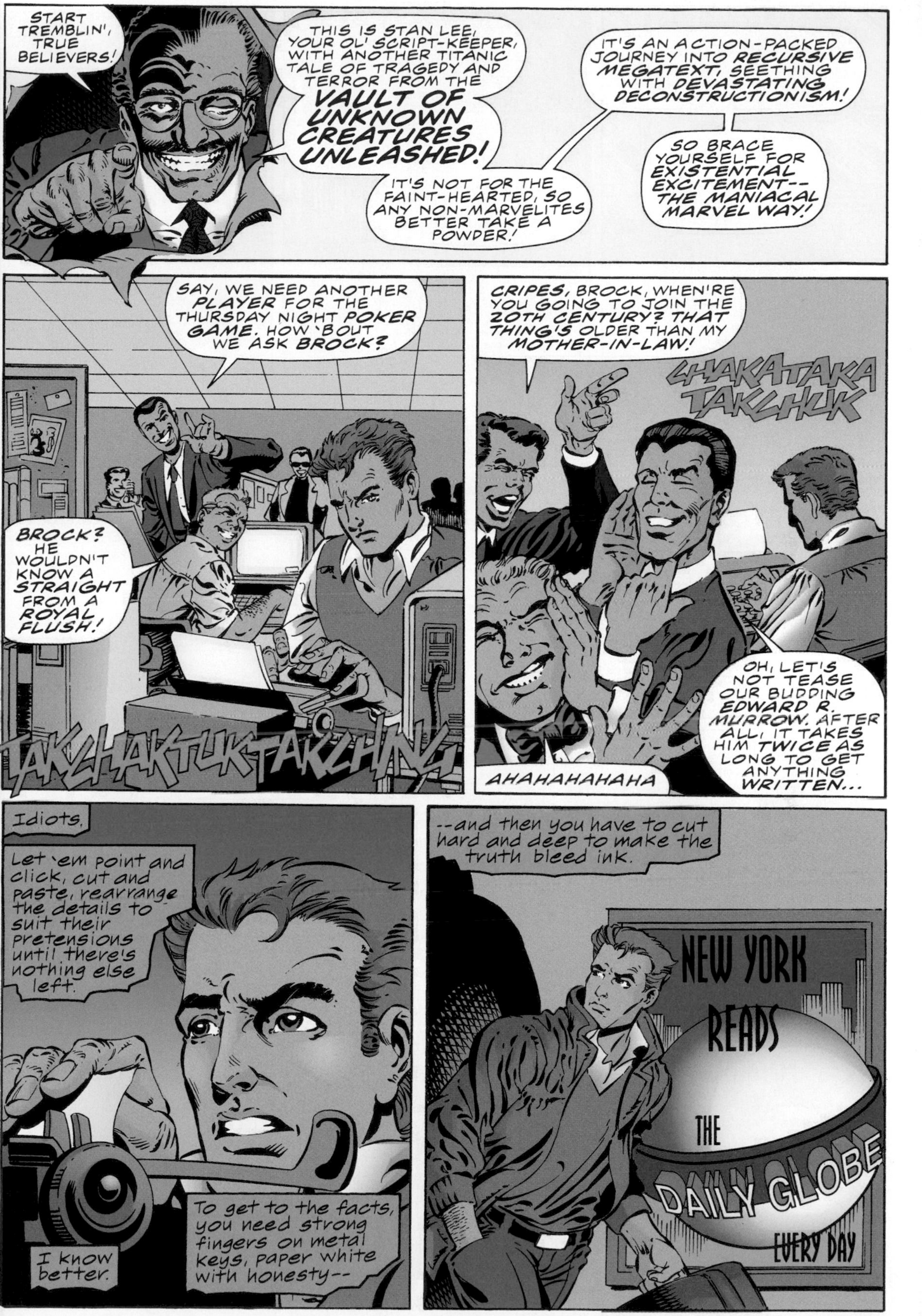
START TREMBLIN', TRUE BELIEVERS!
THIS IS STAN LEE, YOUR OL' SCRIPT-KEEPER, WITH ANOTHER TITANIC TALE OF TRAGEDY AND TERROR FROM THE VAULT OF UNKNOWN CREATURES UNLEASHED!
IT'S NOT FOR THE FAINT-HEARTED, SO ANY NON-MARVELITES BETTER TAKE A POWDER!
IT'S AN ACTION-PACKED JOURNEY INTO RECURSIVE MEGATEXT, SEETHING WITH DEVASTATING DECONSTRUCTIONISM!
SO BRACE YOURSELF FOR EXISTENTIAL EXCITEMENT-- THE MANIACAL MARVEL WAY!
SAY, WE NEED ANOTHER PLAYER FOR THE THURSDAY NIGHT POKER GAME. HOW 'BOUT WE ASK BROCK?
BROCK? HE WOULDN'T KNOW A STRAIGHT FROM A ROYAL FLUSH!
TAKCHAKTUKTAKCHING
CRIPES, BROCK, WHEN'RE YOU GOING TO JOIN THE 20TH CENTURY? THAT THING'S OLDER THAN MY MOTHER-IN-LAW!
CHAKATAKA TAKCHUK
OH, LET'S NOT TEASE OUR BUDDING EDWARD R. MURROW. AFTER ALL, IT TAKES HIM TWICE AS LONG TO GET ANYTHING WRITTEN...
AHAHAHAHAHA
Idiots.
Let 'em point and click, cut and paste, rearrange the details to suit their pretensions until there's nothing else left.
I know better.
To get to the facts, you need strong fingers on metal keys, paper white with honesty--
--and then you have to cut hard and deep to make the truth bleed ink.
NEW YORK READS THE DAILY GLOBE EVERY DAY

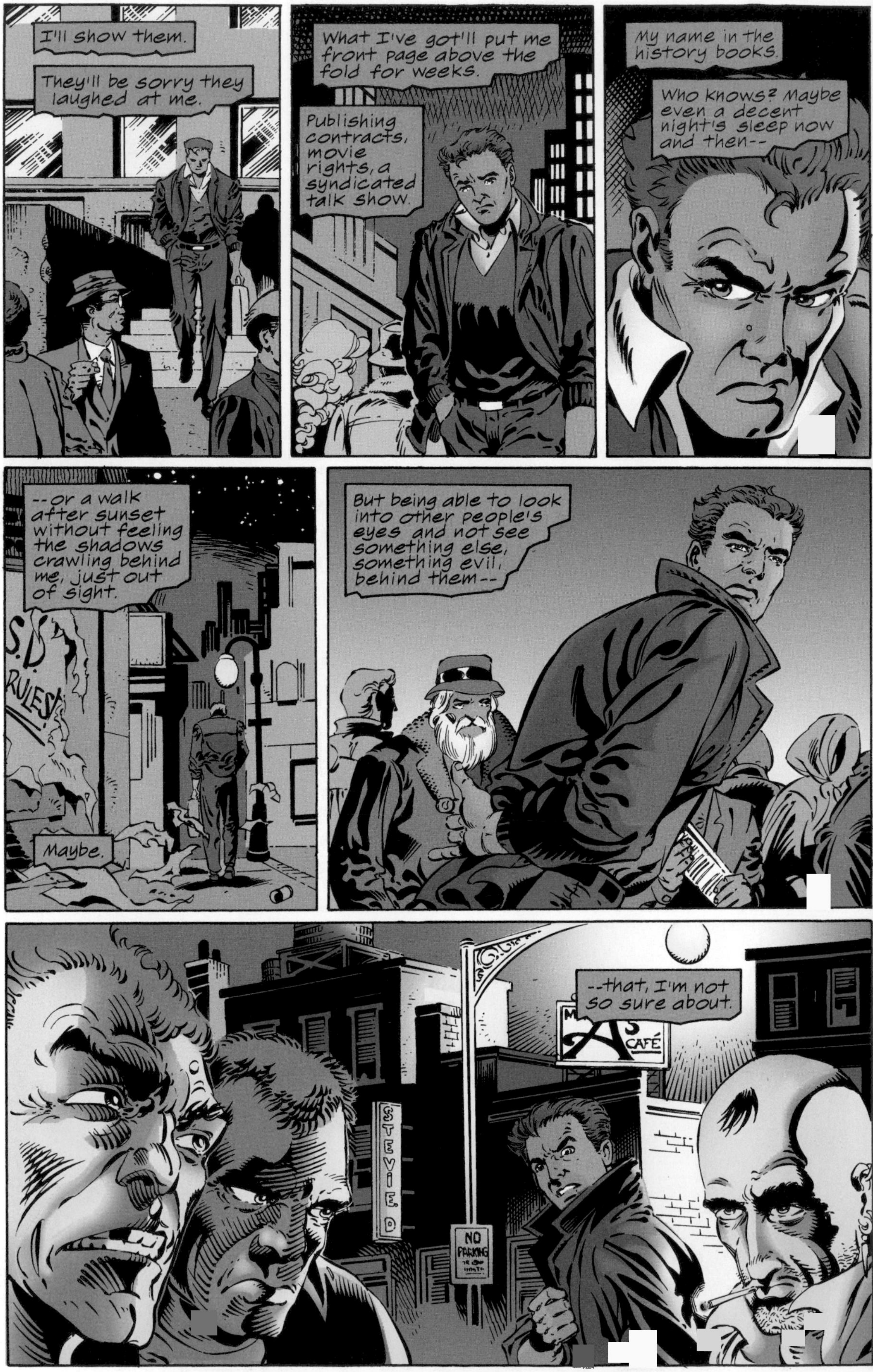
I'll show them.
They'll be sorry they laughed at me.
What I've got'll put me front page above the fold for weeks.
Publishing contracts, movie rights, a syndicated talk show.
My name in the history books.
Who knows? Maybe even a decent night's sleep now and then--
--or a walk after sunset without feeling the shadows crawling behind me, just out of sight.
S.D. RULES!
Maybe.
But being able to look into other people's eyes and not see something else, something evil, behind them--
--that, I'm not so sure about.
CAFÉ
STEVIE D
NO PARKING

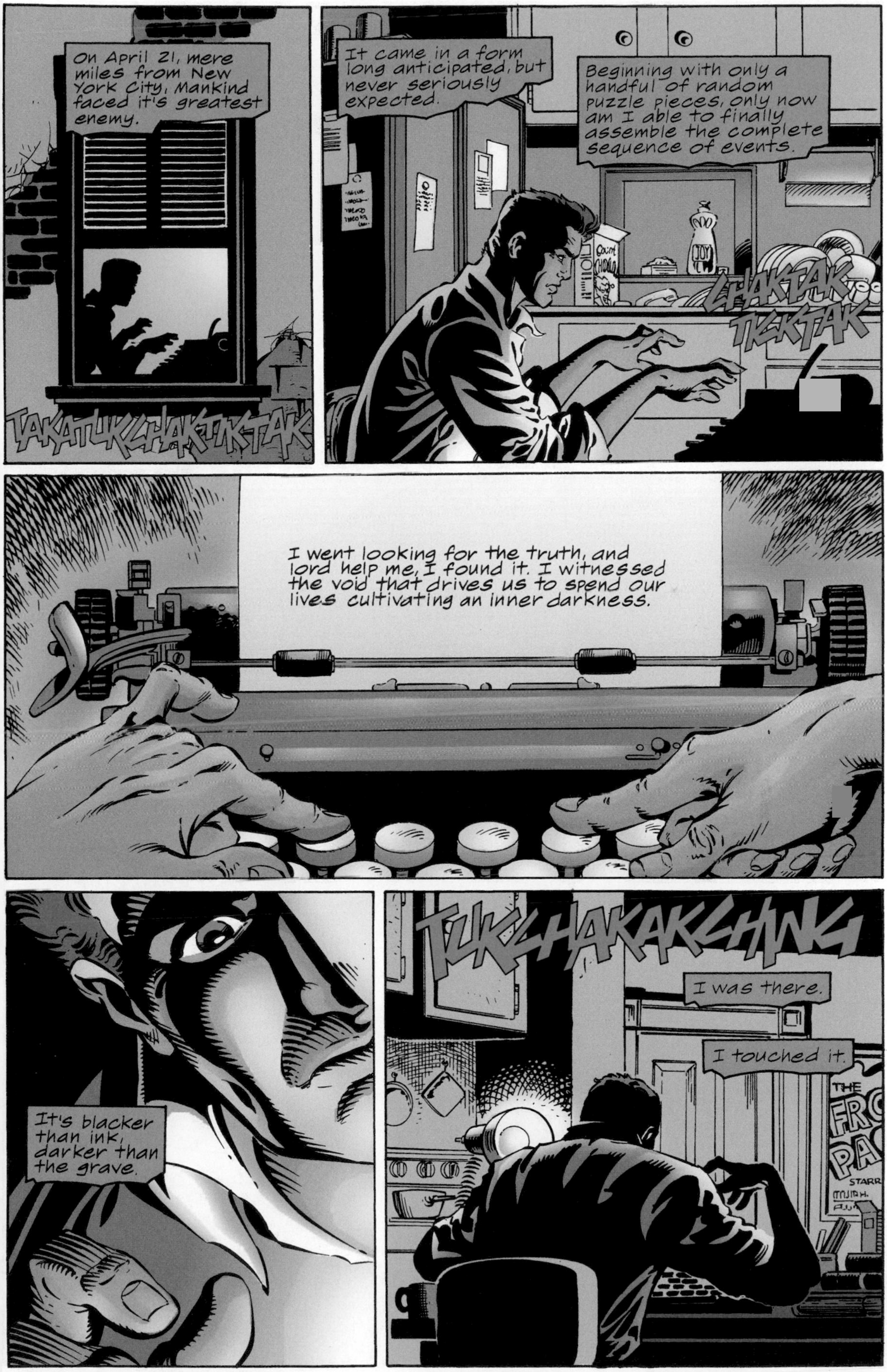
On April 21, mere miles from New York City, Mankind faced it's greatest enemy.
TAKATUKCHAKTIKTAK
It came in a form long anticipated, but never seriously expected.
Beginning with only a handful of random puzzle pieces, only now am I able to finally assemble the complete sequence of events.
CHAKTAK
TIKTAK
I went looking for the truth, and lord help me, I found it. I witnessed the void that drives us to spend our lives cultivating an inner darkness.
It's blacker than ink, darker than the grave.
TUKCHAKAKCHING
I was there.
I touched it.

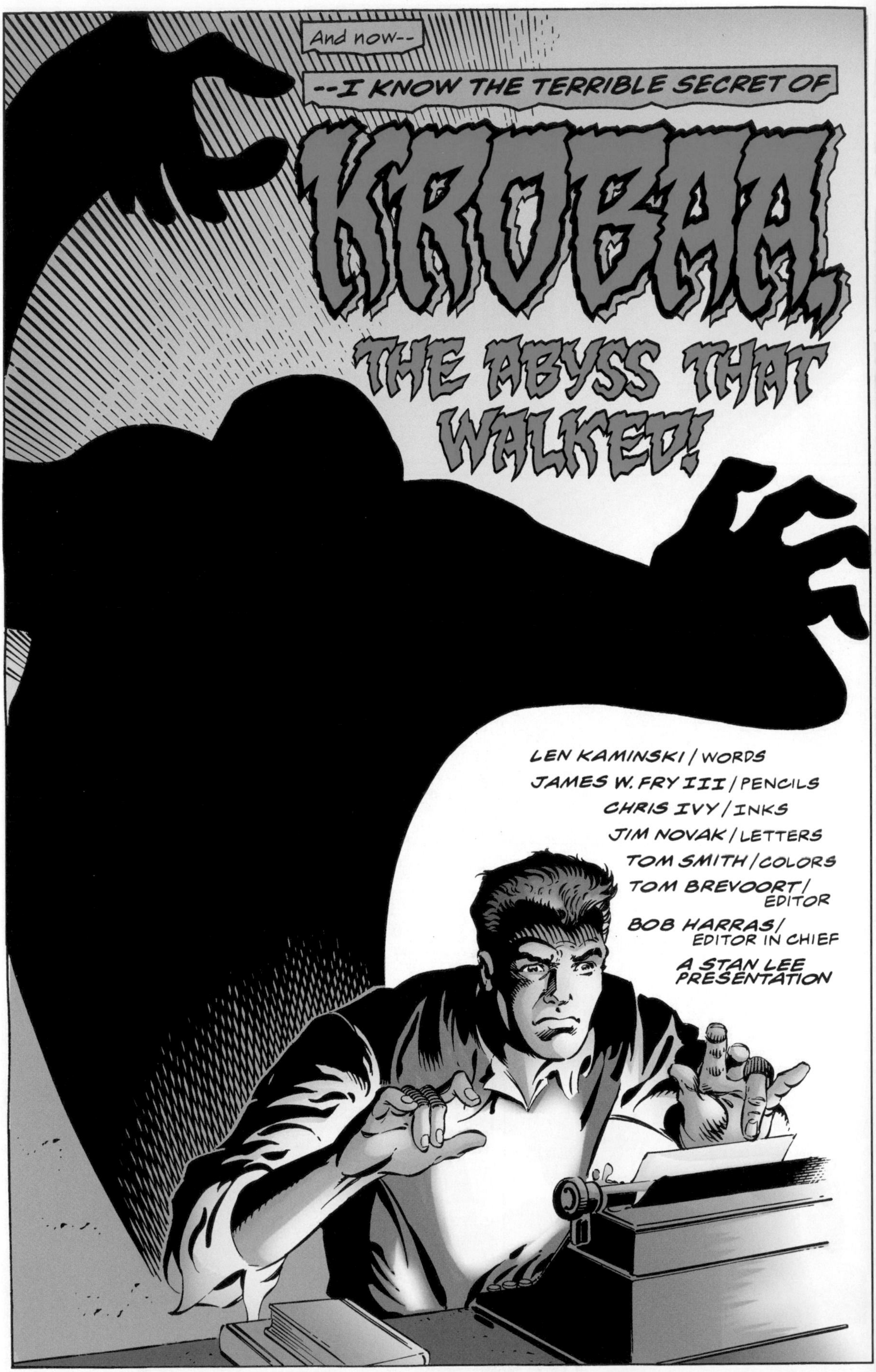
And now--
--I KNOW THE TERRIBLE SECRET OF
KROBAA, THE ABYSS THAT WALKED!
LEN KAMINSKI / WORDS
JAMES W. FRY III / PENCILS
CHRIS IVY / INKS
JIM NOVAK / LETTERS
TOM SMITH / COLORS
TOM BREVOORT / EDITOR
BOB HARRAS / EDITOR IN CHIEF
A STAN LEE PRESENTATION

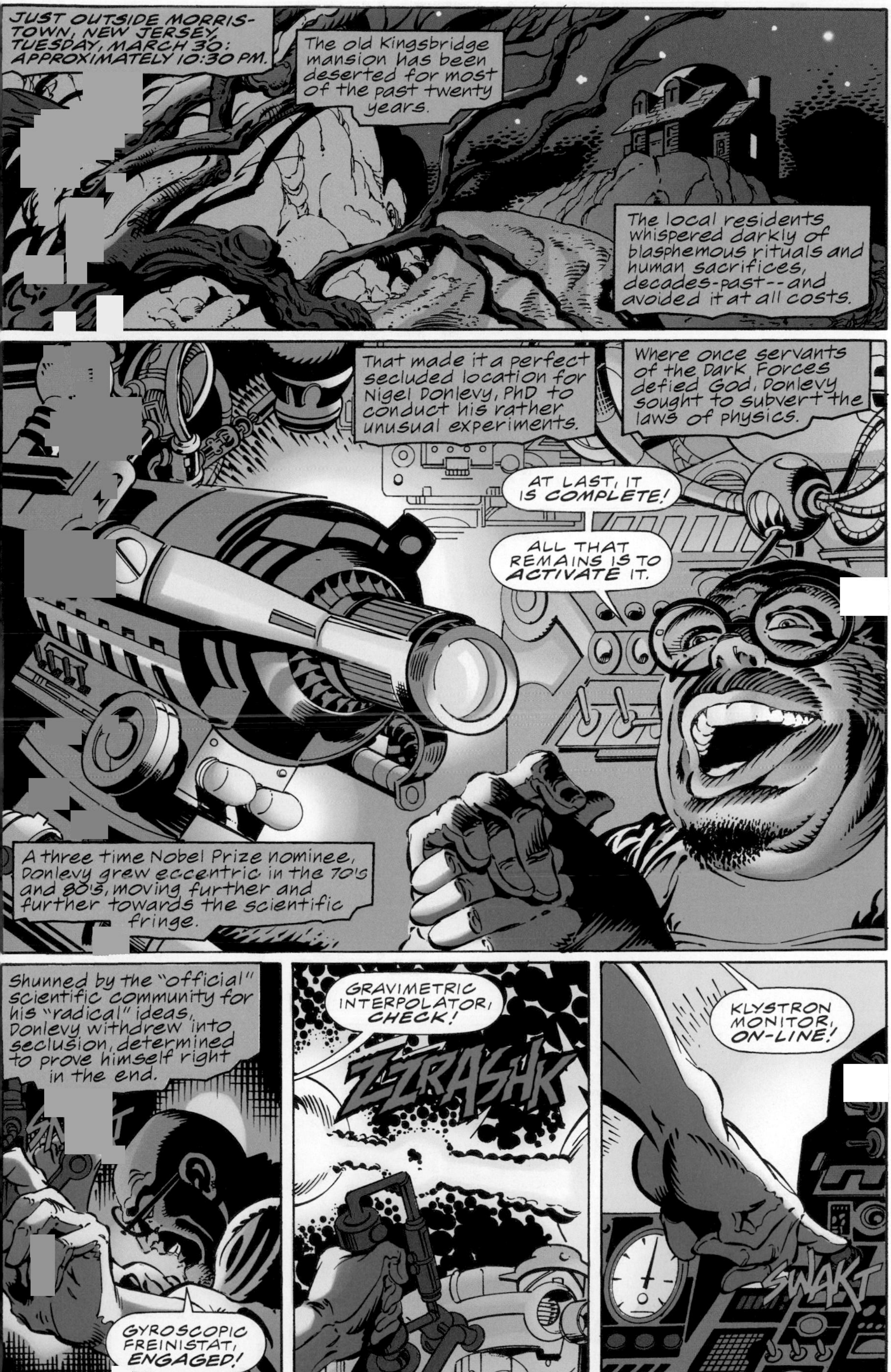
JUST OUTSIDE MORRISTOWN, NEW JERSEY, TUESDAY, MARCH 30: APPROXIMATELY 10:30 PM.
The old Kingsbridge mansion has been deserted for most of the past twenty years.
The local residents whispered darkly of blasphemous rituals and human sacrifices, decades-past--and avoided it at all costs.
That made it a perfect secluded location for Nigel Donlevy, PhD to conduct his rather unusual experiments.
Where once servants of the Dark Forces defied God, Donlevy sought to subvert the laws of physics.
AT LAST, IT IS COMPLETE!
ALL THAT REMAINS IS TO ACTIVATE IT.
A three time Nobel Prize nominee, Donlevy grew eccentric in the 70's and 80's, moving further and further towards the scientific fringe.
Shunned by the "official" scientific community for his "radical" ideas, Donlevy withdrew into seclusion, determined to prove himself right in the end.
GYROSCOPIC FREINISTAT, ENGAGED!
GRAVIMETRIC INTERPOLATOR, CHECK!
ZZRASHK
KLYSTRON MONITOR, ON-LINE!
SWAKT

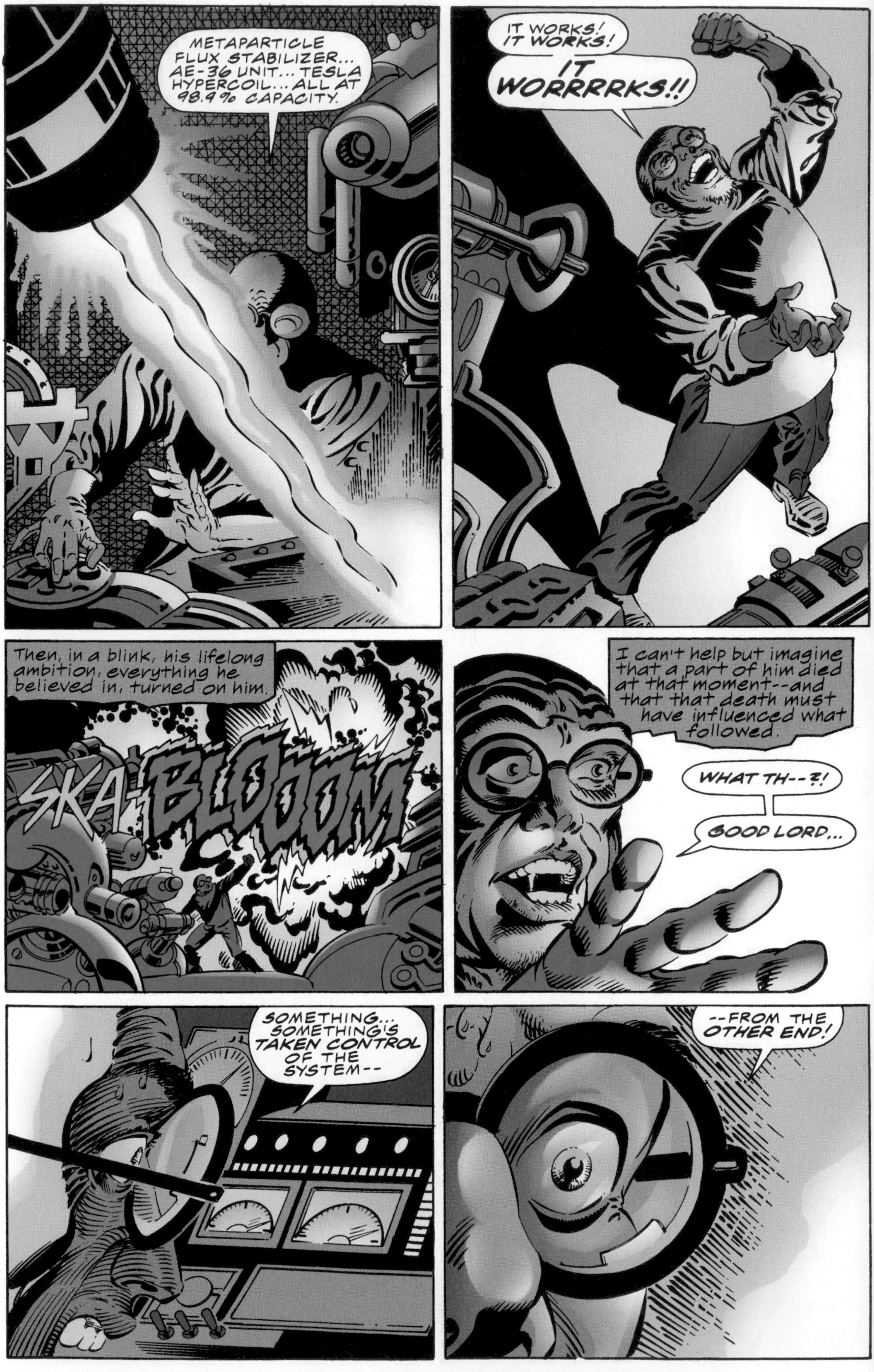

METAPARTICLE FLUX STABILIZER... AE-36 UNIT... TESLA HYPERCOIL... ALL AT 98.9% CAPACITY.
IT WORKS! IT WORKS!
IT WORRRRKS!!
Then, in a blink, his lifelong ambition, everything he believed in, turned on him.
SKA-BLOOOM
I can't help but imagine that a part of him died at that moment--and that that death must have influenced what followed.
WHAT TH--?!
GOOD LORD...
SOMETHING... SOMETHING'S TAKEN CONTROL OF THE SYSTEM--
--FROM THE OTHER END!

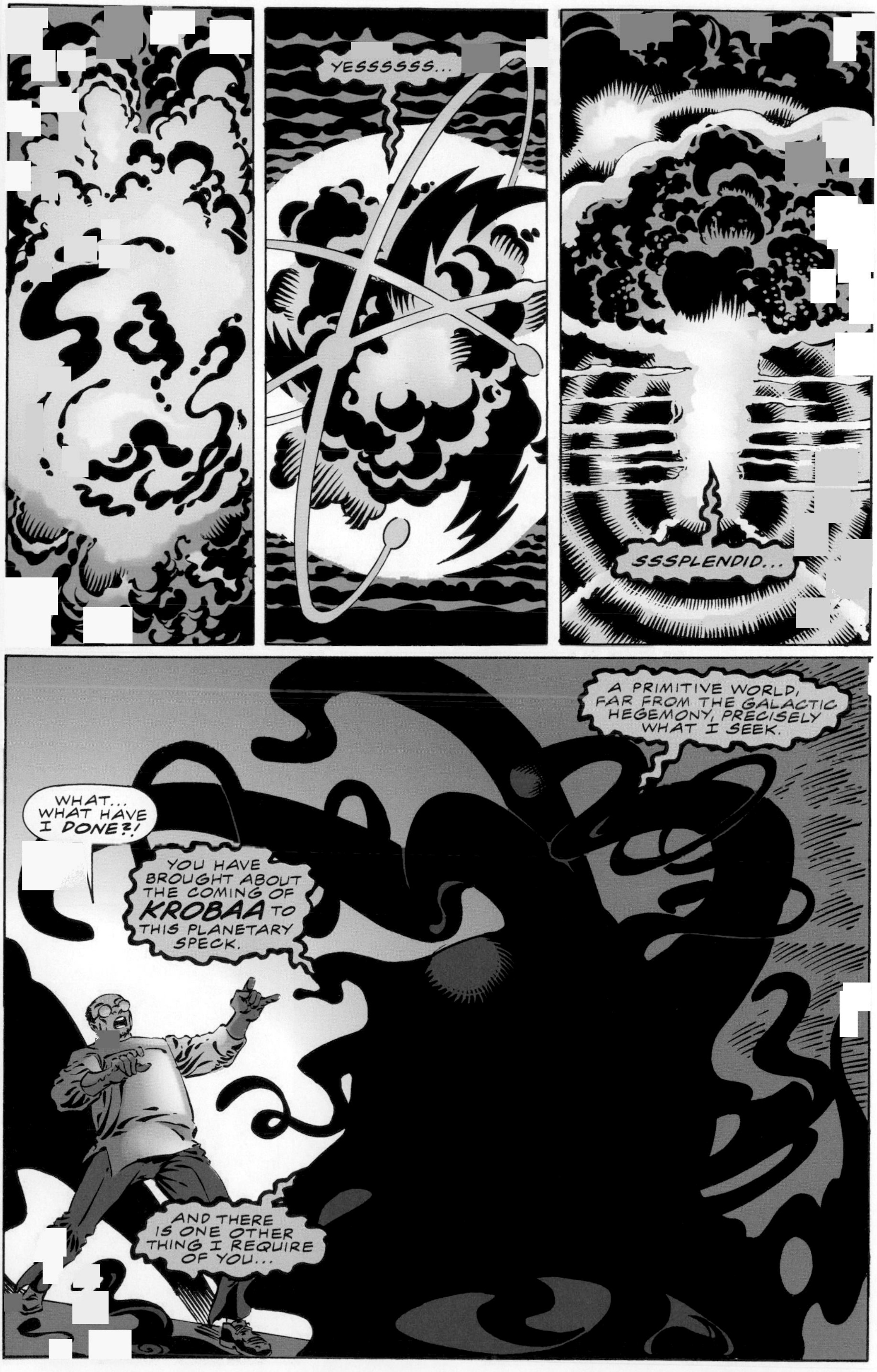
YESSSSSS...
SSSPLENDID...
A PRIMITIVE WORLD, FAR FROM THE GALACTIC HEGEMONY, PRECISELY WHAT I SEEK.
WHAT... WHAT HAVE I DONE?!
YOU HAVE BROUGHT ABOUT THE COMING OF KROBAA TO THIS PLANETARY SPECK.
AND THERE IS ONE OTHER THING I REQUIRE OF YOU...

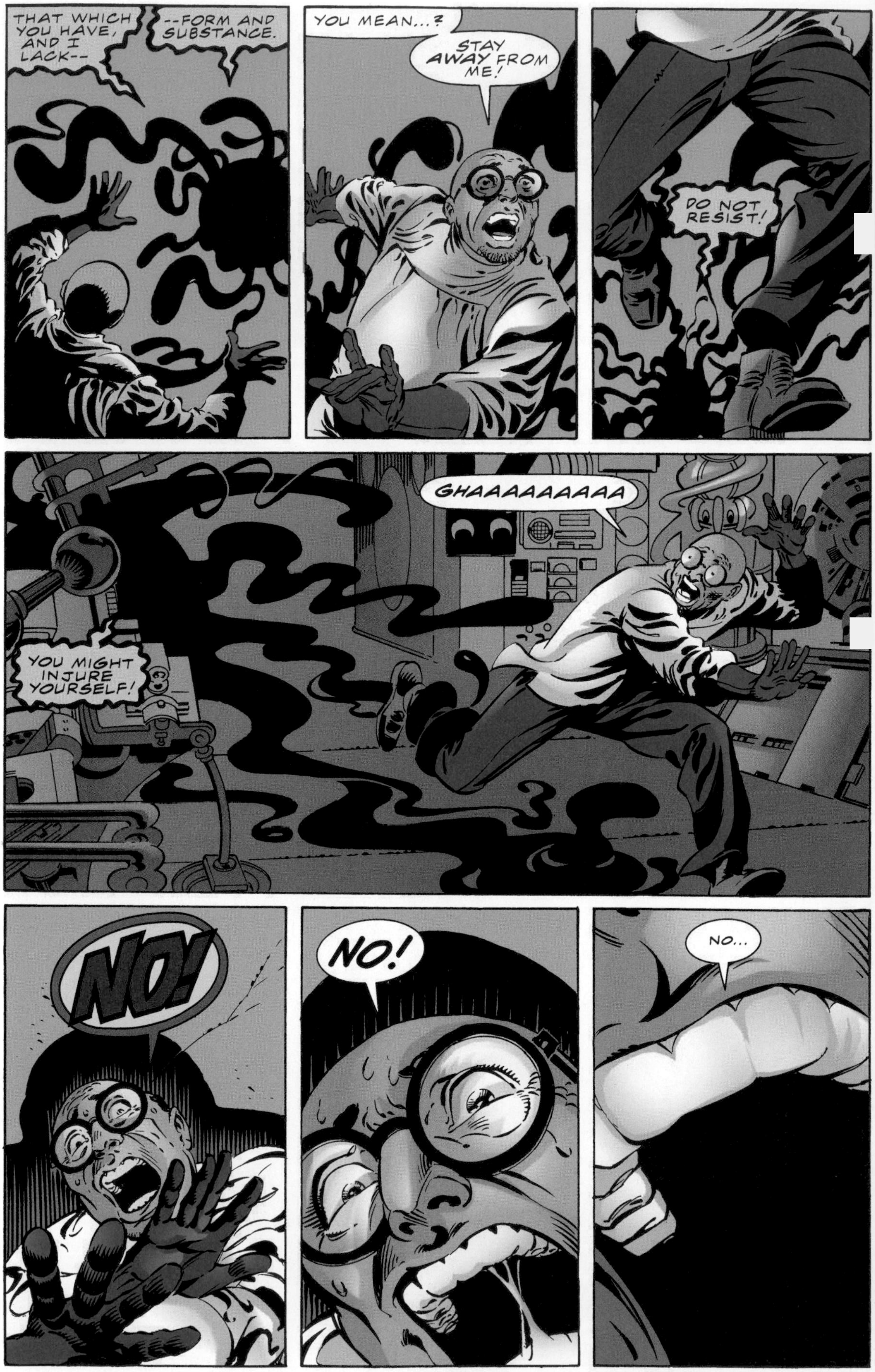
THAT WHICH YOU HAVE, AND I LACK--
--FORM AND SUBSTANCE.
YOU MEAN...?
STAY AWAY FROM ME!
DO NOT RESIST!
GHAAAAAAAAAA
YOU MIGHT INJURE YOURSELF!
NO!
NO!
NO...

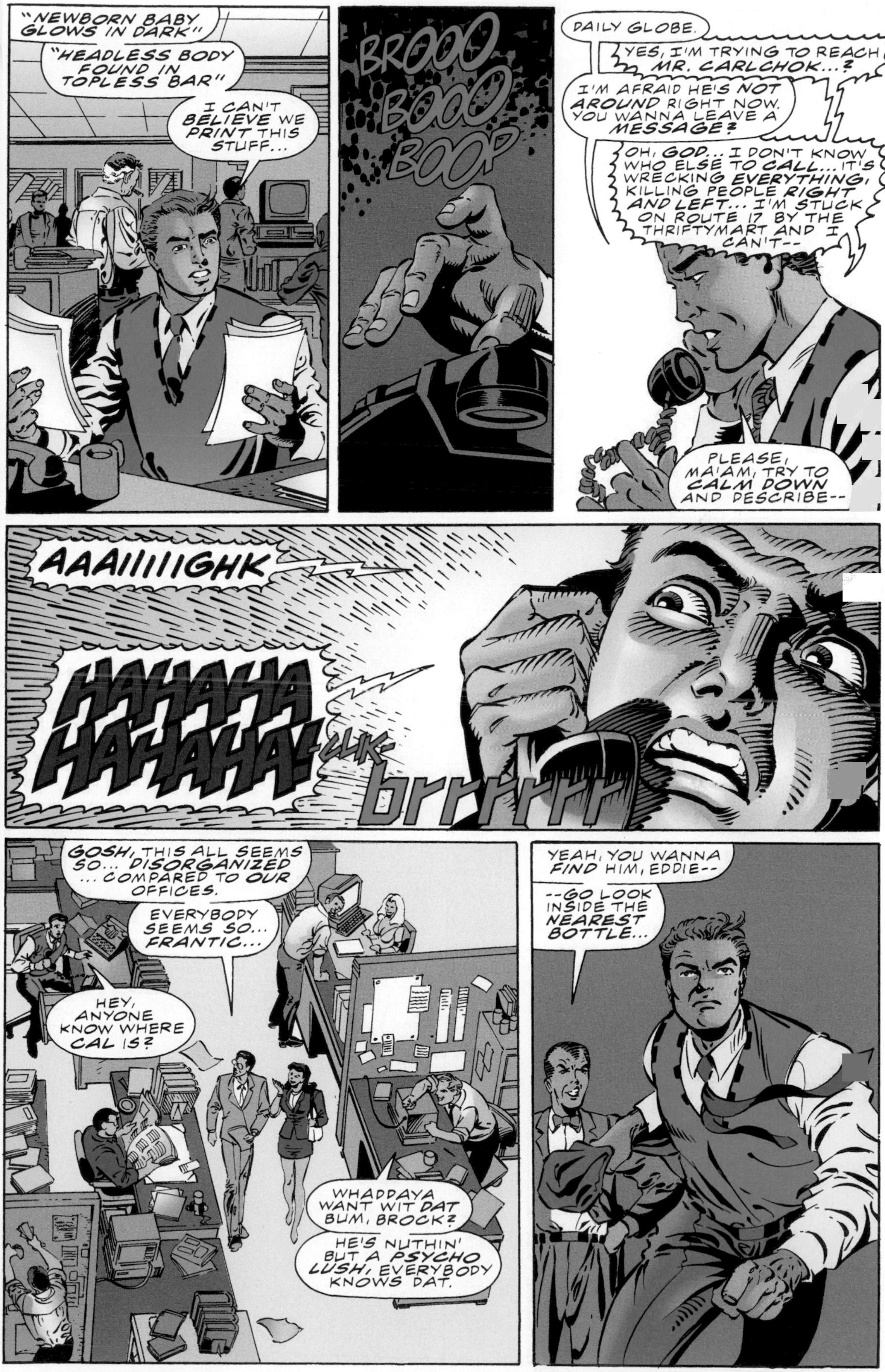
"NEWBORN BABY GLOWS IN DARK"
"HEADLESS BODY FOUND IN TOPLESS BAR"
I CAN'T BELIEVE WE PRINT THIS STUFF...
BROOO BOOO BOOP
DAILY GLOBE.
YES, I'M TRYING TO REACH MR. CARLCHOK...?
I'M AFRAID HE'S NOT AROUND RIGHT NOW. YOU WANNA LEAVE A MESSAGE?
OH, GOD... I DON'T KNOW WHO ELSE TO CALL... IT'S WRECKING EVERYTHING, KILLING PEOPLE RIGHT AND LEFT... I'M STUCK ON ROUTE 17 BY THE THRIFTYMART AND I CAN'T--
PLEASE, MA'AM, TRY TO CALM DOWN AND DESCRIBE--
AAAIIIIIGHK
HAHAHA HAHAHA!
CLIK
brrrrrr
GOSH, THIS ALL SEEMS SO... DISORGANIZED ... COMPARED TO OUR OFFICES.
EVERYBODY SEEMS SO... FRANTIC...
HEY, ANYONE KNOW WHERE CAL IS?
WHADDAYA WANT WIT DAT BUM, BROCK?
HE'S NUTHIN' BUT A PSYCHO LUSH, EVERYBODY KNOWS DAT.
YEAH, YOU WANNA FIND HIM, EDDIE--
--GO LOOK INSIDE THE NEAREST BOTTLE...

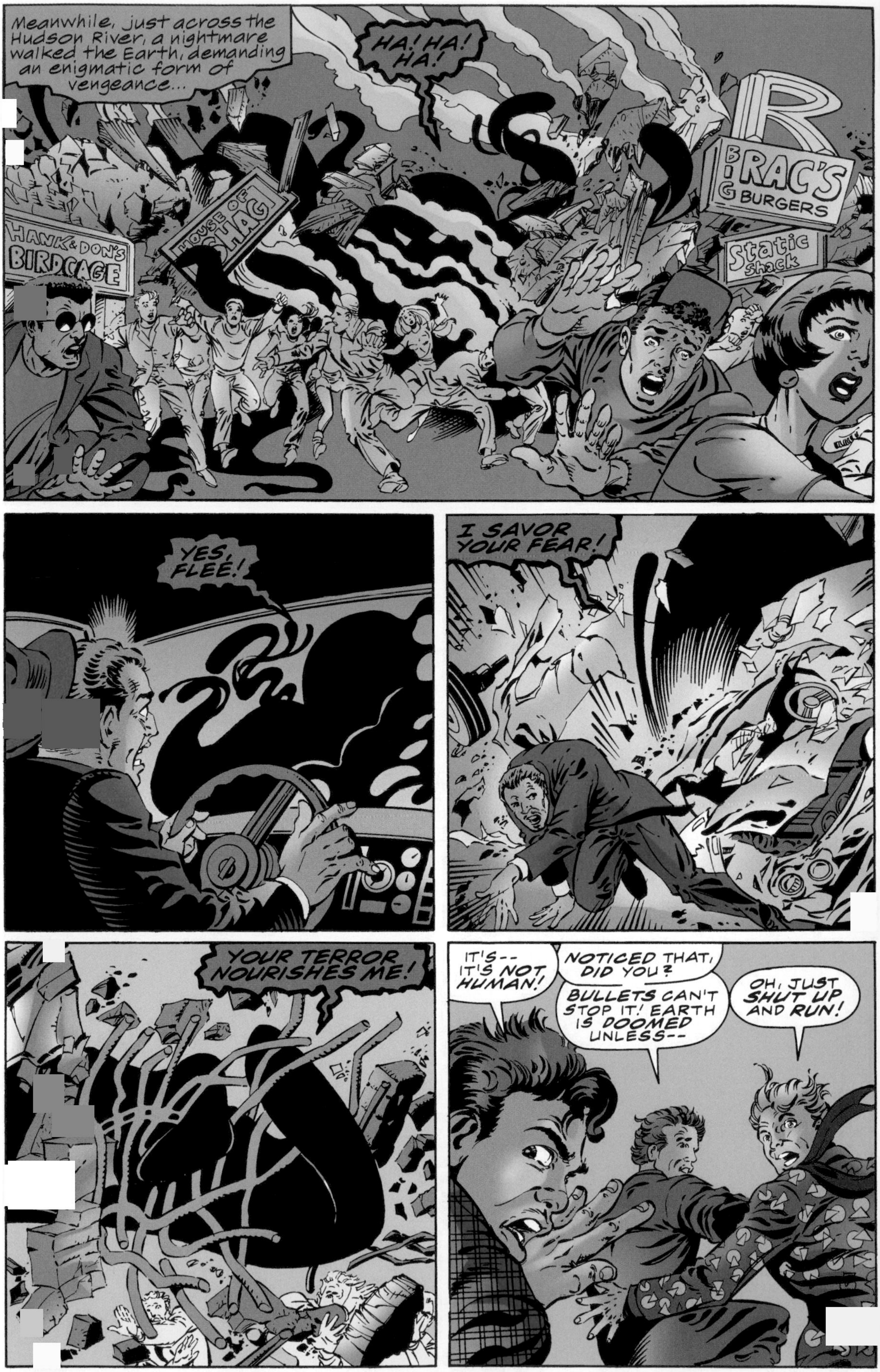
Meanwhile, just across the Hudson River, a nightmare walked the Earth, demanding an enigmatic form of vengeance...
HA! HA! HA!
HANK & DON'S BIRDCAGE
HOUSE OF SHAG
BIG RAC'S BURGERS
Static Shack
YES, FLEE!
I SAVOR YOUR FEAR!
YOUR TERROR NOURISHES ME!
IT'S-- IT'S NOT HUMAN!
NOTICED THAT, DID YOU?
BULLETS CAN'T STOP IT! EARTH IS DOOMED UNLESS--
OH, JUST SHUT UP AND RUN!

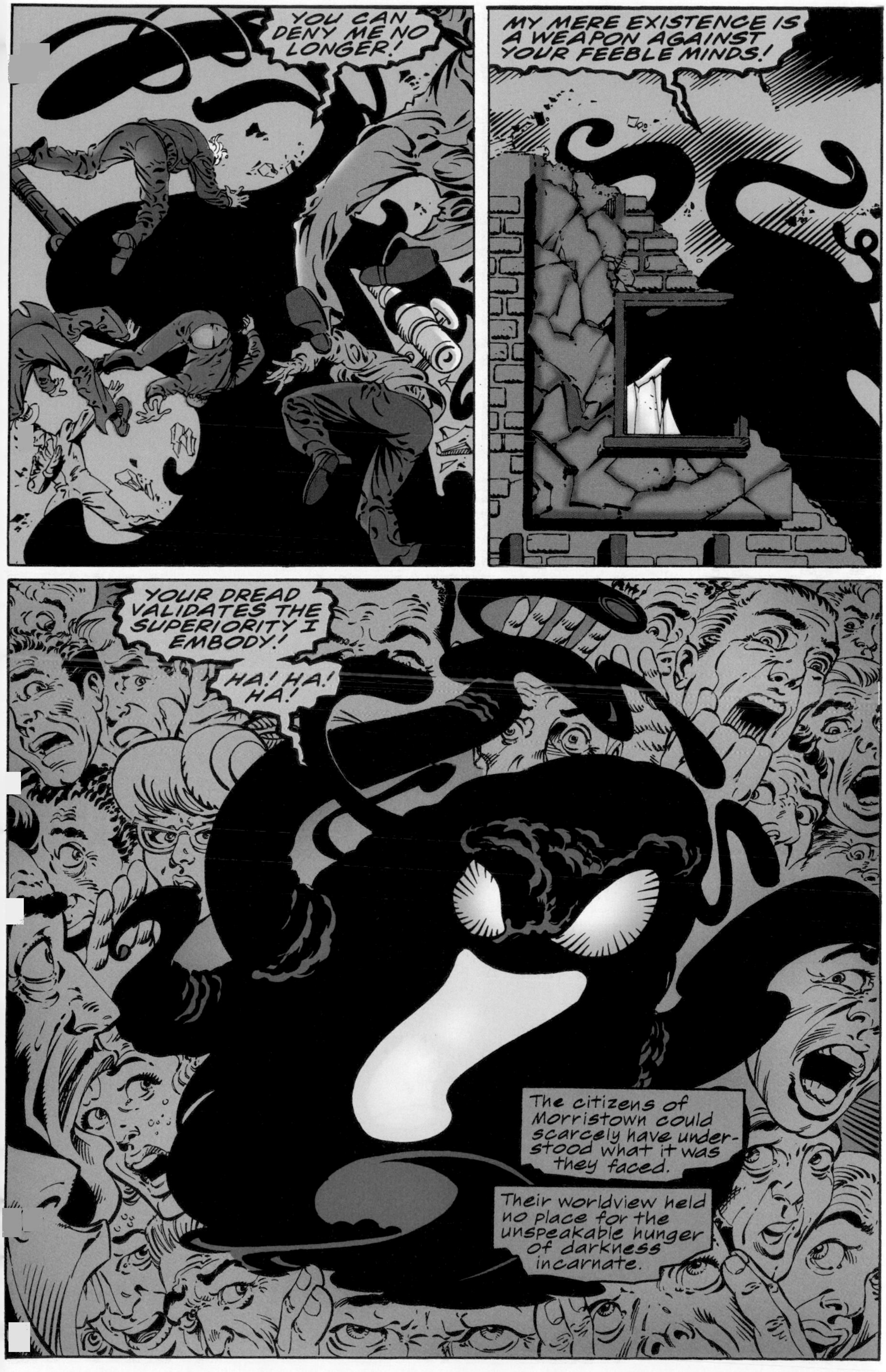
YOU CAN DENY ME NO LONGER!
MY MERE EXISTENCE IS A WEAPON AGAINST YOUR FEEBLE MINDS!
YOUR DREAD VALIDATES THE SUPERIORITY I EMBODY!
HA! HA! HA!
The citizens of Morristown could scarcely have understood what it was they faced.
Their worldview held no place for the unspeakable hunger of darkness incarnate.

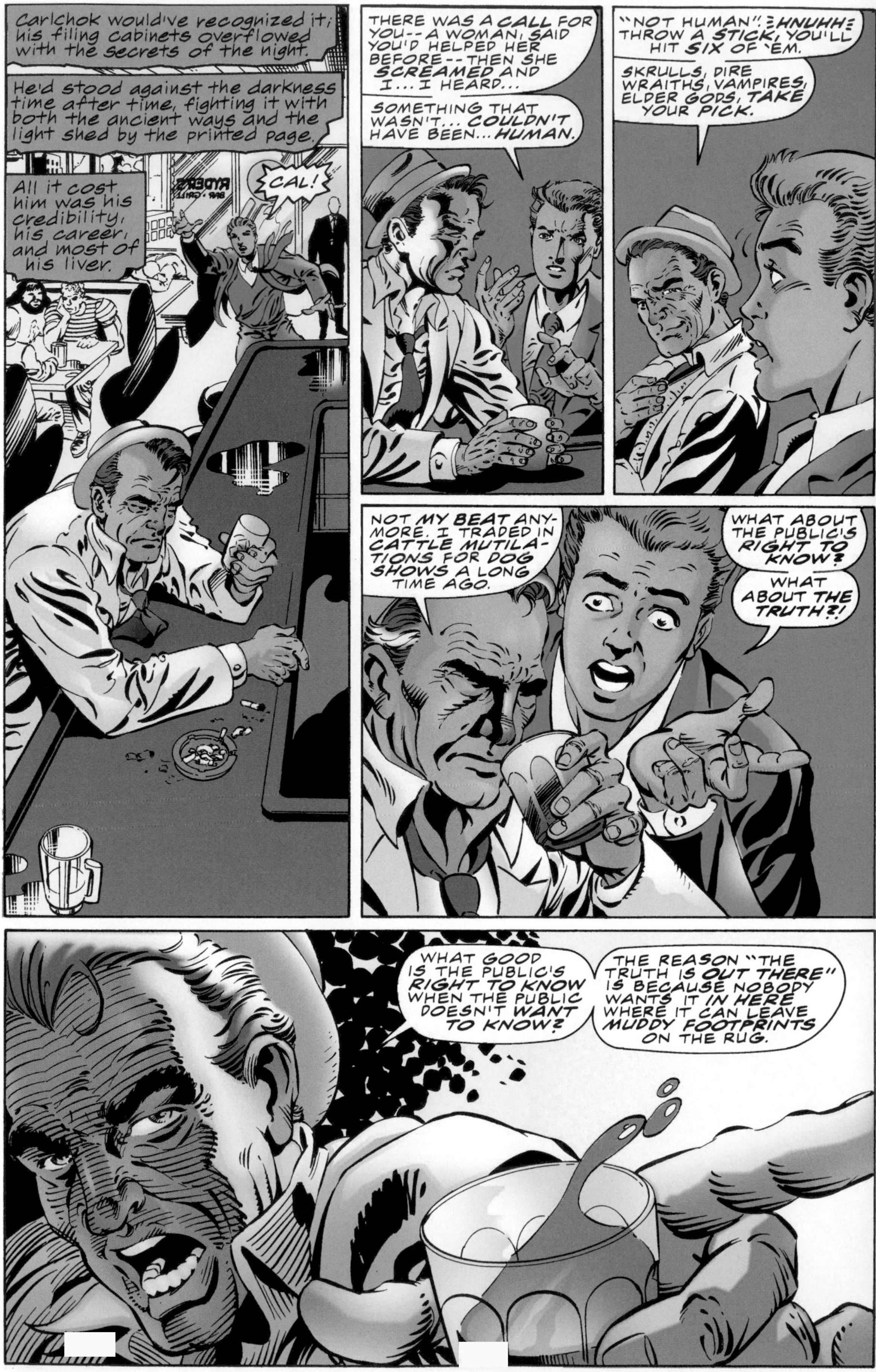
Carlchok would've recognized it; his filing cabinets overflowed with the secrets of the night.
He'd stood against the darkness time after time, fighting it with both the ancient ways and the light shed by the printed page.
All it cost him was his credibility, his career, and most of his liver.
CAL!
THERE WAS A CALL FOR YOU-- A WOMAN, SAID YOU'D HELPED HER BEFORE-- THEN SHE SCREAMED AND I... I HEARD...
SOMETHING THAT WASN'T... COULDN'T HAVE BEEN... HUMAN.
"NOT HUMAN". HNUHH. THROW A STICK, YOU'LL HIT SIX OF 'EM.
SKRULLS, DIRE WRAITHS, VAMPIRES, ELDER GODS, TAKE YOUR PICK.
NOT MY BEAT ANYMORE. I TRADED IN CATTLE MUTILATIONS FOR DOG SHOWS A LONG TIME AGO.
WHAT ABOUT THE PUBLIC'S RIGHT TO KNOW?
WHAT ABOUT THE TRUTH?!
WHAT GOOD IS THE PUBLIC'S RIGHT TO KNOW WHEN THE PUBLIC DOESN'T WANT TO KNOW?
THE REASON "THE TRUTH IS OUT THERE" IS BECAUSE NOBODY WANTS IT IN HERE WHERE IT CAN LEAVE MUDDY FOOTPRINTS ON THE RUG.

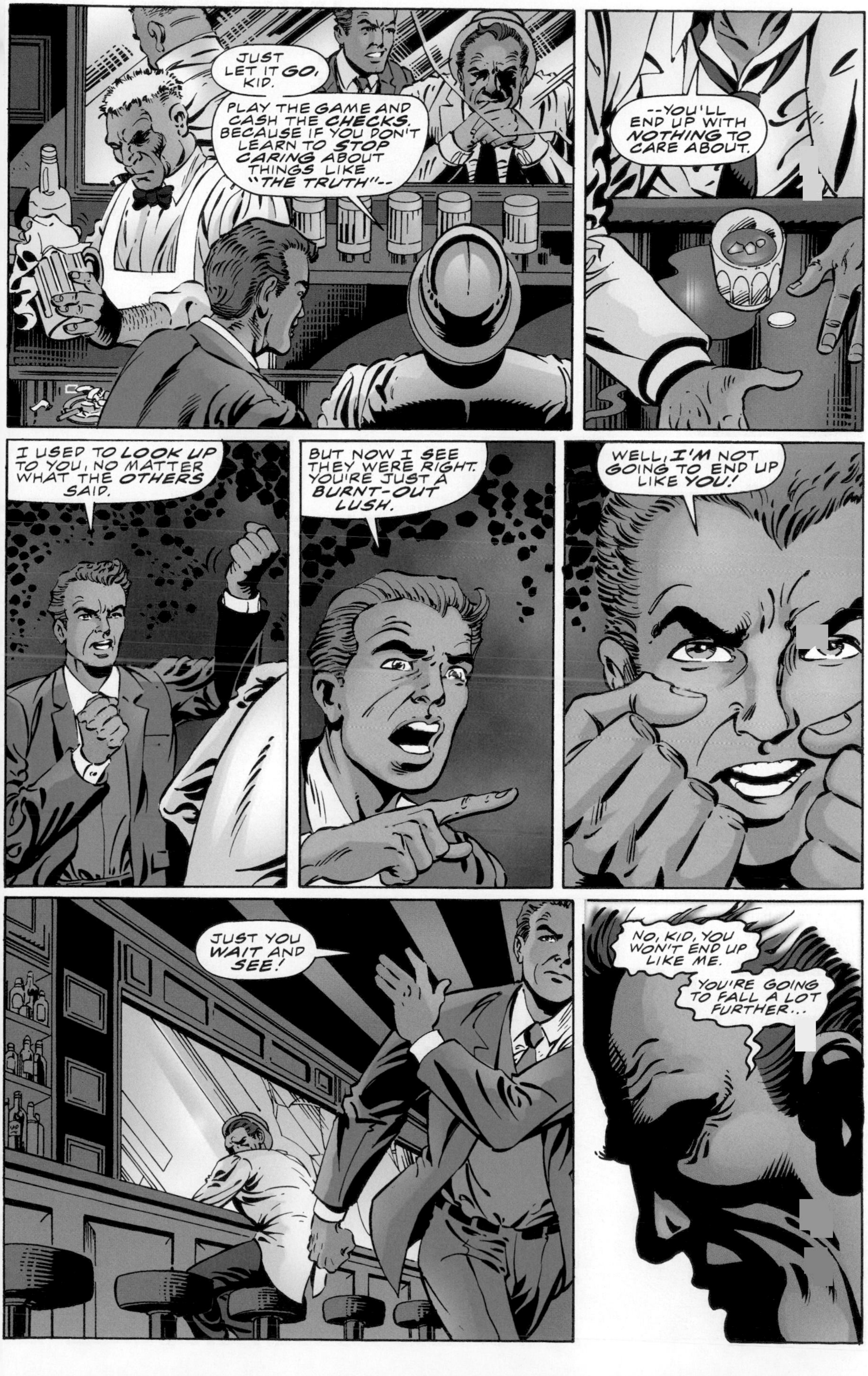
JUST LET IT GO, KID.
PLAY THE GAME AND CASH THE CHECKS. BECAUSE IF YOU DON'T LEARN TO STOP CARING ABOUT THINGS LIKE "THE TRUTH"--
--YOU'LL END UP WITH NOTHING TO CARE ABOUT.
I USED TO LOOK UP TO YOU, NO MATTER WHAT THE OTHERS SAID.
BUT NOW I SEE THEY WERE RIGHT. YOU'RE JUST A BURNT-OUT LUSH.
WELL, I'M NOT GOING TO END UP LIKE YOU!
JUST YOU WAIT AND SEE!
NO, KID, YOU WON'T END UP LIKE ME.
YOU'RE GOING TO FALL A LOT FURTHER...

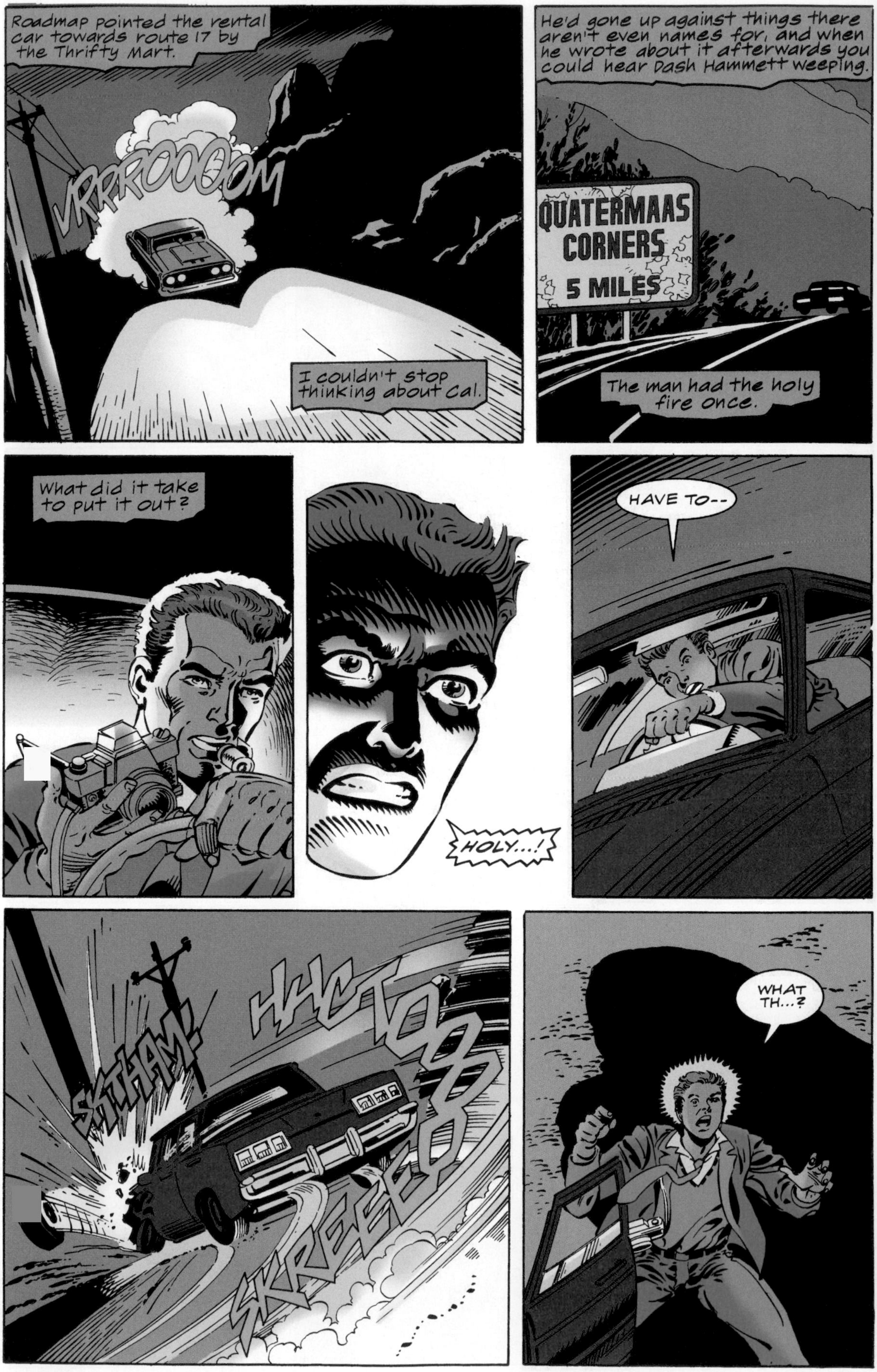
Roadmap pointed the rental car towards route 17 by the Thrifty Mart.
VRRROOOOOM
I couldn't stop thinking about Cal.
He'd gone up against things there aren't even names for, and when he wrote about it afterwards you could hear Dash Hammett weeping.
QUATERMAAS CORNERS 5 MILES
The man had the holy fire once.
What did it take to put it out?
HOLY...!
HAVE TO--
SKTHAM!
HHCTOOO
SKREEEEE
WHAT TH...?

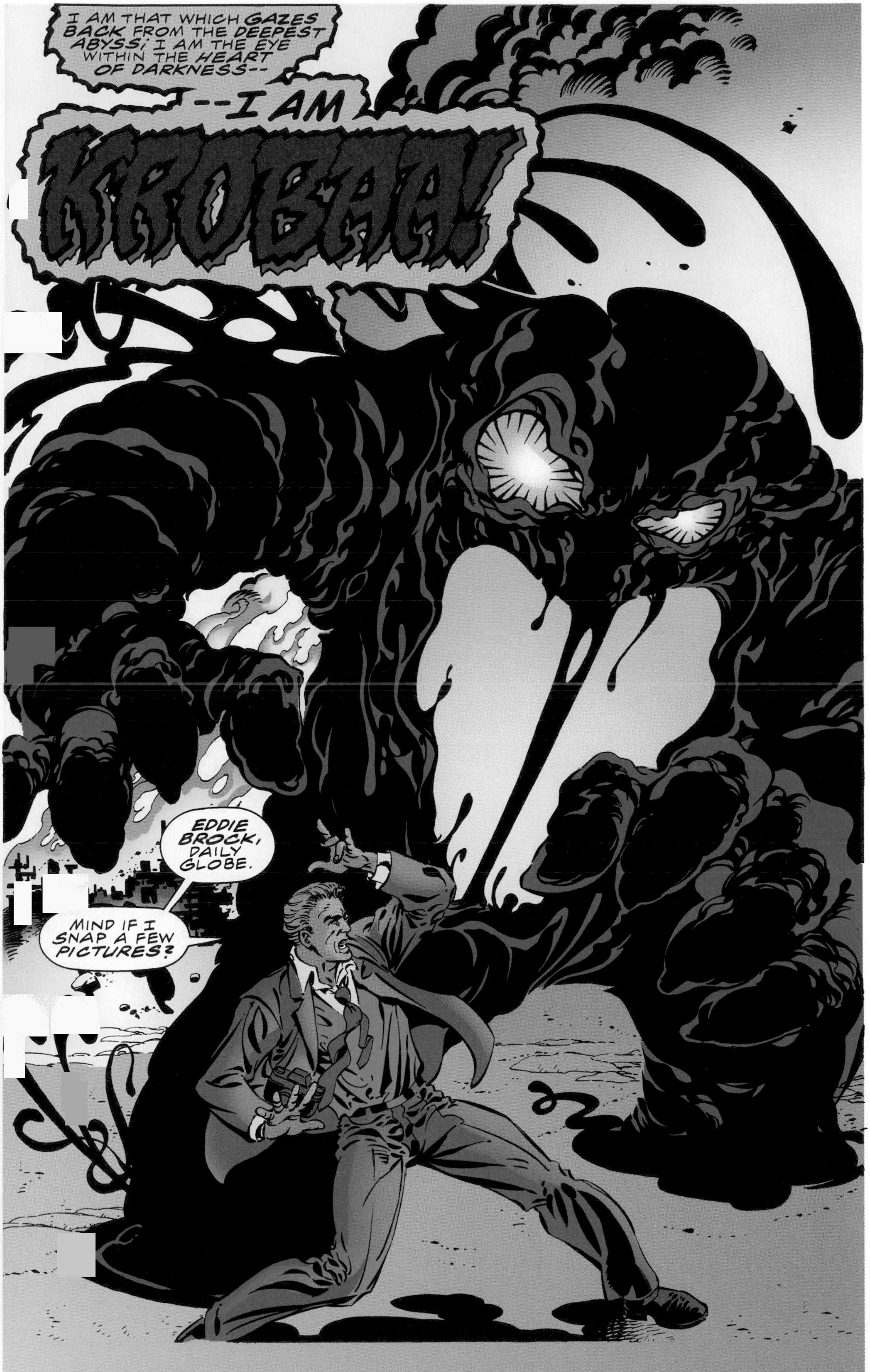
I AM THAT WHICH GAZES BACK FROM THE DEEPEST ABYSS; I AM THE EYE WITHIN THE HEART OF DARKNESS--
--I AM
KROBAA!
EDDIE BROCK, DAILY GLOBE.
MIND IF I SNAP A FEW PICTURES?

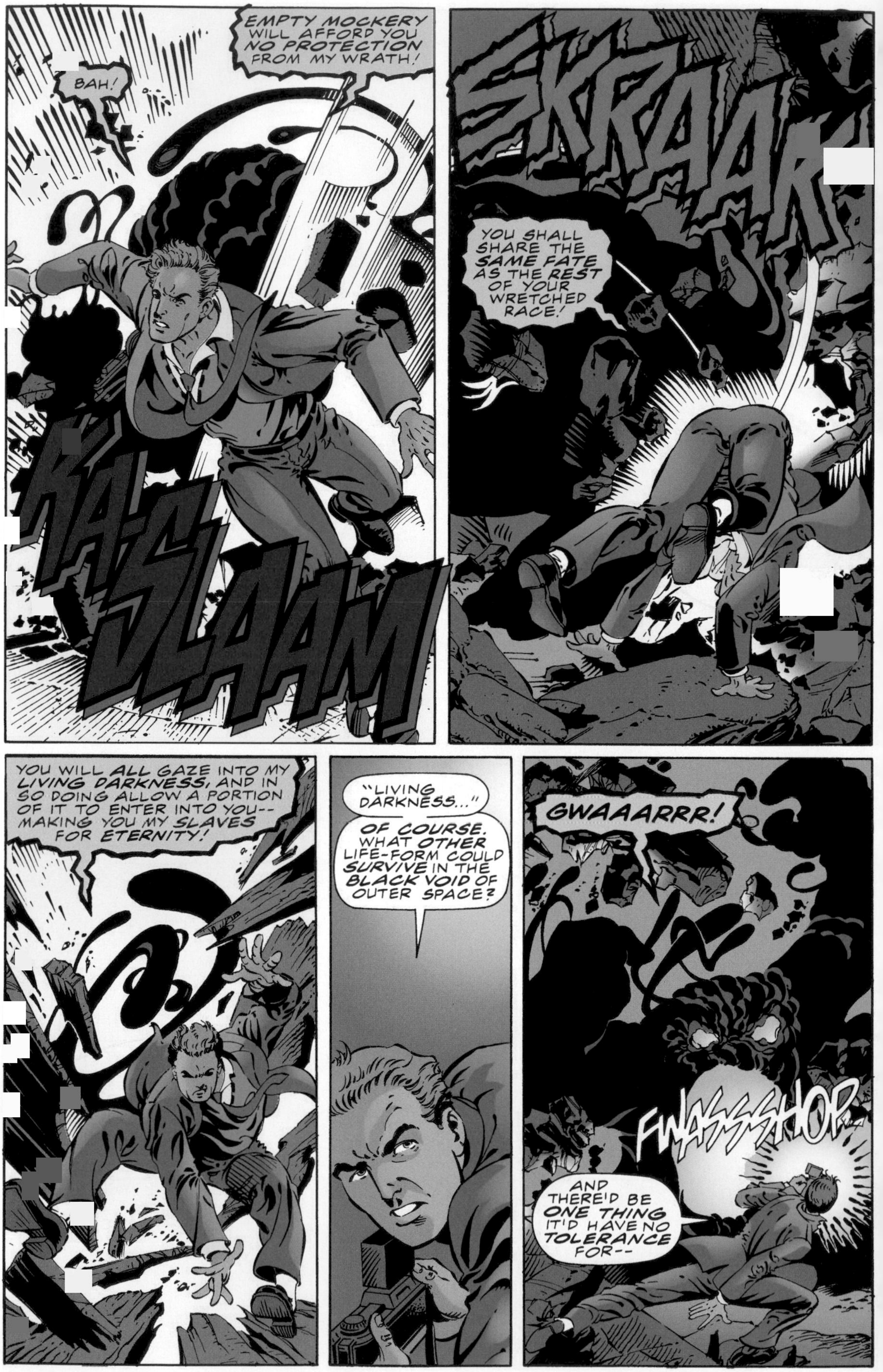
EMPTY MOCKERY WILL AFFORD YOU NO PROTECTION FROM MY WRATH!
BAH!
KA-SLAAM
SKRAAAK
YOU SHALL SHARE THE SAME FATE AS THE REST OF YOUR WRETCHED RACE!
YOU WILL ALL GAZE INTO MY LIVING DARKNESS, AND IN SO DOING ALLOW A PORTION OF IT TO ENTER INTO YOU-- MAKING YOU MY SLAVES FOR ETERNITY!
"LIVING DARKNESS..."
OF COURSE. WHAT OTHER LIFE-FORM COULD SURVIVE IN THE BLACK VOID OF OUTER SPACE?
GWAAARRR!
FWASSHOP
AND THERE'D BE ONE THING IT'D HAVE NO TOLERANCE FOR--

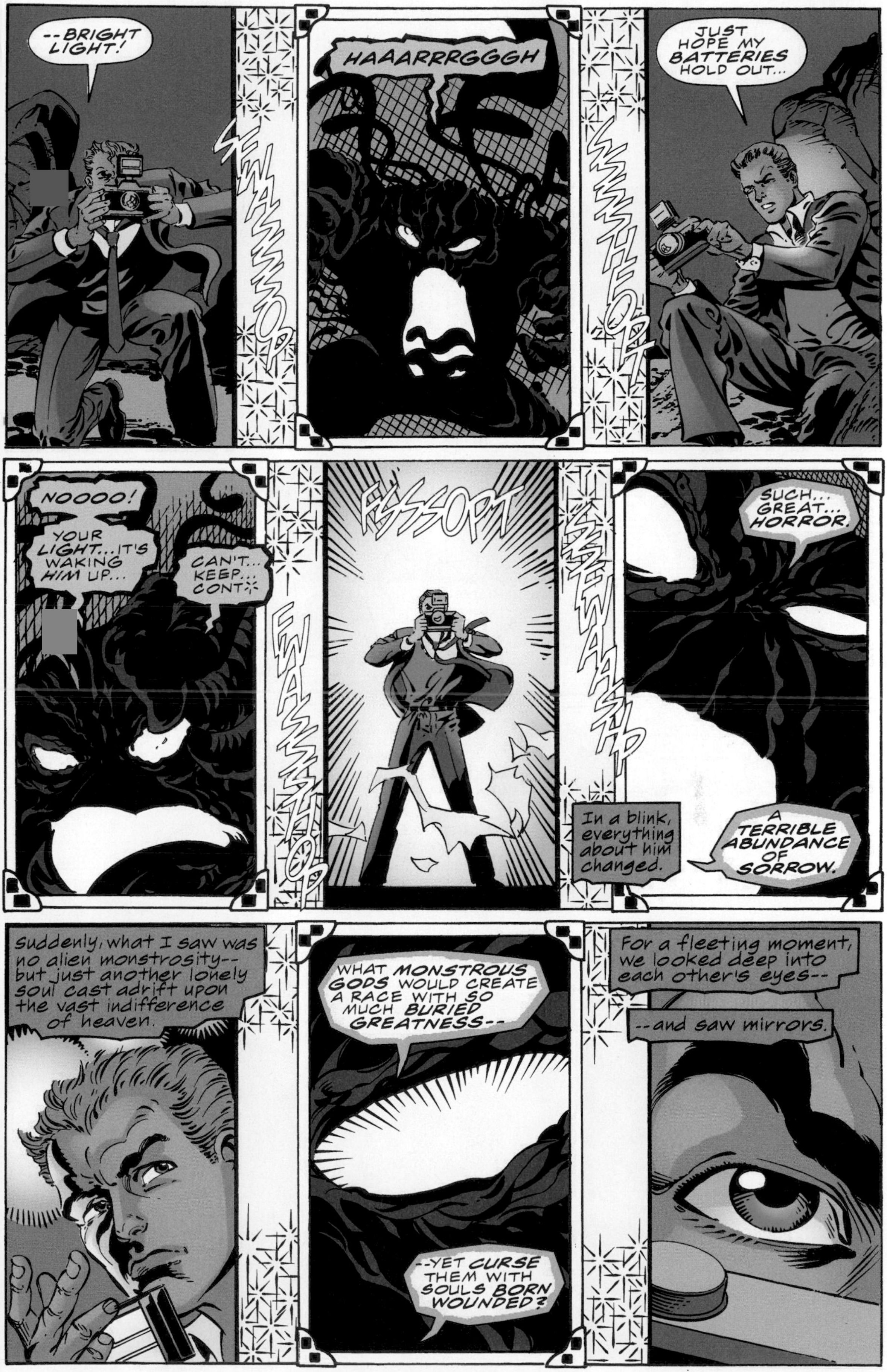
--BRIGHT LIGHT!
HAAARRRGGGH
JUST HOPE MY BATTERIES HOLD OUT...
NOOOO!
YOUR LIGHT...IT'S WAKING HIM UP...
CAN'T... KEEP... CONT
SUCH... GREAT... HORROR.
In a blink, everything about him changed.
A TERRIBLE ABUNDANCE OF SORROW.
Suddenly, what I saw was no alien monstrosity--but just another lonely soul cast adrift upon the vast indifference of heaven.
WHAT MONSTROUS GODS WOULD CREATE A RACE WITH SO MUCH BURIED GREATNESS--
--YET CURSE THEM WITH SOULS BORN WOUNDED?
For a fleeting moment, we looked deep into each other's eyes--
--and saw mirrors.

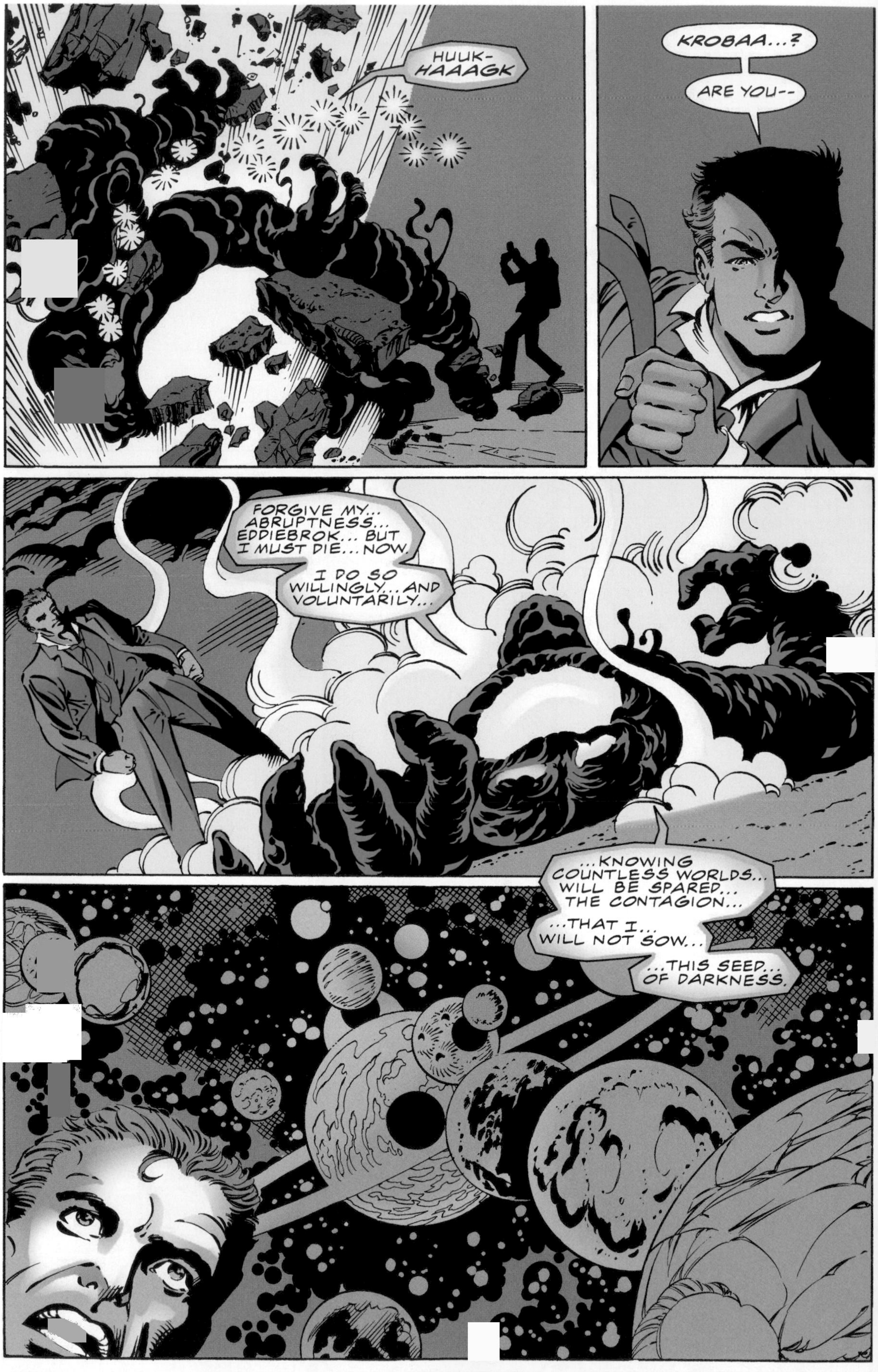
HUUK-
HAAAGK
KROBAA...?
ARE YOU--
FORGIVE MY... ABRUPTNESS... EDDIEBROK... BUT I MUST DIE... NOW.
I DO SO WILLINGLY... AND VOLUNTARILY...
...KNOWING COUNTLESS WORLDS... WILL BE SPARED... THE CONTAGION...
...THAT I... WILL NOT SOW...
...THIS SEED... OF DARKNESS.

MNNNNGGH! HHG!

WHAT TH--?

SKRUPT! KRITCH

AAAAH-HHHGG! GET IT OFF! GET IT OFF ME!

≡HHHHH-UUUUH≡ ≡HHHHH-UUUUH≡

I DIDN'T UNDERSTAND! I DIDN'T KNOW! HE THOUGHT I'D INVITED HIM!

HE WAS AN EXPLORER, SEEKING OUT NEW WORLDS AND CIVILIZATIONS, LEARNING THE UNIQUE FORM OF THEIR THOUGHTS THROUGH TEMPORARY SYMBIOSIS--

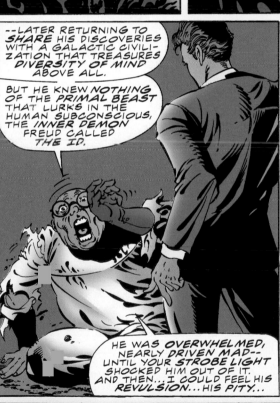

--LATER RETURNING TO SHARE HIS DISCOVERIES WITH A GALACTIC CIVILIZATION THAT TREASURES DIVERSITY OF MIND ABOVE ALL.

BUT HE KNEW NOTHING OF THE PRIMAL BEAST THAT LURKS IN THE HUMAN SUBCONSCIOUS, THE INNER DEMON FREUD CALLED THE ID.

HE WAS OVERWHELMED, NEARLY DRIVEN MAD-- UNTIL YOUR STROBE LIGHT SHOCKED HIM OUT OF IT. AND THEN... I COULD FEEL HIS REVULSION... HIS PITY...

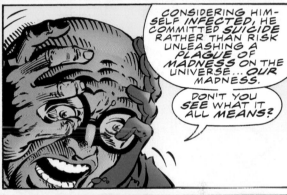

CONSIDERING HIMSELF INFECTED, HE COMMITTED SUICIDE RATHER THAN RISK UNLEASHING A PLAGUE OF MADNESS ON THE UNIVERSE... OUR MADNESS.

DON'T YOU SEE WHAT IT ALL MEANS?

WE'RE MONSTERS! EVERY LAST ONE OF US! MONSTERS!

≡AHUUNHK≡

≡AHUUNHK≡ ≡AHUUNHK≡ ≡AHUUNHK≡

The wind gathered the ebon dust which was all that remained of Krobaa in its fleeting embrace, then scattered it in all directions.

The nights've seemed a little darker ever since.

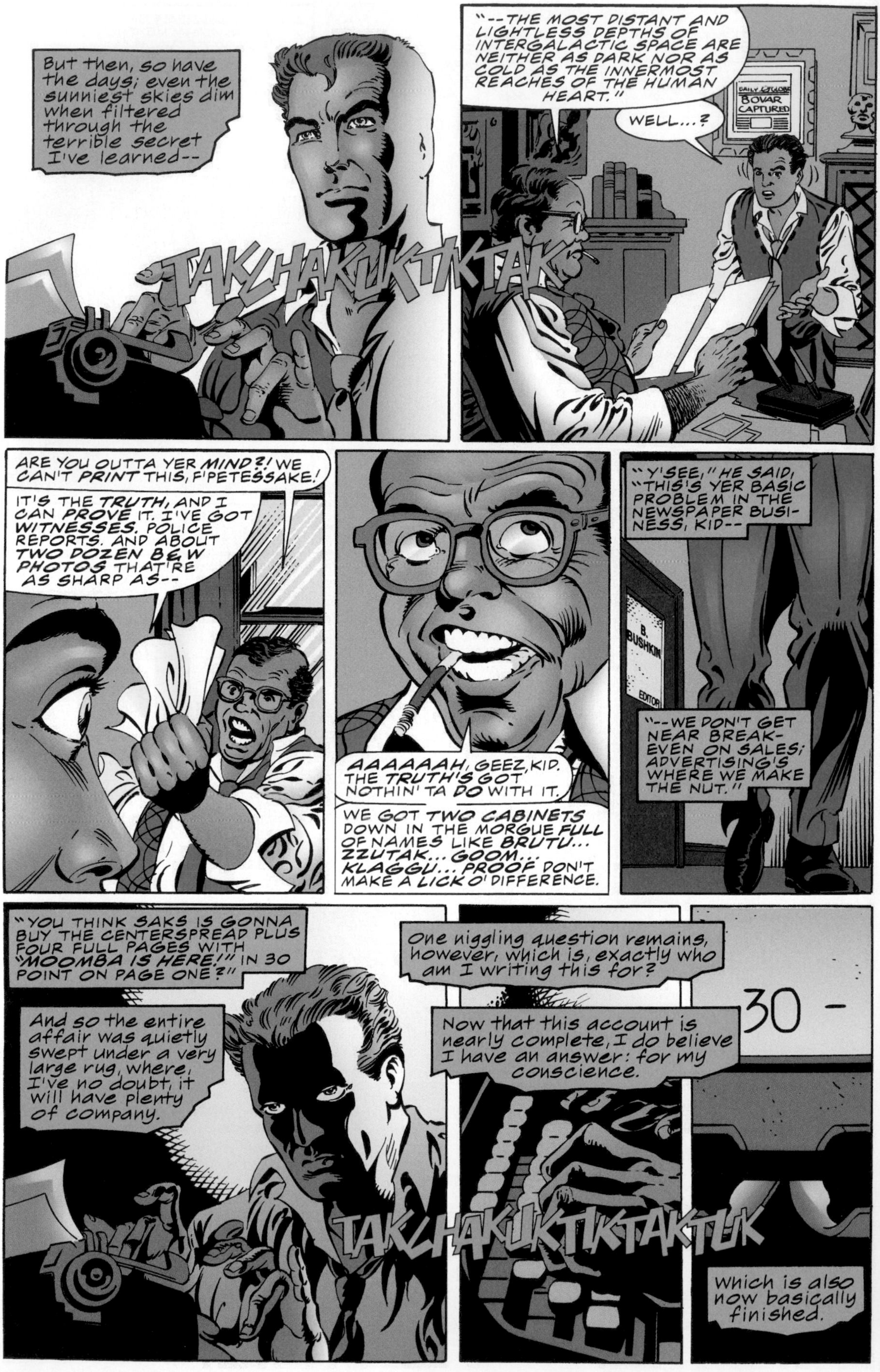
But then, so have the days; even the sunniest skies dim when filtered through the terrible secret I've learned--
TAKCHAKCLIKTIKTAK
"--THE MOST DISTANT AND LIGHTLESS DEPTHS OF INTERGALACTIC SPACE ARE NEITHER AS DARK NOR AS COLD AS THE INNERMOST REACHES OF THE HUMAN HEART."
WELL...?
DAILY GLOBE
BOVAR CAPTURED
ARE YOU OUTTA YER MIND?! WE CAN'T PRINT THIS, F'PETESSAKE!
IT'S THE TRUTH, AND I CAN PROVE IT. I'VE GOT WITNESSES. POLICE REPORTS. AND ABOUT TWO DOZEN B&W PHOTOS THAT'RE AS SHARP AS--
AAAAAAH, GEEZ, KID. THE TRUTH'S GOT NOTHIN' TA DO WITH IT.
WE GOT TWO CABINETS DOWN IN THE MORGUE FULL OF NAMES LIKE BRUTU... ZZUTAK... GOOM... KLAGGU... PROOF DON'T MAKE A LICK O' DIFFERENCE.
"Y'SEE," HE SAID, "THIS'S YER BASIC PROBLEM IN THE NEWSPAPER BUSINESS, KID--
B. BUSHKIN
EDITOR
"--WE DON'T GET NEAR BREAK-EVEN ON SALES; ADVERTISING'S WHERE WE MAKE THE NUT."
"YOU THINK SAKS IS GONNA BUY THE CENTERSPREAD PLUS FOUR FULL PAGES WITH "MOOMBA IS HERE!" IN 30 POINT ON PAGE ONE?"
And so the entire affair was quietly swept under a very large rug, where, I've no doubt, it will have plenty of company.
One niggling question remains, however, which is, exactly who am I writing this for?
Now that this account is nearly complete, I do believe I have an answer: for my conscience.
30 -
TAKCHAKCLIKTIKTAKTUK
Which is also now basically finished.

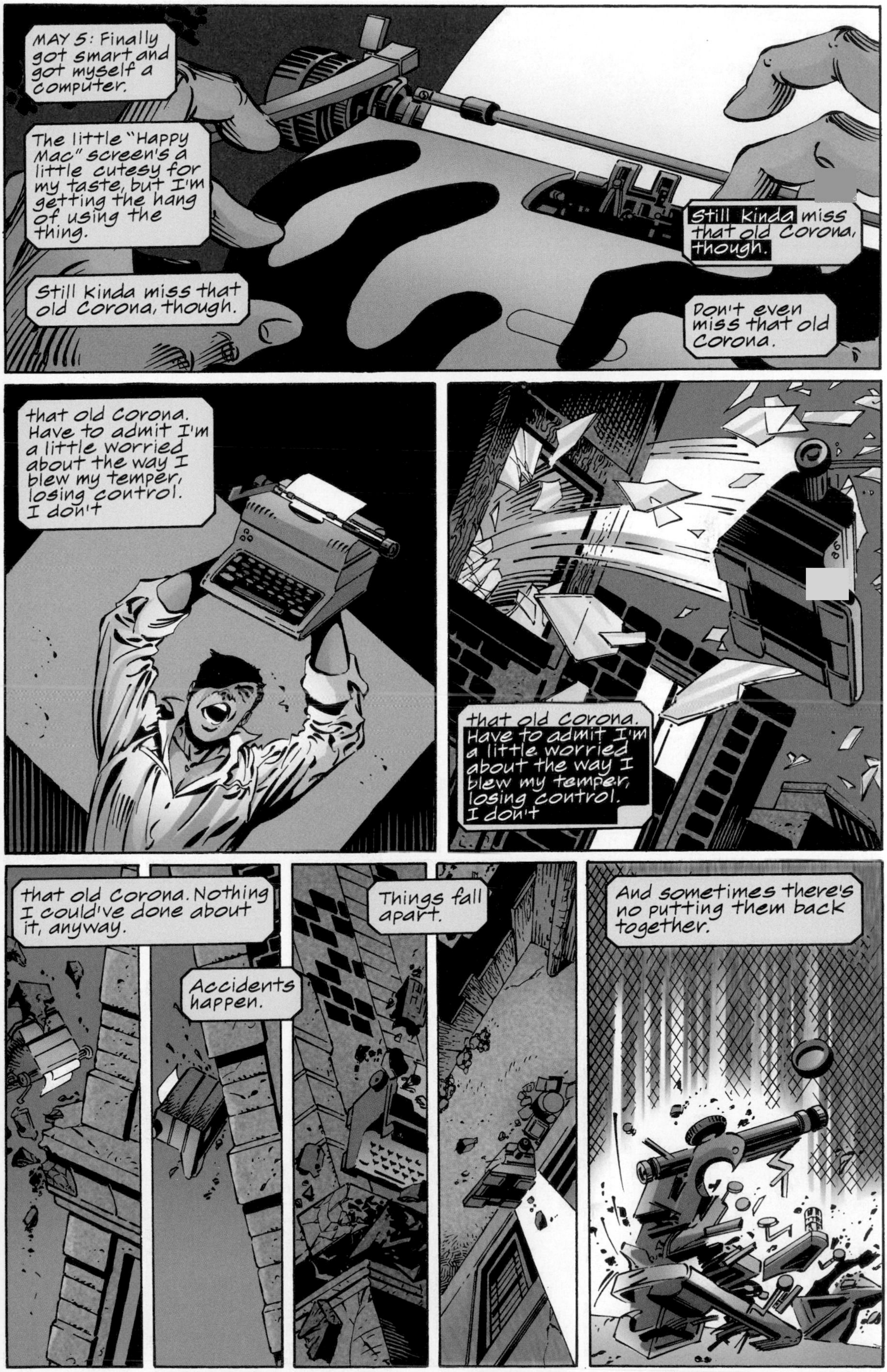
MAY 5: Finally got smart and got myself a computer.
The little "Happy Mac" screen's a little cutesy for my taste, but I'm getting the hang of using the thing.
Still kinda miss that old Corona, though.
Still kinda miss that old Corona, though.
Don't even miss that old Corona.
that old Corona. Have to admit I'm a little worried about the way I blew my temper, losing control. I don't
that old Corona. Have to admit I'm a little worried about the way I blew my temper, losing control. I don't
that old Corona. Nothing I could've done about it, anyway.
Accidents happen.
Things fall apart.
And sometimes there's no putting them back together.

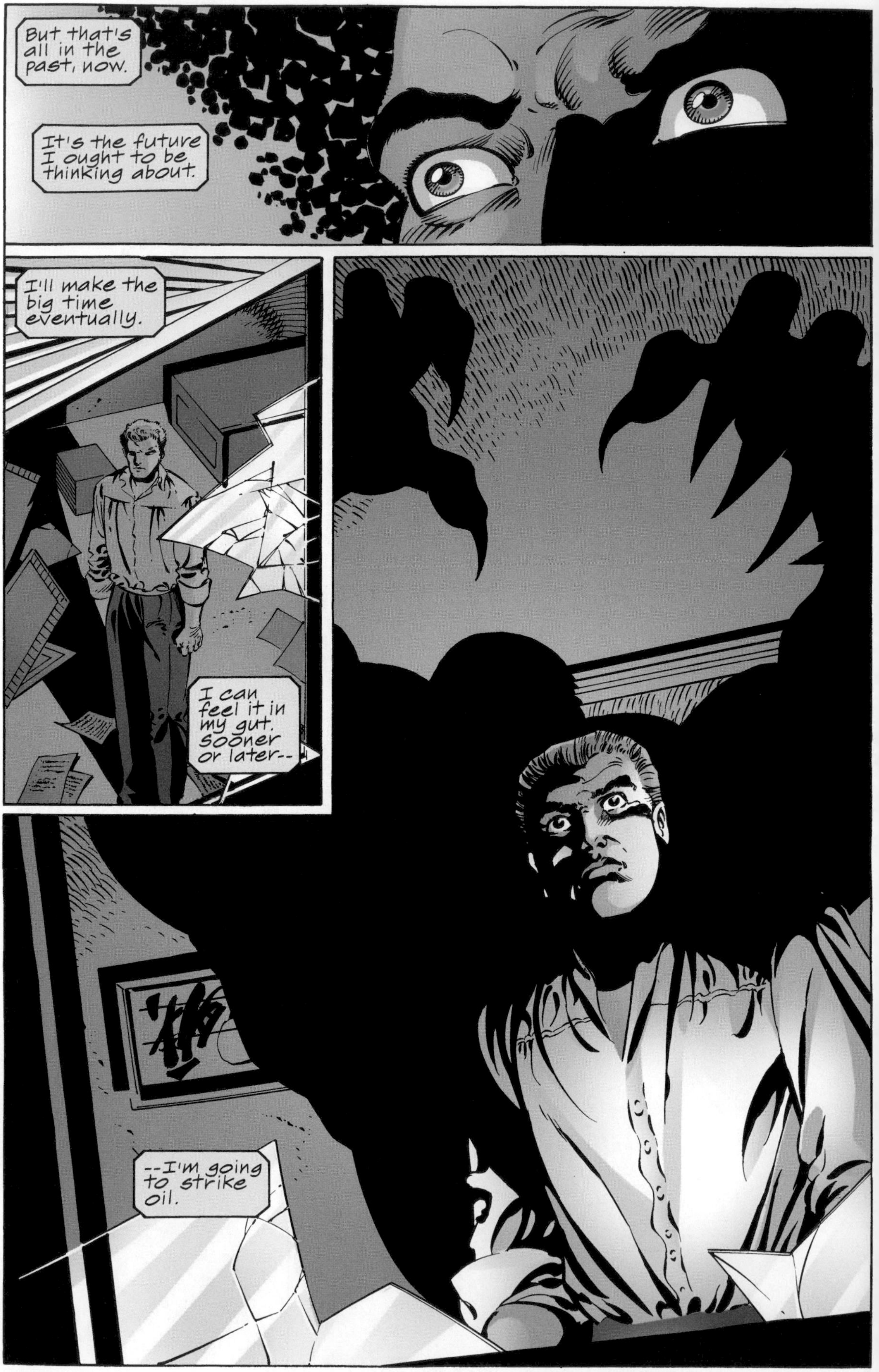

But that's all in the past, now.
It's the future I ought to be thinking about.
I'll make the big time eventually.
I can feel it in my gut. Sooner or later--
--I'm going to strike oil.

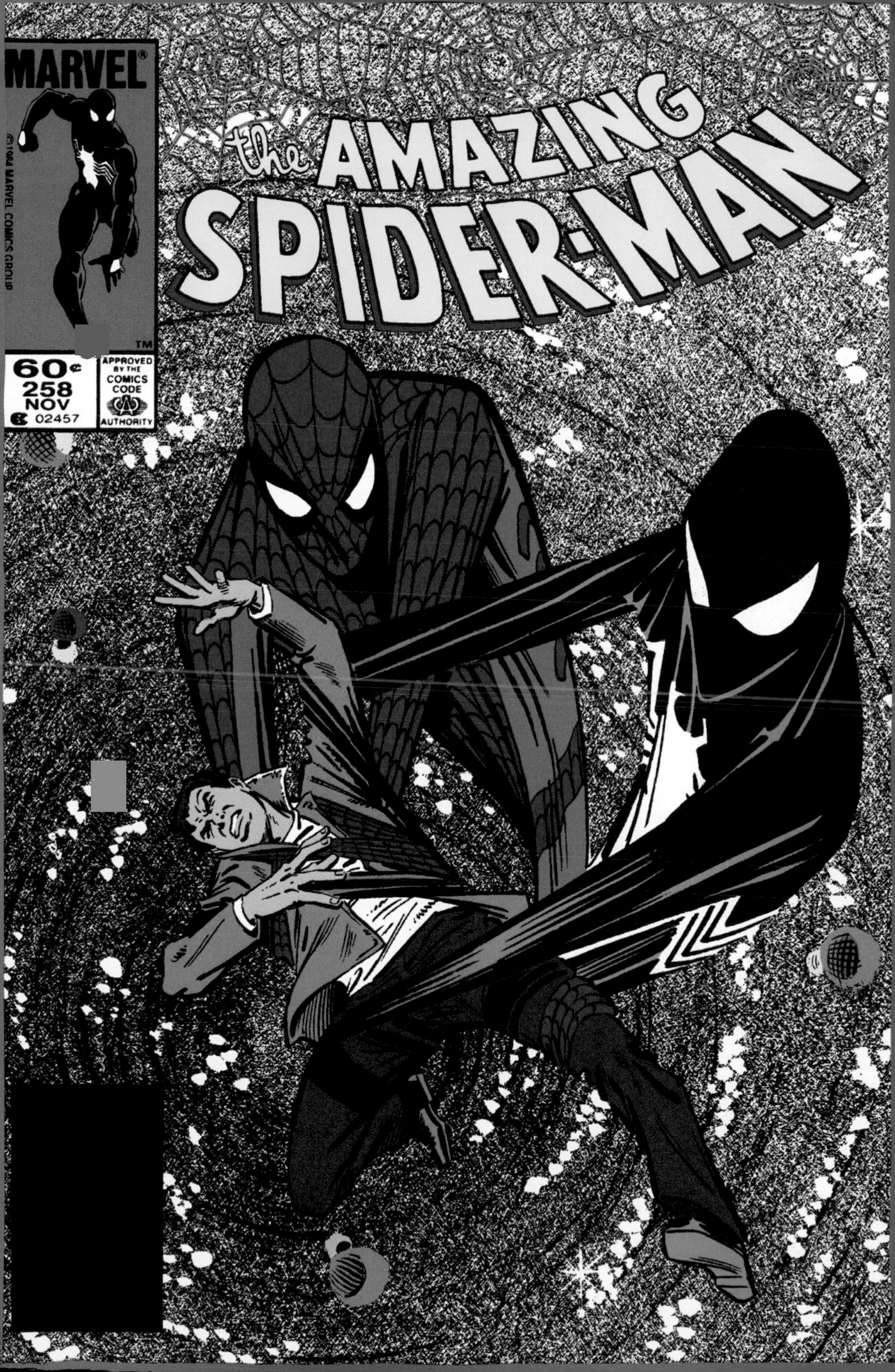
MARVEL®
the AMAZING SPIDER-MAN
TM
©1984 MARVEL COMICS GROUP
60¢
258
NOV
02457
APPROVED BY THE COMICS CODE AUTHORITY

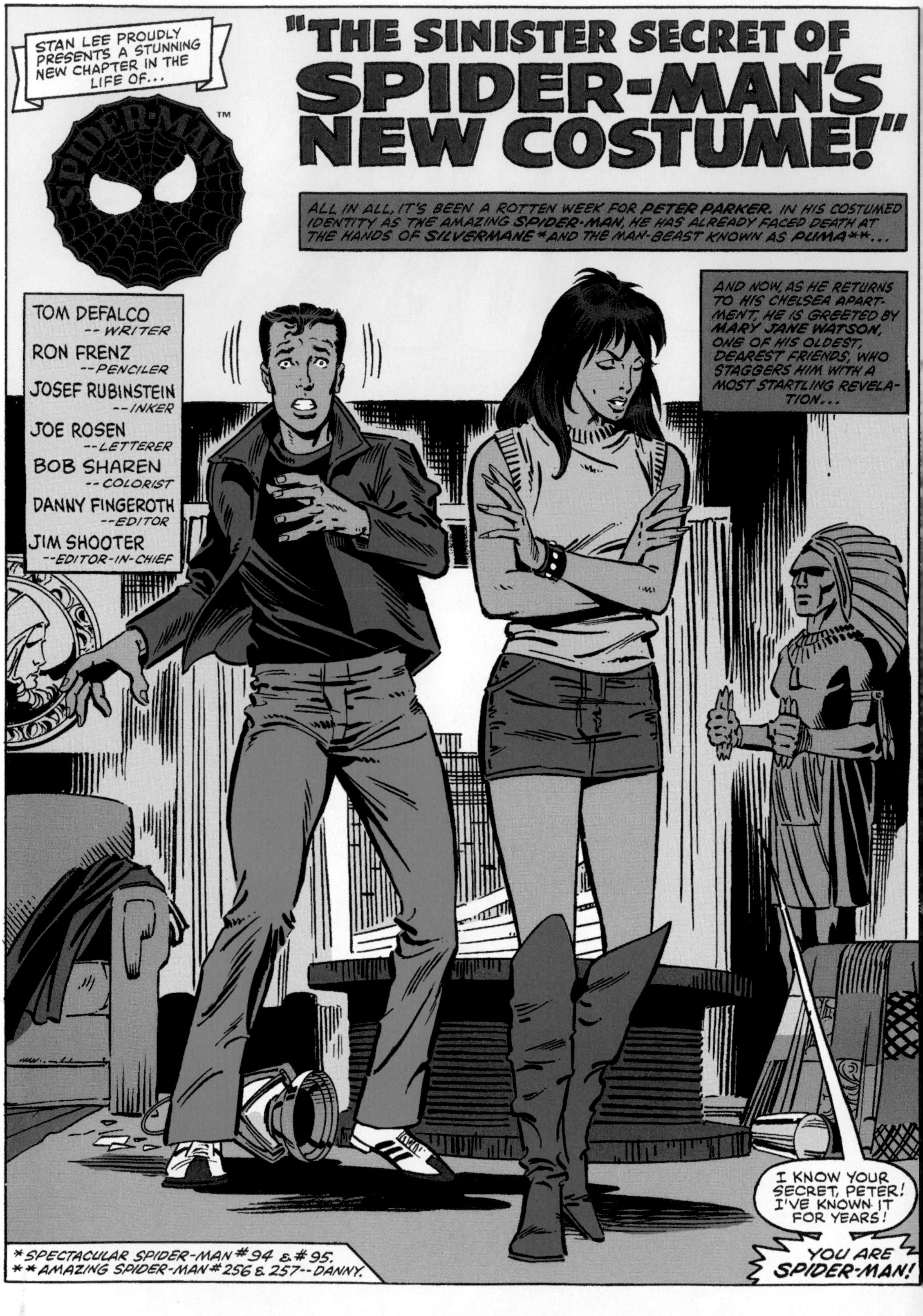
STAN LEE PROUDLY PRESENTS A STUNNING NEW CHAPTER IN THE LIFE OF...
SPIDER-MAN ™
"THE SINISTER SECRET OF SPIDER-MAN'S NEW COSTUME!"
ALL IN ALL, IT'S BEEN A ROTTEN WEEK FOR PETER PARKER. IN HIS COSTUMED IDENTITY AS THE AMAZING SPIDER-MAN, HE HAS ALREADY FACED DEATH AT THE HANDS OF SILVERMANE* AND THE MAN-BEAST KNOWN AS PUMA**...
AND NOW, AS HE RETURNS TO HIS CHELSEA APARTMENT, HE IS GREETED BY MARY JANE WATSON, ONE OF HIS OLDEST, DEAREST FRIENDS, WHO STAGGERS HIM WITH A MOST STARTLING REVELATION...
TOM DEFALCO -- WRITER
RON FRENZ -- PENCILER
JOSEF RUBINSTEIN -- INKER
JOE ROSEN -- LETTERER
BOB SHAREN -- COLORIST
DANNY FINGEROTH -- EDITOR
JIM SHOOTER -- EDITOR-IN-CHIEF
I KNOW YOUR SECRET, PETER! I'VE KNOWN IT FOR YEARS!
YOU ARE SPIDER-MAN!
*SPECTACULAR SPIDER-MAN #94 & #95.
**AMAZING SPIDER-MAN #256 & 257--DANNY.

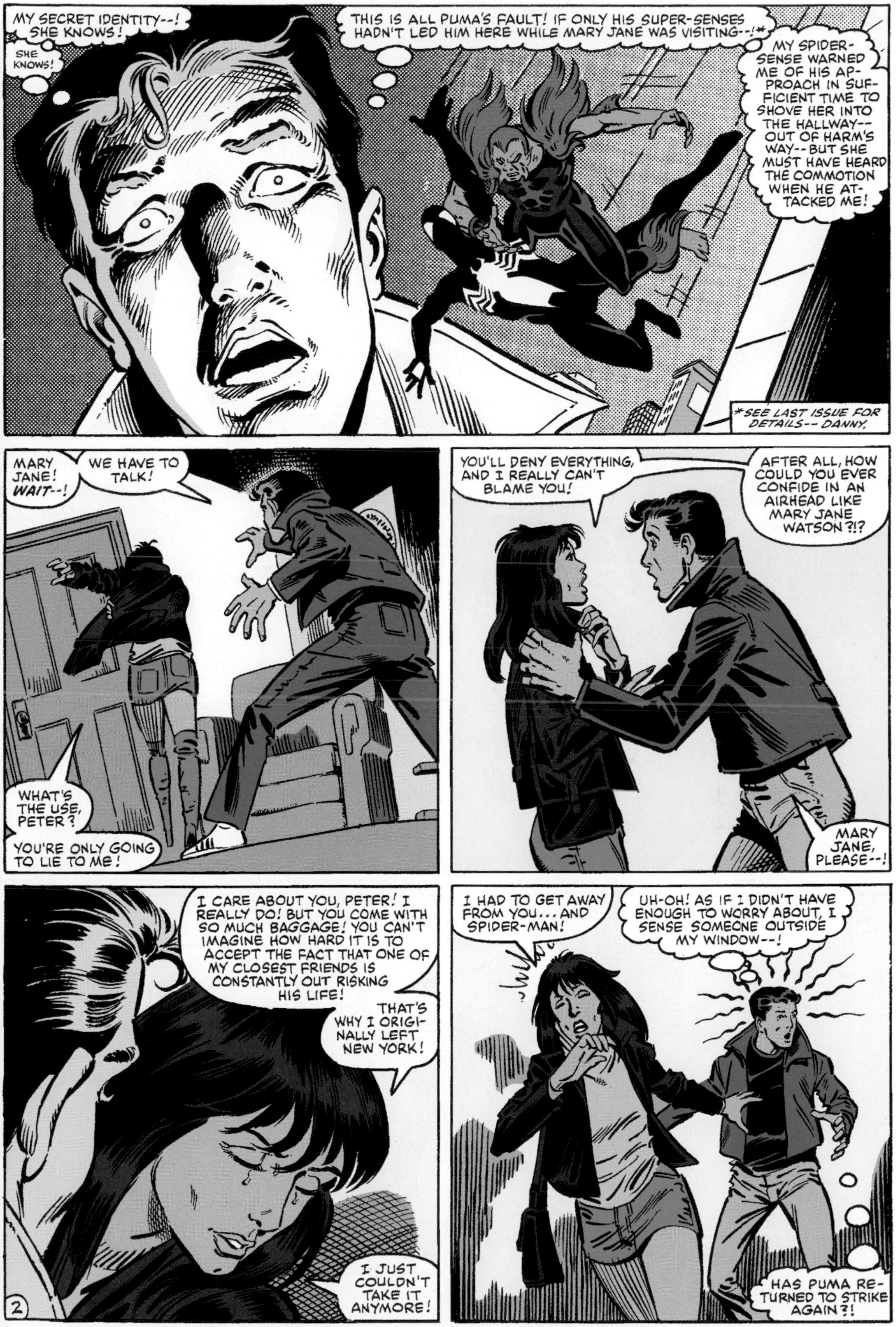
MY SECRET IDENTITY--! SHE KNOWS!
SHE KNOWS!
THIS IS ALL PUMA'S FAULT! IF ONLY HIS SUPER-SENSES HADN'T LED HIM HERE WHILE MARY JANE WAS VISITING--!*
MY SPIDER-SENSE WARNED ME OF HIS APPROACH IN SUFFICIENT TIME TO SHOVE HER INTO THE HALLWAY--OUT OF HARM'S WAY--BUT SHE MUST HAVE HEARD THE COMMOTION WHEN HE ATTACKED ME!
*SEE LAST ISSUE FOR DETAILS-- DANNY.
MARY JANE! WAIT--!
WE HAVE TO TALK!
WHAT'S THE USE, PETER?
YOU'RE ONLY GOING TO LIE TO ME!
YOU'LL DENY EVERYTHING, AND I REALLY CAN'T BLAME YOU!
AFTER ALL, HOW COULD YOU EVER CONFIDE IN AN AIRHEAD LIKE MARY JANE WATSON?!?
MARY JANE, PLEASE--!
I CARE ABOUT YOU, PETER! I REALLY DO! BUT YOU COME WITH SO MUCH BAGGAGE! YOU CAN'T IMAGINE HOW HARD IT IS TO ACCEPT THE FACT THAT ONE OF MY CLOSEST FRIENDS IS CONSTANTLY OUT RISKING HIS LIFE!
THAT'S WHY I ORIGINALLY LEFT NEW YORK!
I JUST COULDN'T TAKE IT ANYMORE!
2
I HAD TO GET AWAY FROM YOU... AND SPIDER-MAN!
UH-OH! AS IF I DIDN'T HAVE ENOUGH TO WORRY ABOUT, I SENSE SOMEONE OUTSIDE MY WINDOW--!
HAS PUMA RETURNED TO STRIKE AGAIN?!

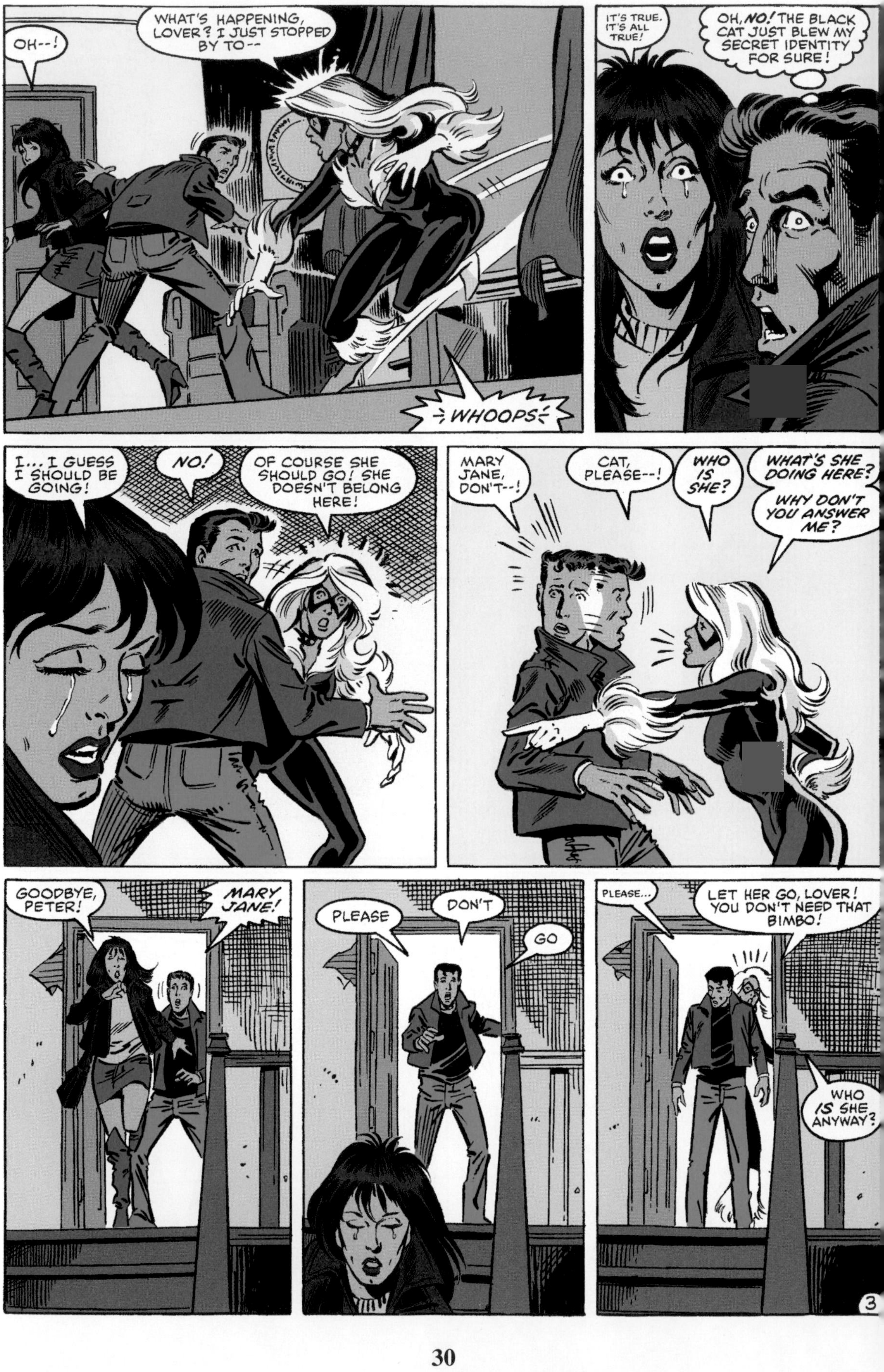
OH--!
WHAT'S HAPPENING, LOVER? I JUST STOPPED BY TO--
WHOOPS
IT'S TRUE. IT'S ALL TRUE!
OH, NO! THE BLACK CAT JUST BLEW MY SECRET IDENTITY FOR SURE!
I... I GUESS I SHOULD BE GOING!
NO!
OF COURSE SHE SHOULD GO! SHE DOESN'T BELONG HERE!
MARY JANE, DON'T--!
CAT, PLEASE--!
WHO IS SHE?
WHAT'S SHE DOING HERE?
WHY DON'T YOU ANSWER ME?
GOODBYE, PETER!
MARY JANE!
PLEASE
DON'T
GO
PLEASE...
LET HER GO, LOVER! YOU DON'T NEED THAT BIMBO!
WHO IS SHE ANYWAY?
3

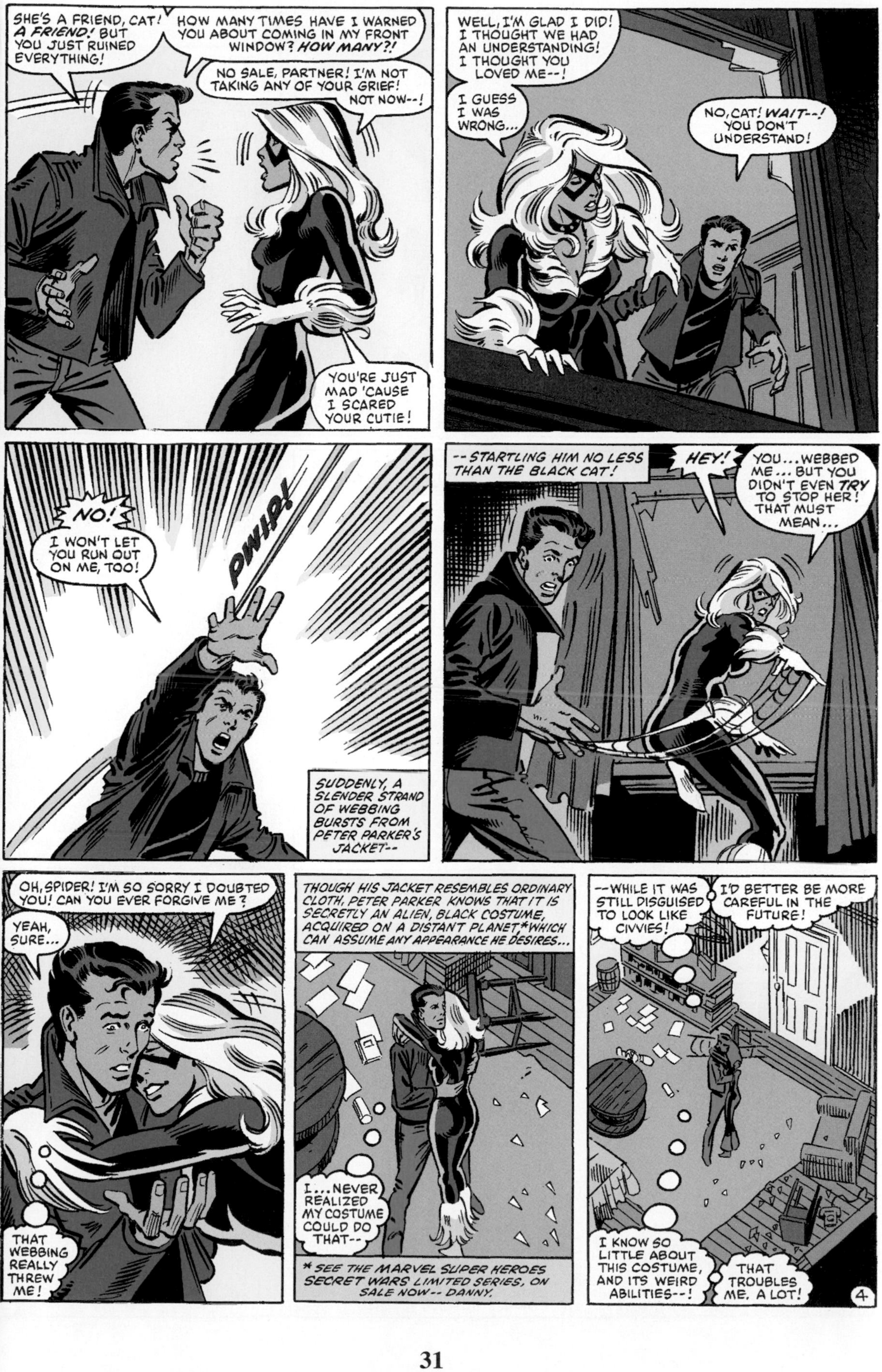

SHE'S A FRIEND, CAT! A FRIEND! BUT YOU JUST RUINED EVERYTHING!
HOW MANY TIMES HAVE I WARNED YOU ABOUT COMING IN MY FRONT WINDOW? HOW MANY?!
NO SALE, PARTNER! I'M NOT TAKING ANY OF YOUR GRIEF! NOT NOW--!
YOU'RE JUST MAD 'CAUSE I SCARED YOUR CUTIE!
WELL, I'M GLAD I DID! I THOUGHT WE HAD AN UNDERSTANDING! I THOUGHT YOU LOVED ME--!
I GUESS I WAS WRONG...
NO, CAT! WAIT--! YOU DON'T UNDERSTAND!
NO!
I WON'T LET YOU RUN OUT ON ME, TOO!
PWIP!
SUDDENLY, A SLENDER STRAND OF WEBBING BURSTS FROM PETER PARKER'S JACKET--
--STARTLING HIM NO LESS THAN THE BLACK CAT!
HEY!
YOU...WEBBED ME... BUT YOU DIDN'T EVEN TRY TO STOP HER! THAT MUST MEAN...
OH, SPIDER! I'M SO SORRY I DOUBTED YOU! CAN YOU EVER FORGIVE ME?
YEAH, SURE...
THAT WEBBING REALLY THREW ME!
THOUGH HIS JACKET RESEMBLES ORDINARY CLOTH, PETER PARKER KNOWS THAT IT IS SECRETLY AN ALIEN, BLACK COSTUME, ACQUIRED ON A DISTANT PLANET,* WHICH CAN ASSUME ANY APPEARANCE HE DESIRES...
I...NEVER REALIZED MY COSTUME COULD DO THAT--
* SEE THE MARVEL SUPER HEROES SECRET WARS LIMITED SERIES, ON SALE NOW -- DANNY.
--WHILE IT WAS STILL DISGUISED TO LOOK LIKE CIVVIES!
I'D BETTER BE MORE CAREFUL IN THE FUTURE!
I KNOW SO LITTLE ABOUT THIS COSTUME, AND ITS WEIRD ABILITIES--!
THAT TROUBLES ME. A LOT!
4

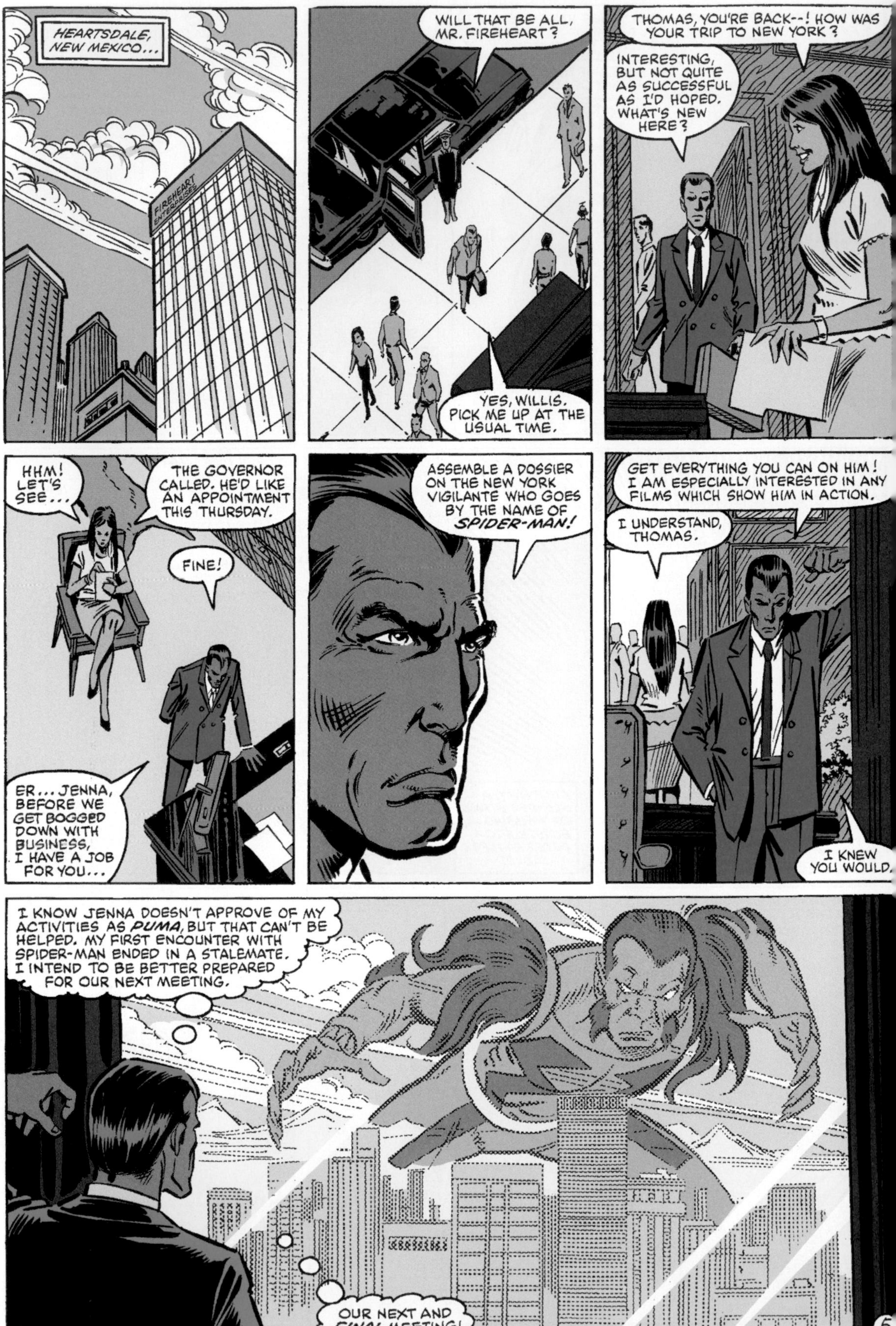

HEARTSDALE, NEW MEXICO...
FIREHEART ENTERPRISES
WILL THAT BE ALL, MR. FIREHEART?
YES, WILLIS. PICK ME UP AT THE USUAL TIME.
THOMAS, YOU'RE BACK--! HOW WAS YOUR TRIP TO NEW YORK?
INTERESTING, BUT NOT QUITE AS SUCCESSFUL AS I'D HOPED. WHAT'S NEW HERE?
HHM! LET'S SEE...
THE GOVERNOR CALLED. HE'D LIKE AN APPOINTMENT THIS THURSDAY.
FINE!
ER... JENNA, BEFORE WE GET BOGGED DOWN WITH BUSINESS, I HAVE A JOB FOR YOU...
ASSEMBLE A DOSSIER ON THE NEW YORK VIGILANTE WHO GOES BY THE NAME OF SPIDER-MAN!
GET EVERYTHING YOU CAN ON HIM! I AM ESPECIALLY INTERESTED IN ANY FILMS WHICH SHOW HIM IN ACTION.
I UNDERSTAND, THOMAS.
I KNEW YOU WOULD.
I KNOW JENNA DOESN'T APPROVE OF MY ACTIVITIES AS PUMA, BUT THAT CAN'T BE HELPED. MY FIRST ENCOUNTER WITH SPIDER-MAN ENDED IN A STALEMATE. I INTEND TO BE BETTER PREPARED FOR OUR NEXT MEETING.
OUR NEXT AND FINAL MEETING!
5

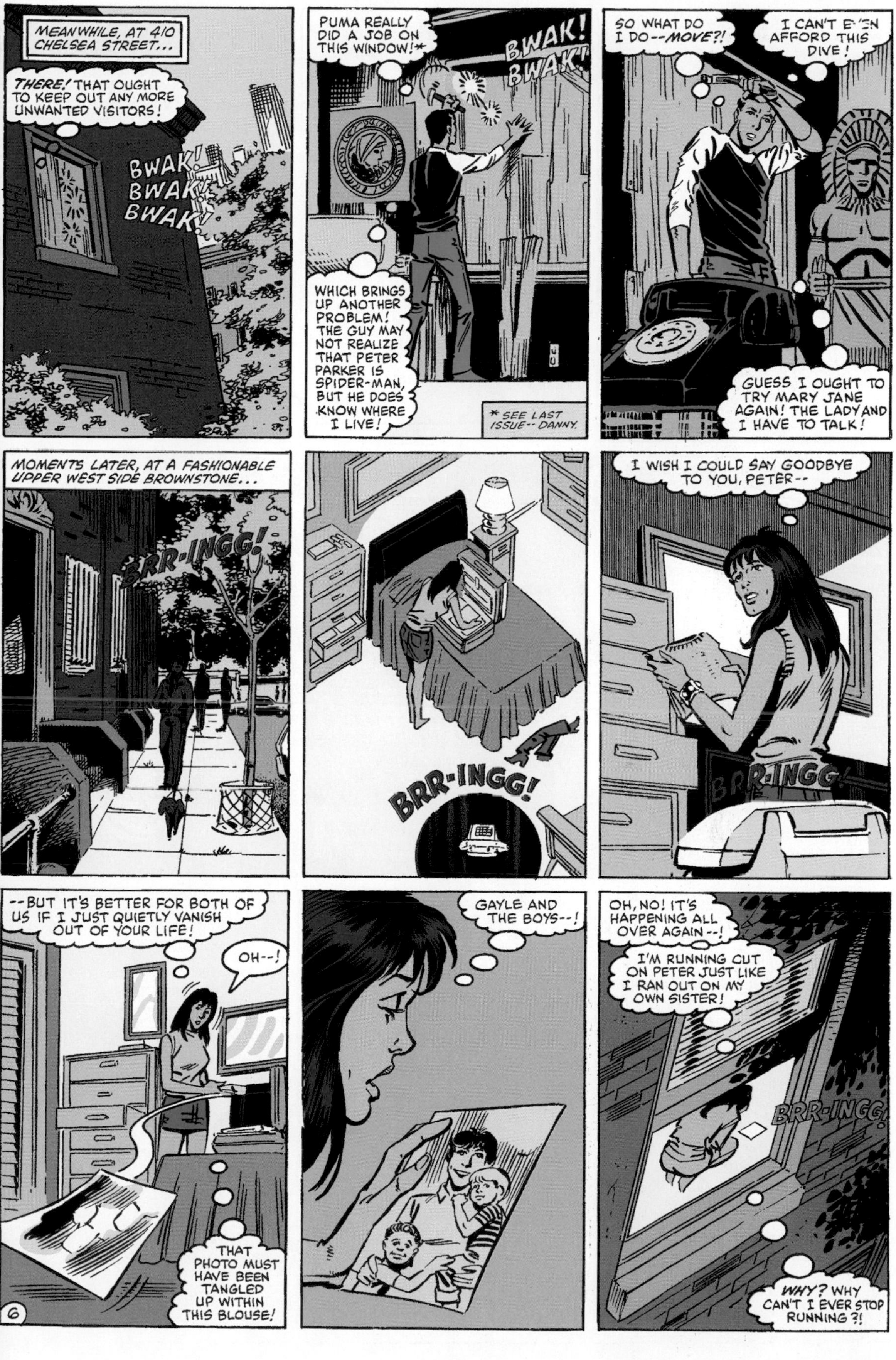

MEANWHILE, AT 410 CHELSEA STREET...
THERE! THAT OUGHT TO KEEP OUT ANY MORE UNWANTED VISITORS!
BWAK! BWAK! BWAK!
PUMA REALLY DID A JOB ON THIS WINDOW!*
BWAK! BWAK!
WHICH BRINGS UP ANOTHER PROBLEM! THE GUY MAY NOT REALIZE THAT PETER PARKER IS SPIDER-MAN, BUT HE DOES KNOW WHERE I LIVE!
* SEE LAST ISSUE-- DANNY.
SO WHAT DO I DO--MOVE?!
I CAN'T EVEN AFFORD THIS DIVE!
GUESS I OUGHT TO TRY MARY JANE AGAIN! THE LADY AND I HAVE TO TALK!
MOMENTS LATER, AT A FASHIONABLE UPPER WEST SIDE BROWNSTONE...
BRR-INGG!
BRR-INGG!
I WISH I COULD SAY GOODBYE TO YOU, PETER--
BRR-INGG!
--BUT IT'S BETTER FOR BOTH OF US IF I JUST QUIETLY VANISH OUT OF YOUR LIFE!
OH--!
THAT PHOTO MUST HAVE BEEN TANGLED UP WITHIN THIS BLOUSE!
6
GAYLE AND THE BOYS--!
OH, NO! IT'S HAPPENING ALL OVER AGAIN--!
I'M RUNNING OUT ON PETER JUST LIKE I RAN OUT ON MY OWN SISTER!
BRR-INGG!
WHY? WHY CAN'T I EVER STOP RUNNING?!

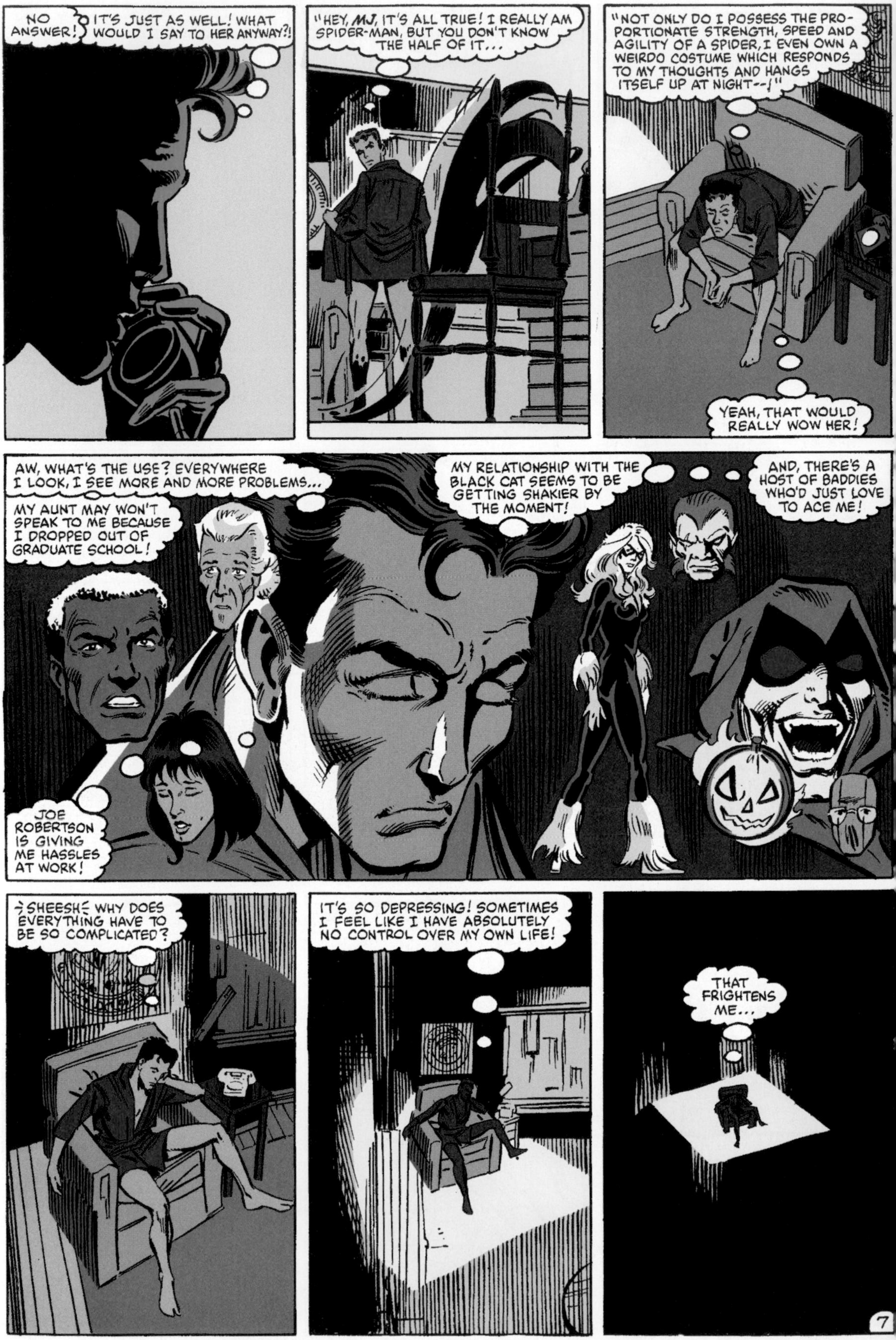

NO ANSWER!
IT'S JUST AS WELL! WHAT WOULD I SAY TO HER ANYWAY?!
"HEY, MJ, IT'S ALL TRUE! I REALLY AM SPIDER-MAN, BUT YOU DON'T KNOW THE HALF OF IT...
"NOT ONLY DO I POSSESS THE PROPORTIONATE STRENGTH, SPEED AND AGILITY OF A SPIDER, I EVEN OWN A WEIRDO COSTUME WHICH RESPONDS TO MY THOUGHTS AND HANGS ITSELF UP AT NIGHT--!"
YEAH, THAT WOULD REALLY WOW HER!
AW, WHAT'S THE USE? EVERYWHERE I LOOK, I SEE MORE AND MORE PROBLEMS...
MY AUNT MAY WON'T SPEAK TO ME BECAUSE I DROPPED OUT OF GRADUATE SCHOOL!
JOE ROBERTSON IS GIVING ME HASSLES AT WORK!
MY RELATIONSHIP WITH THE BLACK CAT SEEMS TO BE GETTING SHAKIER BY THE MOMENT!
AND, THERE'S A HOST OF BADDIES WHO'D JUST LOVE TO ACE ME!
-SHEESH- WHY DOES EVERYTHING HAVE TO BE SO COMPLICATED?
IT'S SO DEPRESSING! SOMETIMES I FEEL LIKE I HAVE ABSOLUTELY NO CONTROL OVER MY OWN LIFE!
THAT FRIGHTENS ME...
7

SOON, A TROUBLED SLEEP CLAIMS THE TIRED, BROODING YOUNG MAN. BUT, SHORTLY AFTER IT DOES...

...HIS UNCANNY COSTUME BEGINS TO STIR!

SERPENTLIKE, IT GLIDES ACROSS THE FLOOR, REACHING FOR HIM--

--FLOWING OVER HIM, UNTIL IT COVERS HIS ENTIRE BODY!

AND THEN...

AND YET, EVEN THOUGH SPIDER-MAN HAUNTS THIS NIGHT, AGILELY SPRINGING FROM ROOFTOP TO ROOFTOP...

...IF WE COULD PEER BENEATH HIS MASK, WE WOULD SEE THAT PETER PARKER IS OBLIVIOUS TO ALL!

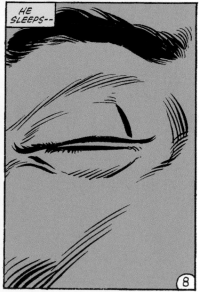

HE SLEEPS--

⑧

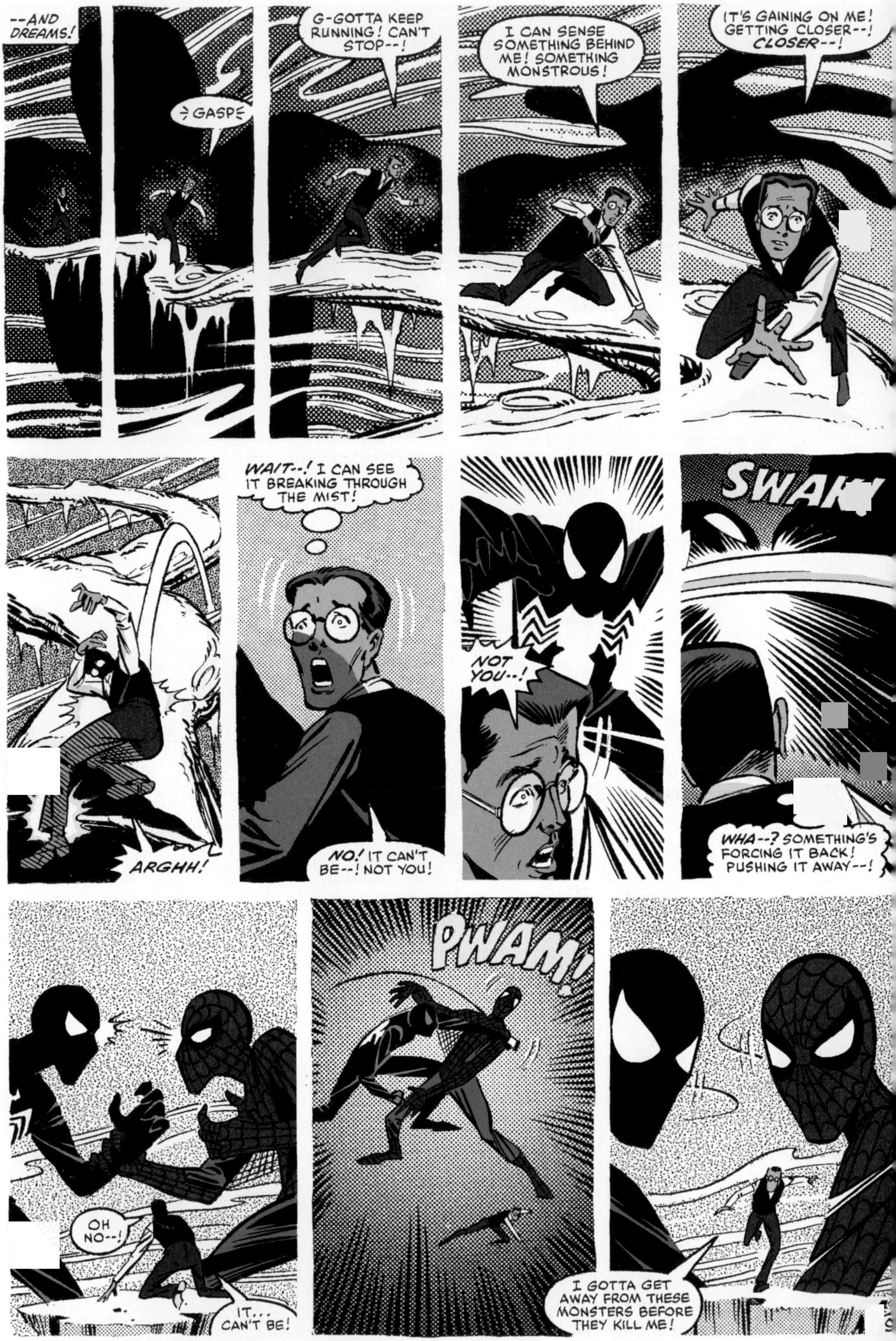
--AND DREAMS!
GASP
G-GOTTA KEEP RUNNING! CAN'T STOP--!
I CAN SENSE SOMETHING BEHIND ME! SOMETHING MONSTROUS!
IT'S GAINING ON ME! GETTING CLOSER--! CLOSER--!
ARGHH!
WAIT--! I CAN SEE IT BREAKING THROUGH THE MIST!
NO! IT CAN'T BE--! NOT YOU!
NOT YOU--!
SWA
WHA--? SOMETHING'S FORCING IT BACK! PUSHING IT AWAY--!
OH NO--!
IT... CAN'T BE!
PWAM!
I GOTTA GET AWAY FROM THESE MONSTERS BEFORE THEY KILL ME!

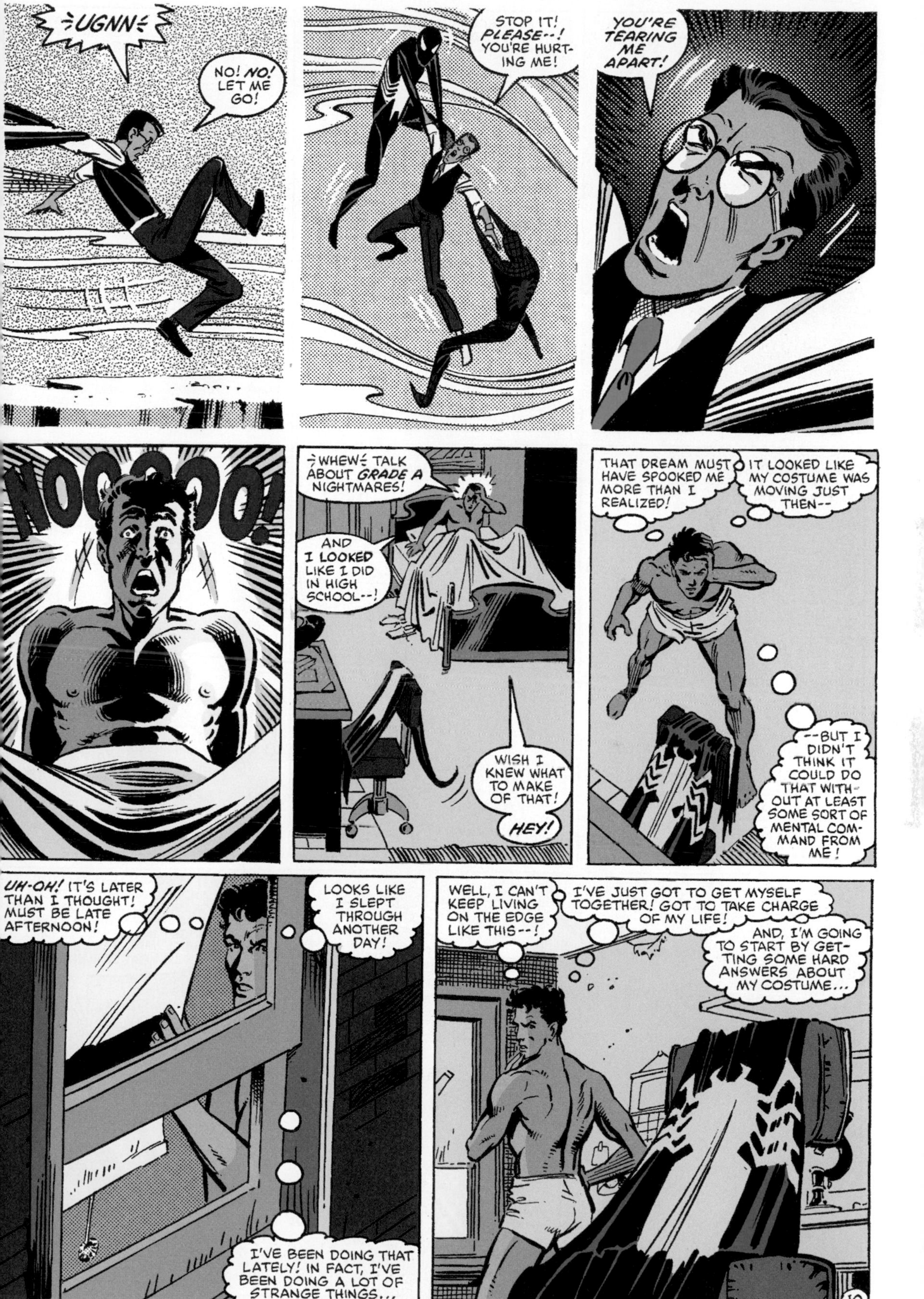
UGNN
NO! NO! LET ME GO!
STOP IT! PLEASE--! YOU'RE HURTING ME!
YOU'RE TEARING ME APART!
NOOOOO!
WHEW TALK ABOUT GRADE A NIGHTMARES!
AND I LOOKED LIKE I DID IN HIGH SCHOOL--!
WISH I KNEW WHAT TO MAKE OF THAT!
HEY!
THAT DREAM MUST HAVE SPOOKED ME MORE THAN I REALIZED!
IT LOOKED LIKE MY COSTUME WAS MOVING JUST THEN--
--BUT I DIDN'T THINK IT COULD DO THAT WITHOUT AT LEAST SOME SORT OF MENTAL COMMAND FROM ME!
UH-OH! IT'S LATER THAN I THOUGHT! MUST BE LATE AFTERNOON!
LOOKS LIKE I SLEPT THROUGH ANOTHER DAY!
I'VE BEEN DOING THAT LATELY! IN FACT, I'VE BEEN DOING A LOT OF STRANGE THINGS...
WELL, I CAN'T KEEP LIVING ON THE EDGE LIKE THIS--!
I'VE JUST GOT TO GET MYSELF TOGETHER! GOT TO TAKE CHARGE OF MY LIFE!
AND, I'M GOING TO START BY GETTING SOME HARD ANSWERS ABOUT MY COSTUME...
10

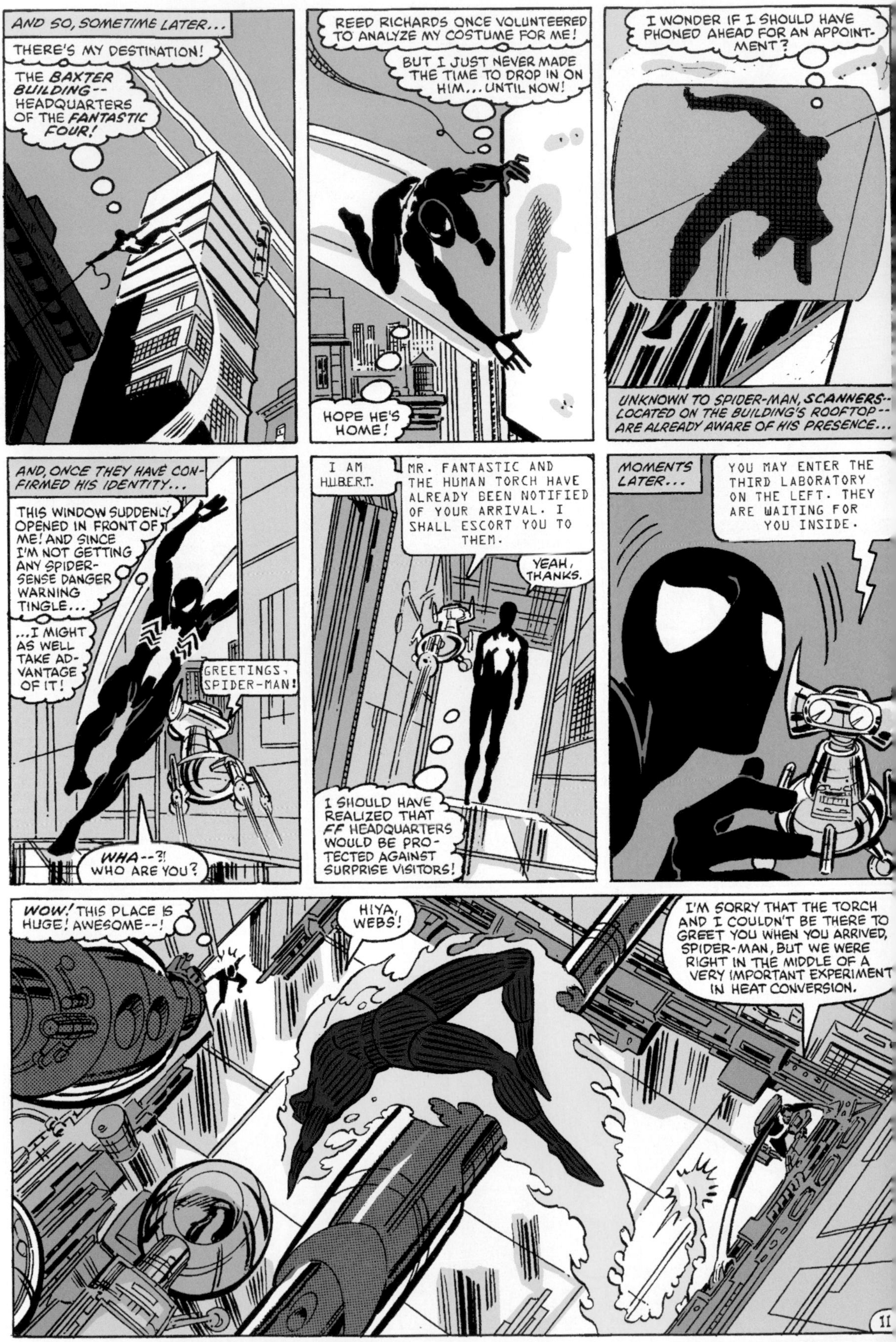
AND SO, SOMETIME LATER...
THERE'S MY DESTINATION!
THE BAXTER BUILDING-- HEADQUARTERS OF THE FANTASTIC FOUR!
REED RICHARDS ONCE VOLUNTEERED TO ANALYZE MY COSTUME FOR ME!
BUT I JUST NEVER MADE THE TIME TO DROP IN ON HIM... UNTIL NOW!
HOPE HE'S HOME!
I WONDER IF I SHOULD HAVE PHONED AHEAD FOR AN APPOINT-MENT?
UNKNOWN TO SPIDER-MAN, SCANNERS-- LOCATED ON THE BUILDING'S ROOFTOP-- ARE ALREADY AWARE OF HIS PRESENCE...
AND, ONCE THEY HAVE CONFIRMED HIS IDENTITY...
THIS WINDOW SUDDENLY OPENED IN FRONT OF ME! AND SINCE I'M NOT GETTING ANY SPIDER-SENSE DANGER WARNING TINGLE...
...I MIGHT AS WELL TAKE ADVANTAGE OF IT!
GREETINGS, SPIDER-MAN!
WHA--?! WHO ARE YOU?
I AM H.U.B.E.R.T.
MR. FANTASTIC AND THE HUMAN TORCH HAVE ALREADY BEEN NOTIFIED OF YOUR ARRIVAL. I SHALL ESCORT YOU TO THEM.
YEAH, THANKS.
I SHOULD HAVE REALIZED THAT FF HEADQUARTERS WOULD BE PROTECTED AGAINST SURPRISE VISITORS!
MOMENTS LATER...
YOU MAY ENTER THE THIRD LABORATORY ON THE LEFT. THEY ARE WAITING FOR YOU INSIDE.
WOW! THIS PLACE IS HUGE! AWESOME--!
HIYA, WEBS!
I'M SORRY THAT THE TORCH AND I COULDN'T BE THERE TO GREET YOU WHEN YOU ARRIVED, SPIDER-MAN, BUT WE WERE RIGHT IN THE MIDDLE OF A VERY IMPORTANT EXPERIMENT IN HEAT CONVERSION.
11

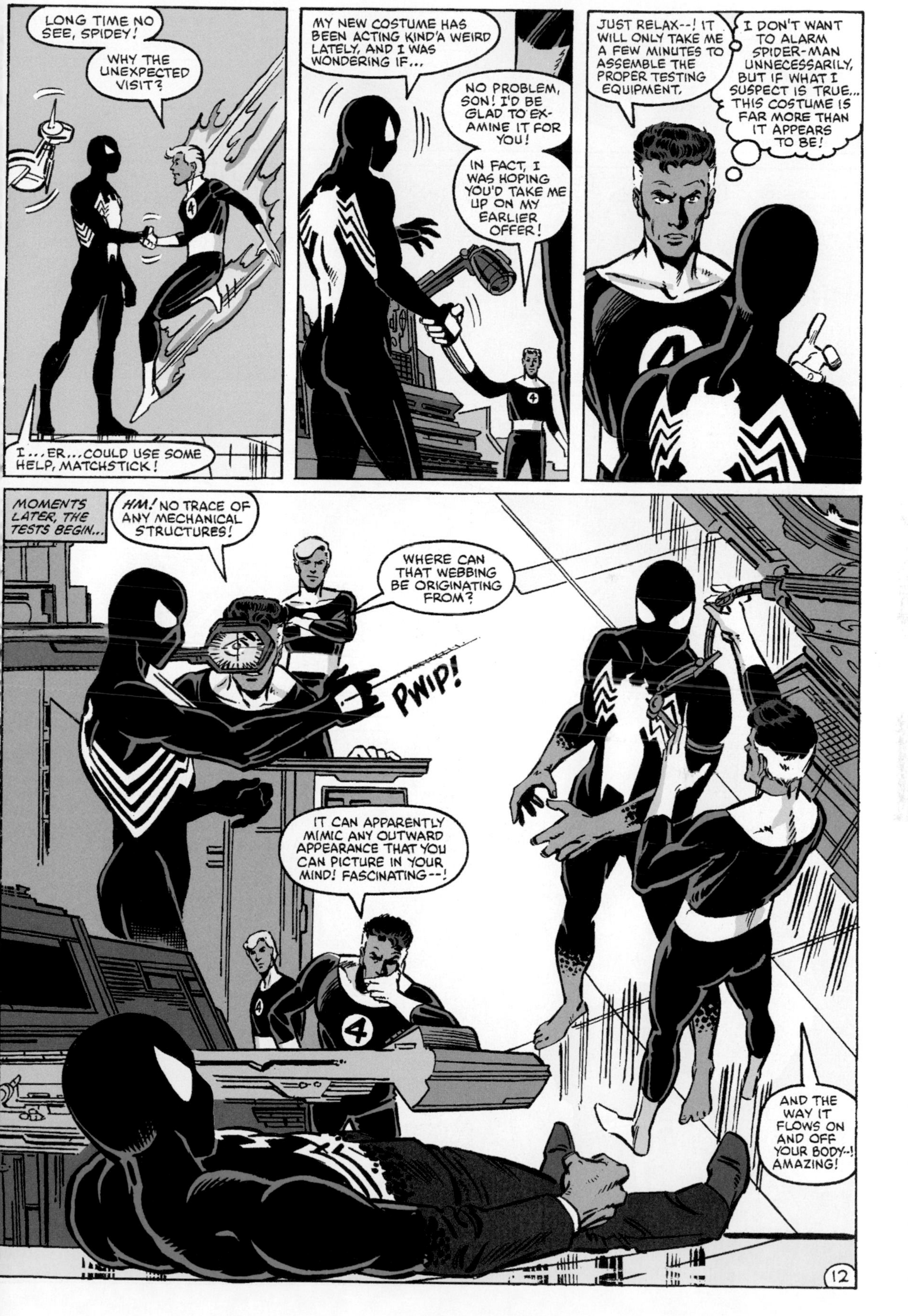
LONG TIME NO SEE, SPIDEY!
WHY THE UNEXPECTED VISIT?
I...ER...COULD USE SOME HELP, MATCHSTICK!
MY NEW COSTUME HAS BEEN ACTING KIND'A WEIRD LATELY, AND I WAS WONDERING IF...
NO PROBLEM, SON! I'D BE GLAD TO EX-AMINE IT FOR YOU!
IN FACT, I WAS HOPING YOU'D TAKE ME UP ON MY EARLIER OFFER!
JUST RELAX--! IT WILL ONLY TAKE ME A FEW MINUTES TO ASSEMBLE THE PROPER TESTING EQUIPMENT.
I DON'T WANT TO ALARM SPIDER-MAN UNNECESSARILY, BUT IF WHAT I SUSPECT IS TRUE... THIS COSTUME IS FAR MORE THAN IT APPEARS TO BE!
MOMENTS LATER, THE TESTS BEGIN...
HM! NO TRACE OF ANY MECHANICAL STRUCTURES!
WHERE CAN THAT WEBBING BE ORIGINATING FROM?
PWIP!
IT CAN APPARENTLY MIMIC ANY OUTWARD APPEARANCE THAT YOU CAN PICTURE IN YOUR MIND! FASCINATING--!
AND THE WAY IT FLOWS ON AND OFF YOUR BODY--! AMAZING!
12

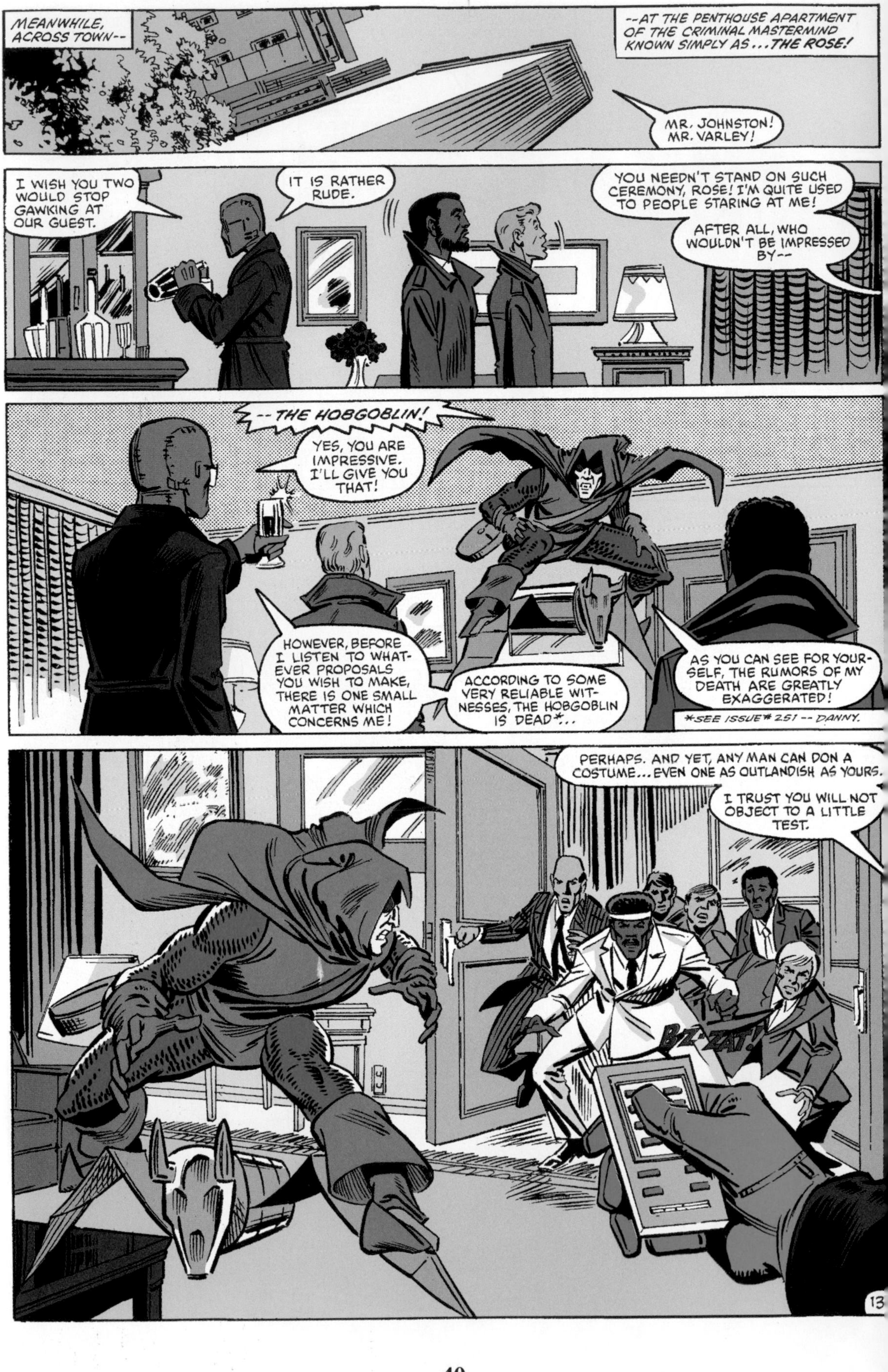
MEANWHILE, ACROSS TOWN--
--AT THE PENTHOUSE APARTMENT OF THE CRIMINAL MASTERMIND KNOWN SIMPLY AS... THE ROSE!
MR. JOHNSTON! MR. VARLEY!
I WISH YOU TWO WOULD STOP GAWKING AT OUR GUEST.
IT IS RATHER RUDE.
YOU NEEDN'T STAND ON SUCH CEREMONY, ROSE! I'M QUITE USED TO PEOPLE STARING AT ME!
AFTER ALL, WHO WOULDN'T BE IMPRESSED BY--
--THE HOBGOBLIN!
YES, YOU ARE IMPRESSIVE. I'LL GIVE YOU THAT!
HOWEVER, BEFORE I LISTEN TO WHATEVER PROPOSALS YOU WISH TO MAKE, THERE IS ONE SMALL MATTER WHICH CONCERNS ME!
ACCORDING TO SOME VERY RELIABLE WITNESSES, THE HOBGOBLIN IS DEAD*...
AS YOU CAN SEE FOR YOURSELF, THE RUMORS OF MY DEATH ARE GREATLY EXAGGERATED!
*SEE ISSUE# 251 -- DANNY.
PERHAPS. AND YET, ANY MAN CAN DON A COSTUME... EVEN ONE AS OUTLANDISH AS YOURS.
I TRUST YOU WILL NOT OBJECT TO A LITTLE TEST.
BZ-ZAT!
13

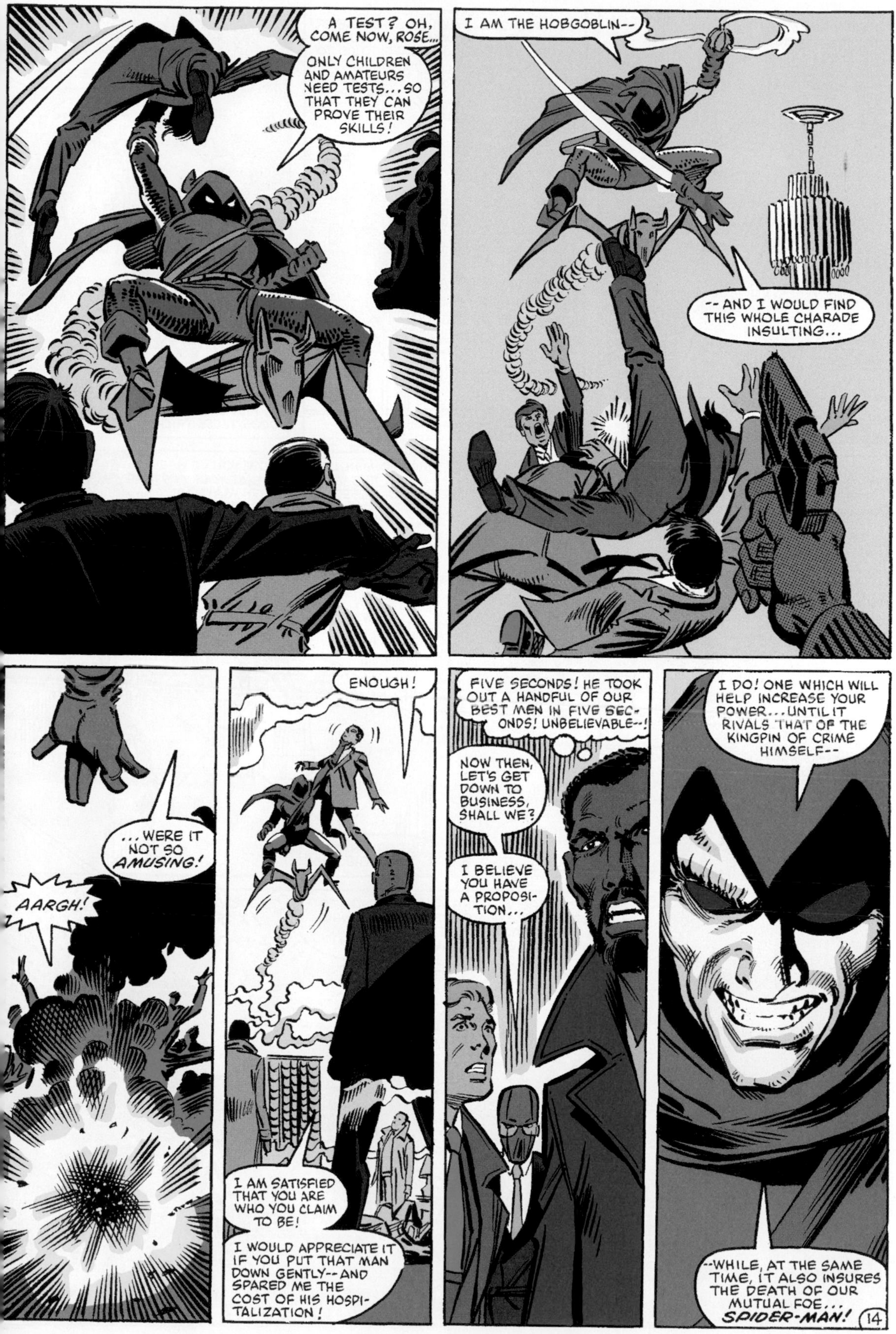
A TEST? OH, COME NOW, ROSE...
ONLY CHILDREN AND AMATEURS NEED TESTS... SO THAT THEY CAN PROVE THEIR SKILLS!
I AM THE HOBGOBLIN--
--AND I WOULD FIND THIS WHOLE CHARADE INSULTING...
...WERE IT NOT SO AMUSING!
AARGH!
ENOUGH!
I AM SATISFIED THAT YOU ARE WHO YOU CLAIM TO BE!
I WOULD APPRECIATE IT IF YOU PUT THAT MAN DOWN GENTLY--AND SPARED ME THE COST OF HIS HOSPITALIZATION!
FIVE SECONDS! HE TOOK OUT A HANDFUL OF OUR BEST MEN IN FIVE SECONDS! UNBELIEVABLE--!
NOW THEN, LET'S GET DOWN TO BUSINESS, SHALL WE?
I BELIEVE YOU HAVE A PROPOSITION...
I DO! ONE WHICH WILL HELP INCREASE YOUR POWER... UNTIL IT RIVALS THAT OF THE KINGPIN OF CRIME HIMSELF--
--WHILE, AT THE SAME TIME, IT ALSO INSURES THE DEATH OF OUR MUTUAL FOE... SPIDER-MAN!
14

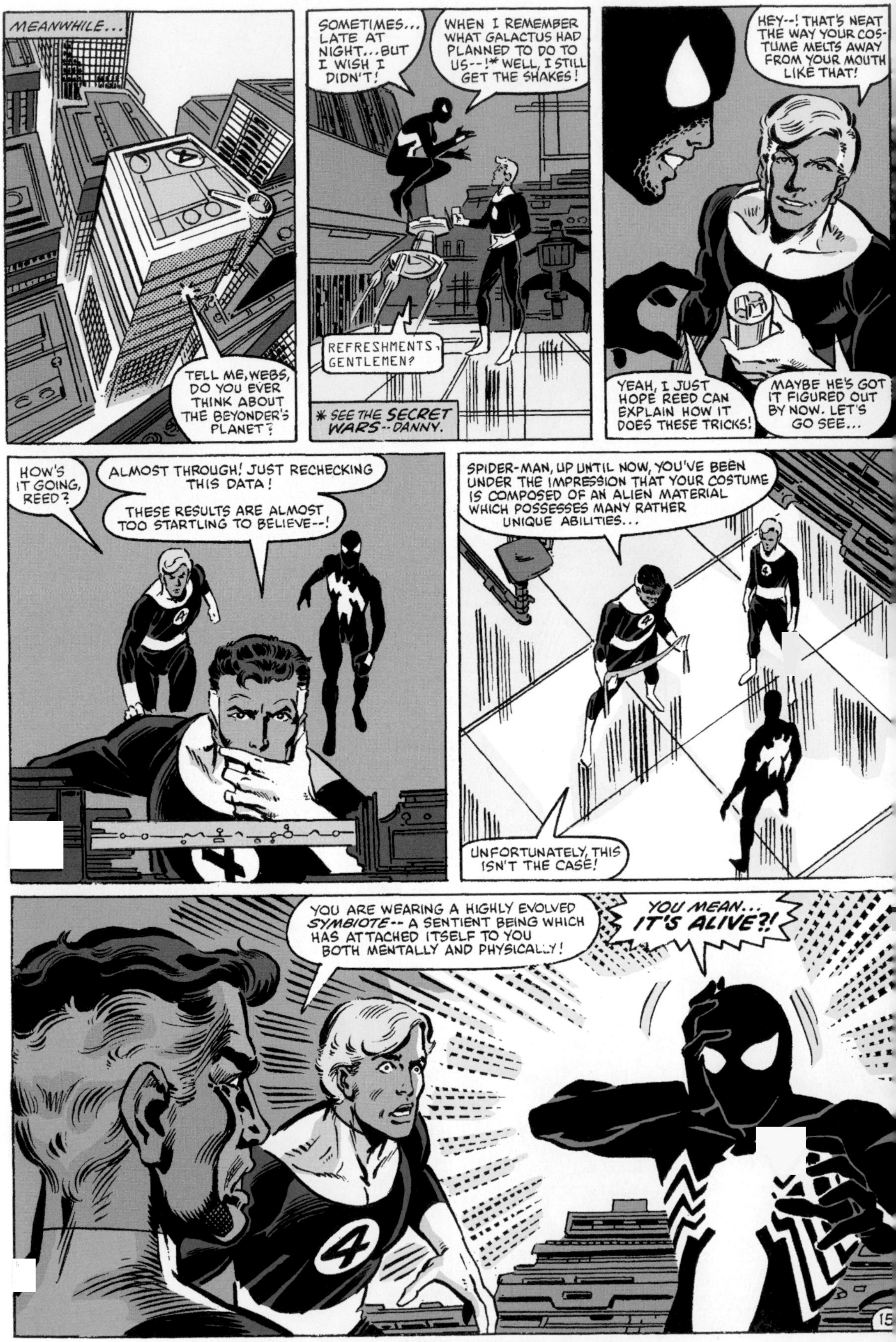
MEANWHILE...
TELL ME, WEBS, DO YOU EVER THINK ABOUT THE BEYONDER'S PLANET?
SOMETIMES... LATE AT NIGHT... BUT I WISH I DIDN'T!
WHEN I REMEMBER WHAT GALACTUS HAD PLANNED TO DO TO US--!* WELL, I STILL GET THE SHAKES!
REFRESHMENTS, GENTLEMEN?
* SEE THE SECRET WARS--DANNY.
HEY--! THAT'S NEAT THE WAY YOUR COSTUME MELTS AWAY FROM YOUR MOUTH LIKE THAT!
YEAH, I JUST HOPE REED CAN EXPLAIN HOW IT DOES THESE TRICKS!
MAYBE HE'S GOT IT FIGURED OUT BY NOW. LET'S GO SEE...
HOW'S IT GOING, REED?
ALMOST THROUGH! JUST RECHECKING THIS DATA!
THESE RESULTS ARE ALMOST TOO STARTLING TO BELIEVE--!
SPIDER-MAN, UP UNTIL NOW, YOU'VE BEEN UNDER THE IMPRESSION THAT YOUR COSTUME IS COMPOSED OF AN ALIEN MATERIAL WHICH POSSESSES MANY RATHER UNIQUE ABILITIES...
UNFORTUNATELY, THIS ISN'T THE CASE!
YOU ARE WEARING A HIGHLY EVOLVED SYMBIOTE-- A SENTIENT BEING WHICH HAS ATTACHED ITSELF TO YOU BOTH MENTALLY AND PHYSICALLY!
YOU MEAN... IT'S ALIVE?!
15

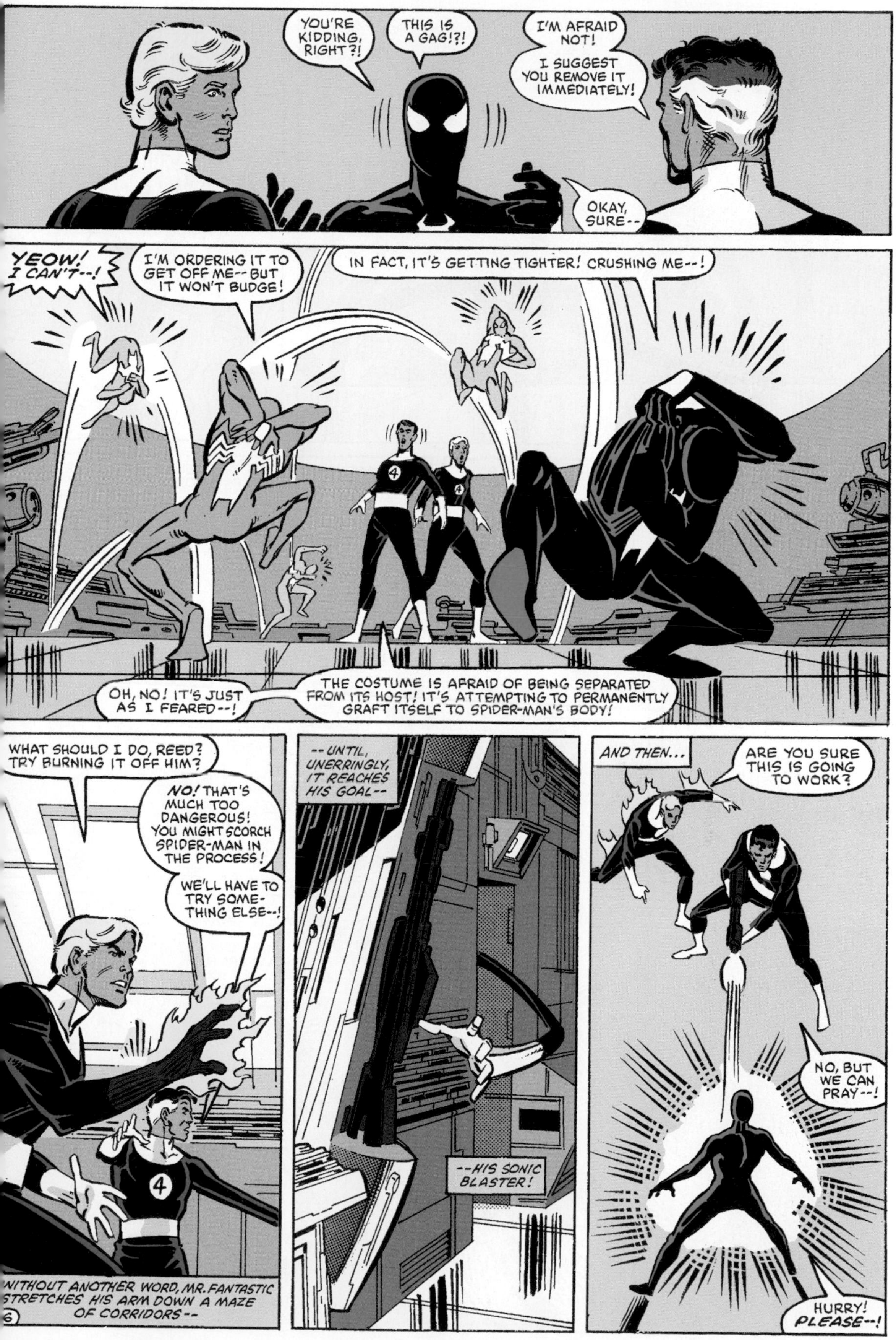

YOU'RE KIDDING, RIGHT?!
THIS IS A GAG!?!
I'M AFRAID NOT!
I SUGGEST YOU REMOVE IT IMMEDIATELY!
OKAY, SURE--
YEOW! I CAN'T--!
I'M ORDERING IT TO GET OFF ME-- BUT IT WON'T BUDGE!
IN FACT, IT'S GETTING TIGHTER! CRUSHING ME--!
OH, NO! IT'S JUST AS I FEARED--!
THE COSTUME IS AFRAID OF BEING SEPARATED FROM ITS HOST! IT'S ATTEMPTING TO PERMANENTLY GRAFT ITSELF TO SPIDER-MAN'S BODY!
WHAT SHOULD I DO, REED? TRY BURNING IT OFF HIM?
NO! THAT'S MUCH TOO DANGEROUS! YOU MIGHT SCORCH SPIDER-MAN IN THE PROCESS!
WE'LL HAVE TO TRY SOME-THING ELSE--!
WITHOUT ANOTHER WORD, MR. FANTASTIC STRETCHES HIS ARM DOWN A MAZE OF CORRIDORS--
6
--UNTIL, UNERRINGLY, IT REACHES HIS GOAL--
--HIS SONIC BLASTER!
AND THEN...
ARE YOU SURE THIS IS GOING TO WORK?
NO, BUT WE CAN PRAY--!
HURRY! PLEASE--!

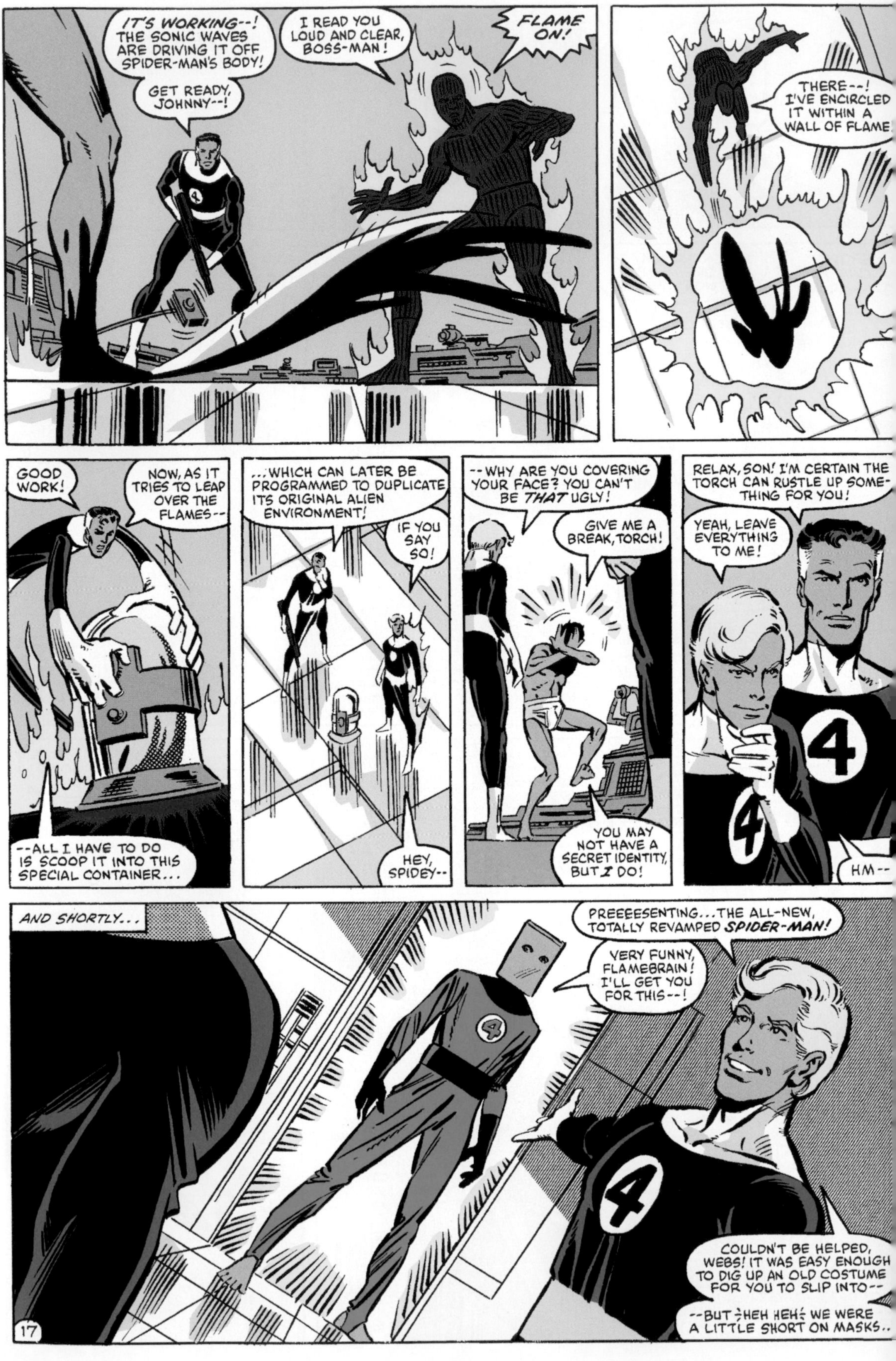
IT'S WORKING--! THE SONIC WAVES ARE DRIVING IT OFF SPIDER-MAN'S BODY!
GET READY, JOHNNY--!
I READ YOU LOUD AND CLEAR, BOSS-MAN!
FLAME ON!
THERE--! I'VE ENCIRCLED IT WITHIN A WALL OF FLAME
GOOD WORK!
NOW, AS IT TRIES TO LEAP OVER THE FLAMES--
--ALL I HAVE TO DO IS SCOOP IT INTO THIS SPECIAL CONTAINER...
...WHICH CAN LATER BE PROGRAMMED TO DUPLICATE ITS ORIGINAL ALIEN ENVIRONMENT!
IF YOU SAY SO!
HEY, SPIDEY--
--WHY ARE YOU COVERING YOUR FACE? YOU CAN'T BE THAT UGLY!
GIVE ME A BREAK, TORCH!
YOU MAY NOT HAVE A SECRET IDENTITY, BUT I DO!
RELAX, SON! I'M CERTAIN THE TORCH CAN RUSTLE UP SOMETHING FOR YOU!
YEAH, LEAVE EVERYTHING TO ME!
HM--
AND SHORTLY...
PREEEESENTING...THE ALL-NEW, TOTALLY REVAMPED SPIDER-MAN!
VERY FUNNY, FLAMEBRAIN! I'LL GET YOU FOR THIS--!
COULDN'T BE HELPED, WEBS! IT WAS EASY ENOUGH TO DIG UP AN OLD COSTUME FOR YOU TO SLIP INTO--
--BUT -HEH HEH- WE WERE A LITTLE SHORT ON MASKS..
17

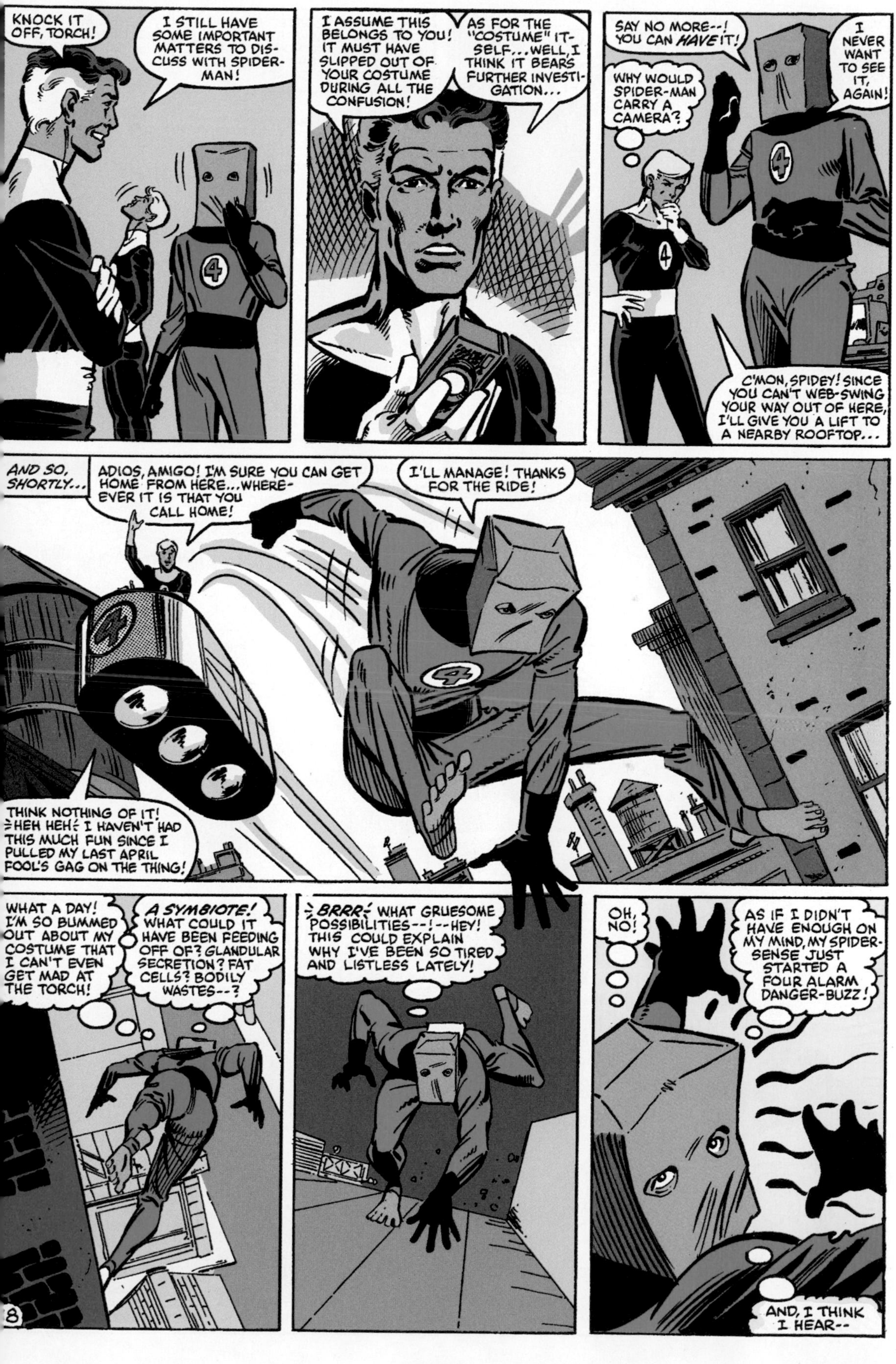
KNOCK IT OFF, TORCH!
I STILL HAVE SOME IMPORTANT MATTERS TO DISCUSS WITH SPIDER-MAN!
I ASSUME THIS BELONGS TO YOU! IT MUST HAVE SLIPPED OUT OF YOUR COSTUME DURING ALL THE CONFUSION!
AS FOR THE "COSTUME" IT-SELF...WELL, I THINK IT BEARS FURTHER INVESTIGATION...
SAY NO MORE--! YOU CAN HAVE IT!
I NEVER WANT TO SEE IT, AGAIN!
WHY WOULD SPIDER-MAN CARRY A CAMERA?
C'MON, SPIDEY! SINCE YOU CAN'T WEB-SWING YOUR WAY OUT OF HERE, I'LL GIVE YOU A LIFT TO A NEARBY ROOFTOP...
AND SO, SHORTLY...
ADIOS, AMIGO! I'M SURE YOU CAN GET HOME FROM HERE...WHERE-EVER IT IS THAT YOU CALL HOME!
I'LL MANAGE! THANKS FOR THE RIDE!
THINK NOTHING OF IT! =HEH HEH= I HAVEN'T HAD THIS MUCH FUN SINCE I PULLED MY LAST APRIL FOOL'S GAG ON THE THING!
WHAT A DAY! I'M SO BUMMED OUT ABOUT MY COSTUME THAT I CAN'T EVEN GET MAD AT THE TORCH!
A SYMBIOTE! WHAT COULD IT HAVE BEEN FEEDING OFF OF? GLANDULAR SECRETION? FAT CELLS? BODILY WASTES--?
8
=BRRR= WHAT GRUESOME POSSIBILITIES--!--HEY! THIS COULD EXPLAIN WHY I'VE BEEN SO TIRED AND LISTLESS LATELY!
OH, NO!
AS IF I DIDN'T HAVE ENOUGH ON MY MIND, MY SPIDER-SENSE JUST STARTED A FOUR ALARM DANGER-BUZZ!
AND, I THINK I HEAR--

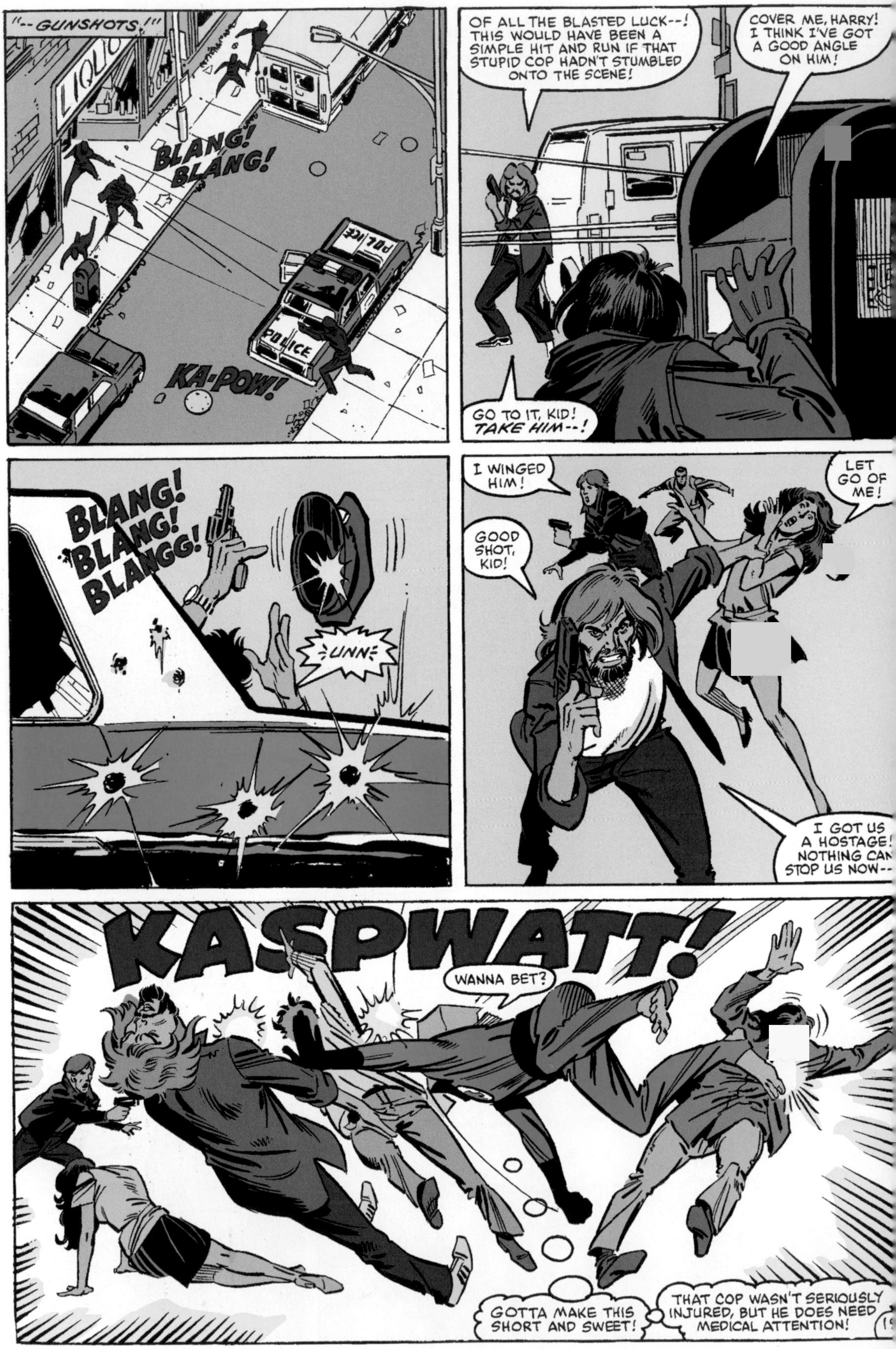
"--GUNSHOTS!"
BLANG! BLANG!
POLICE
KA-POW!
OF ALL THE BLASTED LUCK--! THIS WOULD HAVE BEEN A SIMPLE HIT AND RUN IF THAT STUPID COP HADN'T STUMBLED ONTO THE SCENE!
COVER ME, HARRY! I THINK I'VE GOT A GOOD ANGLE ON HIM!
GO TO IT, KID! TAKE HIM--!
BLANG! BLANG! BLANGG!
UNN
I WINGED HIM!
GOOD SHOT, KID!
LET GO OF ME!
I GOT US A HOSTAGE! NOTHING CAN STOP US NOW--
KASPWATT!
WANNA BET?
GOTTA MAKE THIS SHORT AND SWEET!
THAT COP WASN'T SERIOUSLY INJURED, BUT HE DOES NEED MEDICAL ATTENTION!

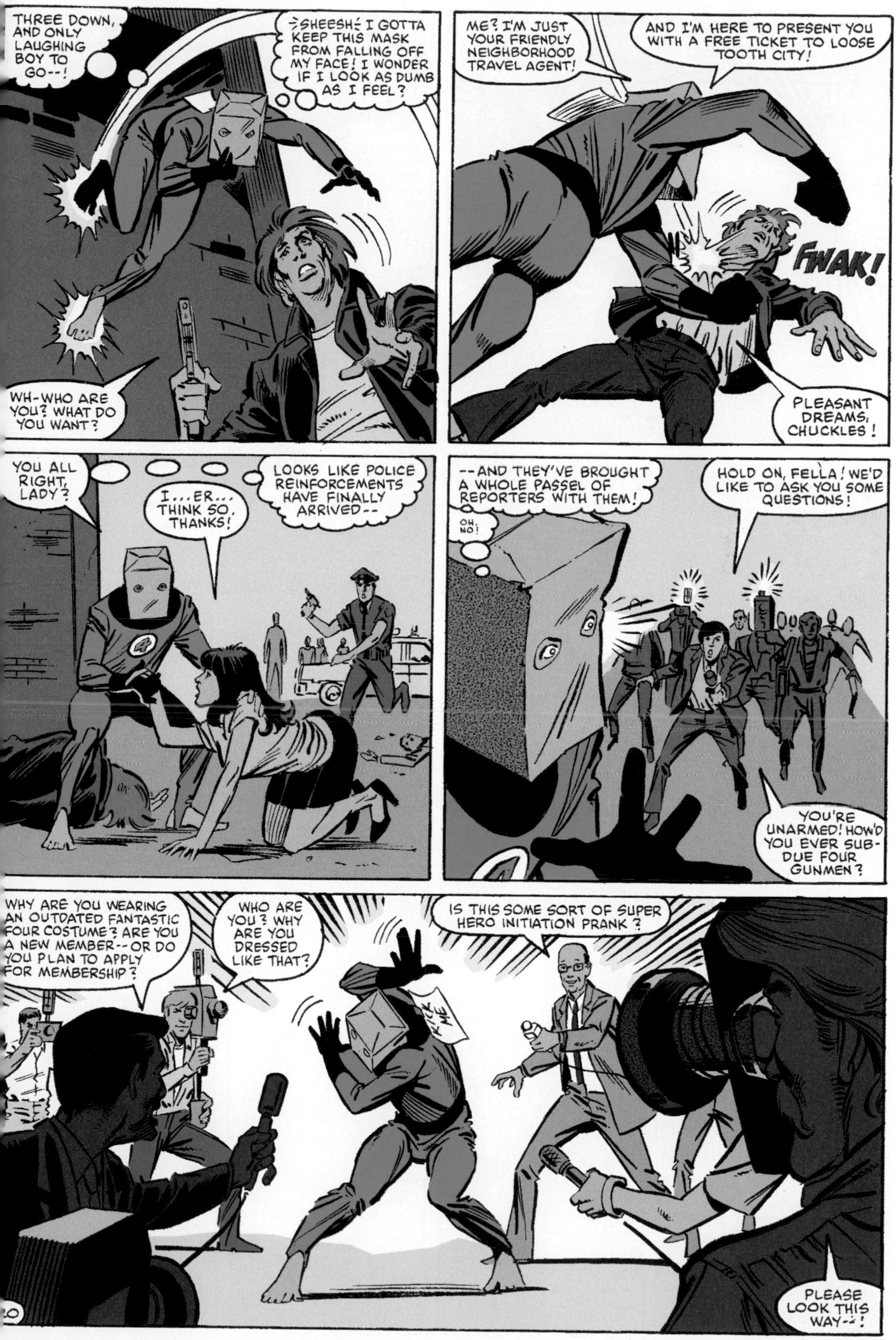

THREE DOWN, AND ONLY LAUGHING BOY TO GO--!
=SHEESH= I GOTTA KEEP THIS MASK FROM FALLING OFF MY FACE! I WONDER IF I LOOK AS DUMB AS I FEEL?
WH-WHO ARE YOU? WHAT DO YOU WANT?
ME? I'M JUST YOUR FRIENDLY NEIGHBORHOOD TRAVEL AGENT!
AND I'M HERE TO PRESENT YOU WITH A FREE TICKET TO LOOSE TOOTH CITY!
FWAK!
PLEASANT DREAMS, CHUCKLES!
YOU ALL RIGHT, LADY?
I...ER... THINK SO. THANKS!
LOOKS LIKE POLICE REINFORCEMENTS HAVE FINALLY ARRIVED--
--AND THEY'VE BROUGHT A WHOLE PASSEL OF REPORTERS WITH THEM!
OH, NO!
HOLD ON, FELLA! WE'D LIKE TO ASK YOU SOME QUESTIONS!
YOU'RE UNARMED! HOW'D YOU EVER SUB-DUE FOUR GUNMEN?
WHY ARE YOU WEARING AN OUTDATED FANTASTIC FOUR COSTUME? ARE YOU A NEW MEMBER--OR DO YOU PLAN TO APPLY FOR MEMBERSHIP?
WHO ARE YOU? WHY ARE YOU DRESSED LIKE THAT?
IS THIS SOME SORT OF SUPER HERO INITIATION PRANK?
KICK ME
PLEASE LOOK THIS WAY--!

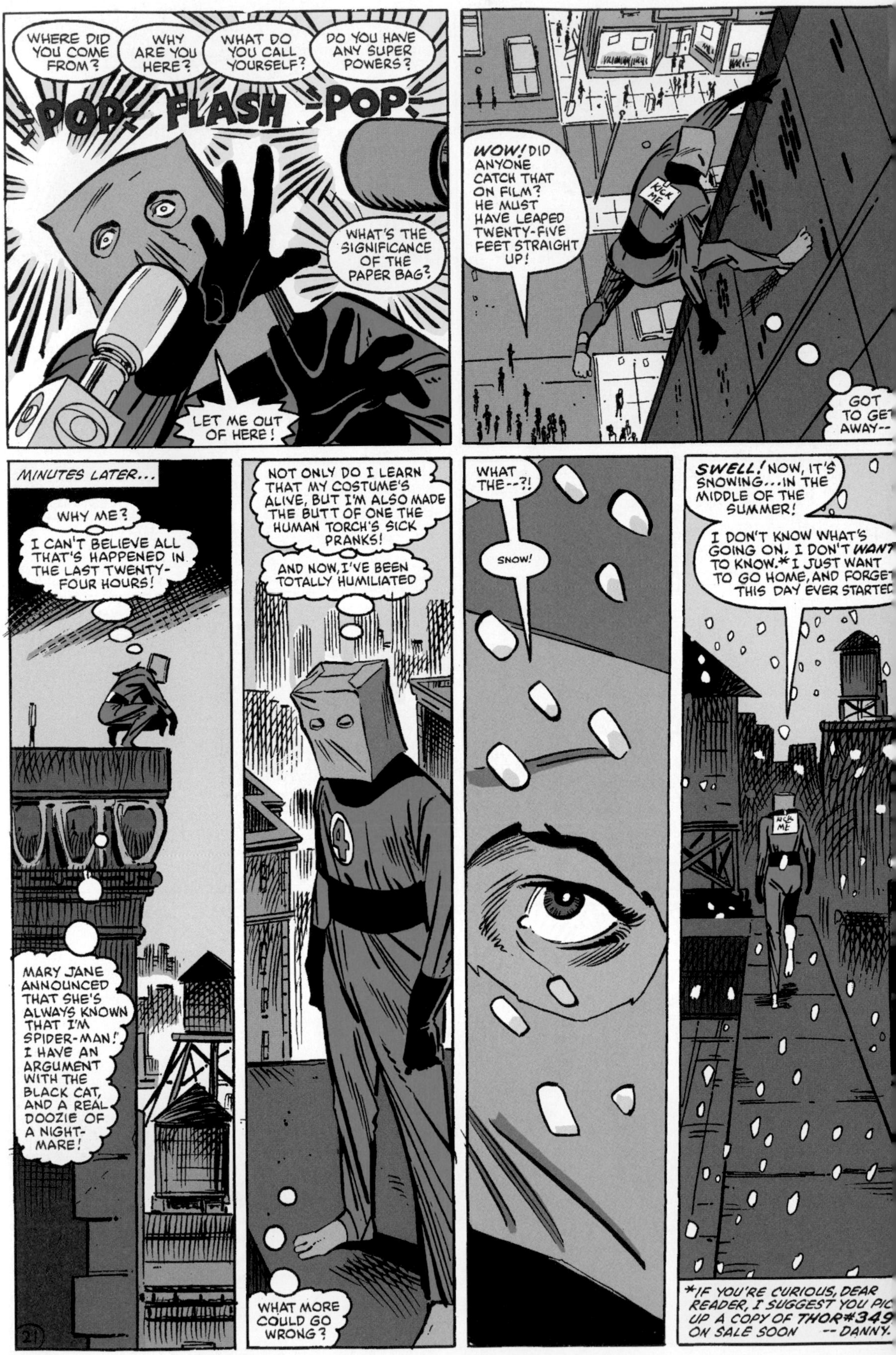
WHERE DID YOU COME FROM?
WHY ARE YOU HERE?
WHAT DO YOU CALL YOURSELF?
DO YOU HAVE ANY SUPER POWERS?
POP FLASH POP
WHAT'S THE SIGNIFICANCE OF THE PAPER BAG?
LET ME OUT OF HERE!
WOW! DID ANYONE CATCH THAT ON FILM? HE MUST HAVE LEAPED TWENTY-FIVE FEET STRAIGHT UP!
KICK ME
GOT TO GET AWAY--
MINUTES LATER...
WHY ME?
I CAN'T BELIEVE ALL THAT'S HAPPENED IN THE LAST TWENTY-FOUR HOURS!
MARY JANE ANNOUNCED THAT SHE'S ALWAYS KNOWN THAT I'M SPIDER-MAN! I HAVE AN ARGUMENT WITH THE BLACK CAT, AND A REAL DOOZIE OF A NIGHT-MARE!
NOT ONLY DO I LEARN THAT MY COSTUME'S ALIVE, BUT I'M ALSO MADE THE BUTT OF ONE THE HUMAN TORCH'S SICK PRANKS!
AND NOW, I'VE BEEN TOTALLY HUMILIATED
WHAT MORE COULD GO WRONG?
WHAT THE--?!
SNOW!
SWELL! NOW, IT'S SNOWING...IN THE MIDDLE OF THE SUMMER!
I DON'T KNOW WHAT'S GOING ON. I DON'T WANT TO KNOW.* I JUST WANT TO GO HOME, AND FORGET THIS DAY EVER STARTED
KICK ME
*IF YOU'RE CURIOUS, DEAR READER, I SUGGEST YOU PICK UP A COPY OF THOR #349 ON SALE SOON --DANNY.
21

MUCH LATER...

...A SPOKESMAN FOR THE FANTASTIC FOUR DECLINED TO COMMENT TODAY ON THE SUDDEN APPEARANCE OF A NEW MASKED ADVENTURER! DUBBED THE "UNKNOWN SUPER HERO" BY THE PRESS--

-- HE WAS INSTRUMENTAL IN THE ARREST OF FOUR GUNMEN WHO WERE ALLEGEDLY ROBBING A LIQUOR STORE THIS AFTERNOON!

OFFICER WILLIAM SLATTERY, WHO WAS WOUNDED AT THE SCENE, IS PRESENTLY LISTED IN SATISFACTORY CONDITION...

DAY IN EVE WAY I AM GETTIN BETTE AND BETTE BURMA S

GOOD! I'M GLAD TO HEAR HE'S DOING OKAY!

HMMM... THESE OLD WEB-SHOOTERS ARE IN A SORRY STATE!

NOW THAT I'VE LOST MY BLACK COSTUME, IT'S GONNA TAKE ME AWHILE TO OUTFIT MYSELF AS SPIDER-MAN AGAIN...

LUCKILY, I STILL HAVE AN OLD RED AND BLUE COSTUME WHICH I CAN WEAR UNTIL... UH-OH!

KNOCK! KNOCK!

I'M COMING--!

MARY JANE--?!

HELLO, PETER, CAN I COME IN?

HAVE YOU SEEN THE WEATHER OUTSIDE? REAL WEIRD, HUH?

YEAH, BUT WE CAN TALK ABOUT THE WEATHER SOME OTHER TIME... I'VE, ER, BEEN TRYING TO CALL YOU!

I KNOW.

LOOK, PETER, I'M REAL SORRY I RAN OUT ON YOU YESTERDAY. IT WAS A ROTTEN THING TO DO.

MARY JANE, I...

NO, PETER. PLEASE LET ME FINISH...YOU SEE, I'VE BEEN DOING A LOT OF THINKING ABOUT YOU...ABOUT US...AND I'VE COME TO A DECISION.

I'VE KNOWN YOUR SECRETS FOR QUITE SOME TIME, BUT YOU'VE NEVER KNOWN MINE. WELL, I GUESS IT'S ONLY FAIR THAT YOU DO...

22

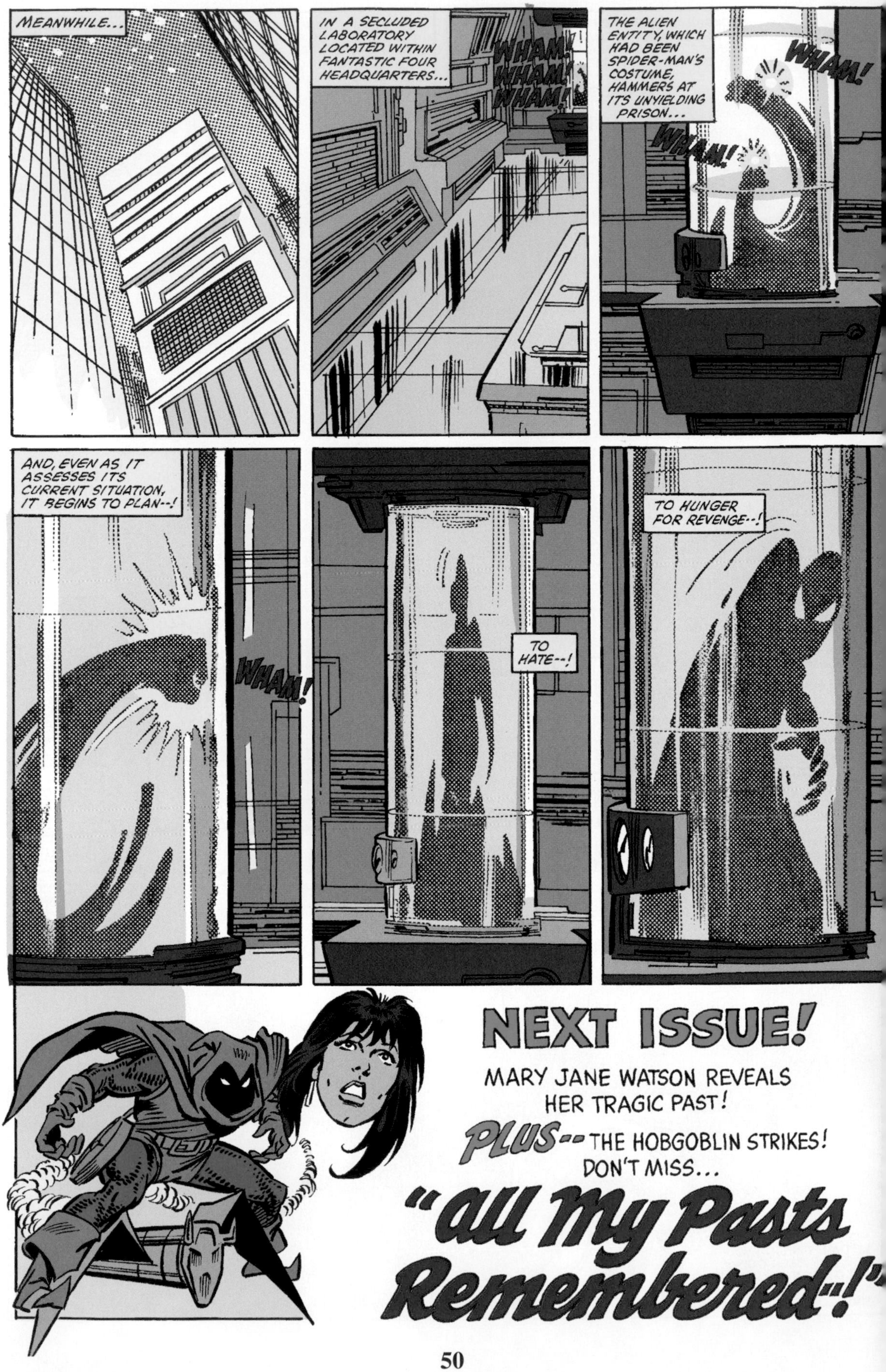
MEANWHILE...
IN A SECLUDED LABORATORY LOCATED WITHIN FANTASTIC FOUR HEADQUARTERS...
WHAM! WHAM! WHAM!
THE ALIEN ENTITY, WHICH HAD BEEN SPIDER-MAN'S COSTUME, HAMMERS AT ITS UNYIELDING PRISON...
WHAM!
WHAM!
AND, EVEN AS IT ASSESSES ITS CURRENT SITUATION, IT BEGINS TO PLAN--!
WHAM!
TO HATE--!
TO HUNGER FOR REVENGE--!
NEXT ISSUE!
MARY JANE WATSON REVEALS HER TRAGIC PAST!
PLUS-- THE HOBGOBLIN STRIKES!
DON'T MISS...
"All My Pasts Remembered--!"

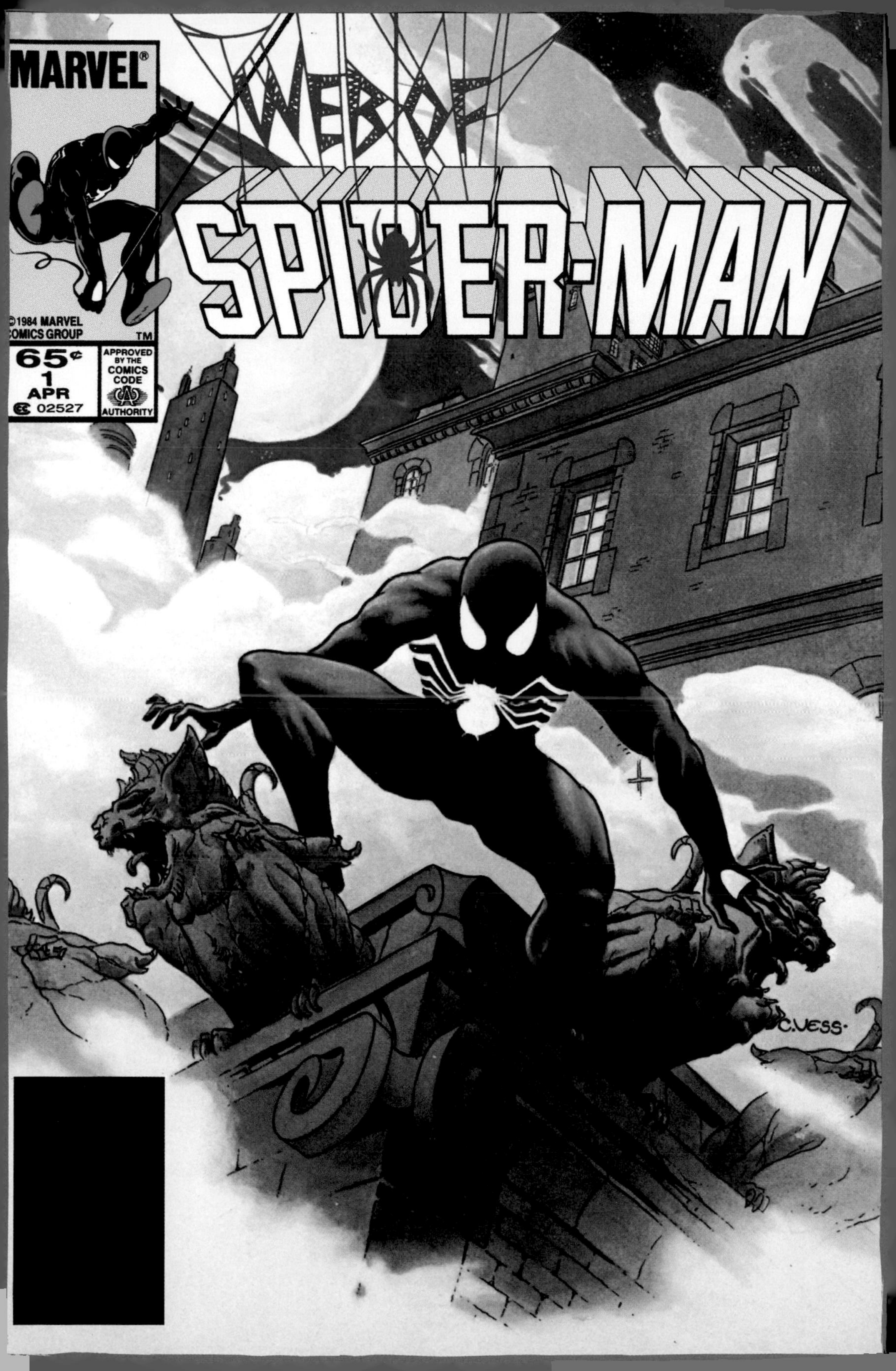
MARVEL®
©1984 MARVEL
COMICS GROUP
TM
65¢
1
APR
02527
APPROVED BY THE COMICS CODE AUTHORITY
WEB OF
SPIDER-MAN
TM
C.VESS·

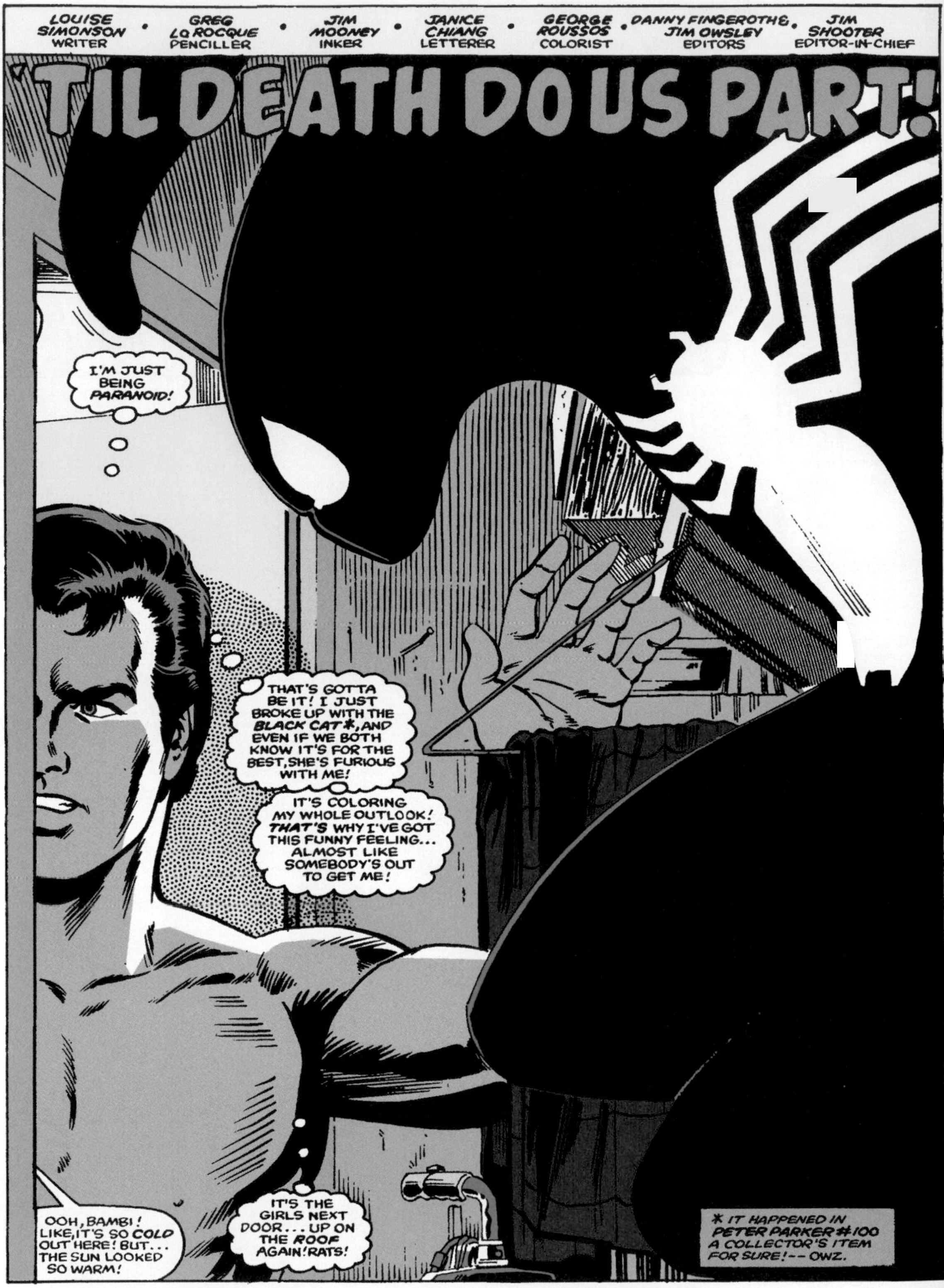
LOUISE SIMONSON WRITER • GREG LaROCQUE PENCILLER • JIM MOONEY INKER • JANICE CHIANG LETTERER • GEORGE ROUSSOS COLORIST • DANNY FINGEROTH & JIM OWSLEY EDITORS • JIM SHOOTER EDITOR-IN-CHIEF
'TIL DEATH DO US PART!
I'M JUST BEING PARANOID!
THAT'S GOTTA BE IT! I JUST BROKE UP WITH THE BLACK CAT*, AND EVEN IF WE BOTH KNOW IT'S FOR THE BEST, SHE'S FURIOUS WITH ME!
IT'S COLORING MY WHOLE OUTLOOK! THAT'S WHY I'VE GOT THIS FUNNY FEELING... ALMOST LIKE SOMEBODY'S OUT TO GET ME!
OOH, BAMBI! LIKE, IT'S SO COLD OUT HERE! BUT... THE SUN LOOKED SO WARM!
IT'S THE GIRLS NEXT DOOR... UP ON THE ROOF AGAIN! RATS!
* IT HAPPENED IN PETER PARKER #100 A COLLECTOR'S ITEM FOR SURE!-- OWZ.

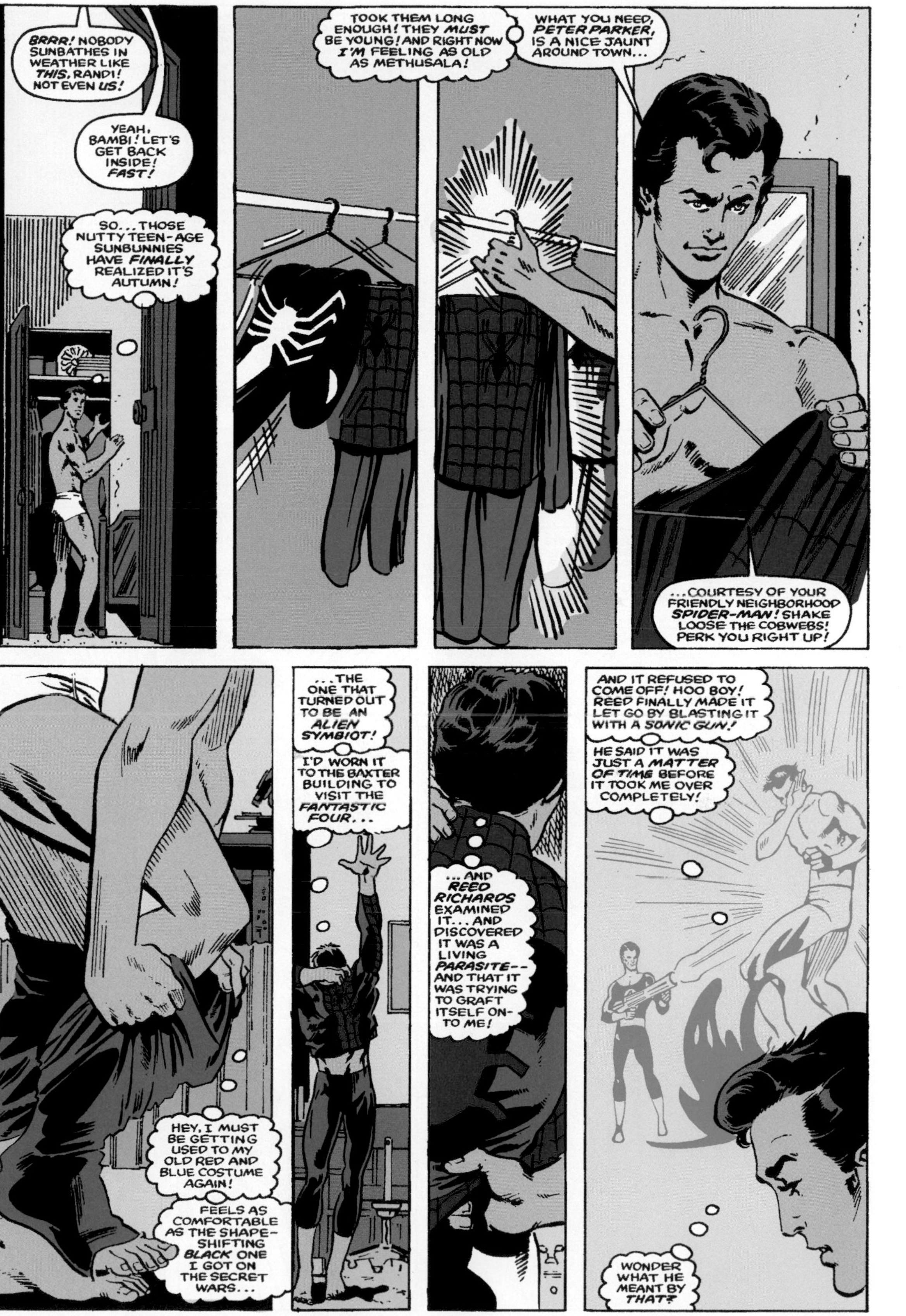
BRRR! NOBODY SUNBATHES IN WEATHER LIKE THIS, RANDI! NOT EVEN US!
YEAH, BAMBI! LET'S GET BACK INSIDE! FAST!
SO... THOSE NUTTY TEEN-AGE SUNBUNNIES HAVE FINALLY REALIZED IT'S AUTUMN!
TOOK THEM LONG ENOUGH! THEY MUST BE YOUNG! AND RIGHT NOW I'M FEELING AS OLD AS METHUSALA!
WHAT YOU NEED, PETER PARKER, IS A NICE JAUNT AROUND TOWN...
...COURTESY OF YOUR FRIENDLY NEIGHBORHOOD SPIDER-MAN! SHAKE LOOSE THE COBWEBS! PERK YOU RIGHT UP!
HEY, I MUST BE GETTING USED TO MY OLD RED AND BLUE COSTUME AGAIN!
FEELS AS COMFORTABLE AS THE SHAPE-SHIFTING BLACK ONE I GOT ON THE SECRET WARS...
...THE ONE THAT TURNED OUT TO BE AN ALIEN SYMBIOT!
I'D WORN IT TO THE BAXTER BUILDING TO VISIT THE FANTASTIC FOUR...
...AND REED RICHARDS EXAMINED IT... AND DISCOVERED IT WAS A LIVING PARASITE-- AND THAT IT WAS TRYING TO GRAFT ITSELF ONTO ME!
AND IT REFUSED TO COME OFF! HOO BOY! REED FINALLY MADE IT LET GO BY BLASTING IT WITH A SONIC GUN!
HE SAID IT WAS JUST A MATTER OF TIME BEFORE IT TOOK ME OVER COMPLETELY!
WONDER WHAT HE MEANT BY THAT?

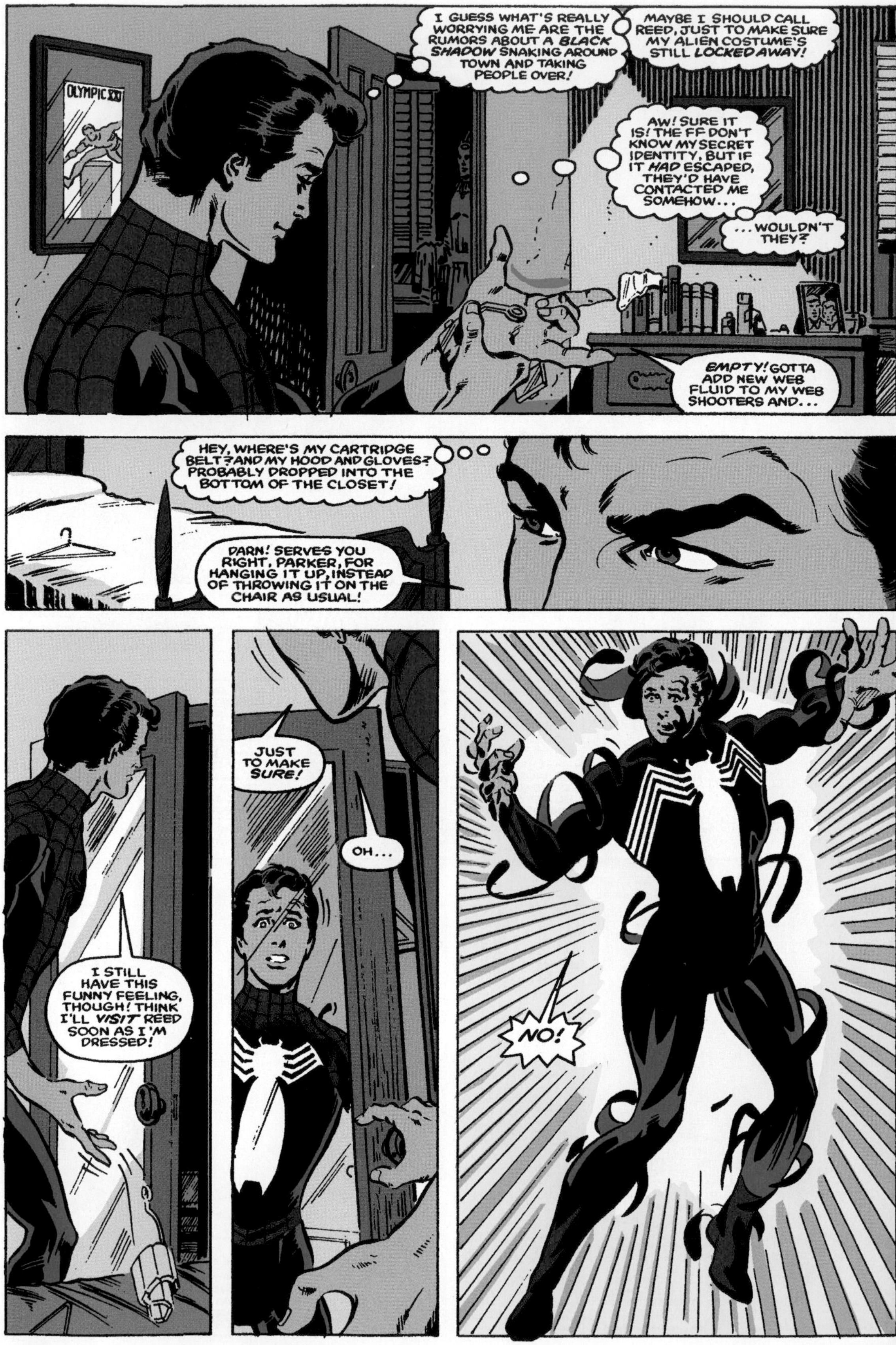
OLYMPIC
I GUESS WHAT'S REALLY WORRYING ME ARE THE RUMORS ABOUT A *BLACK SHADOW* SNAKING AROUND TOWN AND TAKING PEOPLE OVER!
MAYBE I SHOULD CALL REED, JUST TO MAKE SURE MY ALIEN COSTUME'S STILL *LOCKED AWAY!*
AW! SURE IT IS! THE FF DON'T KNOW MY SECRET IDENTITY, BUT IF IT *HAD* ESCAPED, THEY'D HAVE CONTACTED ME SOMEHOW...
...WOULDN'T THEY?
EMPTY! GOTTA ADD NEW WEB FLUID TO MY WEB SHOOTERS AND...
HEY, WHERE'S MY CARTRIDGE BELT? AND MY HOOD AND GLOVES? PROBABLY DROPPED INTO THE BOTTOM OF THE CLOSET!
DARN! SERVES YOU RIGHT, PARKER, FOR HANGING IT UP, INSTEAD OF THROWING IT ON THE CHAIR AS USUAL!
I STILL HAVE THIS FUNNY FEELING, THOUGH! THINK I'LL *VISIT* REED SOON AS I'M DRESSED!
JUST TO MAKE *SURE!*
OH...
NO!

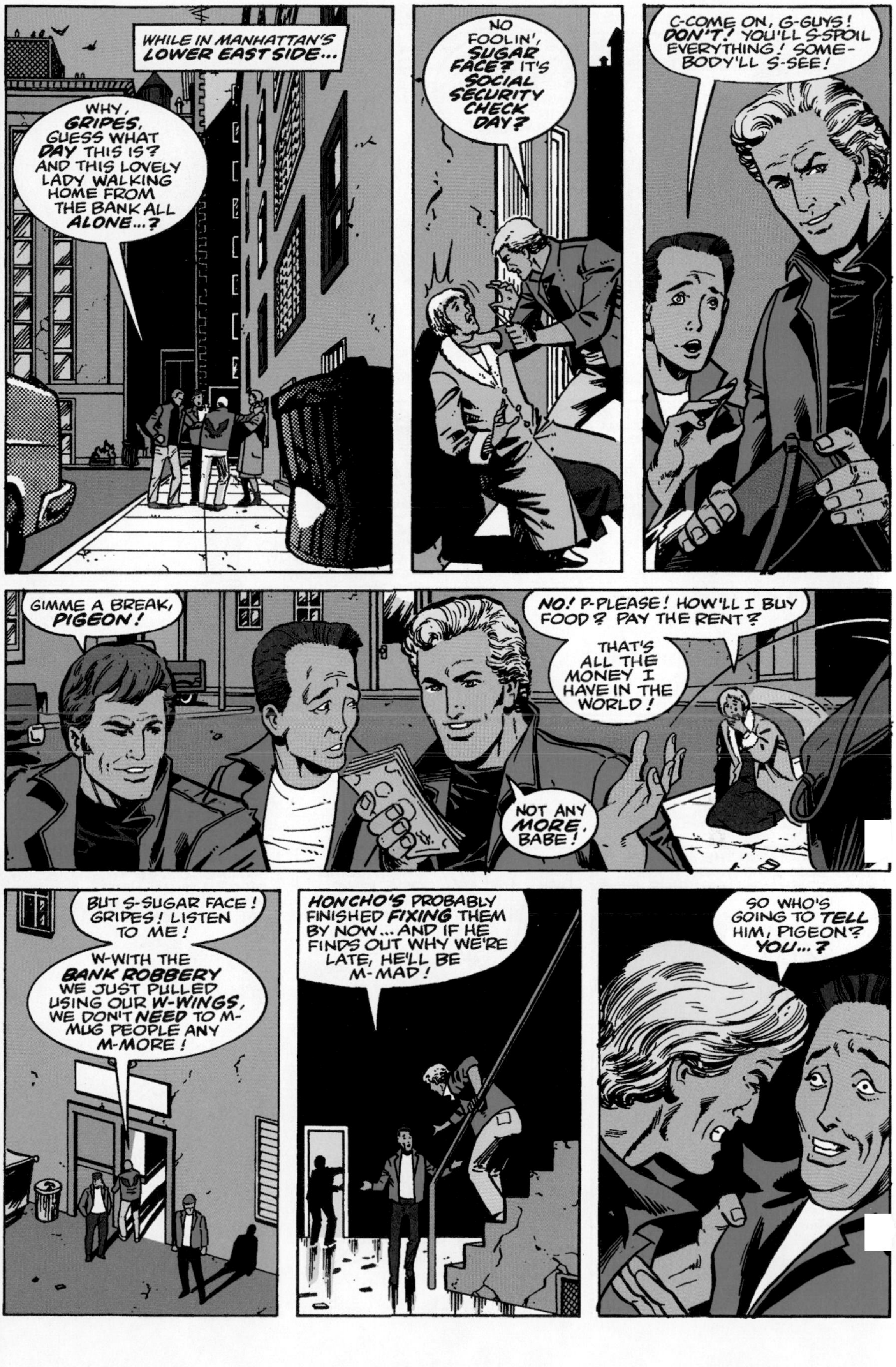
WHILE IN MANHATTAN'S LOWER EAST SIDE...
WHY, GRIPES, GUESS WHAT DAY THIS IS? AND THIS LOVELY LADY WALKING HOME FROM THE BANK ALL ALONE...?
NO FOOLIN', SUGAR FACE? IT'S SOCIAL SECURITY CHECK DAY?
C-COME ON, G-GUYS! DON'T! YOU'LL S-SPOIL EVERYTHING! SOMEBODY'LL S-SEE!
GIMME A BREAK, PIGEON!
NO! P-PLEASE! HOW'LL I BUY FOOD? PAY THE RENT?
THAT'S ALL THE MONEY I HAVE IN THE WORLD!
NOT ANY MORE, BABE!
BUT S-SUGAR FACE! GRIPES! LISTEN TO ME!
W-WITH THE BANK ROBBERY WE JUST PULLED USING OUR W-WINGS, WE DON'T NEED TO M-MUG PEOPLE ANY M-MORE!
HONCHO'S PROBABLY FINISHED FIXING THEM BY NOW... AND IF HE FINDS OUT WHY WE'RE LATE, HE'LL BE M-MAD!
SO WHO'S GOING TO TELL HIM, PIGEON? YOU...?

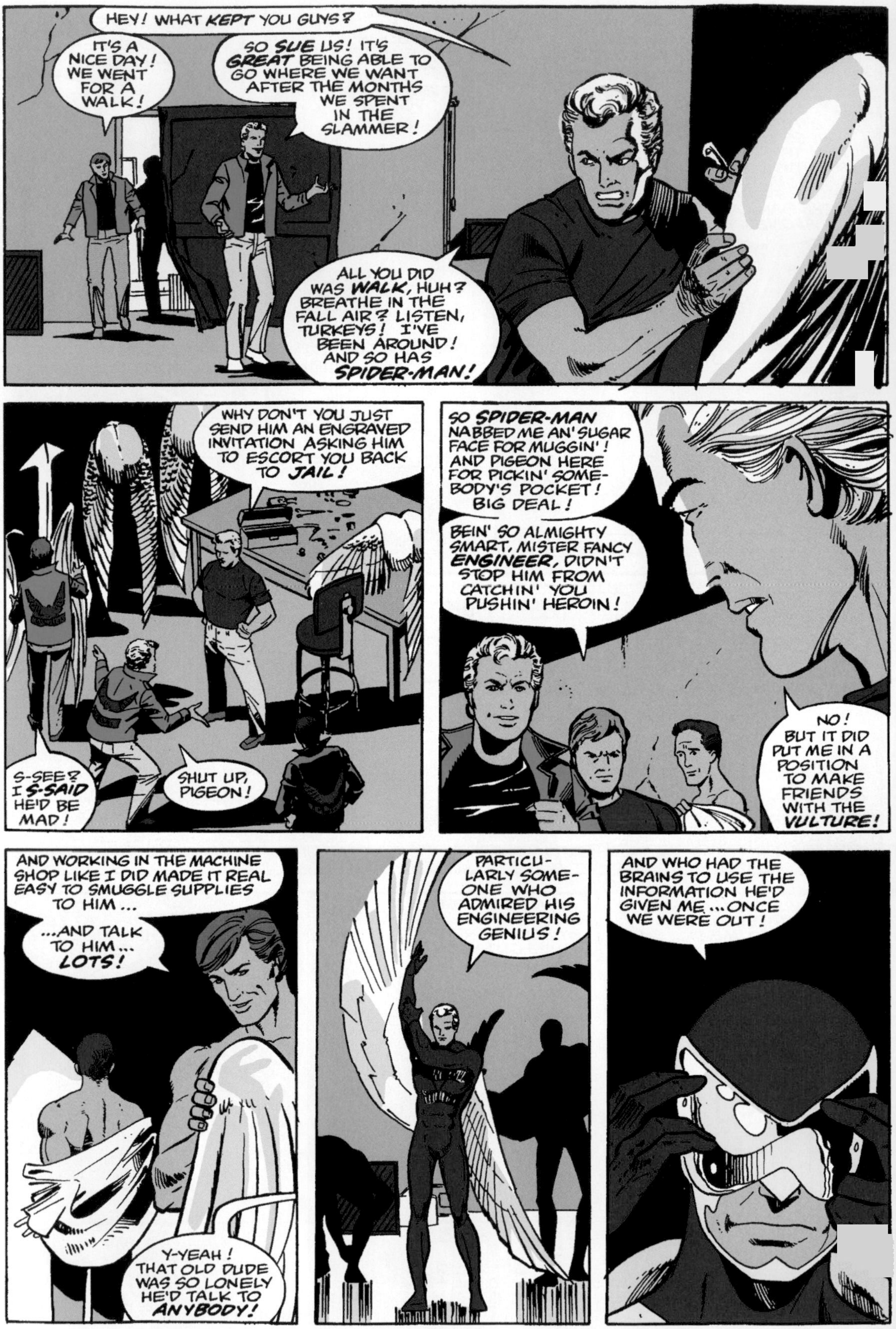
HEY! WHAT KEPT YOU GUYS?
IT'S A NICE DAY! WE WENT FOR A WALK!
SO SUE US! IT'S GREAT BEING ABLE TO GO WHERE WE WANT AFTER THE MONTHS WE SPENT IN THE SLAMMER!
ALL YOU DID WAS WALK, HUH? BREATHE IN THE FALL AIR? LISTEN, TURKEYS! I'VE BEEN AROUND! AND SO HAS SPIDER-MAN!
WHY DON'T YOU JUST SEND HIM AN ENGRAVED INVITATION ASKING HIM TO ESCORT YOU BACK TO JAIL!
S-SEE? I S-SAID HE'D BE MAD!
SHUT UP, PIGEON!
SO SPIDER-MAN NABBED ME AN' SUGAR FACE FOR MUGGIN'! AND PIGEON HERE FOR PICKIN' SOMEBODY'S POCKET! BIG DEAL!
BEIN' SO ALMIGHTY SMART, MISTER FANCY ENGINEER, DIDN'T STOP HIM FROM CATCHIN' YOU PUSHIN' HEROIN!
NO! BUT IT DID PUT ME IN A POSITION TO MAKE FRIENDS WITH THE VULTURE!
AND WORKING IN THE MACHINE SHOP LIKE I DID MADE IT REAL EASY TO SMUGGLE SUPPLIES TO HIM...
...AND TALK TO HIM... LOTS!
Y-YEAH! THAT OLD DUDE WAS SO LONELY HE'D TALK TO ANYBODY!
PARTICULARLY SOMEONE WHO ADMIRED HIS ENGINEERING GENIUS!
AND WHO HAD THE BRAINS TO USE THE INFORMATION HE'D GIVEN ME...ONCE WE WERE OUT!

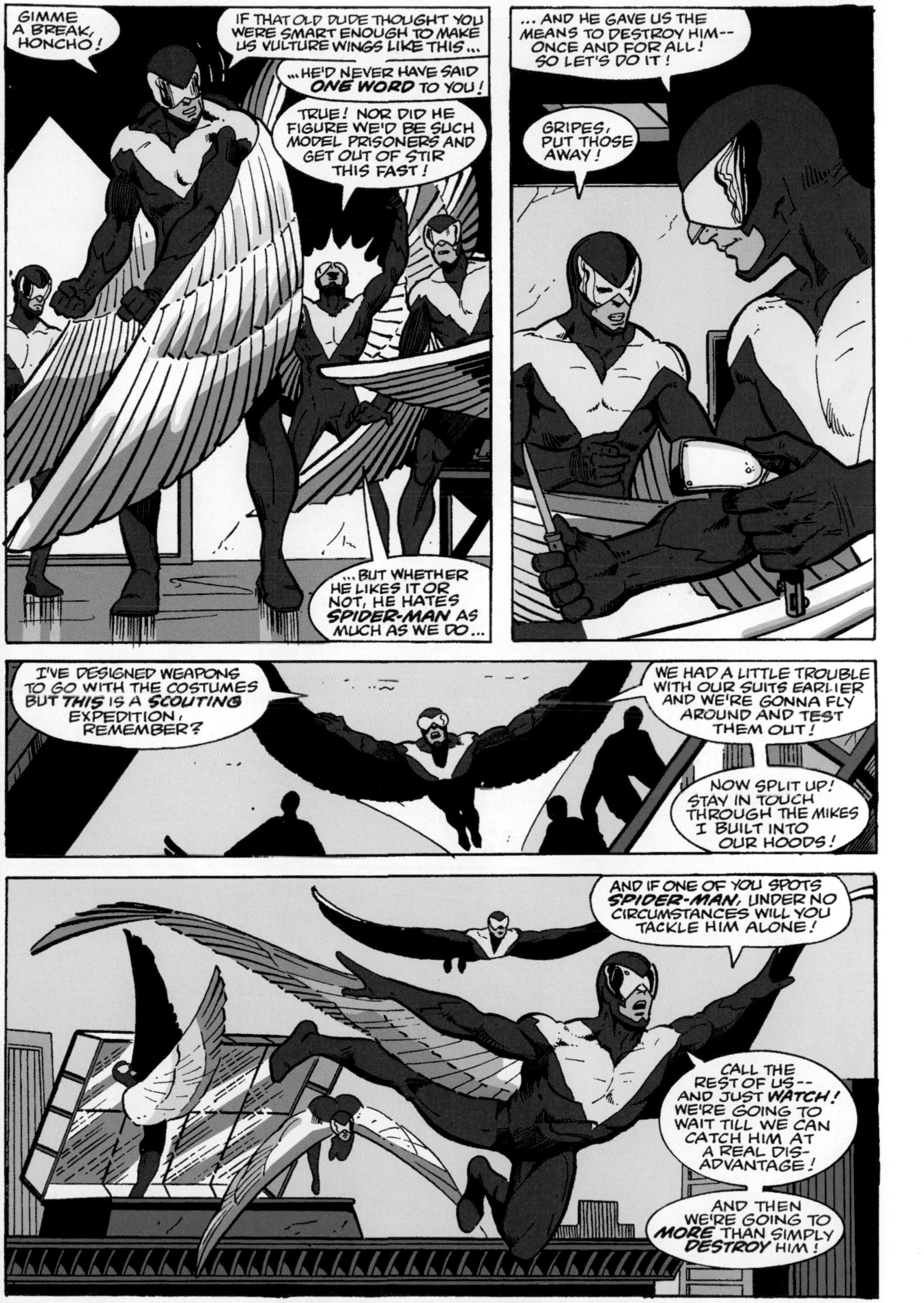
GIMME A BREAK, HONCHO!
IF THAT OLD DUDE THOUGHT YOU WERE SMART ENOUGH TO MAKE US VULTURE WINGS LIKE THIS...
...HE'D NEVER HAVE SAID ONE WORD TO YOU!
TRUE! NOR DID HE FIGURE WE'D BE SUCH MODEL PRISONERS AND GET OUT OF STIR THIS FAST!
...BUT WHETHER HE LIKES IT OR NOT, HE HATES SPIDER-MAN AS MUCH AS WE DO...
...AND HE GAVE US THE MEANS TO DESTROY HIM-- ONCE AND FOR ALL! SO LET'S DO IT!
GRIPES, PUT THOSE AWAY!
I'VE DESIGNED WEAPONS TO GO WITH THE COSTUMES BUT THIS IS A SCOUTING EXPEDITION, REMEMBER?
WE HAD A LITTLE TROUBLE WITH OUR SUITS EARLIER AND WE'RE GONNA FLY AROUND AND TEST THEM OUT!
NOW SPLIT UP! STAY IN TOUCH THROUGH THE MIKES I BUILT INTO OUR HOODS!
AND IF ONE OF YOU SPOTS SPIDER-MAN, UNDER NO CIRCUMSTANCES WILL YOU TACKLE HIM ALONE!
CALL THE REST OF US-- AND JUST WATCH! WE'RE GOING TO WAIT TILL WE CAN CATCH HIM AT A REAL DIS-ADVANTAGE!
AND THEN WE'RE GOING TO MORE THAN SIMPLY DESTROY HIM!

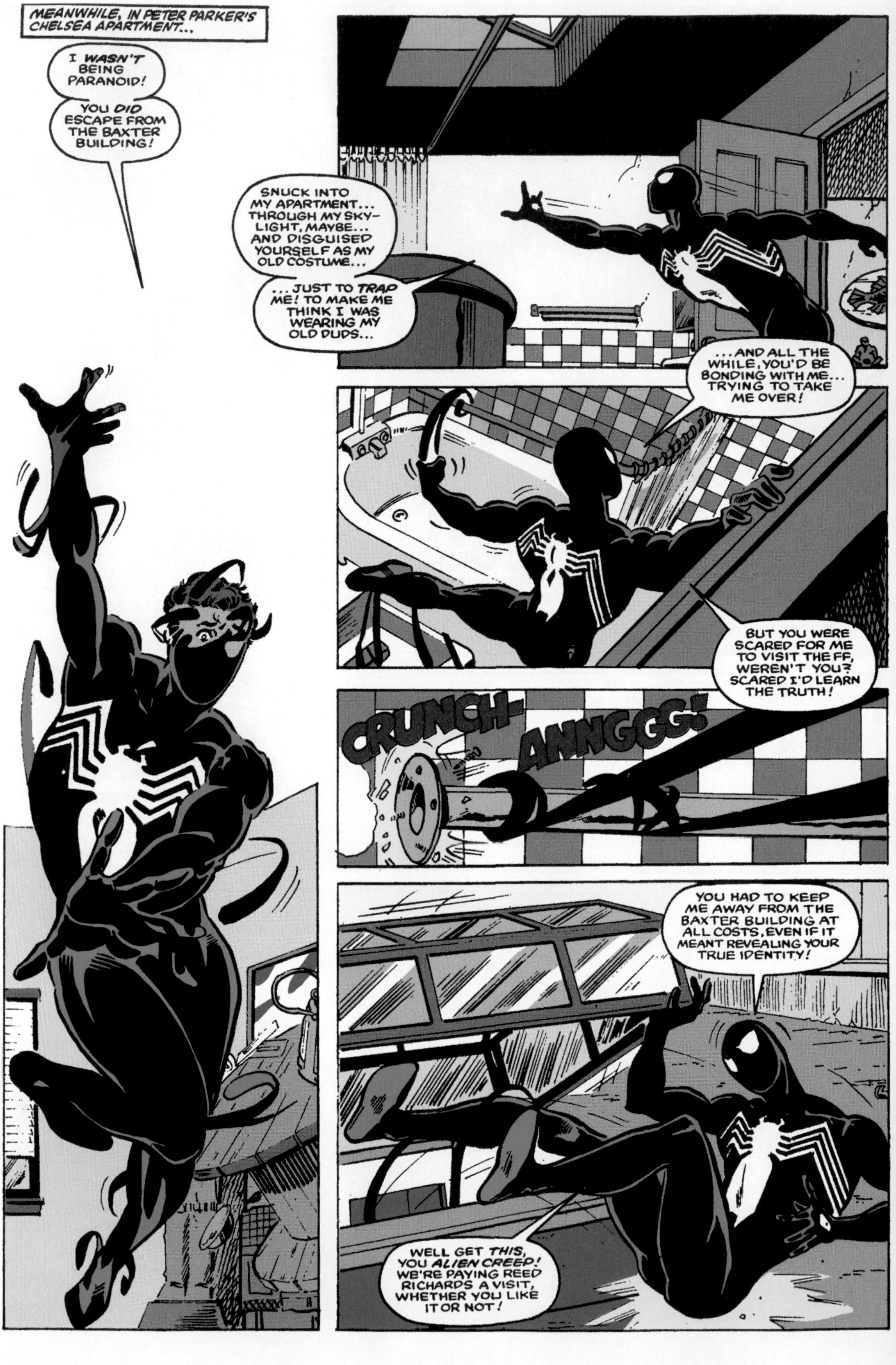
MEANWHILE, IN PETER PARKER'S CHELSEA APARTMENT...
I WASN'T BEING PARANOID!
YOU DID ESCAPE FROM THE BAXTER BUILDING!
SNUCK INTO MY APARTMENT... THROUGH MY SKY-LIGHT, MAYBE... AND DISGUISED YOURSELF AS MY OLD COSTUME...
...JUST TO TRAP ME! TO MAKE ME THINK I WAS WEARING MY OLD DUDS...
...AND ALL THE WHILE, YOU'D BE BONDING WITH ME... TRYING TO TAKE ME OVER!
BUT YOU WERE SCARED FOR ME TO VISIT THE FF, WEREN'T YOU? SCARED I'D LEARN THE TRUTH!
CRUNCH-ANNGGG!
YOU HAD TO KEEP ME AWAY FROM THE BAXTER BUILDING AT ALL COSTS, EVEN IF IT MEANT REVEALING YOUR TRUE IDENTITY!
WELL GET THIS, YOU ALIEN CREEP! WE'RE PAYING REED RICHARDS A VISIT, WHETHER YOU LIKE IT OR NOT!

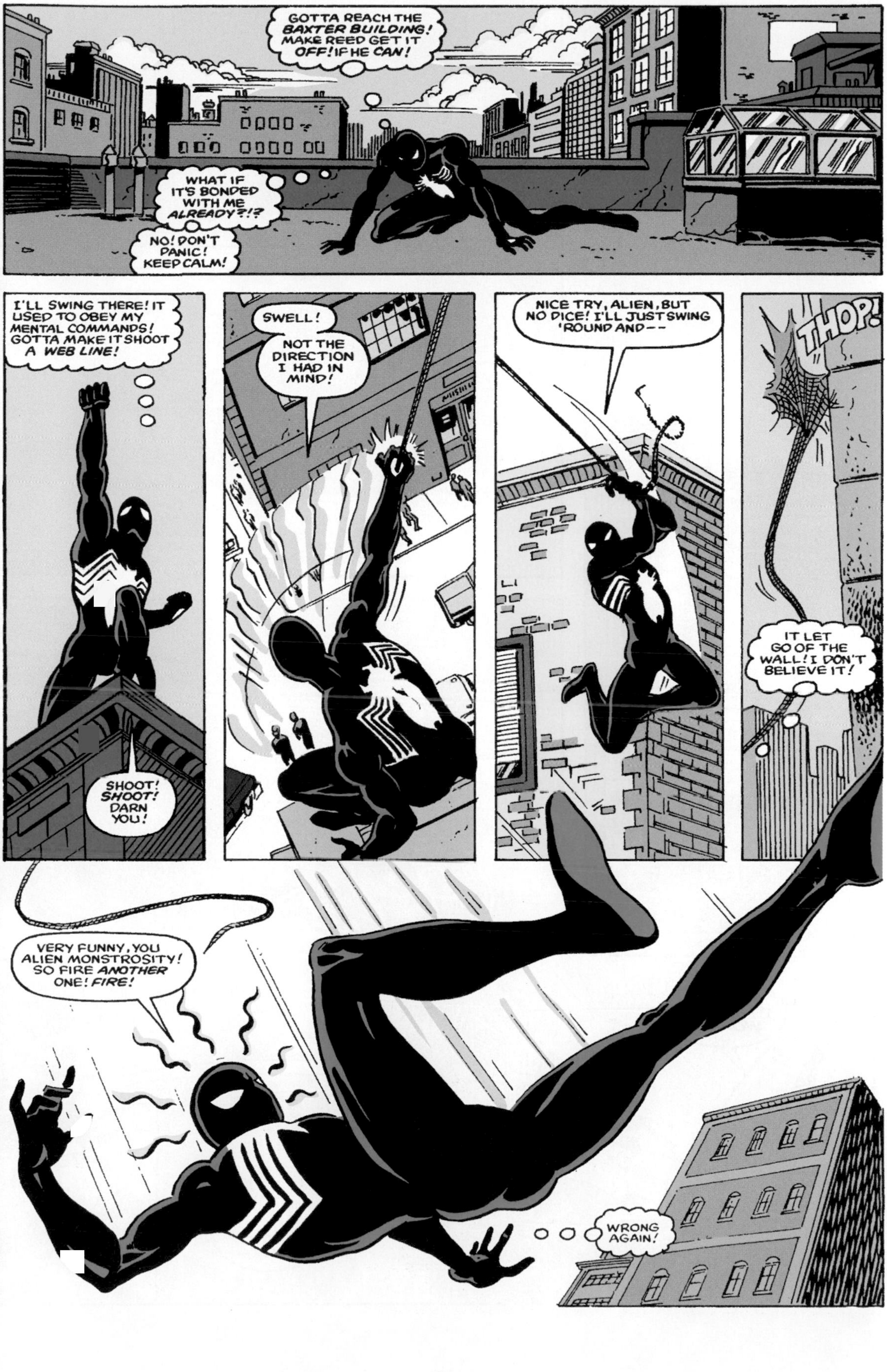
GOTTA REACH THE BAXTER BUILDING! MAKE REED GET IT OFF! IF HE CAN!
WHAT IF IT'S BONDED WITH ME ALREADY?!?
NO! DON'T PANIC! KEEP CALM!
I'LL SWING THERE! IT USED TO OBEY MY MENTAL COMMANDS! GOTTA MAKE IT SHOOT A WEB LINE!
SHOOT! SHOOT! DARN YOU!
SWELL!
NOT THE DIRECTION I HAD IN MIND!
NICE TRY, ALIEN, BUT NO DICE! I'LL JUST SWING 'ROUND AND--
THOP!
IT LET GO OF THE WALL! I DON'T BELIEVE IT!
VERY FUNNY, YOU ALIEN MONSTROSITY! SO FIRE ANOTHER ONE! FIRE!
WRONG AGAIN!

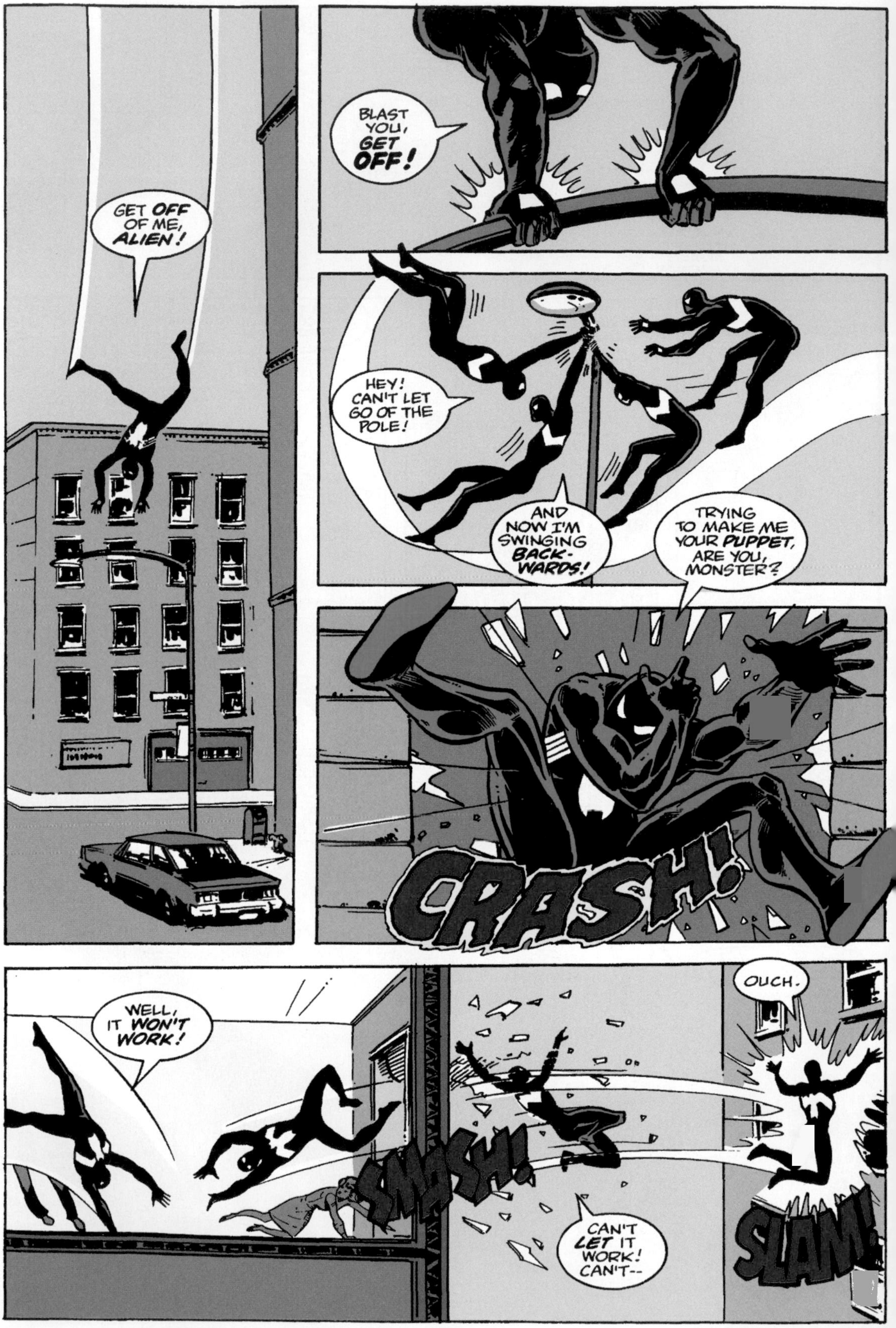
GET OFF OF ME, ALIEN!
BLAST YOU, GET OFF!
HEY! CAN'T LET GO OF THE POLE!
AND NOW I'M SWINGING BACK-WARDS!
TRYING TO MAKE ME YOUR PUPPET, ARE YOU, MONSTER?
CRASH!
WELL, IT WON'T WORK!
SMASH!
CAN'T LET IT WORK! CAN'T--
OUCH.
SLAM!

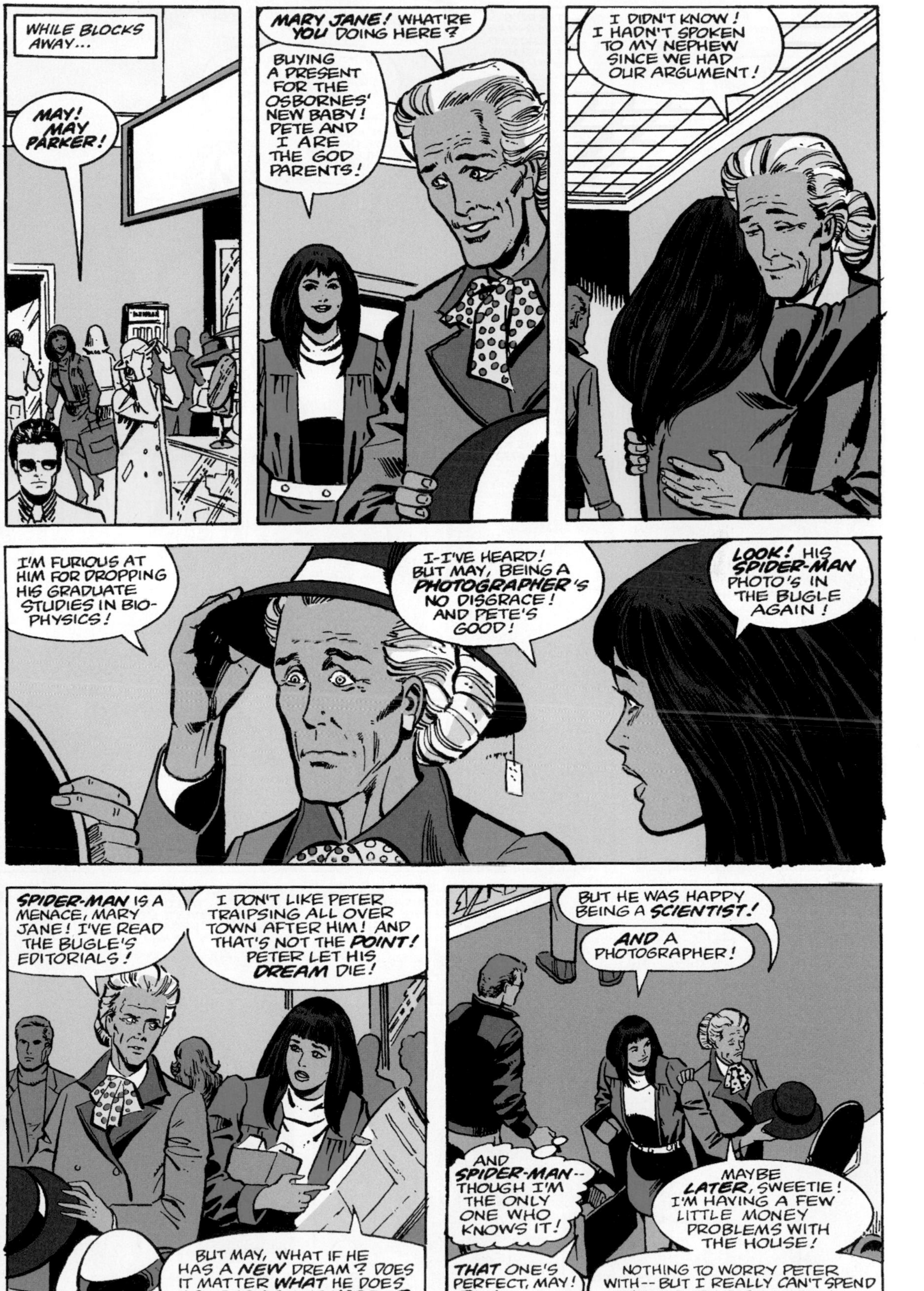
WHILE BLOCKS AWAY...
MAY! MAY PARKER!
MARY JANE! WHAT'RE YOU DOING HERE?
BUYING A PRESENT FOR THE OSBORNES' NEW BABY! PETE AND I ARE THE GOD PARENTS!
I DIDN'T KNOW! I HADN'T SPOKEN TO MY NEPHEW SINCE WE HAD OUR ARGUMENT!
I'M FURIOUS AT HIM FOR DROPPING HIS GRADUATE STUDIES IN BIO-PHYSICS!
I-I'VE HEARD! BUT MAY, BEING A PHOTOGRAPHER'S NO DISGRACE! AND PETE'S GOOD!
LOOK! HIS SPIDER-MAN PHOTO'S IN THE BUGLE AGAIN!
SPIDER-MAN IS A MENACE, MARY JANE! I'VE READ THE BUGLE'S EDITORIALS!
I DON'T LIKE PETER TRAIPSING ALL OVER TOWN AFTER HIM! AND THAT'S NOT THE POINT! PETER LET HIS DREAM DIE!
BUT MAY, WHAT IF HE HAS A NEW DREAM? DOES IT MATTER WHAT HE DOES AS LONG AS HE'S HAPPY?
BUT HE WAS HAPPY BEING A SCIENTIST!
AND A PHOTOGRAPHER!
AND SPIDER-MAN-- THOUGH I'M THE ONLY ONE WHO KNOWS IT!
THAT ONE'S PERFECT, MAY! BUY IT!
MAYBE LATER, SWEETIE! I'M HAVING A FEW LITTLE MONEY PROBLEMS WITH THE HOUSE!
NOTHING TO WORRY PETER WITH-- BUT I REALLY CAN'T SPEND THE MONEY RIGHT NOW!

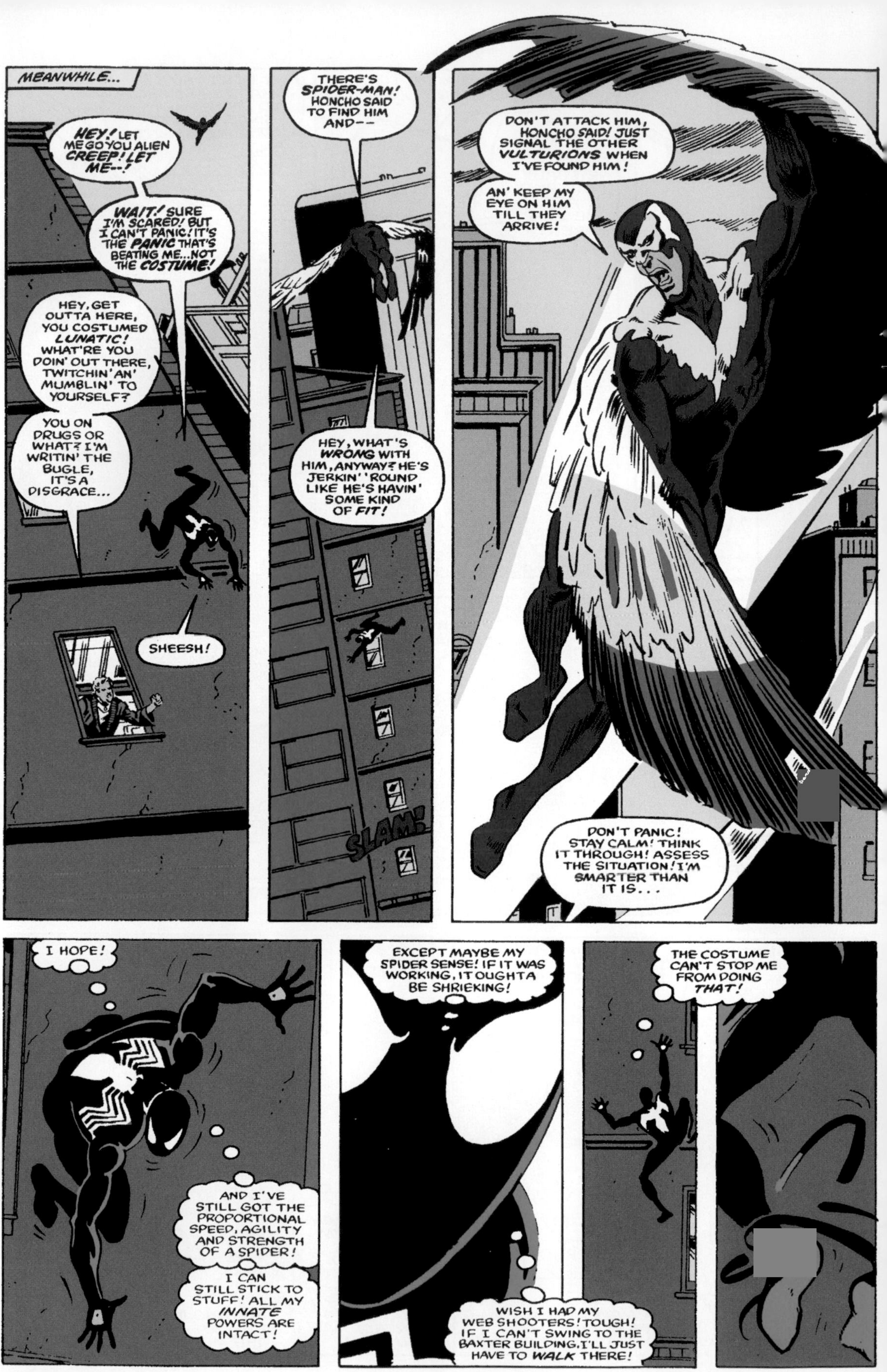
MEANWHILE...
HEY! LET ME GO YOU ALIEN CREEP! LET ME--!
WAIT! SURE I'M SCARED! BUT I CAN'T PANIC! IT'S THE PANIC THAT'S BEATING ME...NOT THE COSTUME!
HEY, GET OUTTA HERE, YOU COSTUMED LUNATIC! WHAT'RE YOU DOIN' OUT THERE, TWITCHIN' AN' MUMBLIN' TO YOURSELF?
YOU ON DRUGS OR WHAT? I'M WRITIN' THE BUGLE, IT'S A DISGRACE...
SHEESH!
THERE'S SPIDER-MAN! HONCHO SAID TO FIND HIM AND--
HEY, WHAT'S WRONG WITH HIM, ANYWAY? HE'S JERKIN' 'ROUND LIKE HE'S HAVIN' SOME KIND OF FIT!
SLAM!
DON'T ATTACK HIM, HONCHO SAID! JUST SIGNAL THE OTHER VULTURIONS WHEN I'VE FOUND HIM!
AN' KEEP MY EYE ON HIM TILL THEY ARRIVE!
DON'T PANIC! STAY CALM! THINK IT THROUGH! ASSESS THE SITUATION! I'M SMARTER THAN IT IS...
I HOPE!
AND I'VE STILL GOT THE PROPORTIONAL SPEED, AGILITY AND STRENGTH OF A SPIDER!
I CAN STILL STICK TO STUFF! ALL MY INNATE POWERS ARE INTACT!
EXCEPT MAYBE MY SPIDER SENSE! IF IT WAS WORKING, IT OUGHTA BE SHRIEKING!
WISH I HAD MY WEB SHOOTERS! TOUGH! IF I CAN'T SWING TO THE BAXTER BUILDING, I'LL JUST HAVE TO WALK THERE!
THE COSTUME CAN'T STOP ME FROM DOING THAT!

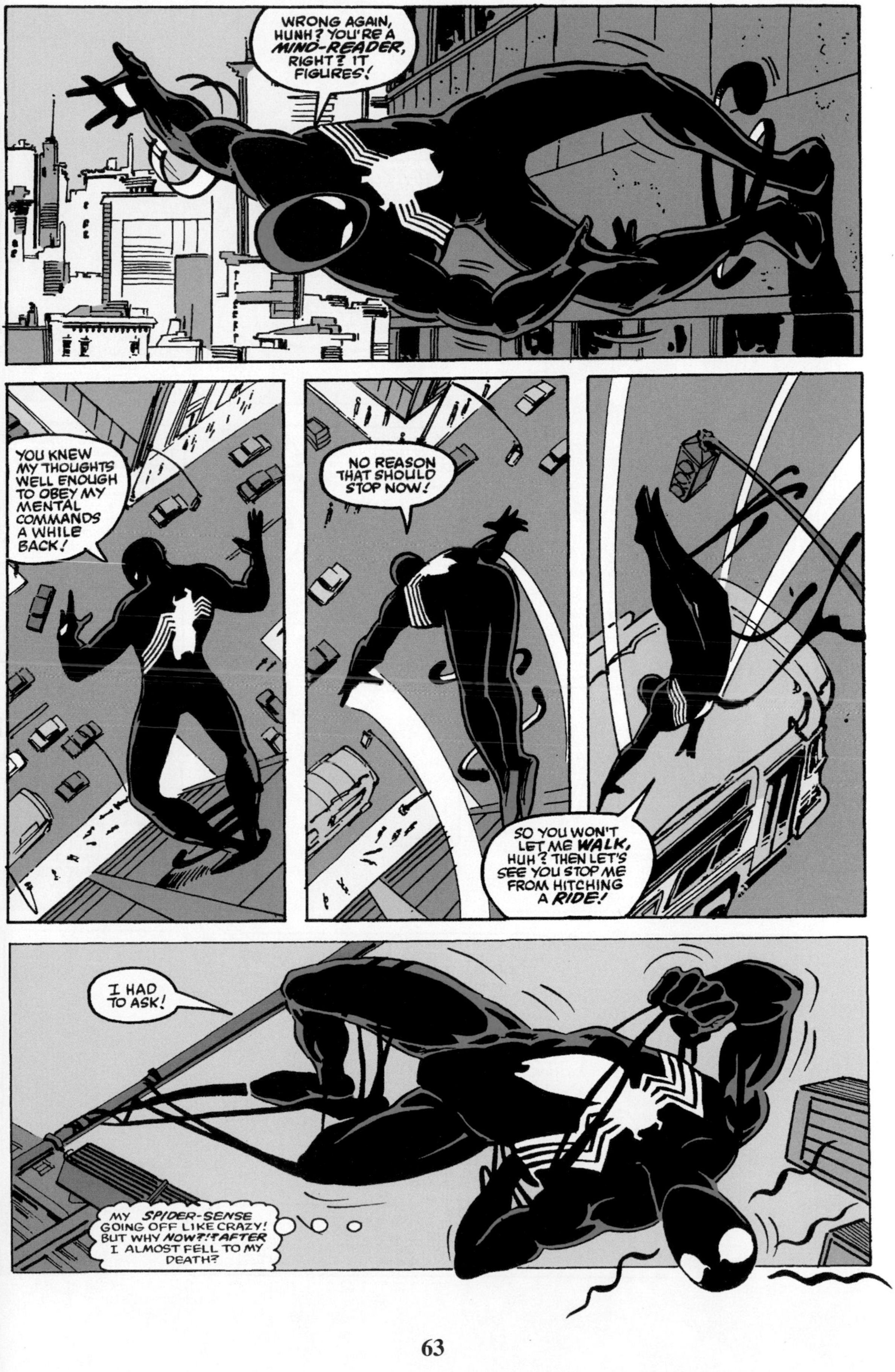
WRONG AGAIN, HUNH? YOU'RE A MIND-READER, RIGHT? IT FIGURES!
YOU KNEW MY THOUGHTS WELL ENOUGH TO OBEY MY MENTAL COMMANDS A WHILE BACK!
NO REASON THAT SHOULD STOP NOW!
SO YOU WON'T LET ME WALK, HUH? THEN LET'S SEE YOU STOP ME FROM HITCHING A RIDE!
I HAD TO ASK!
MY SPIDER-SENSE GOING OFF LIKE CRAZY! BUT WHY NOW?!?AFTER I ALMOST FELL TO MY DEATH?

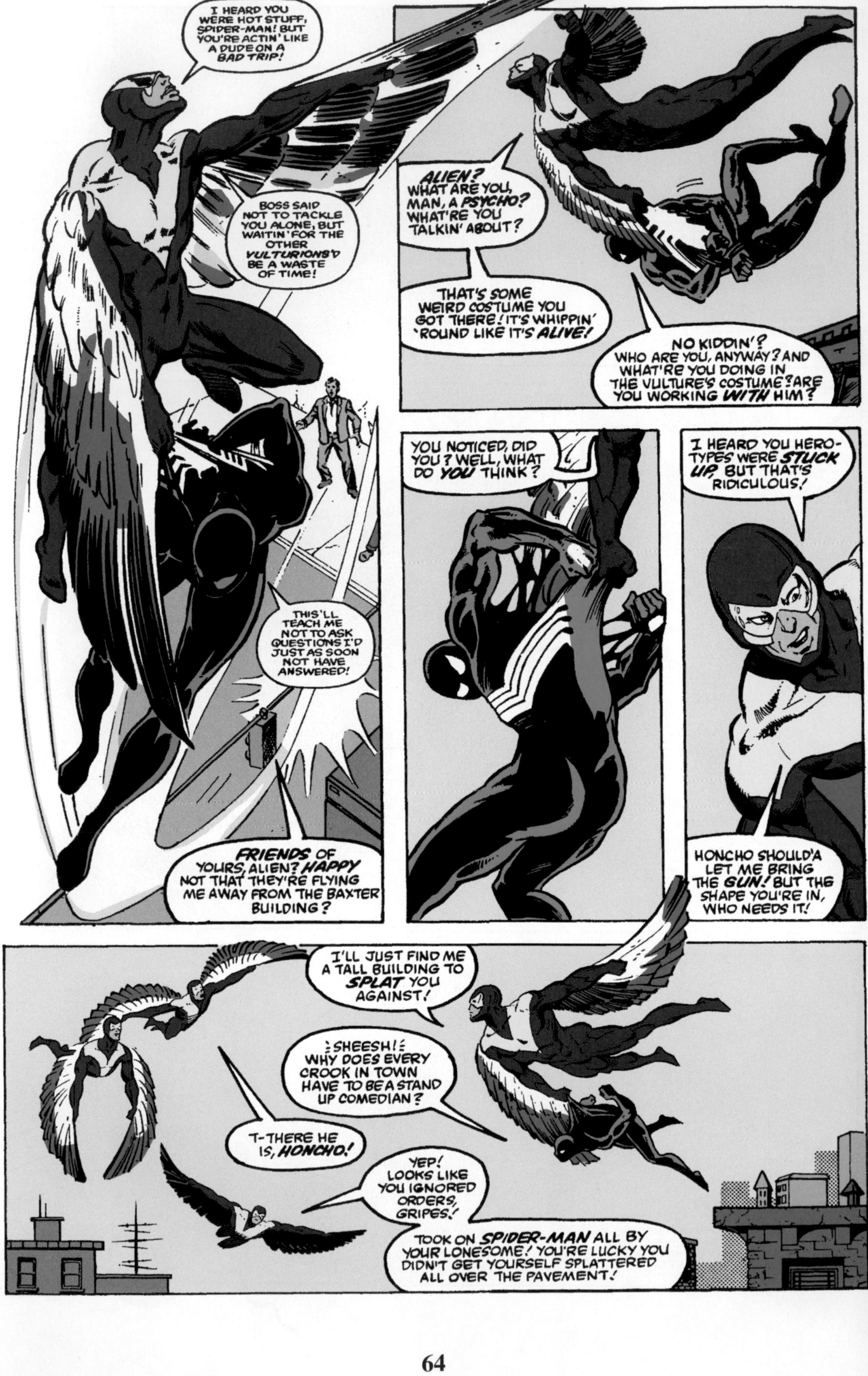

I HEARD YOU WERE HOT STUFF, SPIDER-MAN! BUT YOU'RE ACTIN' LIKE A DUDE ON A BAD TRIP!
BOSS SAID NOT TO TACKLE YOU ALONE, BUT WAITIN' FOR THE OTHER VULTURIONS'D BE A WASTE OF TIME!
THIS'LL TEACH ME NOT TO ASK QUESTIONS I'D JUST AS SOON NOT HAVE ANSWERED!
FRIENDS OF YOURS, ALIEN? HAPPY NOT THAT THEY'RE FLYING ME AWAY FROM THE BAXTER BUILDING?
ALIEN? WHAT ARE YOU, MAN, A PSYCHO? WHAT'RE YOU TALKIN' ABOUT?
THAT'S SOME WEIRD COSTUME YOU GOT THERE! IT'S WHIPPIN' 'ROUND LIKE IT'S ALIVE!
NO KIDDIN'? WHO ARE YOU, ANYWAY? AND WHAT'RE YOU DOING IN THE VULTURE'S COSTUME? ARE YOU WORKING WITH HIM?
YOU NOTICED, DID YOU? WELL, WHAT DO YOU THINK?
I HEARD YOU HERO-TYPES WERE STUCK UP, BUT THAT'S RIDICULOUS!
HONCHO SHOULD'A LET ME BRING THE GUN! BUT THE SHAPE YOU'RE IN, WHO NEEDS IT!
I'LL JUST FIND ME A TALL BUILDING TO SPLAT YOU AGAINST!
SHEESH! WHY DOES EVERY CROOK IN TOWN HAVE TO BE A STAND UP COMEDIAN?
T-THERE HE IS, HONCHO!
YEP! LOOKS LIKE YOU IGNORED ORDERS, GRIPES!
TOOK ON SPIDER-MAN ALL BY YOUR LONESOME! YOU'RE LUCKY YOU DIDN'T GET YOURSELF SPLATTERED ALL OVER THE PAVEMENT!

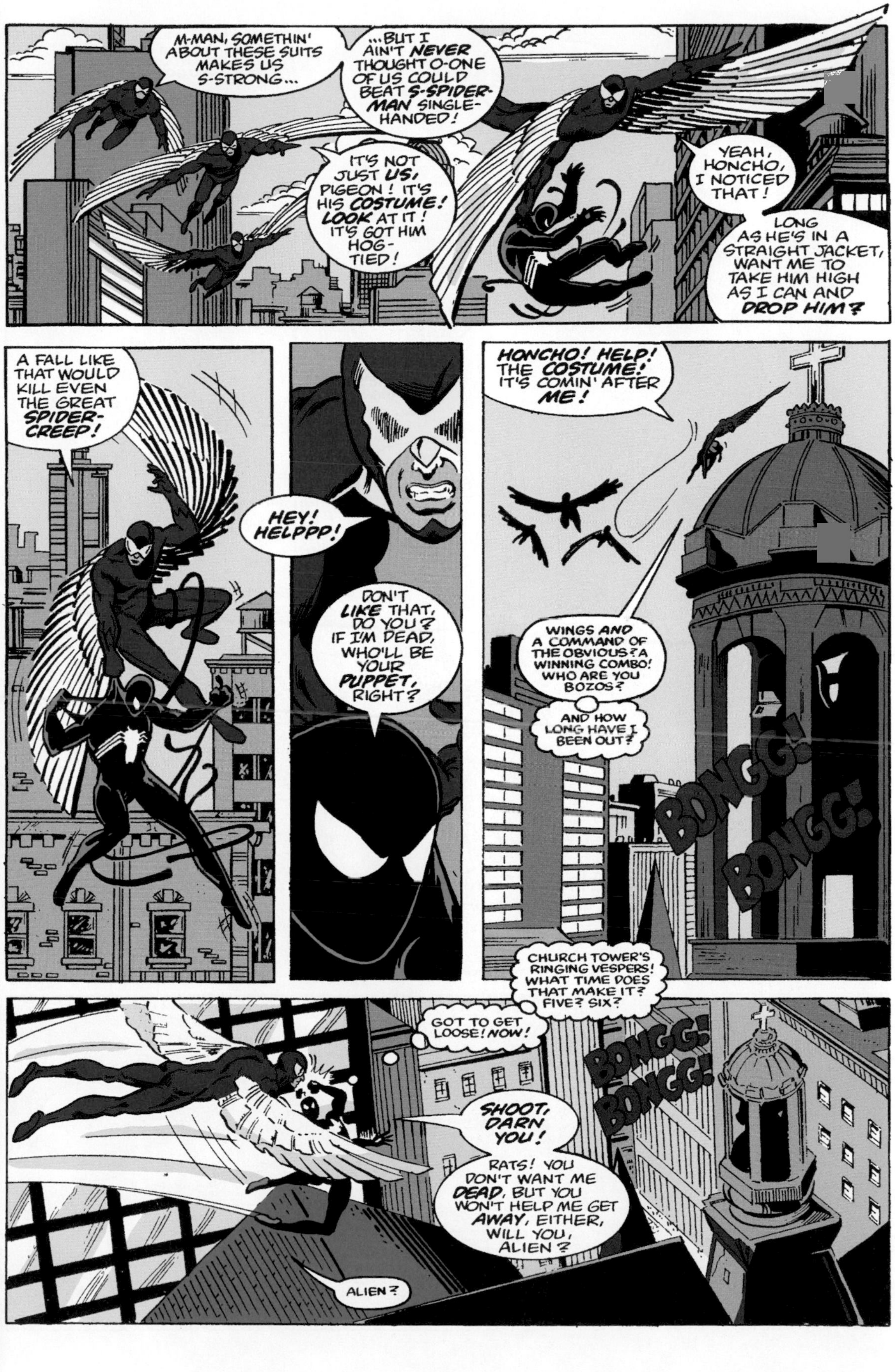
M-MAN, SOMETHIN' ABOUT THESE SUITS MAKES US S-STRONG...
...BUT I AIN'T NEVER THOUGHT O-ONE OF US COULD BEAT S-SPIDER-MAN SINGLE-HANDED!
IT'S NOT JUST US, PIGEON! IT'S HIS COSTUME! LOOK AT IT! IT'S GOT HIM HOG-TIED!
YEAH, HONCHO, I NOTICED THAT!
LONG AS HE'S IN A STRAIGHT JACKET, WANT ME TO TAKE HIM HIGH AS I CAN AND DROP HIM?
A FALL LIKE THAT WOULD KILL EVEN THE GREAT SPIDER-CREEP!
HEY! HELPPP!
DON'T LIKE THAT, DO YOU? IF I'M DEAD, WHO'LL BE YOUR PUPPET, RIGHT?
HONCHO! HELP! THE COSTUME! IT'S COMIN' AFTER ME!
WINGS AND A COMMAND OF THE OBVIOUS? A WINNING COMBO! WHO ARE YOU BOZOS?
AND HOW LONG HAVE I BEEN OUT?
BONGG! BONGG!
CHURCH TOWER'S RINGING VESPERS! WHAT TIME DOES THAT MAKE IT? FIVE? SIX?
GOT TO GET LOOSE! NOW!
BONGG! BONGG!
SHOOT, DARN YOU!
RATS! YOU DON'T WANT ME DEAD, BUT YOU WON'T HELP ME GET AWAY, EITHER, WILL YOU, ALIEN?
ALIEN?

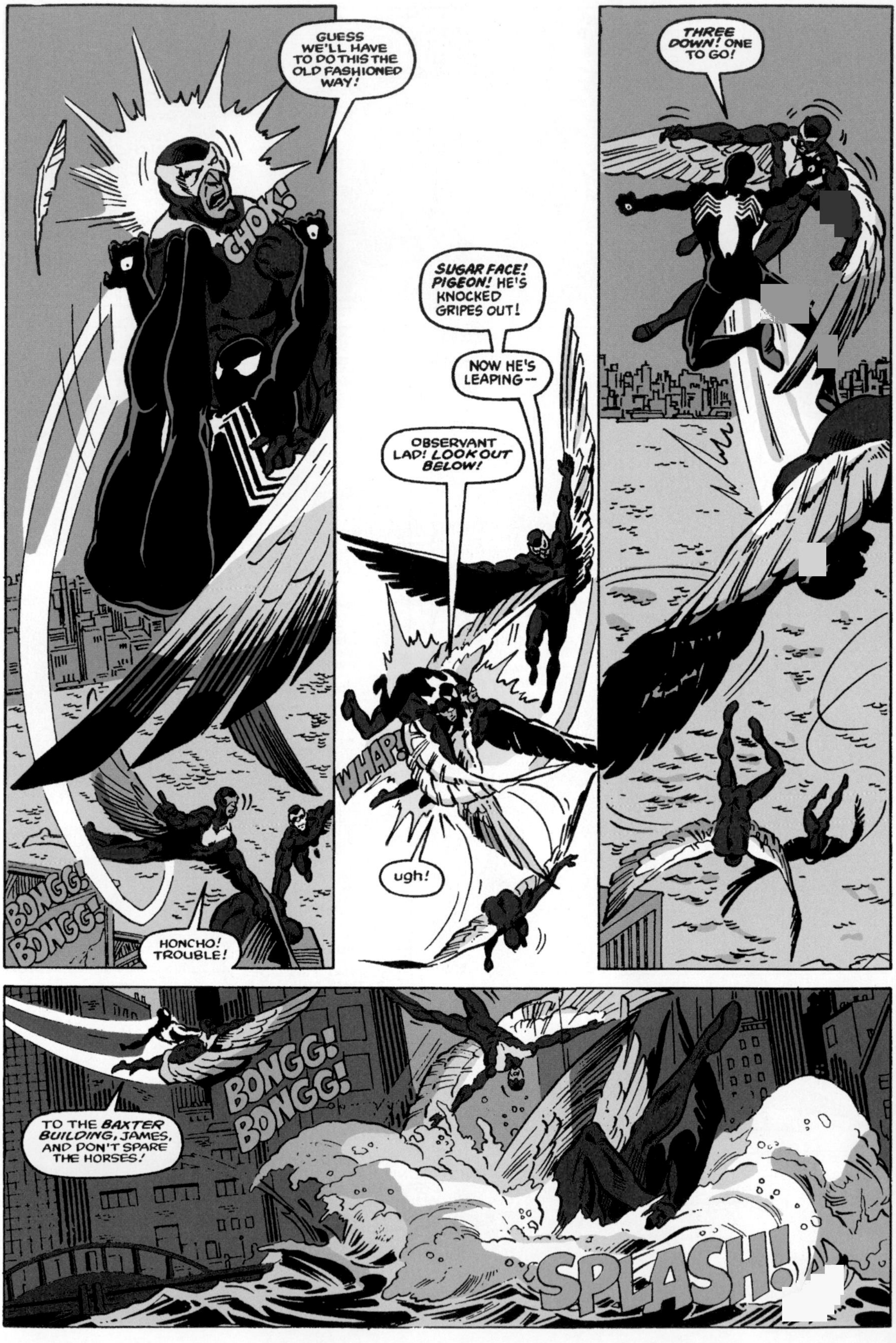
GUESS WE'LL HAVE TO DO THIS THE OLD FASHIONED WAY!
CHOK!
BONGG! BONGG!
HONCHO! TROUBLE!
SUGAR FACE! PIGEON! HE'S KNOCKED GRIPES OUT!
NOW HE'S LEAPING--
OBSERVANT LAD! LOOK OUT BELOW!
WHAP!
ugh!
THREE DOWN! ONE TO GO!
TO THE BAXTER BUILDING, JAMES, AND DON'T SPARE THE HORSES!
BONGG! BONGG!
SPLASH!

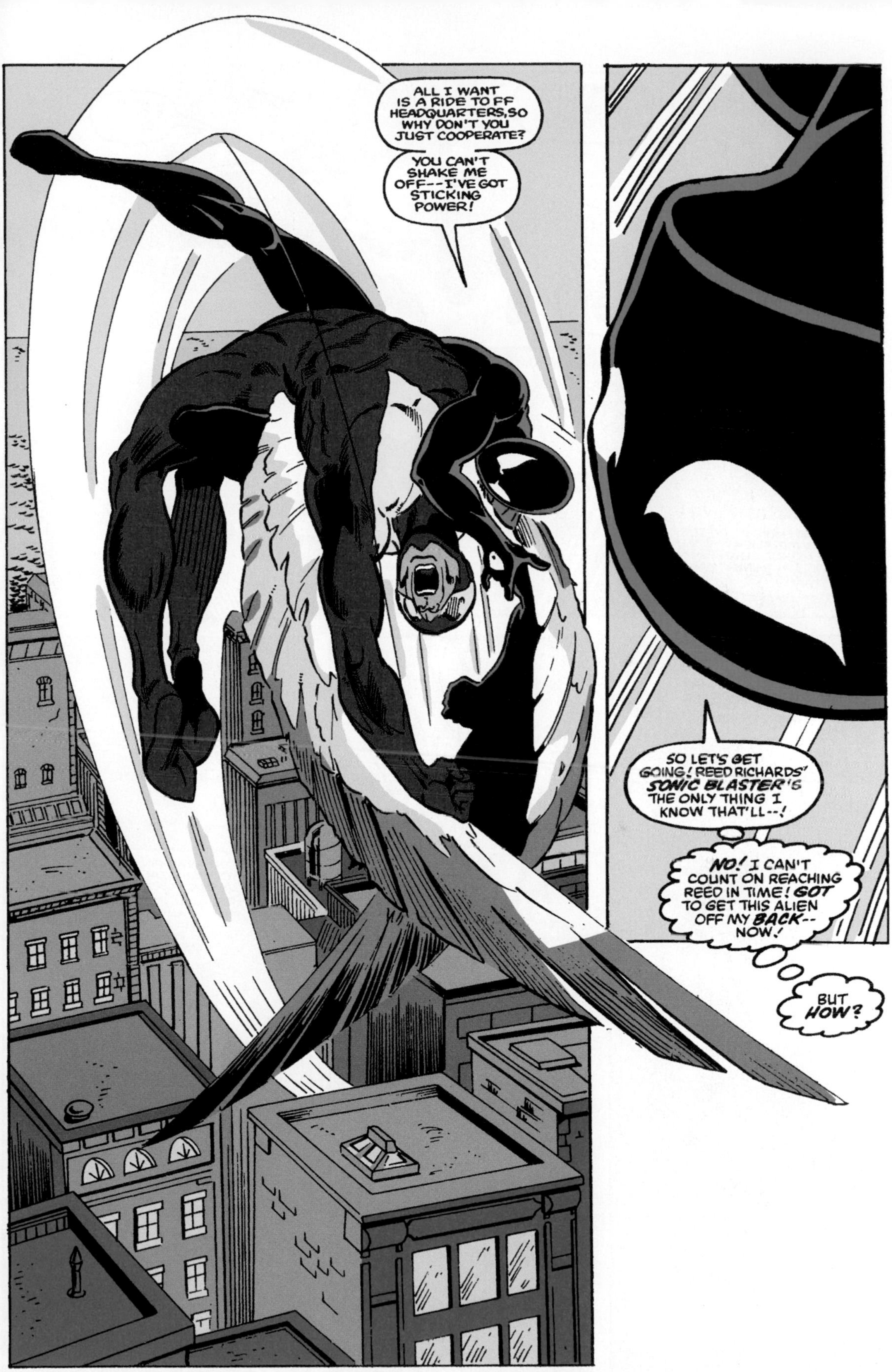
ALL I WANT IS A RIDE TO FF HEADQUARTERS, SO WHY DON'T YOU JUST COOPERATE?
YOU CAN'T SHAKE ME OFF--I'VE GOT STICKING POWER!
SO LET'S GET GOING! REED RICHARDS' SONIC BLASTER'S THE ONLY THING I KNOW THAT'LL--!
NO! I CAN'T COUNT ON REACHING REED IN TIME! GOT TO GET THIS ALIEN OFF MY BACK-- NOW!
BUT HOW?

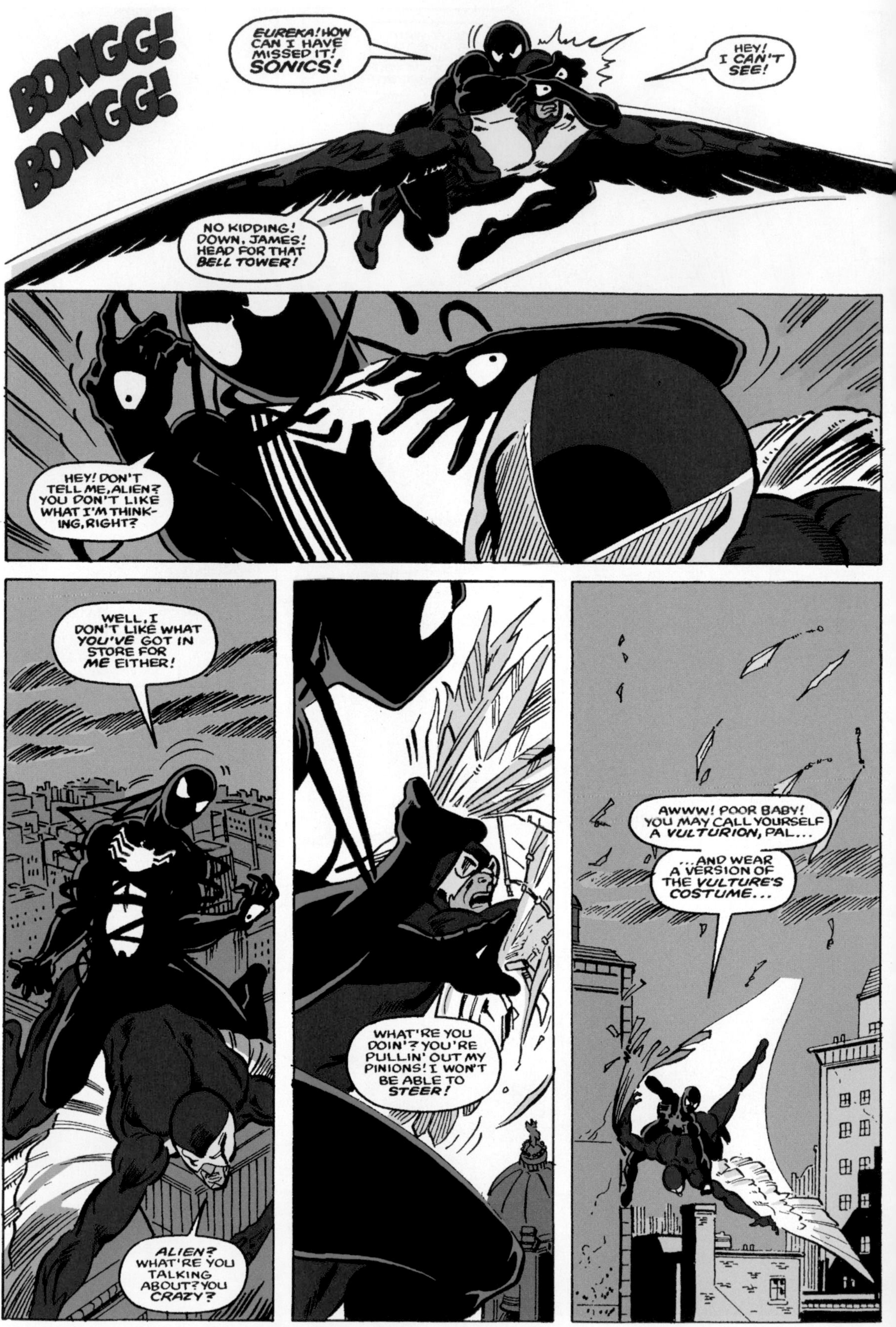
BONGG! BONGG!
EUREKA! HOW CAN I HAVE MISSED IT! SONICS!
HEY! I CAN'T SEE!
NO KIDDING! DOWN, JAMES! HEAD FOR THAT BELL TOWER!
HEY! DON'T TELL ME, ALIEN? YOU DON'T LIKE WHAT I'M THINKING, RIGHT?
WELL, I DON'T LIKE WHAT YOU'VE GOT IN STORE FOR ME EITHER!
ALIEN? WHAT'RE YOU TALKING ABOUT? YOU CRAZY?
WHAT'RE YOU DOIN'? YOU'RE PULLIN' OUT MY PINIONS! I WON'T BE ABLE TO STEER!
AWWW! POOR BABY! YOU MAY CALL YOURSELF A VULTURION, PAL...
...AND WEAR A VERSION OF THE VULTURE'S COSTUME...

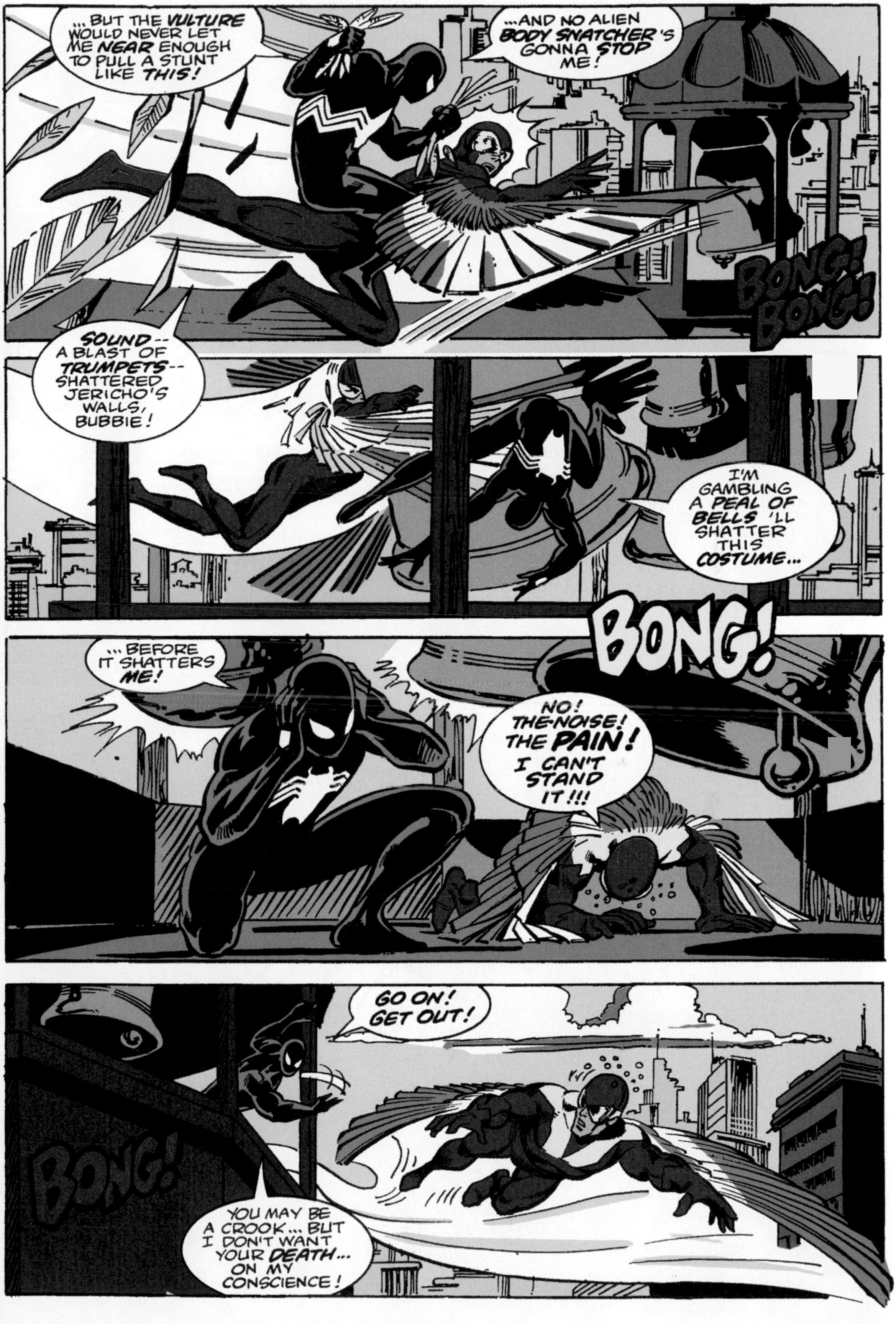

... BUT THE VULTURE WOULD NEVER LET ME NEAR ENOUGH TO PULL A STUNT LIKE THIS!
...AND NO ALIEN BODY SNATCHER'S GONNA STOP ME!
BONG! BONG!
SOUND -- A BLAST OF TRUMPETS -- SHATTERED JERICHO'S WALLS, BUBBIE!
I'M GAMBLING A PEAL OF BELLS 'LL SHATTER THIS COSTUME...
BONG!
... BEFORE IT SHATTERS ME!
NO! THE NOISE! THE PAIN! I CAN'T STAND IT!!!
GO ON! GET OUT!
BONG!
YOU MAY BE A CROOK... BUT I DON'T WANT YOUR DEATH... ON MY CONSCIENCE!

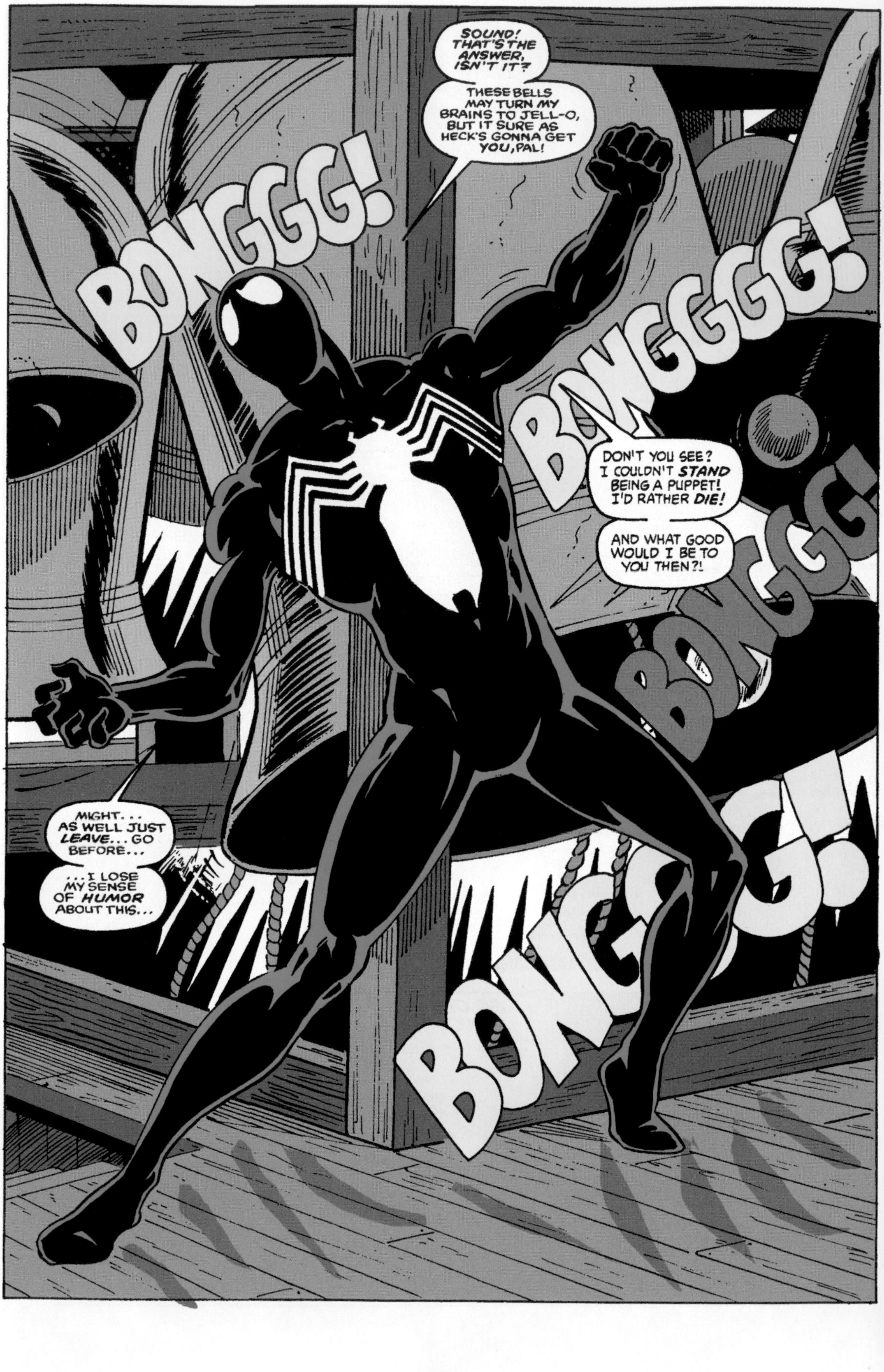
SOUND! THAT'S THE ANSWER, ISN'T IT?
THESE BELLS MAY TURN MY BRAINS TO JELL-O, BUT IT SURE AS HECK'S GONNA GET YOU, PAL!
BONGGG!
BONGGGGG!
DON'T YOU SEE? I COULDN'T STAND BEING A PUPPET! I'D RATHER DIE!
AND WHAT GOOD WOULD I BE TO YOU THEN?!
BONGGG!
MIGHT... AS WELL JUST LEAVE... GO BEFORE...
...I LOSE MY SENSE OF HUMOR ABOUT THIS...

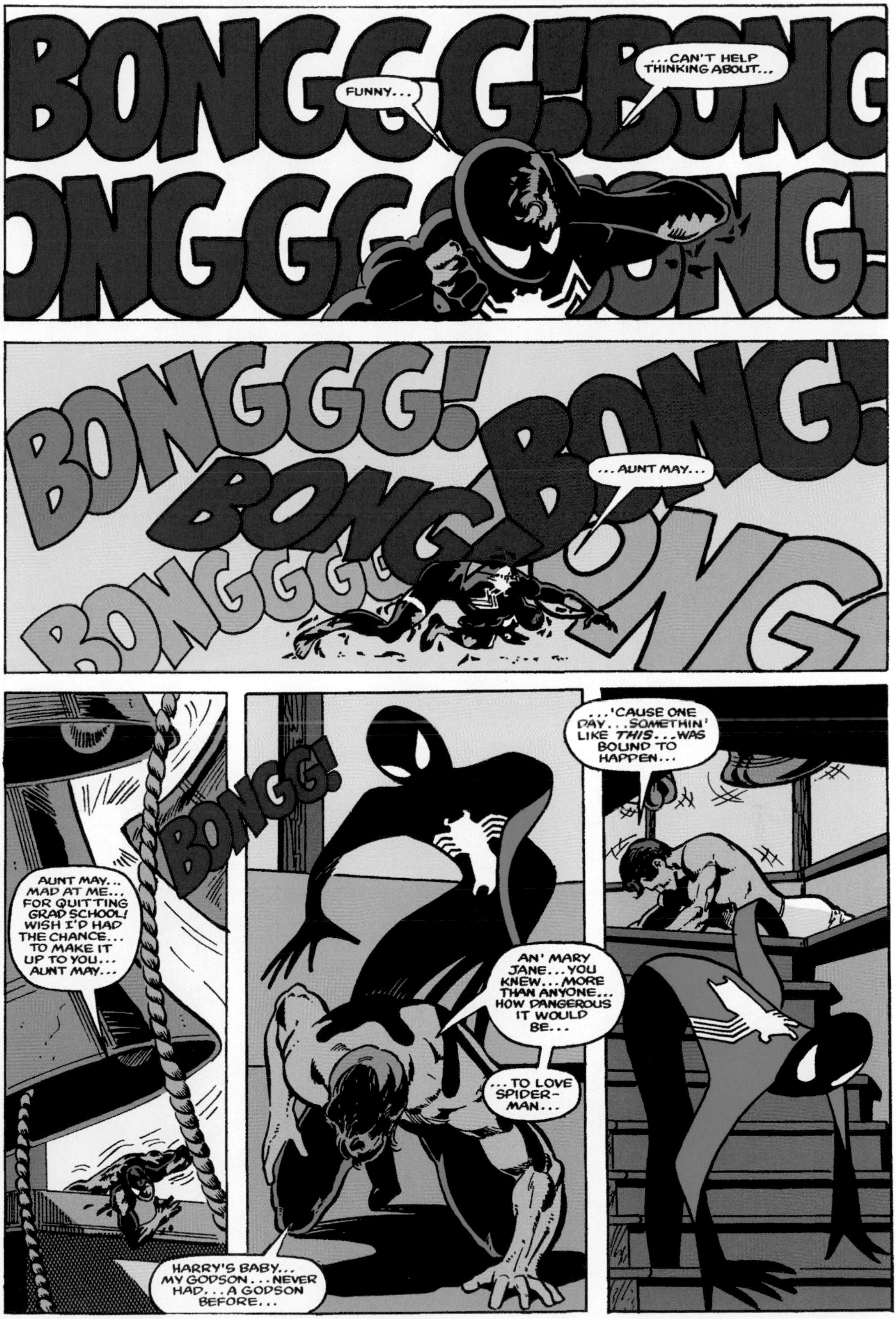

BONGGG! BONG
FUNNY...
...CAN'T HELP THINKING ABOUT...
ONGGG BONG!
BONGGG!
BONG
BONG!
...AUNT MAY...
BONGGGG
BONG
BONGG!
AUNT MAY... MAD AT ME... FOR QUITTING GRAD SCHOOL! WISH I'D HAD THE CHANCE... TO MAKE IT UP TO YOU... AUNT MAY...
HARRY'S BABY... MY GODSON... NEVER HAD... A GODSON BEFORE...
AN' MARY JANE... YOU KNEW... MORE THAN ANYONE... HOW DANGEROUS IT WOULD BE...
...TO LOVE SPIDER-MAN...
...'CAUSE ONE DAY... SOMETHIN' LIKE THIS... WAS BOUND TO HAPPEN...

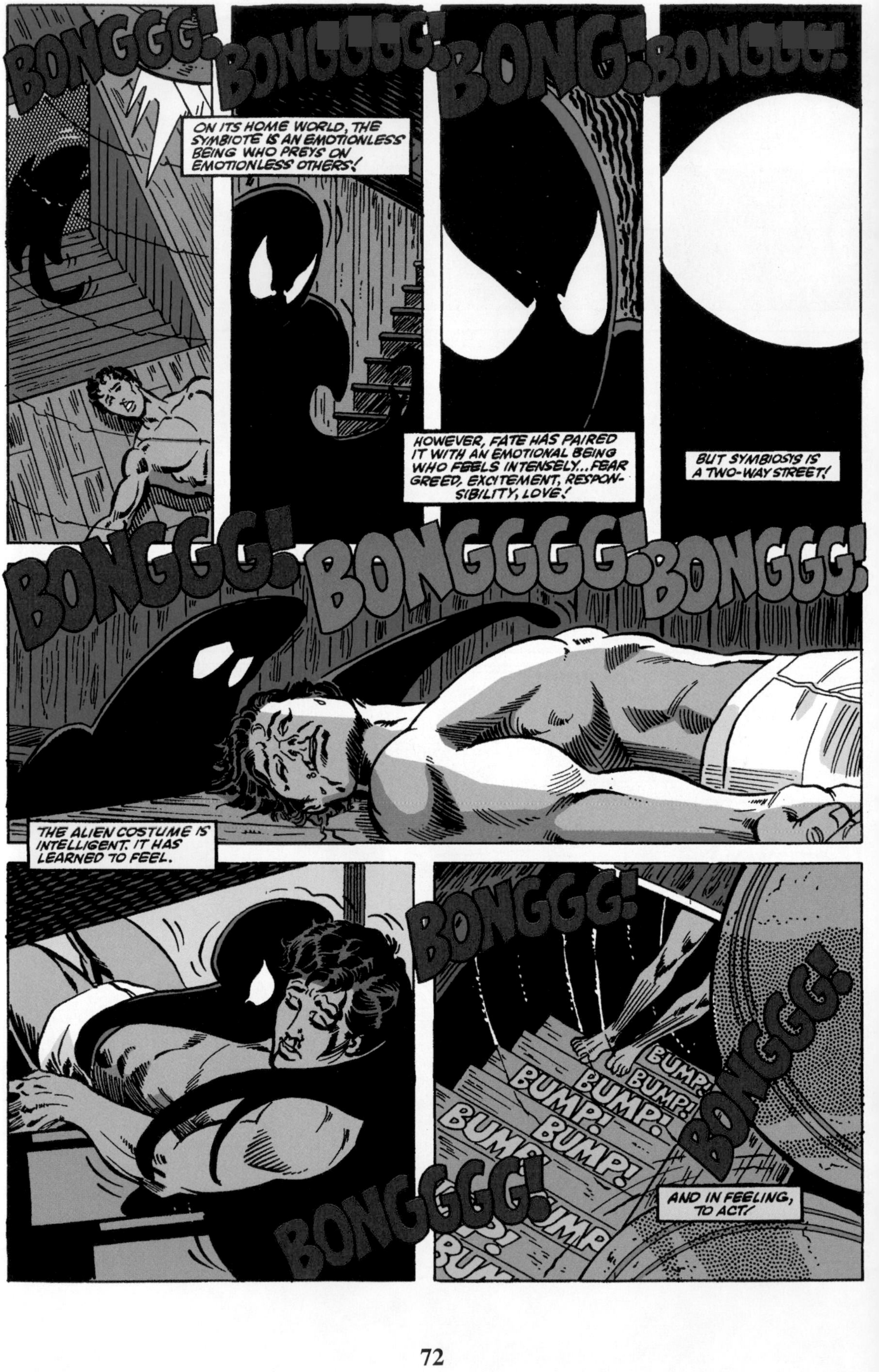
BONGGG!
ON ITS HOME WORLD, THE SYMBIOTE IS AN EMOTIONLESS BEING WHO PREYS ON EMOTIONLESS OTHERS!
BONG!
HOWEVER, FATE HAS PAIRED IT WITH AN EMOTIONAL BEING WHO FEELS INTENSELY... FEAR GREED, EXCITEMENT, RESPONSIBILITY, LOVE!
BUT SYMBIOSYS IS A TWO-WAY STREET!
BONGGG!
BONGGGG!
BONGGG!
THE ALIEN COSTUME IS INTELLIGENT. IT HAS LEARNED TO FEEL.
BONGGGG!
BONGGG!
BUMP! BUMP! BUMP! BUMP! BUMP! BUMP!
BONGGG!
AND IN FEELING, TO ACT!

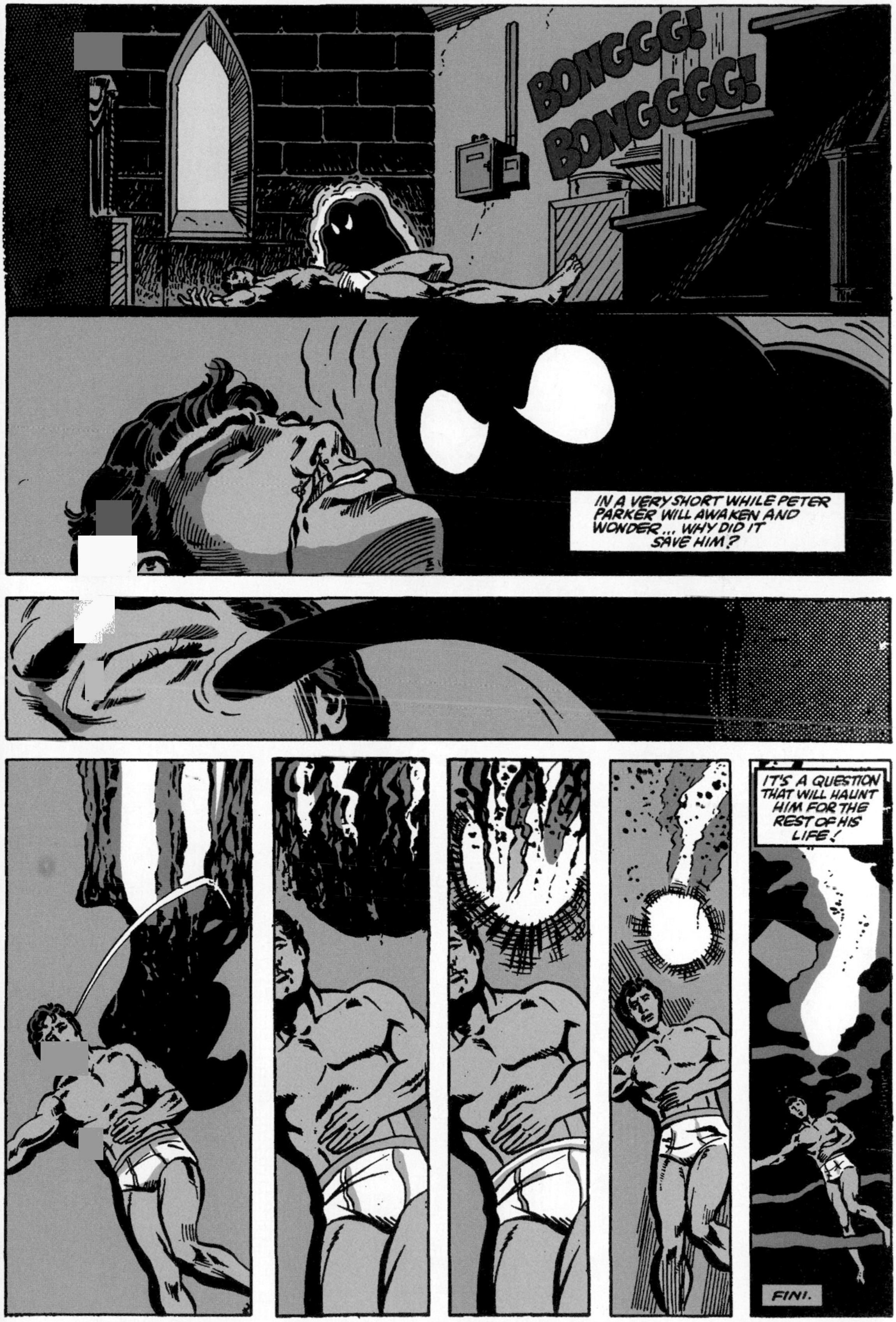
BONGGG!
BONGGGG!
IN A VERY SHORT WHILE PETER PARKER WILL AWAKEN AND WONDER... WHY DID IT SAVE HIM?
IT'S A QUESTION THAT WILL HAUNT HIM FOR THE REST OF HIS LIFE!
FINI.

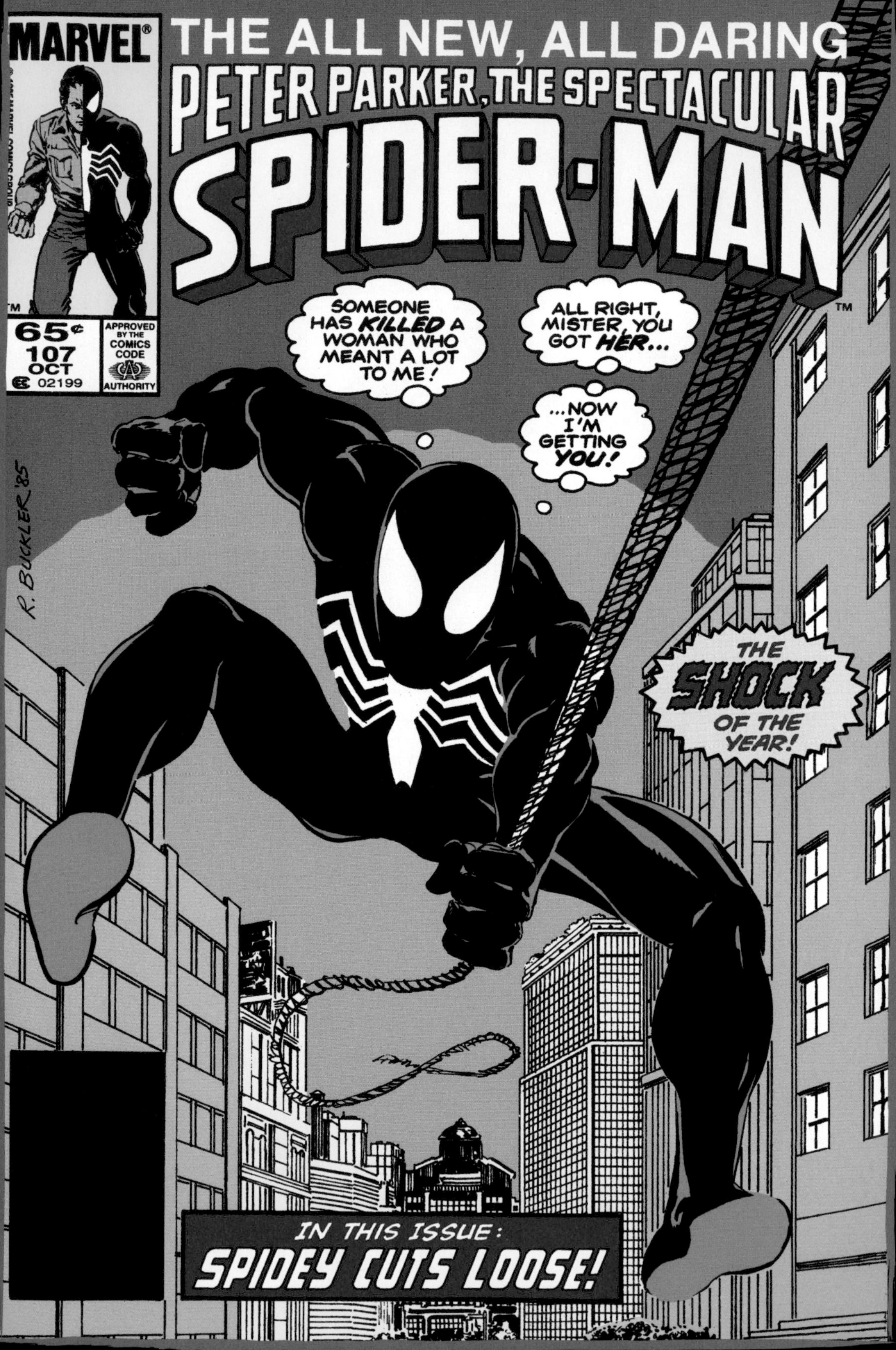

MARVEL®
THE ALL NEW, ALL DARING
PETER PARKER, THE SPECTACULAR
SPIDER-MAN
TM
65¢
107
OCT
02199
APPROVED BY THE COMICS CODE AUTHORITY
SOMEONE HAS KILLED A WOMAN WHO MEANT A LOT TO ME!
ALL RIGHT, MISTER, YOU GOT HER...
...NOW I'M GETTING YOU!
R. BUCKLER '85
THE SHOCK OF THE YEAR!
IN THIS ISSUE:
SPIDEY CUTS LOOSE!

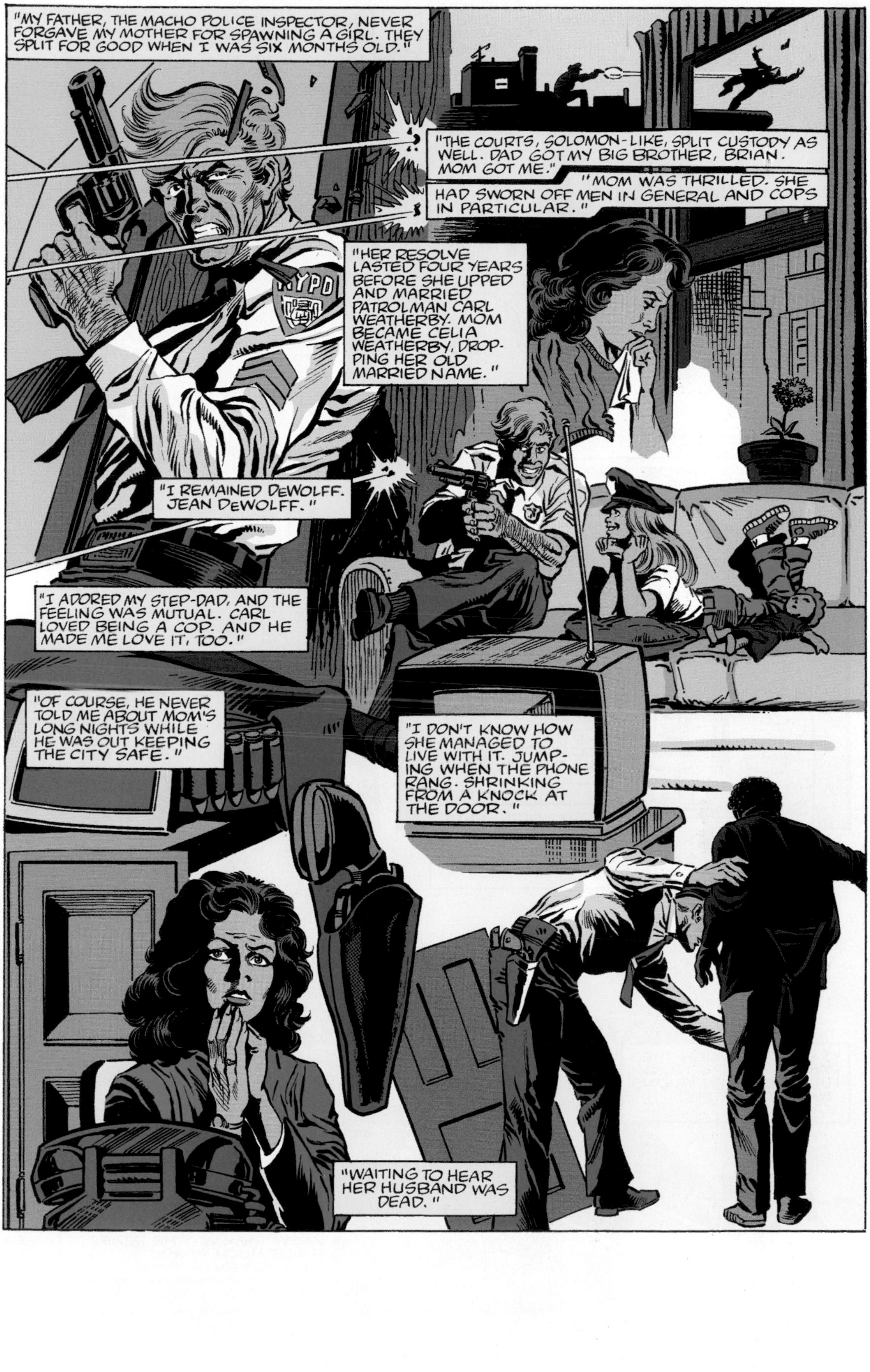
"MY FATHER, THE MACHO POLICE INSPECTOR, NEVER FORGAVE MY MOTHER FOR SPAWNING A GIRL. THEY SPLIT FOR GOOD WHEN I WAS SIX MONTHS OLD."
"THE COURTS, SOLOMON-LIKE, SPLIT CUSTODY AS WELL. DAD GOT MY BIG BROTHER, BRIAN. MOM GOT ME."
"MOM WAS THRILLED. SHE HAD SWORN OFF MEN IN GENERAL AND COPS IN PARTICULAR."
"HER RESOLVE LASTED FOUR YEARS BEFORE SHE UPPED AND MARRIED PATROLMAN CARL WEATHERBY. MOM BECAME CELIA WEATHERBY, DROPPING HER OLD MARRIED NAME."
"I REMAINED DEWOLFF. JEAN DEWOLFF."
"I ADORED MY STEP-DAD, AND THE FEELING WAS MUTUAL. CARL LOVED BEING A COP. AND HE MADE ME LOVE IT, TOO."
"OF COURSE, HE NEVER TOLD ME ABOUT MOM'S LONG NIGHTS WHILE HE WAS OUT KEEPING THE CITY SAFE."
"I DON'T KNOW HOW SHE MANAGED TO LIVE WITH IT. JUMPING WHEN THE PHONE RANG. SHRINKING FROM A KNOCK AT THE DOOR."
"WAITING TO HEAR HER HUSBAND WAS DEAD."
NYPD

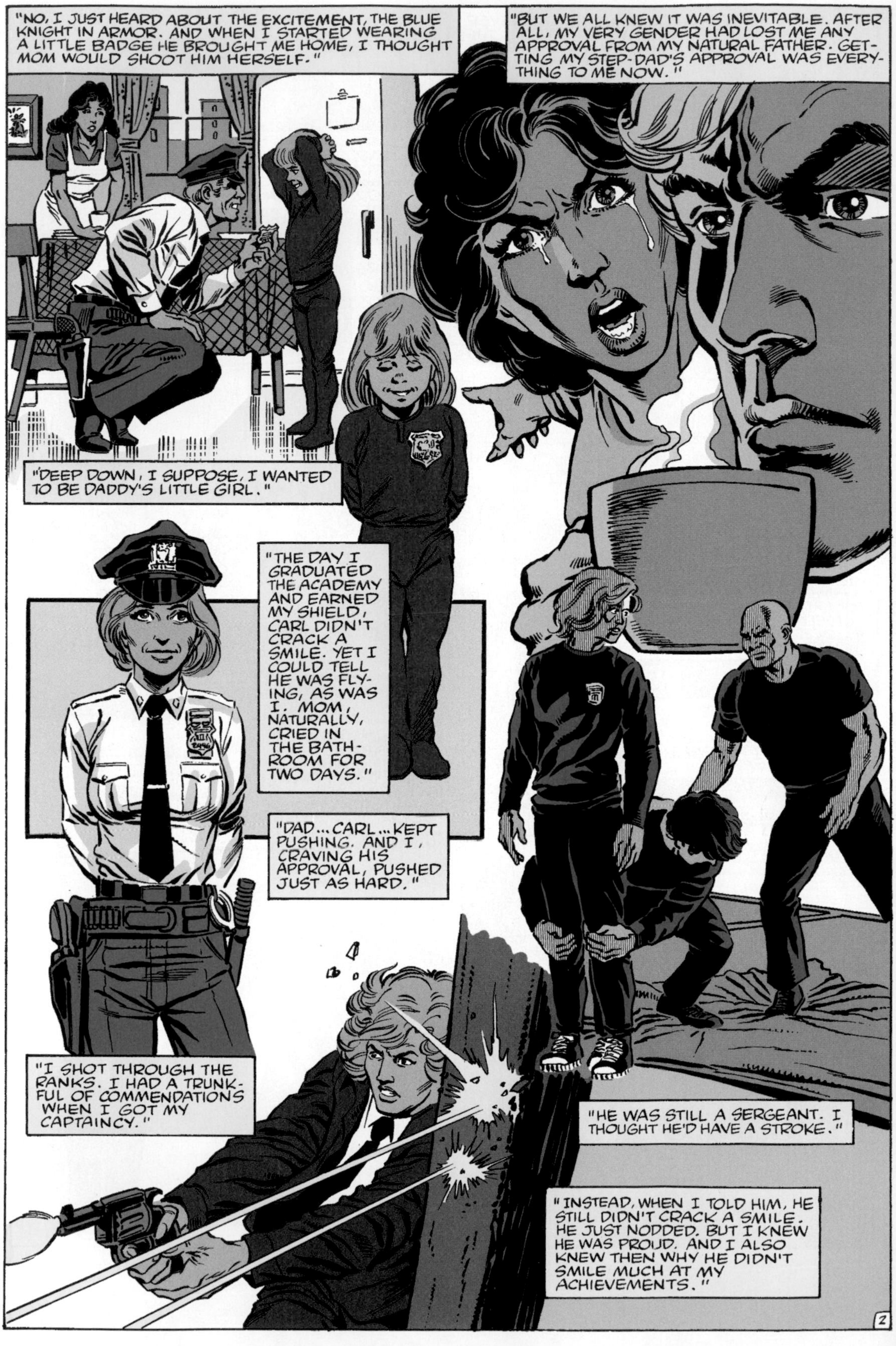
"NO, I JUST HEARD ABOUT THE EXCITEMENT, THE BLUE KNIGHT IN ARMOR. AND WHEN I STARTED WEARING A LITTLE BADGE HE BROUGHT ME HOME, I THOUGHT MOM WOULD SHOOT HIM HERSELF."
"DEEP DOWN, I SUPPOSE, I WANTED TO BE DADDY'S LITTLE GIRL."
"BUT WE ALL KNEW IT WAS INEVITABLE. AFTER ALL, MY VERY GENDER HAD LOST ME ANY APPROVAL FROM MY NATURAL FATHER. GETTING MY STEP-DAD'S APPROVAL WAS EVERYTHING TO ME NOW."
"THE DAY I GRADUATED THE ACADEMY AND EARNED MY SHIELD, CARL DIDN'T CRACK A SMILE. YET I COULD TELL HE WAS FLYING, AS WAS I. MOM, NATURALLY, CRIED IN THE BATHROOM FOR TWO DAYS."
"DAD... CARL... KEPT PUSHING. AND I, CRAVING HIS APPROVAL, PUSHED JUST AS HARD."
"I SHOT THROUGH THE RANKS. I HAD A TRUNKFUL OF COMMENDATIONS WHEN I GOT MY CAPTAINCY."
"HE WAS STILL A SERGEANT. I THOUGHT HE'D HAVE A STROKE."
"INSTEAD, WHEN I TOLD HIM, HE STILL DIDN'T CRACK A SMILE. HE JUST NODDED. BUT I KNEW HE WAS PROUD. AND I ALSO KNEW THEN WHY HE DIDN'T SMILE MUCH AT MY ACHIEVEMENTS."
2

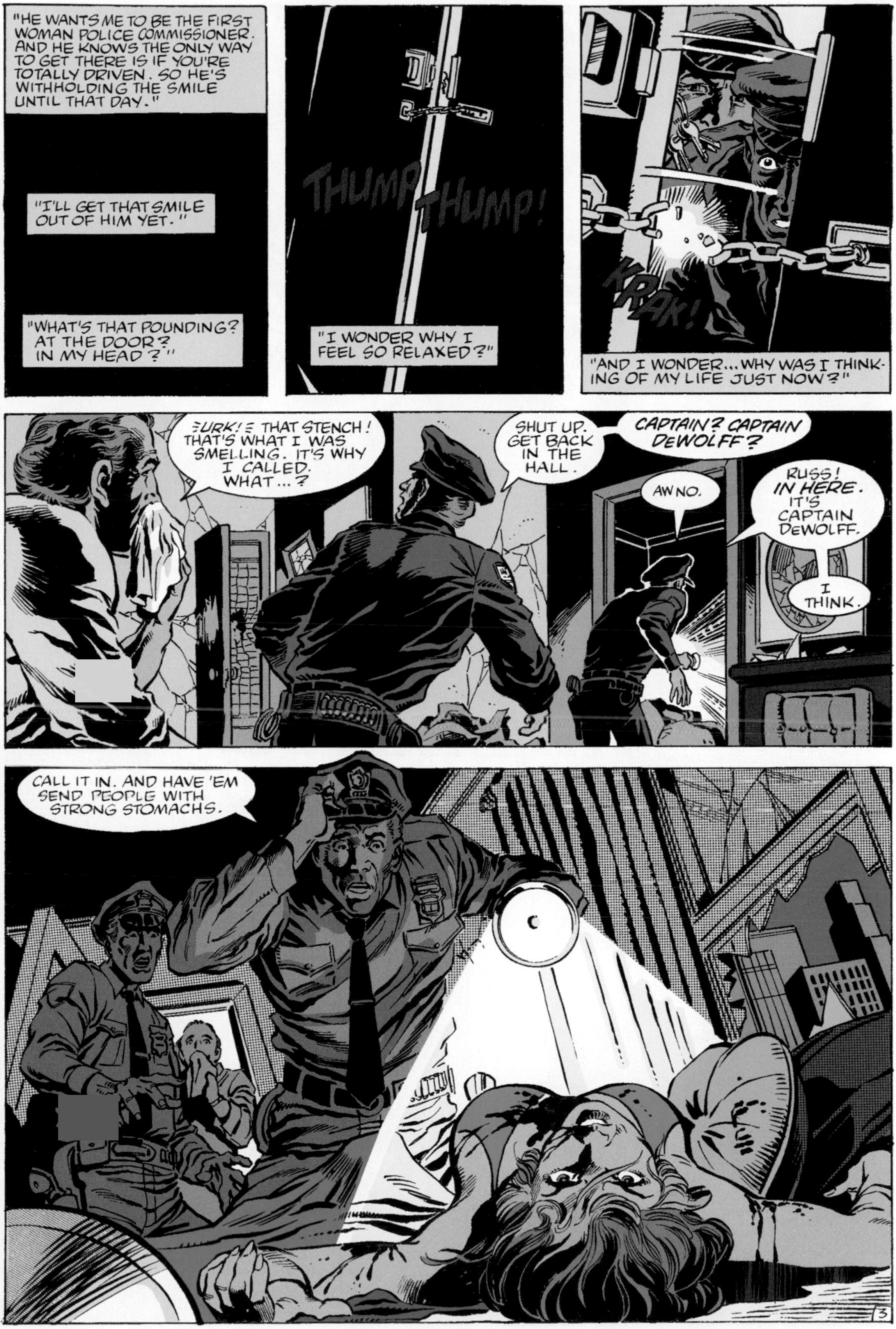
"HE WANTS ME TO BE THE FIRST WOMAN POLICE COMMISSIONER. AND HE KNOWS THE ONLY WAY TO GET THERE IS IF YOU'RE TOTALLY DRIVEN. SO HE'S WITHHOLDING THE SMILE UNTIL THAT DAY."
"I'LL GET THAT SMILE OUT OF HIM YET."
"WHAT'S THAT POUNDING? AT THE DOOR? IN MY HEAD?"
THUMP
THUMP!
"I WONDER WHY I FEEL SO RELAXED?"
KRAK!
"AND I WONDER... WHY WAS I THINKING OF MY LIFE JUST NOW?"
URK! THAT STENCH! THAT'S WHAT I WAS SMELLING. IT'S WHY I CALLED. WHAT...?
SHUT UP. GET BACK IN THE HALL.
CAPTAIN? CAPTAIN DeWOLFF?
AW NO.
RUSS! IN HERE. IT'S CAPTAIN DeWOLFF.
I THINK.
CALL IT IN. AND HAVE 'EM SEND PEOPLE WITH STRONG STOMACHS.
3

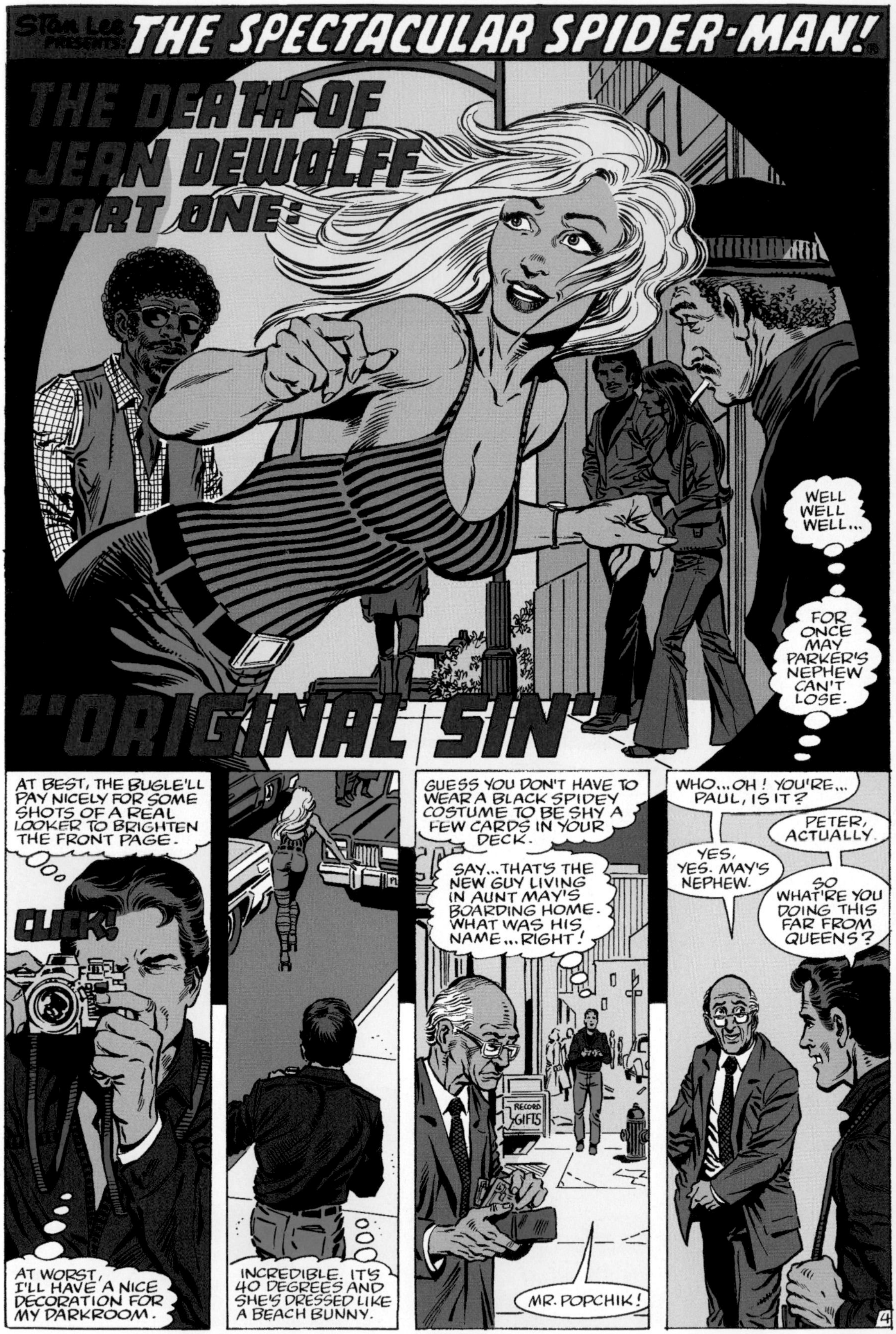
Stan Lee presents: THE SPECTACULAR SPIDER-MAN!
THE DEATH OF JEAN DEWOLFF PART ONE:
"ORIGINAL SIN"
WELL WELL WELL...
FOR ONCE MAY PARKER'S NEPHEW CAN'T LOSE.
AT BEST, THE BUGLE'LL PAY NICELY FOR SOME SHOTS OF A REAL LOOKER TO BRIGHTEN THE FRONT PAGE.
CLICK!
AT WORST, I'LL HAVE A NICE DECORATION FOR MY DARKROOM.
INCREDIBLE. IT'S 40 DEGREES AND SHE'S DRESSED LIKE A BEACH BUNNY.
GUESS YOU DON'T HAVE TO WEAR A BLACK SPIDEY COSTUME TO BE SHY A FEW CARDS IN YOUR DECK.
SAY...THAT'S THE NEW GUY LIVING IN AUNT MAY'S BOARDING HOME. WHAT WAS HIS NAME...RIGHT!
RECORD GIFTS
MR. POPCHIK!
WHO...OH! YOU'RE... PAUL, IS IT?
PETER, ACTUALLY.
YES, YES. MAY'S NEPHEW.
SO WHAT'RE YOU DOING THIS FAR FROM QUEENS?
4

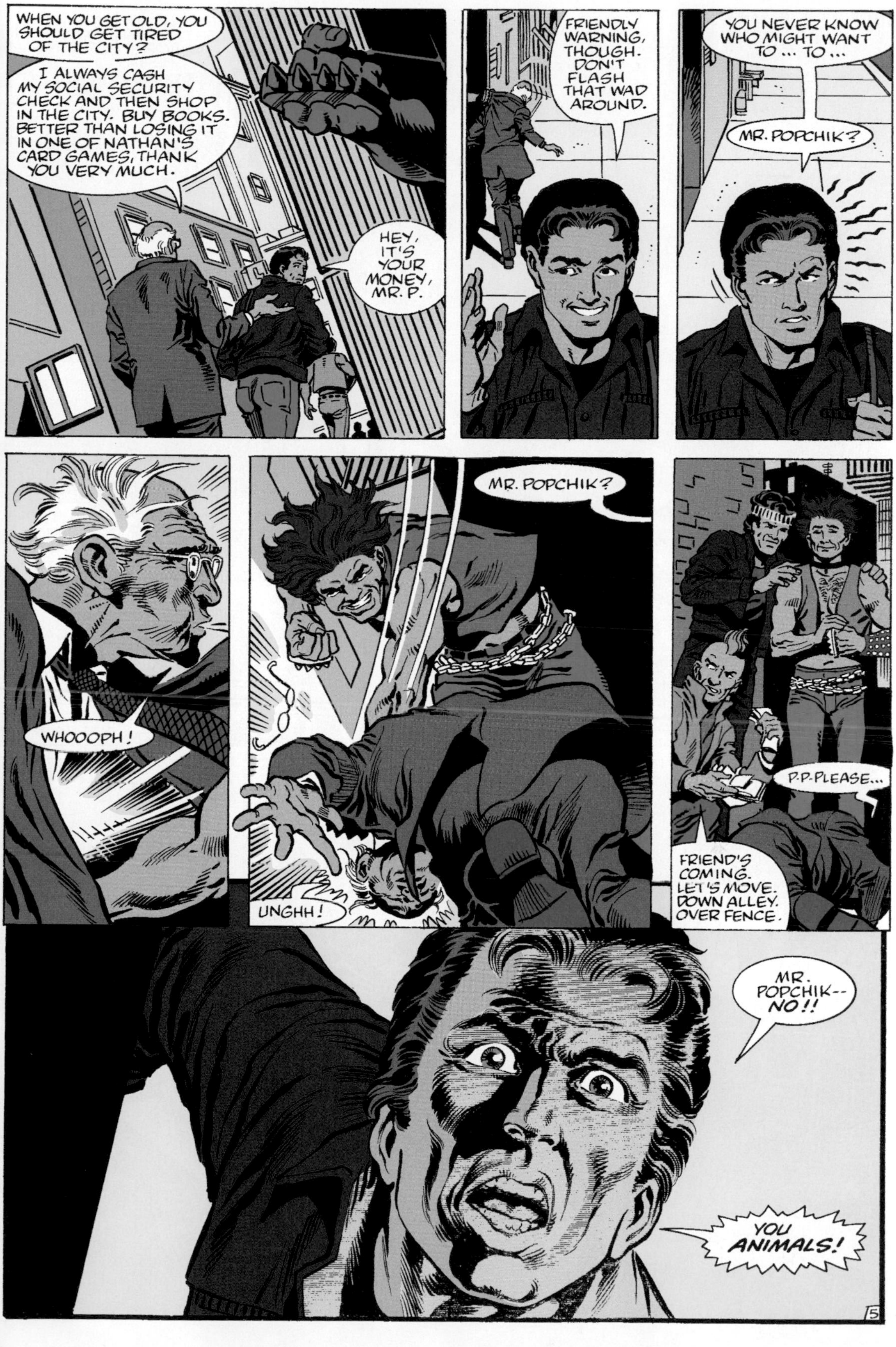
WHEN YOU GET OLD, YOU SHOULD GET TIRED OF THE CITY?
I ALWAYS CASH MY SOCIAL SECURITY CHECK AND THEN SHOP IN THE CITY. BUY BOOKS. BETTER THAN LOSING IT IN ONE OF NATHAN'S CARD GAMES, THANK YOU VERY MUCH.
HEY, IT'S YOUR MONEY, MR. P.
FRIENDLY WARNING, THOUGH. DON'T FLASH THAT WAD AROUND.
YOU NEVER KNOW WHO MIGHT WANT TO ... TO ...
MR. POPCHIK?
WHOOOPH!
MR. POPCHIK?
UNGHH!
P-P-PLEASE...
FRIEND'S COMING. LET'S MOVE. DOWN ALLEY. OVER FENCE.
MR. POPCHIK-- NO!!
YOU ANIMALS!
5

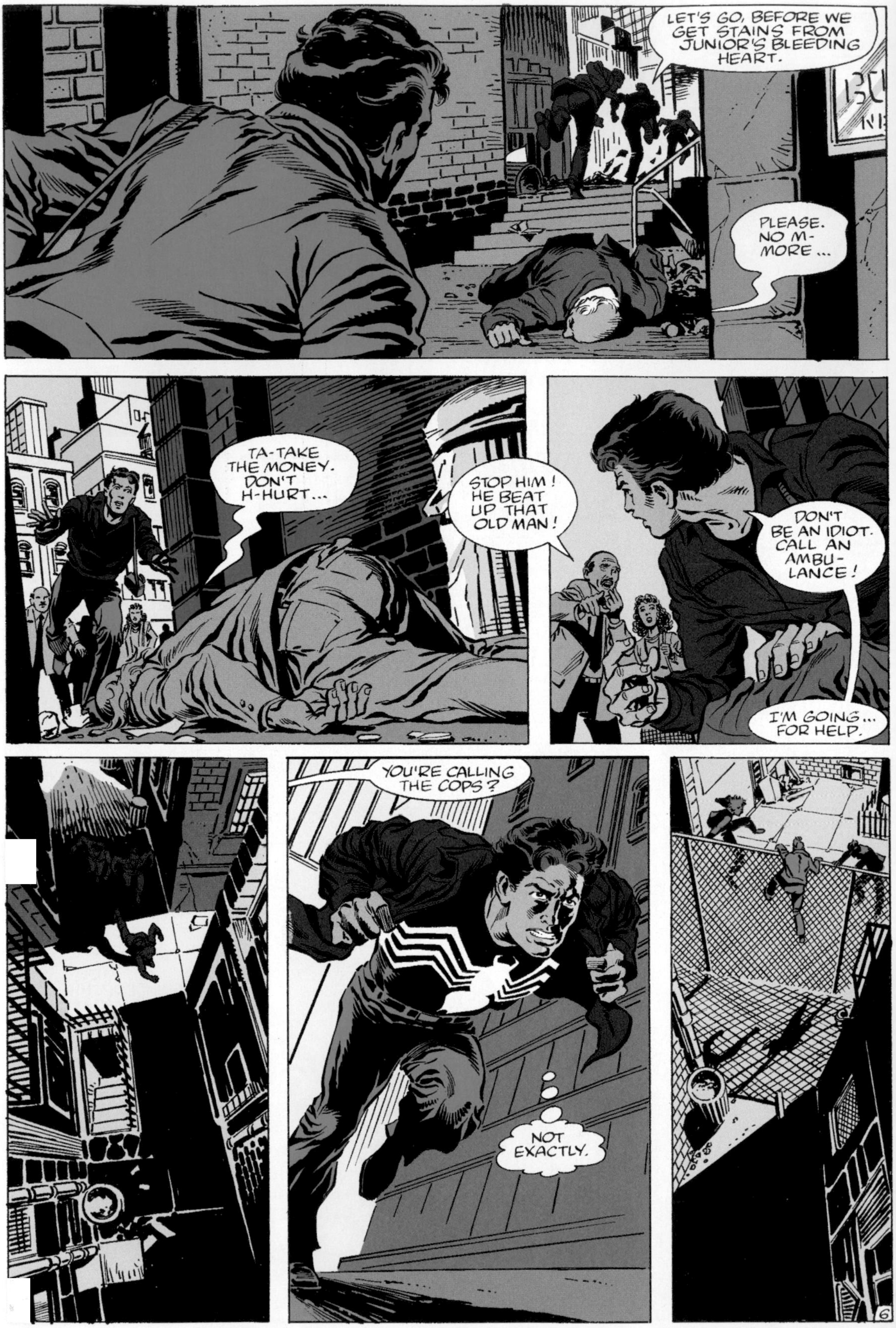
LET'S GO, BEFORE WE GET STAINS FROM JUNIOR'S BLEEDING HEART.
PLEASE. NO M-MORE...
TA-TAKE THE MONEY. DON'T H-HURT...
STOP HIM! HE BEAT UP THAT OLD MAN!
DON'T BE AN IDIOT. CALL AN AMBULANCE!
I'M GOING... FOR HELP.
YOU'RE CALLING THE COPS?
NOT EXACTLY.
6

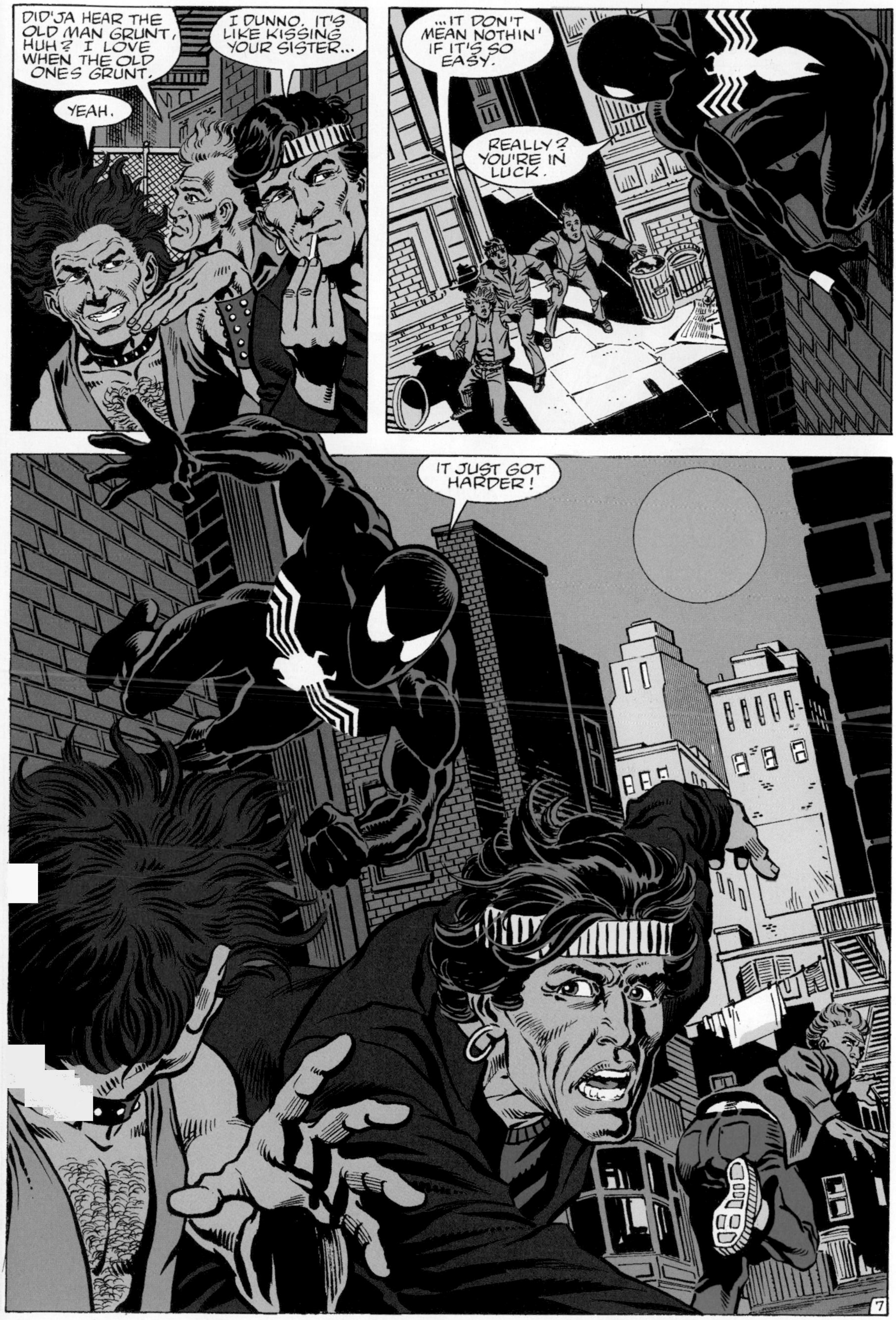
DID'JA HEAR THE OLD MAN GRUNT, HUH? I LOVE WHEN THE OLD ONES GRUNT.
YEAH.
I DUNNO. IT'S LIKE KISSING YOUR SISTER...
...IT DON'T MEAN NOTHIN' IF IT'S SO EASY.
REALLY? YOU'RE IN LUCK.
IT JUST GOT HARDER!
7

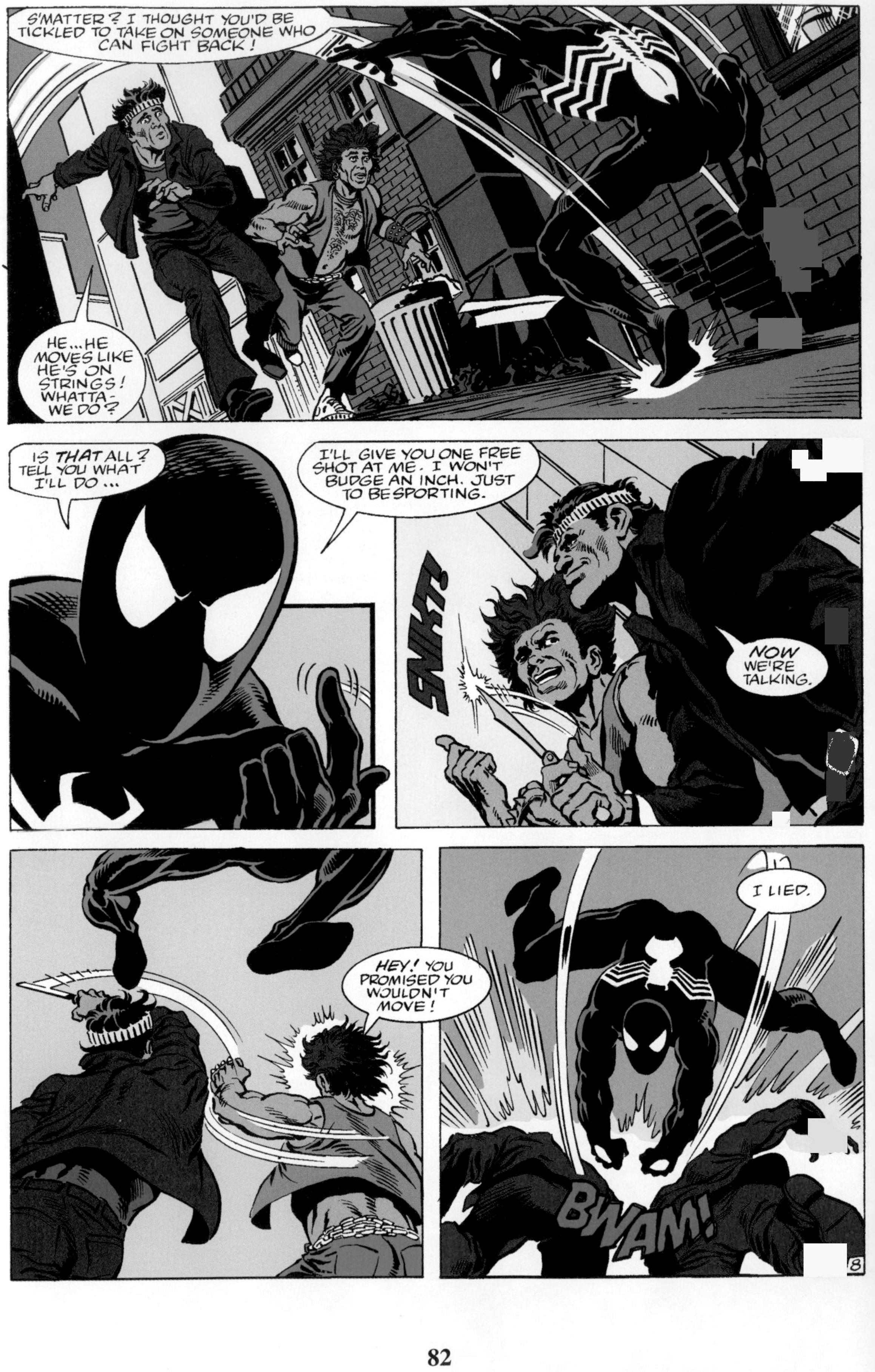
S'MATTER? I THOUGHT YOU'D BE TICKLED TO TAKE ON SOMEONE WHO CAN FIGHT BACK!
HE...HE MOVES LIKE HE'S ON STRINGS! WHATTA-WE DO?
IS THAT ALL? TELL YOU WHAT I'LL DO...
I'LL GIVE YOU ONE FREE SHOT AT ME. I WON'T BUDGE AN INCH. JUST TO BE SPORTING.
SNIKT!
NOW WE'RE TALKING.
HEY! YOU PROMISED YOU WOULDN'T MOVE!
I LIED.
BWAM!
8

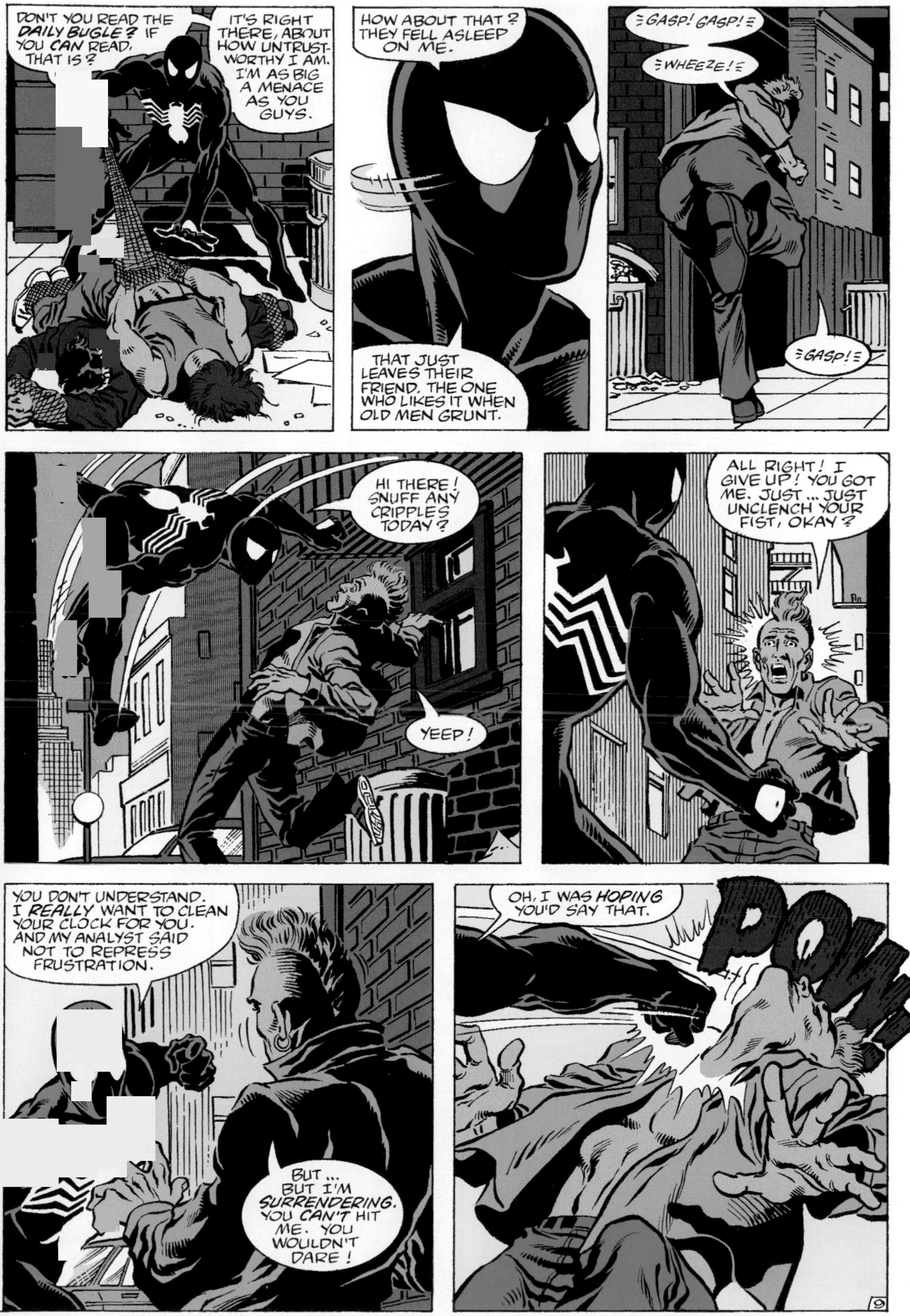
DON'T YOU READ THE DAILY BUGLE? IF YOU CAN READ, THAT IS?
IT'S RIGHT THERE, ABOUT HOW UNTRUSTWORTHY I AM. I'M AS BIG A MENACE AS YOU GUYS.
HOW ABOUT THAT? THEY FELL ASLEEP ON ME.
THAT JUST LEAVES THEIR FRIEND. THE ONE WHO LIKES IT WHEN OLD MEN GRUNT.
GASP! GASP!
WHEEZE!
GASP!
HI THERE! SNUFF ANY CRIPPLES TODAY?
YEEP!
ALL RIGHT! I GIVE UP! YOU GOT ME. JUST... JUST UNCLENCH YOUR FIST, OKAY?
YOU DON'T UNDERSTAND. I REALLY WANT TO CLEAN YOUR CLOCK FOR YOU. AND MY ANALYST SAID NOT TO REPRESS FRUSTRATION.
BUT... BUT I'M SURRENDERING. YOU CAN'T HIT ME. YOU WOULDN'T DARE!
OH, I WAS HOPING YOU'D SAY THAT.
POW
9

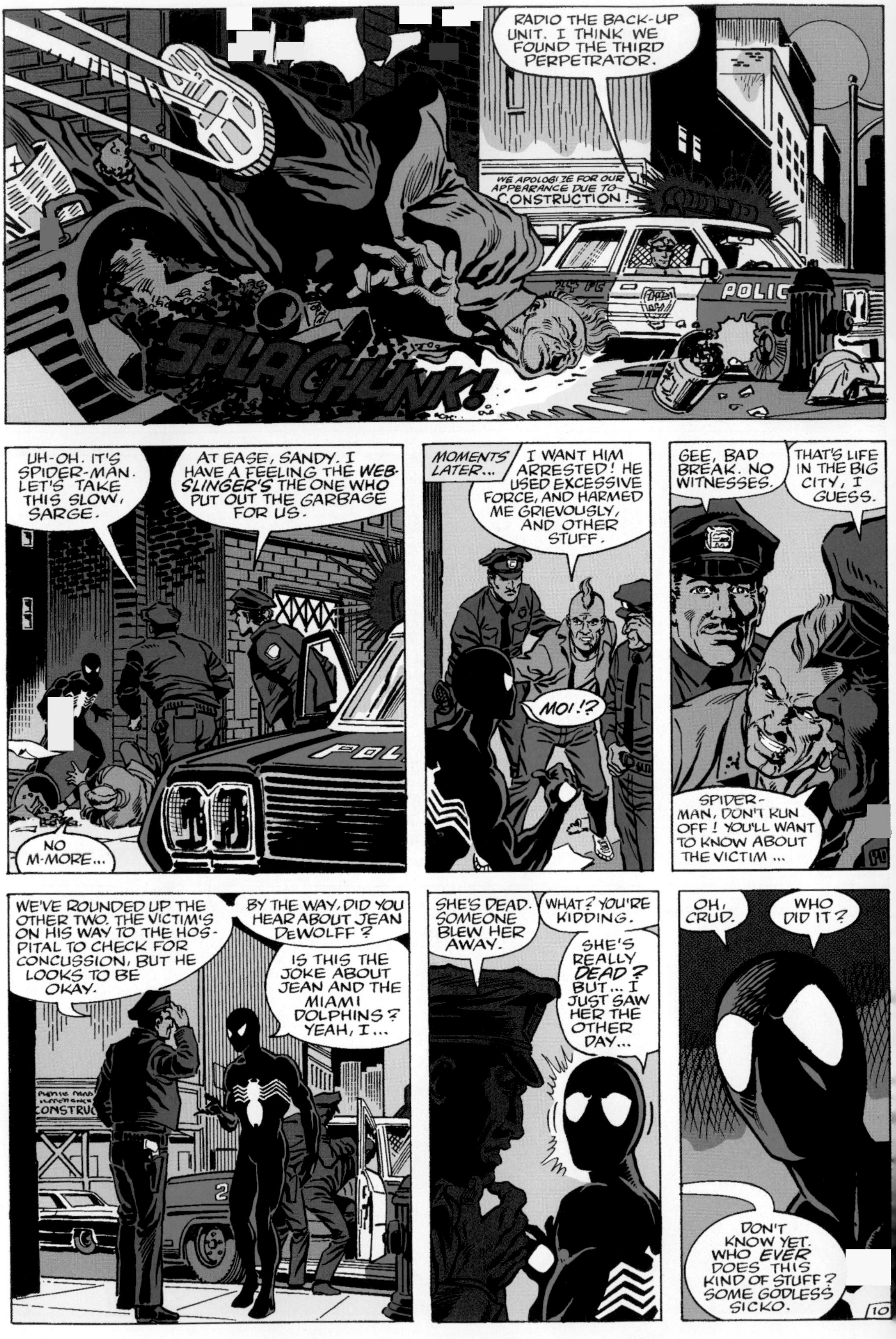
RADIO THE BACK-UP UNIT. I THINK WE FOUND THE THIRD PERPETRATOR.
WE APOLOGIZE FOR OUR APPEARANCE DUE TO CONSTRUCTION!
SPLACHUNK!
POLIC
UH-OH. IT'S SPIDER-MAN. LET'S TAKE THIS SLOW, SARGE.
AT EASE, SANDY. I HAVE A FEELING THE WEB-SLINGER'S THE ONE WHO PUT OUT THE GARBAGE FOR US.
NO M-MORE...
MOMENTS LATER...
I WANT HIM ARRESTED! HE USED EXCESSIVE FORCE, AND HARMED ME GRIEVOUSLY, AND OTHER STUFF.
MOI!?
GEE, BAD BREAK. NO WITNESSES.
THAT'S LIFE IN THE BIG CITY, I GUESS.
SPIDER-MAN, DON'T RUN OFF! YOU'LL WANT TO KNOW ABOUT THE VICTIM ...
WE'VE ROUNDED UP THE OTHER TWO. THE VICTIM'S ON HIS WAY TO THE HOSPITAL TO CHECK FOR CONCUSSION, BUT HE LOOKS TO BE OKAY.
BY THE WAY, DID YOU HEAR ABOUT JEAN DEWOLFF?
IS THIS THE JOKE ABOUT JEAN AND THE MIAMI DOLPHINS? YEAH, I...
SHE'S DEAD. SOMEONE BLEW HER AWAY.
WHAT? YOU'RE KIDDING.
SHE'S REALLY DEAD? BUT... I JUST SAW HER THE OTHER DAY...
OH, CRUD.
WHO DID IT?
DON'T KNOW YET. WHO EVER DOES THIS KIND OF STUFF? SOME GODLESS SICKO.
10

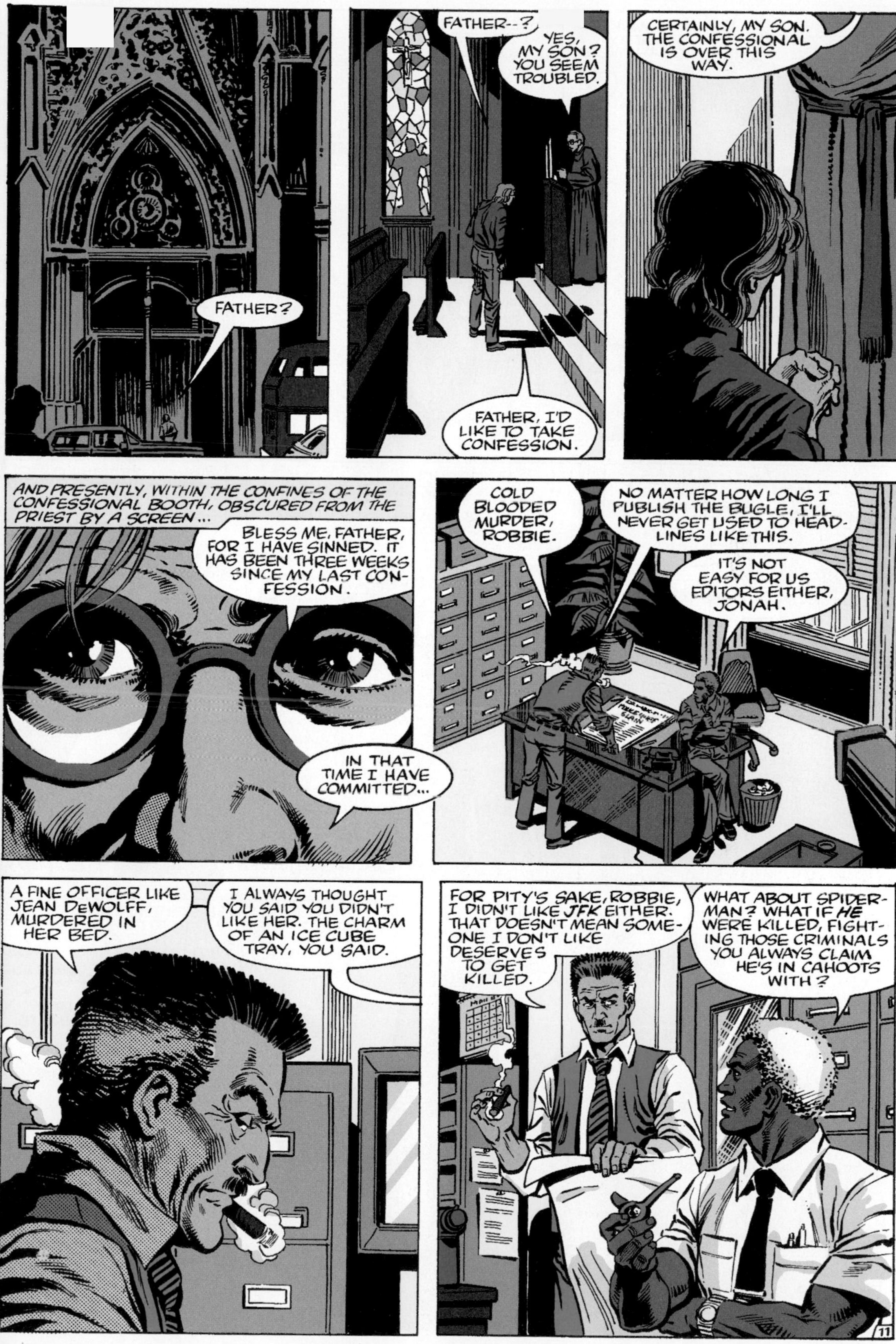
FATHER?
FATHER--?
YES, MY SON? YOU SEEM TROUBLED.
FATHER, I'D LIKE TO TAKE CONFESSION.
CERTAINLY, MY SON. THE CONFESSIONAL IS OVER THIS WAY.
AND PRESENTLY, WITHIN THE CONFINES OF THE CONFESSIONAL BOOTH, OBSCURED FROM THE PRIEST BY A SCREEN...
BLESS ME, FATHER, FOR I HAVE SINNED. IT HAS BEEN THREE WEEKS SINCE MY LAST CONFESSION.
IN THAT TIME I HAVE COMMITTED...
COLD BLOODED MURDER, ROBBIE.
NO MATTER HOW LONG I PUBLISH THE BUGLE, I'LL NEVER GET USED TO HEADLINES LIKE THIS.
IT'S NOT EASY FOR US EDITORS EITHER, JONAH.
A FINE OFFICER LIKE JEAN DEWOLFF, MURDERED IN HER BED.
I ALWAYS THOUGHT YOU SAID YOU DIDN'T LIKE HER. THE CHARM OF AN ICE CUBE TRAY, YOU SAID.
FOR PITY'S SAKE, ROBBIE, I DIDN'T LIKE JFK EITHER. THAT DOESN'T MEAN SOMEONE I DON'T LIKE DESERVES TO GET KILLED.
WHAT ABOUT SPIDER-MAN? WHAT IF HE WERE KILLED, FIGHTING THOSE CRIMINALS YOU ALWAYS CLAIM HE'S IN CAHOOTS WITH?
11

YOU'RE BEING BLASTED MORBID, ROBBIE.

IT'S A MORBID NEWSDAY, JONAH. WELL?

WELL... HITLER DESERVED TO DIE...

AND SO DO ASSASSINS AND COP KILLERS. SCUM LIKE THAT. WHATEVER ELSE HE IS, SPIDER-MAN IS *NOT* ONE OF THOSE.

WHY JONAH, THAT'S THE NICEST THING YOU'VE EVER SAID ABOUT SPIDER-MAN IN YOUR LIFE.

YEAH, BUT DON'T QUOTE ME.

MR. ROBERTSON? AH... SORRY TO BREAK IN. I'M REVEREND JACKSON TOLLIVER.

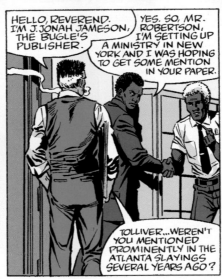

HELLO, REVEREND. I'M J. JONAH JAMESON, THE BUGLE'S PUBLISHER.

YES. SO, MR. ROBERTSON, I'M SETTING UP A MINISTRY IN NEW YORK AND I WAS HOPING TO GET SOME MENTION IN YOUR PAPER.

TOLLIVER... WEREN'T YOU MENTIONED PROMINENTLY IN THE ATLANTA SLAYINGS SEVERAL YEARS AGO?

WHY, I'M SURPRISED, SIR, THAT A WHITE MAN WOULD CARE SO ABOUT THE SLAYINGS OF YOUNG BLACK CHILDREN.

WHY, REVEREND TOLLIVER... ARE YOU A RACIST?

MY APOLOGIES, SIR.

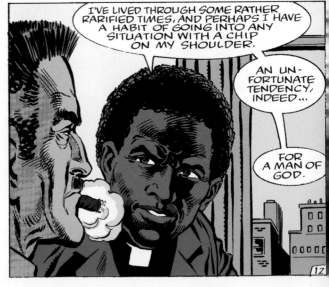

I'VE LIVED THROUGH SOME RATHER RARIFIED TIMES, AND PERHAPS I HAVE A HABIT OF GOING INTO ANY SITUATION WITH A CHIP ON MY SHOULDER.

AN UNFORTUNATE TENDENCY, INDEED...

FOR A MAN OF GOD.

12

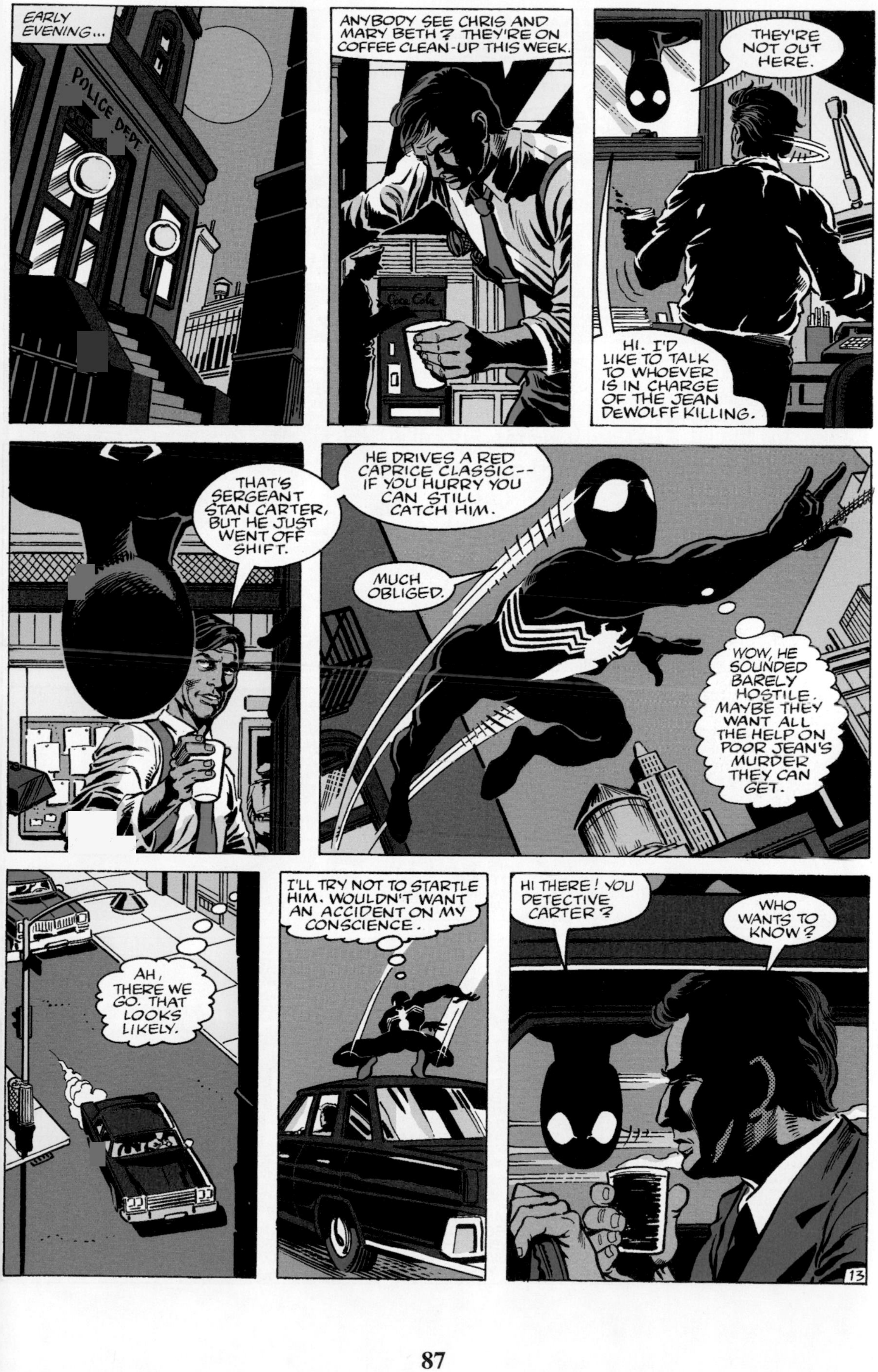
EARLY EVENING...
POLICE DEPT.
ANYBODY SEE CHRIS AND MARY BETH? THEY'RE ON COFFEE CLEAN-UP THIS WEEK.
THEY'RE NOT OUT HERE.
HI. I'D LIKE TO TALK TO WHOEVER IS IN CHARGE OF THE JEAN DEWOLFF KILLING.
THAT'S SERGEANT STAN CARTER, BUT HE JUST WENT OFF SHIFT.
HE DRIVES A RED CAPRICE CLASSIC-- IF YOU HURRY YOU CAN STILL CATCH HIM.
MUCH OBLIGED.
WOW, HE SOUNDED BARELY HOSTILE. MAYBE THEY WANT ALL THE HELP ON POOR JEAN'S MURDER THEY CAN GET.
AH, THERE WE GO. THAT LOOKS LIKELY.
I'LL TRY NOT TO STARTLE HIM. WOULDN'T WANT AN ACCIDENT ON MY CONSCIENCE.
HI THERE! YOU DETECTIVE CARTER?
WHO WANTS TO KNOW?
13

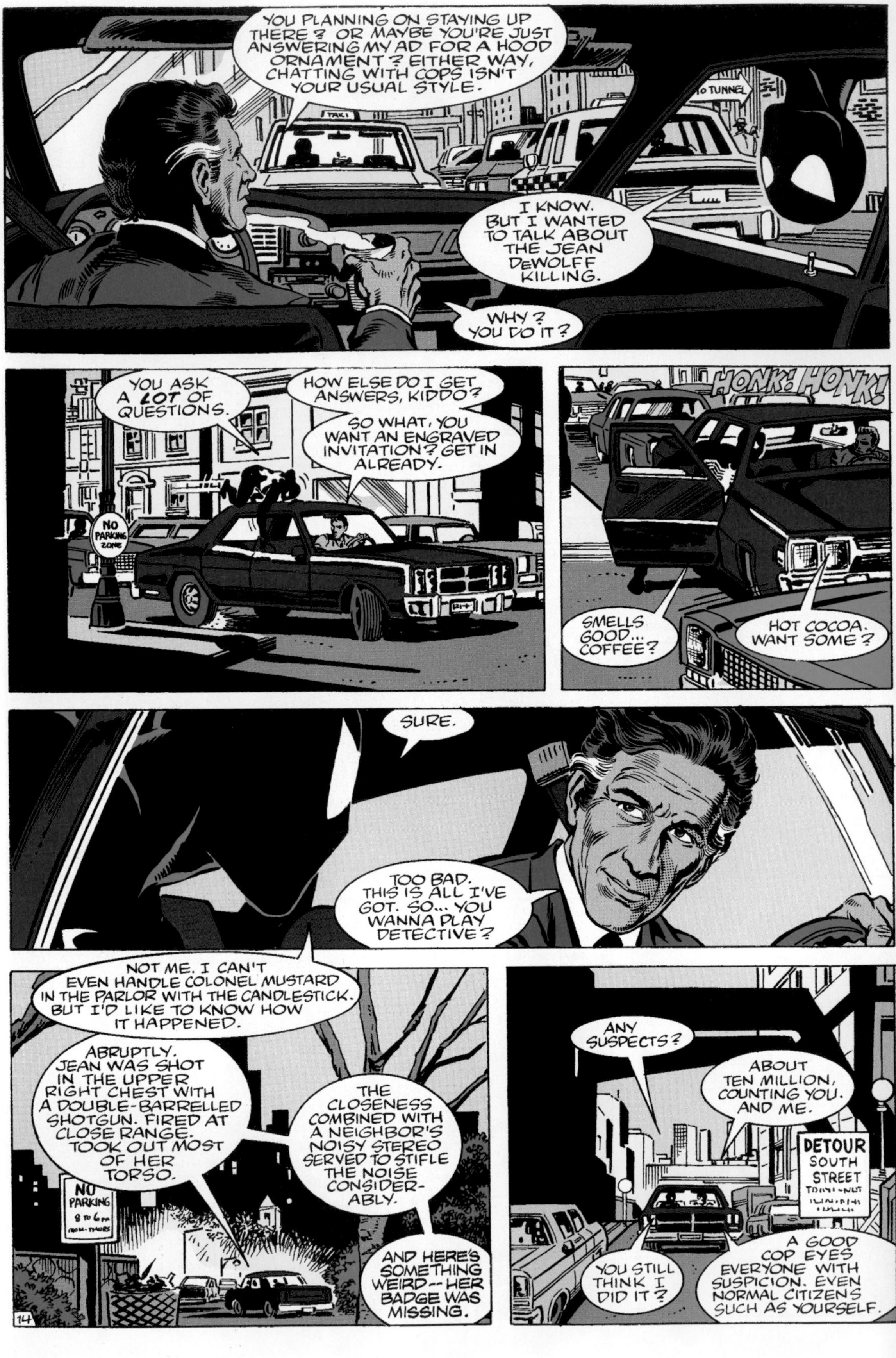

YOU PLANNING ON STAYING UP THERE ? OR MAYBE YOU'RE JUST ANSWERING MY AD FOR A HOOD ORNAMENT ? EITHER WAY, CHATTING WITH COPS ISN'T YOUR USUAL STYLE.
TO TUNNEL
I KNOW. BUT I WANTED TO TALK ABOUT THE JEAN DEWOLFF KILLING.
WHY ? YOU DO IT ?
YOU ASK A LOT OF QUESTIONS.
HOW ELSE DO I GET ANSWERS, KIDDO ?
SO WHAT, YOU WANT AN ENGRAVED INVITATION ? GET IN ALREADY.
NO PARKING ZONE
HONK! HONK!
SMELLS GOOD... COFFEE?
HOT COCOA. WANT SOME ?
SURE.
TOO BAD. THIS IS ALL I'VE GOT. SO... YOU WANNA PLAY DETECTIVE ?
NOT ME. I CAN'T EVEN HANDLE COLONEL MUSTARD IN THE PARLOR WITH THE CANDLESTICK. BUT I'D LIKE TO KNOW HOW IT HAPPENED.
ABRUPTLY. JEAN WAS SHOT IN THE UPPER RIGHT CHEST WITH A DOUBLE-BARRELLED SHOTGUN. FIRED AT CLOSE RANGE. TOOK OUT MOST OF HER TORSO.
THE CLOSENESS COMBINED WITH A NEIGHBOR'S NOISY STEREO SERVED TO STIFLE THE NOISE CONSIDER-ABLY.
NO PARKING 8 TO 6 PM
AND HERE'S SOMETHING WEIRD-- HER BADGE WAS MISSING.
14
ANY SUSPECTS ?
ABOUT TEN MILLION, COUNTING YOU. AND ME.
DETOUR SOUTH STREET
YOU STILL THINK I DID IT ?
A GOOD COP EYES EVERYONE WITH SUSPICION. EVEN NORMAL CITIZENS SUCH AS YOURSELF.

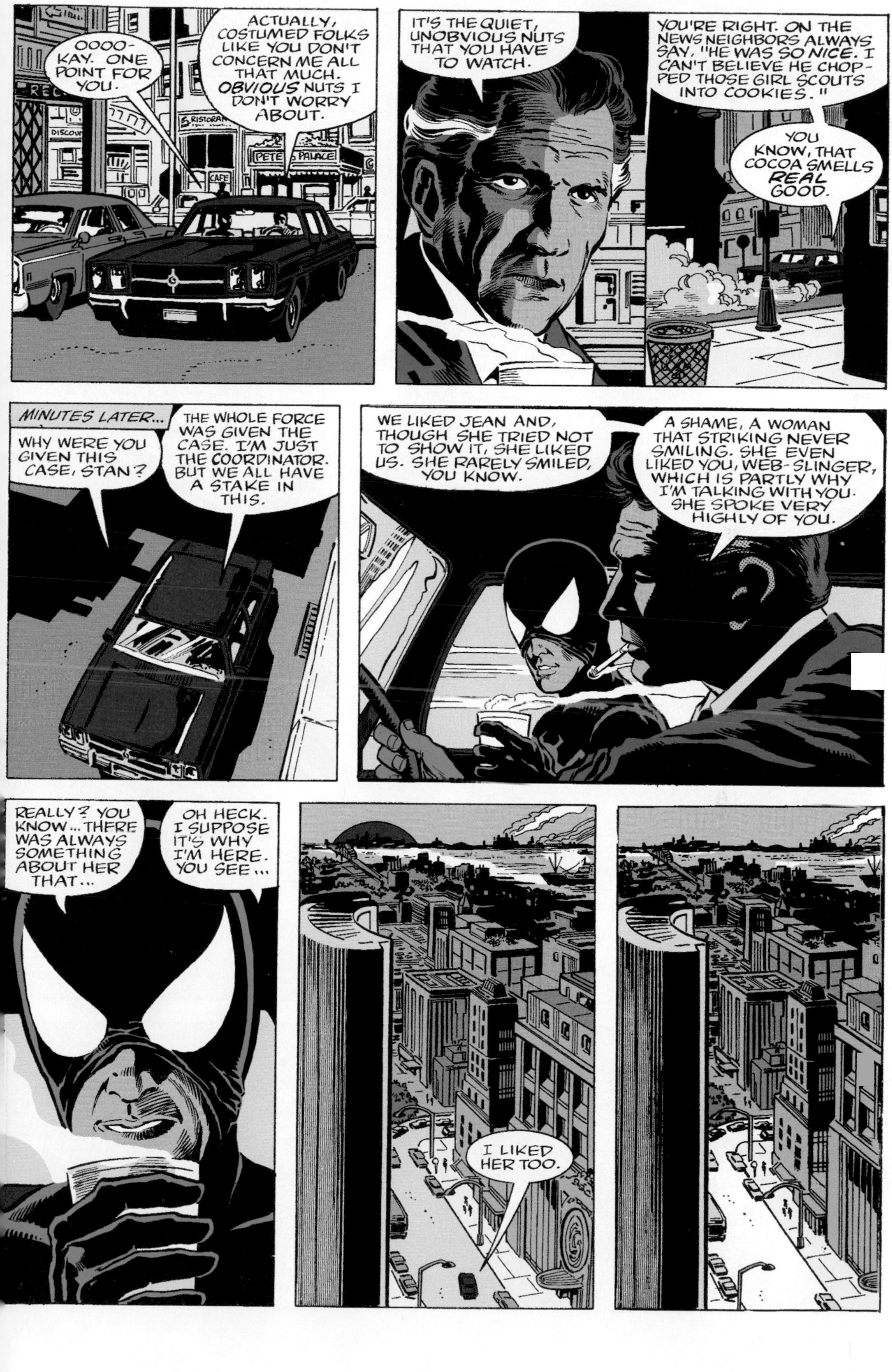
OOOO-KAY. ONE POINT FOR YOU.
ACTUALLY, COSTUMED FOLKS LIKE YOU DON'T CONCERN ME ALL THAT MUCH. OBVIOUS NUTS I DON'T WORRY ABOUT.
IT'S THE QUIET, UNOBVIOUS NUTS THAT YOU HAVE TO WATCH.
YOU'RE RIGHT. ON THE NEWS NEIGHBORS ALWAYS SAY, "HE WAS SO NICE. I CAN'T BELIEVE HE CHOPPED THOSE GIRL SCOUTS INTO COOKIES."
YOU KNOW, THAT COCOA SMELLS REAL GOOD.
MINUTES LATER...
WHY WERE YOU GIVEN THIS CASE, STAN?
THE WHOLE FORCE WAS GIVEN THE CASE. I'M JUST THE COORDINATOR. BUT WE ALL HAVE A STAKE IN THIS.
WE LIKED JEAN AND, THOUGH SHE TRIED NOT TO SHOW IT, SHE LIKED US. SHE RARELY SMILED, YOU KNOW.
A SHAME, A WOMAN THAT STRIKING NEVER SMILING. SHE EVEN LIKED YOU, WEB-SLINGER, WHICH IS PARTLY WHY I'M TALKING WITH YOU. SHE SPOKE VERY HIGHLY OF YOU.
REALLY? YOU KNOW... THERE WAS ALWAYS SOMETHING ABOUT HER THAT...
OH HECK. I SUPPOSE IT'S WHY I'M HERE. YOU SEE...
I LIKED HER TOO.

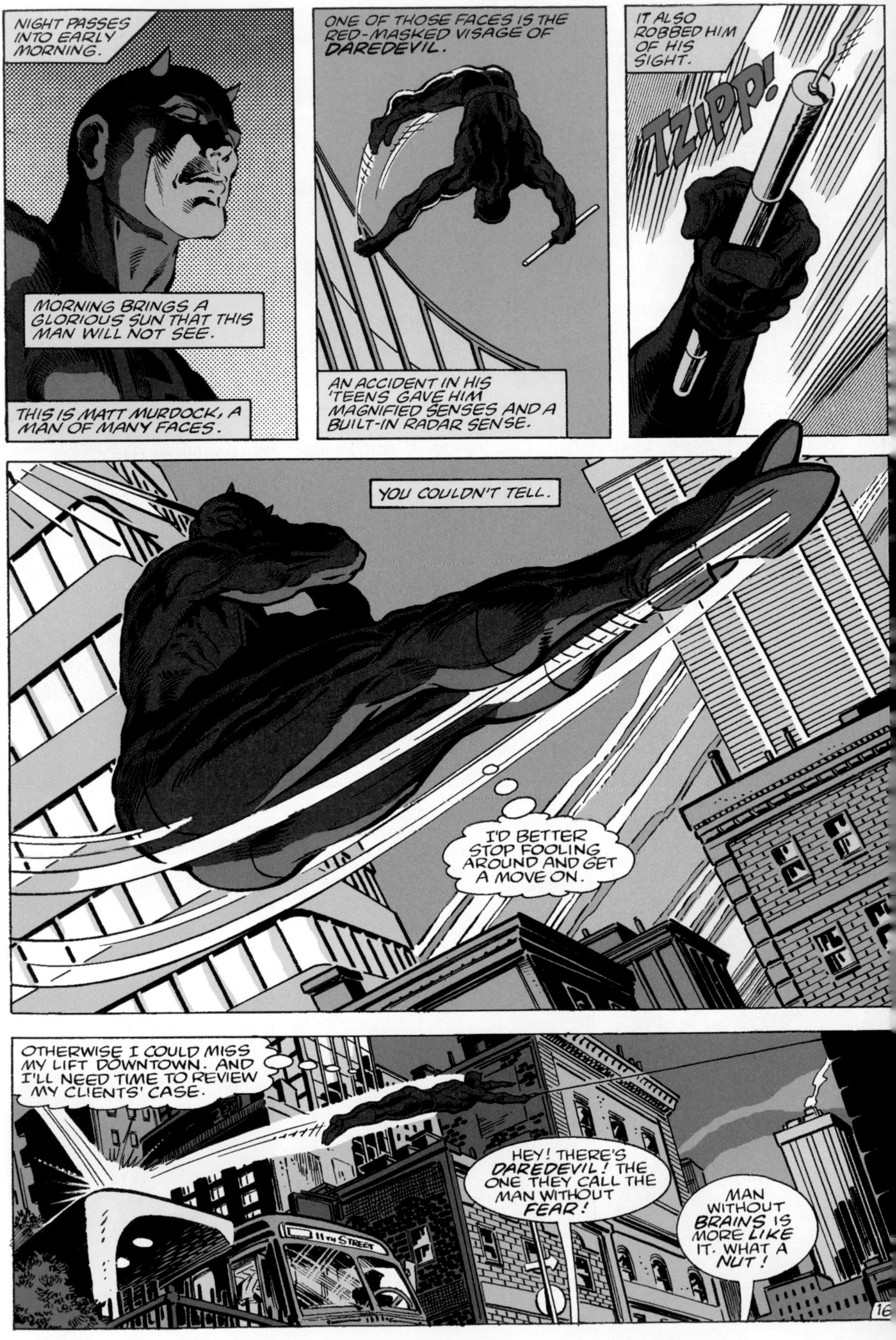
NIGHT PASSES INTO EARLY MORNING.
MORNING BRINGS A GLORIOUS SUN THAT THIS MAN WILL NOT SEE.
THIS IS MATT MURDOCK, A MAN OF MANY FACES.
ONE OF THOSE FACES IS THE RED-MASKED VISAGE OF DAREDEVIL.
AN ACCIDENT IN HIS 'TEENS GAVE HIM MAGNIFIED SENSES AND A BUILT-IN RADAR SENSE.
IT ALSO ROBBED HIM OF HIS SIGHT.
TZIPP!
YOU COULDN'T TELL.
I'D BETTER STOP FOOLING AROUND AND GET A MOVE ON.
OTHERWISE I COULD MISS MY LIFT DOWNTOWN. AND I'LL NEED TIME TO REVIEW MY CLIENTS' CASE.
11TH STREET
HEY! THERE'S DAREDEVIL! THE ONE THEY CALL THE MAN WITHOUT FEAR!
MAN WITHOUT BRAINS IS MORE LIKE IT. WHAT A NUT!
16

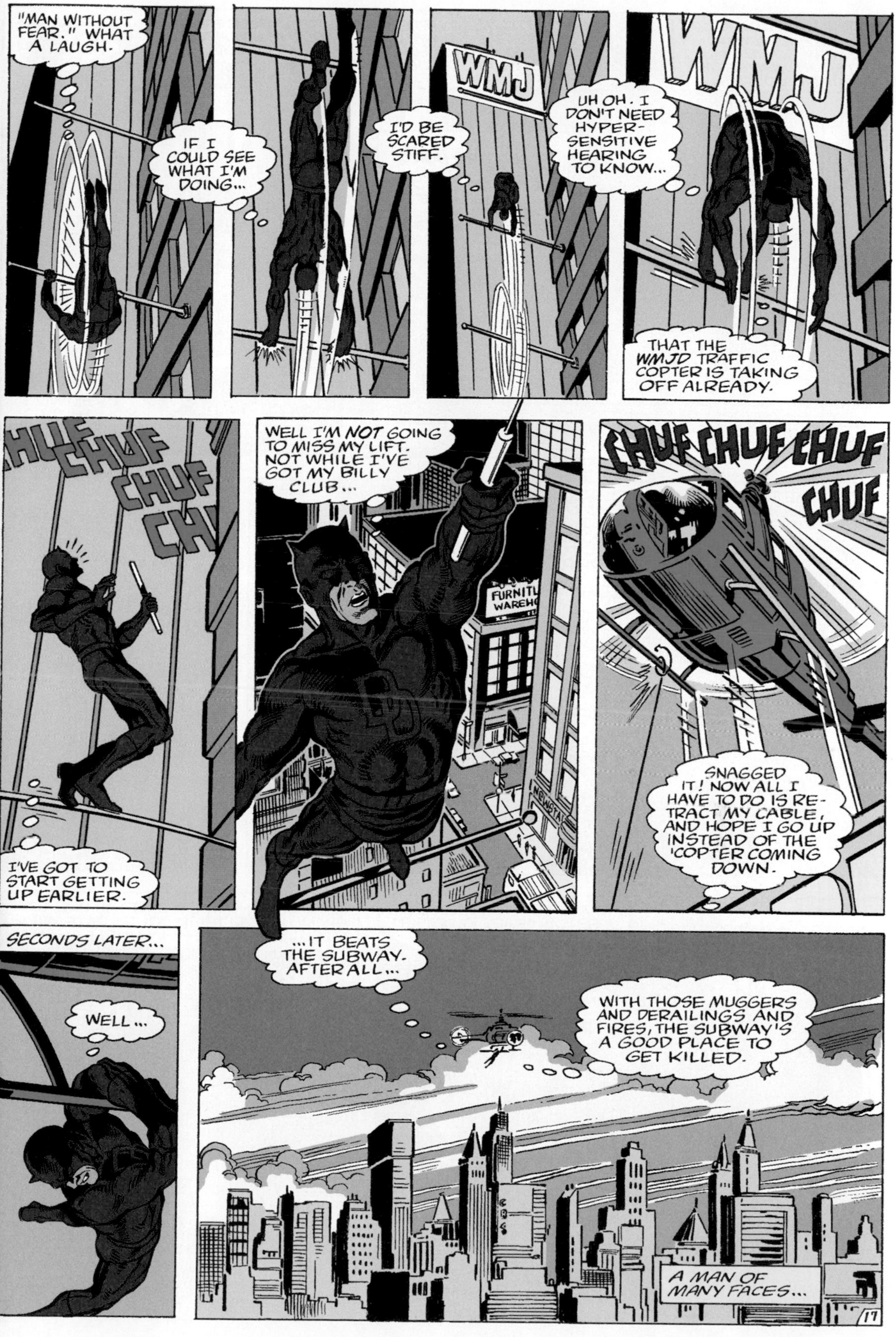
"MAN WITHOUT FEAR." WHAT A LAUGH.
IF I COULD SEE WHAT I'M DOING...
I'D BE SCARED STIFF.
UH OH. I DON'T NEED HYPER-SENSITIVE HEARING TO KNOW...
WMJ
WMJ
THAT THE WMJD TRAFFIC COPTER IS TAKING OFF ALREADY.
CHUF CHUF CHUF CHU
I'VE GOT TO START GETTING UP EARLIER.
WELL I'M NOT GOING TO MISS MY LIFT. NOT WHILE I'VE GOT MY BILLY CLUB...
CHUF CHUF CHUF CHUF
SNAGGED IT! NOW ALL I HAVE TO DO IS RETRACT MY CABLE, AND HOPE I GO UP INSTEAD OF THE 'COPTER COMING DOWN.
SECONDS LATER...
WELL...
...IT BEATS THE SUBWAY. AFTER ALL...
WITH THOSE MUGGERS AND DERAILINGS AND FIRES, THE SUBWAY'S A GOOD PLACE TO GET KILLED.
A MAN OF MANY FACES...
17

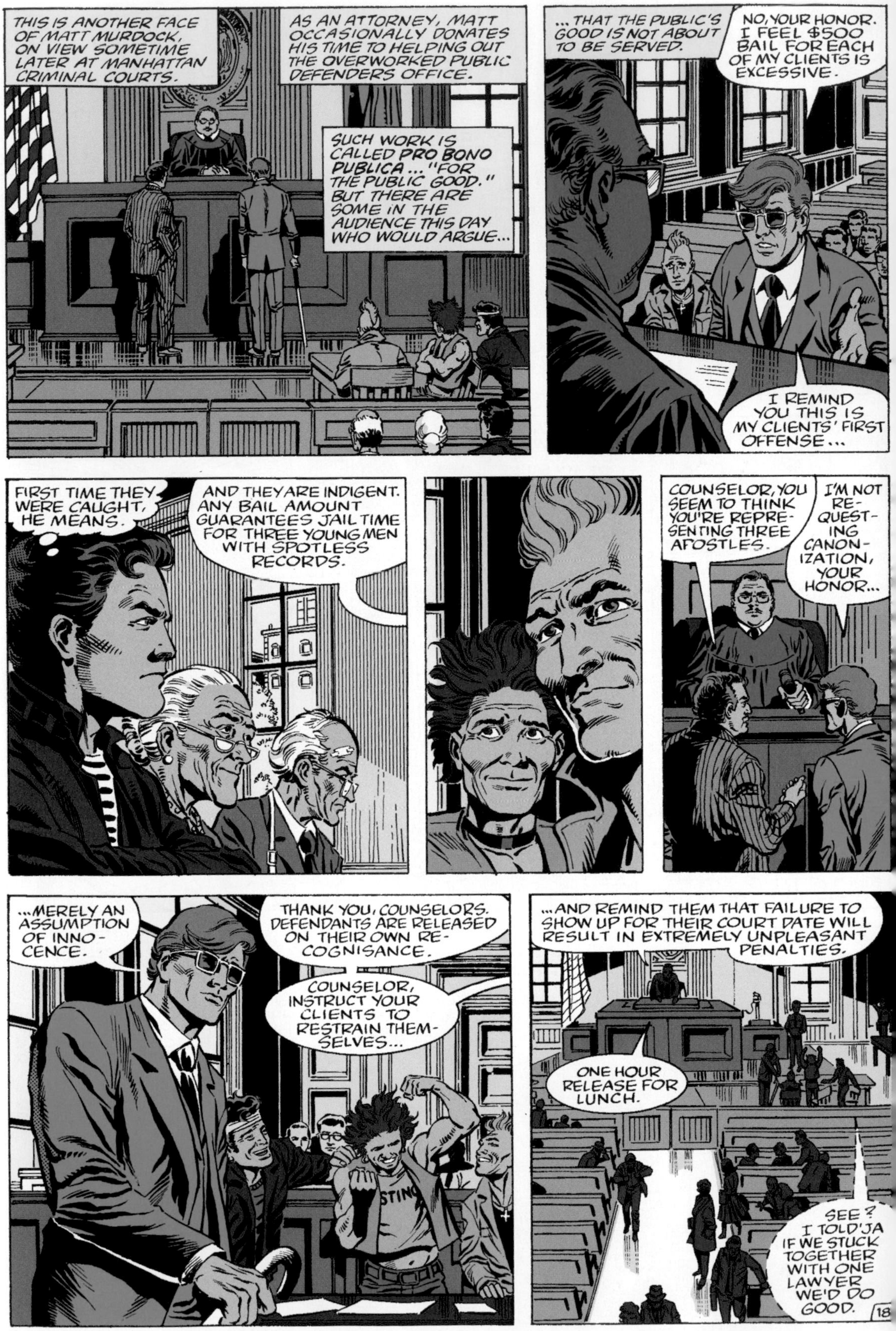
THIS IS ANOTHER FACE OF MATT MURDOCK, ON VIEW SOMETIME LATER AT MANHATTAN CRIMINAL COURTS.
AS AN ATTORNEY, MATT OCCASIONALLY DONATES HIS TIME TO HELPING OUT THE OVERWORKED PUBLIC DEFENDERS OFFICE.
SUCH WORK IS CALLED PRO BONO PUBLICA ... "FOR THE PUBLIC GOOD." BUT THERE ARE SOME IN THE AUDIENCE THIS DAY WHO WOULD ARGUE...
...THAT THE PUBLIC'S GOOD IS NOT ABOUT TO BE SERVED.
NO, YOUR HONOR. I FEEL $500 BAIL FOR EACH OF MY CLIENTS IS EXCESSIVE.
I REMIND YOU THIS IS MY CLIENTS' FIRST OFFENSE...
FIRST TIME THEY WERE CAUGHT, HE MEANS.
AND THEY ARE INDIGENT. ANY BAIL AMOUNT GUARANTEES JAIL TIME FOR THREE YOUNG MEN WITH SPOTLESS RECORDS.
COUNSELOR, YOU SEEM TO THINK YOU'RE REPRESENTING THREE APOSTLES.
I'M NOT REQUESTING CANONIZATION, YOUR HONOR...
...MERELY AN ASSUMPTION OF INNOCENCE.
THANK YOU, COUNSELORS. DEFENDANTS ARE RELEASED ON THEIR OWN RECOGNISANCE.
COUNSELOR, INSTRUCT YOUR CLIENTS TO RESTRAIN THEMSELVES...
STING
...AND REMIND THEM THAT FAILURE TO SHOW UP FOR THEIR COURT DATE WILL RESULT IN EXTREMELY UNPLEASANT PENALTIES.
ONE HOUR RELEASE FOR LUNCH.
SEE? I TOLD'JA IF WE STUCK TOGETHER WITH ONE LAWYER WE'D DO GOOD.
18

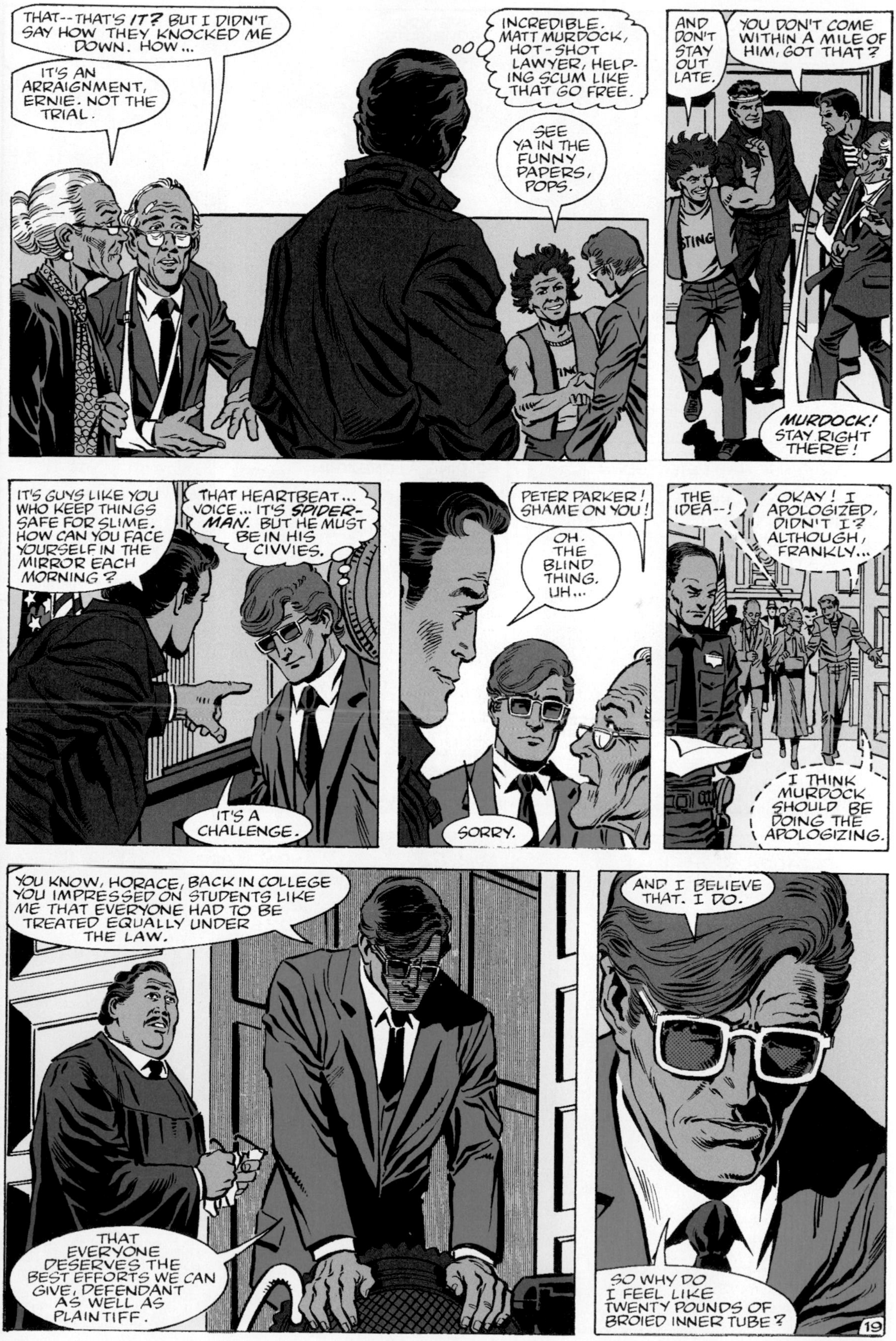
THAT--THAT'S IT? BUT I DIDN'T SAY HOW THEY KNOCKED ME DOWN. HOW...
IT'S AN ARRAIGNMENT, ERNIE. NOT THE TRIAL.
INCREDIBLE. MATT MURDOCK, HOT-SHOT LAWYER, HELPING SCUM LIKE THAT GO FREE.
SEE YA IN THE FUNNY PAPERS, POPS.
AND DON'T STAY OUT LATE.
YOU DON'T COME WITHIN A MILE OF HIM, GOT THAT?
MURDOCK! STAY RIGHT THERE!
IT'S GUYS LIKE YOU WHO KEEP THINGS SAFE FOR SLIME. HOW CAN YOU FACE YOURSELF IN THE MIRROR EACH MORNING?
THAT HEARTBEAT... VOICE... IT'S SPIDER-MAN. BUT HE MUST BE IN HIS CIVVIES.
IT'S A CHALLENGE.
PETER PARKER! SHAME ON YOU!
OH. THE BLIND THING. UH...
SORRY.
THE IDEA--!
OKAY! I APOLOGIZED, DIDN'T I? ALTHOUGH, FRANKLY...
I THINK MURDOCK SHOULD BE DOING THE APOLOGIZING.
YOU KNOW, HORACE, BACK IN COLLEGE YOU IMPRESSED ON STUDENTS LIKE ME THAT EVERYONE HAD TO BE TREATED EQUALLY UNDER THE LAW.
THAT EVERYONE DESERVES THE BEST EFFORTS WE CAN GIVE, DEFENDANT AS WELL AS PLAINTIFF.
AND I BELIEVE THAT. I DO.
SO WHY DO I FEEL LIKE TWENTY POUNDS OF BROIED INNER TUBE?
19

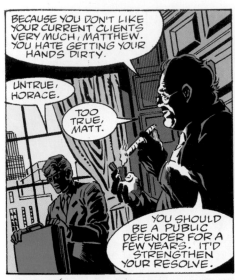

BECAUSE YOU DON'T LIKE YOUR CURRENT CLIENTS VERY MUCH, MATTHEW. YOU HATE GETTING YOUR HANDS DIRTY.

UNTRUE, HORACE.

TOO TRUE, MATT.

YOU SHOULD BE A PUBLIC DEFENDER FOR A FEW YEARS. IT'D STRENGTHEN YOUR RESOLVE.

GIVE YOU SOME GUTS.

LET ME HAVE A MINUTE TO USE THE LITTLE JUDGE'S ROOM, AND THEN WE'LL GRAB SOME LUNCH.

UH... FINE.

GOOD, HORACE, MAKE A CONVENIENT EXIT...

...SO I CAN CHECK OUT JUST WHO MY RADAR SENSE HAS DETECTED IN YOUR STUDY.

IF IT WEREN'T FOR HORACE, I'D CHANGE TO DD. AS IT IS...

...I MIGHT NOT HAVE THE TIME.

ONE PERSON... BULKY, MALE. HOLDING A LONG, THIN OBJECT...

A SHOTGUN.

HIS PULSE IS RACING WILDLY. PERSPERATION SO THICK... I THINK HE'S ON DRUGS.

WHO'S THERE? WHO IS IT?

I AM THE SIN-EATER. AND YOU ARE--?

HIS VOICE--! HIS AURA IS LIKE DECAYING VERMIN.

DON'T HURT ME. I'M BLIND.

20

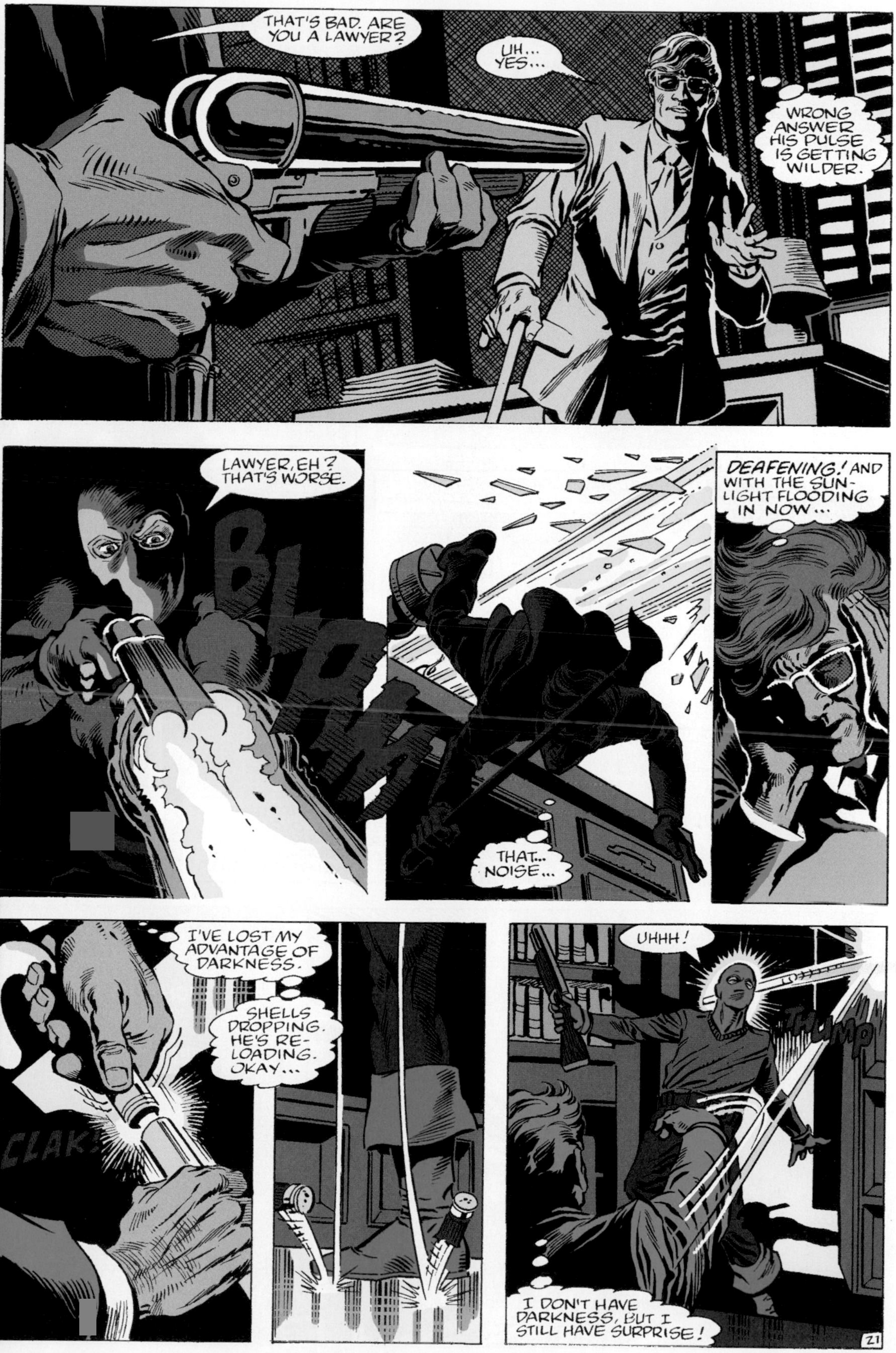
THAT'S BAD. ARE YOU A LAWYER?
UH... YES...
WRONG ANSWER HIS PULSE IS GETTING WILDER.
LAWYER, EH? THAT'S WORSE.
DEAFENING! AND WITH THE SUN-LIGHT FLOODING IN NOW...
THAT... NOISE...
I'VE LOST MY ADVANTAGE OF DARKNESS.
SHELLS DROPPING. HE'S RE-LOADING. OKAY...
UHHH!
THUMP
I DON'T HAVE DARKNESS, BUT I STILL HAVE SURPRISE!
21

WHAT THE DEVIL *WAS* THAT?

MY BILLY CLUB, YOU LUNATIC. AND NOW...

MATT? WHAT'S GOING--

ON?

ONE MOMENT IN TIME, FROZEN FOR *MATT MURDOCK.*

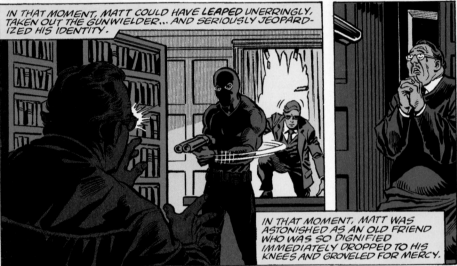

IN THAT MOMENT, MATT COULD HAVE *LEAPED* UNERRINGLY, TAKEN OUT THE GUNWIELDER... AND SERIOUSLY JEOPARDIZED HIS IDENTITY.

IN THAT MOMENT, MATT WAS ASTONISHED AS AN OLD FRIEND WHO WAS SO DIGNIFIED IMMEDIATELY DROPPED TO HIS KNEES AND GROVELED FOR MERCY.

THE FACE OF *MATT MURDOCK...* FROZEN ONLY A MOMENT IN SURPRISE AND INDECISION.

A MOMENT TOO LONG.

BLAM!

PETER DAVID
Writer

RICH BUCKLER
Penciler

BRETT BREEDING
Inker

PHIL FELIX
Letterer

BOB SHAREN
Colorist

JIM OWSLEY
Editor

JIM SHOOTER
Editor In Chief

96

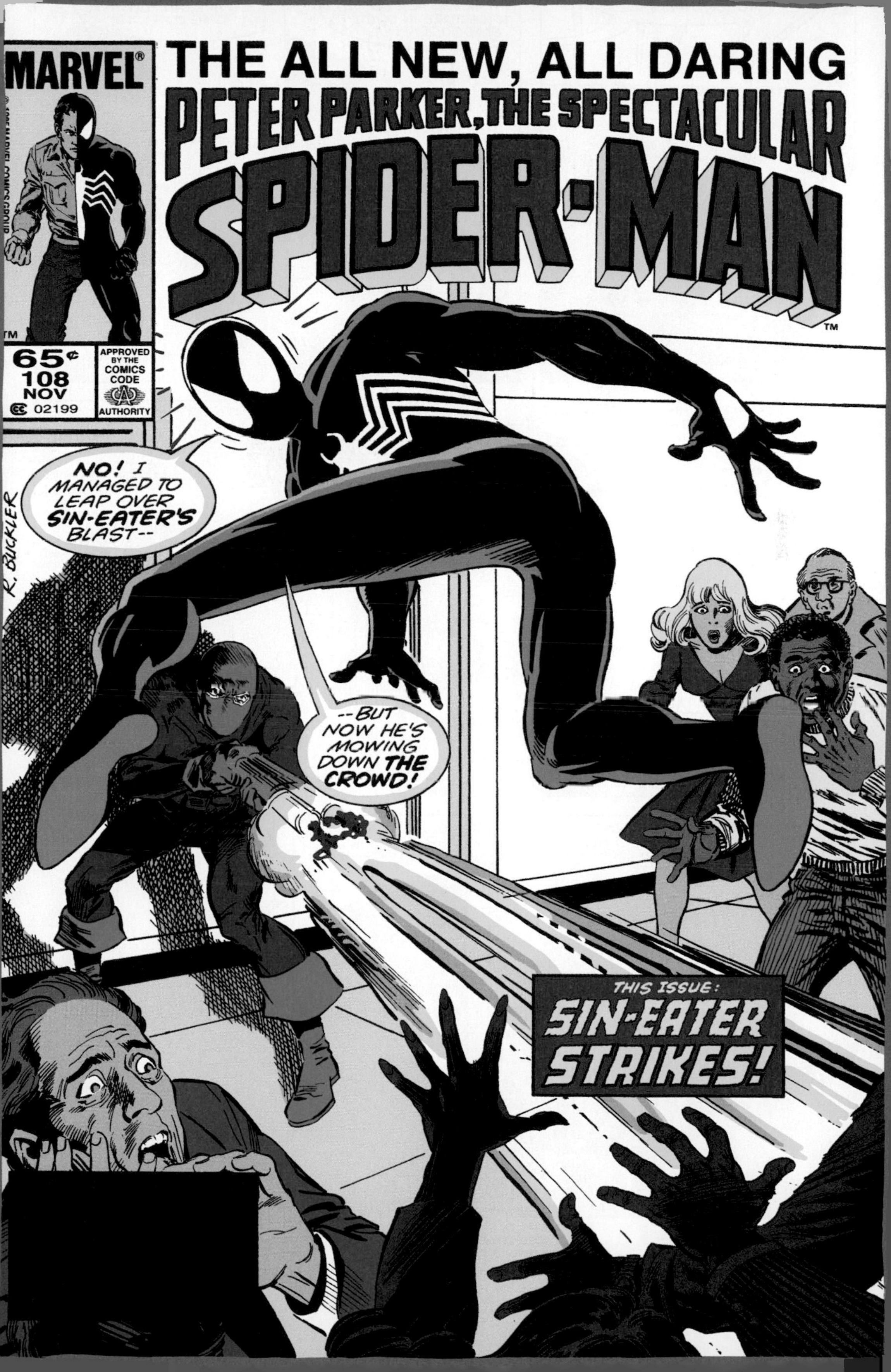
MARVEL®
THE ALL NEW, ALL DARING
PETER PARKER, THE SPECTACULAR
SPIDER-MAN™
65¢
108
NOV
02199
APPROVED BY THE COMICS CODE AUTHORITY
NO! I MANAGED TO LEAP OVER SIN-EATER'S BLAST--
--BUT NOW HE'S MOWING DOWN THE CROWD!
R. BUCKLER
THIS ISSUE: SIN-EATER STRIKES!

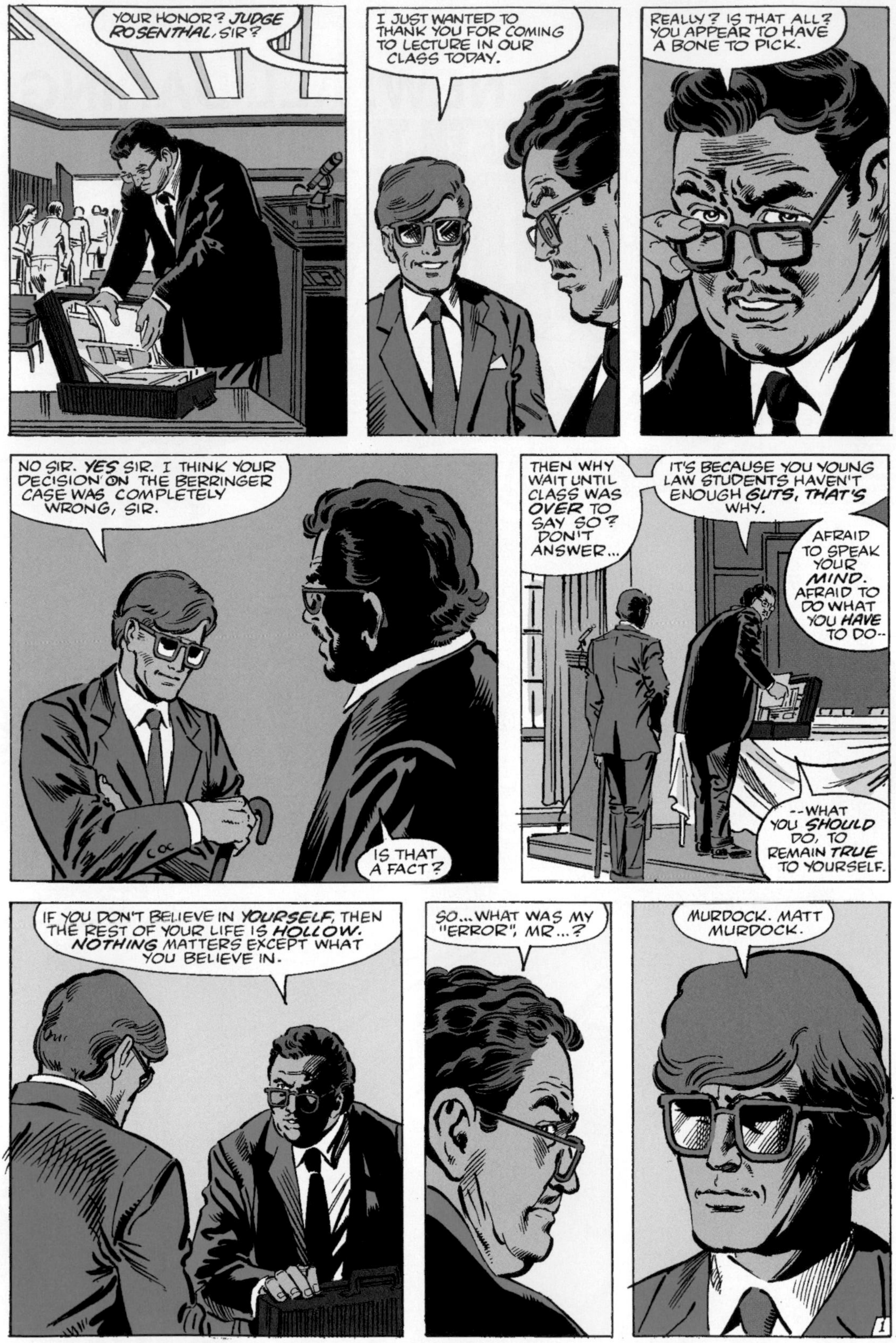
YOUR HONOR? JUDGE ROSENTHAL, SIR?
I JUST WANTED TO THANK YOU FOR COMING TO LECTURE IN OUR CLASS TODAY.
REALLY? IS THAT ALL? YOU APPEAR TO HAVE A BONE TO PICK.
NO SIR. YES SIR. I THINK YOUR DECISION ON THE BERRINGER CASE WAS COMPLETELY WRONG, SIR.
IS THAT A FACT?
THEN WHY WAIT UNTIL CLASS WAS OVER TO SAY SO? DON'T ANSWER...
IT'S BECAUSE YOU YOUNG LAW STUDENTS HAVEN'T ENOUGH GUTS, THAT'S WHY.
AFRAID TO SPEAK YOUR MIND. AFRAID TO DO WHAT YOU HAVE TO DO--
--WHAT YOU SHOULD DO, TO REMAIN TRUE TO YOURSELF.
IF YOU DON'T BELIEVE IN YOURSELF, THEN THE REST OF YOUR LIFE IS HOLLOW. NOTHING MATTERS EXCEPT WHAT YOU BELIEVE IN.
SO...WHAT WAS MY "ERROR", MR...?
MURDOCK. MATT MURDOCK.
1

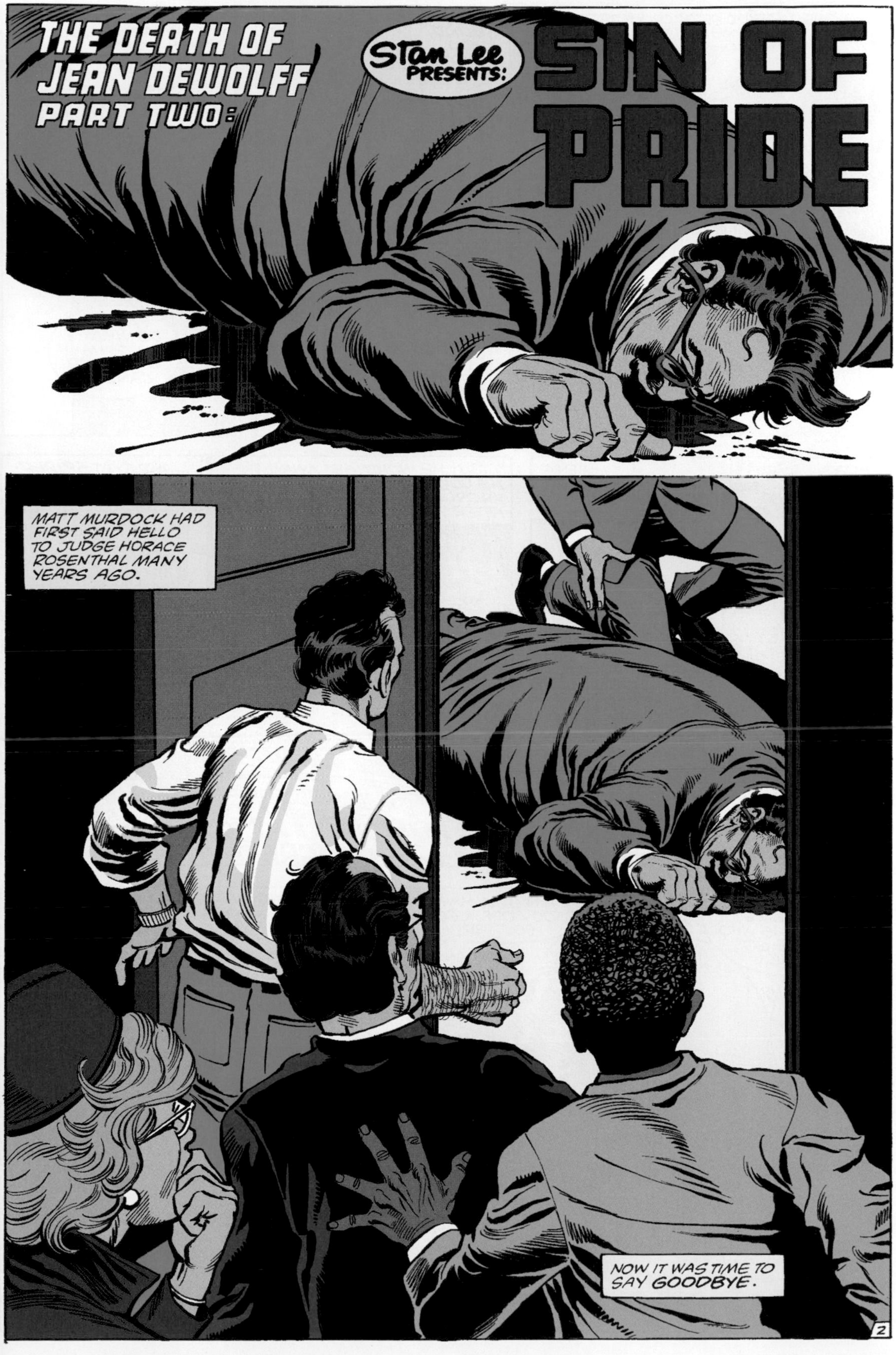
THE DEATH OF JEAN DEWOLFF PART TWO:
STAN LEE PRESENTS:
SIN OF PRIDE
MATT MURDOCK HAD FIRST SAID HELLO TO JUDGE HORACE ROSENTHAL MANY YEARS AGO.
NOW IT WAS TIME TO SAY GOODBYE.
2

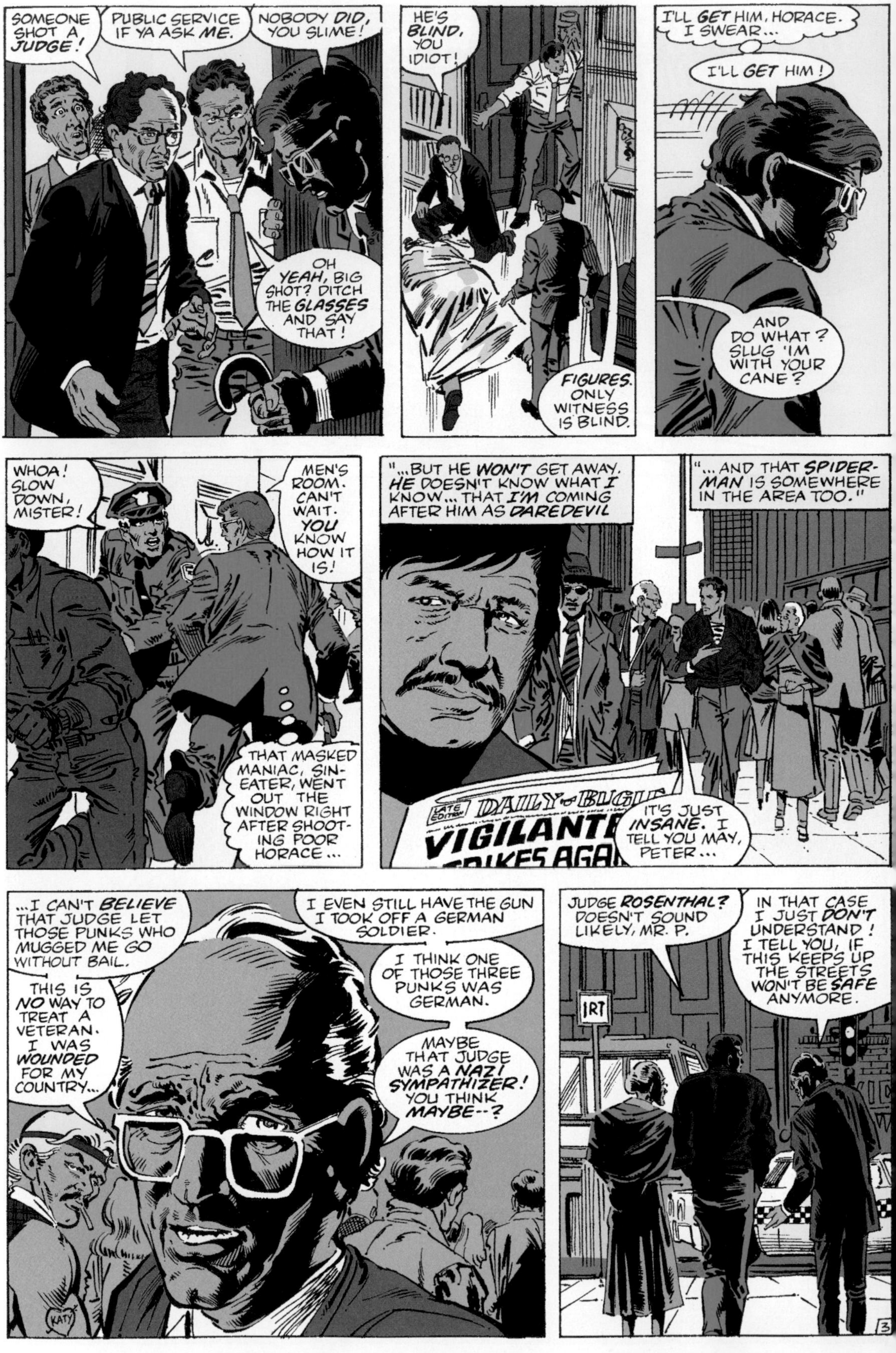
SOMEONE SHOT A JUDGE!
PUBLIC SERVICE IF YA ASK ME.
NOBODY DID, YOU SLIME!
OH YEAH, BIG SHOT? DITCH THE GLASSES AND SAY THAT!
HE'S BLIND, YOU IDIOT!
FIGURES. ONLY WITNESS IS BLIND.
I'LL GET HIM, HORACE. I SWEAR...
I'LL GET HIM!
AND DO WHAT? SLUG 'IM WITH YOUR CANE?
WHOA! SLOW DOWN, MISTER!
MEN'S ROOM. CAN'T WAIT. YOU KNOW HOW IT IS!
THAT MASKED MANIAC, SIN-EATER, WENT OUT THE WINDOW RIGHT AFTER SHOOTING POOR HORACE...
"...BUT HE WON'T GET AWAY. HE DOESN'T KNOW WHAT I KNOW... THAT I'M COMING AFTER HIM AS DAREDEVIL
"...AND THAT SPIDER-MAN IS SOMEWHERE IN THE AREA TOO."
DAILY BUGLE
LATE EDITION
VIGILANTE
IT'S JUST INSANE. I TELL YOU MAY, PETER...
...I CAN'T BELIEVE THAT JUDGE LET THOSE PUNKS WHO MUGGED ME GO WITHOUT BAIL.
THIS IS NO WAY TO TREAT A VETERAN. I WAS WOUNDED FOR MY COUNTRY...
I EVEN STILL HAVE THE GUN I TOOK OFF A GERMAN SOLDIER.
I THINK ONE OF THOSE THREE PUNKS WAS GERMAN.
MAYBE THAT JUDGE WAS A NAZI SYMPATHIZER! YOU THINK MAYBE--?
KATY
JUDGE ROSENTHAL? DOESN'T SOUND LIKELY, MR. P.
IN THAT CASE I JUST DON'T UNDERSTAND! I TELL YOU, IF THIS KEEPS UP THE STREETS WON'T BE SAFE ANYMORE.
IRT
3

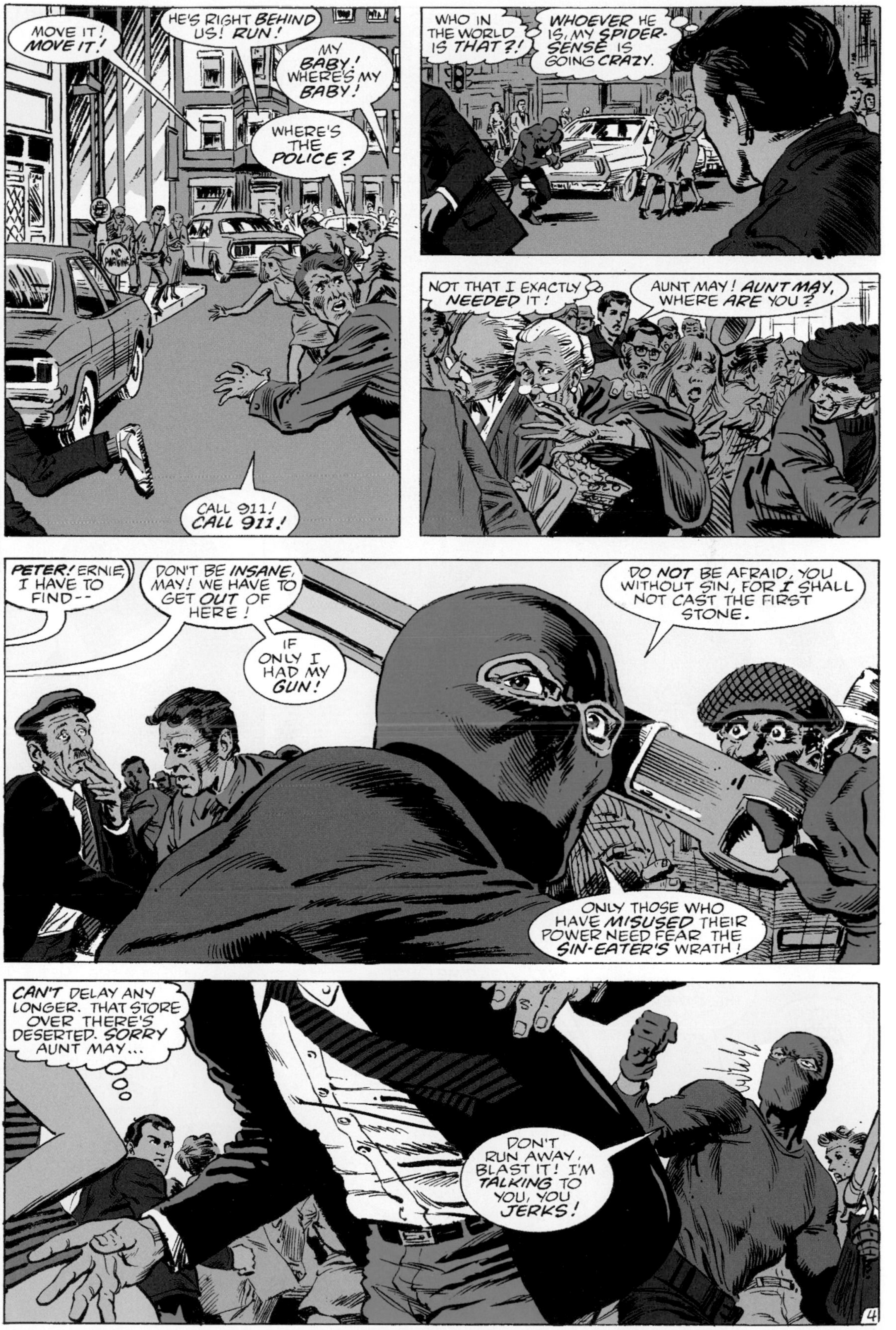
MOVE IT! MOVE IT!
HE'S RIGHT BEHIND US! RUN!
MY BABY! WHERE'S MY BABY!
WHERE'S THE POLICE?
CALL 911! CALL 911!
WHO IN THE WORLD IS THAT?!
WHOEVER HE IS, MY SPIDER-SENSE IS GOING CRAZY.
NOT THAT I EXACTLY NEEDED IT!
AUNT MAY! AUNT MAY, WHERE ARE YOU?
PETER! ERNIE, I HAVE TO FIND--
DON'T BE INSANE, MAY! WE HAVE TO GET OUT OF HERE!
IF ONLY I HAD MY GUN!
DO NOT BE AFRAID, YOU WITHOUT SIN, FOR I SHALL NOT CAST THE FIRST STONE.
ONLY THOSE WHO HAVE MISUSED THEIR POWER NEED FEAR THE SIN-EATER'S WRATH!
CAN'T DELAY ANY LONGER. THAT STORE OVER THERE'S DESERTED. SORRY AUNT MAY...
DON'T RUN AWAY, BLAST IT! I'M TALKING TO YOU, YOU JERKS!
4

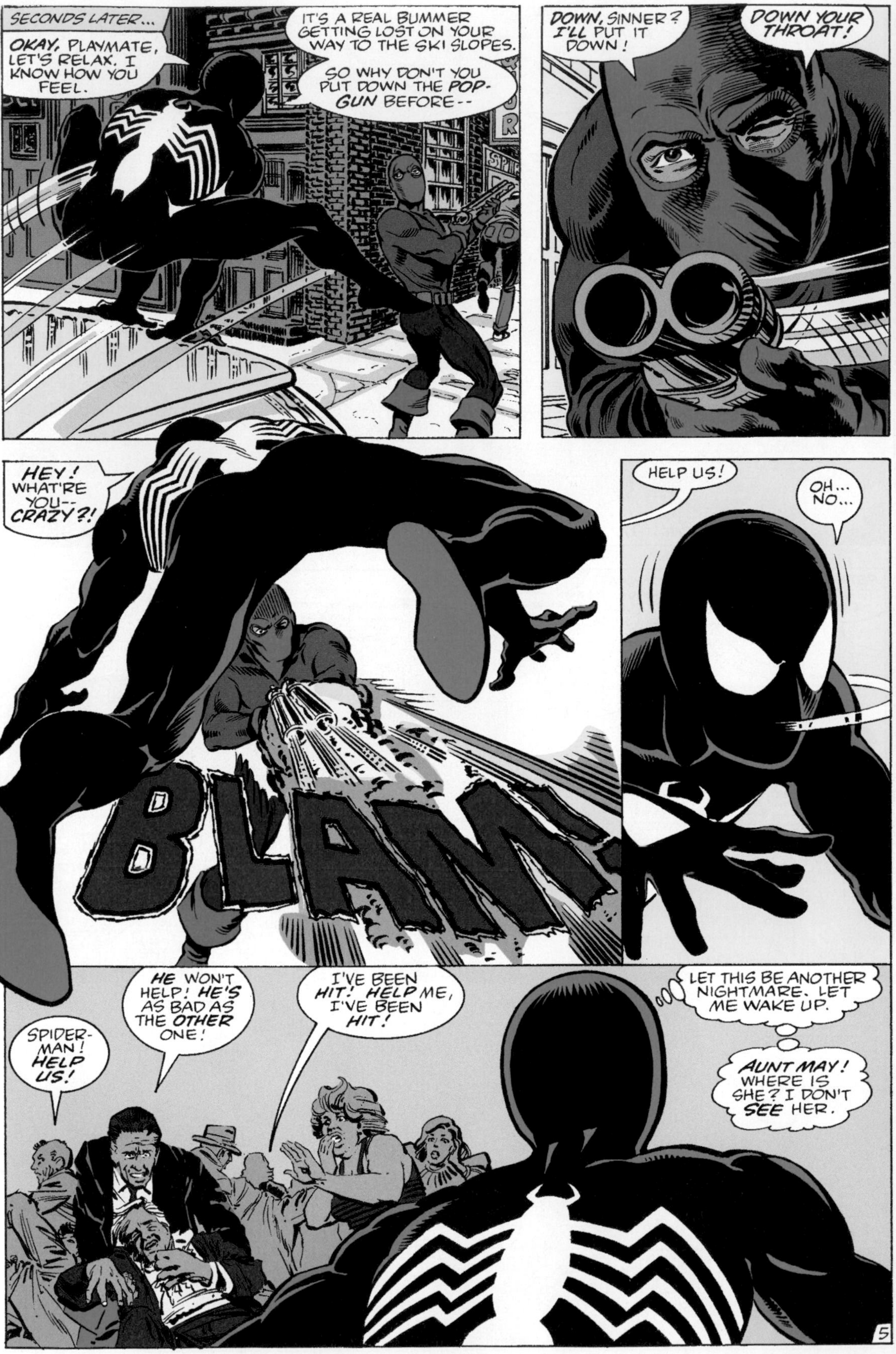

SECONDS LATER...
OKAY, PLAYMATE, LET'S RELAX. I KNOW HOW YOU FEEL.
IT'S A REAL BUMMER GETTING LOST ON YOUR WAY TO THE SKI SLOPES.
SO WHY DON'T YOU PUT DOWN THE POP-GUN BEFORE--
DOWN, SINNER? I'LL PUT IT DOWN!
DOWN YOUR THROAT!
HEY! WHAT'RE YOU-- CRAZY?!
BLAM!
HELP US!
OH... NO...
SPIDER-MAN! HELP US!
HE WON'T HELP! HE'S AS BAD AS THE OTHER ONE!
I'VE BEEN HIT! HELP ME, I'VE BEEN HIT!
LET THIS BE ANOTHER NIGHTMARE. LET ME WAKE UP.
AUNT MAY! WHERE IS SHE? I DON'T SEE HER.
5

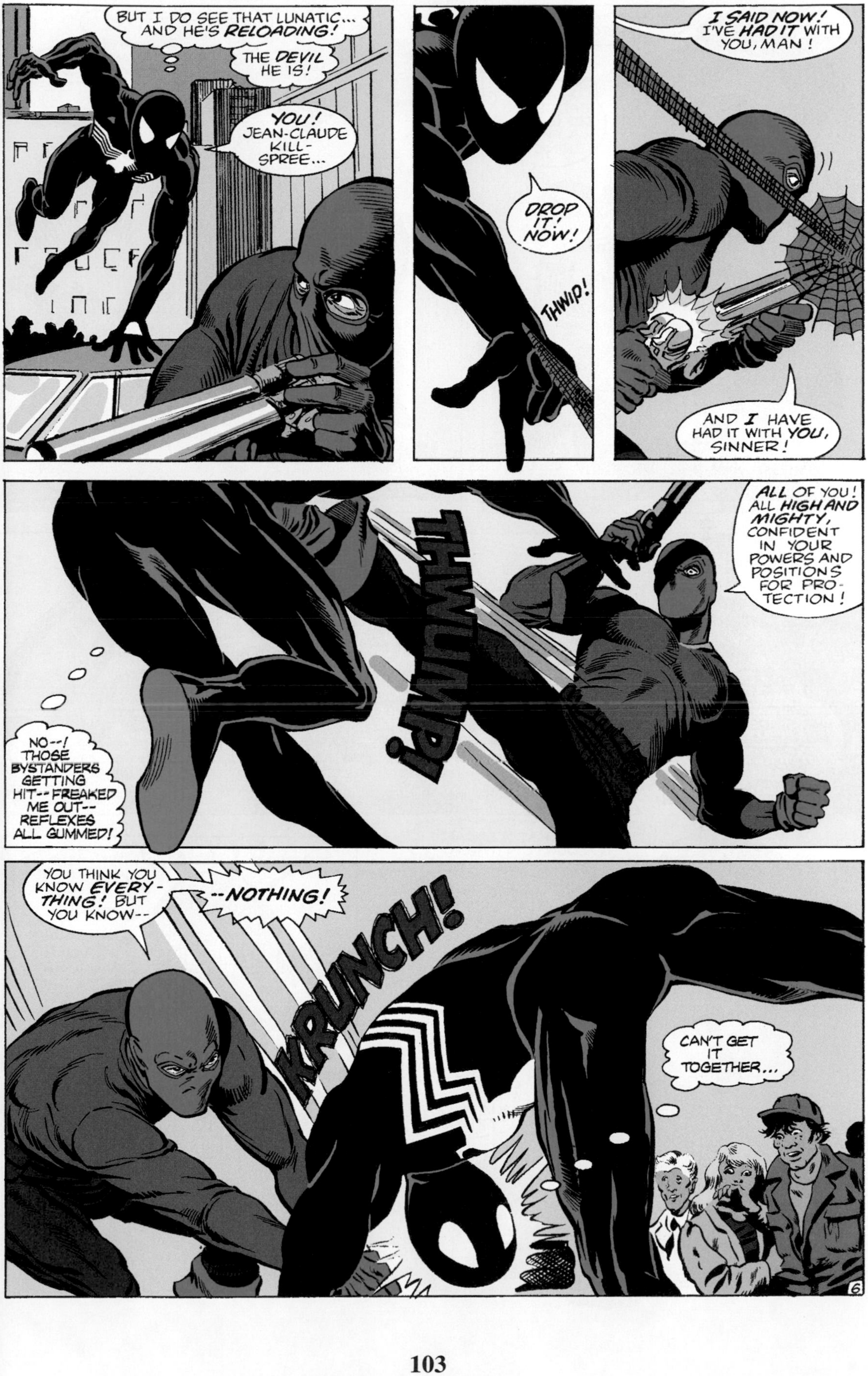
BUT I DO SEE THAT LUNATIC... AND HE'S RELOADING!
THE DEVIL HE IS!
YOU! JEAN-CLAUDE KILL-SPREE...
DROP IT! NOW!
THWIP!
I SAID NOW! I'VE HAD IT WITH YOU, MAN!
AND I HAVE HAD IT WITH YOU, SINNER!
ALL OF YOU! ALL HIGH AND MIGHTY, CONFIDENT IN YOUR POWERS AND POSITIONS FOR PRO-TECTION!
THWUMP!
NO--! THOSE BYSTANDERS GETTING HIT--FREAKED ME OUT--REFLEXES ALL GUMMED!
YOU THINK YOU KNOW EVERY-THING! BUT YOU KNOW--
--NOTHING!
KRUNCH!
CAN'T GET IT TOGETHER...
6

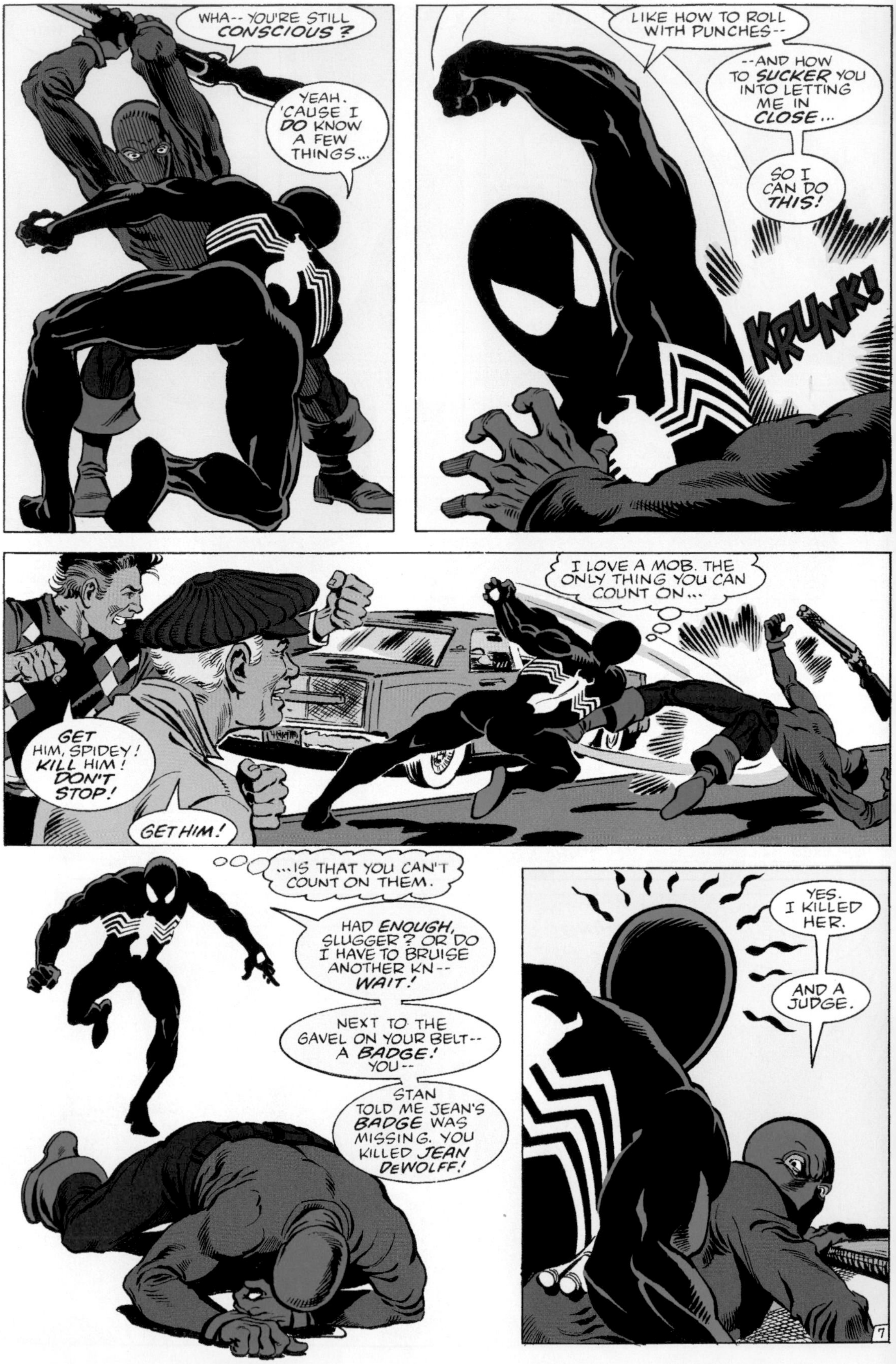
WHA-- YOU'RE STILL CONSCIOUS?
YEAH. 'CAUSE I DO KNOW A FEW THINGS...
LIKE HOW TO ROLL WITH PUNCHES--
--AND HOW TO SUCKER YOU INTO LETTING ME IN CLOSE...
SO I CAN DO THIS!
KRUNK!
I LOVE A MOB. THE ONLY THING YOU CAN COUNT ON...
GET HIM, SPIDEY! KILL HIM! DON'T STOP!
GET HIM!
...IS THAT YOU CAN'T COUNT ON THEM.
HAD ENOUGH, SLUGGER? OR DO I HAVE TO BRUISE ANOTHER KN-- WAIT!
NEXT TO THE GAVEL ON YOUR BELT-- A BADGE! YOU--
STAN TOLD ME JEAN'S BADGE WAS MISSING. YOU KILLED JEAN DEWOLFF!
YES. I KILLED HER.
AND A JUDGE.
7

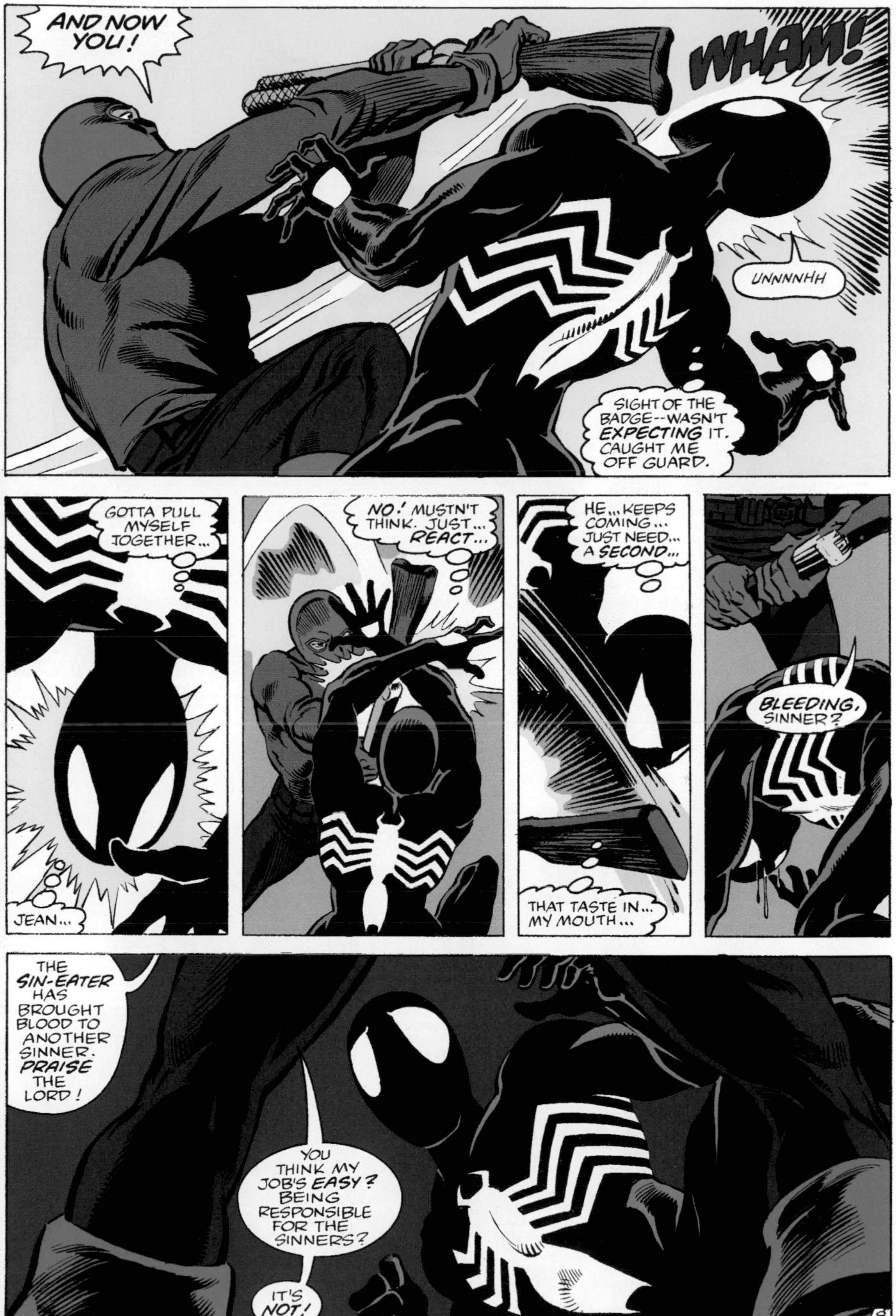
AND NOW YOU!
WHAM!
UNNNNHH
SIGHT OF THE BADGE--WASN'T EXPECTING IT. CAUGHT ME OFF GUARD.
GOTTA PULL MYSELF TOGETHER...
JEAN...
NO! MUSTN'T THINK. JUST... REACT...
HE... KEEPS COMING... JUST NEED... A SECOND...
THAT TASTE IN... MY MOUTH...
BLEEDING, SINNER?
THE SIN-EATER HAS BROUGHT BLOOD TO ANOTHER SINNER. PRAISE THE LORD!
YOU THINK MY JOB'S EASY? BEING RESPONSIBLE FOR THE SINNERS?
IT'S NOT!
8

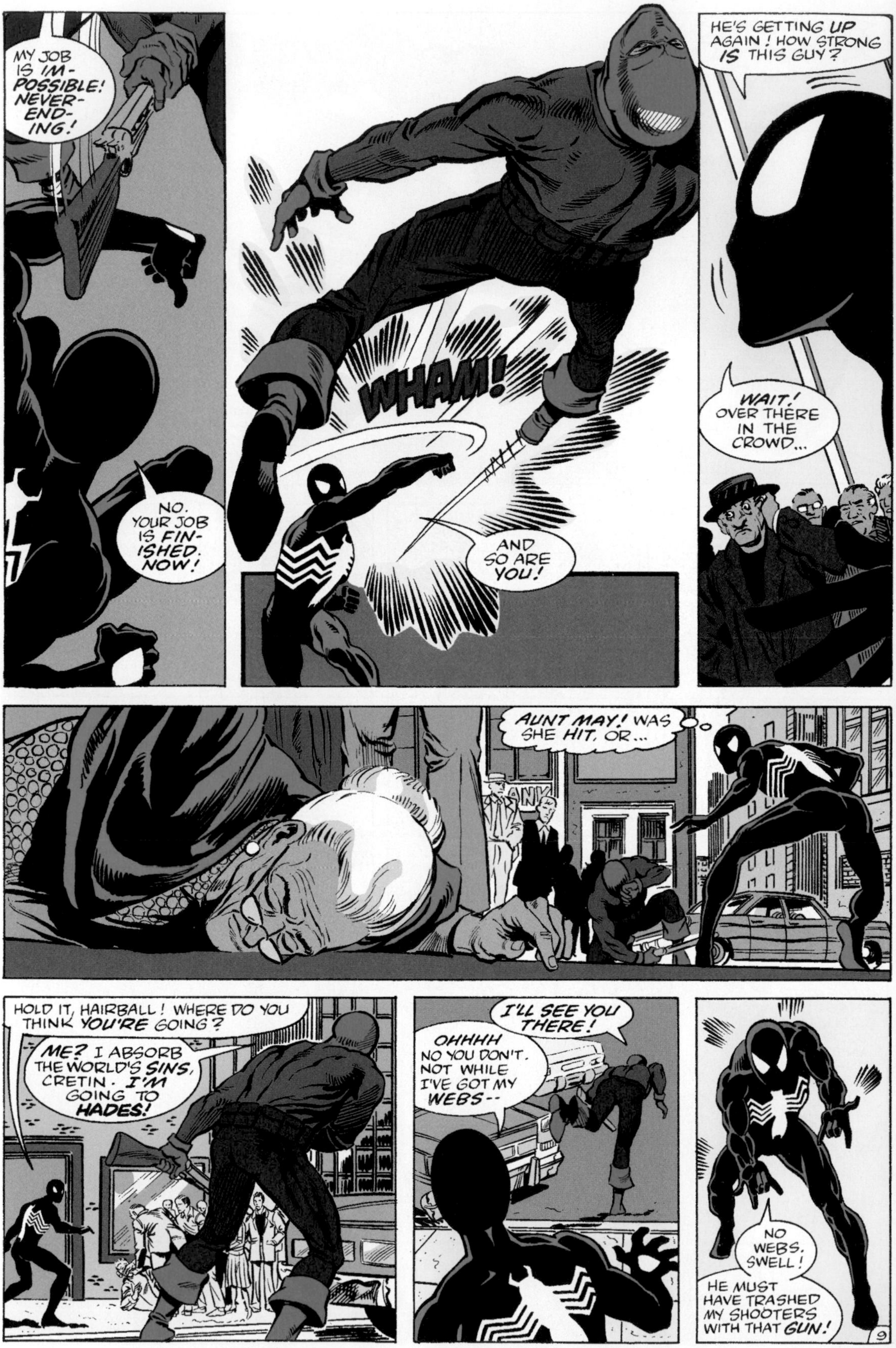
MY JOB IS IM-POSSIBLE! NEVER-END-ING!
NO. YOUR JOB IS FIN-ISHED NOW!
WHAM!
AND SO ARE YOU!
HE'S GETTING UP AGAIN! HOW STRONG IS THIS GUY?
WAIT! OVER THERE IN THE CROWD...
AUNT MAY! WAS SHE HIT, OR...
HOLD IT, HAIRBALL! WHERE DO YOU THINK YOU'RE GOING?
ME? I ABSORB THE WORLD'S SINS, CRETIN. I'M GOING TO HADES!
I'LL SEE YOU THERE!
OHHHH NO YOU DON'T. NOT WHILE I'VE GOT MY WEBS--
NO WEBS. SWELL!
HE MUST HAVE TRASHED MY SHOOTERS WITH THAT GUN!
9

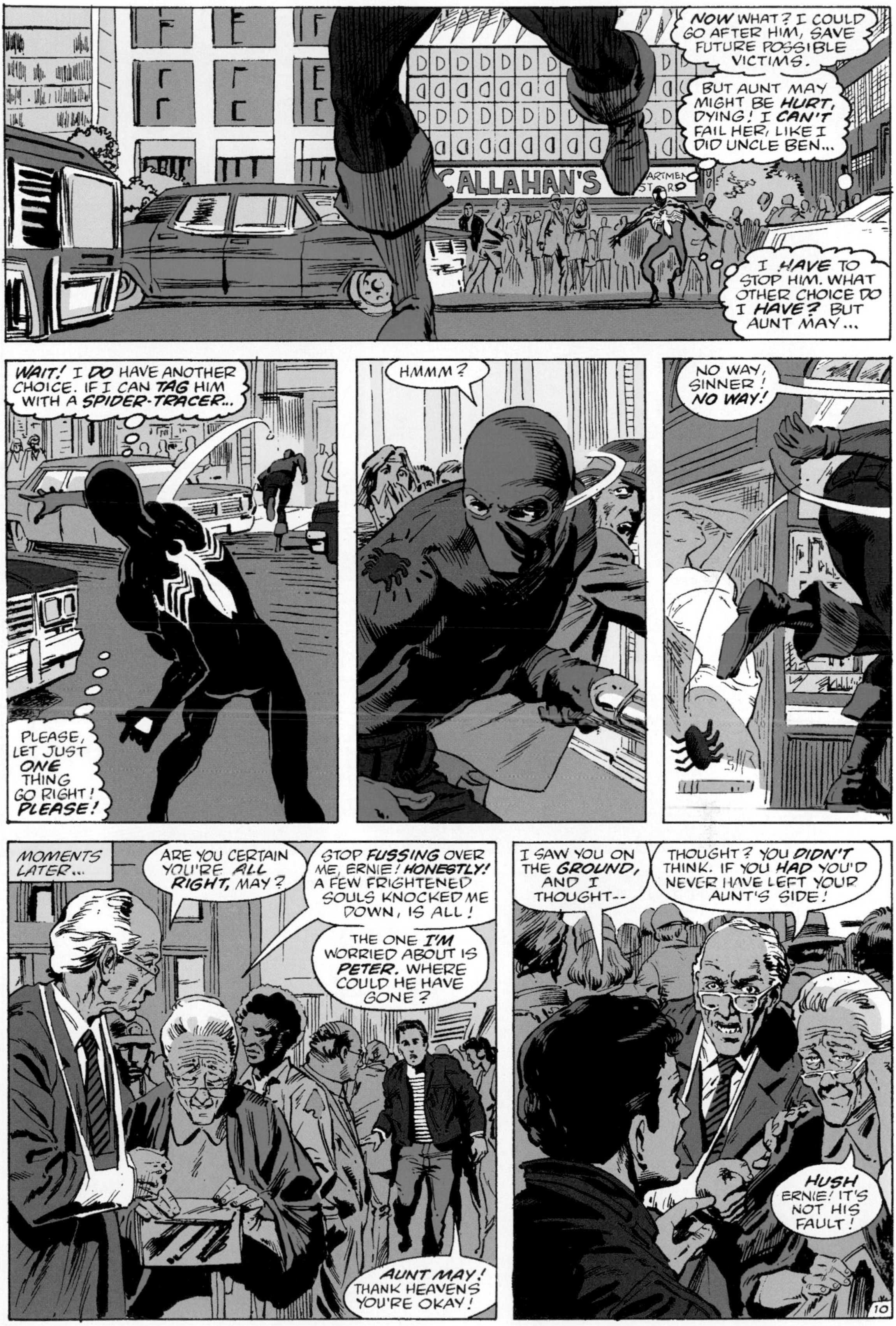
NOW WHAT? I COULD GO AFTER HIM, SAVE FUTURE POSSIBLE VICTIMS.
BUT AUNT MAY MIGHT BE HURT, DYING! I CAN'T FAIL HER, LIKE I DID UNCLE BEN...
CALLAHAN'S
I HAVE TO STOP HIM. WHAT OTHER CHOICE DO I HAVE? BUT AUNT MAY...
WAIT! I DO HAVE ANOTHER CHOICE. IF I CAN TAG HIM WITH A SPIDER-TRACER...
PLEASE, LET JUST ONE THING GO RIGHT! PLEASE!
HMMM?
NO WAY, SINNER! NO WAY!
MOMENTS LATER...
ARE YOU CERTAIN YOU'RE ALL RIGHT, MAY?
STOP FUSSING OVER ME, ERNIE! HONESTLY! A FEW FRIGHTENED SOULS KNOCKED ME DOWN, IS ALL!
THE ONE I'M WORRIED ABOUT IS PETER. WHERE COULD HE HAVE GONE?
AUNT MAY! THANK HEAVENS YOU'RE OKAY!
I SAW YOU ON THE GROUND, AND I THOUGHT--
THOUGHT? YOU DIDN'T THINK. IF YOU HAD YOU'D NEVER HAVE LEFT YOUR AUNT'S SIDE!
HUSH ERNIE! IT'S NOT HIS FAULT!
10

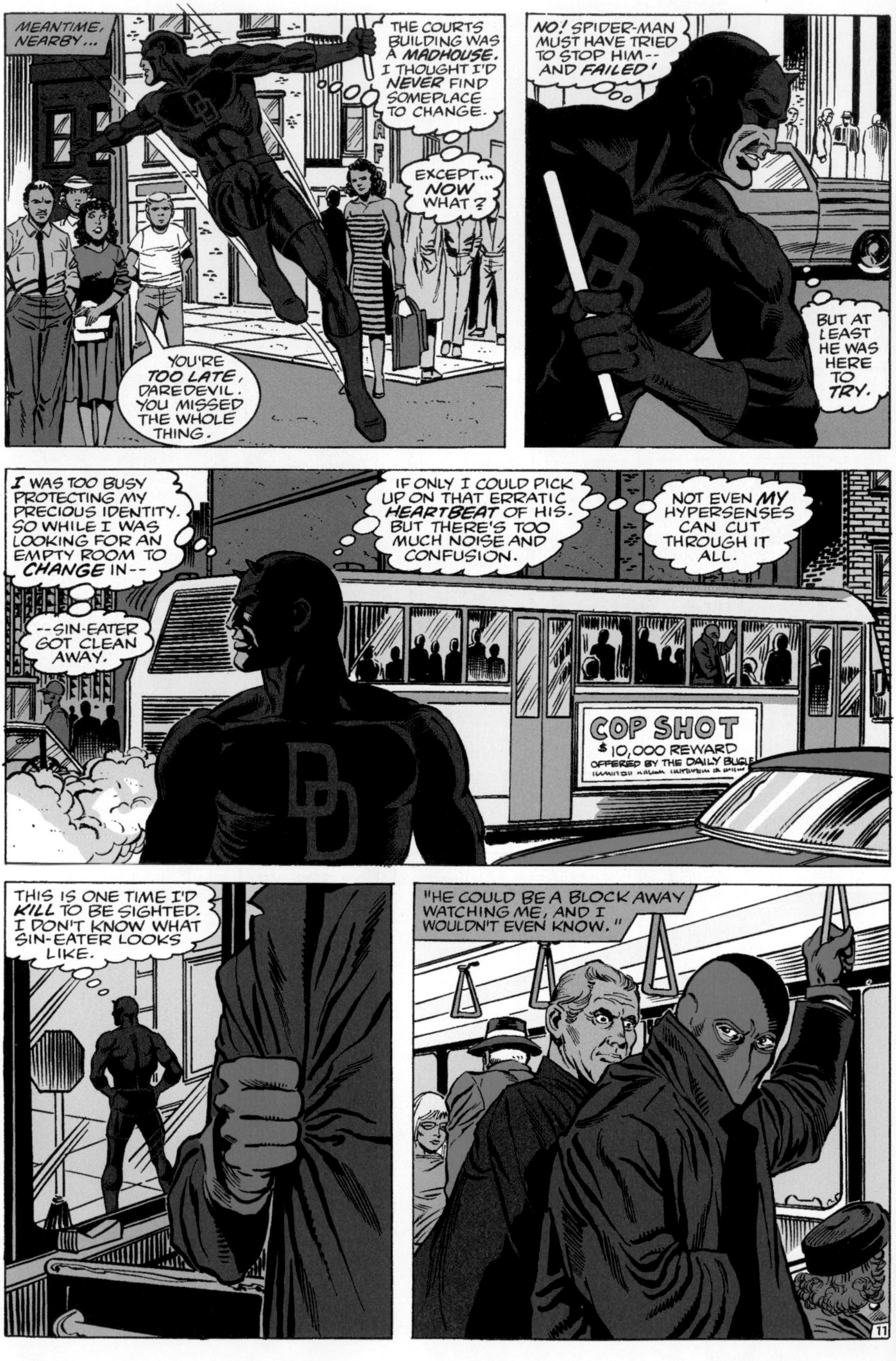
MEANTIME, NEARBY...
THE COURTS BUILDING WAS A MADHOUSE. I THOUGHT I'D NEVER FIND SOMEPLACE TO CHANGE.
EXCEPT... NOW WHAT?
YOU'RE TOO LATE, DAREDEVIL. YOU MISSED THE WHOLE THING.
NO! SPIDER-MAN MUST HAVE TRIED TO STOP HIM-- AND FAILED!
BUT AT LEAST HE WAS HERE TO TRY.
I WAS TOO BUSY PROTECTING MY PRECIOUS IDENTITY. SO WHILE I WAS LOOKING FOR AN EMPTY ROOM TO CHANGE IN--
--SIN-EATER GOT CLEAN AWAY.
IF ONLY I COULD PICK UP ON THAT ERRATIC HEARTBEAT OF HIS. BUT THERE'S TOO MUCH NOISE AND CONFUSION.
NOT EVEN MY HYPERSENSES CAN CUT THROUGH IT ALL.
COP SHOT
$10,000 REWARD
OFFERED BY THE DAILY BUGLE
THIS IS ONE TIME I'D KILL TO BE SIGHTED. I DON'T KNOW WHAT SIN-EATER LOOKS LIKE.
"HE COULD BE A BLOCK AWAY WATCHING ME, AND I WOULDN'T EVEN KNOW."
11

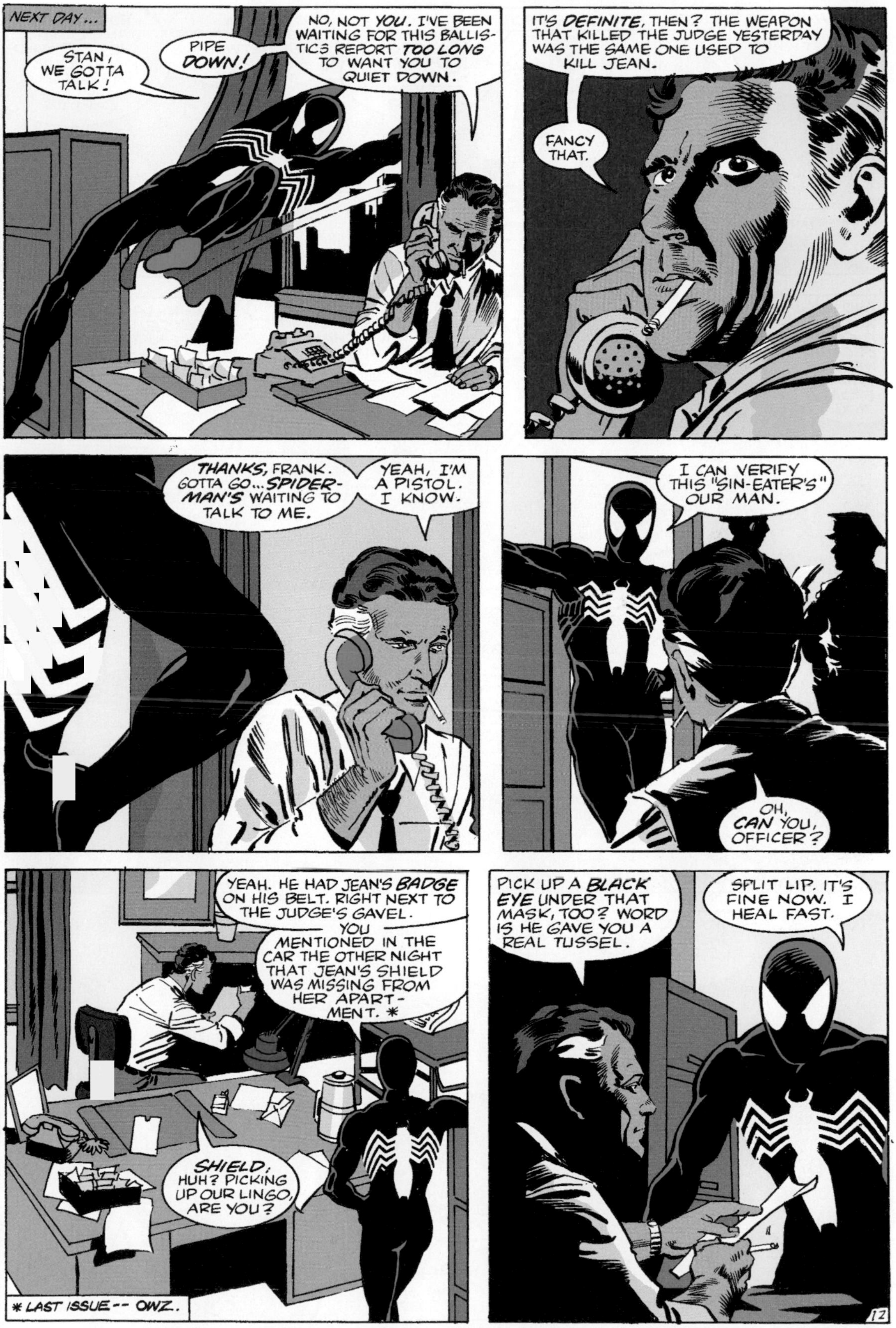
NEXT DAY...
STAN, WE GOTTA TALK!
PIPE DOWN!
NO, NOT YOU. I'VE BEEN WAITING FOR THIS BALLISTICS REPORT TOO LONG TO WANT YOU TO QUIET DOWN.
IT'S DEFINITE, THEN? THE WEAPON THAT KILLED THE JUDGE YESTERDAY WAS THE SAME ONE USED TO KILL JEAN.
FANCY THAT.
THANKS, FRANK. GOTTA GO... SPIDER-MAN'S WAITING TO TALK TO ME.
YEAH, I'M A PISTOL. I KNOW.
I CAN VERIFY THIS "SIN-EATER'S" OUR MAN.
OH, CAN YOU, OFFICER?
YEAH. HE HAD JEAN'S BADGE ON HIS BELT. RIGHT NEXT TO THE JUDGE'S GAVEL.
YOU MENTIONED IN THE CAR THE OTHER NIGHT THAT JEAN'S SHIELD WAS MISSING FROM HER APARTMENT. *
SHIELD, HUH? PICKING UP OUR LINGO, ARE YOU?
* LAST ISSUE -- OWZ.
PICK UP A BLACK EYE UNDER THAT MASK, TOO? WORD IS HE GAVE YOU A REAL TUSSEL.
SPLIT LIP. IT'S FINE NOW. I HEAL FAST.
12

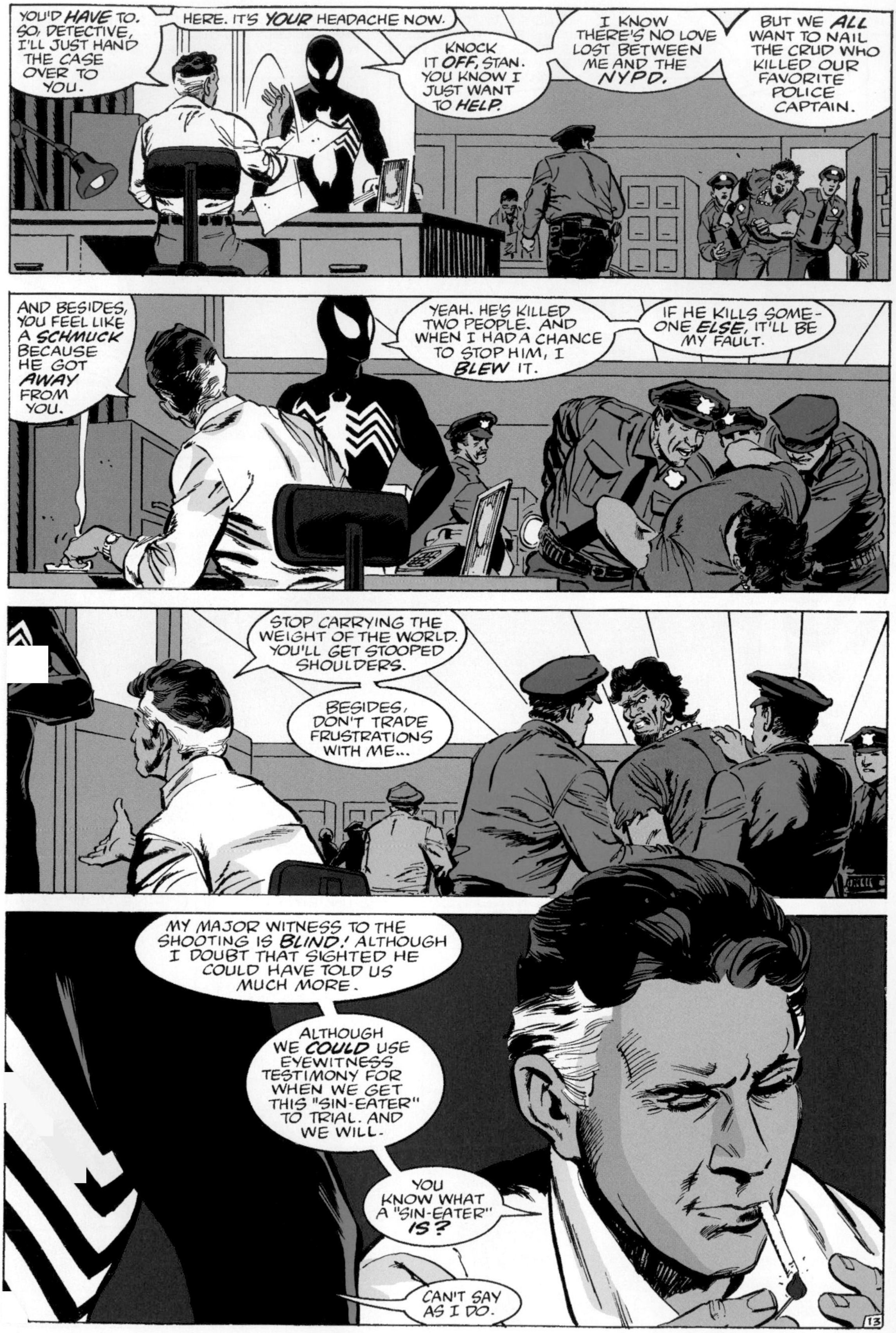
YOU'D HAVE TO. SO, DETECTIVE, I'LL JUST HAND THE CASE OVER TO YOU.
HERE. IT'S YOUR HEADACHE NOW.
KNOCK IT OFF, STAN. YOU KNOW I JUST WANT TO HELP.
I KNOW THERE'S NO LOVE LOST BETWEEN ME AND THE NYPD.
BUT WE ALL WANT TO NAIL THE CRUD WHO KILLED OUR FAVORITE POLICE CAPTAIN.
AND BESIDES, YOU FEEL LIKE A SCHMUCK BECAUSE HE GOT AWAY FROM YOU.
YEAH. HE'S KILLED TWO PEOPLE. AND WHEN I HAD A CHANCE TO STOP HIM, I BLEW IT.
IF HE KILLS SOME-ONE ELSE, IT'LL BE MY FAULT.
STOP CARRYING THE WEIGHT OF THE WORLD. YOU'LL GET STOOPED SHOULDERS.
BESIDES, DON'T TRADE FRUSTRATIONS WITH ME...
MY MAJOR WITNESS TO THE SHOOTING IS BLIND! ALTHOUGH I DOUBT THAT SIGHTED HE COULD HAVE TOLD US MUCH MORE.
ALTHOUGH WE COULD USE EYEWITNESS TESTIMONY FOR WHEN WE GET THIS "SIN-EATER" TO TRIAL. AND WE WILL.
YOU KNOW WHAT A "SIN-EATER" IS?
CAN'T SAY AS I DO.
13

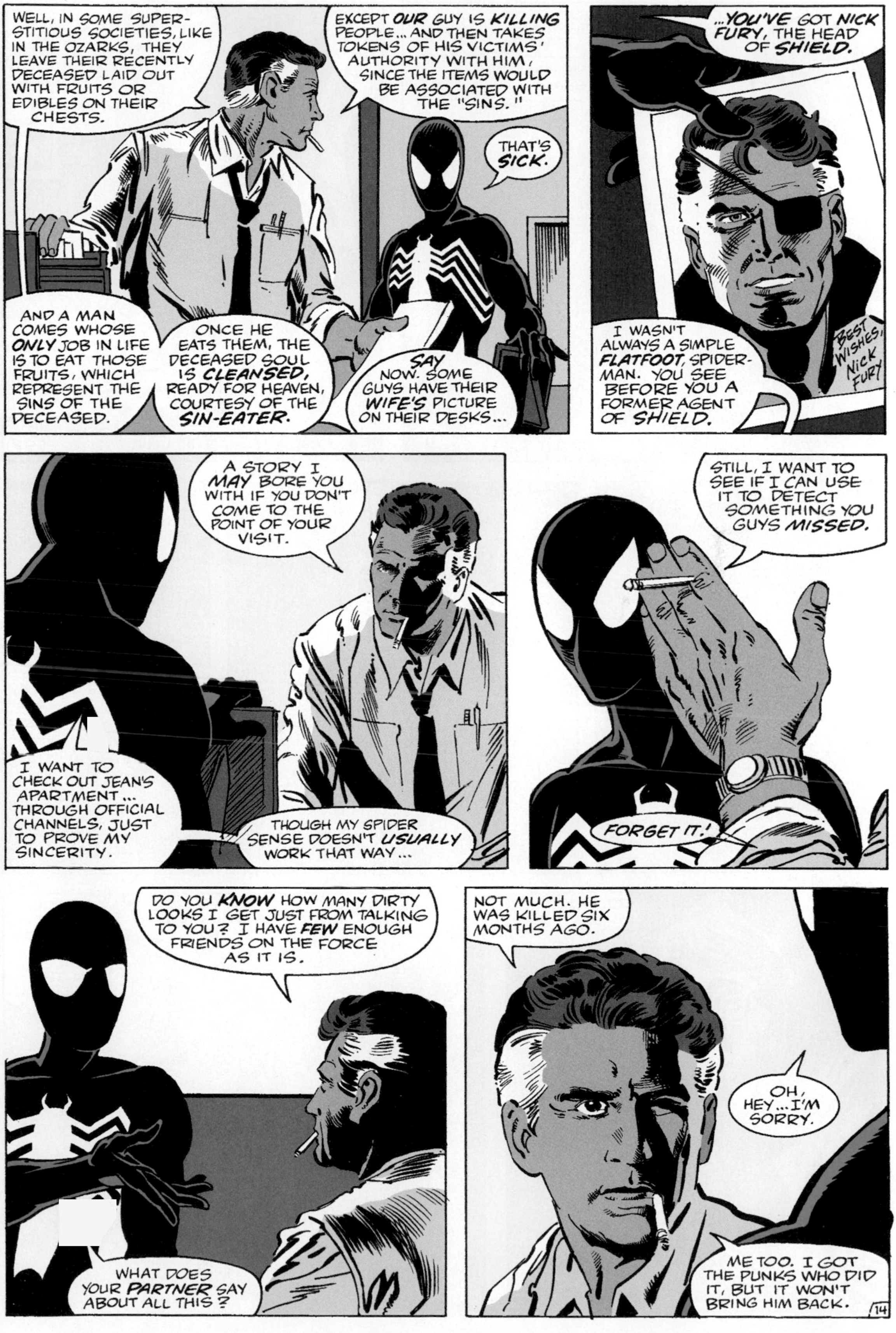
WELL, IN SOME SUPERSTITIOUS SOCIETIES, LIKE IN THE OZARKS, THEY LEAVE THEIR RECENTLY DECEASED LAID OUT WITH FRUITS OR EDIBLES ON THEIR CHESTS.
AND A MAN COMES WHOSE ONLY JOB IN LIFE IS TO EAT THOSE FRUITS, WHICH REPRESENT THE SINS OF THE DECEASED.
ONCE HE EATS THEM, THE DECEASED SOUL IS CLEANSED, READY FOR HEAVEN, COURTESY OF THE SIN-EATER.
EXCEPT OUR GUY IS KILLING PEOPLE... AND THEN TAKES TOKENS OF HIS VICTIMS' AUTHORITY WITH HIM, SINCE THE ITEMS WOULD BE ASSOCIATED WITH THE "SINS."
THAT'S SICK.
SAY NOW. SOME GUYS HAVE THEIR WIFE'S PICTURE ON THEIR DESKS...
...YOU'VE GOT NICK FURY, THE HEAD OF SHIELD.
BEST WISHES, NICK FURY
I WASN'T ALWAYS A SIMPLE FLATFOOT, SPIDER-MAN. YOU SEE BEFORE YOU A FORMER AGENT OF SHIELD.
A STORY I MAY BORE YOU WITH IF YOU DON'T COME TO THE POINT OF YOUR VISIT.
I WANT TO CHECK OUT JEAN'S APARTMENT... THROUGH OFFICIAL CHANNELS, JUST TO PROVE MY SINCERITY.
THOUGH MY SPIDER SENSE DOESN'T USUALLY WORK THAT WAY...
STILL, I WANT TO SEE IF I CAN USE IT TO DETECT SOMETHING YOU GUYS MISSED.
FORGET IT!
DO YOU KNOW HOW MANY DIRTY LOOKS I GET JUST FROM TALKING TO YOU? I HAVE FEW ENOUGH FRIENDS ON THE FORCE AS IT IS.
WHAT DOES YOUR PARTNER SAY ABOUT ALL THIS?
NOT MUCH. HE WAS KILLED SIX MONTHS AGO.
OH, HEY... I'M SORRY.
ME TOO. I GOT THE PUNKS WHO DID IT, BUT IT WON'T BRING HIM BACK.
14

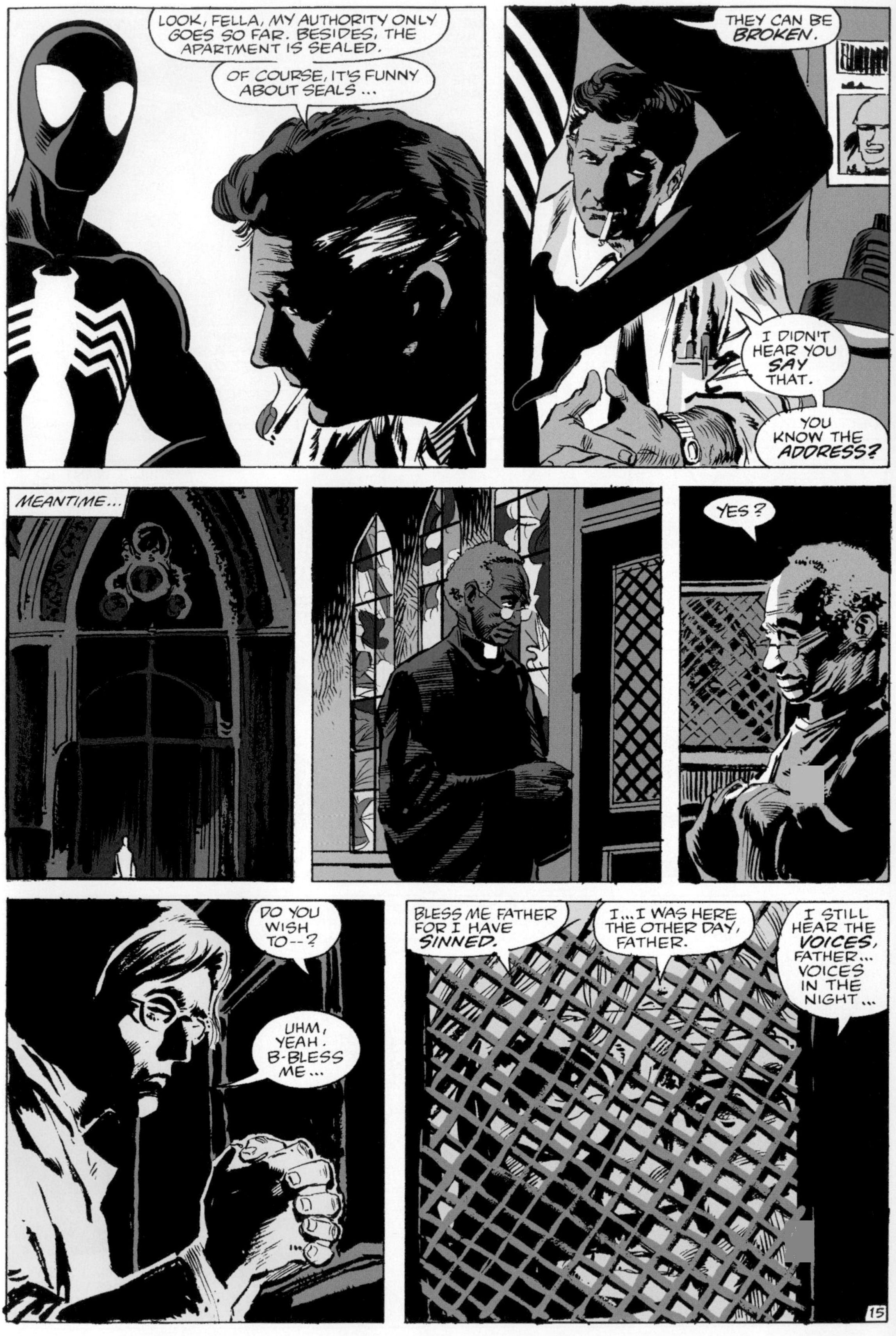
LOOK, FELLA, MY AUTHORITY ONLY GOES SO FAR. BESIDES, THE APARTMENT IS SEALED.
OF COURSE, IT'S FUNNY ABOUT SEALS ...
THEY CAN BE BROKEN.
I DIDN'T HEAR YOU SAY THAT.
YOU KNOW THE ADDRESS?
MEANTIME...
YES?
DO YOU WISH TO--?
UHM, YEAH. B-BLESS ME ...
BLESS ME FATHER FOR I HAVE SINNED.
I...I WAS HERE THE OTHER DAY, FATHER.
I STILL HEAR THE VOICES, FATHER... VOICES IN THE NIGHT...
15

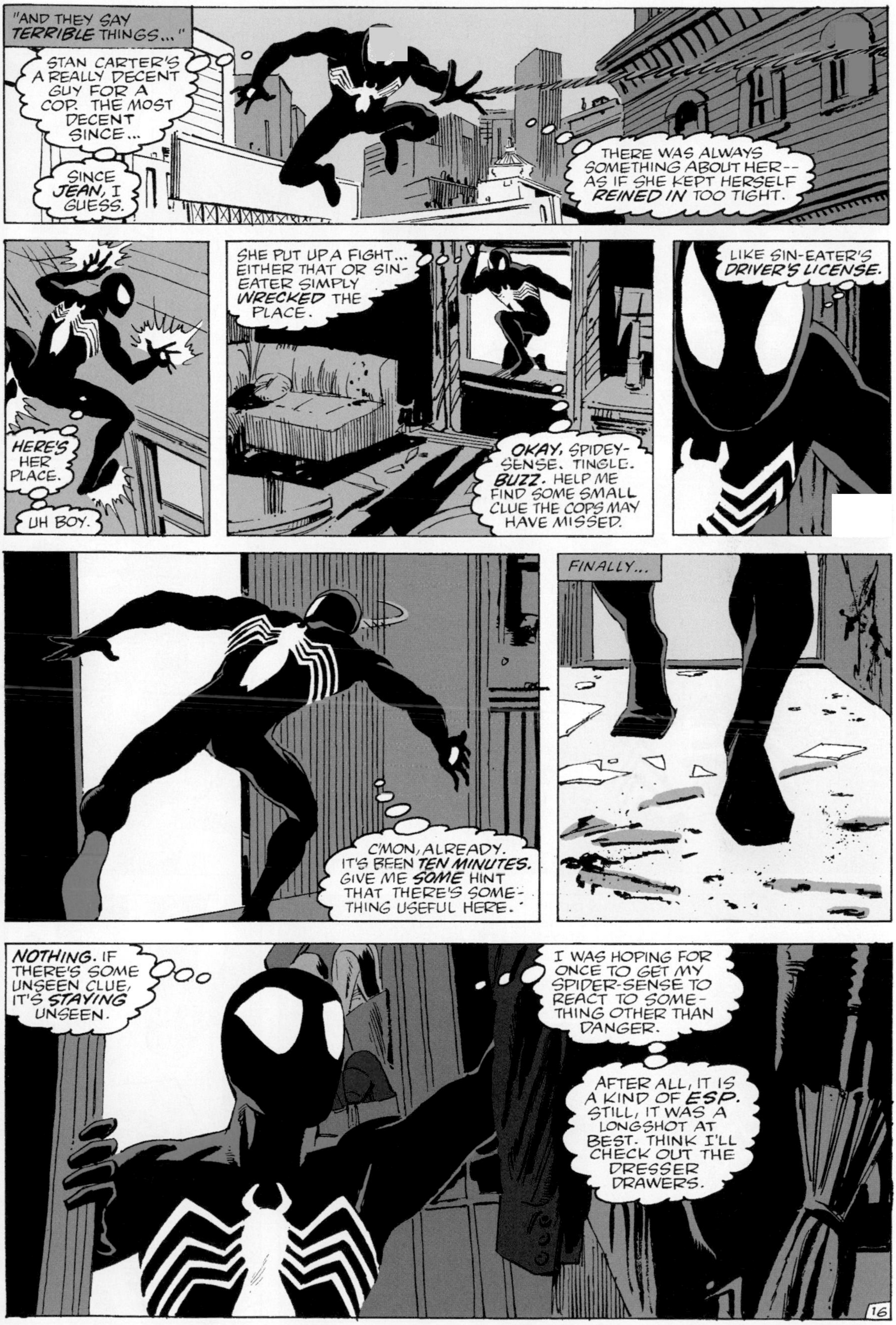
"AND THEY SAY TERRIBLE THINGS..."
STAN CARTER'S A REALLY DECENT GUY FOR A COP. THE MOST DECENT SINCE...
SINCE JEAN, I GUESS.
THERE WAS ALWAYS SOMETHING ABOUT HER-- AS IF SHE KEPT HERSELF REINED IN TOO TIGHT.
HERE'S HER PLACE.
UH BOY.
SHE PUT UP A FIGHT... EITHER THAT OR SIN-EATER SIMPLY WRECKED THE PLACE.
OKAY, SPIDEY-SENSE. TINGLE. BUZZ. HELP ME FIND SOME SMALL CLUE THE COPS MAY HAVE MISSED.
LIKE SIN-EATER'S DRIVER'S LICENSE.
C'MON, ALREADY. IT'S BEEN TEN MINUTES. GIVE ME SOME HINT THAT THERE'S SOMETHING USEFUL HERE.
FINALLY...
NOTHING. IF THERE'S SOME UNSEEN CLUE, IT'S STAYING UNSEEN.
I WAS HOPING FOR ONCE TO GET MY SPIDER-SENSE TO REACT TO SOMETHING OTHER THAN DANGER.
AFTER ALL, IT IS A KIND OF ESP. STILL, IT WAS A LONGSHOT AT BEST. THINK I'LL CHECK OUT THE DRESSER DRAWERS.
16

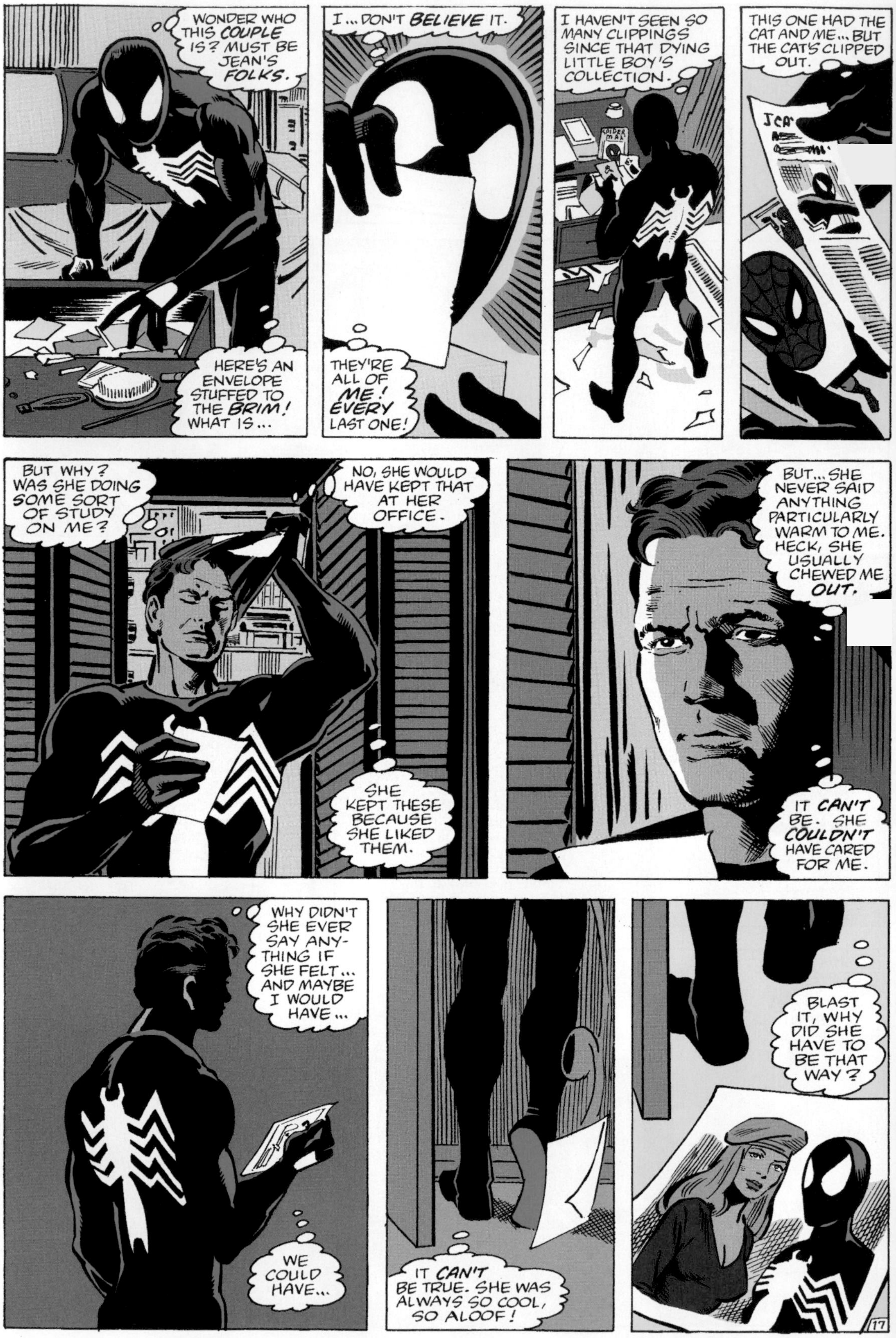
WONDER WHO THIS COUPLE IS? MUST BE JEAN'S FOLKS.
HERE'S AN ENVELOPE STUFFED TO THE BRIM! WHAT IS...
I... DON'T BELIEVE IT.
THEY'RE ALL OF ME! EVERY LAST ONE!
I HAVEN'T SEEN SO MANY CLIPPINGS SINCE THAT DYING LITTLE BOY'S COLLECTION.
THIS ONE HAD THE CAT AND ME... BUT THE CAT'S CLIPPED OUT.
BUT WHY? WAS SHE DOING SOME SORT OF STUDY ON ME?
NO, SHE WOULD HAVE KEPT THAT AT HER OFFICE.
SHE KEPT THESE BECAUSE SHE LIKED THEM.
BUT... SHE NEVER SAID ANYTHING PARTICULARLY WARM TO ME. HECK, SHE USUALLY CHEWED ME OUT.
IT CAN'T BE. SHE COULDN'T HAVE CARED FOR ME.
WHY DIDN'T SHE EVER SAY ANY-THING IF SHE FELT... AND MAYBE I WOULD HAVE...
WE COULD HAVE...
IT CAN'T BE TRUE. SHE WAS ALWAYS SO COOL, SO ALOOF!
BLAST IT, WHY DID SHE HAVE TO BE THAT WAY?
17

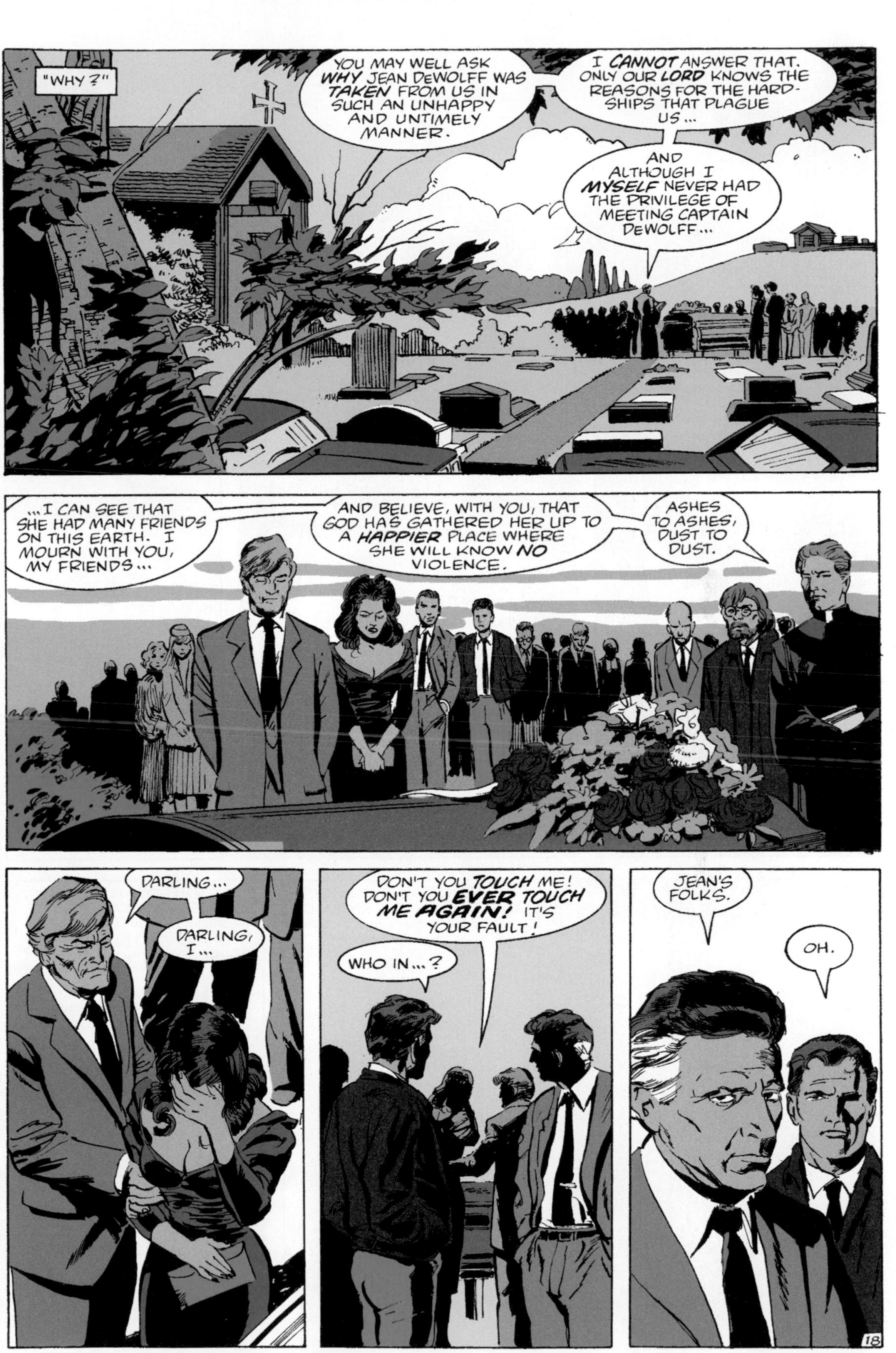
"WHY?"
YOU MAY WELL ASK WHY JEAN DeWOLFF WAS TAKEN FROM US IN SUCH AN UNHAPPY AND UNTIMELY MANNER.
I CANNOT ANSWER THAT. ONLY OUR LORD KNOWS THE REASONS FOR THE HARDSHIPS THAT PLAGUE US...
AND ALTHOUGH I MYSELF NEVER HAD THE PRIVILEGE OF MEETING CAPTAIN DeWOLFF...
...I CAN SEE THAT SHE HAD MANY FRIENDS ON THIS EARTH. I MOURN WITH YOU, MY FRIENDS...
AND BELIEVE, WITH YOU, THAT GOD HAS GATHERED HER UP TO A HAPPIER PLACE WHERE SHE WILL KNOW NO VIOLENCE.
ASHES TO ASHES, DUST TO DUST.
DARLING...
DARLING, I...
DON'T YOU TOUCH ME! DON'T YOU EVER TOUCH ME AGAIN! IT'S YOUR FAULT!
WHO IN...?
JEAN'S FOLKS.
OH.
18

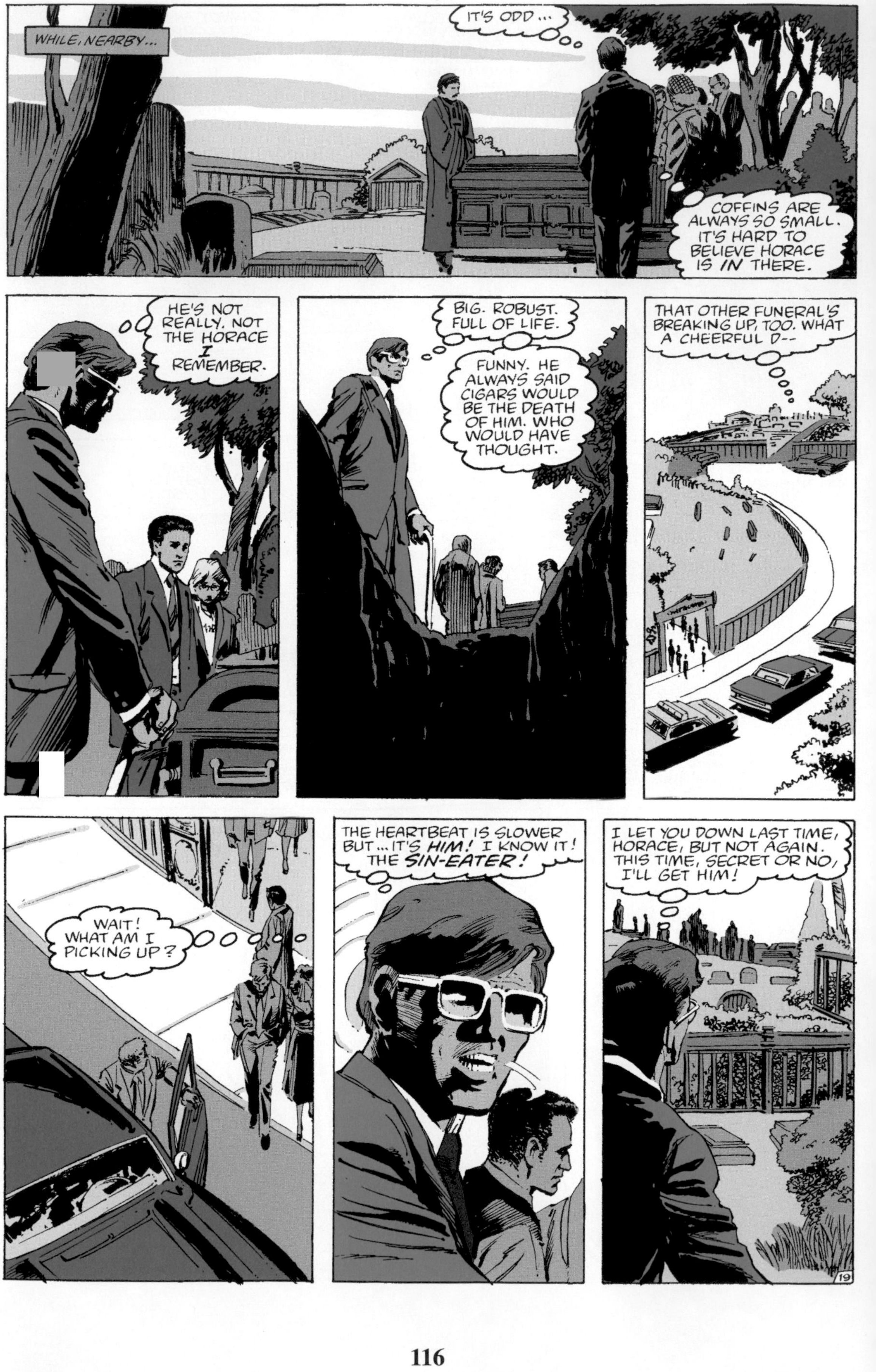
WHILE, NEARBY...
IT'S ODD...
COFFINS ARE ALWAYS SO SMALL. IT'S HARD TO BELIEVE HORACE IS IN THERE.
HE'S NOT REALLY. NOT THE HORACE I REMEMBER.
BIG. ROBUST. FULL OF LIFE.
FUNNY. HE ALWAYS SAID CIGARS WOULD BE THE DEATH OF HIM. WHO WOULD HAVE THOUGHT.
THAT OTHER FUNERAL'S BREAKING UP, TOO. WHAT A CHEERFUL D--
WAIT! WHAT AM I PICKING UP?
THE HEARTBEAT IS SLOWER BUT... IT'S HIM! I KNOW IT! THE SIN-EATER!
I LET YOU DOWN LAST TIME, HORACE, BUT NOT AGAIN. THIS TIME, SECRET OR NO, I'LL GET HIM!
19

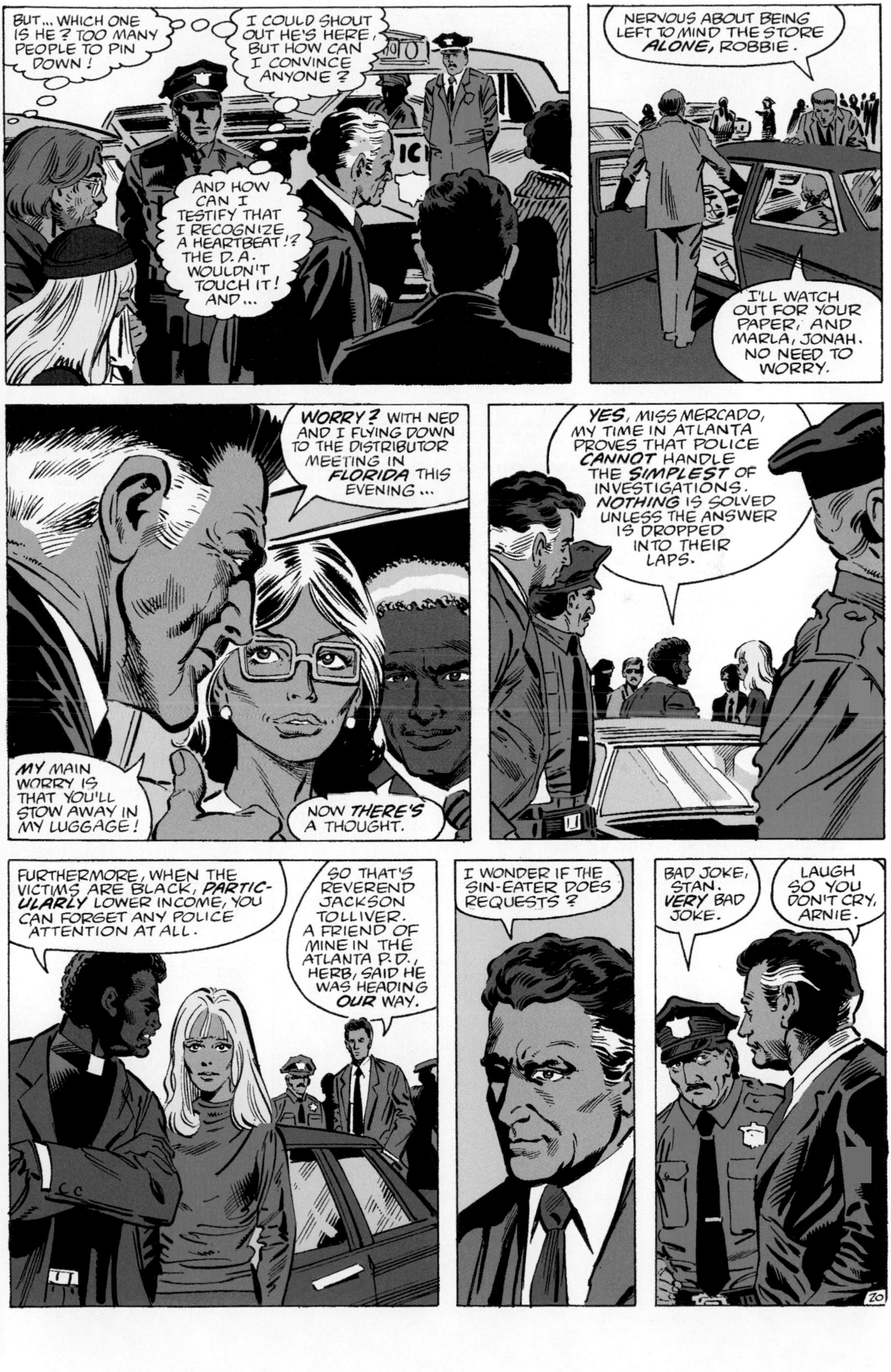
BUT... WHICH ONE IS HE? TOO MANY PEOPLE TO PIN DOWN!
I COULD SHOUT OUT HE'S HERE, BUT HOW CAN I CONVINCE ANYONE?
AND HOW CAN I TESTIFY THAT I RECOGNIZE A HEARTBEAT!? THE D.A. WOULDN'T TOUCH IT! AND...
NERVOUS ABOUT BEING LEFT TO MIND THE STORE ALONE, ROBBIE.
I'LL WATCH OUT FOR YOUR PAPER, AND MARLA, JONAH. NO NEED TO WORRY.
WORRY? WITH NED AND I FLYING DOWN TO THE DISTRIBUTOR MEETING IN FLORIDA THIS EVENING...
MY MAIN WORRY IS THAT YOU'LL STOW AWAY IN MY LUGGAGE!
NOW THERE'S A THOUGHT.
YES, MISS MERCADO, MY TIME IN ATLANTA PROVES THAT POLICE CANNOT HANDLE THE SIMPLEST OF INVESTIGATIONS. NOTHING IS SOLVED UNLESS THE ANSWER IS DROPPED INTO THEIR LAPS.
FURTHERMORE, WHEN THE VICTIMS ARE BLACK, PARTICULARLY LOWER INCOME, YOU CAN FORGET ANY POLICE ATTENTION AT ALL.
SO THAT'S REVEREND JACKSON TOLLIVER. A FRIEND OF MINE IN THE ATLANTA P.D., HERB, SAID HE WAS HEADING OUR WAY.
I WONDER IF THE SIN-EATER DOES REQUESTS?
BAD JOKE, STAN. VERY BAD JOKE.
LAUGH SO YOU DON'T CRY, ARNIE.
20

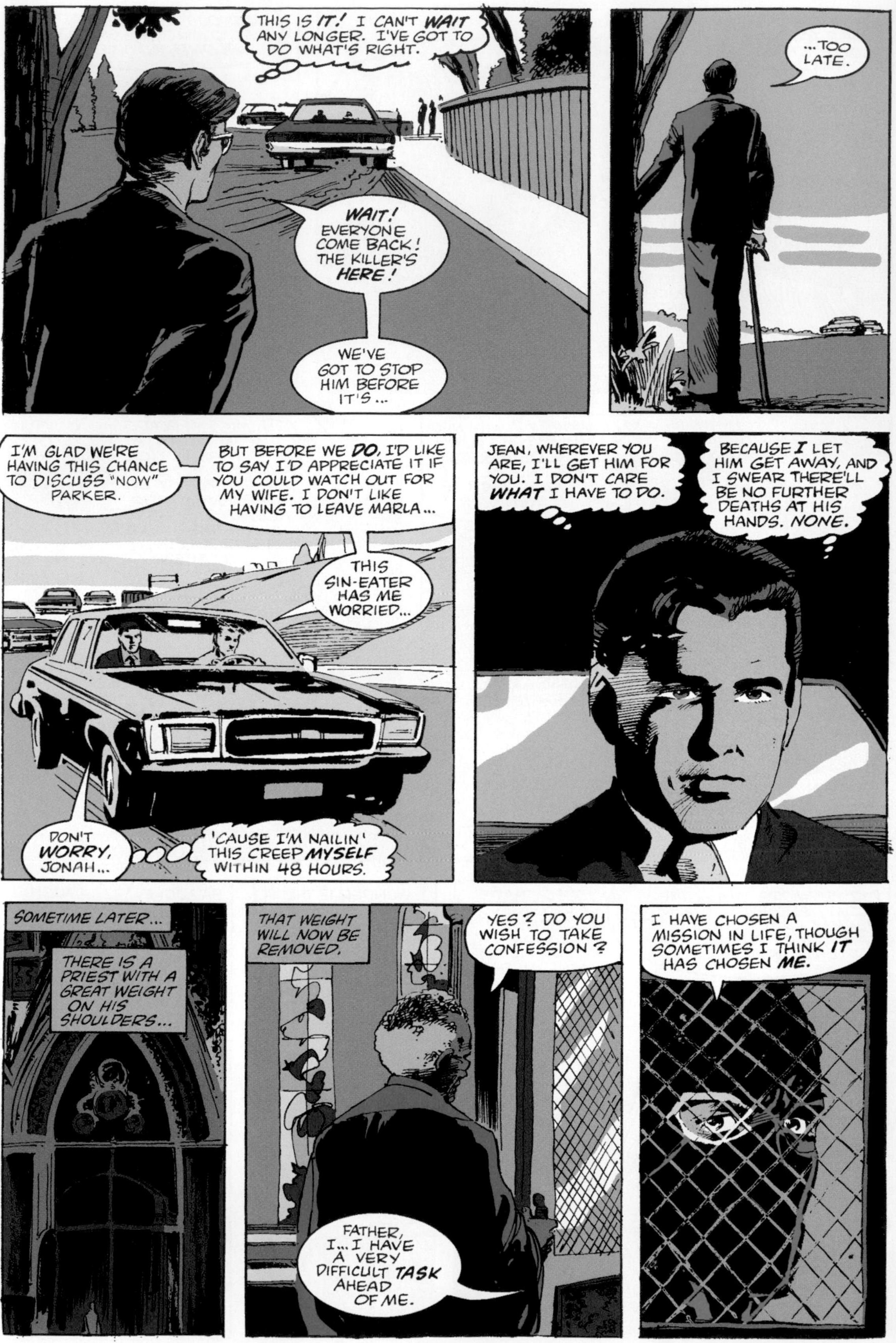
THIS IS IT! I CAN'T WAIT ANY LONGER. I'VE GOT TO DO WHAT'S RIGHT.
WAIT! EVERYONE COME BACK! THE KILLER'S HERE!
WE'VE GOT TO STOP HIM BEFORE IT'S...
...TOO LATE.
I'M GLAD WE'RE HAVING THIS CHANCE TO DISCUSS "NOW" PARKER.
BUT BEFORE WE DO, I'D LIKE TO SAY I'D APPRECIATE IT IF YOU COULD WATCH OUT FOR MY WIFE. I DON'T LIKE HAVING TO LEAVE MARLA...
THIS SIN-EATER HAS ME WORRIED...
DON'T WORRY, JONAH...
'CAUSE I'M NAILIN' THIS CREEP MYSELF WITHIN 48 HOURS.
JEAN, WHEREVER YOU ARE, I'LL GET HIM FOR YOU. I DON'T CARE WHAT I HAVE TO DO.
BECAUSE I LET HIM GET AWAY, AND I SWEAR THERE'LL BE NO FURTHER DEATHS AT HIS HANDS. NONE.
SOMETIME LATER...
THERE IS A PRIEST WITH A GREAT WEIGHT ON HIS SHOULDERS...
THAT WEIGHT WILL NOW BE REMOVED.
FATHER, I... I HAVE A VERY DIFFICULT TASK AHEAD OF ME.
YES? DO YOU WISH TO TAKE CONFESSION?
I HAVE CHOSEN A MISSION IN LIFE, THOUGH SOMETIMES I THINK IT HAS CHOSEN ME.

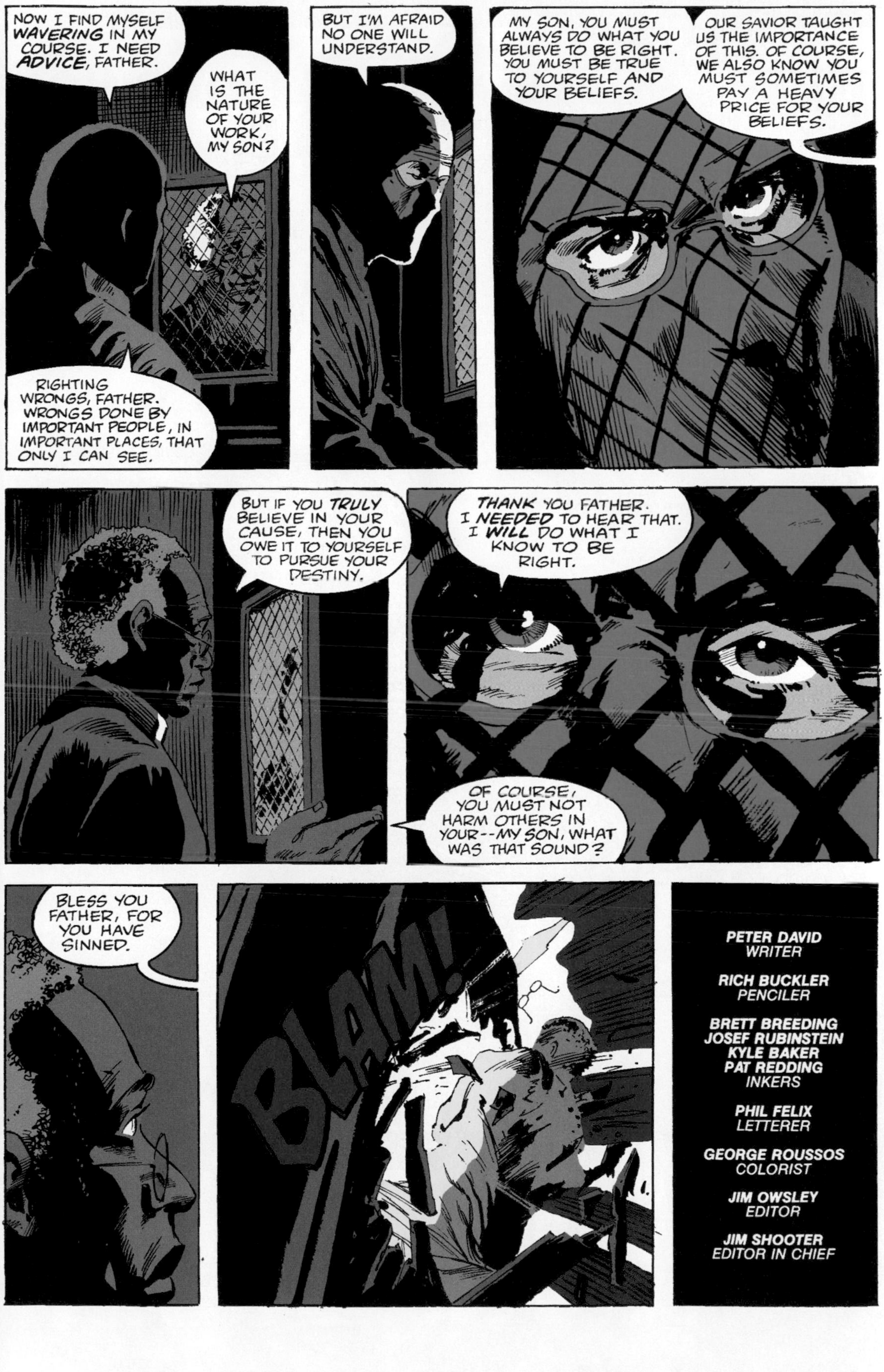
NOW I FIND MYSELF WAVERING IN MY COURSE. I NEED ADVICE, FATHER.
WHAT IS THE NATURE OF YOUR WORK, MY SON?
RIGHTING WRONGS, FATHER. WRONGS DONE BY IMPORTANT PEOPLE, IN IMPORTANT PLACES, THAT ONLY I CAN SEE.
BUT I'M AFRAID NO ONE WILL UNDERSTAND.
MY SON, YOU MUST ALWAYS DO WHAT YOU BELIEVE TO BE RIGHT. YOU MUST BE TRUE TO YOURSELF AND YOUR BELIEFS.
OUR SAVIOR TAUGHT US THE IMPORTANCE OF THIS. OF COURSE, WE ALSO KNOW YOU MUST SOMETIMES PAY A HEAVY PRICE FOR YOUR BELIEFS.
BUT IF YOU TRULY BELIEVE IN YOUR CAUSE, THEN YOU OWE IT TO YOURSELF TO PURSUE YOUR DESTINY.
THANK YOU FATHER. I NEEDED TO HEAR THAT. I WILL DO WHAT I KNOW TO BE RIGHT.
OF COURSE, YOU MUST NOT HARM OTHERS IN YOUR--MY SON, WHAT WAS THAT SOUND?
BLESS YOU FATHER, FOR YOU HAVE SINNED.
BLAM!
PETER DAVID
WRITER
RICH BUCKLER
PENCILER
BRETT BREEDING
JOSEF RUBINSTEIN
KYLE BAKER
PAT REDDING
INKERS
PHIL FELIX
LETTERER
GEORGE ROUSSOS
COLORIST
JIM OWSLEY
EDITOR
JIM SHOOTER
EDITOR IN CHIEF

MARVEL®
THE ALL NEW. ALL DARING
PETER PARKER, THE SPECTACULAR
SPIDER-MAN™
65¢
109
DEC
APPROVED BY THE COMICS CODE AUTHORITY
02199
HE WHO IS
WITHOUT SIN

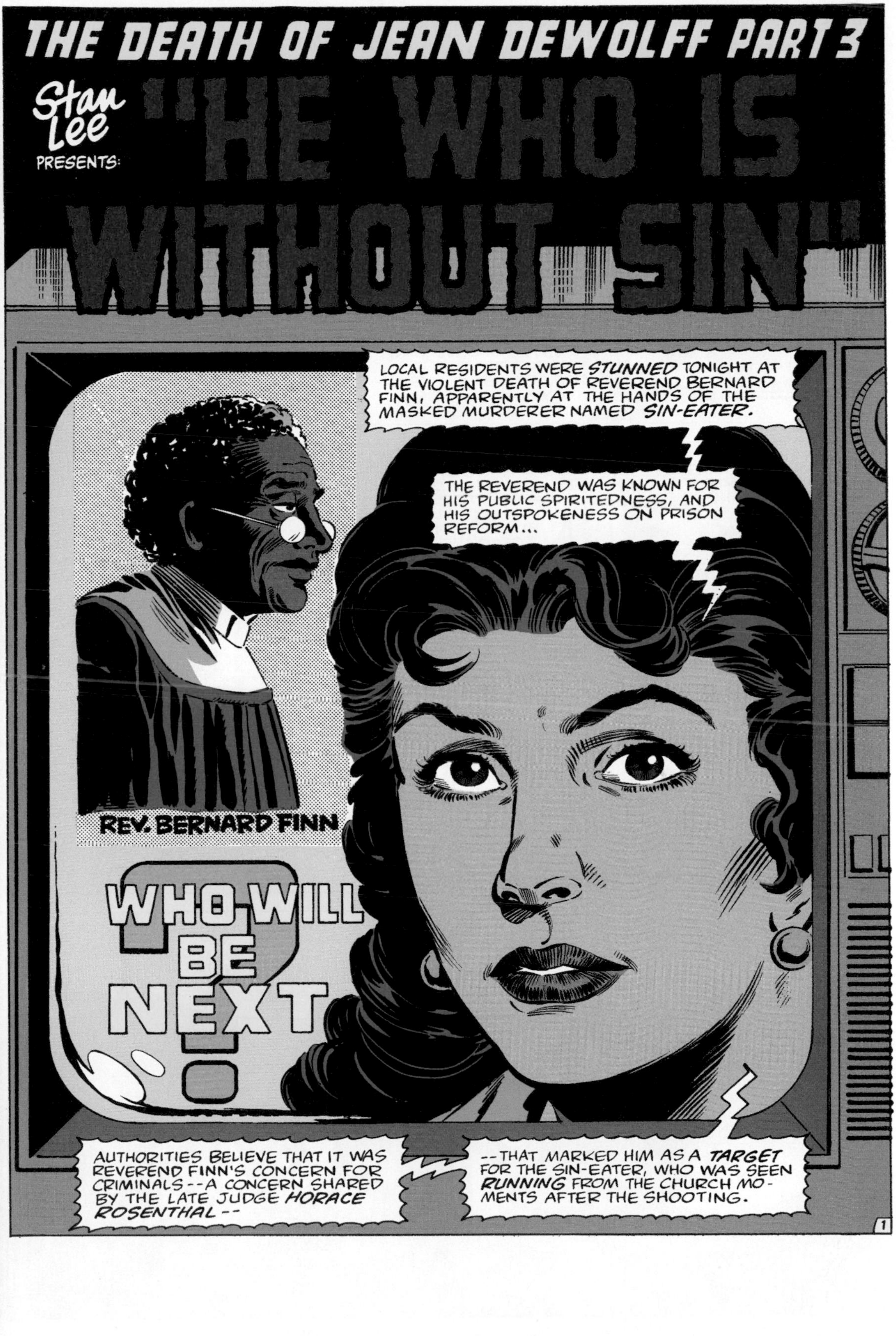
THE DEATH OF JEAN DEWOLFF PART 3
Stan Lee PRESENTS:
"HE WHO IS WITHOUT SIN"
LOCAL RESIDENTS WERE STUNNED TONIGHT AT THE VIOLENT DEATH OF REVEREND BERNARD FINN, APPARENTLY AT THE HANDS OF THE MASKED MURDERER NAMED SIN-EATER.
THE REVEREND WAS KNOWN FOR HIS PUBLIC SPIRITEDNESS, AND HIS OUTSPOKENESS ON PRISON REFORM...
REV. BERNARD FINN
WHO WILL BE NEXT?
AUTHORITIES BELIEVE THAT IT WAS REVEREND FINN'S CONCERN FOR CRIMINALS--A CONCERN SHARED BY THE LATE JUDGE HORACE ROSENTHAL--
--THAT MARKED HIM AS A TARGET FOR THE SIN-EATER, WHO WAS SEEN RUNNING FROM THE CHURCH MOMENTS AFTER THE SHOOTING.
1

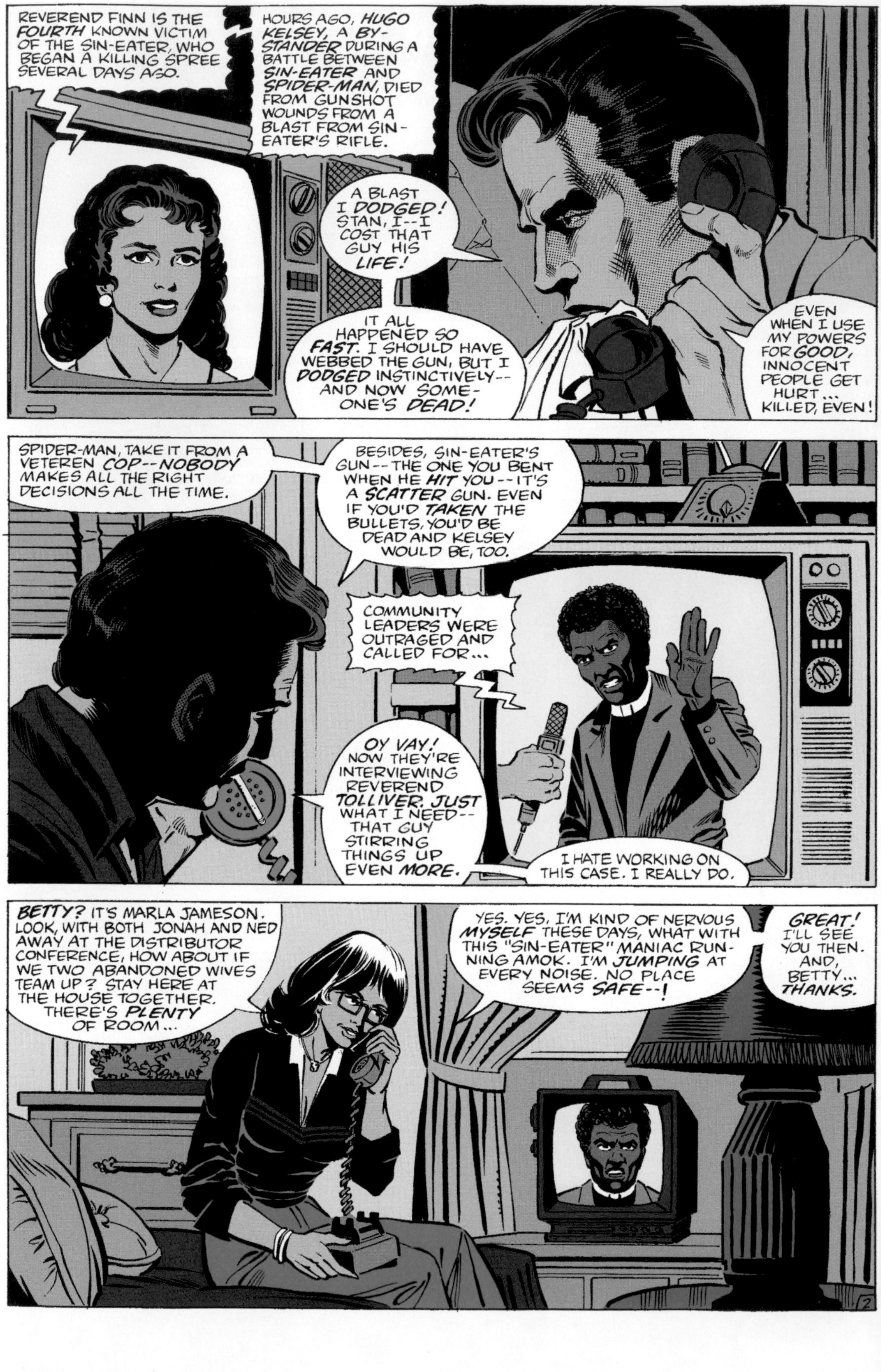
REVEREND FINN IS THE FOURTH KNOWN VICTIM OF THE SIN-EATER, WHO BEGAN A KILLING SPREE SEVERAL DAYS AGO.
HOURS AGO, HUGO KELSEY, A BY-STANDER DURING A BATTLE BETWEEN SIN-EATER AND SPIDER-MAN, DIED FROM GUNSHOT WOUNDS FROM A BLAST FROM SIN-EATER'S RIFLE.
A BLAST I DODGED! STAN, I--I COST THAT GUY HIS LIFE!
IT ALL HAPPENED SO FAST. I SHOULD HAVE WEBBED THE GUN, BUT I DODGED INSTINCTIVELY-- AND NOW SOME-ONE'S DEAD!
EVEN WHEN I USE MY POWERS FOR GOOD, INNOCENT PEOPLE GET HURT... KILLED, EVEN!
SPIDER-MAN, TAKE IT FROM A VETEREN COP--NOBODY MAKES ALL THE RIGHT DECISIONS ALL THE TIME.
BESIDES, SIN-EATER'S GUN--THE ONE YOU BENT WHEN HE HIT YOU--IT'S A SCATTER GUN. EVEN IF YOU'D TAKEN THE BULLETS, YOU'D BE DEAD AND KELSEY WOULD BE, TOO.
COMMUNITY LEADERS WERE OUTRAGED AND CALLED FOR...
OY VAY! NOW THEY'RE INTERVIEWING REVEREND TOLLIVER. JUST WHAT I NEED-- THAT GUY STIRRING THINGS UP EVEN MORE.
I HATE WORKING ON THIS CASE. I REALLY DO.
BETTY? IT'S MARLA JAMESON. LOOK, WITH BOTH JONAH AND NED AWAY AT THE DISTRIBUTOR CONFERENCE, HOW ABOUT IF WE TWO ABANDONED WIVES TEAM UP? STAY HERE AT THE HOUSE TOGETHER. THERE'S PLENTY OF ROOM...
YES. YES, I'M KIND OF NERVOUS MYSELF THESE DAYS, WHAT WITH THIS "SIN-EATER" MANIAC RUN-NING AMOK. I'M JUMPING AT EVERY NOISE. NO PLACE SEEMS SAFE--!
GREAT! I'LL SEE YOU THEN. AND, BETTY... THANKS.
2

I AM *STUNNED* THAT THE POLICE ARE UNABLE TO PROTECT EVEN A HOLY MAN IN THIS CITY. I JUST HOPE THAT, SINCE REVEREND FINN WAS *BLACK*, HE WILL NOT RECEIVE SHORT SHRIFT AT THE HANDS OF THE DETECTIVES.

WELL-SPOKEN, REV-- *IF* I SAY SO *MYSELF*.

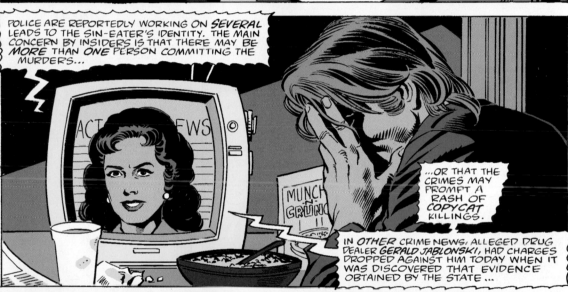

POLICE ARE REPORTEDLY WORKING ON *SEVERAL* LEADS TO THE SIN-EATER'S IDENTITY. THE MAIN CONCERN BY INSIDERS IS THAT THERE MAY BE *MORE* THAN *ONE* PERSON COMMITTING THE MURDERS...

...OR THAT THE CRIMES MAY PROMPT A *RASH* OF *COPYCAT* KILLINGS.

IN *OTHER* CRIME NEWS, ALLEGED DRUG DEALER *GERALD JABLONSKI*, HAD CHARGES DROPPED AGAINST HIM TODAY WHEN IT WAS DISCOVERED THAT EVIDENCE OBTAINED BY THE STATE ...

...WAS DONE SO *IMPROPERLY*, AND THAT EVIDENCE WAS RULED *INADMISSIBLE*. JABLONSKI IS QUOTED AS SAYING, "THANK HEAVENS, THE SYSTEM *WORKS*."

POLICE ARE *ALSO* PUZZLED BY A SERIES OF *BURGLARIES* ON THE *EAST SIDE* RECENTLY...

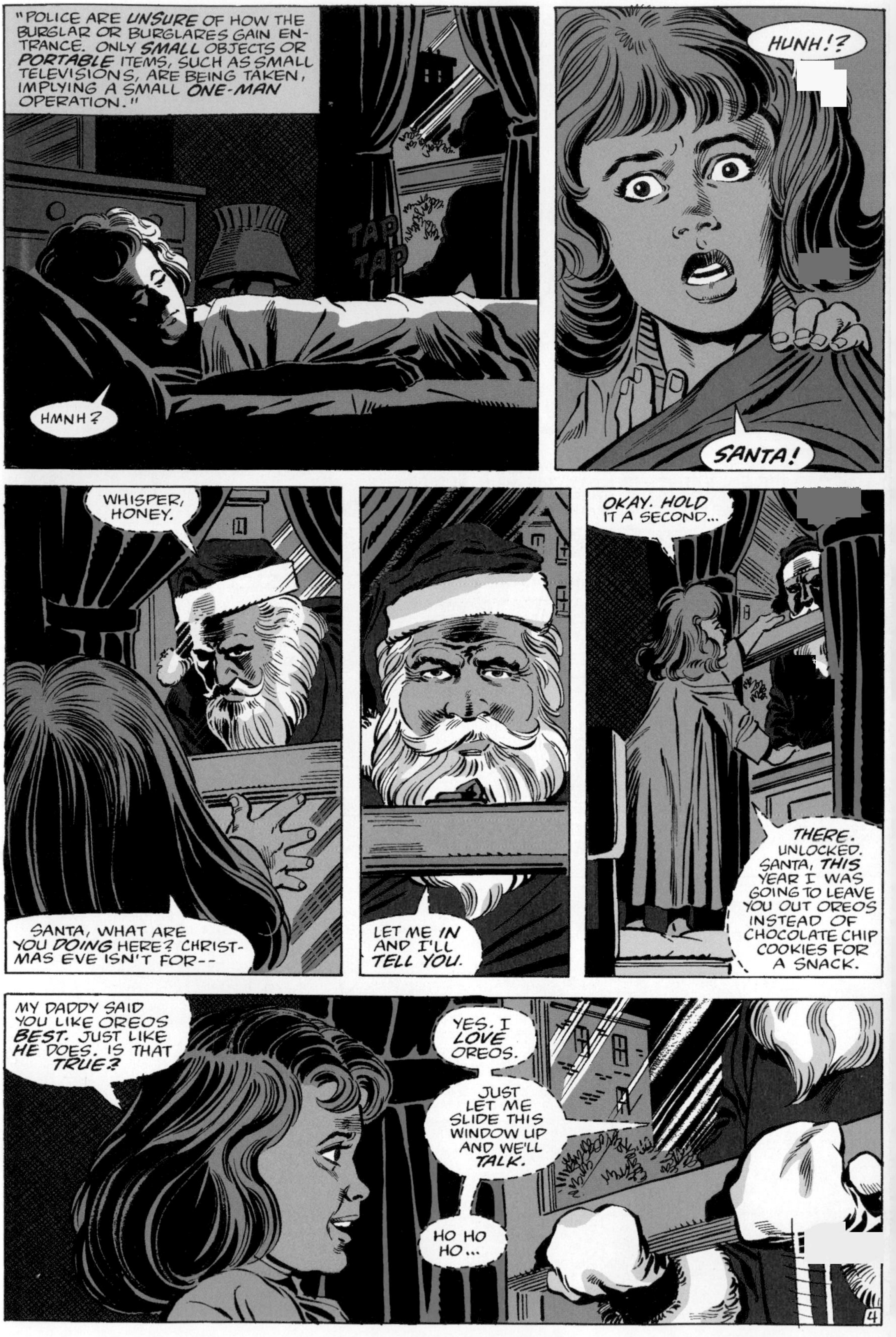
"POLICE ARE UNSURE OF HOW THE BURGLAR OR BURGLARES GAIN ENTRANCE. ONLY SMALL OBJECTS OR PORTABLE ITEMS, SUCH AS SMALL TELEVISIONS, ARE BEING TAKEN, IMPLYING A SMALL ONE-MAN OPERATION."
TAP TAP
HMNH?
HUNH!?
SANTA!
WHISPER, HONEY.
SANTA, WHAT ARE YOU DOING HERE? CHRISTMAS EVE ISN'T FOR--
LET ME IN AND I'LL TELL YOU.
OKAY. HOLD IT A SECOND...
THERE. UNLOCKED. SANTA, THIS YEAR I WAS GOING TO LEAVE YOU OUT OREOS INSTEAD OF CHOCOLATE CHIP COOKIES FOR A SNACK.
MY DADDY SAID YOU LIKE OREOS BEST. JUST LIKE HE DOES. IS THAT TRUE?
YES. I LOVE OREOS.
JUST LET ME SLIDE THIS WINDOW UP AND WE'LL TALK.
HO HO HO...
4

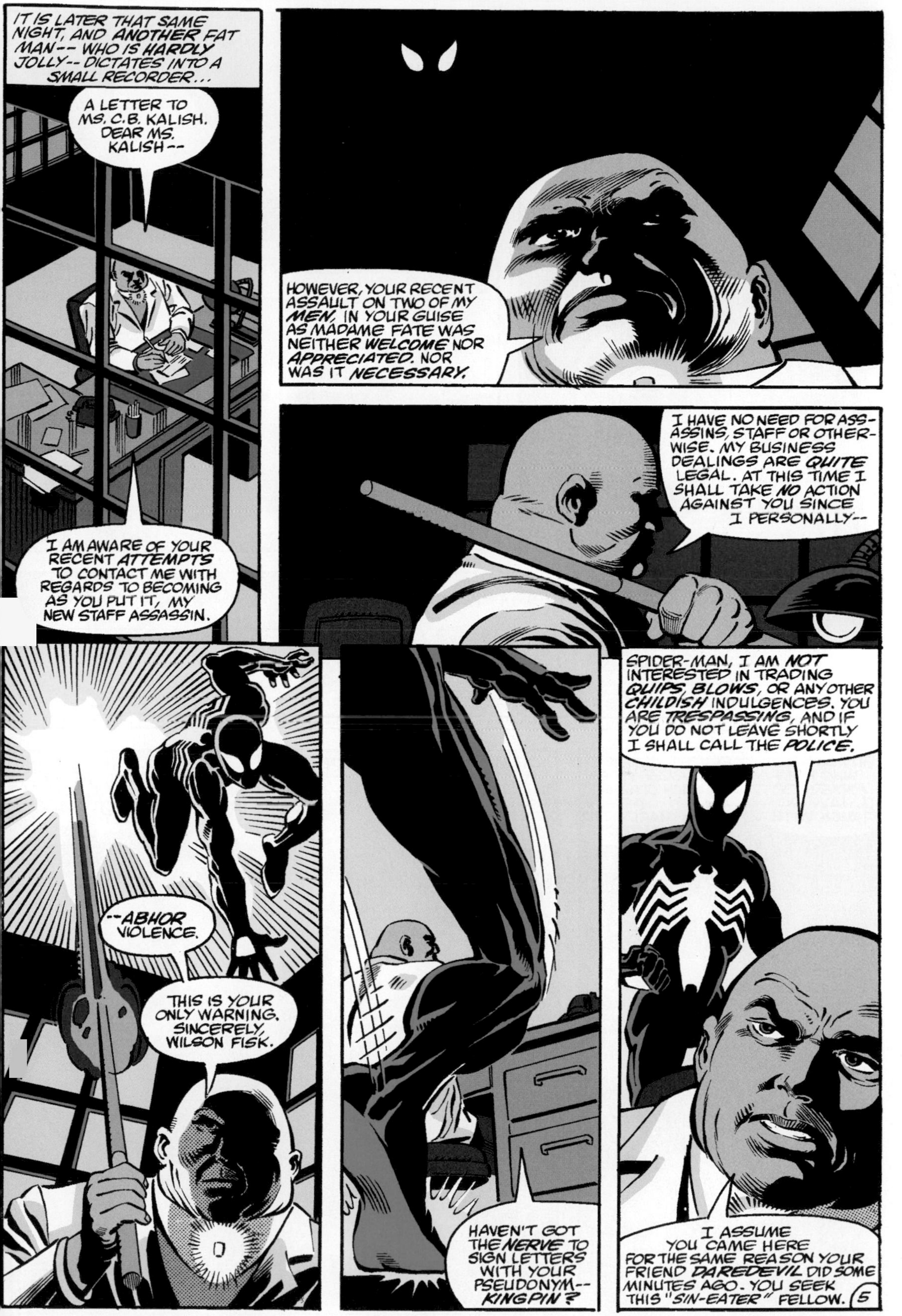
IT IS LATER THAT SAME NIGHT, AND ANOTHER FAT MAN-- WHO IS HARDLY JOLLY-- DICTATES INTO A SMALL RECORDER...
A LETTER TO MS. C.B. KALISH. DEAR MS. KALISH--
I AM AWARE OF YOUR RECENT ATTEMPTS TO CONTACT ME WITH REGARDS TO BECOMING AS YOU PUT IT, MY NEW STAFF ASSASSIN.
HOWEVER, YOUR RECENT ASSAULT ON TWO OF MY MEN, IN YOUR GUISE AS MADAME FATE WAS NEITHER WELCOME NOR APPRECIATED. NOR WAS IT NECESSARY.
I HAVE NO NEED FOR ASSASSINS, STAFF OR OTHERWISE. MY BUSINESS DEALINGS ARE QUITE LEGAL. AT THIS TIME I SHALL TAKE NO ACTION AGAINST YOU SINCE I PERSONALLY--
--ABHOR VIOLENCE.
THIS IS YOUR ONLY WARNING. SINCERELY, WILSON FISK.
HAVEN'T GOT THE NERVE TO SIGN LETTERS WITH YOUR PSEUDONYM-- KINGPIN?
SPIDER-MAN, I AM NOT INTERESTED IN TRADING QUIPS, BLOWS, OR ANY OTHER CHILDISH INDULGENCES. YOU ARE TRESPASSING, AND IF YOU DO NOT LEAVE SHORTLY I SHALL CALL THE POLICE.
I ASSUME YOU CAME HERE FOR THE SAME REASON YOUR FRIEND DAREDEVIL DID SOME MINUTES AGO. YOU SEEK THIS "SIN-EATER" FELLOW.
5

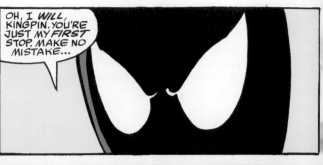

I CANNOT HELP YOU IN THIS.

I SUGGEST YOU MIGHT CHECK WITH THE *LOWER* RUNGS OF GARBAGE THAT EXIST IN THE SHADOWY WORLD OF THE CRIMINAL -- PERHAPS *THEY* HAVE THE INFORMATION YOU WANT.

OH, I *WILL*, KINGPIN. YOU'RE JUST MY *FIRST* STOP. MAKE NO MISTAKE...

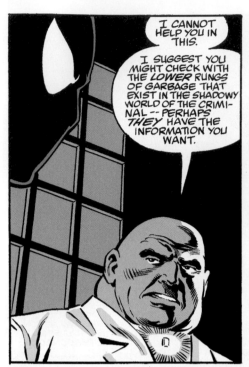

I'M GETTING THE MONSTER WHO KILLED JEAN DeWOLFF.

I DID NOT LIKE CAPTAIN DeWOLFF, NOR JUDGE ROSENTHAL. THEY WERE BOTH HONEST...

AND, HONEST PEOPLE BORE ME.

BUT SOMEONE WHO KILLS *PRIESTS* I HAVE NO TRUCK WITH.

PRIEST KILLERS *POLARIZE* CITIES, AND SUCH CITIES ARE HARDER TO *CONTROL.*

YOU MAY LEAVE NOW, SPIDER-MAN. AND, BY THE WAY--

--I TRUST YOU WILL NOT FIND IT NECESSARY TO RENDER ANY MORE OF MY GUARDS UNCONSCIOUS ON YOUR WAY OUT.

6

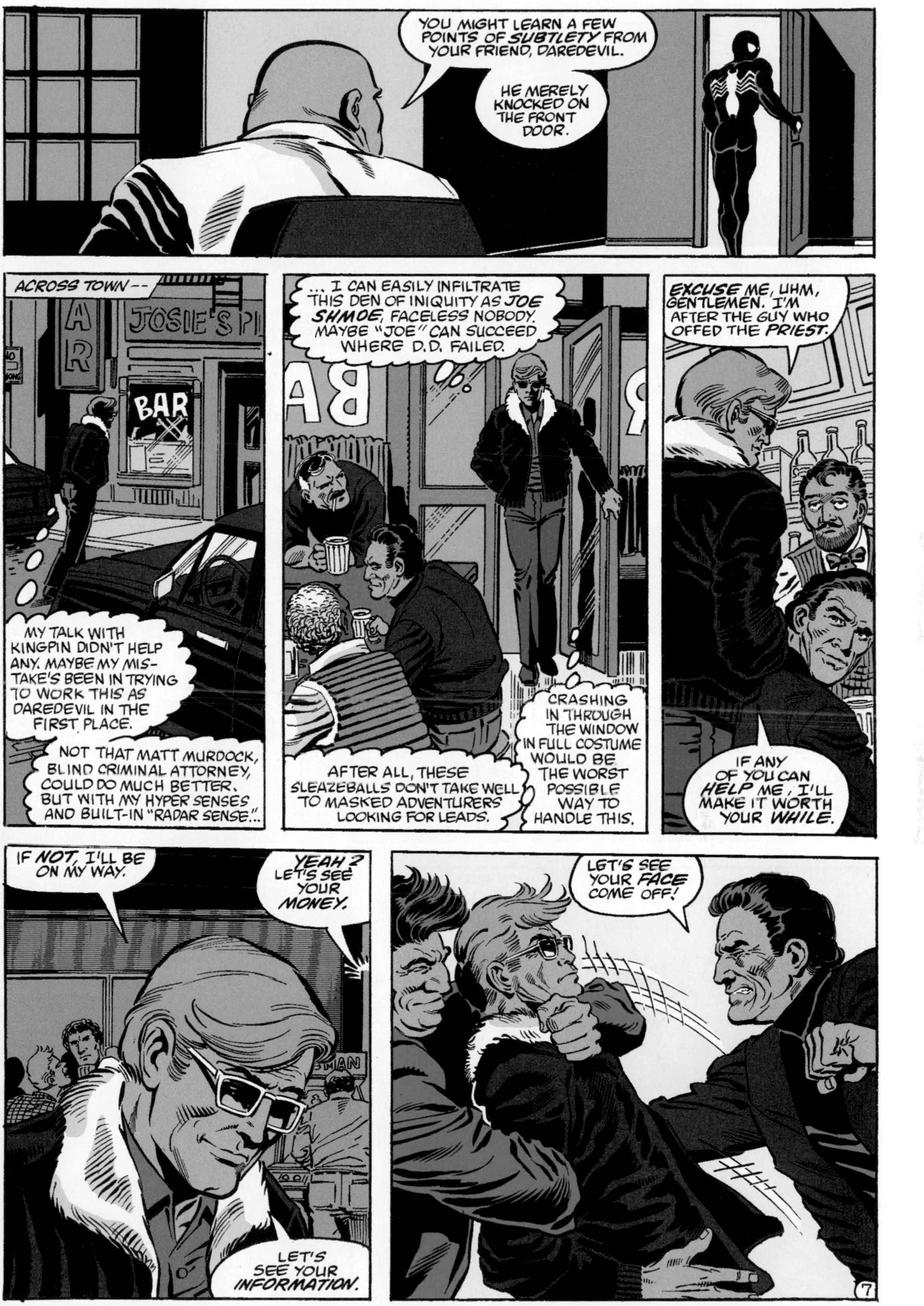
YOU MIGHT LEARN A FEW POINTS OF SUBTLETY FROM YOUR FRIEND, DAREDEVIL.
HE MERELY KNOCKED ON THE FRONT DOOR.
ACROSS TOWN --
JOSIE'S
BAR
MY TALK WITH KINGPIN DIDN'T HELP ANY. MAYBE MY MISTAKE'S BEEN IN TRYING TO WORK THIS AS DAREDEVIL IN THE FIRST PLACE.
NOT THAT MATT MURDOCK, BLIND CRIMINAL ATTORNEY, COULD DO MUCH BETTER. BUT WITH MY HYPER SENSES AND BUILT-IN "RADAR SENSE"...
... I CAN EASILY INFILTRATE THIS DEN OF INIQUITY AS JOE SHMOE, FACELESS NOBODY. MAYBE "JOE" CAN SUCCEED WHERE D.D. FAILED.
AFTER ALL, THESE SLEAZEBALLS DON'T TAKE WELL TO MASKED ADVENTURERS LOOKING FOR LEADS.
CRASHING IN THROUGH THE WINDOW IN FULL COSTUME WOULD BE THE WORST POSSIBLE WAY TO HANDLE THIS.
EXCUSE ME, UHM, GENTLEMEN. I'M AFTER THE GUY WHO OFFED THE PRIEST.
IF ANY OF YOU CAN HELP ME, I'LL MAKE IT WORTH YOUR WHILE.
IF NOT, I'LL BE ON MY WAY.
YEAH? LET'S SEE YOUR MONEY.
LET'S SEE YOUR INFORMATION.
LET'S SEE YOUR FACE COME OFF!
7

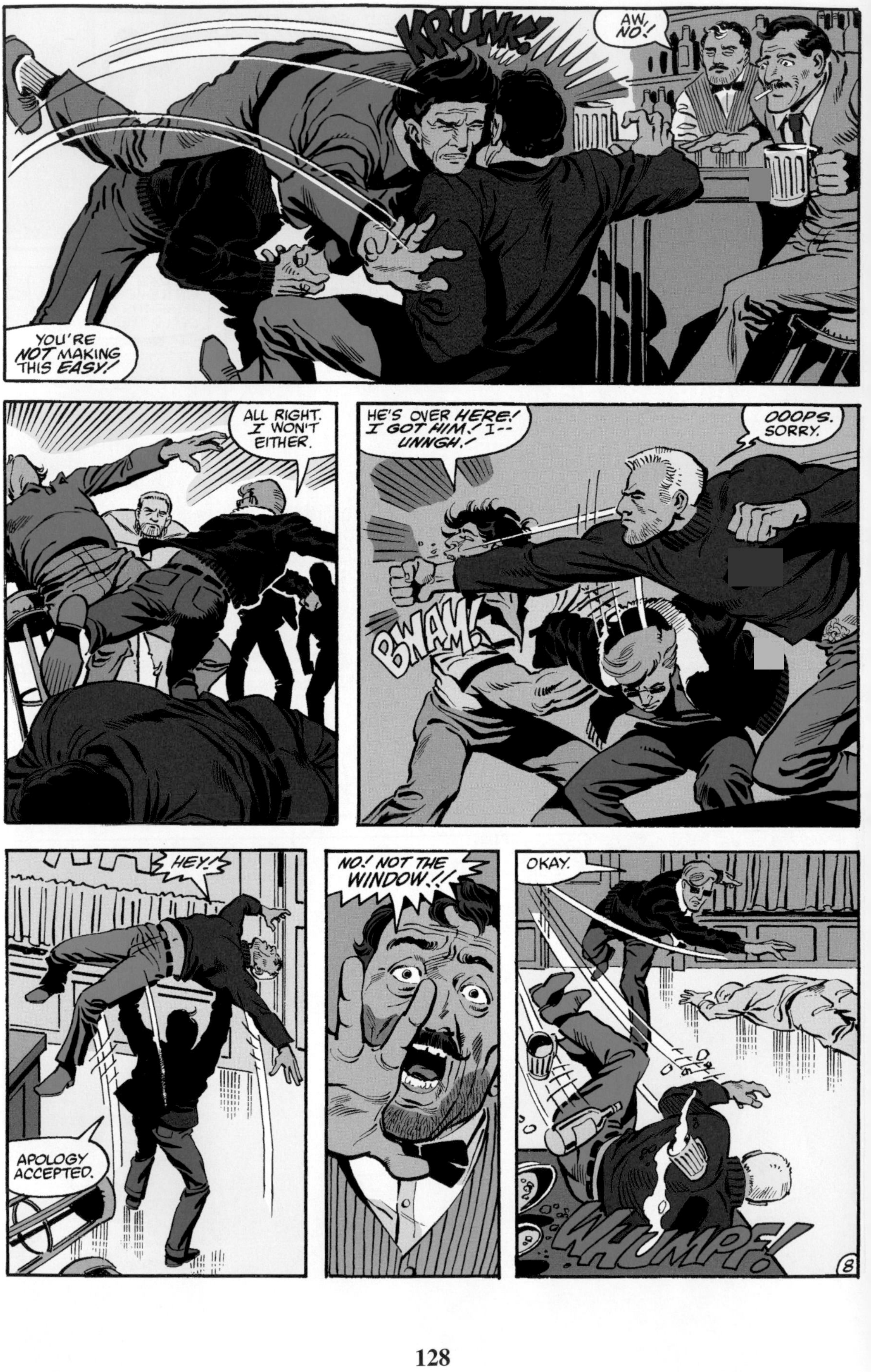
KRUNK!
AW, NO!
YOU'RE NOT MAKING THIS EASY!
ALL RIGHT. I WON'T EITHER.
HE'S OVER HERE! I GOT HIM! I-- UNNGH!
OOOPS. SORRY.
BWAM!
HEY!
APOLOGY ACCEPTED.
NO! NOT THE WINDOW!!
OKAY.
WHUMPF!
8

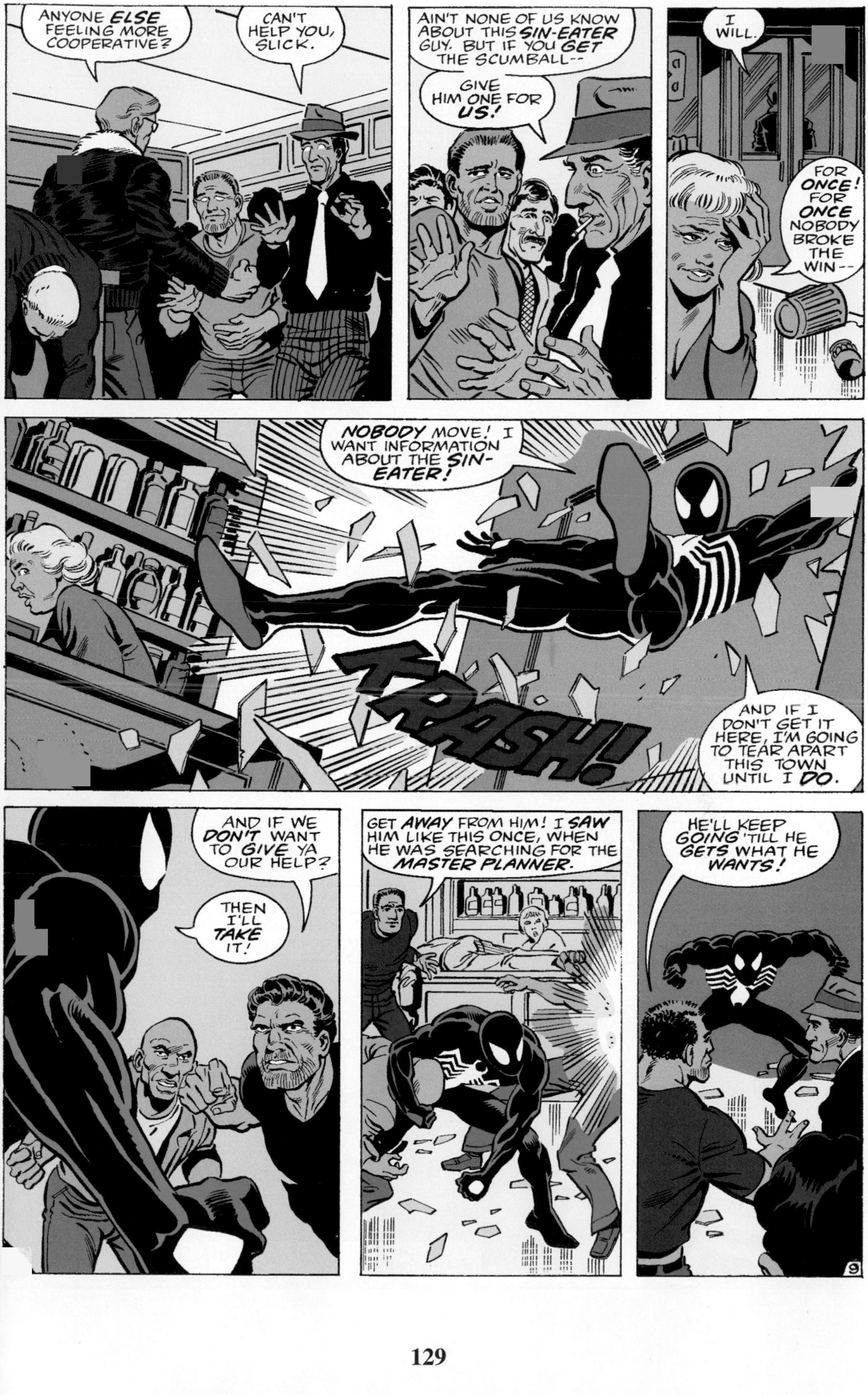
ANYONE ELSE FEELING MORE COOPERATIVE?
CAN'T HELP YOU, SLICK.
AIN'T NONE OF US KNOW ABOUT THIS SIN-EATER GUY. BUT IF YOU GET THE SCUMBALL--
GIVE HIM ONE FOR US!
I WILL.
FOR ONCE! FOR ONCE NOBODY BROKE THE WIN--
NOBODY MOVE! I WANT INFORMATION ABOUT THE SIN-EATER!
KRASH!
AND IF I DON'T GET IT HERE, I'M GOING TO TEAR APART THIS TOWN UNTIL I DO.
AND IF WE DON'T WANT TO GIVE YA OUR HELP?
THEN I'LL TAKE IT!
GET AWAY FROM HIM! I SAW HIM LIKE THIS ONCE, WHEN HE WAS SEARCHING FOR THE MASTER PLANNER.
HE'LL KEEP GOING 'TILL HE GETS WHAT HE WANTS!
9

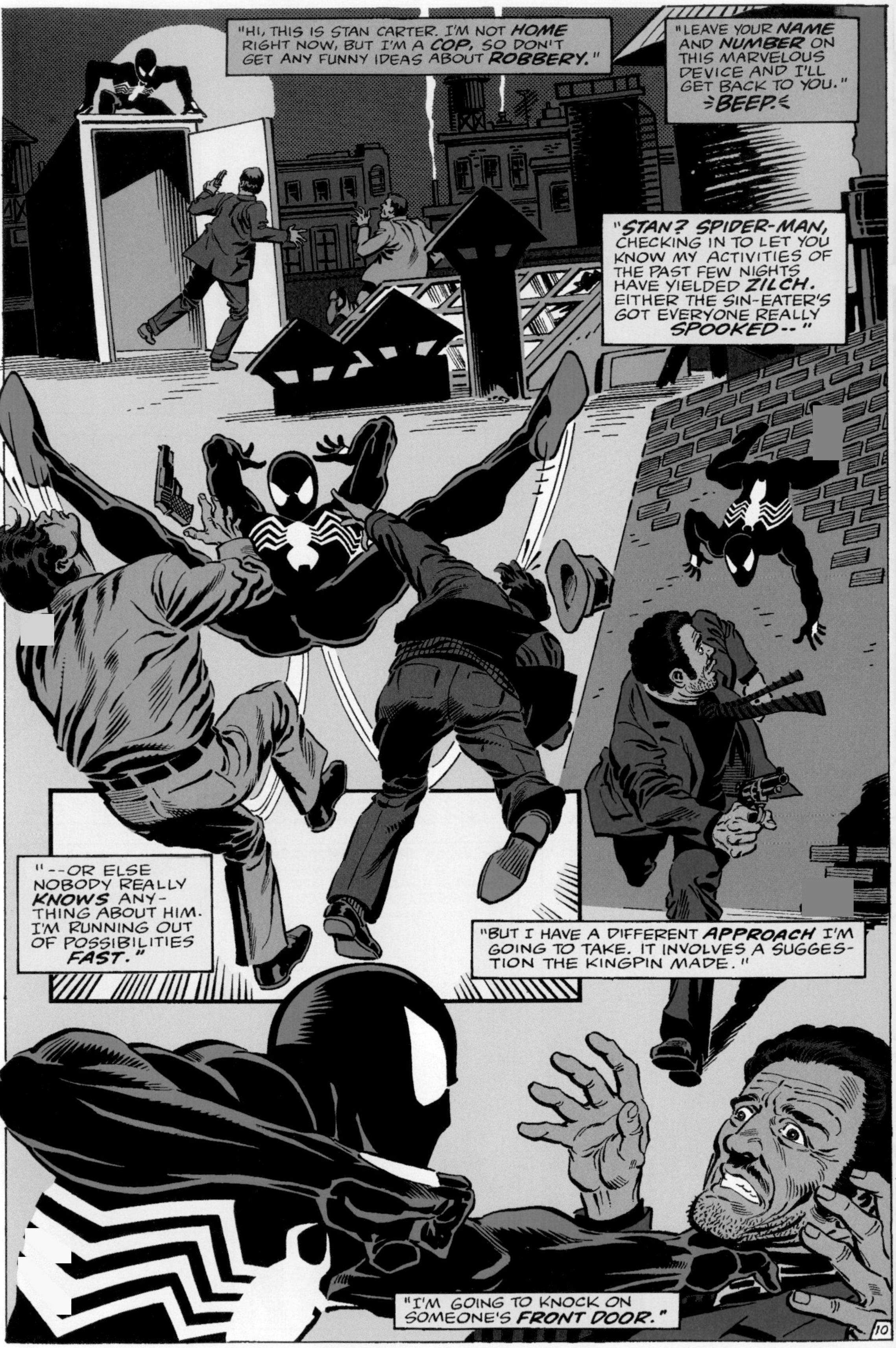
"HI, THIS IS STAN CARTER. I'M NOT HOME RIGHT NOW, BUT I'M A COP, SO DON'T GET ANY FUNNY IDEAS ABOUT ROBBERY."
"LEAVE YOUR NAME AND NUMBER ON THIS MARVELOUS DEVICE AND I'LL GET BACK TO YOU."
BEEP.
"STAN? SPIDER-MAN, CHECKING IN TO LET YOU KNOW MY ACTIVITIES OF THE PAST FEW NIGHTS HAVE YIELDED ZILCH. EITHER THE SIN-EATER'S GOT EVERYONE REALLY SPOOKED--"
"--OR ELSE NOBODY REALLY KNOWS ANYTHING ABOUT HIM. I'M RUNNING OUT OF POSSIBILITIES FAST."
"BUT I HAVE A DIFFERENT APPROACH I'M GOING TO TAKE. IT INVOLVES A SUGGESTION THE KINGPIN MADE."
"I'M GOING TO KNOCK ON SOMEONE'S FRONT DOOR."
10

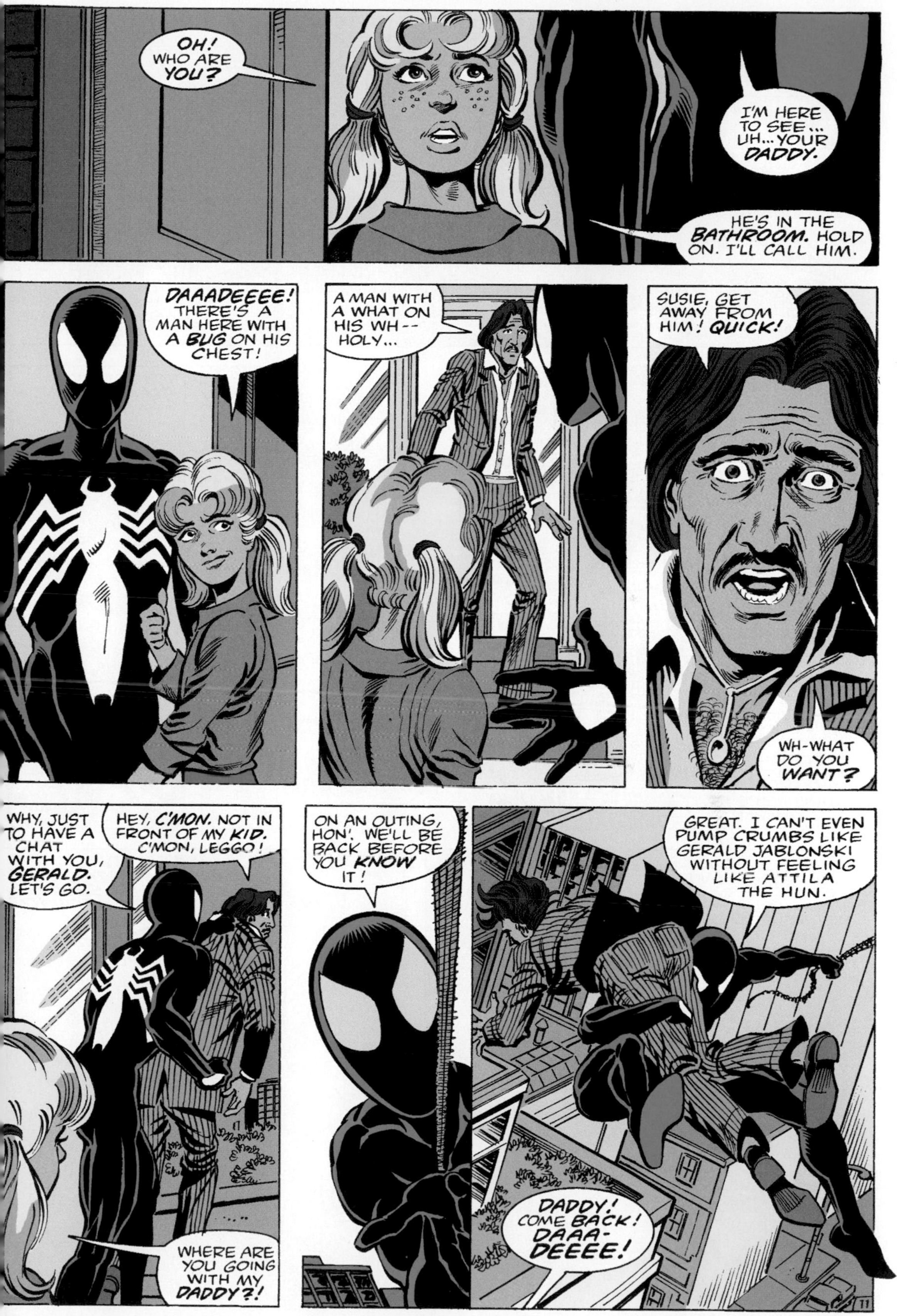
OH! WHO ARE YOU?
I'M HERE TO SEE... UH... YOUR DADDY.
HE'S IN THE BATHROOM. HOLD ON. I'LL CALL HIM.
DAAADEEEE! THERE'S A MAN HERE WITH A BUG ON HIS CHEST!
A MAN WITH A WHAT ON HIS WH-- HOLY...
SUSIE, GET AWAY FROM HIM! QUICK!
WH-WHAT DO YOU WANT?
WHY, JUST TO HAVE A CHAT WITH YOU, GERALD. LET'S GO.
HEY, C'MON. NOT IN FRONT OF MY KID. C'MON, LEGGO!
...
WHERE ARE YOU GOING WITH MY DADDY?!
ON AN OUTING, HON'. WE'LL BE BACK BEFORE YOU KNOW IT!
GREAT. I CAN'T EVEN PUMP CRUMBS LIKE GERALD JABLONSKI WITHOUT FEELING LIKE ATTILA THE HUN.
DADDY! COME BACK! DAAA-DEEEE!
11

I HEARD ABOUT YOU ON THE *NEWS* THE OTHER DAY, GERRY. ABOUT HOW YOU BEAT THAT *DRUG RAP.*

SO I SAID TO MYSELF, *"SELF,"* I SAID, "GERRY DESERVES TO GO OUT AND *CELEBRATE* HIS WIN.

BUT, YOU'RE SUCH A HARD WORKER I KNEW YOU'D HAVE TO BE, WELL, *FORCED.*

HOW COULD YOU BRING ME *HERE?!* HALF THE HIRED THUGS IN THE CITY HANG OUT HERE !!

SURE! I'VE EVEN WALTZED MOST OF 'EM *AROUND* THE PAST FEW DAYS, SO THEY'LL LEAVE *ME* ALONE.

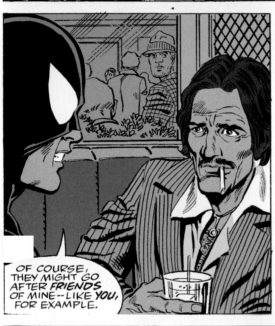

OF COURSE, THEY MIGHT GO AFTER *FRIENDS* OF MINE-- LIKE *YOU,* FOR EXAMPLE.

M-ME?

YOU *GOT* A BAD *STAMMER,* KNOW THAT, GERRY?

AND *YES,* I MEAN YOU! WE'RE PALS, AREN'T WE, GERRY? I MEAN, I'VE BEEN TO YOUR HOUSE, MET YOUR LOVELY SUSIE...

HECK, WE'RE PRACTICALLY *RELATED!*

FOR P-PITY'S SAKE, KEEP YOUR VOICE *DOWN!*

WELL, I'M *GLAD* WE HAD THIS CHAT. I'LL BE SEEING YOU AROUND, *PAL!*

12

132

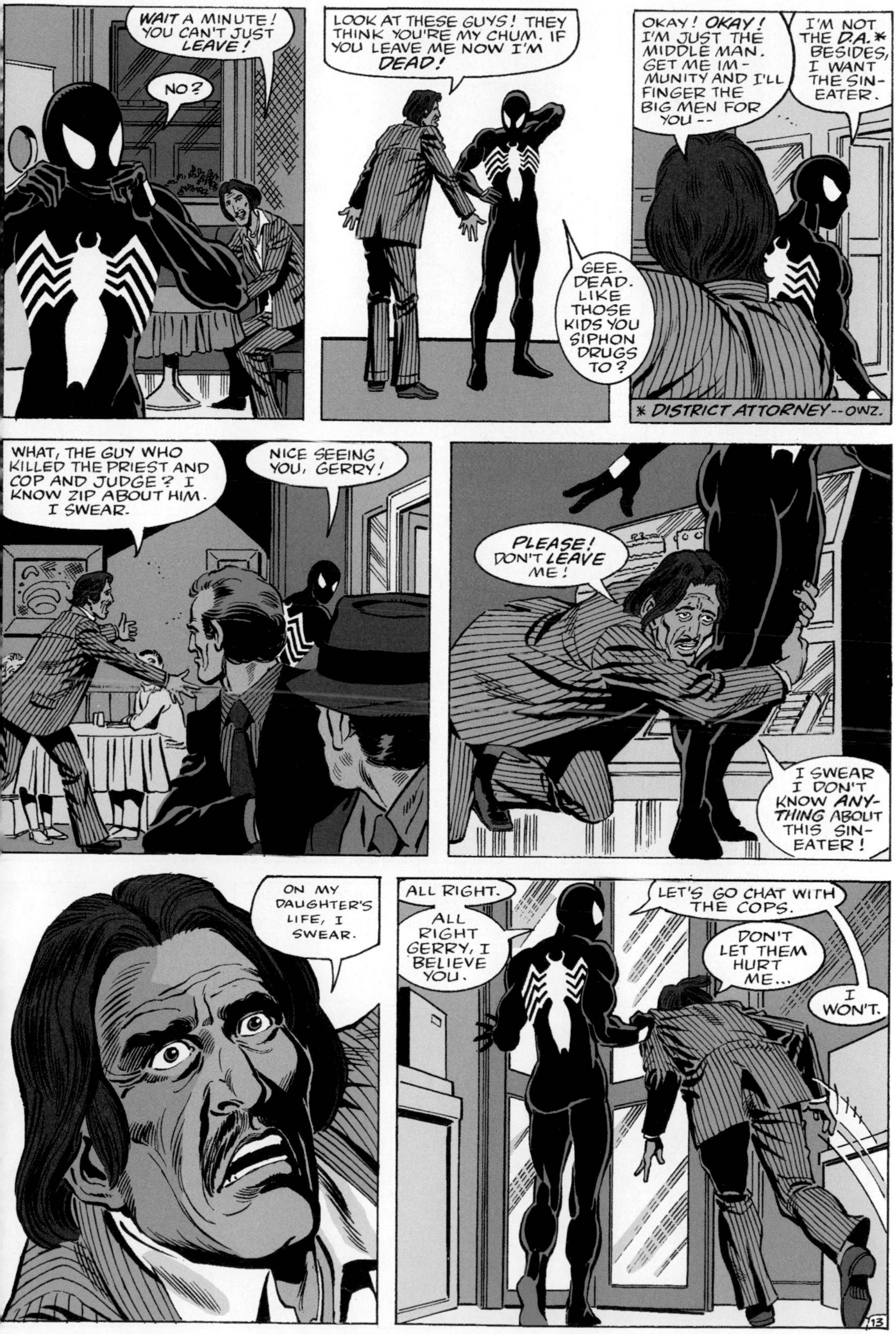
WAIT A MINUTE! YOU CAN'T JUST LEAVE!
NO?
LOOK AT THESE GUYS! THEY THINK YOU'RE MY CHUM. IF YOU LEAVE ME NOW I'M DEAD!
GEE. DEAD. LIKE THOSE KIDS YOU SIPHON DRUGS TO?
OKAY! OKAY! I'M JUST THE MIDDLE MAN. GET ME IM-MUNITY AND I'LL FINGER THE BIG MEN FOR YOU --
I'M NOT THE D.A.* BESIDES, I WANT THE SIN-EATER.
* DISTRICT ATTORNEY -- OWZ.
WHAT, THE GUY WHO KILLED THE PRIEST AND COP AND JUDGE? I KNOW ZIP ABOUT HIM. I SWEAR.
NICE SEEING YOU, GERRY!
PLEASE! DON'T LEAVE ME!
I SWEAR I DON'T KNOW ANYTHING ABOUT THIS SIN-EATER!
ON MY DAUGHTER'S LIFE, I SWEAR.
ALL RIGHT.
ALL RIGHT GERRY, I BELIEVE YOU.
LET'S GO CHAT WITH THE COPS.
DON'T LET THEM HURT ME...
I WON'T.
13

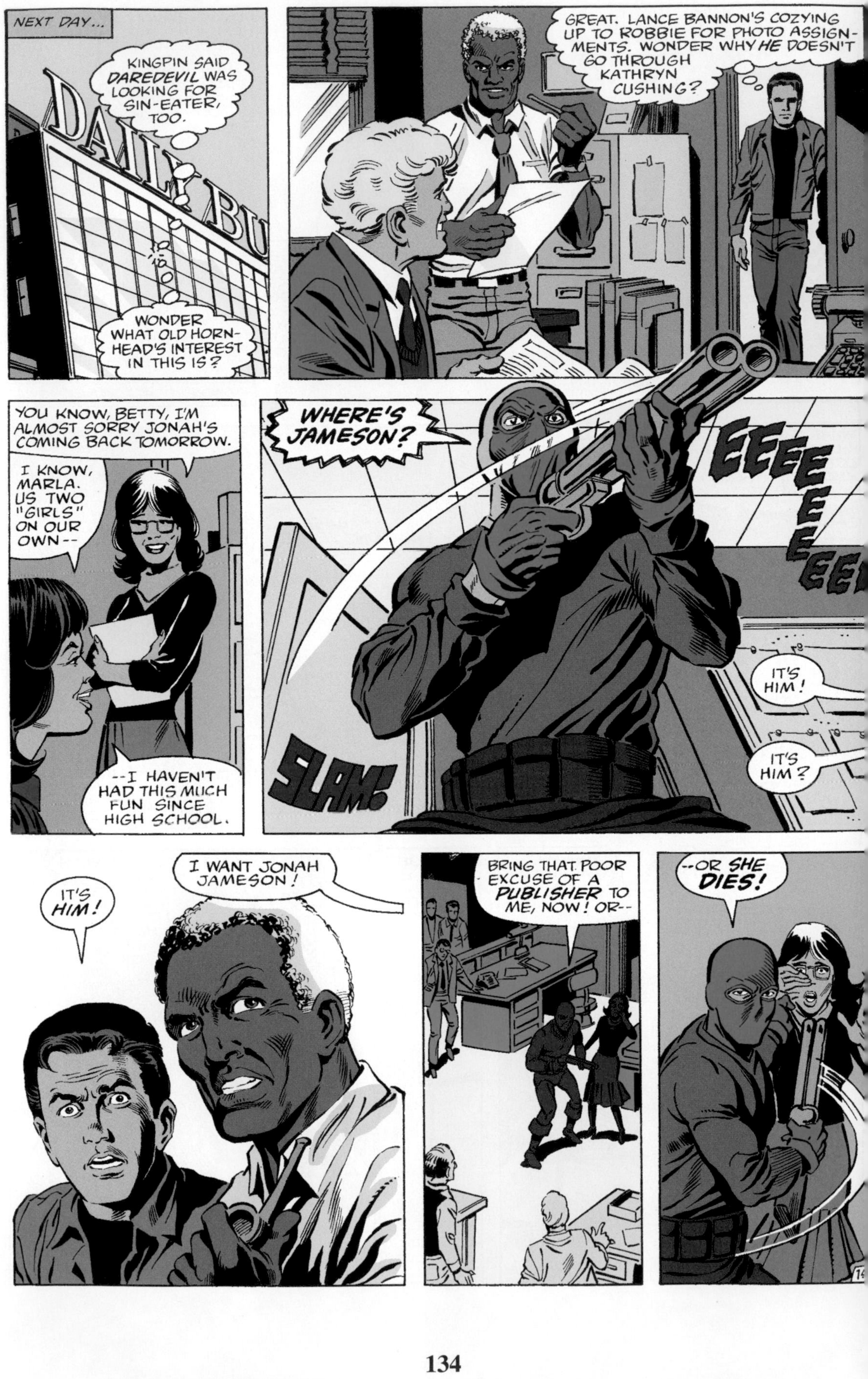
NEXT DAY...
DAILY BU
KINGPIN SAID *DAREDEVIL* WAS LOOKING FOR SIN-EATER, TOO.
WONDER WHAT OLD HORN-HEAD'S INTEREST IN THIS IS?
GREAT. LANCE BANNON'S COZYING UP TO ROBBIE FOR PHOTO ASSIGNMENTS. WONDER WHY *HE* DOESN'T GO THROUGH KATHRYN CUSHING?
YOU KNOW, BETTY, I'M ALMOST SORRY JONAH'S COMING BACK TOMORROW.
I KNOW, MARLA. US TWO "GIRLS" ON OUR OWN--
--I HAVEN'T HAD THIS MUCH FUN SINCE HIGH SCHOOL.
WHERE'S JAMESON?
SLAM!
IT'S HIM!
IT'S HIM?
IT'S *HIM!*
I WANT JONAH JAMESON!
BRING THAT POOR EXCUSE OF A *PUBLISHER* TO ME, NOW! OR--
--OR *SHE DIES!*

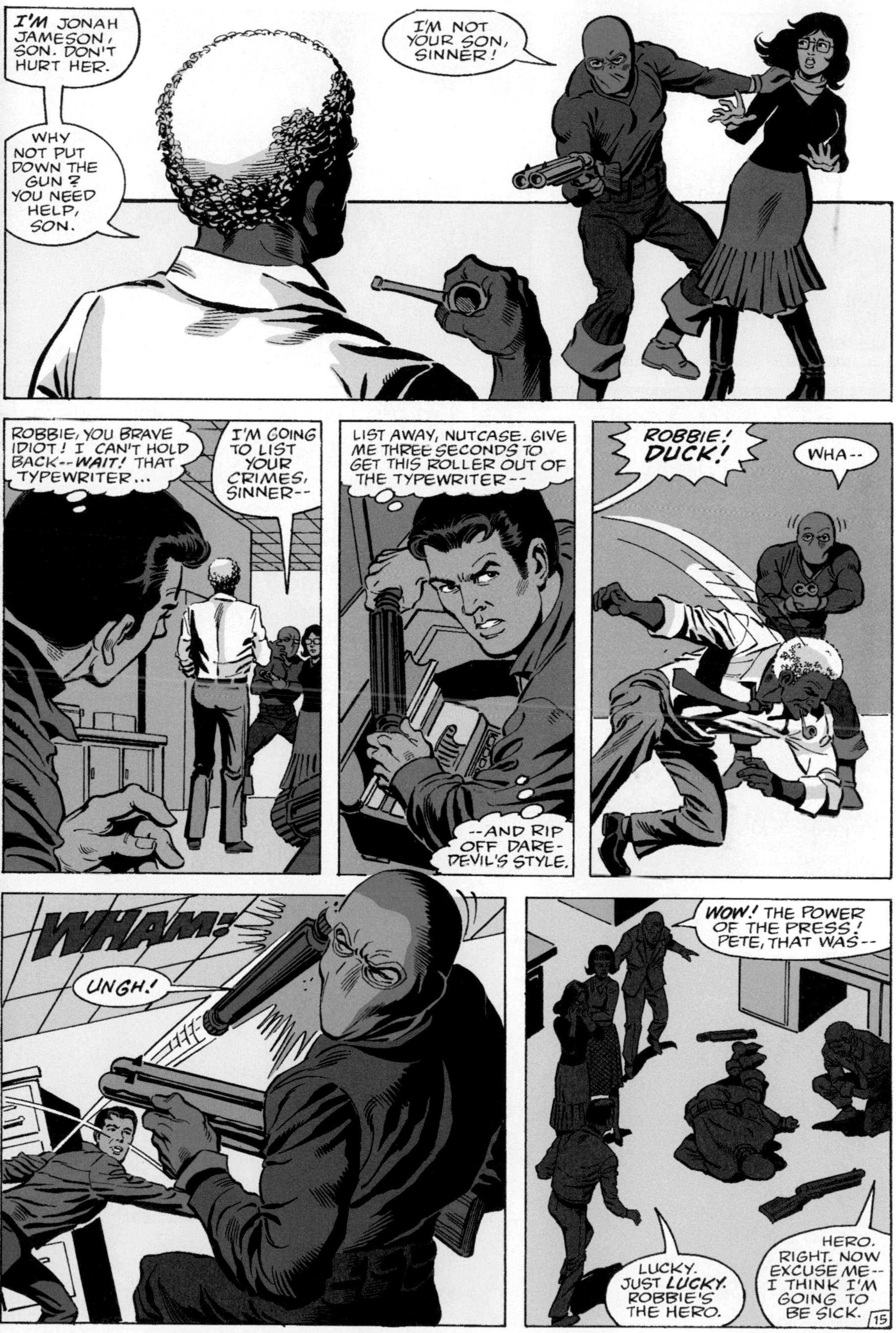
I'M JONAH JAMESON, SON. DON'T HURT HER.
WHY NOT PUT DOWN THE GUN? YOU NEED HELP, SON.
I'M NOT YOUR SON, SINNER!
ROBBIE, YOU BRAVE IDIOT! I CAN'T HOLD BACK--WAIT! THAT TYPEWRITER...
I'M GOING TO LIST YOUR CRIMES, SINNER--
LIST AWAY, NUTCASE. GIVE ME THREE SECONDS TO GET THIS ROLLER OUT OF THE TYPEWRITER--
--AND RIP OFF DAREDEVIL'S STYLE.
ROBBIE! DUCK!
WHA--
WHAM!
UNGH!
WOW! THE POWER OF THE PRESS! PETE, THAT WAS--
LUCKY. JUST LUCKY. ROBBIE'S THE HERO.
HERO. RIGHT. NOW EXCUSE ME-- I THINK I'M GOING TO BE SICK.
15

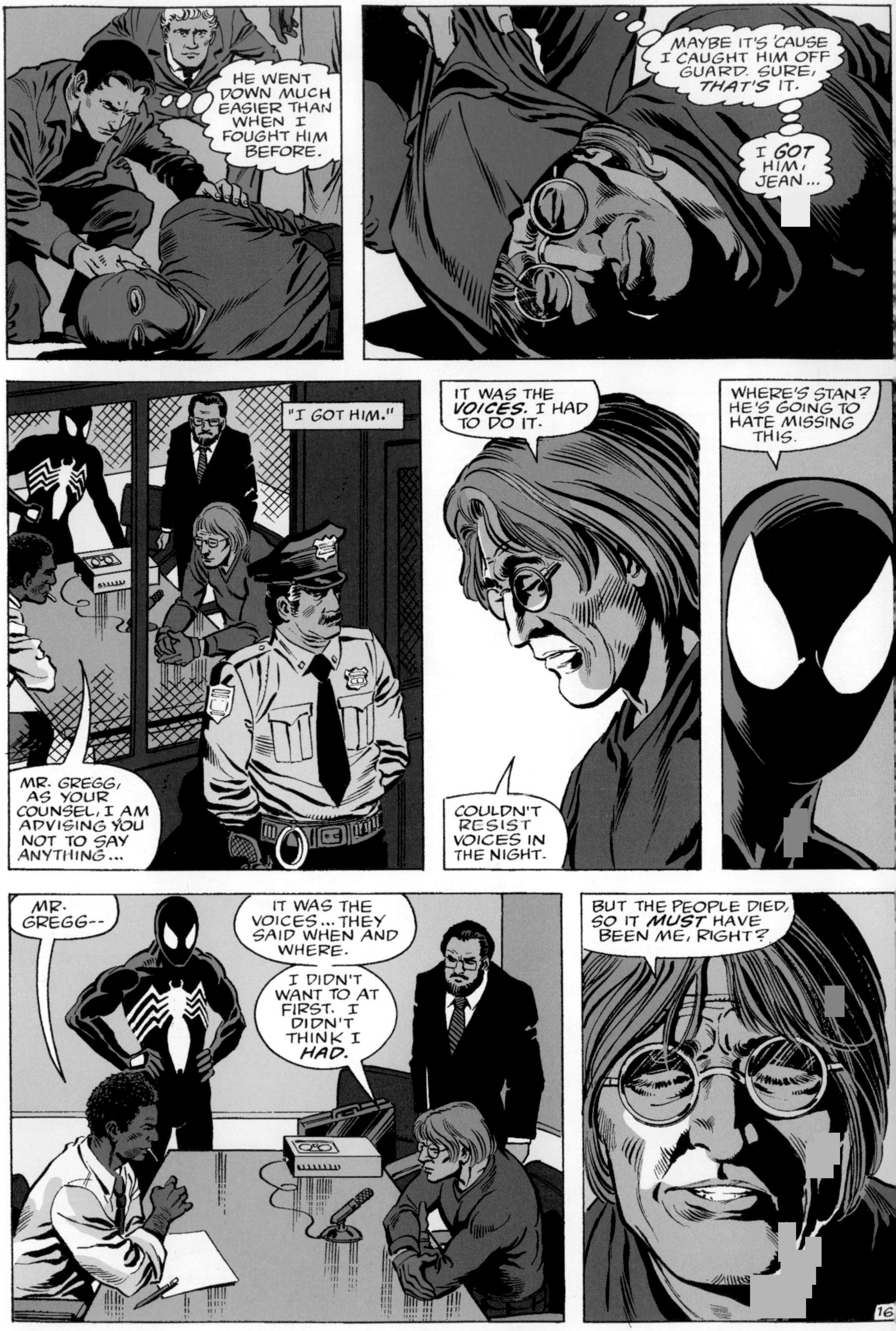
HE WENT DOWN MUCH EASIER THAN WHEN I FOUGHT HIM BEFORE.
MAYBE IT'S 'CAUSE I CAUGHT HIM OFF GUARD. SURE, THAT'S IT.
I GOT HIM, JEAN...
"I GOT HIM."
MR. GREGG, AS YOUR COUNSEL, I AM ADVISING YOU NOT TO SAY ANYTHING...
IT WAS THE VOICES. I HAD TO DO IT.
COULDN'T RESIST VOICES IN THE NIGHT.
WHERE'S STAN? HE'S GOING TO HATE MISSING THIS.
MR. GREGG--
IT WAS THE VOICES... THEY SAID WHEN AND WHERE.
I DIDN'T WANT TO AT FIRST. I DIDN'T THINK I HAD.
BUT THE PEOPLE DIED, SO IT MUST HAVE BEEN ME, RIGHT?
16

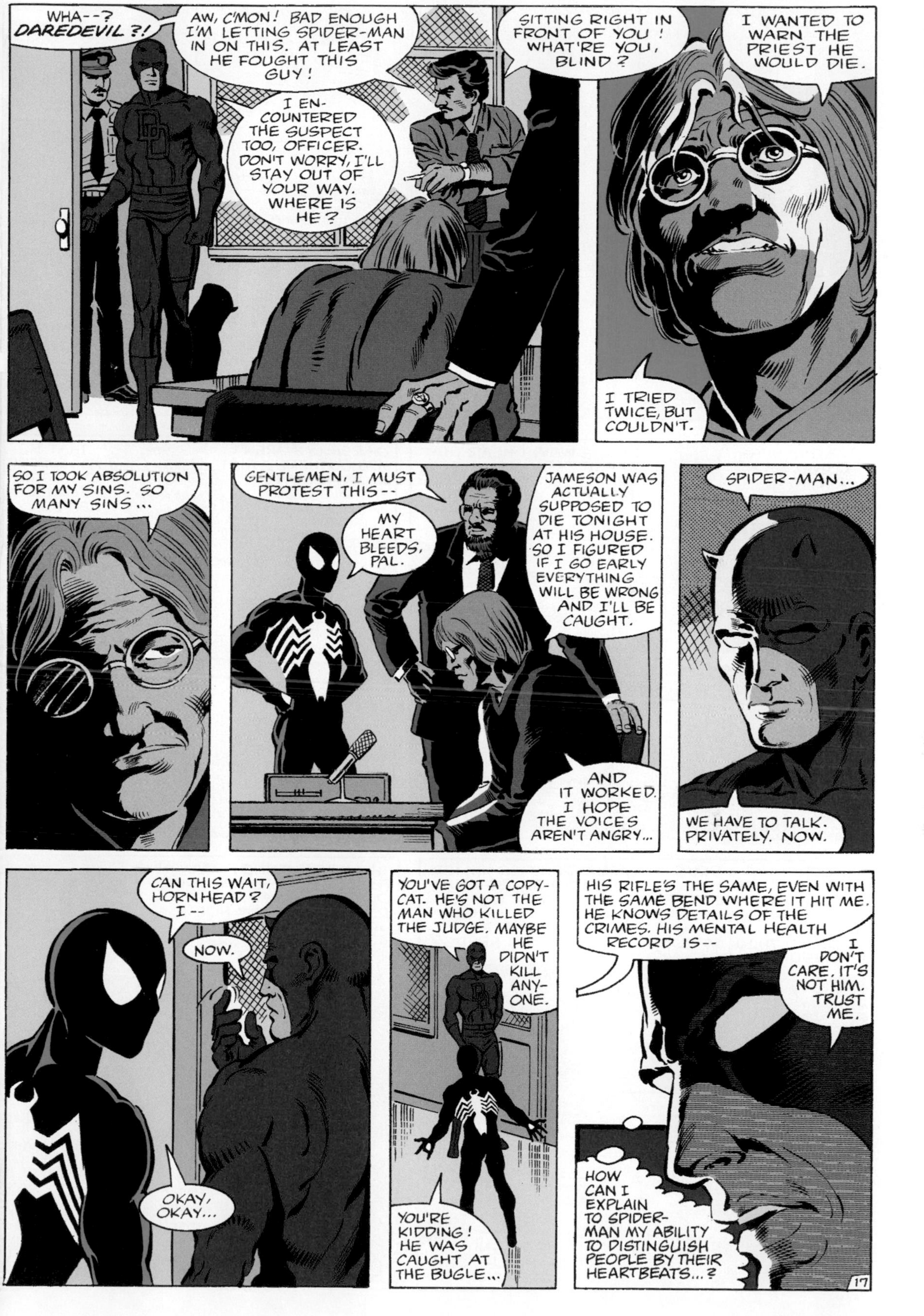
WHA--? DAREDEVIL ?!
AW, C'MON! BAD ENOUGH I'M LETTING SPIDER-MAN IN ON THIS. AT LEAST HE FOUGHT THIS GUY!
I EN-COUNTERED THE SUSPECT TOO, OFFICER. DON'T WORRY, I'LL STAY OUT OF YOUR WAY. WHERE IS HE?
SITTING RIGHT IN FRONT OF YOU! WHAT'RE YOU, BLIND?
I WANTED TO WARN THE PRIEST HE WOULD DIE.
I TRIED TWICE, BUT COULDN'T.
SO I TOOK ABSOLUTION FOR MY SINS. SO MANY SINS...
GENTLEMEN, I MUST PROTEST THIS--
MY HEART BLEEDS, PAL.
JAMESON WAS ACTUALLY SUPPOSED TO DIE TONIGHT AT HIS HOUSE. SO I FIGURED IF I GO EARLY EVERYTHING WILL BE WRONG AND I'LL BE CAUGHT.
AND IT WORKED. I HOPE THE VOICES AREN'T ANGRY...
SPIDER-MAN...
WE HAVE TO TALK. PRIVATELY. NOW.
CAN THIS WAIT, HORNHEAD? I--
NOW.
OKAY, OKAY...
YOU'VE GOT A COPY-CAT. HE'S NOT THE MAN WHO KILLED THE JUDGE. MAYBE HE DIDN'T KILL ANY-ONE.
YOU'RE KIDDING! HE WAS CAUGHT AT THE BUGLE...
HIS RIFLE'S THE SAME, EVEN WITH THE SAME BEND WHERE IT HIT ME. HE KNOWS DETAILS OF THE CRIMES. HIS MENTAL HEALTH RECORD IS--
I DON'T CARE. IT'S NOT HIM. TRUST ME.
HOW CAN I EXPLAIN TO SPIDER-MAN MY ABILITY TO DISTINGUISH PEOPLE BY THEIR HEARTBEATS...?
17

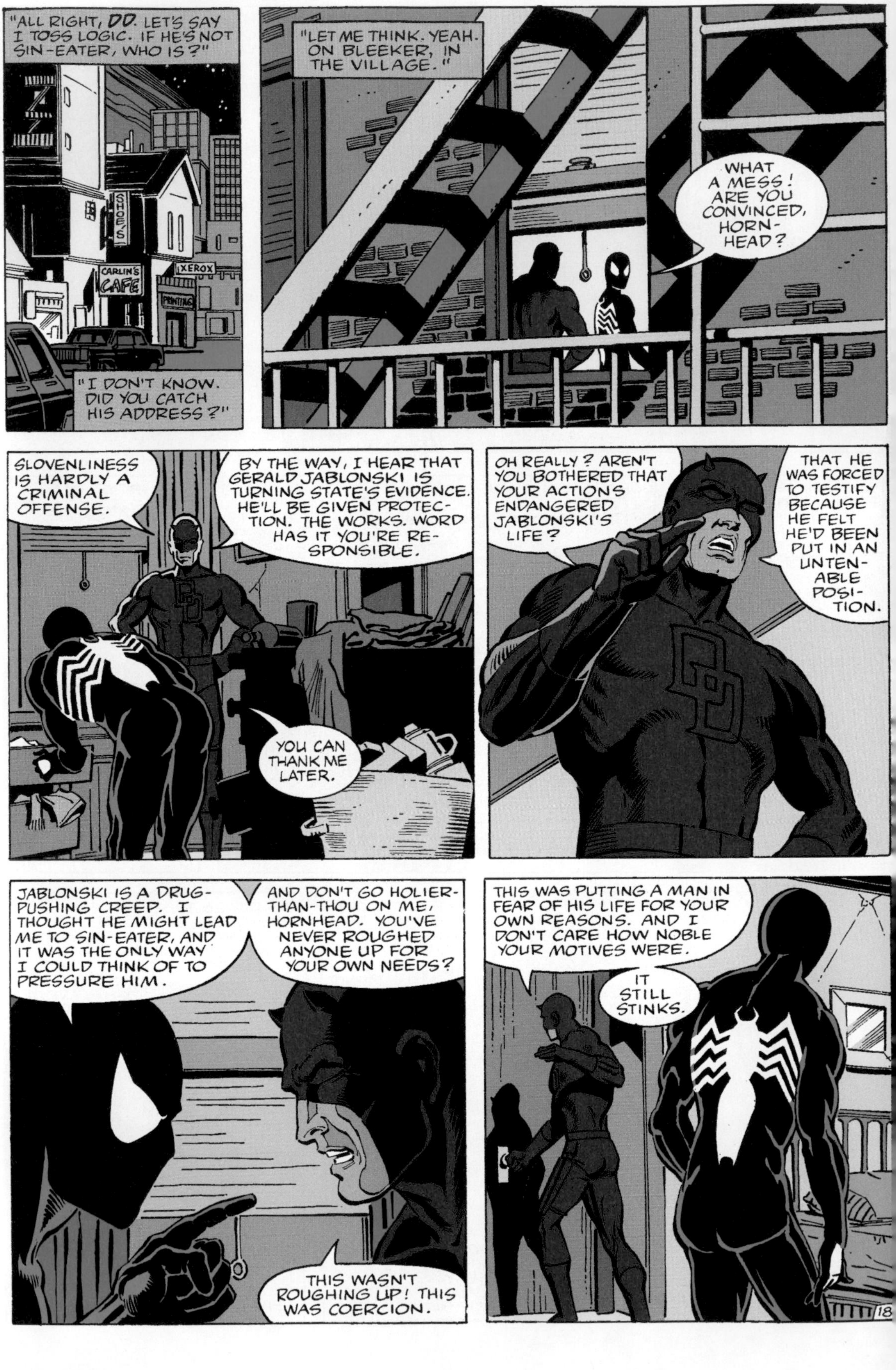
"ALL RIGHT, DD. LET'S SAY I TOSS LOGIC. IF HE'S NOT SIN-EATER, WHO IS?"
SHOES
CARLIN'S CAFE
XEROX
PRINTING
"I DON'T KNOW. DID YOU CATCH HIS ADDRESS?"
"LET ME THINK. YEAH. ON BLEEKER, IN THE VILLAGE."
WHAT A MESS! ARE YOU CONVINCED, HORN-HEAD?
SLOVENLINESS IS HARDLY A CRIMINAL OFFENSE.
BY THE WAY, I HEAR THAT GERALD JABLONSKI IS TURNING STATE'S EVIDENCE. HE'LL BE GIVEN PROTEC-TION. THE WORKS. WORD HAS IT YOU'RE RE-SPONSIBLE.
YOU CAN THANK ME LATER.
OH REALLY? AREN'T YOU BOTHERED THAT YOUR ACTIONS ENDANGERED JABLONSKI'S LIFE?
THAT HE WAS FORCED TO TESTIFY BECAUSE HE FELT HE'D BEEN PUT IN AN UNTEN-ABLE POSI-TION.
JABLONSKI IS A DRUG-PUSHING CREEP. I THOUGHT HE MIGHT LEAD ME TO SIN-EATER, AND IT WAS THE ONLY WAY I COULD THINK OF TO PRESSURE HIM.
AND DON'T GO HOLIER-THAN-THOU ON ME, HORNHEAD. YOU'VE NEVER ROUGHED ANYONE UP FOR YOUR OWN NEEDS?
THIS WASN'T ROUGHING UP! THIS WAS COERCION.
THIS WAS PUTTING A MAN IN FEAR OF HIS LIFE FOR YOUR OWN REASONS. AND I DON'T CARE HOW NOBLE YOUR MOTIVES WERE.
IT STILL STINKS.
18

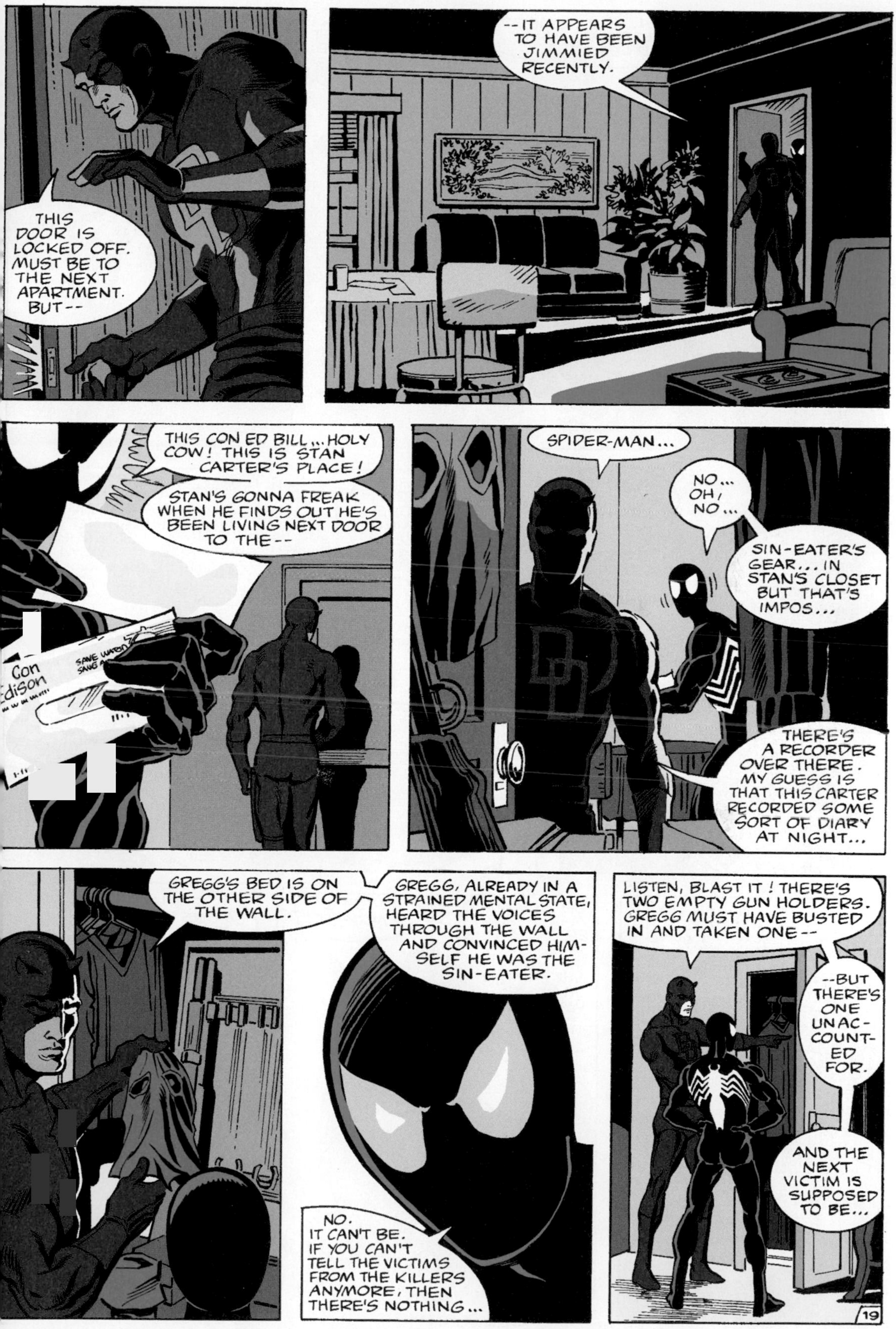

THIS DOOR IS LOCKED OFF. MUST BE TO THE NEXT APARTMENT. BUT--
--IT APPEARS TO HAVE BEEN JIMMIED RECENTLY.
THIS CON ED BILL... HOLY COW! THIS IS STAN CARTER'S PLACE!
STAN'S GONNA FREAK WHEN HE FINDS OUT HE'S BEEN LIVING NEXT DOOR TO THE--
Con Edison
SPIDER-MAN...
NO... OH, NO...
SIN-EATER'S GEAR... IN STAN'S CLOSET BUT THAT'S IMPOS...
THERE'S A RECORDER OVER THERE. MY GUESS IS THAT THIS CARTER RECORDED SOME SORT OF DIARY AT NIGHT...
GREGG'S BED IS ON THE OTHER SIDE OF THE WALL.
GREGG, ALREADY IN A STRAINED MENTAL STATE, HEARD THE VOICES THROUGH THE WALL AND CONVINCED HIMSELF HE WAS THE SIN-EATER.
NO. IT CAN'T BE. IF YOU CAN'T TELL THE VICTIMS FROM THE KILLERS ANYMORE, THEN THERE'S NOTHING...
LISTEN, BLAST IT! THERE'S TWO EMPTY GUN HOLDERS. GREGG MUST HAVE BUSTED IN AND TAKEN ONE--
--BUT THERE'S ONE UNACCOUNTED FOR.
AND THE NEXT VICTIM IS SUPPOSED TO BE...
19

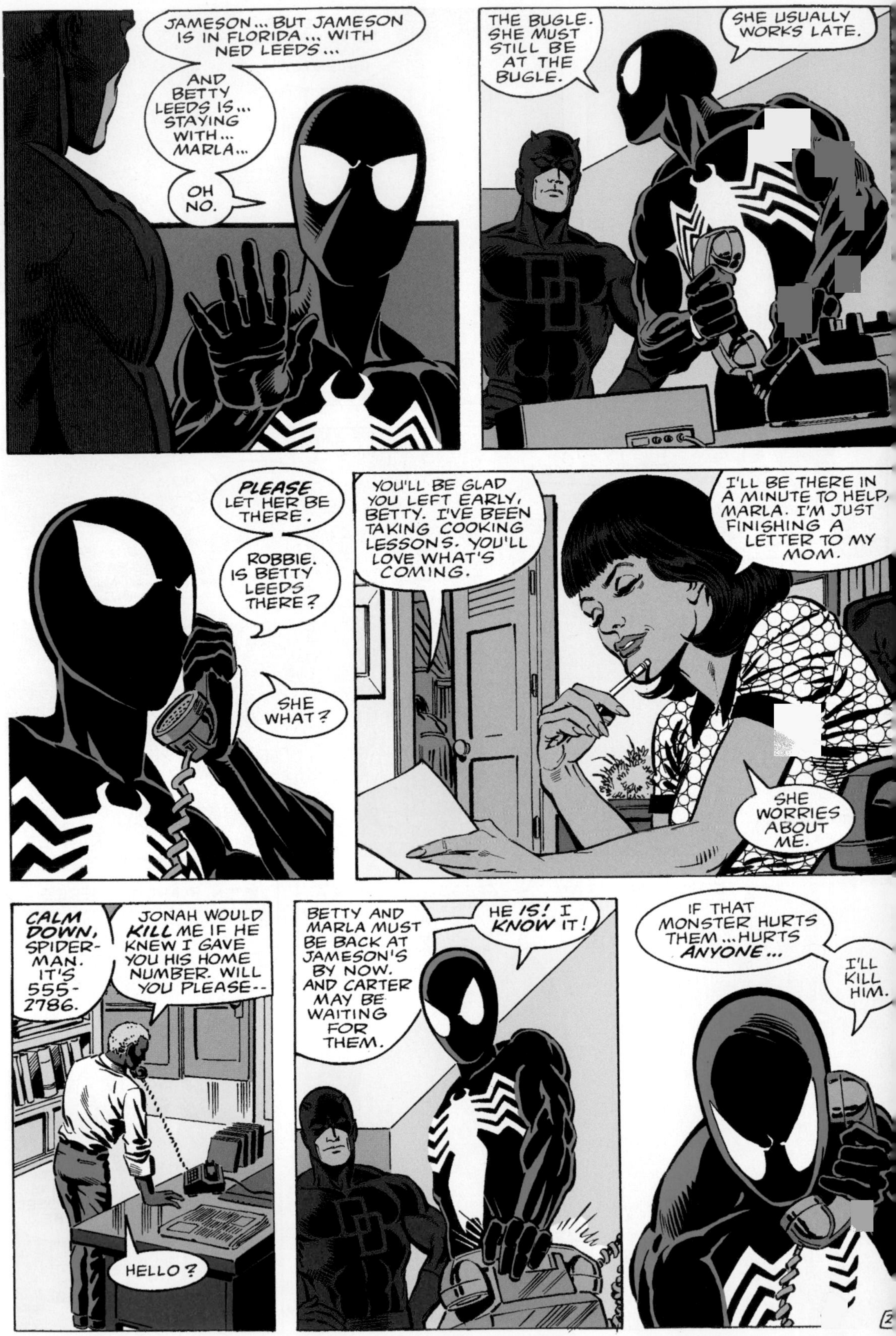
JAMESON... BUT JAMESON IS IN FLORIDA... WITH NED LEEDS...
AND BETTY LEEDS IS... STAYING WITH... MARLA...
OH NO.
THE BUGLE. SHE MUST STILL BE AT THE BUGLE.
SHE USUALLY WORKS LATE.
PLEASE LET HER BE THERE.
ROBBIE. IS BETTY LEEDS THERE?
SHE WHAT?
YOU'LL BE GLAD YOU LEFT EARLY, BETTY. I'VE BEEN TAKING COOKING LESSONS. YOU'LL LOVE WHAT'S COMING.
I'LL BE THERE IN A MINUTE TO HELP, MARLA. I'M JUST FINISHING A LETTER TO MY MOM.
SHE WORRIES ABOUT ME.
CALM DOWN, SPIDER-MAN. IT'S 555-2786.
JONAH WOULD KILL ME IF HE KNEW I GAVE YOU HIS HOME NUMBER. WILL YOU PLEASE--
HELLO?
BETTY AND MARLA MUST BE BACK AT JAMESON'S BY NOW. AND CARTER MAY BE WAITING FOR THEM.
HE IS! I KNOW IT!
IF THAT MONSTER HURTS THEM... HURTS ANYONE...
I'LL KILL HIM.

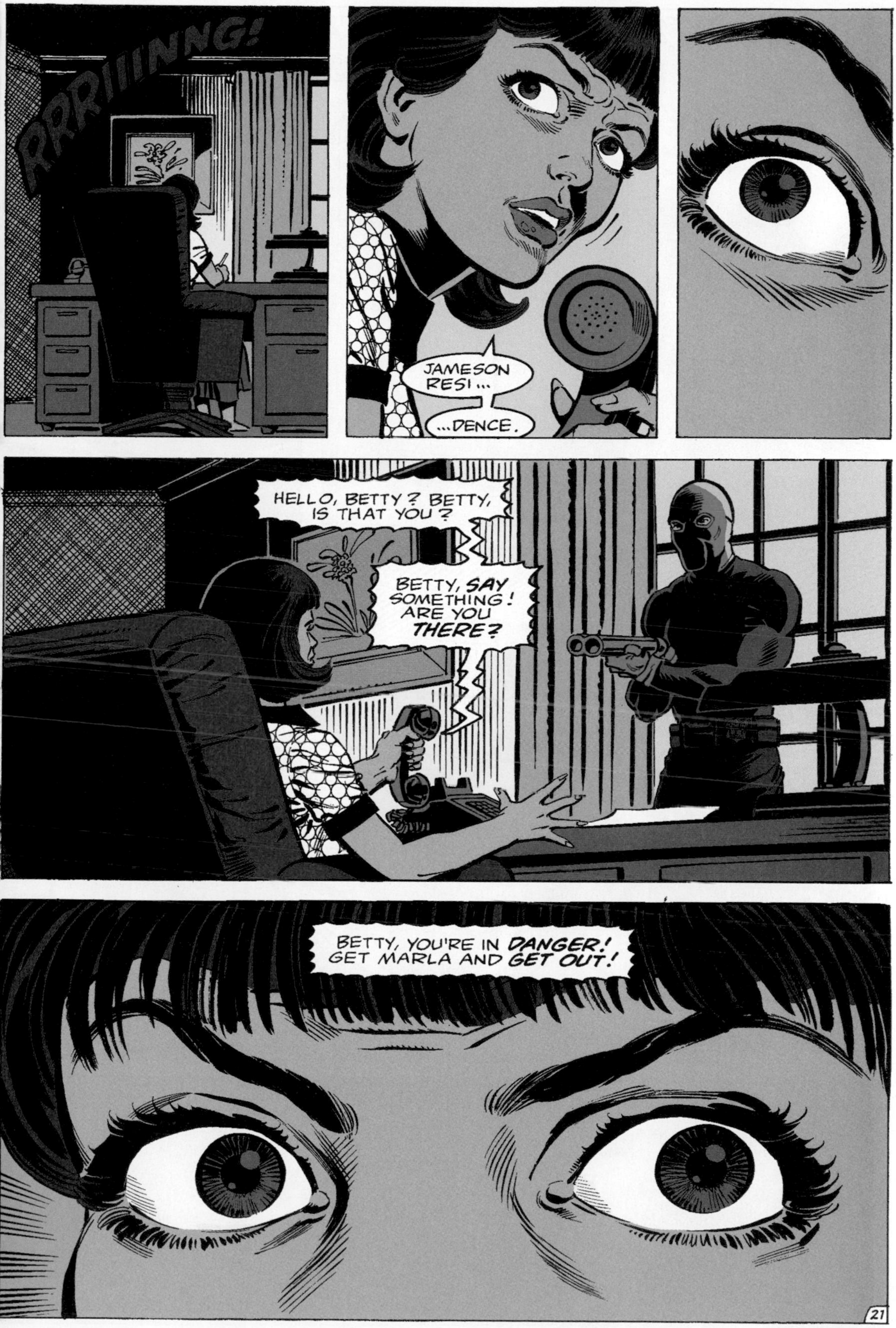
RRRIIIINNG!
JAMESON RESI...
...DENCE.
HELLO, BETTY? BETTY, IS THAT YOU?
BETTY, SAY SOMETHING! ARE YOU THERE?
BETTY, YOU'RE IN DANGER! GET MARLA AND GET OUT!
21

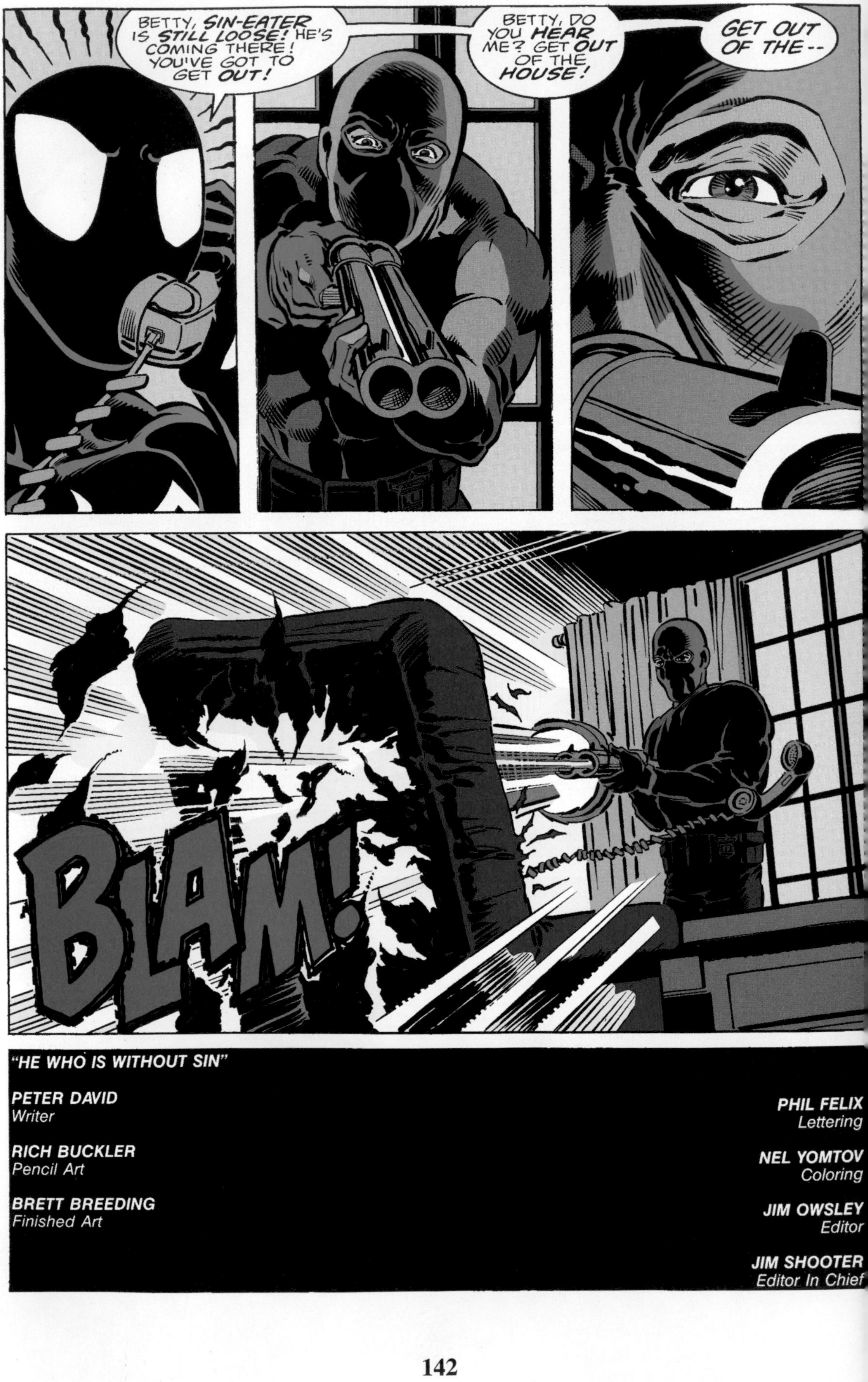
BETTY, SIN-EATER IS STILL LOOSE! HE'S COMING THERE! YOU'VE GOT TO GET OUT!
BETTY, DO YOU HEAR ME? GET OUT OF THE HOUSE!
GET OUT OF THE--
BLAM!

"HE WHO IS WITHOUT SIN"

PETER DAVID
Writer

RICH BUCKLER
Pencil Art

BRETT BREEDING
Finished Art

PHIL FELIX
Lettering

NEL YOMTOV
Coloring

JIM OWSLEY
Editor

JIM SHOOTER
Editor In Chief

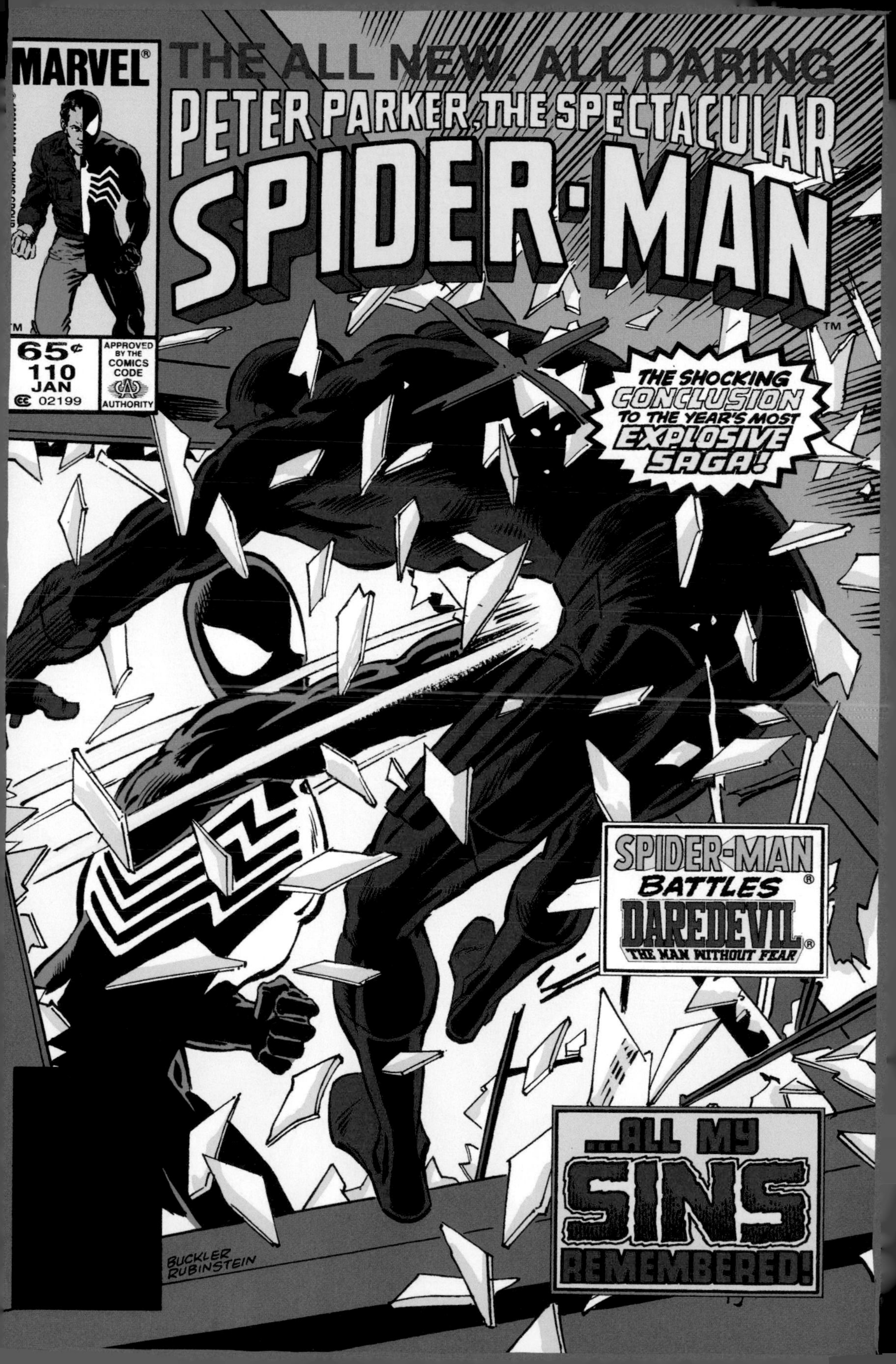

MARVEL
THE ALL NEW, ALL DARING
PETER PARKER, THE SPECTACULAR
SPIDER-MAN
65¢
110
JAN
APPROVED BY THE COMICS CODE AUTHORITY
02199
THE SHOCKING CONCLUSION TO THE YEAR'S MOST EXPLOSIVE SAGA!
SPIDER-MAN BATTLES DAREDEVIL THE MAN WITHOUT FEAR
...ALL MY SINS REMEMBERED!
BUCKLER RUBINSTEIN

WHEN I FIRST MET BETTY BRANT, I WAS A SHY, BESPECTACLED BOOKWORM.

NO GIRL HAD EVER GLANCED AT ME BEFORE, AND THEN BETTY...

BETTY JUMP-STARTED MY HEART.

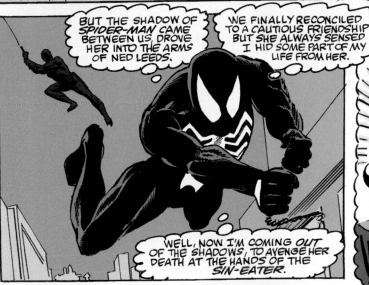

BUT THE SHADOW OF *SPIDER-MAN* CAME BETWEEN US, DROVE HER INTO THE ARMS OF NED LEEDS.

WE FINALLY RECONCILED TO A CAUTIOUS FRIENDSHIP-- BUT SHE ALWAYS SENSED I HID SOME PART OF MY LIFE FROM HER.

WELL, NOW I'M COMING *OUT* OF THE SHADOWS, TO AVENGE HER DEATH AT THE HANDS OF THE *SIN-EATER.*

AND HEAVEN *HELP* HIM, BECAUSE NOTHING'S GOING TO SAVE HIM NOW.

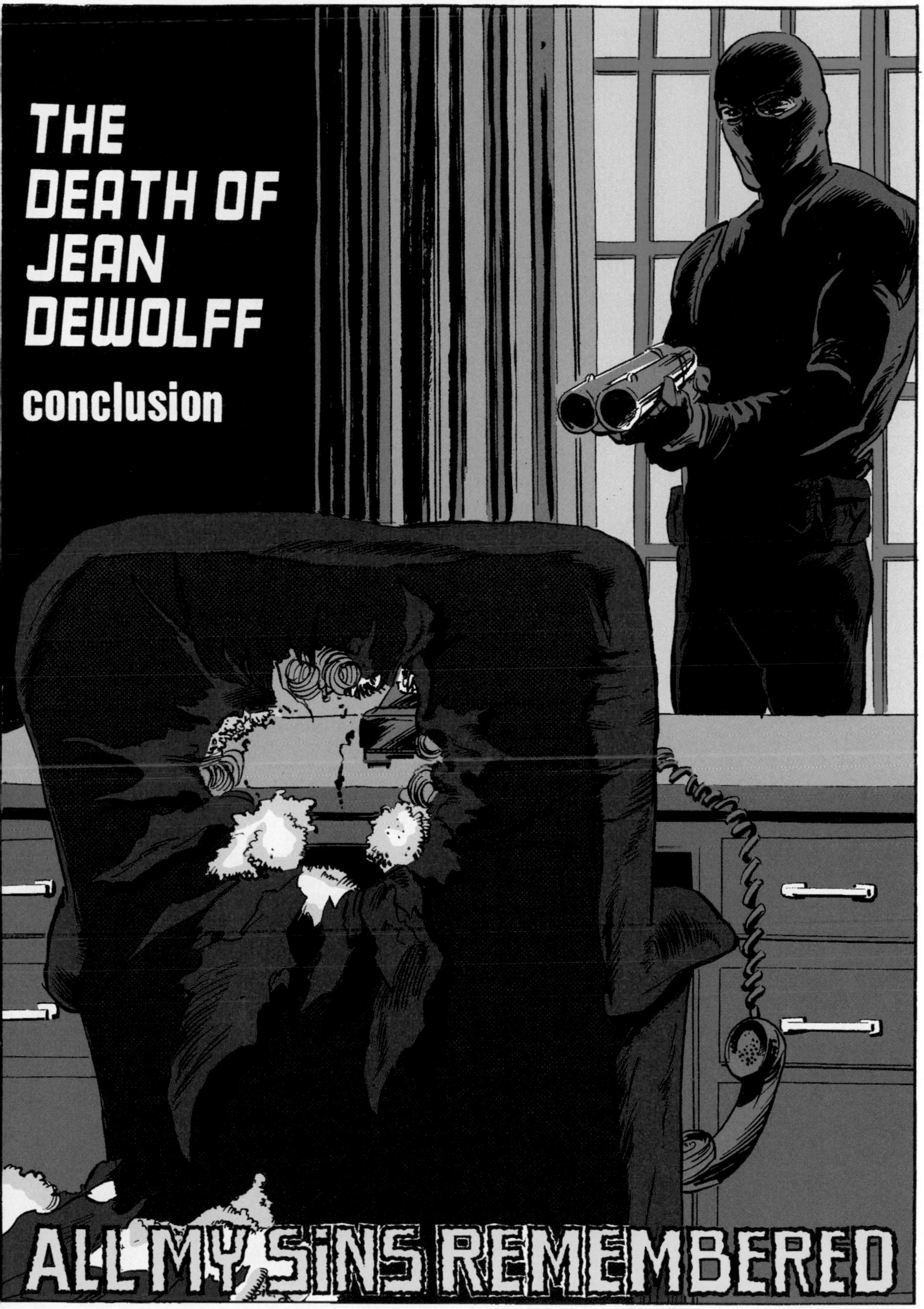
THE DEATH OF JEAN DEWOLFF
conclusion
ALL MY SINS REMEMBERED

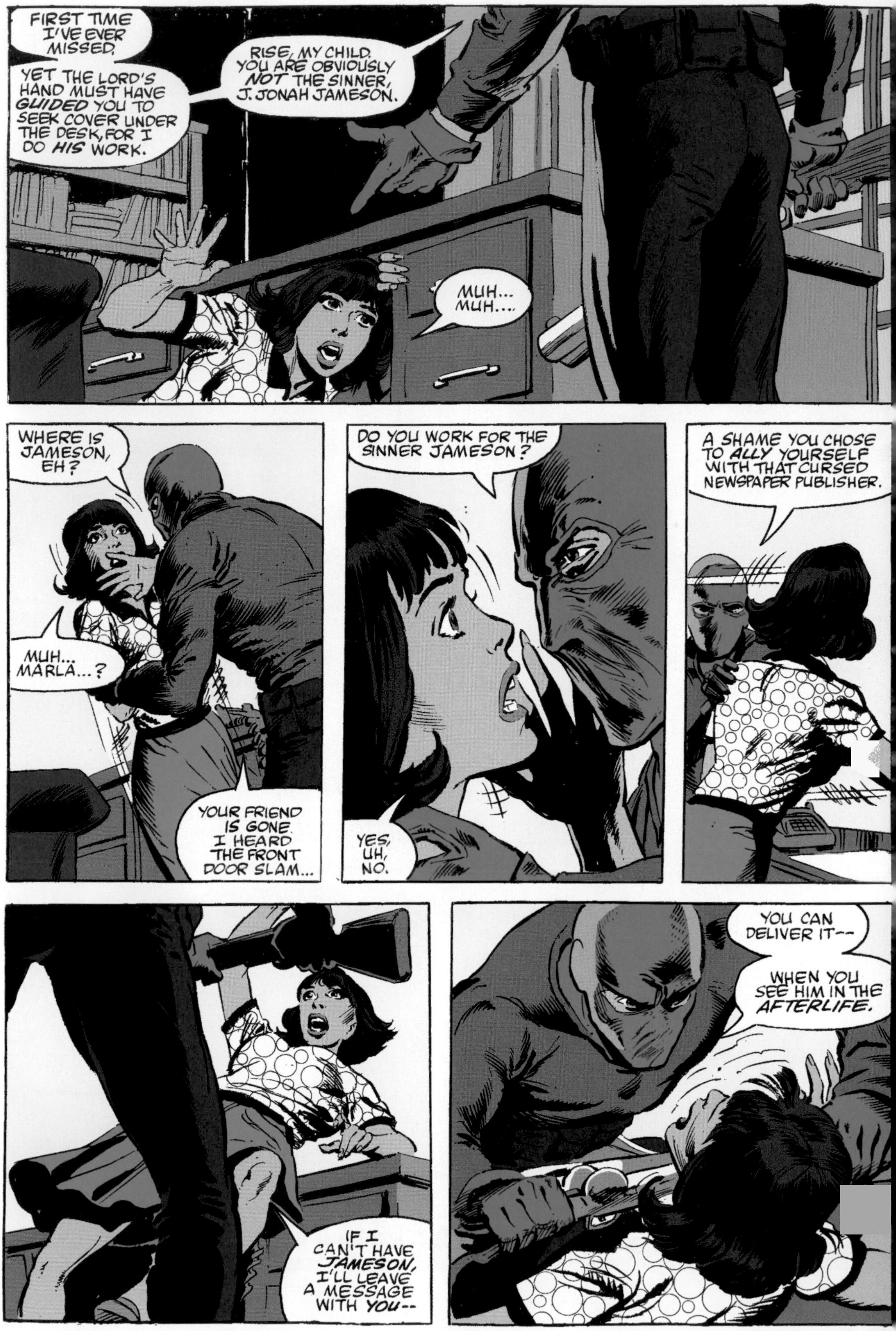

FIRST TIME I'VE EVER MISSED.
YET THE LORD'S HAND MUST HAVE GUIDED YOU TO SEEK COVER UNDER THE DESK, FOR I DO HIS WORK.
RISE, MY CHILD. YOU ARE OBVIOUSLY NOT THE SINNER, J. JONAH JAMESON.
MUH... MUH....
WHERE IS JAMESON, EH?
MUH... MARLA...?
YOUR FRIEND IS GONE. I HEARD THE FRONT DOOR SLAM...
DO YOU WORK FOR THE SINNER JAMESON?
YES, UH, NO.
A SHAME YOU CHOSE TO ALLY YOURSELF WITH THAT CURSED NEWSPAPER PUBLISHER.
IF I CAN'T HAVE JAMESON, I'LL LEAVE A MESSAGE WITH YOU--
YOU CAN DELIVER IT--
WHEN YOU SEE HIM IN THE AFTERLIFE.

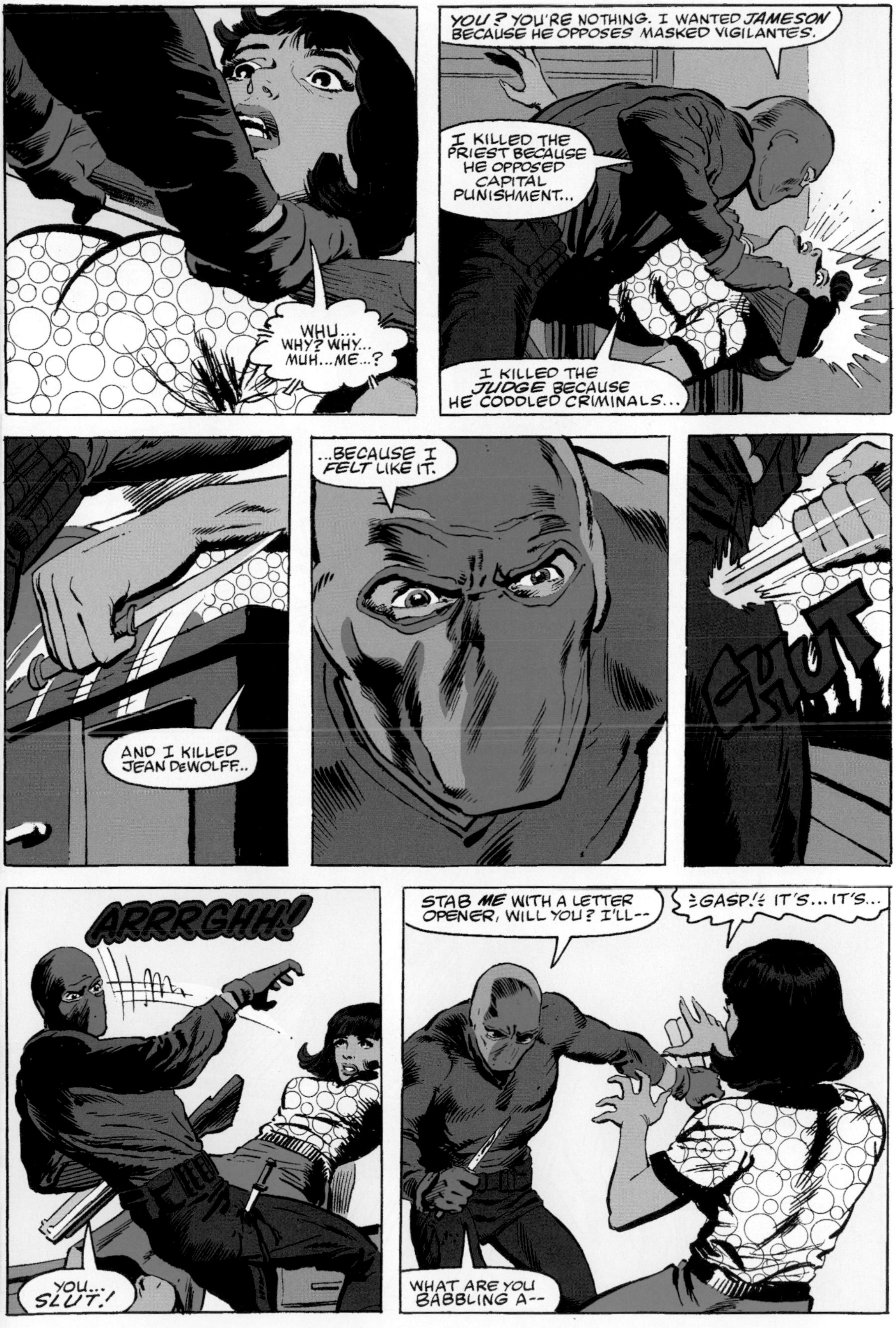
WHU... WHY? WHY... MUH...ME...?
YOU? YOU'RE NOTHING. I WANTED JAMESON BECAUSE HE OPPOSES MASKED VIGILANTES.
I KILLED THE PRIEST BECAUSE HE OPPOSED CAPITAL PUNISHMENT...
I KILLED THE JUDGE BECAUSE HE CODDLED CRIMINALS...
AND I KILLED JEAN DeWOLFF..
...BECAUSE I FELT LIKE IT.
CHUT
ARRRGHH!
YOU... SLUT!
STAB ME WITH A LETTER OPENER, WILL YOU? I'LL--
≷GASP!≶ IT'S...IT'S...
WHAT ARE YOU BABBLING A--

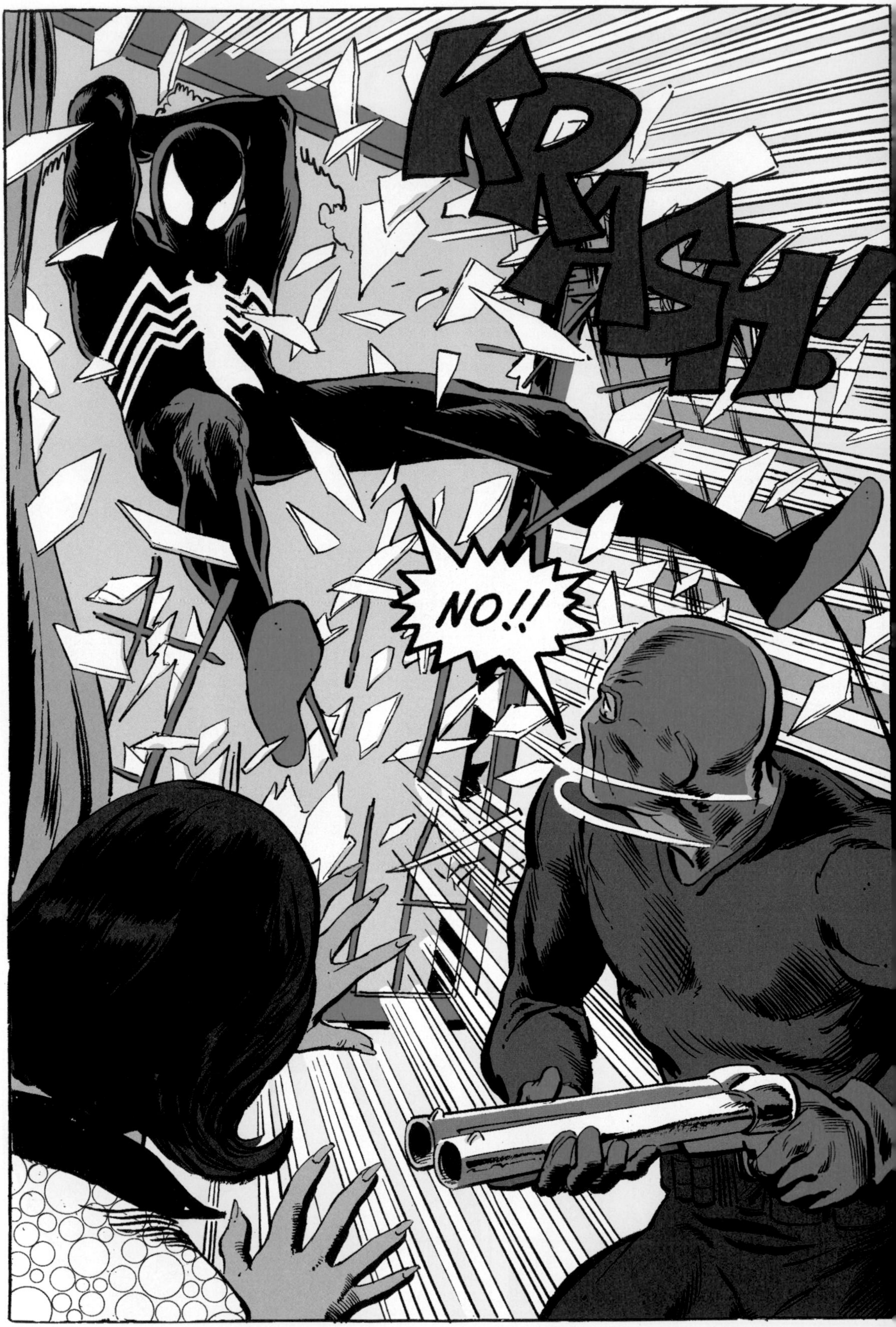
KRASH!
NO!!

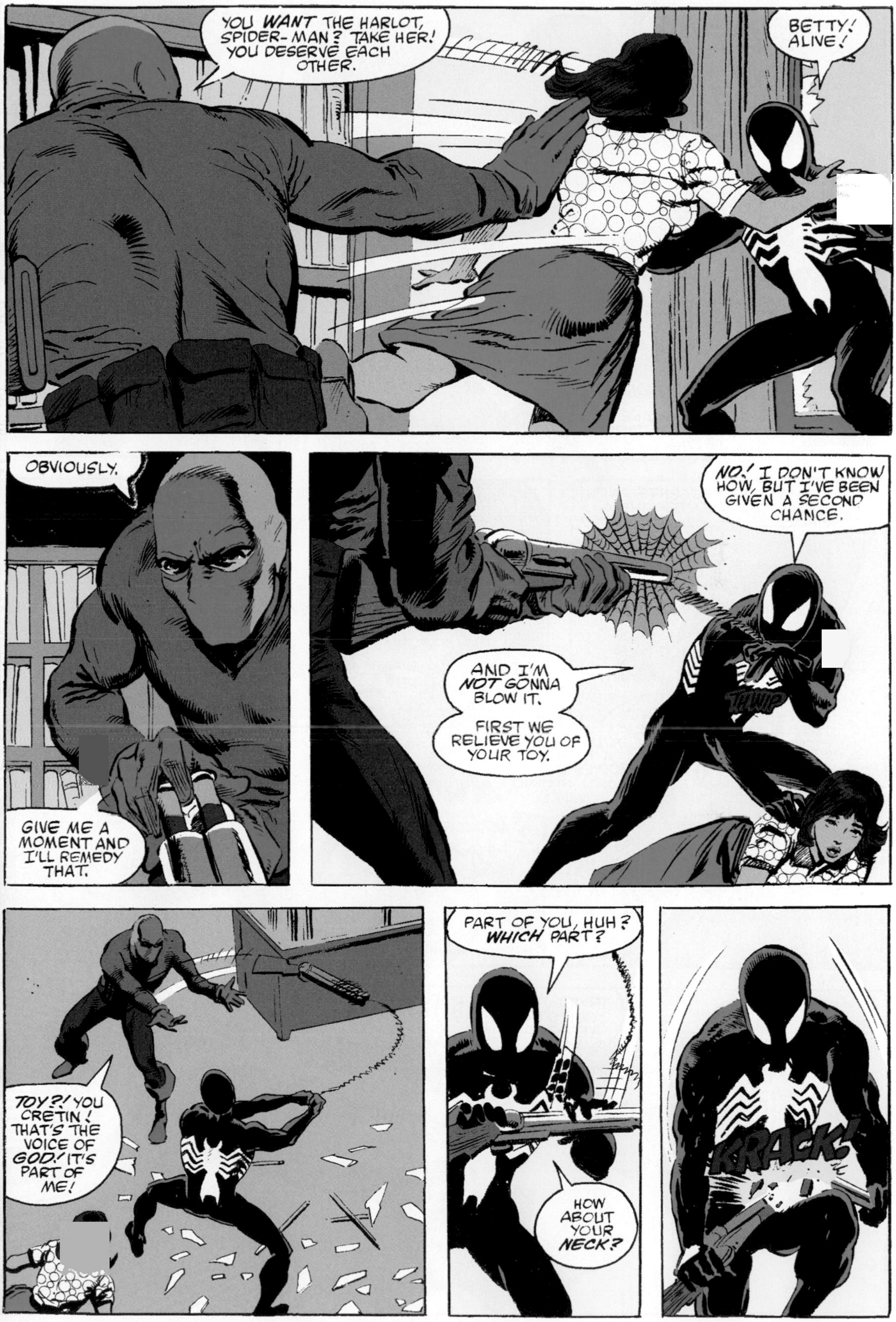
YOU WANT THE HARLOT, SPIDER-MAN? TAKE HER! YOU DESERVE EACH OTHER.
BETTY! ALIVE!
OBVIOUSLY.
GIVE ME A MOMENT AND I'LL REMEDY THAT.
NO! I DON'T KNOW HOW, BUT I'VE BEEN GIVEN A SECOND CHANCE.
AND I'M NOT GONNA BLOW IT.
FIRST WE RELIEVE YOU OF YOUR TOY.
THWIP
TOY?! YOU CRETIN! THAT'S THE VOICE OF GOD! IT'S PART OF ME!
PART OF YOU, HUH? WHICH PART?
HOW ABOUT YOUR NECK?
KRACK!

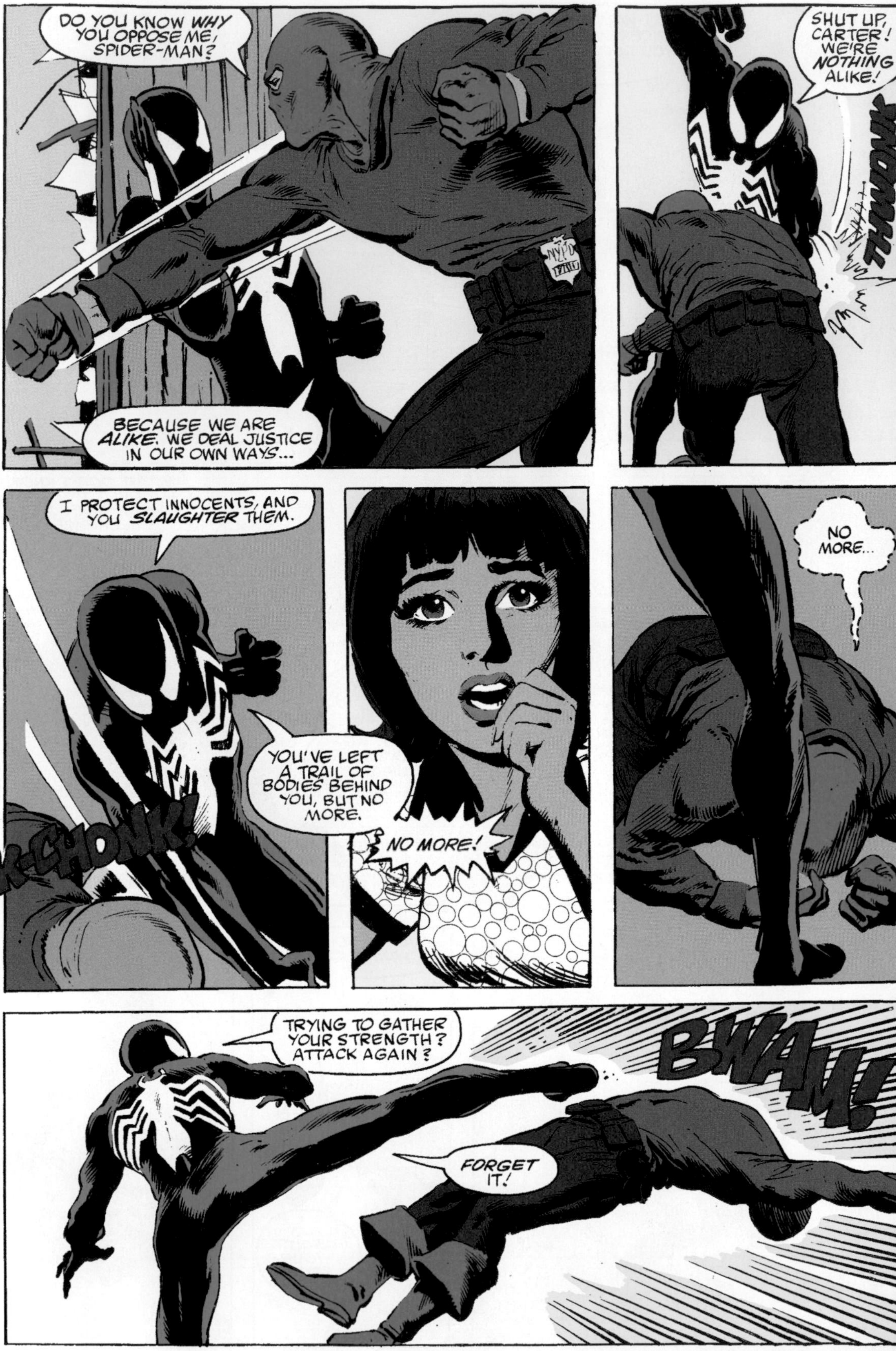
DO YOU KNOW WHY YOU OPPOSE ME, SPIDER-MAN?
BECAUSE WE ARE ALIKE. WE DEAL JUSTICE IN OUR OWN WAYS...
SHUT UP, CARTER! WE'RE NOTHING ALIKE!
THWONK
I PROTECT INNOCENTS, AND YOU SLAUGHTER THEM.
YOU'VE LEFT A TRAIL OF BODIES BEHIND YOU, BUT NO MORE.
K-CHONK!
NO MORE!
NO MORE...
TRYING TO GATHER YOUR STRENGTH? ATTACK AGAIN?
BWAM!
FORGET IT!

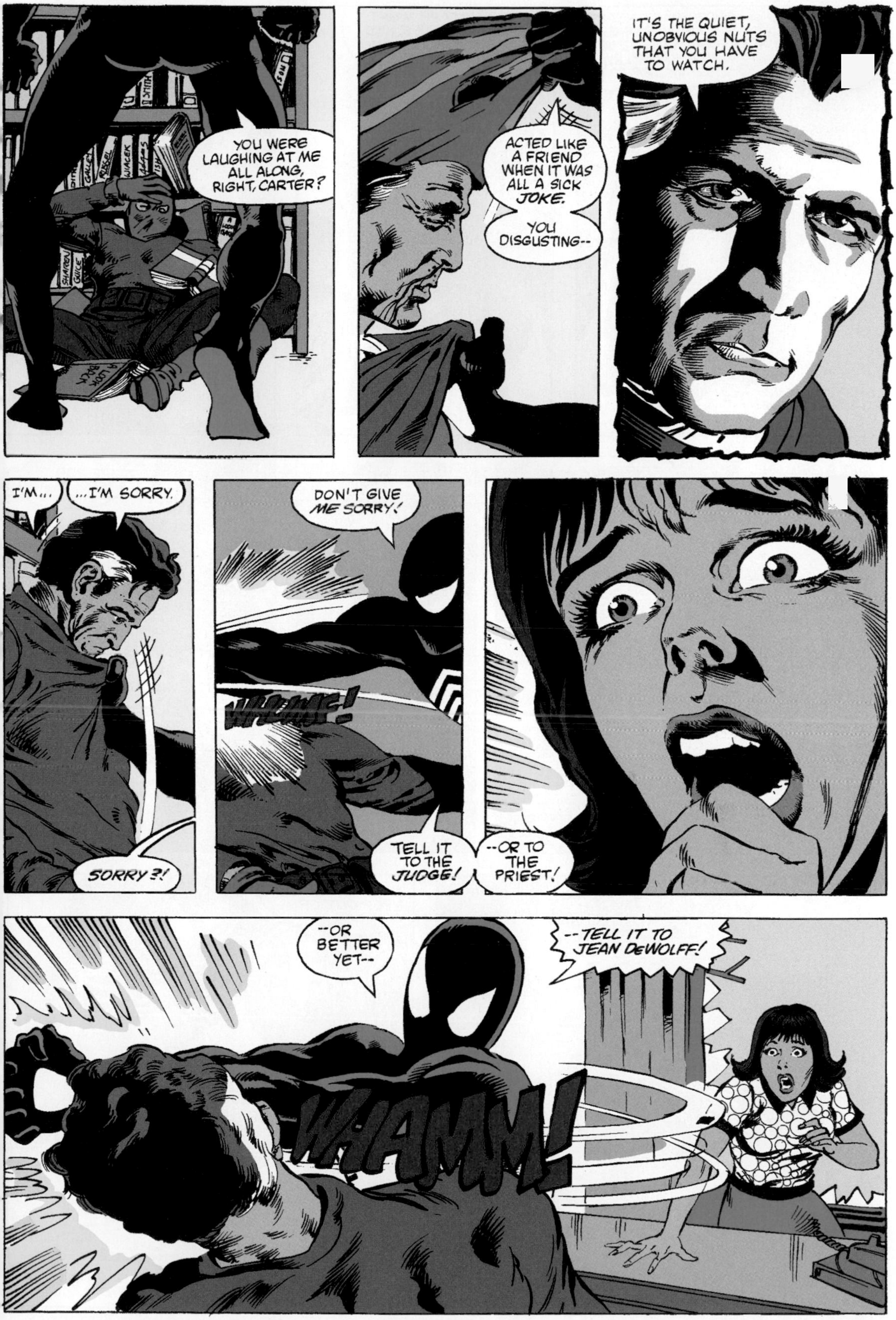
YOU WERE LAUGHING AT ME ALL ALONG, RIGHT, CARTER?
ACTED LIKE A FRIEND WHEN IT WAS ALL A SICK JOKE.
YOU DISGUSTING--
IT'S THE QUIET, UNOBVIOUS NUTS THAT YOU HAVE TO WATCH.
I'M...
...I'M SORRY.
SORRY?!
DON'T GIVE ME SORRY!
WHAMM!
TELL IT TO THE JUDGE!
--OR TO THE PRIEST!
--OR BETTER YET--
--TELL IT TO JEAN DeWOLFF!
WHAMM!

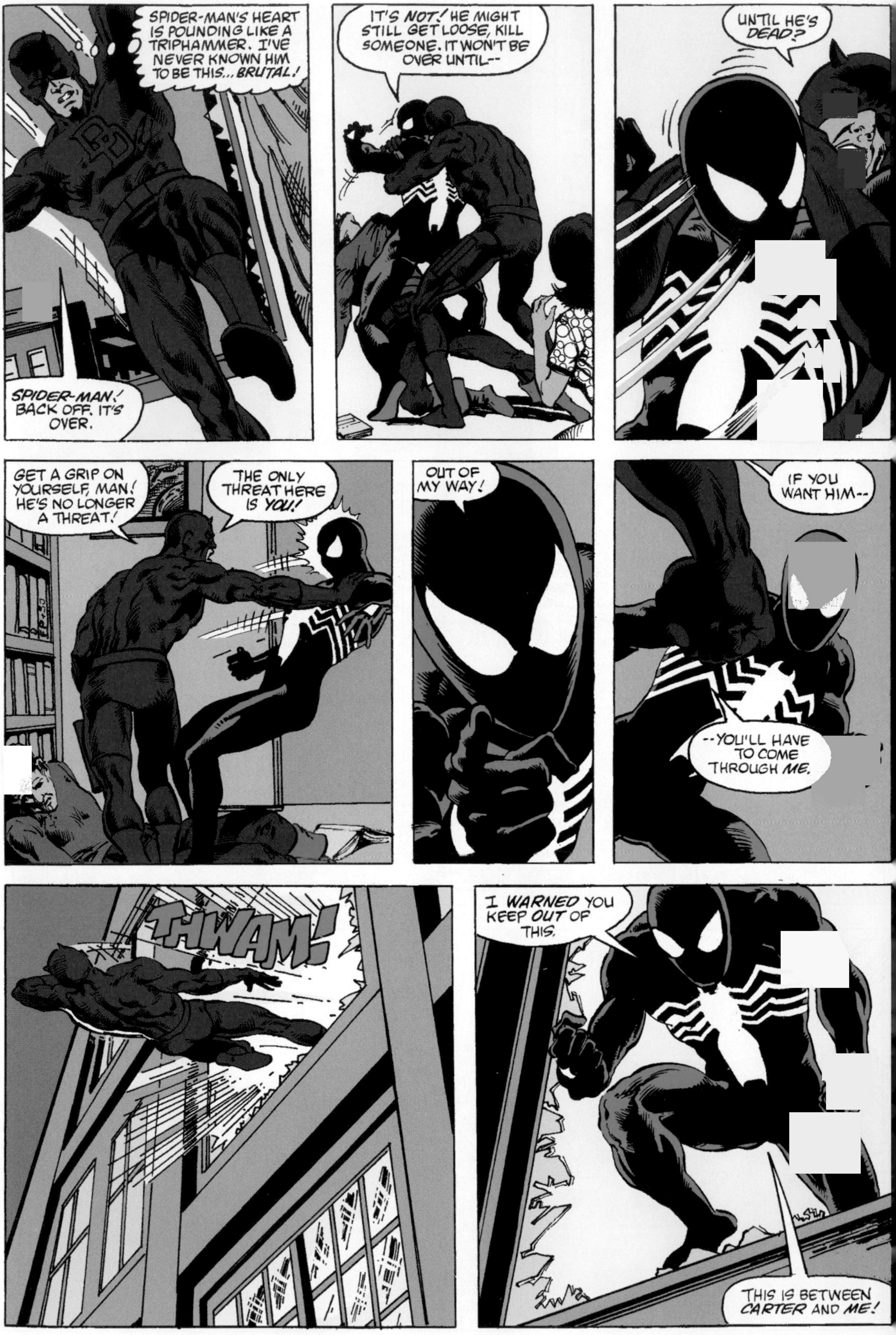
SPIDER-MAN'S HEART IS POUNDING LIKE A TRIPHAMMER. I'VE NEVER KNOWN HIM TO BE THIS... BRUTAL!
SPIDER-MAN! BACK OFF. IT'S OVER.
IT'S NOT! HE MIGHT STILL GET LOOSE, KILL SOMEONE. IT WON'T BE OVER UNTIL--
UNTIL HE'S DEAD?
GET A GRIP ON YOURSELF, MAN! HE'S NO LONGER A THREAT!
THE ONLY THREAT HERE IS YOU!
OUT OF MY WAY!
IF YOU WANT HIM--
--YOU'LL HAVE TO COME THROUGH ME.
THWAM!
I WARNED YOU KEEP OUT OF THIS.
THIS IS BETWEEN CARTER AND ME!

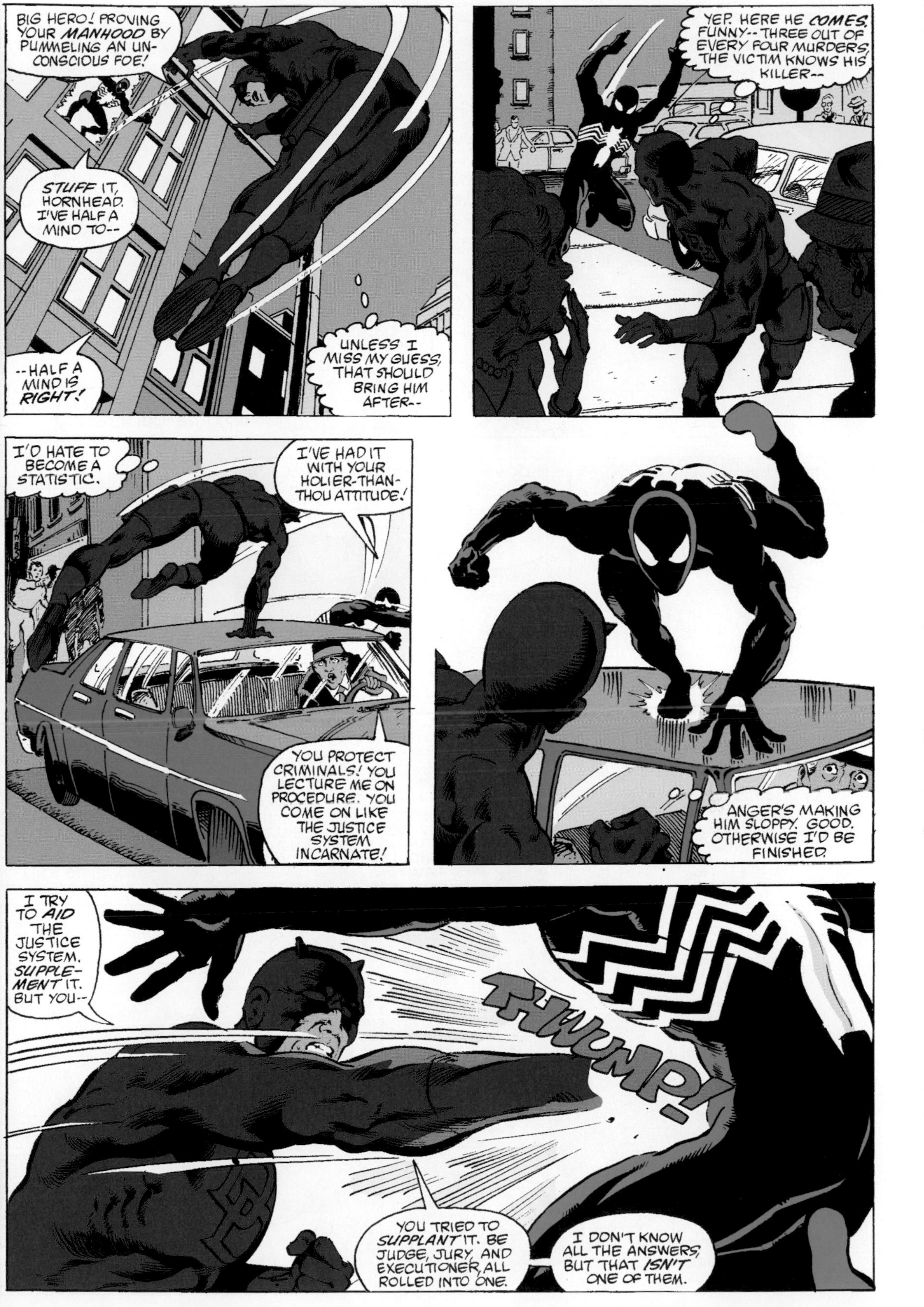
BIG HERO! PROVING YOUR MANHOOD BY PUMMELING AN UN-CONSCIOUS FOE!
STUFF IT, HORNHEAD. I'VE HALF A MIND TO--
--HALF A MIND IS RIGHT!
UNLESS I MISS MY GUESS, THAT SHOULD BRING HIM AFTER--
YEP. HERE HE COMES. FUNNY-- THREE OUT OF EVERY FOUR MURDERS, THE VICTIM KNOWS HIS KILLER--
I'D HATE TO BECOME A STATISTIC.
I'VE HAD IT WITH YOUR HOLIER-THAN-THOU ATTITUDE!
YOU PROTECT CRIMINALS! YOU LECTURE ME ON PROCEDURE. YOU COME ON LIKE THE JUSTICE SYSTEM INCARNATE!
ANGER'S MAKING HIM SLOPPY. GOOD. OTHERWISE I'D BE FINISHED.
I TRY TO AID THE JUSTICE SYSTEM. SUPPLE-MENT IT. BUT YOU--
THWUMP!
YOU TRIED TO SUPPLANT IT. BE JUDGE, JURY, AND EXECUTIONER, ALL ROLLED INTO ONE.
I DON'T KNOW ALL THE ANSWERS, BUT THAT ISN'T ONE OF THEM.

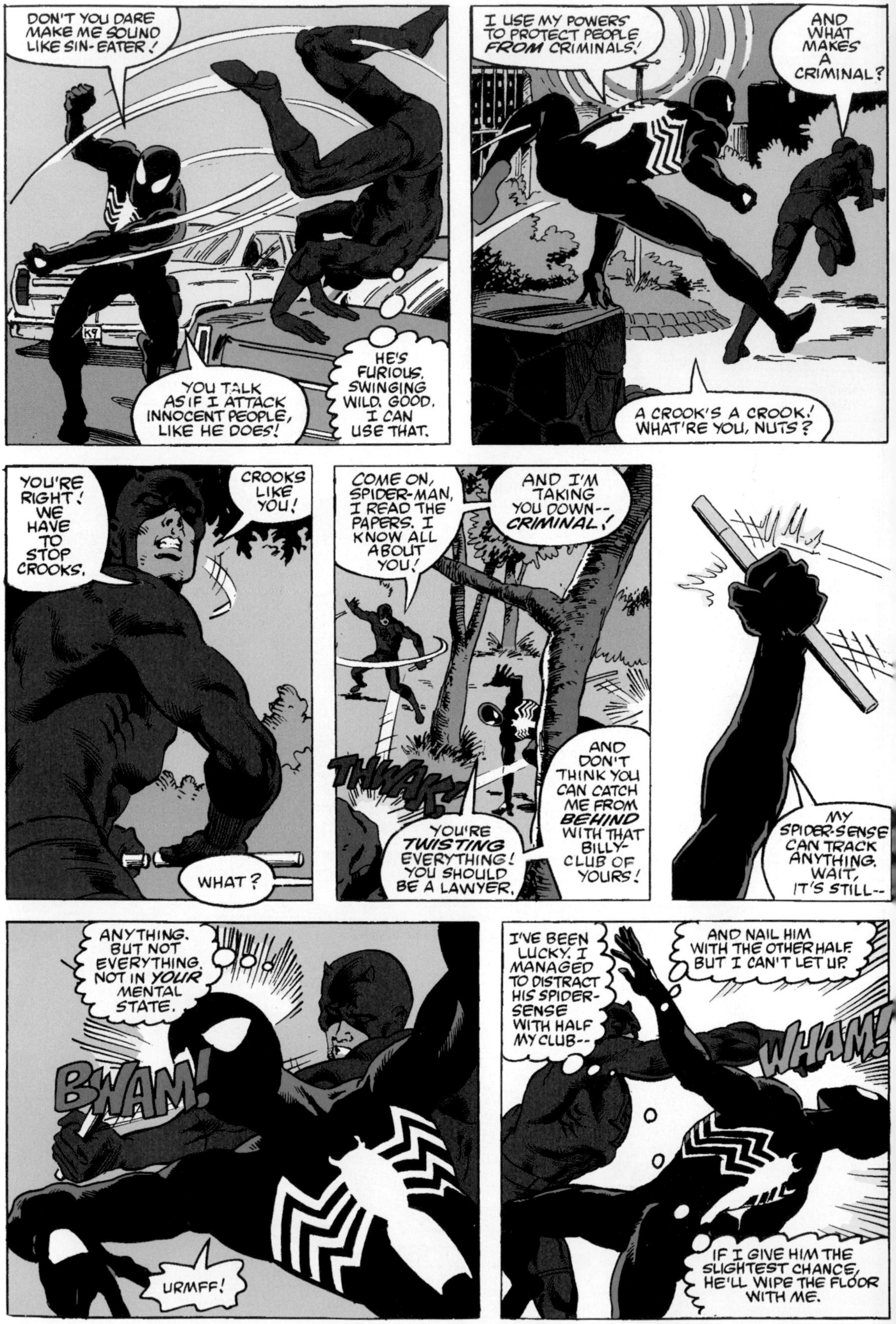
DON'T YOU DARE MAKE ME SOUND LIKE SIN-EATER!
YOU TALK AS IF I ATTACK INNOCENT PEOPLE, LIKE HE DOES!
HE'S FURIOUS. SWINGING WILD. GOOD. I CAN USE THAT.
I USE MY POWERS TO PROTECT PEOPLE FROM CRIMINALS!
AND WHAT MAKES A CRIMINAL?
A CROOK'S A CROOK! WHAT'RE YOU, NUTS?
YOU'RE RIGHT! WE HAVE TO STOP CROOKS.
CROOKS LIKE YOU!
WHAT?
COME ON, SPIDER-MAN, I READ THE PAPERS. I KNOW ALL ABOUT YOU!
AND I'M TAKING YOU DOWN-- CRIMINAL!
THWAK!
YOU'RE TWISTING EVERYTHING! YOU SHOULD BE A LAWYER.
AND DON'T THINK YOU CAN CATCH ME FROM BEHIND WITH THAT BILLY-CLUB OF YOURS!
MY SPIDER-SENSE CAN TRACK ANYTHING. WAIT, IT'S STILL--
ANYTHING. BUT NOT EVERYTHING. NOT IN YOUR MENTAL STATE.
BWAM!
URMFF!
I'VE BEEN LUCKY. I MANAGED TO DISTRACT HIS SPIDER-SENSE WITH HALF MY CLUB--
AND NAIL HIM WITH THE OTHER HALF. BUT I CAN'T LET UP.
WHAM!
IF I GIVE HIM THE SLIGHTEST CHANCE, HE'LL WIPE THE FLOOR WITH ME.

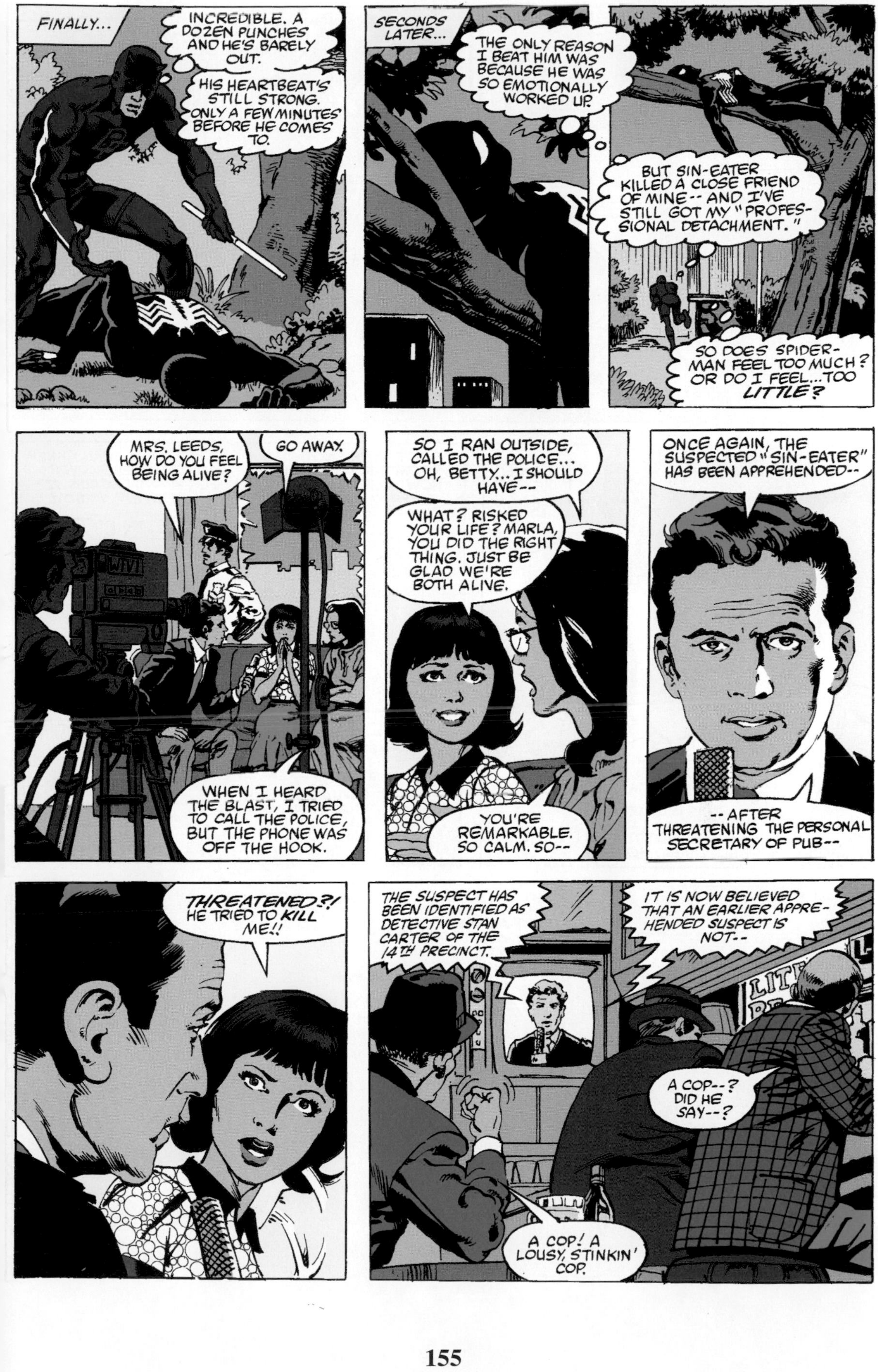
FINALLY...
INCREDIBLE. A DOZEN PUNCHES AND HE'S BARELY OUT.
HIS HEARTBEAT'S STILL STRONG. ONLY A FEW MINUTES BEFORE HE COMES TO.
SECONDS LATER...
THE ONLY REASON I BEAT HIM WAS BECAUSE HE WAS SO EMOTIONALLY WORKED UP.
BUT SIN-EATER KILLED A CLOSE FRIEND OF MINE-- AND I'VE STILL GOT MY "PROFES-SIONAL DETACHMENT."
SO DOES SPIDER-MAN FEEL TOO MUCH? OR DO I FEEL...TOO LITTLE?
MRS. LEEDS, HOW DO YOU FEEL BEING ALIVE?
GO AWAY.
WIVI
WHEN I HEARD THE BLAST, I TRIED TO CALL THE POLICE, BUT THE PHONE WAS OFF THE HOOK.
SO I RAN OUTSIDE, CALLED THE POLICE... OH, BETTY... I SHOULD HAVE--
WHAT? RISKED YOUR LIFE? MARLA, YOU DID THE RIGHT THING. JUST BE GLAD WE'RE BOTH ALIVE.
YOU'RE REMARKABLE. SO CALM. SO--
ONCE AGAIN, THE SUSPECTED "SIN-EATER" HAS BEEN APPREHENDED--
--AFTER THREATENING THE PERSONAL SECRETARY OF PUB--
THREATENED?! HE TRIED TO KILL ME!!
THE SUSPECT HAS BEEN IDENTIFIED AS DETECTIVE STAN CARTER OF THE 14TH PRECINCT.
IT IS NOW BELIEVED THAT AN EARLIER APPRE-HENDED SUSPECT IS NOT--
A COP--? DID HE SAY--?
A COP! A LOUSY, STINKIN' COP.

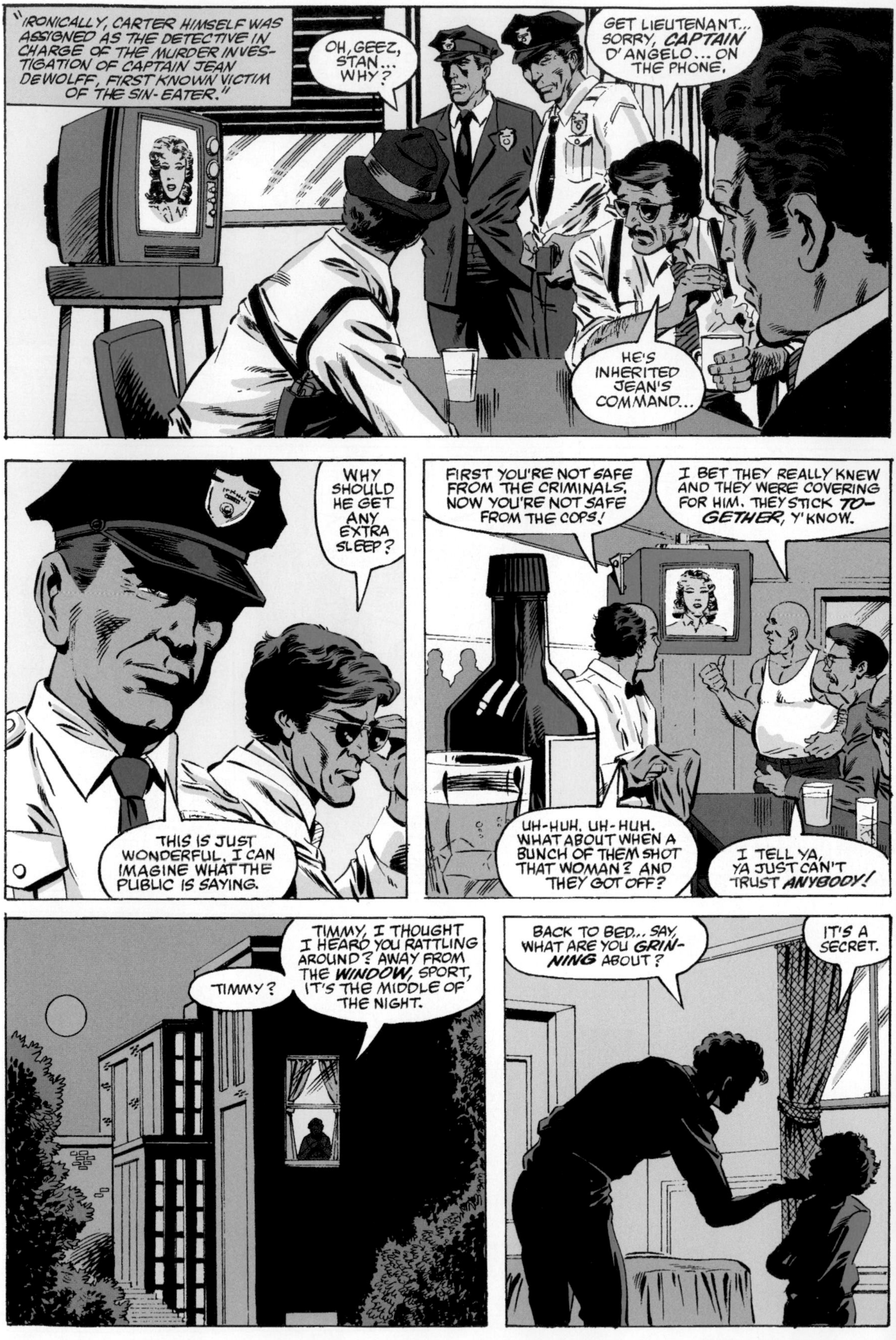
"IRONICALLY, CARTER HIMSELF WAS ASSIGNED AS THE DETECTIVE IN CHARGE OF THE MURDER INVESTIGATION OF CAPTAIN JEAN DEWOLFF, FIRST KNOWN VICTIM OF THE SIN-EATER."
OH, GEEZ, STAN... WHY?
GET LIEUTENANT... SORRY, CAPTAIN D'ANGELO... ON THE PHONE.
HE'S INHERITED JEAN'S COMMAND...
WHY SHOULD HE GET ANY EXTRA SLEEP?
THIS IS JUST WONDERFUL. I CAN IMAGINE WHAT THE PUBLIC IS SAYING.
FIRST YOU'RE NOT SAFE FROM THE CRIMINALS. NOW YOU'RE NOT SAFE FROM THE COPS!
I BET THEY REALLY KNEW AND THEY WERE COVERING FOR HIM. THEY STICK TOGETHER, Y'KNOW.
UH-HUH. UH-HUH. WHAT ABOUT WHEN A BUNCH OF THEM SHOT THAT WOMAN? AND THEY GOT OFF?
I TELL YA, YA JUST CAN'T TRUST ANYBODY!
TIMMY?
TIMMY, I THOUGHT I HEARD YOU RATTLING AROUND? AWAY FROM THE WINDOW, SPORT, IT'S THE MIDDLE OF THE NIGHT.
BACK TO BED... SAY, WHAT ARE YOU GRINNING ABOUT?
IT'S A SECRET.

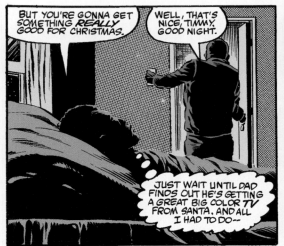

BUT YOU'RE GONNA GET SOMETHING *REALLY* GOOD FOR CHRISTMAS.

WELL, THAT'S NICE, TIMMY. GOOD NIGHT.

JUST WAIT UNTIL DAD FINDS OUT HE'S GETTING A GREAT BIG COLOR *TV* FROM SANTA. AND ALL I HAD TO DO--

HONEY, WHERE'S THE PORTABLE *TV?*

-- IS TRADE SANTA OUR LITTLE ONE.

...ho ho ho...

NEXT MORNING, IN THE LOBBY OF THE DAILY BUGLE...

BOY, THE "TOYS FOR THE UNDERPRIVILEGED" DRIVE IS SURE GETTING A PATHETIC TURNOUT THIS YEAR.

GUESS THE CITY ISN'T IN MUCH OF A GIVING MOOD RECENTLY.

THE OVERWHELMING FEELING SEEMS TO BE ANGER.

OUT OF MY WAY OR YOU'RE FIRED.

BUT I DON'T WORK HERE.

FINE. YOU'RE HIRED.

NOW YOU'RE THROUGH. GET *OUT.*

AND SPEAKING OF ANGRY MOODS... *HI,* JONAH!

HOW DID THE DISTRIBUTOR CONFERENCE GO?

FINE IF YOU ENJOY DEBACLES.

SOME WHOLESALER HATED MY CIGAR. SO NOW "NOW" MAGAZINE WON'T BE CARRIED IN CLEVELAND.

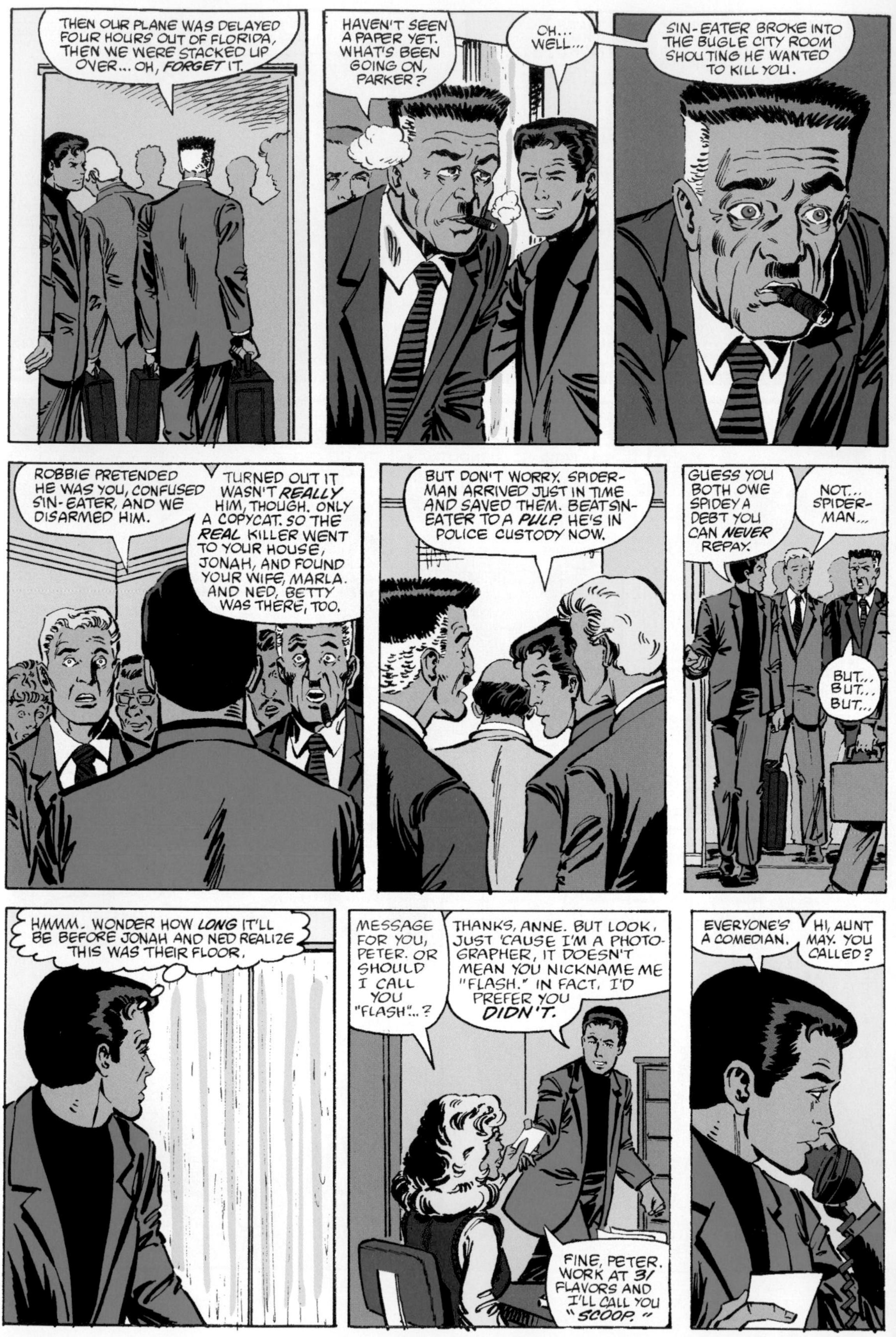
THEN OUR PLANE WAS DELAYED FOUR HOURS OUT OF FLORIDA, THEN WE WERE STACKED UP OVER... OH, FORGET IT.
HAVEN'T SEEN A PAPER YET. WHAT'S BEEN GOING ON, PARKER?
OH... WELL...
SIN-EATER BROKE INTO THE BUGLE CITY ROOM SHOUTING HE WANTED TO KILL YOU.
ROBBIE PRETENDED HE WAS YOU, CONFUSED SIN-EATER, AND WE DISARMED HIM.
TURNED OUT IT WASN'T REALLY HIM, THOUGH. ONLY A COPYCAT. SO THE REAL KILLER WENT TO YOUR HOUSE, JONAH, AND FOUND YOUR WIFE, MARLA. AND NED, BETTY WAS THERE, TOO.
BUT DON'T WORRY. SPIDER-MAN ARRIVED JUST IN TIME AND SAVED THEM. BEAT SIN-EATER TO A PULP. HE'S IN POLICE CUSTODY NOW.
GUESS YOU BOTH OWE SPIDEY A DEBT YOU CAN NEVER REPAY.
NOT... SPIDER-MAN...
BUT... BUT... BUT...
HMMM. WONDER HOW LONG IT'LL BE BEFORE JONAH AND NED REALIZE THIS WAS THEIR FLOOR.
MESSAGE FOR YOU, PETER. OR SHOULD I CALL YOU "FLASH"...?
THANKS, ANNE. BUT LOOK, JUST 'CAUSE I'M A PHOTOGRAPHER, IT DOESN'T MEAN YOU NICKNAME ME "FLASH." IN FACT, I'D PREFER YOU DIDN'T.
FINE, PETER. WORK AT 31 FLAVORS AND I'LL CALL YOU "SCOOP."
EVERYONE'S A COMEDIAN.
HI, AUNT MAY. YOU CALLED?

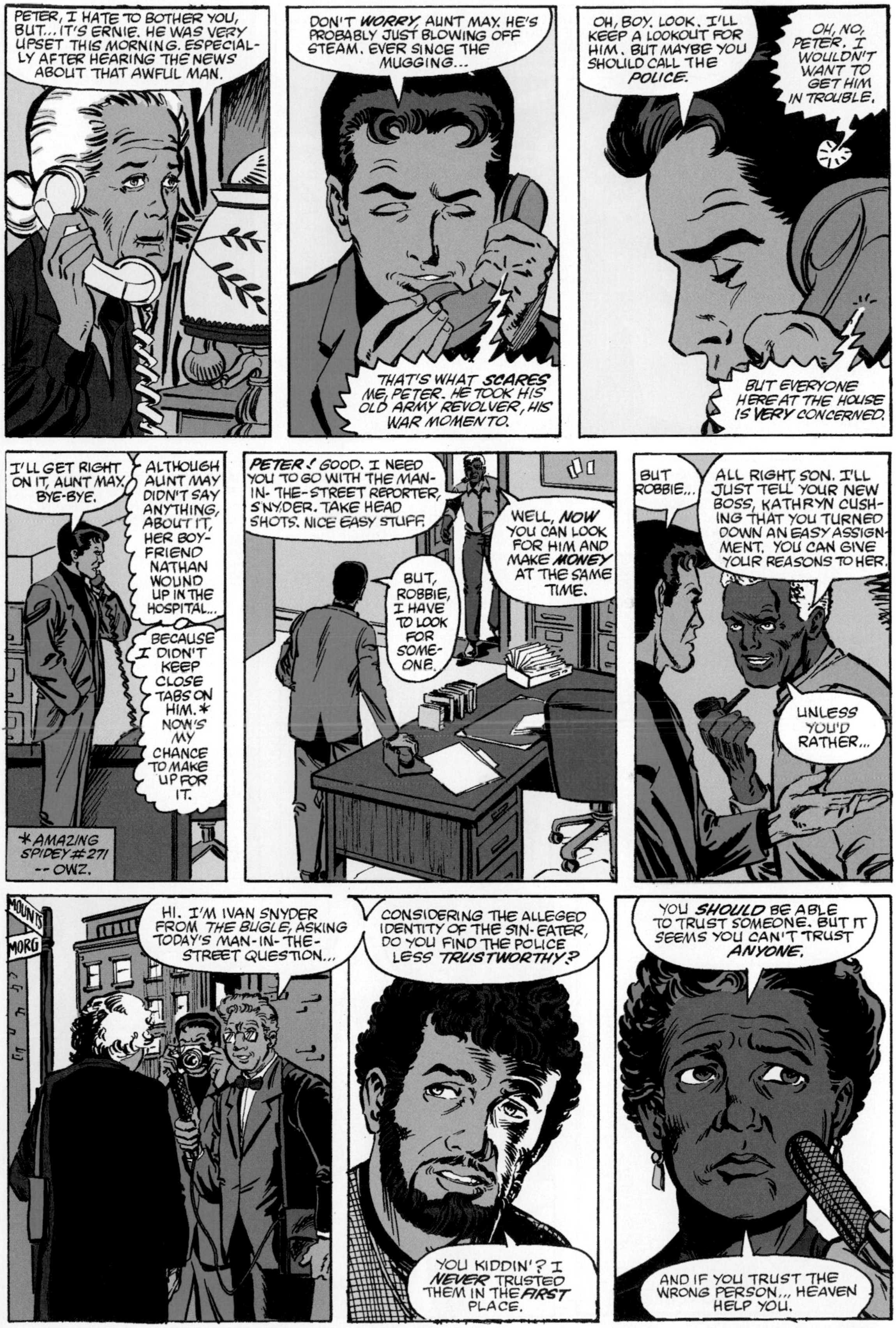
PETER, I HATE TO BOTHER YOU, BUT... IT'S ERNIE. HE WAS VERY UPSET THIS MORNING. ESPECIALLY AFTER HEARING THE NEWS ABOUT THAT AWFUL MAN.
DON'T WORRY, AUNT MAY. HE'S PROBABLY JUST BLOWING OFF STEAM. EVER SINCE THE MUGGING...
THAT'S WHAT SCARES ME, PETER. HE TOOK HIS OLD ARMY REVOLVER, HIS WAR MOMENTO.
OH, BOY. LOOK. I'LL KEEP A LOOKOUT FOR HIM. BUT MAYBE YOU SHOULD CALL THE POLICE.
OH, NO, PETER. I WOULDN'T WANT TO GET HIM IN TROUBLE.
BUT EVERYONE HERE AT THE HOUSE IS VERY CONCERNED.
I'LL GET RIGHT ON IT, AUNT MAY. BYE-BYE.
ALTHOUGH AUNT MAY DIDN'T SAY ANYTHING, ABOUT IT, HER BOYFRIEND NATHAN WOUND UP IN THE HOSPITAL...
BECAUSE I DIDN'T KEEP CLOSE TABS ON HIM.* NOW'S MY CHANCE TO MAKE UP FOR IT.
*AMAZING SPIDEY #271 -- OWZ.
PETER! GOOD. I NEED YOU TO GO WITH THE MAN-IN-THE-STREET REPORTER, SNYDER. TAKE HEAD SHOTS. NICE EASY STUFF.
BUT, ROBBIE, I HAVE TO LOOK FOR SOMEONE.
WELL, NOW YOU CAN LOOK FOR HIM AND MAKE MONEY AT THE SAME TIME.
BUT ROBBIE...
ALL RIGHT, SON. I'LL JUST TELL YOUR NEW BOSS, KATHRYN CUSHING THAT YOU TURNED DOWN AN EASY ASSIGNMENT. YOU CAN GIVE YOUR REASONS TO HER.
UNLESS YOU'D RATHER...
MOUNTS
MORG
HI. I'M IVAN SNYDER FROM THE BUGLE, ASKING TODAY'S MAN-IN-THE-STREET QUESTION...
CONSIDERING THE ALLEGED IDENTITY OF THE SIN-EATER, DO YOU FIND THE POLICE LESS TRUSTWORTHY?
YOU KIDDIN'? I NEVER TRUSTED THEM IN THE FIRST PLACE.
YOU SHOULD BE ABLE TO TRUST SOMEONE. BUT IT SEEMS YOU CAN'T TRUST ANYONE.
AND IF YOU TRUST THE WRONG PERSON,,, HEAVEN HELP YOU.

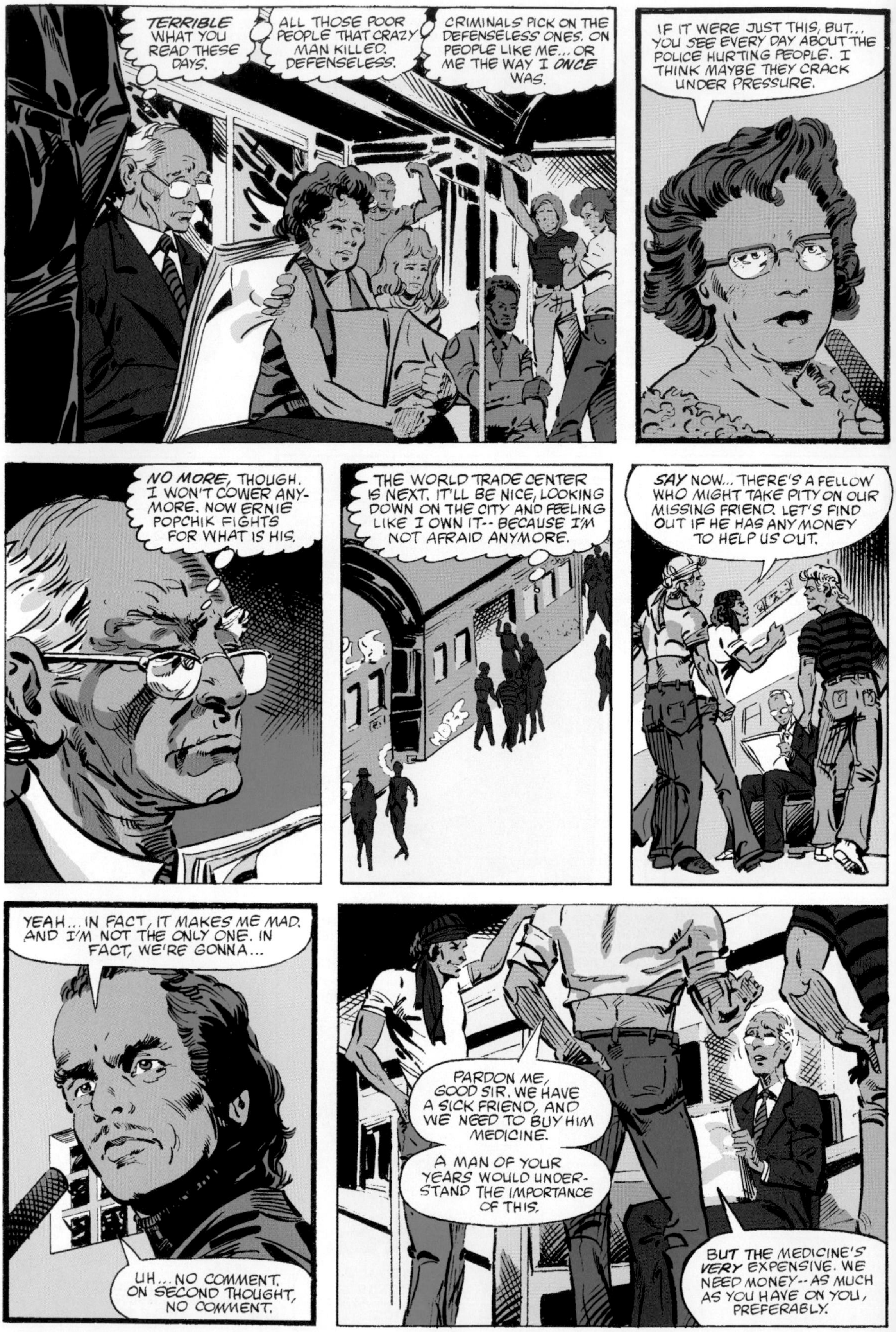
TERRIBLE WHAT YOU READ THESE DAYS.
ALL THOSE POOR PEOPLE THAT CRAZY MAN KILLED. DEFENSELESS.
CRIMINALS PICK ON THE DEFENSELESS ONES. ON PEOPLE LIKE ME... OR ME THE WAY I ONCE WAS.
IF IT WERE JUST THIS, BUT... YOU SEE EVERY DAY ABOUT THE POLICE HURTING PEOPLE. I THINK MAYBE THEY CRACK UNDER PRESSURE.
NO MORE, THOUGH. I WON'T COWER ANYMORE. NOW ERNIE POPCHIK FIGHTS FOR WHAT IS HIS.
THE WORLD TRADE CENTER IS NEXT. IT'LL BE NICE, LOOKING DOWN ON THE CITY AND FEELING LIKE I OWN IT-- BECAUSE I'M NOT AFRAID ANYMORE.
SAY NOW... THERE'S A FELLOW WHO MIGHT TAKE PITY ON OUR MISSING FRIEND. LET'S FIND OUT IF HE HAS ANY MONEY TO HELP US OUT.
YEAH... IN FACT, IT MAKES ME MAD. AND I'M NOT THE ONLY ONE. IN FACT, WE'RE GONNA...
UH... NO COMMENT. ON SECOND THOUGHT, NO COMMENT.
PARDON ME, GOOD SIR. WE HAVE A SICK FRIEND, AND WE NEED TO BUY HIM MEDICINE.
A MAN OF YOUR YEARS WOULD UNDERSTAND THE IMPORTANCE OF THIS.
BUT THE MEDICINE'S VERY EXPENSIVE. WE NEED MONEY-- AS MUCH AS YOU HAVE ON YOU, PREFERABLY.

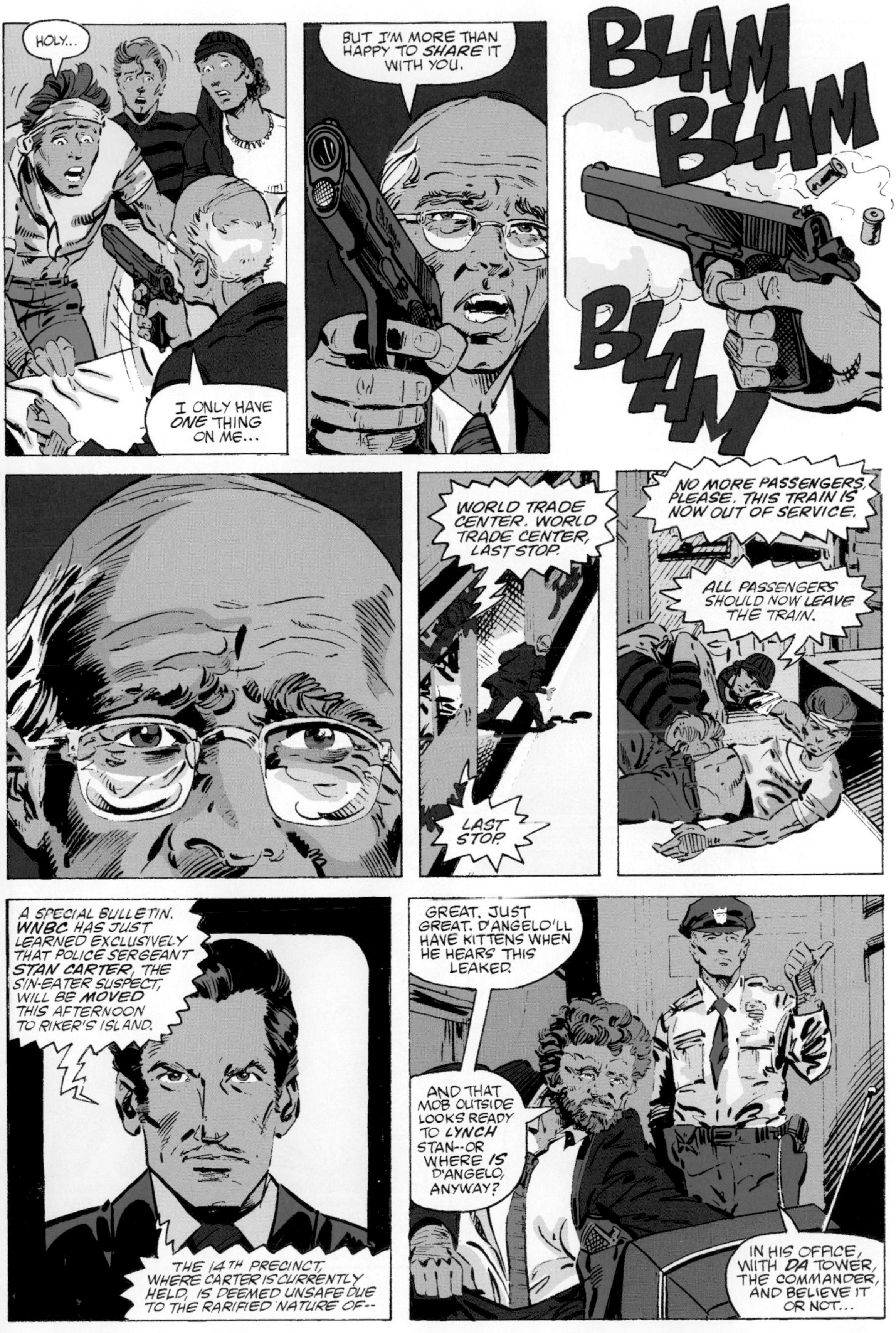
HOLY...
I ONLY HAVE ONE THING ON ME...
BUT I'M MORE THAN HAPPY TO SHARE IT WITH YOU.
BLAM
BLAM
BLAM
WORLD TRADE CENTER. WORLD TRADE CENTER, LAST STOP.
LAST STOP.
NO MORE PASSENGERS, PLEASE. THIS TRAIN IS NOW OUT OF SERVICE.
ALL PASSENGERS SHOULD NOW LEAVE THE TRAIN.
A SPECIAL BULLETIN. WNBC HAS JUST LEARNED EXCLUSIVELY THAT POLICE SERGEANT STAN CARTER, THE SIN-EATER SUSPECT, WILL BE MOVED THIS AFTERNOON TO RIKER'S ISLAND.
THE 14TH PRECINCT, WHERE CARTER IS CURRENTLY HELD, IS DEEMED UNSAFE DUE TO THE RARIFIED NATURE OF--
GREAT. JUST GREAT. D'ANGELO'LL HAVE KITTENS WHEN HE HEARS THIS LEAKED.
AND THAT MOB OUTSIDE LOOKS READY TO LYNCH STAN--OR WHERE IS D'ANGELO, ANYWAY?
IN HIS OFFICE, WITH DA TOWER, THE COMMANDER, AND BELIEVE IT OR NOT...

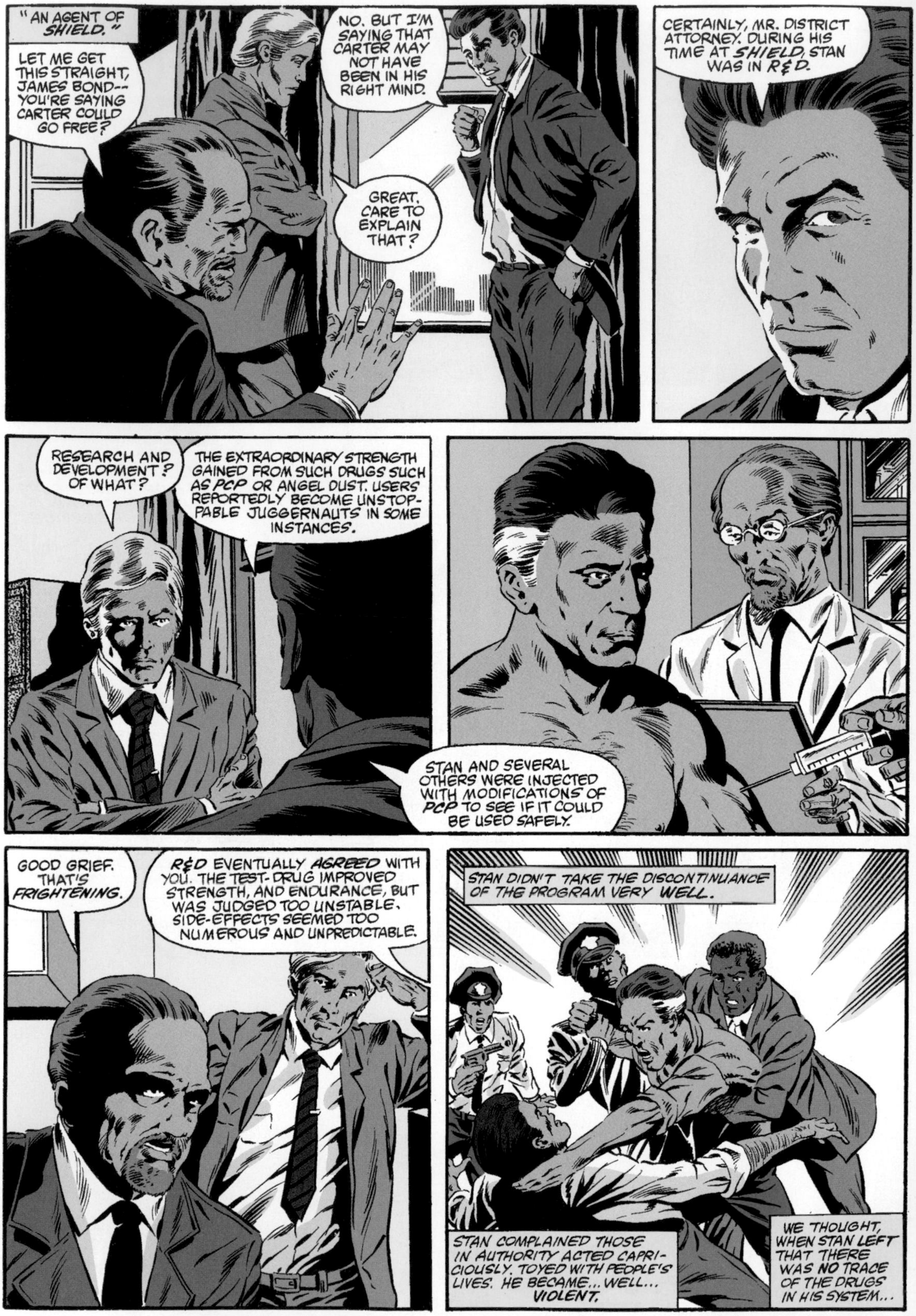
"AN AGENT OF SHIELD."
LET ME GET THIS STRAIGHT, JAMES BOND-- YOU'RE SAYING CARTER COULD GO FREE?
NO. BUT I'M SAYING THAT CARTER MAY NOT HAVE BEEN IN HIS RIGHT MIND.
GREAT. CARE TO EXPLAIN THAT?
CERTAINLY, MR. DISTRICT ATTORNEY. DURING HIS TIME AT SHIELD, STAN WAS IN R&D.
RESEARCH AND DEVELOPMENT? OF WHAT?
THE EXTRAORDINARY STRENGTH GAINED FROM SUCH DRUGS SUCH AS PCP OR ANGEL DUST. USERS REPORTEDLY BECOME UNSTOPPABLE JUGGERNAUTS IN SOME INSTANCES.
STAN AND SEVERAL OTHERS WERE INJECTED WITH MODIFICATIONS OF PCP TO SEE IF IT COULD BE USED SAFELY.
GOOD GRIEF. THAT'S FRIGHTENING.
R&D EVENTUALLY AGREED WITH YOU. THE TEST-DRUG IMPROVED STRENGTH, AND ENDURANCE, BUT WAS JUDGED TOO UNSTABLE. SIDE-EFFECTS SEEMED TOO NUMEROUS AND UNPREDICTABLE.
STAN DIDN'T TAKE THE DISCONTINUANCE OF THE PROGRAM VERY WELL.
STAN COMPLAINED THOSE IN AUTHORITY ACTED CAPRICIOUSLY. TOYED WITH PEOPLE'S LIVES. HE BECAME... WELL... VIOLENT.
WE THOUGHT, WHEN STAN LEFT THAT THERE WAS NO TRACE OF THE DRUGS IN HIS SYSTEM...

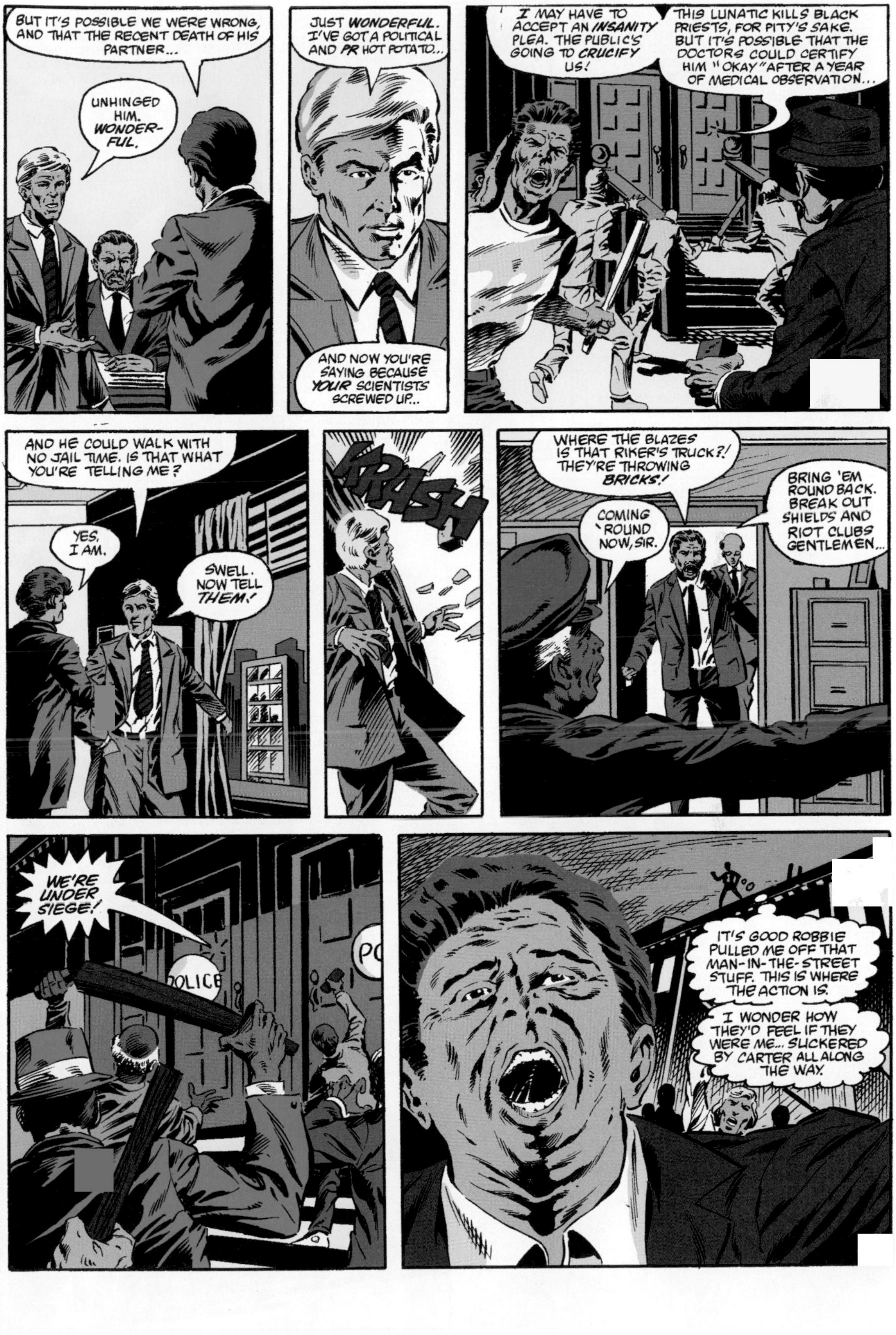
BUT IT'S POSSIBLE WE WERE WRONG, AND THAT THE RECENT DEATH OF HIS PARTNER...
UNHINGED HIM. WONDERFUL.
JUST WONDERFUL. I'VE GOT A POLITICAL AND PR HOT POTATO...
AND NOW YOU'RE SAYING BECAUSE YOUR SCIENTISTS SCREWED UP...
I MAY HAVE TO ACCEPT AN INSANITY PLEA. THE PUBLIC'S GOING TO CRUCIFY US!
THIS LUNATIC KILLS BLACK PRIESTS, FOR PITY'S SAKE. BUT IT'S POSSIBLE THAT THE DOCTORS COULD CERTIFY HIM "OKAY" AFTER A YEAR OF MEDICAL OBSERVATION...
AND HE COULD WALK WITH NO JAIL TIME. IS THAT WHAT YOU'RE TELLING ME?
YES, I AM.
SWELL. NOW TELL THEM!
KRASH
WHERE THE BLAZES IS THAT RIKER'S TRUCK?! THEY'RE THROWING BRICKS!
COMING 'ROUND NOW, SIR.
BRING 'EM ROUND BACK. BREAK OUT SHIELDS AND RIOT CLUBS GENTLEMEN...
WE'RE UNDER SIEGE!
POLICE
IT'S GOOD ROBBIE PULLED ME OFF THAT MAN-IN-THE-STREET STUFF. THIS IS WHERE THE ACTION IS.
I WONDER HOW THEY'D FEEL IF THEY WERE ME... SUCKERED BY CARTER ALL ALONG THE WAY.

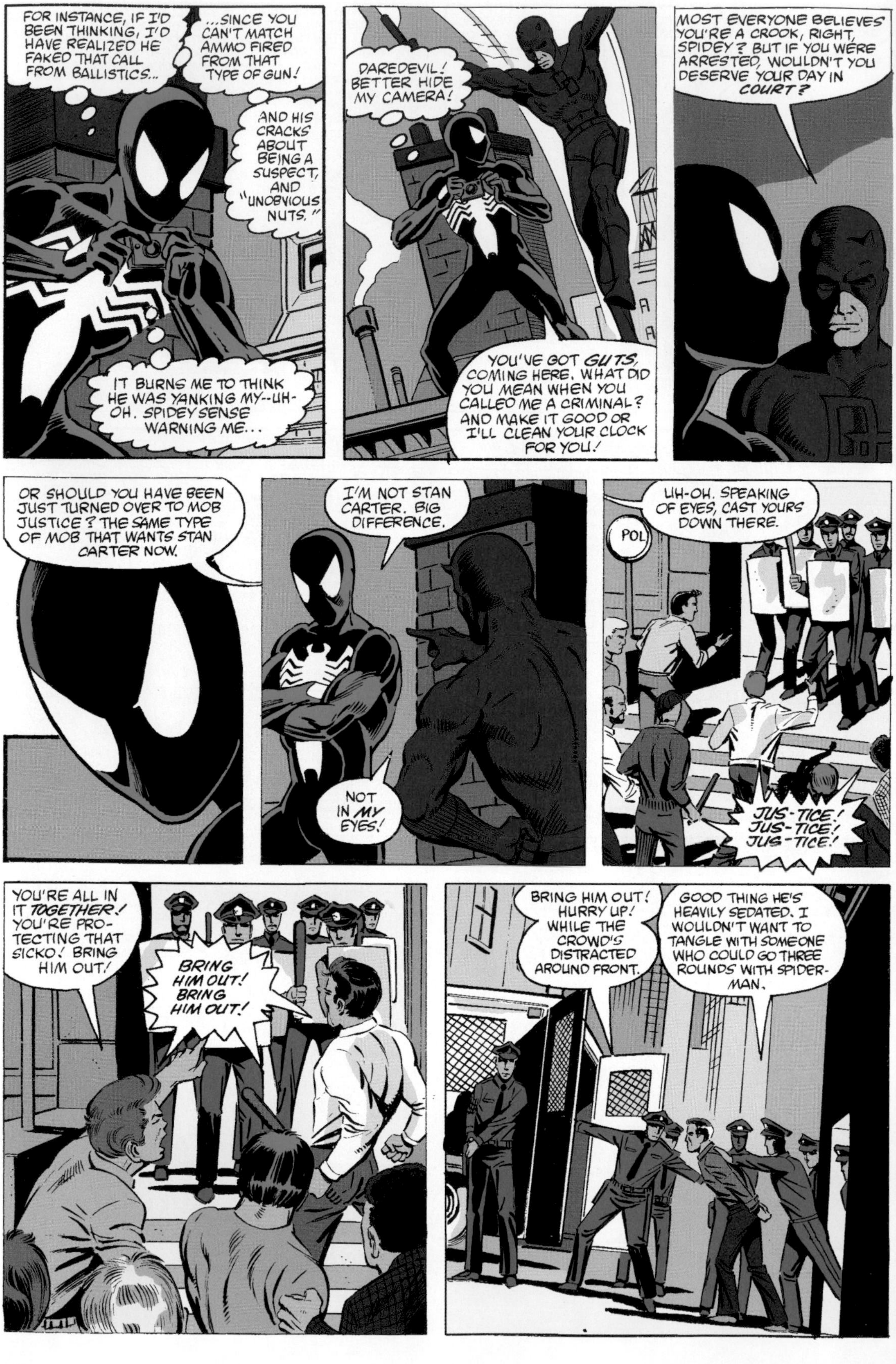
FOR INSTANCE, IF I'D BEEN THINKING, I'D HAVE REALIZED HE FAKED THAT CALL FROM BALLISTICS...
...SINCE YOU CAN'T MATCH AMMO FIRED FROM THAT TYPE OF GUN!
AND HIS CRACKS ABOUT BEING A SUSPECT, AND "UNOBVIOUS NUTS."
IT BURNS ME TO THINK HE WAS YANKING MY--UH-OH. SPIDEY SENSE WARNING ME...
DAREDEVIL! BETTER HIDE MY CAMERA!
YOU'VE GOT GUTS, COMING HERE. WHAT DID YOU MEAN WHEN YOU CALLED ME A CRIMINAL? AND MAKE IT GOOD OR I'LL CLEAN YOUR CLOCK FOR YOU!
MOST EVERYONE BELIEVES YOU'RE A CROOK, RIGHT, SPIDEY? BUT IF YOU WERE ARRESTED, WOULDN'T YOU DESERVE YOUR DAY IN COURT?
OR SHOULD YOU HAVE BEEN JUST TURNED OVER TO MOB JUSTICE? THE SAME TYPE OF MOB THAT WANTS STAN CARTER NOW.
I'M NOT STAN CARTER. BIG DIFFERENCE.
NOT IN MY EYES!
UH-OH. SPEAKING OF EYES, CAST YOURS DOWN THERE.
POL
JUS-TICE! JUS-TICE! JUS-TICE!
YOU'RE ALL IN IT TOGETHER! YOU'RE PROTECTING THAT SICKO! BRING HIM OUT!
BRING HIM OUT! BRING HIM OUT!
BRING HIM OUT! HURRY UP! WHILE THE CROWD'S DISTRACTED AROUND FRONT.
GOOD THING HE'S HEAVILY SEDATED. I WOULDN'T WANT TO TANGLE WITH SOMEONE WHO COULD GO THREE ROUNDS WITH SPIDER-MAN.

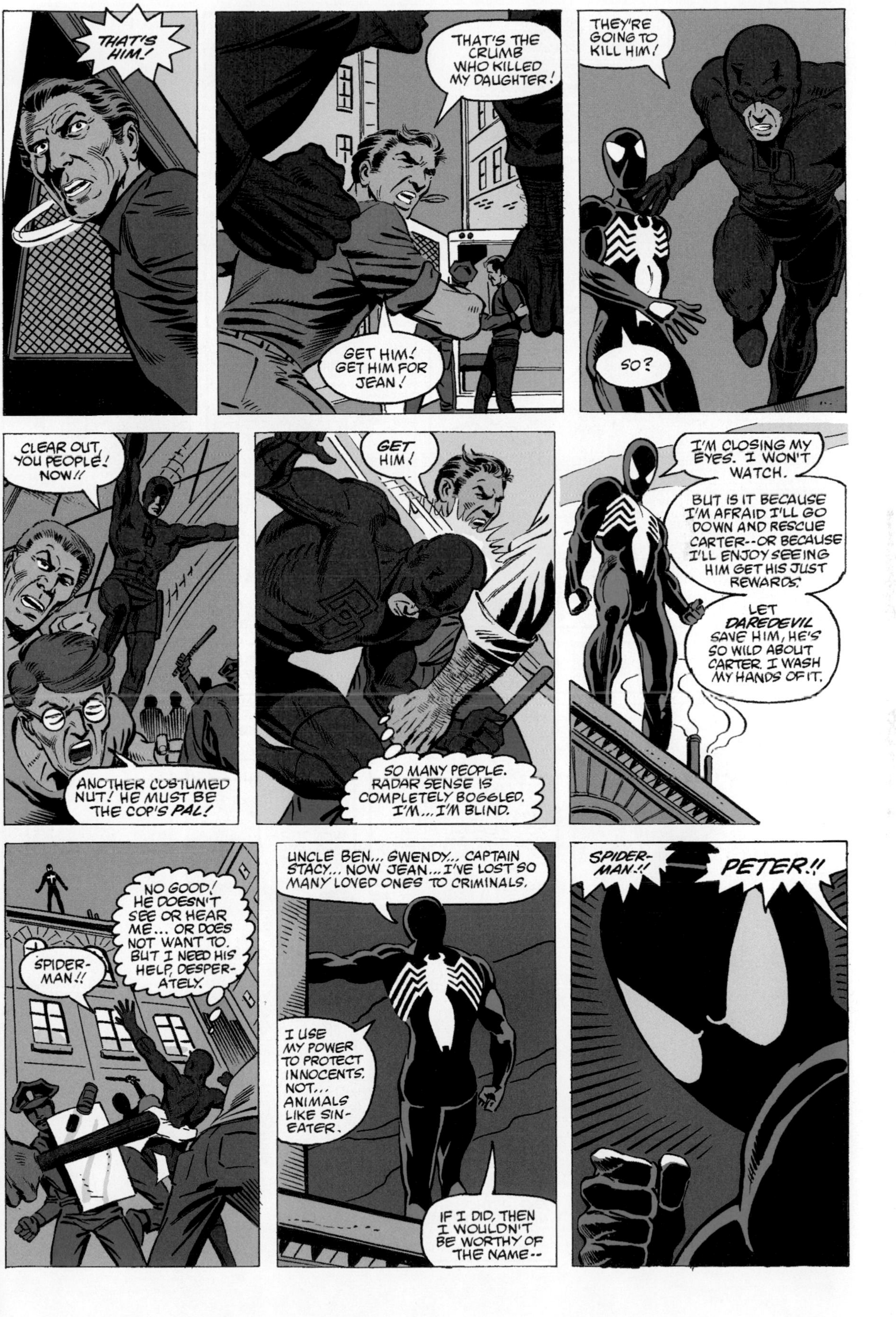
THAT'S HIM!
THAT'S THE CRUMB WHO KILLED MY DAUGHTER!
GET HIM! GET HIM FOR JEAN!
THEY'RE GOING TO KILL HIM!
SO?
CLEAR OUT, YOU PEOPLE! NOW!!
ANOTHER COSTUMED NUT! HE MUST BE THE COP'S PAL!
GET HIM!
SO MANY PEOPLE. RADAR SENSE IS COMPLETELY BOGGLED. I'M... I'M BLIND.
I'M CLOSING MY EYES. I WON'T WATCH.
BUT IS IT BECAUSE I'M AFRAID I'LL GO DOWN AND RESCUE CARTER--OR BECAUSE I'LL ENJOY SEEING HIM GET HIS JUST REWARDS?
LET DAREDEVIL SAVE HIM, HE'S SO WILD ABOUT CARTER. I WASH MY HANDS OF IT.
NO GOOD! HE DOESN'T SEE OR HEAR ME... OR DOES NOT WANT TO. BUT I NEED HIS HELP, DESPERATELY.
SPIDER-MAN!!
UNCLE BEN... GWENDY... CAPTAIN STACY... NOW JEAN... I'VE LOST SO MANY LOVED ONES TO CRIMINALS.
I USE MY POWER TO PROTECT INNOCENTS, NOT... ANIMALS LIKE SIN-EATER.
IF I DID, THEN I WOULDN'T BE WORTHY OF THE NAME--
SPIDER-MAN!!
PETER!!

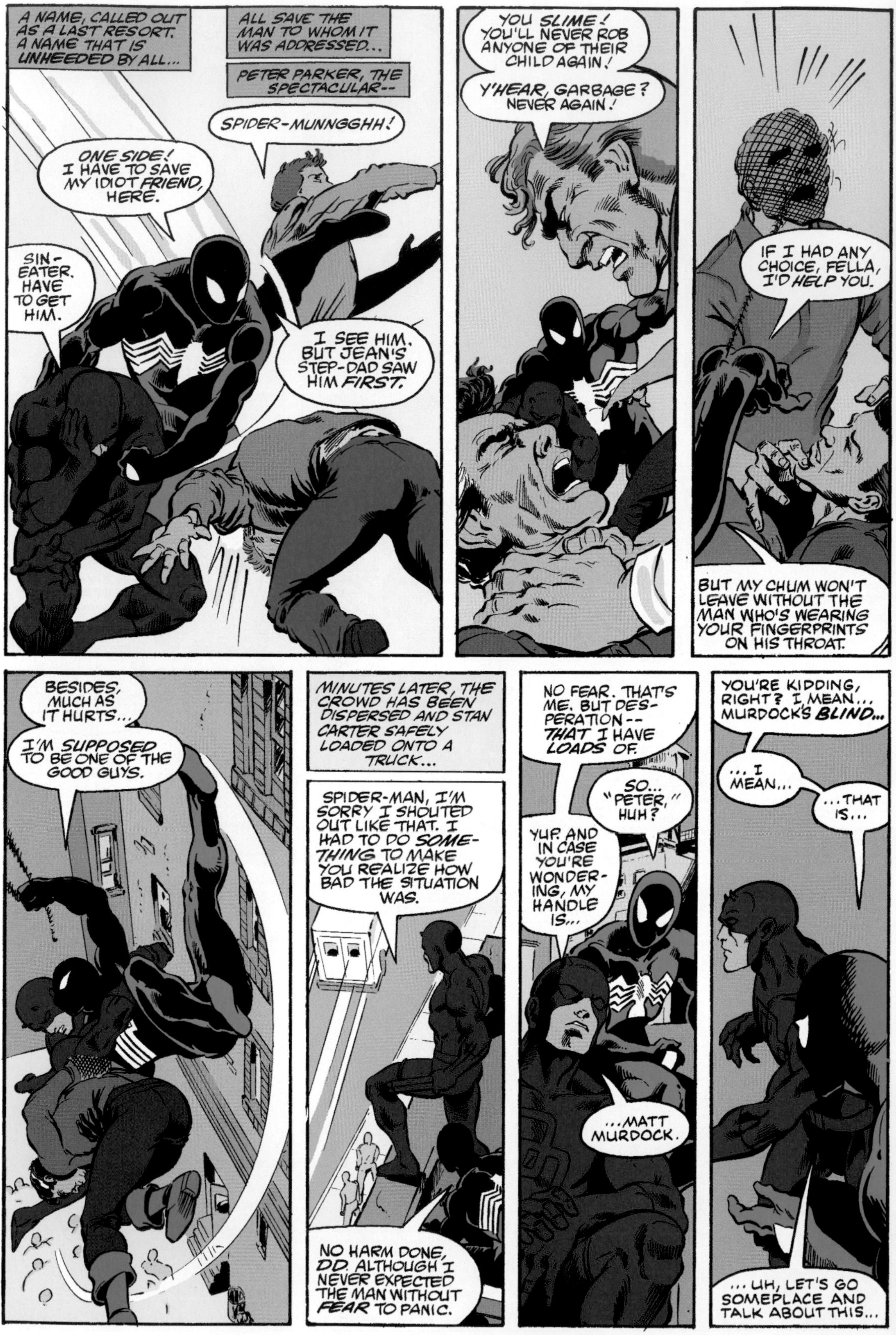
A NAME, CALLED OUT AS A LAST RESORT. A NAME THAT IS UNHEEDED BY ALL...
ALL SAVE THE MAN TO WHOM IT WAS ADDRESSED...
PETER PARKER, THE SPECTACULAR--
SPIDER-MUNNGGHH!
ONE SIDE! I HAVE TO SAVE MY IDIOT FRIEND, HERE.
SIN-EATER. HAVE TO GET HIM.
I SEE HIM. BUT JEAN'S STEP-DAD SAW HIM FIRST.
YOU SLIME! YOU'LL NEVER ROB ANYONE OF THEIR CHILD AGAIN!
Y'HEAR, GARBAGE? NEVER AGAIN!
IF I HAD ANY CHOICE, FELLA, I'D HELP YOU.
BUT MY CHUM WON'T LEAVE WITHOUT THE MAN WHO'S WEARING YOUR FINGERPRINTS ON HIS THROAT.
BESIDES, MUCH AS IT HURTS...
I'M SUPPOSED TO BE ONE OF THE GOOD GUYS.
MINUTES LATER, THE CROWD HAS BEEN DISPERSED AND STAN CARTER SAFELY LOADED ONTO A TRUCK...
SPIDER-MAN, I'M SORRY I SHOUTED OUT LIKE THAT. I HAD TO DO SOMETHING TO MAKE YOU REALIZE HOW BAD THE SITUATION WAS.
NO HARM DONE, DD. ALTHOUGH I NEVER EXPECTED THE MAN WITHOUT FEAR TO PANIC.
NO FEAR. THAT'S ME. BUT DESPERATION -- THAT I HAVE LOADS OF.
SO... "PETER," HUH?
YUP. AND IN CASE YOU'RE WONDERING, MY HANDLE IS...
...MATT MURDOCK.
YOU'RE KIDDING, RIGHT? I MEAN... MURDOCK'S BLIND...
... I MEAN...
...THAT IS...
...UH, LET'S GO SOMEPLACE AND TALK ABOUT THIS...

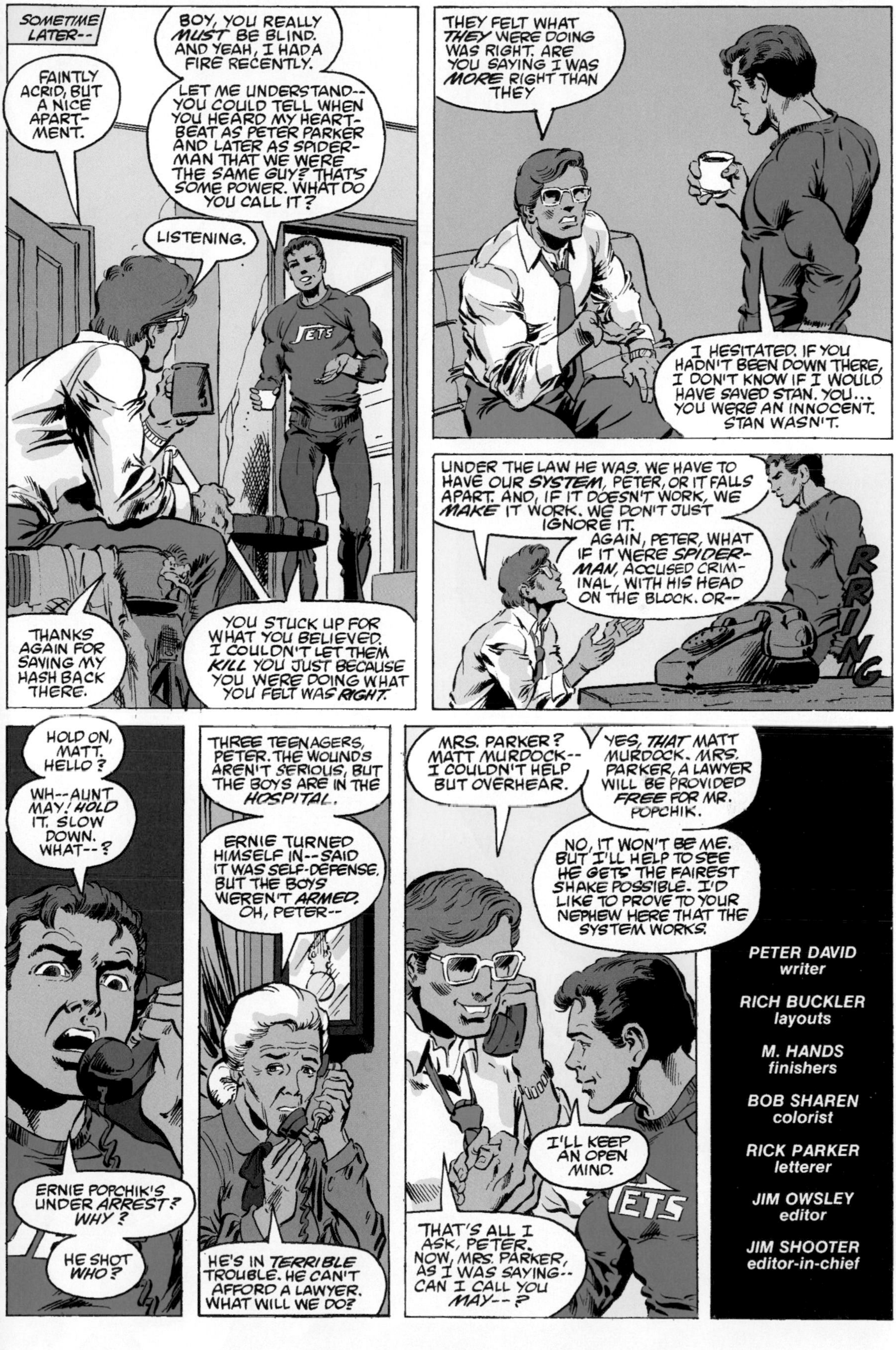
SOMETIME LATER--
FAINTLY ACRID, BUT A NICE APARTMENT.
BOY, YOU REALLY MUST BE BLIND. AND YEAH, I HAD A FIRE RECENTLY.
LET ME UNDERSTAND-- YOU COULD TELL WHEN YOU HEARD MY HEARTBEAT AS PETER PARKER AND LATER AS SPIDER-MAN THAT WE WERE THE SAME GUY? THAT'S SOME POWER. WHAT DO YOU CALL IT?
LISTENING.
THANKS AGAIN FOR SAVING MY HASH BACK THERE.
YOU STUCK UP FOR WHAT YOU BELIEVED. I COULDN'T LET THEM KILL YOU JUST BECAUSE YOU WERE DOING WHAT YOU FELT WAS RIGHT.
THEY FELT WHAT THEY WERE DOING WAS RIGHT. ARE YOU SAYING I WAS MORE RIGHT THAN THEY
I HESITATED. IF YOU HADN'T BEEN DOWN THERE, I DON'T KNOW IF I WOULD HAVE SAVED STAN. YOU... YOU WERE AN INNOCENT. STAN WASN'T.
UNDER THE LAW HE WAS. WE HAVE TO HAVE OUR SYSTEM, PETER, OR IT FALLS APART. AND, IF IT DOESN'T WORK, WE MAKE IT WORK. WE DON'T JUST IGNORE IT.
AGAIN, PETER, WHAT IF IT WERE SPIDER-MAN, ACCUSED CRIMINAL, WITH HIS HEAD ON THE BLOCK. OR--
RRING
HOLD ON, MATT. HELLO?
WH--AUNT MAY! HOLD IT. SLOW DOWN. WHAT--?
ERNIE POPCHIK'S UNDER ARREST? WHY?
HE SHOT WHO?
THREE TEENAGERS, PETER. THE WOUNDS AREN'T SERIOUS, BUT THE BOYS ARE IN THE HOSPITAL.
ERNIE TURNED HIMSELF IN--SAID IT WAS SELF-DEFENSE. BUT THE BOYS WEREN'T ARMED. OH, PETER--
HE'S IN TERRIBLE TROUBLE. HE CAN'T AFFORD A LAWYER. WHAT WILL WE DO?
MRS. PARKER? MATT MURDOCK-- I COULDN'T HELP BUT OVERHEAR.
YES, THAT MATT MURDOCK. MRS. PARKER, A LAWYER WILL BE PROVIDED FREE FOR MR. POPCHIK.
NO, IT WON'T BE ME. BUT I'LL HELP TO SEE HE GETS THE FAIREST SHAKE POSSIBLE. I'D LIKE TO PROVE TO YOUR NEPHEW HERE THAT THE SYSTEM WORKS.
I'LL KEEP AN OPEN MIND.
THAT'S ALL I ASK, PETER. NOW, MRS. PARKER, AS I WAS SAYING-- CAN I CALL YOU MAY--?
PETER DAVID writer
RICH BUCKLER layouts
M. HANDS finishers
BOB SHAREN colorist
RICK PARKER letterer
JIM OWSLEY editor
JIM SHOOTER editor-in-chief

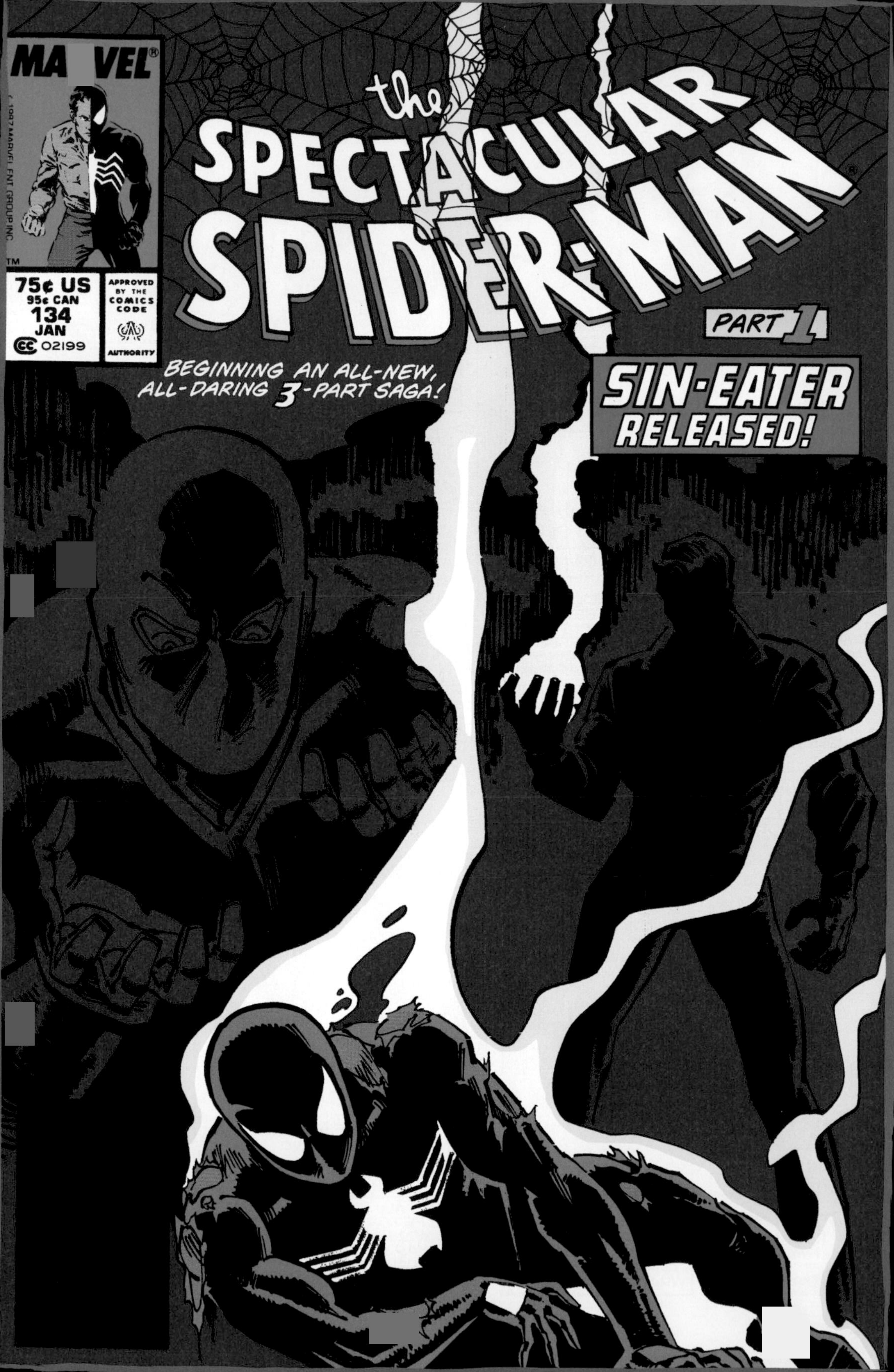

MA VEL
the SPECTACULAR SPIDER-MAN
75¢ US
95¢ CAN
134
JAN
02199
APPROVED BY THE COMICS CODE AUTHORITY
BEGINNING AN ALL-NEW, ALL-DARING 3-PART SAGA!
PART 1
SIN-EATER RELEASED!

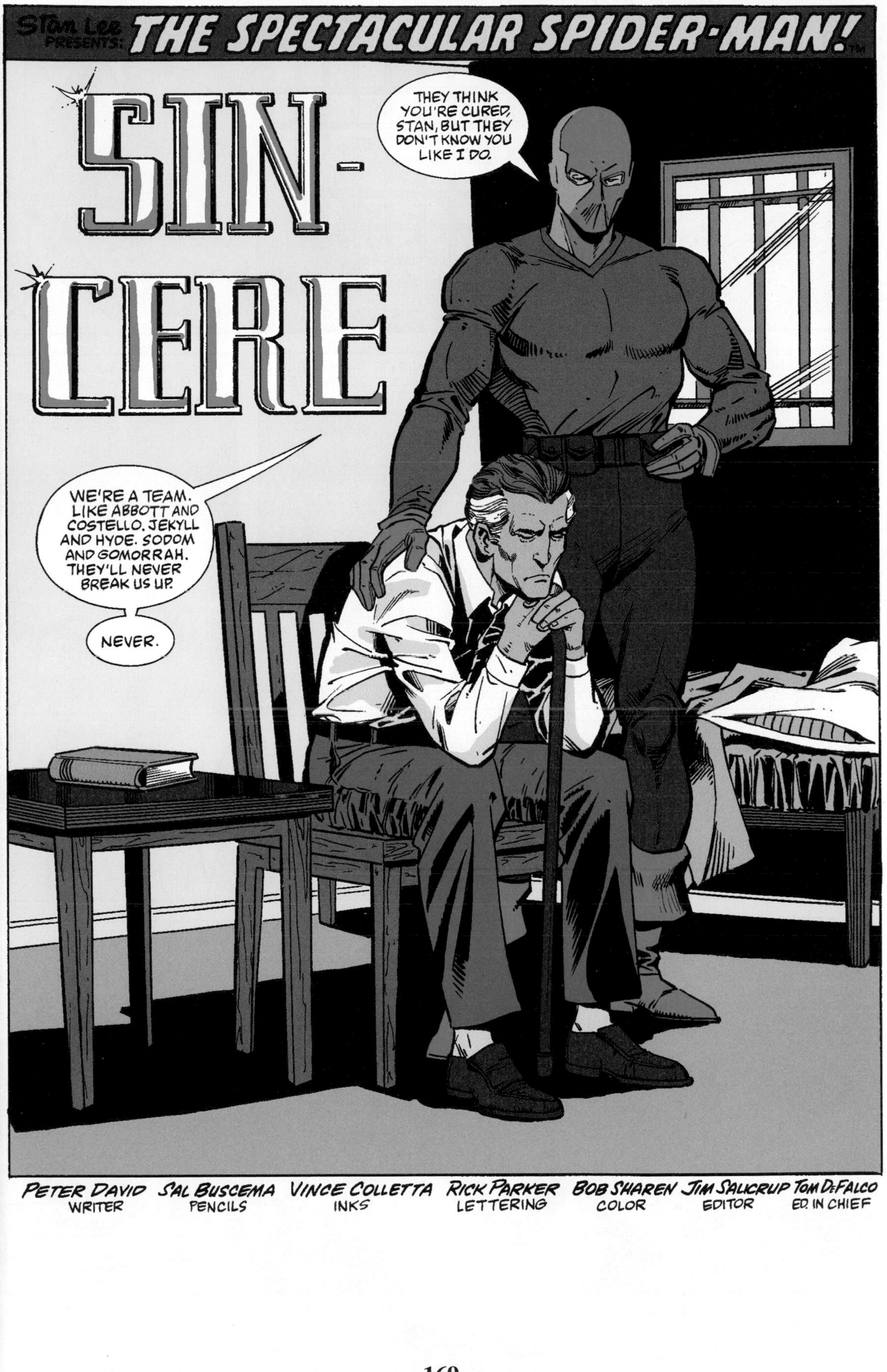
Stan Lee PRESENTS: THE SPECTACULAR SPIDER-MAN! TM
SIN-CERE
THEY THINK YOU'RE CURED, STAN, BUT THEY DON'T KNOW YOU LIKE I DO.
WE'RE A TEAM. LIKE ABBOTT AND COSTELLO. JEKYLL AND HYDE. SODOM AND GOMORRAH. THEY'LL NEVER BREAK US UP.
NEVER.
PETER DAVID WRITER
SAL BUSCEMA PENCILS
VINCE COLLETTA INKS
RICK PARKER LETTERING
BOB SHAREN COLOR
JIM SALICRUP EDITOR
TOM DEFALCO ED. IN CHIEF

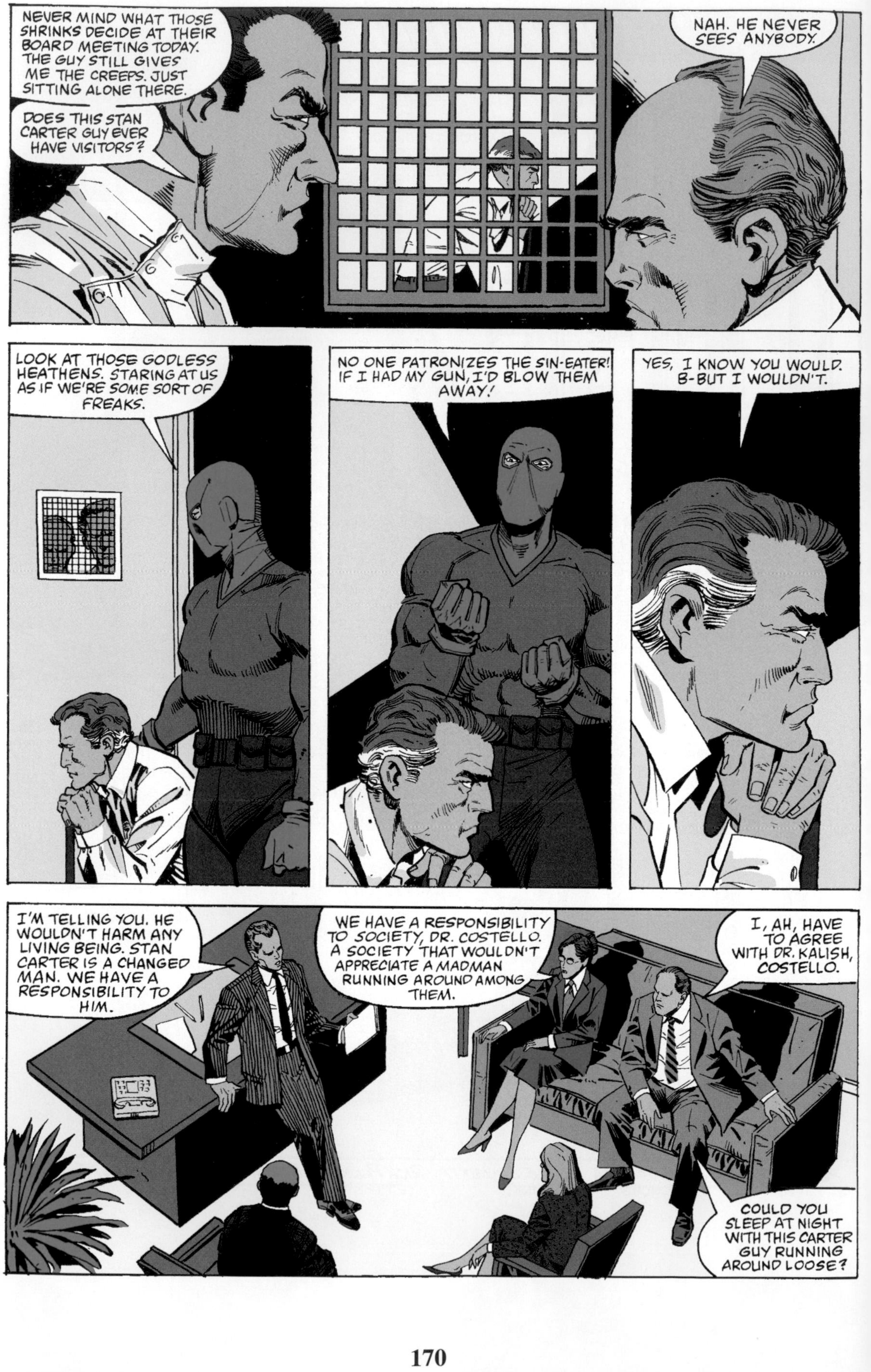

NEVER MIND WHAT THOSE SHRINKS DECIDE AT THEIR BOARD MEETING TODAY. THE GUY STILL GIVES ME THE CREEPS. JUST SITTING ALONE THERE.
DOES THIS STAN CARTER GUY EVER HAVE VISITORS?
NAH. HE NEVER SEES ANYBODY.
LOOK AT THOSE GODLESS HEATHENS. STARING AT US AS IF WE'RE SOME SORT OF FREAKS.
NO ONE PATRONIZES THE SIN-EATER! IF I HAD MY GUN, I'D BLOW THEM AWAY!
YES, I KNOW YOU WOULD. B-BUT I WOULDN'T.
I'M TELLING YOU. HE WOULDN'T HARM ANY LIVING BEING. STAN CARTER IS A CHANGED MAN. WE HAVE A RESPONSIBILITY TO HIM.
WE HAVE A RESPONSIBILITY TO SOCIETY, DR. COSTELLO. A SOCIETY THAT WOULDN'T APPRECIATE A MADMAN RUNNING AROUND AMONG THEM.
I, AH, HAVE TO AGREE WITH DR. KALISH, COSTELLO.
COULD YOU SLEEP AT NIGHT WITH THIS CARTER GUY RUNNING AROUND LOOSE?

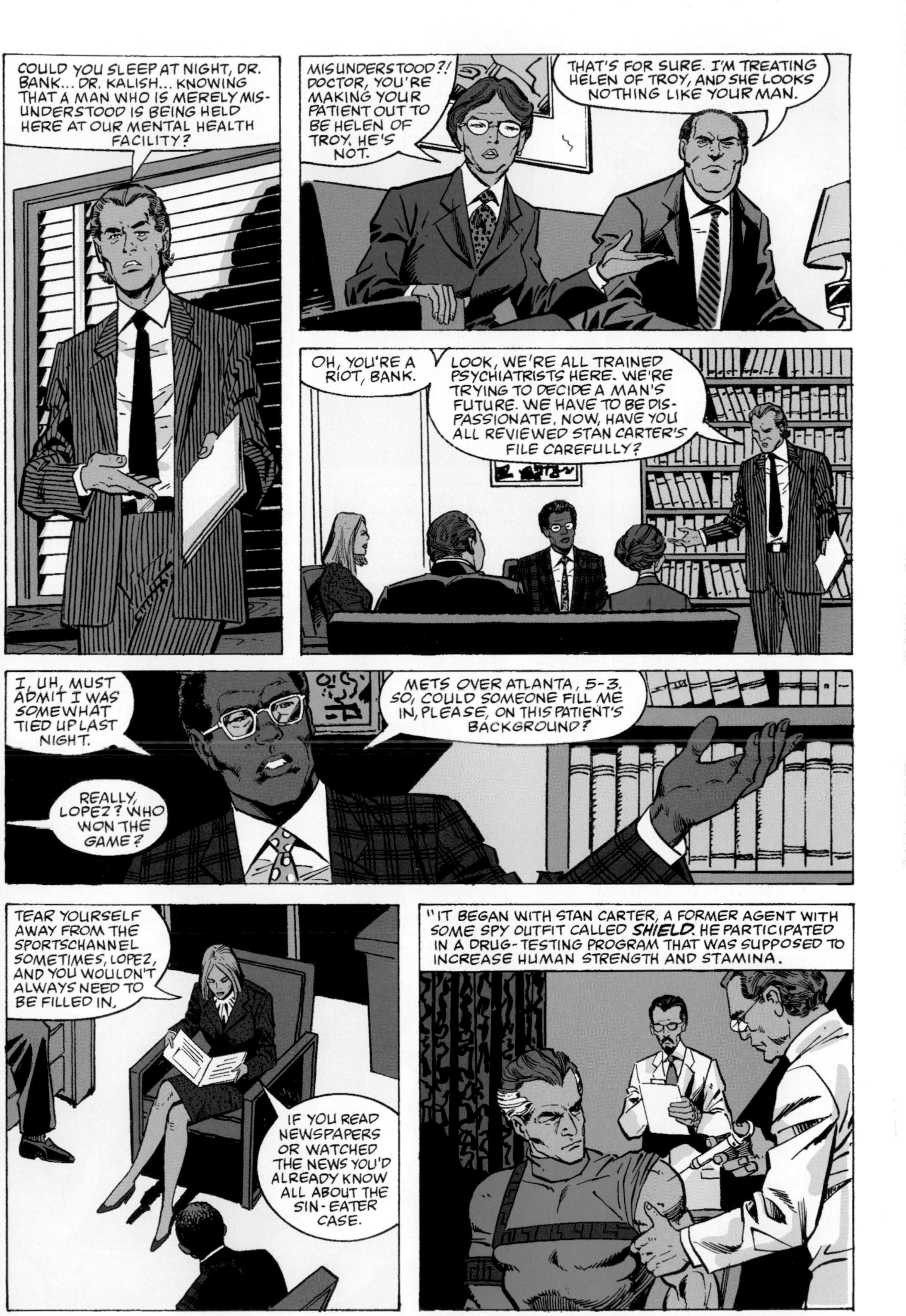

COULD YOU SLEEP AT NIGHT, DR. BANK... DR. KALISH... KNOWING THAT A MAN WHO IS MERELY MIS-UNDERSTOOD IS BEING HELD HERE AT OUR MENTAL HEALTH FACILITY?
MISUNDERSTOOD?! DOCTOR, YOU'RE MAKING YOUR PATIENT OUT TO BE HELEN OF TROY. HE'S NOT.
THAT'S FOR SURE. I'M TREATING HELEN OF TROY, AND SHE LOOKS NOTHING LIKE YOUR MAN.
OH, YOU'RE A RIOT, BANK.
LOOK, WE'RE ALL TRAINED PSYCHIATRISTS HERE. WE'RE TRYING TO DECIDE A MAN'S FUTURE. WE HAVE TO BE DIS-PASSIONATE. NOW, HAVE YOU ALL REVIEWED STAN CARTER'S FILE CAREFULLY?
I, UH, MUST ADMIT I WAS SOMEWHAT TIED UP LAST NIGHT.
REALLY, LOPEZ? WHO WON THE GAME?
METS OVER ATLANTA, 5-3. SO, COULD SOMEONE FILL ME IN, PLEASE, ON THIS PATIENT'S BACKGROUND?
TEAR YOURSELF AWAY FROM THE SPORTSCHANNEL SOMETIMES, LOPEZ, AND YOU WOULDN'T ALWAYS NEED TO BE FILLED IN.
IF YOU READ NEWSPAPERS OR WATCHED THE NEWS YOU'D ALREADY KNOW ALL ABOUT THE SIN-EATER CASE.
"IT BEGAN WITH STAN CARTER, A FORMER AGENT WITH SOME SPY OUTFIT CALLED SHIELD. HE PARTICIPATED IN A DRUG-TESTING PROGRAM THAT WAS SUPPOSED TO INCREASE HUMAN STRENGTH AND STAMINA.

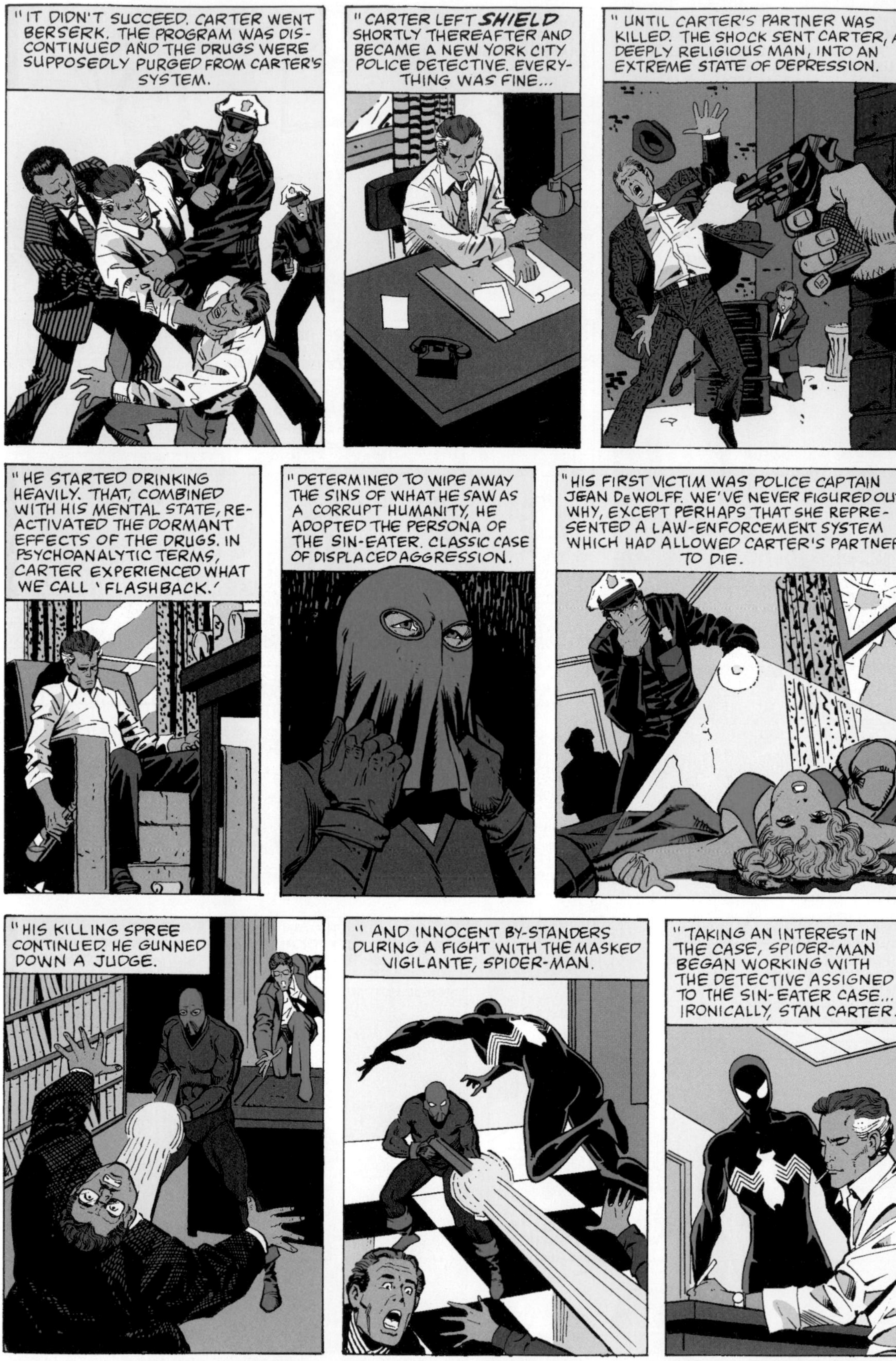
"IT DIDN'T SUCCEED. CARTER WENT BERSERK. THE PROGRAM WAS DIS-CONTINUED AND THE DRUGS WERE SUPPOSEDLY PURGED FROM CARTER'S SYSTEM.
"CARTER LEFT SHIELD SHORTLY THEREAFTER AND BECAME A NEW YORK CITY POLICE DETECTIVE. EVERY-THING WAS FINE...
"UNTIL CARTER'S PARTNER WAS KILLED. THE SHOCK SENT CARTER, A DEEPLY RELIGIOUS MAN, INTO AN EXTREME STATE OF DEPRESSION.
"HE STARTED DRINKING HEAVILY. THAT, COMBINED WITH HIS MENTAL STATE, RE-ACTIVATED THE DORMANT EFFECTS OF THE DRUGS. IN PSYCHOANALYTIC TERMS, CARTER EXPERIENCED WHAT WE CALL 'FLASHBACK.'
"DETERMINED TO WIPE AWAY THE SINS OF WHAT HE SAW AS A CORRUPT HUMANITY, HE ADOPTED THE PERSONA OF THE SIN-EATER. CLASSIC CASE OF DISPLACED AGGRESSION.
"HIS FIRST VICTIM WAS POLICE CAPTAIN JEAN DeWOLFF. WE'VE NEVER FIGURED OUT WHY, EXCEPT PERHAPS THAT SHE REPRE-SENTED A LAW-ENFORCEMENT SYSTEM WHICH HAD ALLOWED CARTER'S PARTNER TO DIE.
"HIS KILLING SPREE CONTINUED. HE GUNNED DOWN A JUDGE.
" AND INNOCENT BY-STANDERS DURING A FIGHT WITH THE MASKED VIGILANTE, SPIDER-MAN.
"TAKING AN INTEREST IN THE CASE, SPIDER-MAN BEGAN WORKING WITH THE DETECTIVE ASSIGNED TO THE SIN-EATER CASE... IRONICALLY, STAN CARTER.

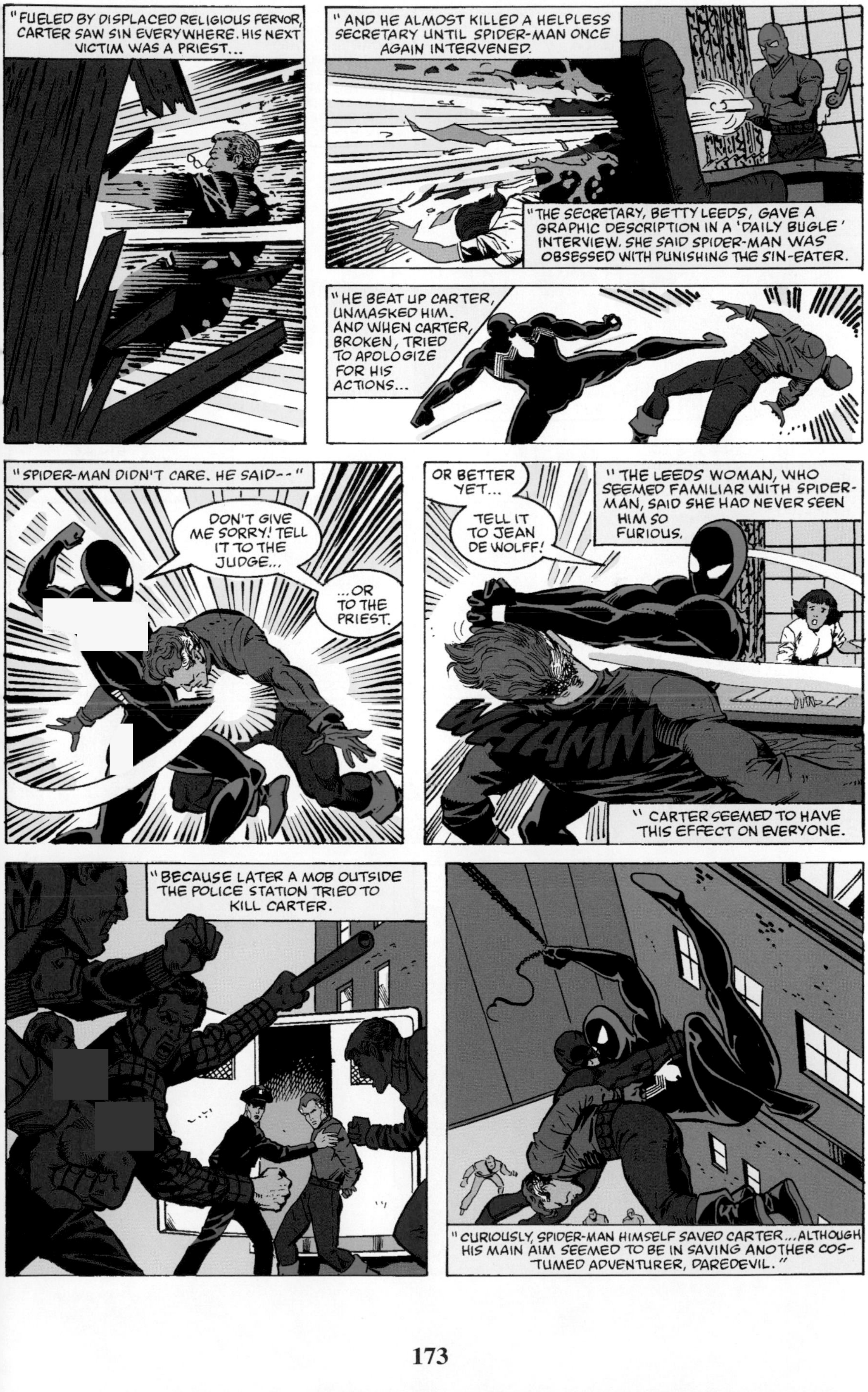
"FUELED BY DISPLACED RELIGIOUS FERVOR, CARTER SAW SIN EVERYWHERE. HIS NEXT VICTIM WAS A PRIEST...
"AND HE ALMOST KILLED A HELPLESS SECRETARY UNTIL SPIDER-MAN ONCE AGAIN INTERVENED.
"THE SECRETARY, BETTY LEEDS, GAVE A GRAPHIC DESCRIPTION IN A 'DAILY BUGLE' INTERVIEW. SHE SAID SPIDER-MAN WAS OBSESSED WITH PUNISHING THE SIN-EATER.
"HE BEAT UP CARTER, UNMASKED HIM. AND WHEN CARTER, BROKEN, TRIED TO APOLOGIZE FOR HIS ACTIONS...
"SPIDER-MAN DIDN'T CARE. HE SAID--"
DON'T GIVE ME SORRY! TELL IT TO THE JUDGE...
...OR TO THE PRIEST.
OR BETTER YET...
TELL IT TO JEAN DE WOLFF!
"THE LEEDS WOMAN, WHO SEEMED FAMILIAR WITH SPIDER-MAN, SAID SHE HAD NEVER SEEN HIM SO FURIOUS.
WHAMM
"CARTER SEEMED TO HAVE THIS EFFECT ON EVERYONE.
"BECAUSE LATER A MOB OUTSIDE THE POLICE STATION TRIED TO KILL CARTER.
"CURIOUSLY, SPIDER-MAN HIMSELF SAVED CARTER... ALTHOUGH HIS MAIN AIM SEEMED TO BE IN SAVING ANOTHER COSTUMED ADVENTURER, DAREDEVIL."

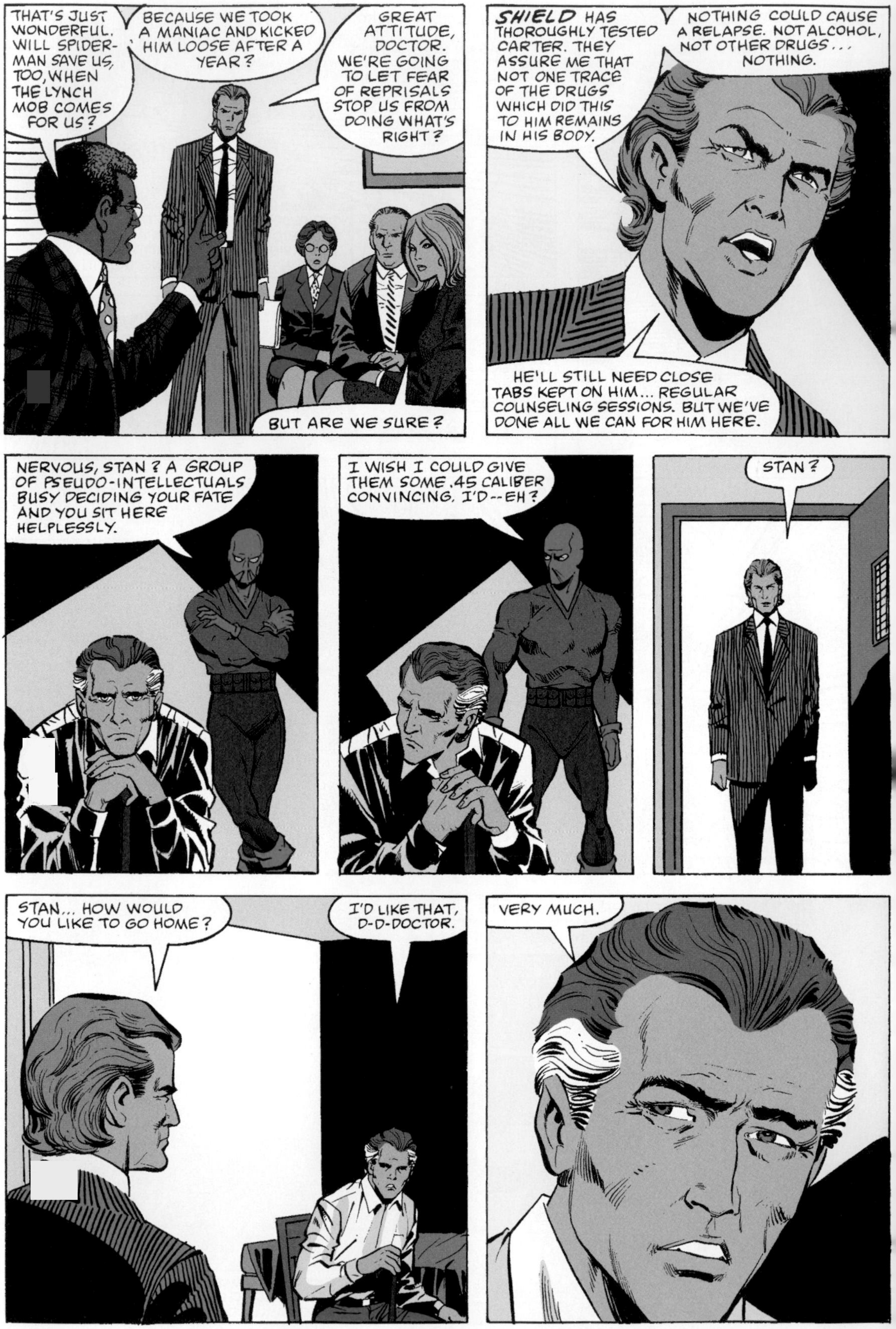

THAT'S JUST WONDERFUL. WILL SPIDER-MAN SAVE US, TOO, WHEN THE LYNCH MOB COMES FOR US?
BECAUSE WE TOOK A MANIAC AND KICKED HIM LOOSE AFTER A YEAR?
GREAT ATTITUDE, DOCTOR. WE'RE GOING TO LET FEAR OF REPRISALS STOP US FROM DOING WHAT'S RIGHT?
BUT ARE WE SURE?
SHIELD HAS THOROUGHLY TESTED CARTER. THEY ASSURE ME THAT NOT ONE TRACE OF THE DRUGS WHICH DID THIS TO HIM REMAINS IN HIS BODY.
NOTHING COULD CAUSE A RELAPSE. NOT ALCOHOL, NOT OTHER DRUGS... NOTHING.
HE'LL STILL NEED CLOSE TABS KEPT ON HIM... REGULAR COUNSELING SESSIONS. BUT WE'VE DONE ALL WE CAN FOR HIM HERE.
NERVOUS, STAN? A GROUP OF PSEUDO-INTELLECTUALS BUSY DECIDING YOUR FATE AND YOU SIT HERE HELPLESSLY.
I WISH I COULD GIVE THEM SOME .45 CALIBER CONVINCING. I'D--EH?
STAN?
STAN... HOW WOULD YOU LIKE TO GO HOME?
I'D LIKE THAT, D-D-DOCTOR.
VERY MUCH.

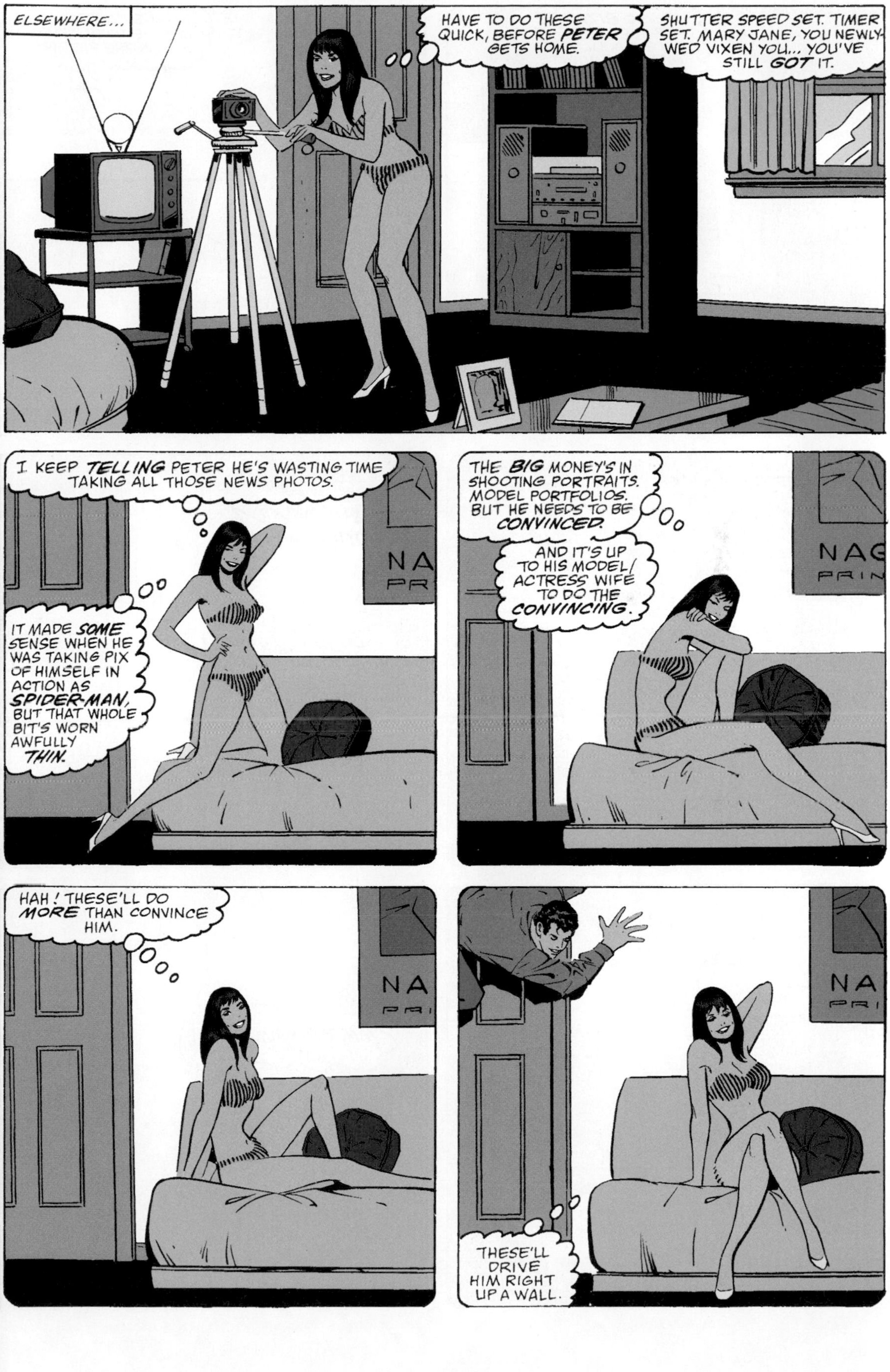
ELSEWHERE...
HAVE TO DO THESE QUICK, BEFORE PETER GETS HOME.
SHUTTER SPEED SET. TIMER SET. MARY JANE, YOU NEWLY-WED VIXEN YOU... YOU'VE STILL GOT IT.
I KEEP TELLING PETER HE'S WASTING TIME TAKING ALL THOSE NEWS PHOTOS.
IT MADE SOME SENSE WHEN HE WAS TAKING PIX OF HIMSELF IN ACTION AS SPIDER-MAN, BUT THAT WHOLE BIT'S WORN AWFULLY THIN.
THE BIG MONEY'S IN SHOOTING PORTRAITS. MODEL PORTFOLIOS. BUT HE NEEDS TO BE CONVINCED.
AND IT'S UP TO HIS MODEL/ ACTRESS WIFE TO DO THE CONVINCING.
HAH! THESE'LL DO MORE THAN CONVINCE HIM.
THESE'LL DRIVE HIM RIGHT UP A WALL.

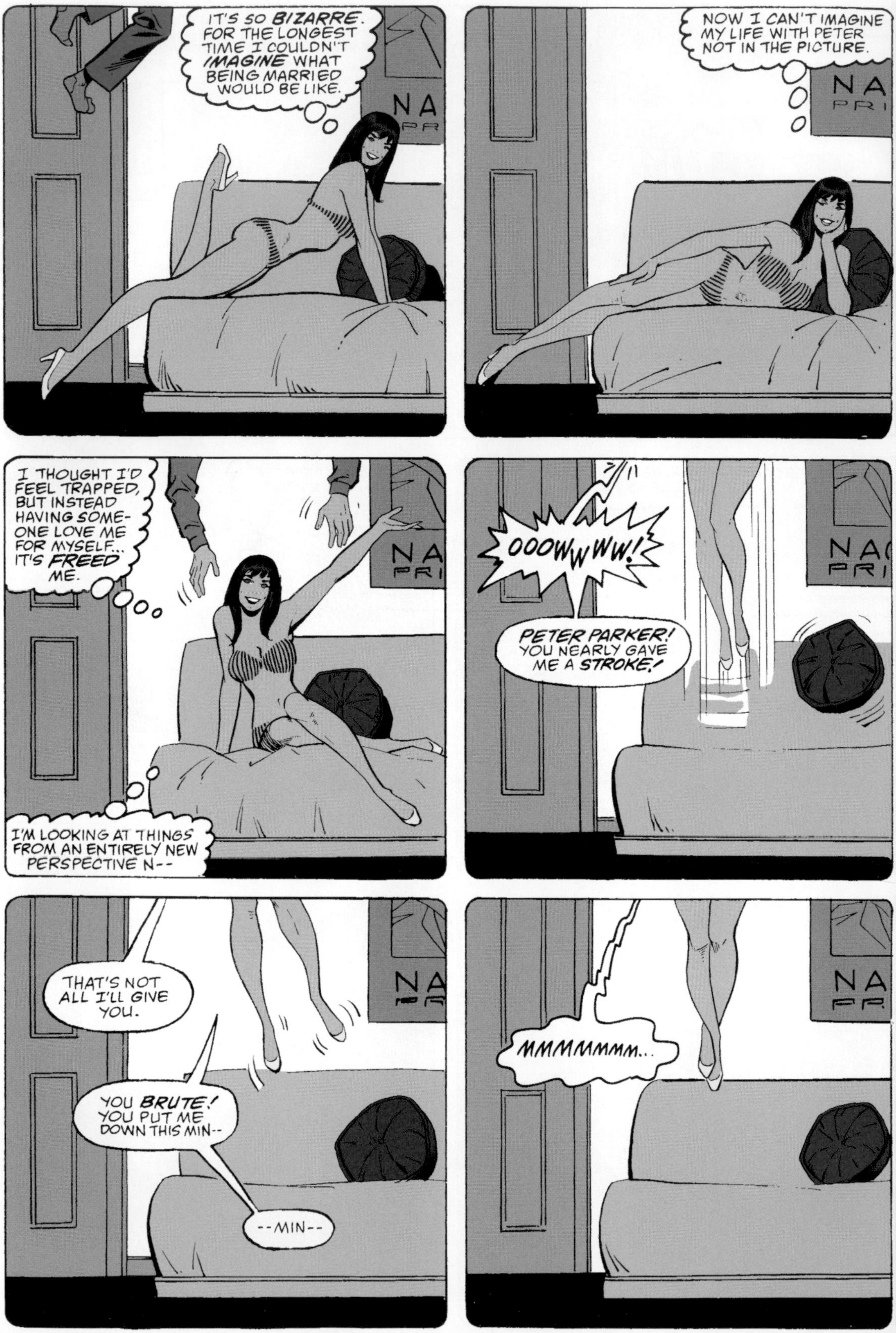
IT'S SO BIZARRE. FOR THE LONGEST TIME I COULDN'T IMAGINE WHAT BEING MARRIED WOULD BE LIKE.
NOW I CAN'T IMAGINE MY LIFE WITH PETER NOT IN THE PICTURE.
I THOUGHT I'D FEEL TRAPPED, BUT INSTEAD HAVING SOME-ONE LOVE ME FOR MYSELF... IT'S FREED ME.
I'M LOOKING AT THINGS FROM AN ENTIRELY NEW PERSPECTIVE N--
OOOWWWW!
PETER PARKER! YOU NEARLY GAVE ME A STROKE!
THAT'S NOT ALL I'LL GIVE YOU.
YOU BRUTE! YOU PUT ME DOWN THIS MIN--
--MIN--
MMMMMMM...

MEANWHILE...

THEY THOUGHT THEY COULD HOLD ME. THE IDIOTS. *NO ONE* HOLDS MAX DILLON.

EVER SINCE THE FREAK ACCIDENT THAT GAVE ME CONTROL OVER ELECTRICITY, I'VE CALLED ALL THE SHOTS.

AW, CRIPES. WHO AM I *KIDDING?* EVERY TIME I PUT ON THAT STUPID YELLOW AND GREEN COSTUME OF MINE, EVERY TIME I BECOME *ELECTRO...*

" ... SPIDER-MAN CLEANS MY CLOCK.

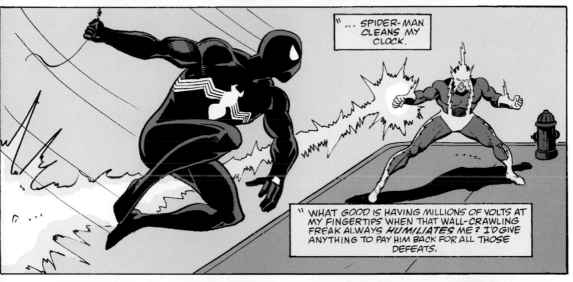

" WHAT *GOOD* IS HAVING MILLIONS OF VOLTS AT MY FINGERTIPS WHEN THAT WALL-CRAWLING FREAK ALWAYS *HUMILIATES* ME? I'D GIVE ANYTHING TO PAY HIM BACK FOR ALL THOSE DEFEATS.

IF I HAD HIM AT MY MERCY I WOULDN'T KILL HIM. THAT WOULD BE TOO *QUICK.* HE'D HAVE TO SUFFER...

BUT WHY *THINK* ABOUT IT? I'M GETTING SOME QUICK BUCKS AND GETTING OUT OF TOWN.

CROWN JEWELERS

AND SINCE MY COSTUME ALWAYS BRINGS SPIDER-MAN OR THOSE SUPER-TYPES RUNNING, THIS TIME, I'LL BE... *SUBTLE.*

MAY I *HELP* YOU, SIR?

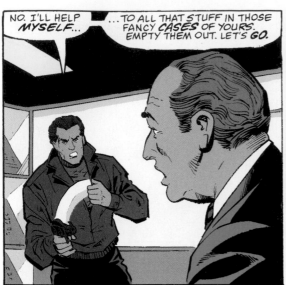

NO. I'LL HELP *MYSELF*...

...TO ALL THAT STUFF IN THOSE FANCY *CASES* OF YOURS. EMPTY THEM OUT. LET'S *GO*.

OH, COME *ON*, SIR. THIS IS A RESPECTABLE ESTABLISHMENT. YOU COULD AT *LEAST* USE A RESPECTABLE WEAPON.

ZZAP!

HE WAS HALF-RIGHT. THE GUN'S HARMLESS. BUT THE ELECTRICITY I'M FUNNELING THROUGH IT ISN'T.

OH, MY LORD! *MYRON!*

KUD

MYRON MADE JOKES. YOU GONNA MAKE JOKES, TOO?

NO, SIR.

MOVE FASTER.

YES, SIR.

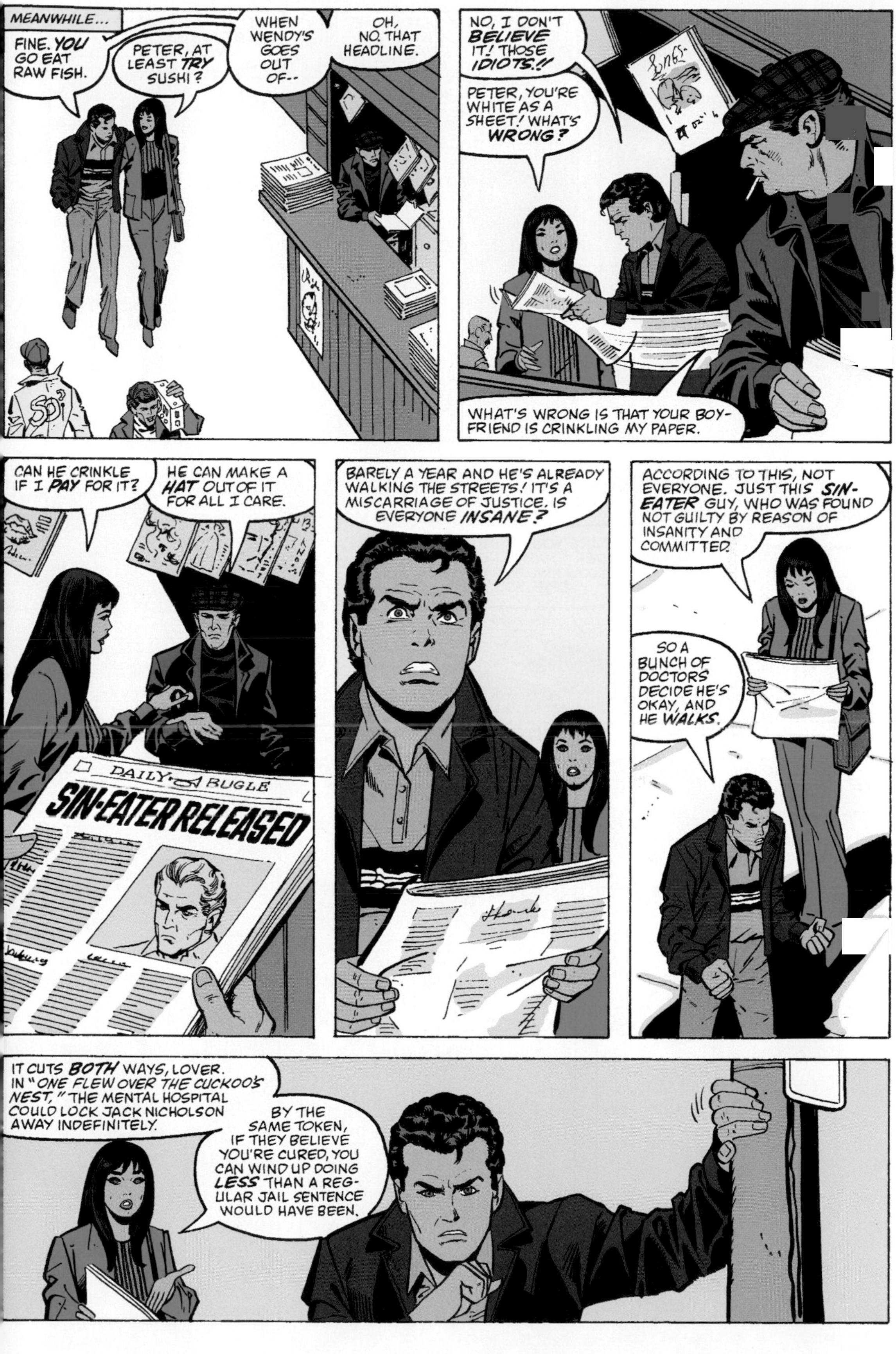
MEANWHILE...
FINE. YOU GO EAT RAW FISH.
PETER, AT LEAST TRY SUSHI?
WHEN WENDY'S GOES OUT OF--
OH, NO. THAT HEADLINE.
NO, I DON'T BELIEVE IT! THOSE IDIOTS!!
PETER, YOU'RE WHITE AS A SHEET! WHAT'S WRONG?
WHAT'S WRONG IS THAT YOUR BOY-FRIEND IS CRINKLING MY PAPER.
CAN HE CRINKLE IF I PAY FOR IT?
HE CAN MAKE A HAT OUT OF IT FOR ALL I CARE.
DAILY BUGLE
SIN-EATER RELEASED
BARELY A YEAR AND HE'S ALREADY WALKING THE STREETS! IT'S A MISCARRIAGE OF JUSTICE. IS EVERYONE INSANE?
ACCORDING TO THIS, NOT EVERYONE. JUST THIS SIN-EATER GUY, WHO WAS FOUND NOT GUILTY BY REASON OF INSANITY AND COMMITTED.
SO A BUNCH OF DOCTORS DECIDE HE'S OKAY, AND HE WALKS.
IT CUTS BOTH WAYS, LOVER. IN "ONE FLEW OVER THE CUCKOO'S NEST," THE MENTAL HOSPITAL COULD LOCK JACK NICHOLSON AWAY INDEFINITELY.
BY THE SAME TOKEN, IF THEY BELIEVE YOU'RE CURED, YOU CAN WIND UP DOING LESS THAN A REG-ULAR JAIL SENTENCE WOULD HAVE BEEN.

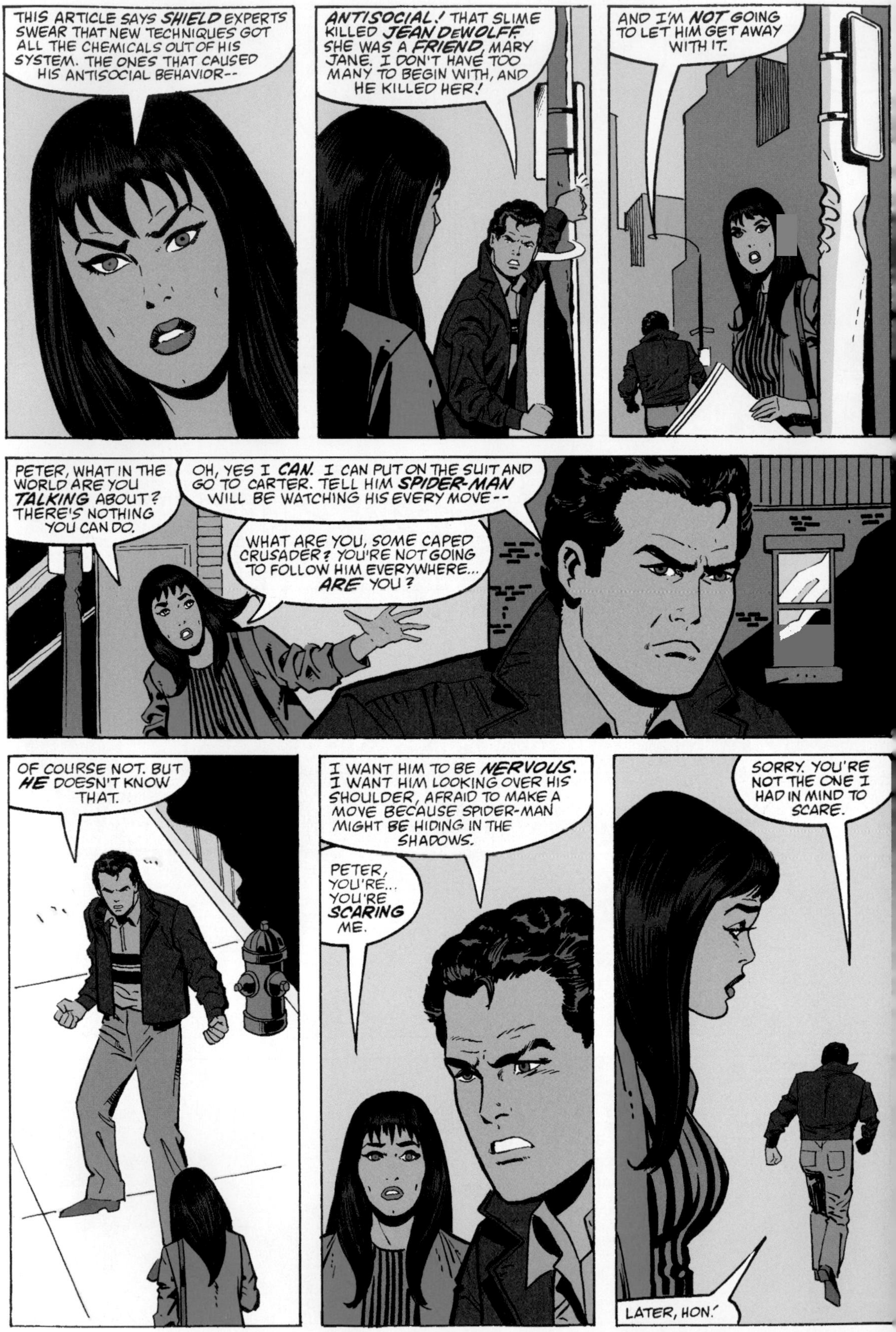
THIS ARTICLE SAYS SHIELD EXPERTS SWEAR THAT NEW TECHNIQUES GOT ALL THE CHEMICALS OUT OF HIS SYSTEM. THE ONES THAT CAUSED HIS ANTISOCIAL BEHAVIOR--
ANTISOCIAL! THAT SLIME KILLED JEAN DeWOLFF. SHE WAS A FRIEND, MARY JANE. I DON'T HAVE TOO MANY TO BEGIN WITH, AND HE KILLED HER!
AND I'M NOT GOING TO LET HIM GET AWAY WITH IT.
PETER, WHAT IN THE WORLD ARE YOU TALKING ABOUT? THERE'S NOTHING YOU CAN DO.
OH, YES I CAN. I CAN PUT ON THE SUIT AND GO TO CARTER. TELL HIM SPIDER-MAN WILL BE WATCHING HIS EVERY MOVE--
WHAT ARE YOU, SOME CAPED CRUSADER? YOU'RE NOT GOING TO FOLLOW HIM EVERYWHERE... ARE YOU?
OF COURSE NOT. BUT HE DOESN'T KNOW THAT.
I WANT HIM TO BE NERVOUS. I WANT HIM LOOKING OVER HIS SHOULDER, AFRAID TO MAKE A MOVE BECAUSE SPIDER-MAN MIGHT BE HIDING IN THE SHADOWS.
PETER, YOU'RE... YOU'RE SCARING ME.
SORRY. YOU'RE NOT THE ONE I HAD IN MIND TO SCARE.
LATER, HON.

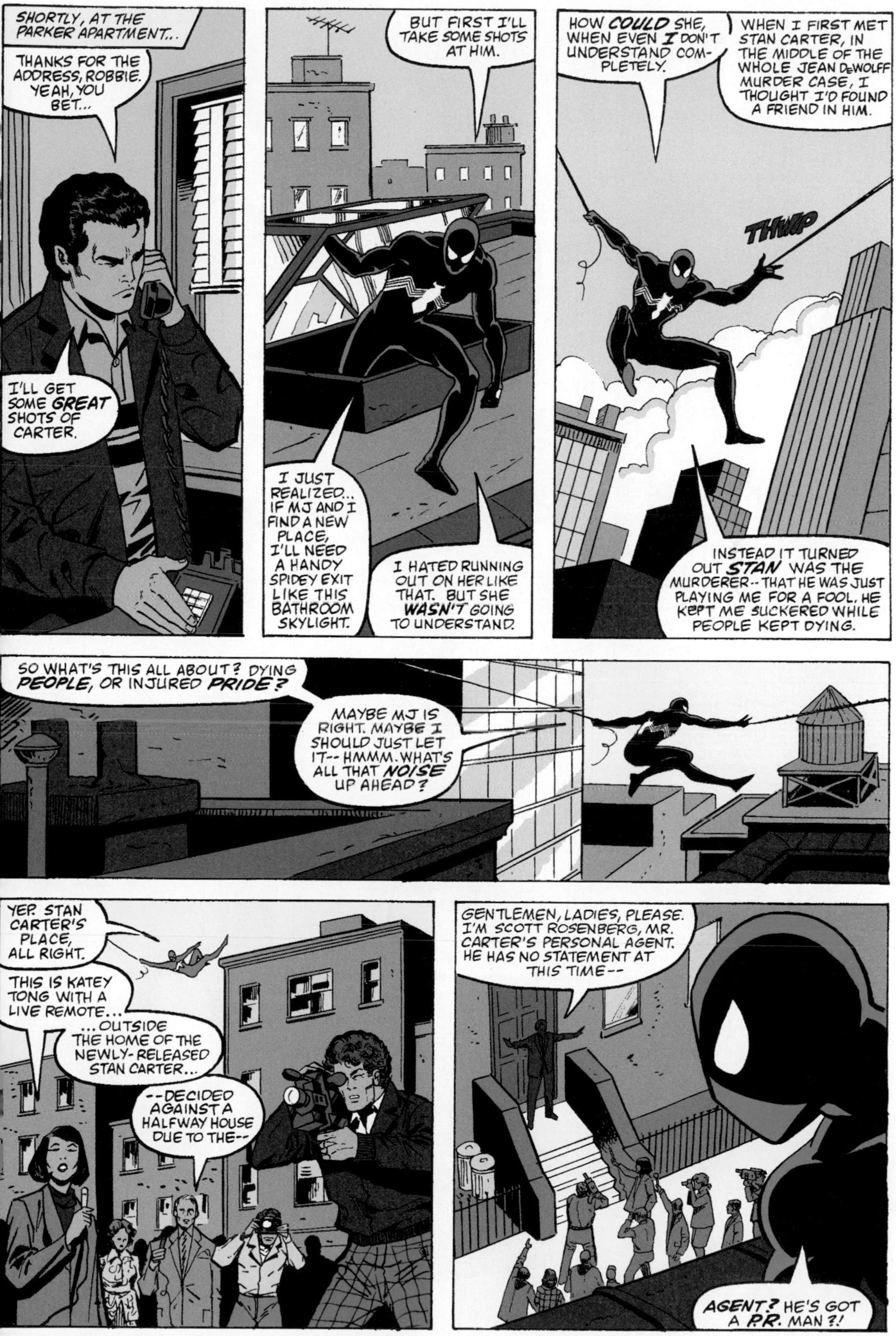
SHORTLY, AT THE PARKER APARTMENT...
THANKS FOR THE ADDRESS, ROBBIE. YEAH, YOU BET...
I'LL GET SOME GREAT SHOTS OF CARTER.
BUT FIRST I'LL TAKE SOME SHOTS AT HIM.
I JUST REALIZED... IF MJ AND I FIND A NEW PLACE, I'LL NEED A HANDY SPIDEY EXIT LIKE THIS BATHROOM SKYLIGHT.
I HATED RUNNING OUT ON HER LIKE THAT. BUT SHE WASN'T GOING TO UNDERSTAND.
HOW COULD SHE, WHEN EVEN I DON'T UNDERSTAND COMPLETELY.
WHEN I FIRST MET STAN CARTER, IN THE MIDDLE OF THE WHOLE JEAN DEWOLFF MURDER CASE, I THOUGHT I'D FOUND A FRIEND IN HIM.
THWIP
INSTEAD IT TURNED OUT STAN WAS THE MURDERER -- THAT HE WAS JUST PLAYING ME FOR A FOOL. HE KEPT ME SUCKERED WHILE PEOPLE KEPT DYING.
SO WHAT'S THIS ALL ABOUT? DYING PEOPLE, OR INJURED PRIDE?
MAYBE MJ IS RIGHT. MAYBE I SHOULD JUST LET IT-- HMMM. WHAT'S ALL THAT NOISE UP AHEAD?
YEP. STAN CARTER'S PLACE, ALL RIGHT.
THIS IS KATEY TONG WITH A LIVE REMOTE...
...OUTSIDE THE HOME OF THE NEWLY-RELEASED STAN CARTER...
--DECIDED AGAINST A HALFWAY HOUSE DUE TO THE--
GENTLEMEN, LADIES, PLEASE. I'M SCOTT ROSENBERG, MR. CARTER'S PERSONAL AGENT. HE HAS NO STATEMENT AT THIS TIME--
AGENT? HE'S GOT A P.R. MAN?!

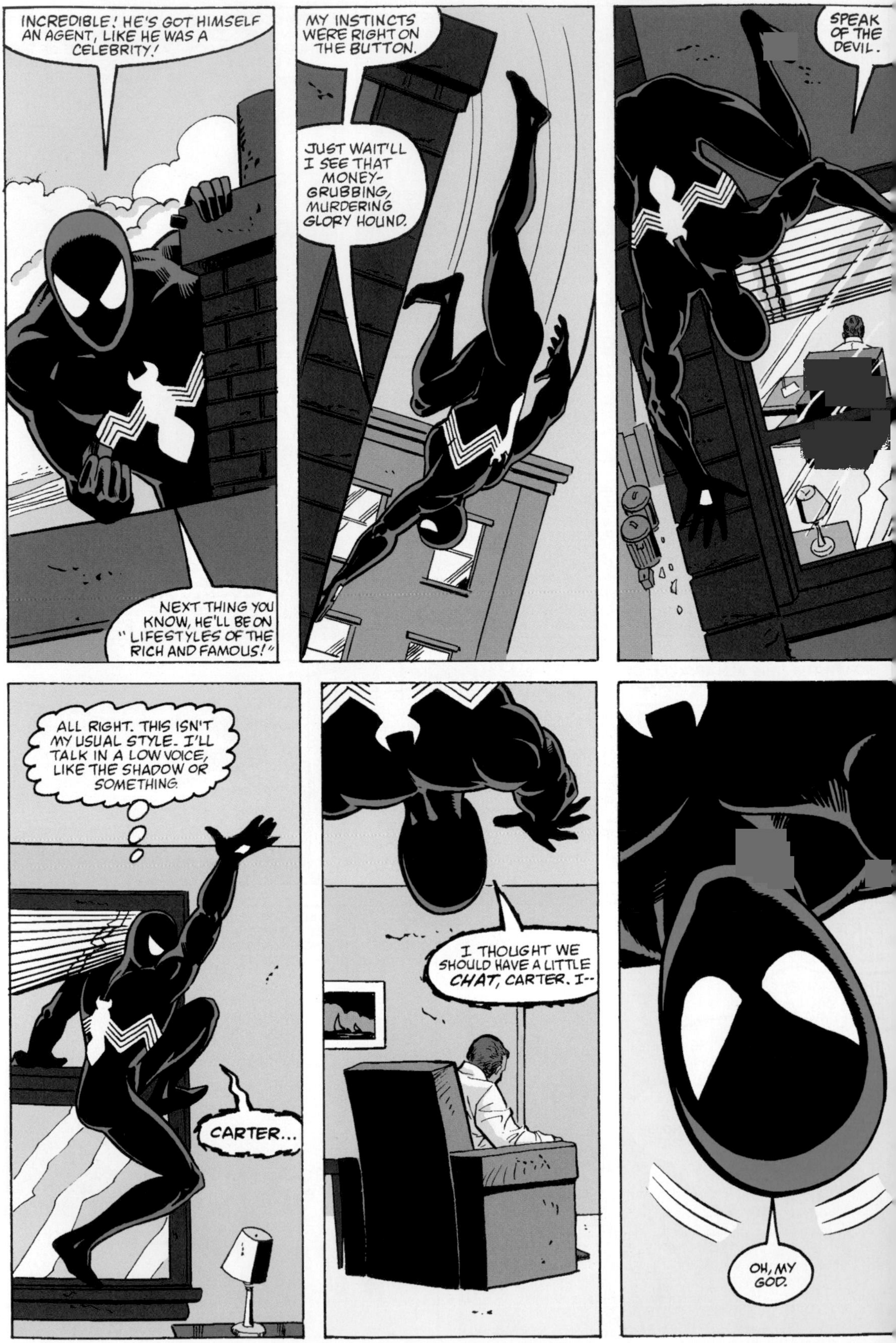

INCREDIBLE! HE'S GOT HIMSELF AN AGENT, LIKE HE WAS A CELEBRITY!
NEXT THING YOU KNOW, HE'LL BE ON "LIFESTYLES OF THE RICH AND FAMOUS!"
MY INSTINCTS WERE RIGHT ON THE BUTTON.
JUST WAIT'LL I SEE THAT MONEY-GRUBBING, MURDERING GLORY HOUND.
SPEAK OF THE DEVIL.
ALL RIGHT. THIS ISN'T MY USUAL STYLE. I'LL TALK IN A LOW VOICE, LIKE THE SHADOW OR SOMETHING.
CARTER...
I THOUGHT WE SHOULD HAVE A LITTLE CHAT, CARTER. I--
OH, MY GOD.

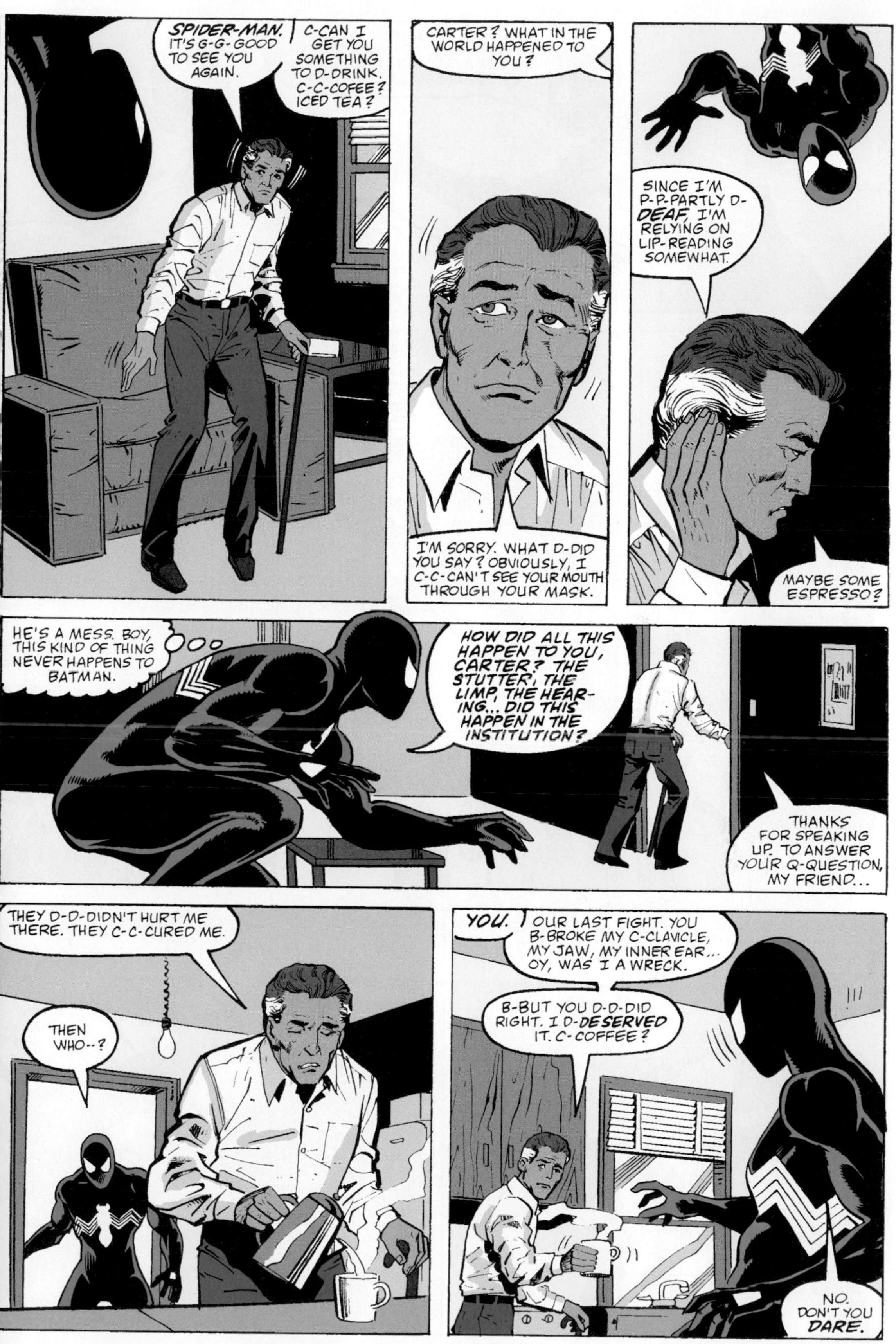
SPIDER-MAN. IT'S G-G-GOOD TO SEE YOU AGAIN.
C-CAN I GET YOU SOMETHING TO D-DRINK. C-C-COFFEE? ICED TEA?
CARTER? WHAT IN THE WORLD HAPPENED TO YOU?
I'M SORRY. WHAT D-DID YOU SAY? OBVIOUSLY, I C-C-CAN'T SEE YOUR MOUTH THROUGH YOUR MASK.
SINCE I'M P-P-PARTLY D-DEAF, I'M RELYING ON LIP-READING SOMEWHAT.
MAYBE SOME ESPRESSO?
HE'S A MESS. BOY, THIS KIND OF THING NEVER HAPPENS TO BATMAN.
HOW DID ALL THIS HAPPEN TO YOU, CARTER? THE STUTTER, THE LIMP, THE HEARING... DID THIS HAPPEN IN THE INSTITUTION?
THANKS FOR SPEAKING UP. TO ANSWER YOUR Q-QUESTION, MY FRIEND...
THEY D-D-DIDN'T HURT ME THERE. THEY C-C-CURED ME.
THEN WHO--?
YOU.
OUR LAST FIGHT. YOU B-BROKE MY C-CLAVICLE, MY JAW, MY INNER EAR... OY, WAS I A WRECK.
B-BUT YOU D-D-DID RIGHT. I D-DESERVED IT. C-COFFEE?
NO. DON'T YOU DARE.

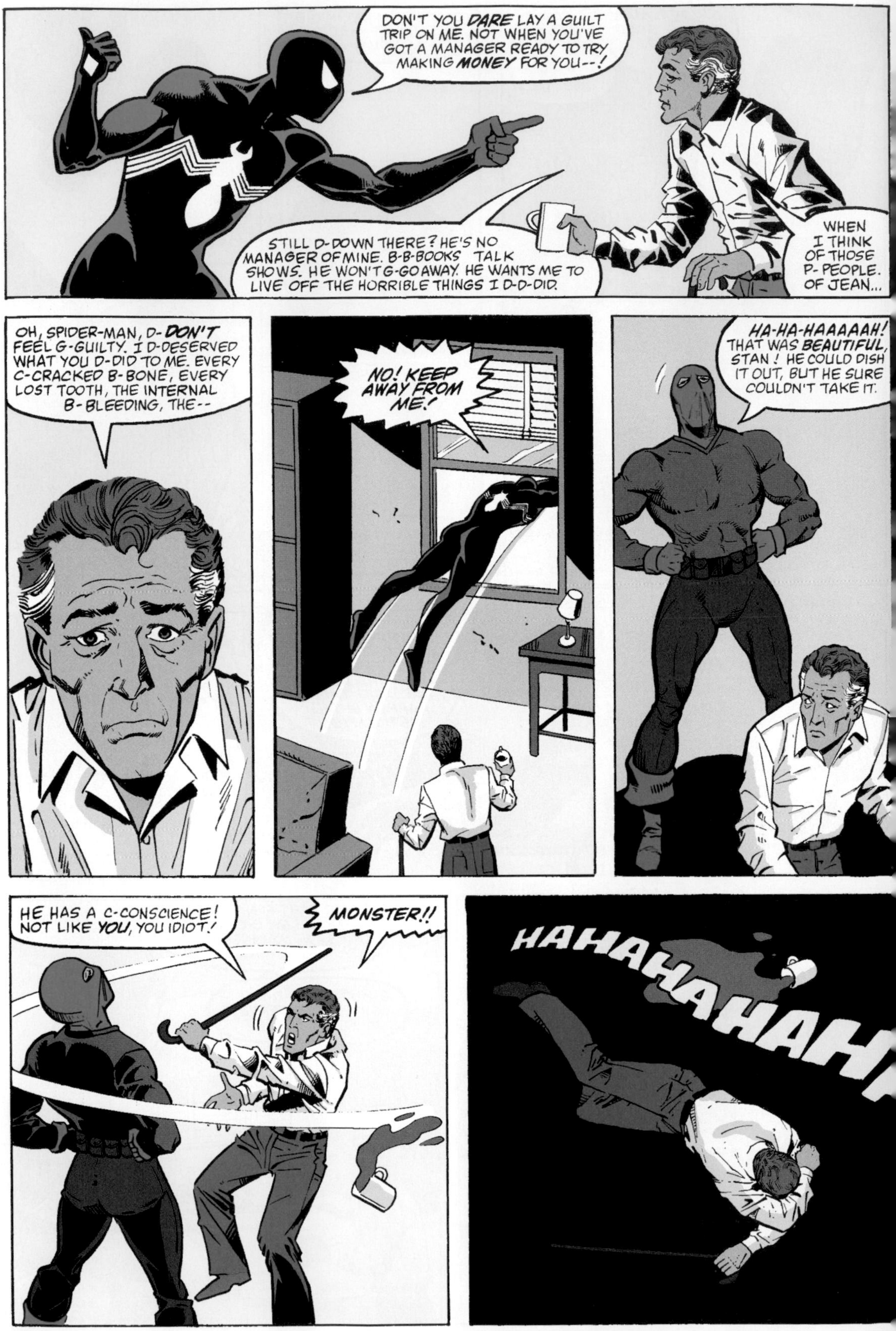
DON'T YOU DARE LAY A GUILT TRIP ON ME. NOT WHEN YOU'VE GOT A MANAGER READY TO TRY MAKING MONEY FOR YOU--!
STILL D-DOWN THERE? HE'S NO MANAGER OF MINE. B-B-BOOKS TALK SHOWS. HE WON'T G-GO AWAY. HE WANTS ME TO LIVE OFF THE HORRIBLE THINGS I D-D-DID.
WHEN I THINK OF THOSE P-PEOPLE. OF JEAN...
OH, SPIDER-MAN, D-DON'T FEEL G-GUILTY. I D-DESERVED WHAT YOU D-DID TO ME. EVERY C-CRACKED B-BONE, EVERY LOST TOOTH, THE INTERNAL B-BLEEDING, THE--
NO! KEEP AWAY FROM ME!
HA-HA-HAAAAAH! THAT WAS BEAUTIFUL, STAN! HE COULD DISH IT OUT, BUT HE SURE COULDN'T TAKE IT.
HE HAS A C-CONSCIENCE! NOT LIKE YOU, YOU IDIOT!
MONSTER!!
HAHAHAHAHAHAH

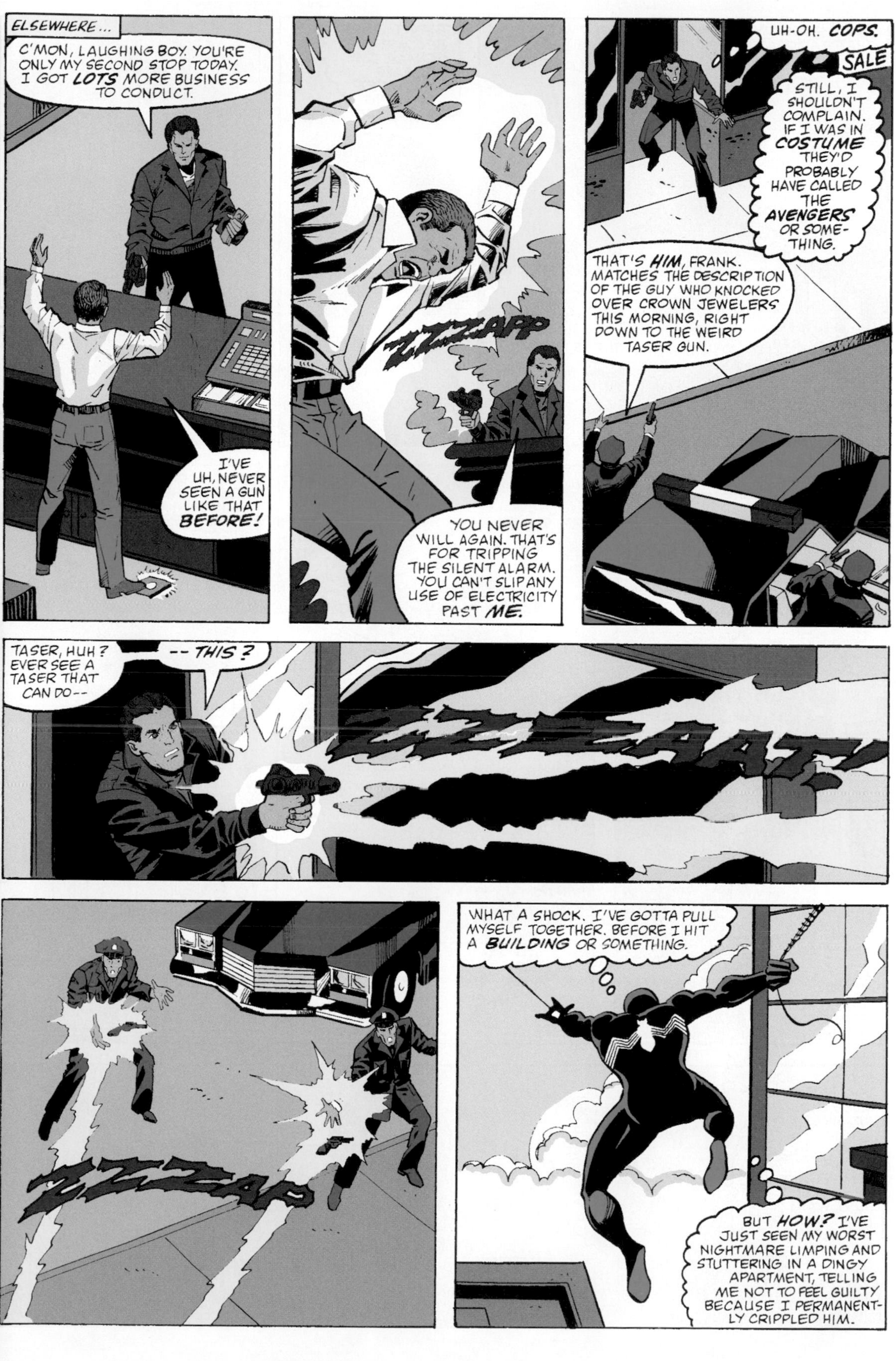

ELSEWHERE...
C'MON, LAUGHING BOY. YOU'RE ONLY MY SECOND STOP TODAY. I GOT LOTS MORE BUSINESS TO CONDUCT.
I'VE UH, NEVER SEEN A GUN LIKE THAT BEFORE!
ZZZAPP
YOU NEVER WILL AGAIN. THAT'S FOR TRIPPING THE SILENT ALARM. YOU CAN'T SLIP ANY USE OF ELECTRICITY PAST ME.
UH-OH. COPS.
SALE
STILL, I SHOULDN'T COMPLAIN. IF I WAS IN COSTUME THEY'D PROBABLY HAVE CALLED THE AVENGERS OR SOMETHING.
THAT'S HIM, FRANK. MATCHES THE DESCRIPTION OF THE GUY WHO KNOCKED OVER CROWN JEWELERS THIS MORNING, RIGHT DOWN TO THE WEIRD TASER GUN.
TASER, HUH? EVER SEE A TASER THAT CAN DO--
-- THIS?
ZZZZAAT!
ZZZZAP
WHAT A SHOCK. I'VE GOTTA PULL MYSELF TOGETHER. BEFORE I HIT A BUILDING OR SOMETHING.
BUT HOW? I'VE JUST SEEN MY WORST NIGHTMARE LIMPING AND STUTTERING IN A DINGY APARTMENT, TELLING ME NOT TO FEEL GUILTY BECAUSE I PERMANENTLY CRIPPLED HIM.

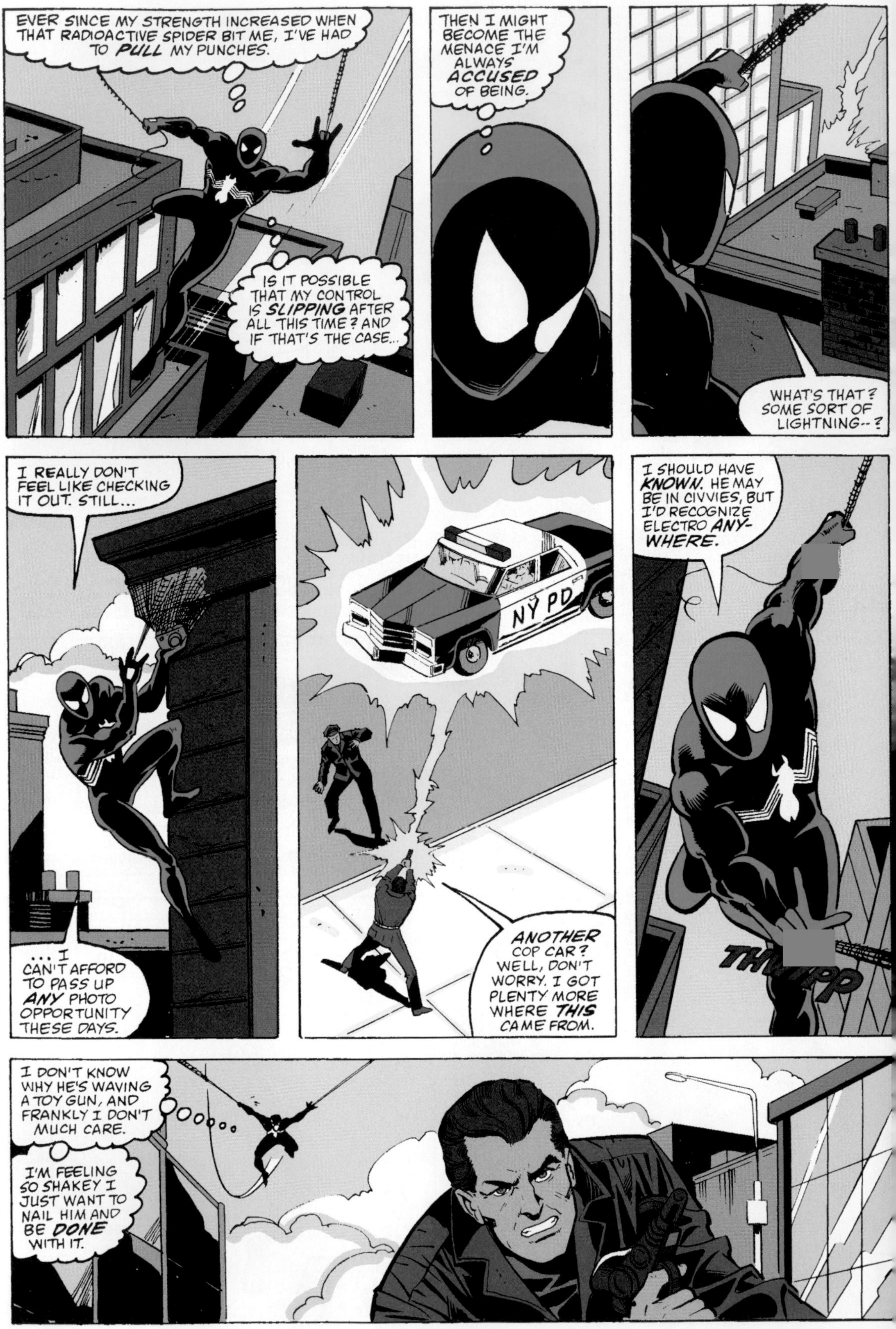
EVER SINCE MY STRENGTH INCREASED WHEN THAT RADIOACTIVE SPIDER BIT ME, I'VE HAD TO PULL MY PUNCHES.
IS IT POSSIBLE THAT MY CONTROL IS SLIPPING AFTER ALL THIS TIME? AND IF THAT'S THE CASE...
THEN I MIGHT BECOME THE MENACE I'M ALWAYS ACCUSED OF BEING.
WHAT'S THAT? SOME SORT OF LIGHTNING--?
I REALLY DON'T FEEL LIKE CHECKING IT OUT. STILL...
... I CAN'T AFFORD TO PASS UP ANY PHOTO OPPORTUNITY THESE DAYS.
NY PD
ANOTHER COP CAR? WELL, DON'T WORRY. I GOT PLENTY MORE WHERE THIS CAME FROM.
I SHOULD HAVE KNOWN. HE MAY BE IN CIVVIES, BUT I'D RECOGNIZE ELECTRO ANYWHERE.
THWIPP
I DON'T KNOW WHY HE'S WAVING A TOY GUN, AND FRANKLY I DON'T MUCH CARE.
I'M FEELING SO SHAKEY I JUST WANT TO NAIL HIM AND BE DONE WITH IT.

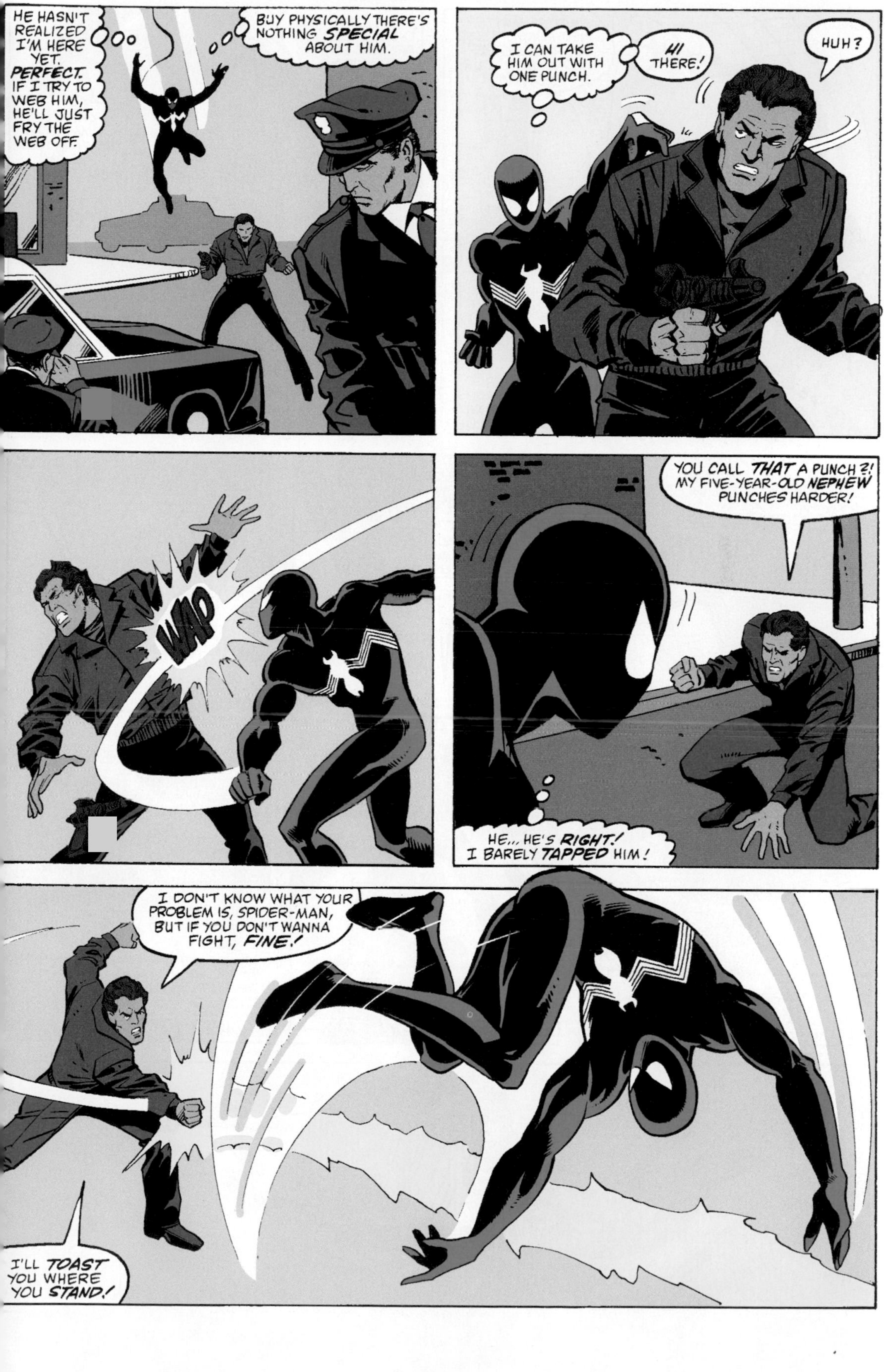
HE HASN'T REALIZED I'M HERE YET. PERFECT. IF I TRY TO WEB HIM, HE'LL JUST FRY THE WEB OFF.
BUT PHYSICALLY THERE'S NOTHING SPECIAL ABOUT HIM.
I CAN TAKE HIM OUT WITH ONE PUNCH.
HI THERE!
HUH?
WAP
YOU CALL THAT A PUNCH?! MY FIVE-YEAR-OLD NEPHEW PUNCHES HARDER!
HE... HE'S RIGHT! I BARELY TAPPED HIM!
I DON'T KNOW WHAT YOUR PROBLEM IS, SPIDER-MAN, BUT IF YOU DON'T WANNA FIGHT, FINE!
I'LL TOAST YOU WHERE YOU STAND!

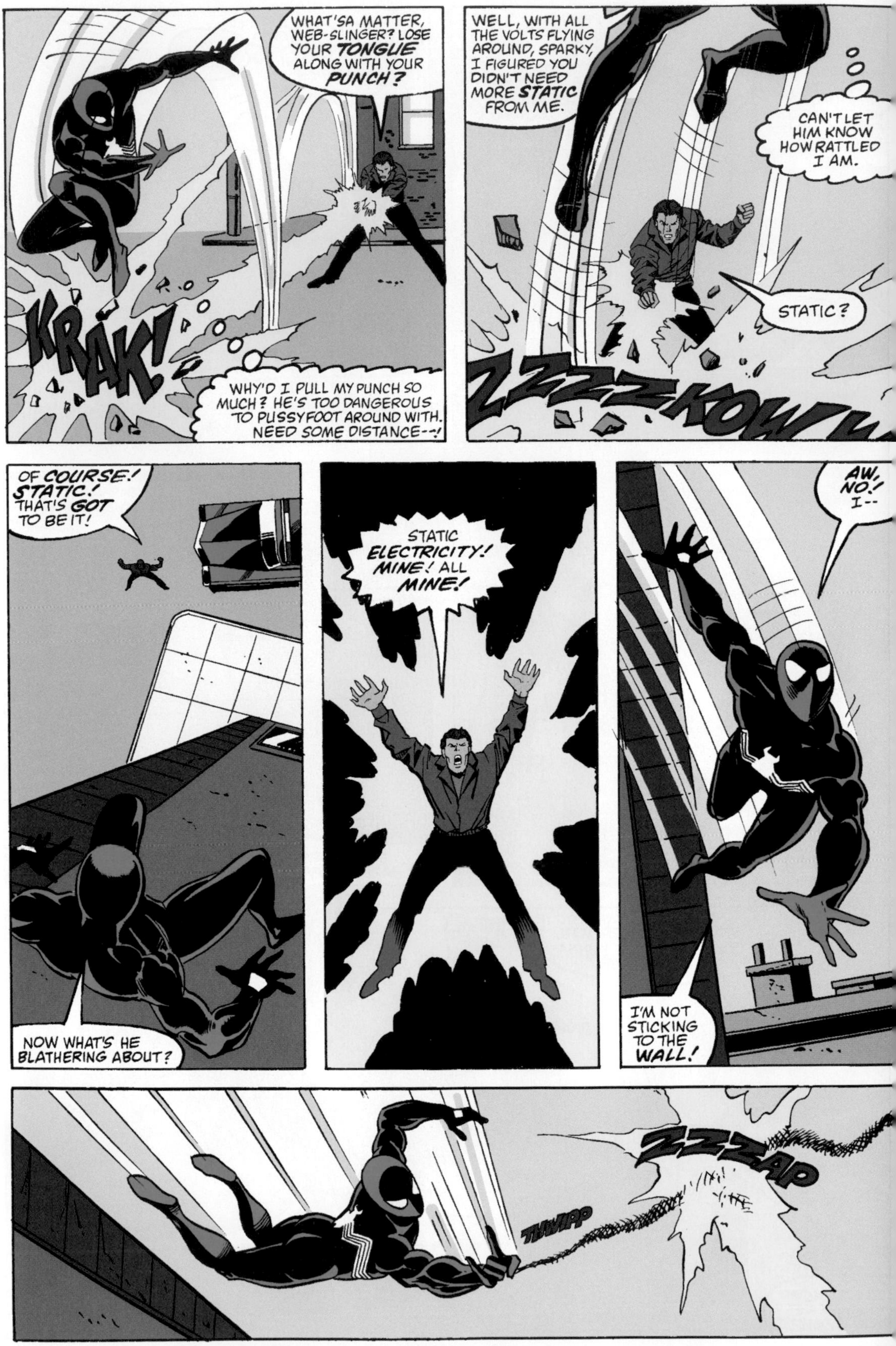
WHAT'SA MATTER, WEB-SLINGER? LOSE YOUR TONGUE ALONG WITH YOUR PUNCH?
KRAK!
WHY'D I PULL MY PUNCH SO MUCH? HE'S TOO DANGEROUS TO PUSSYFOOT AROUND WITH. NEED SOME DISTANCE--!
WELL, WITH ALL THE VOLTS FLYING AROUND, SPARKY, I FIGURED YOU DIDN'T NEED MORE STATIC FROM ME.
CAN'T LET HIM KNOW HOW RATTLED I AM.
STATIC?
OF COURSE! STATIC! THAT'S GOT TO BE IT!
NOW WHAT'S HE BLATHERING ABOUT?
STATIC ELECTRICITY! MINE! ALL MINE!
AW, NO! I--
I'M NOT STICKING TO THE WALL!
THWIPP
ZZZAP

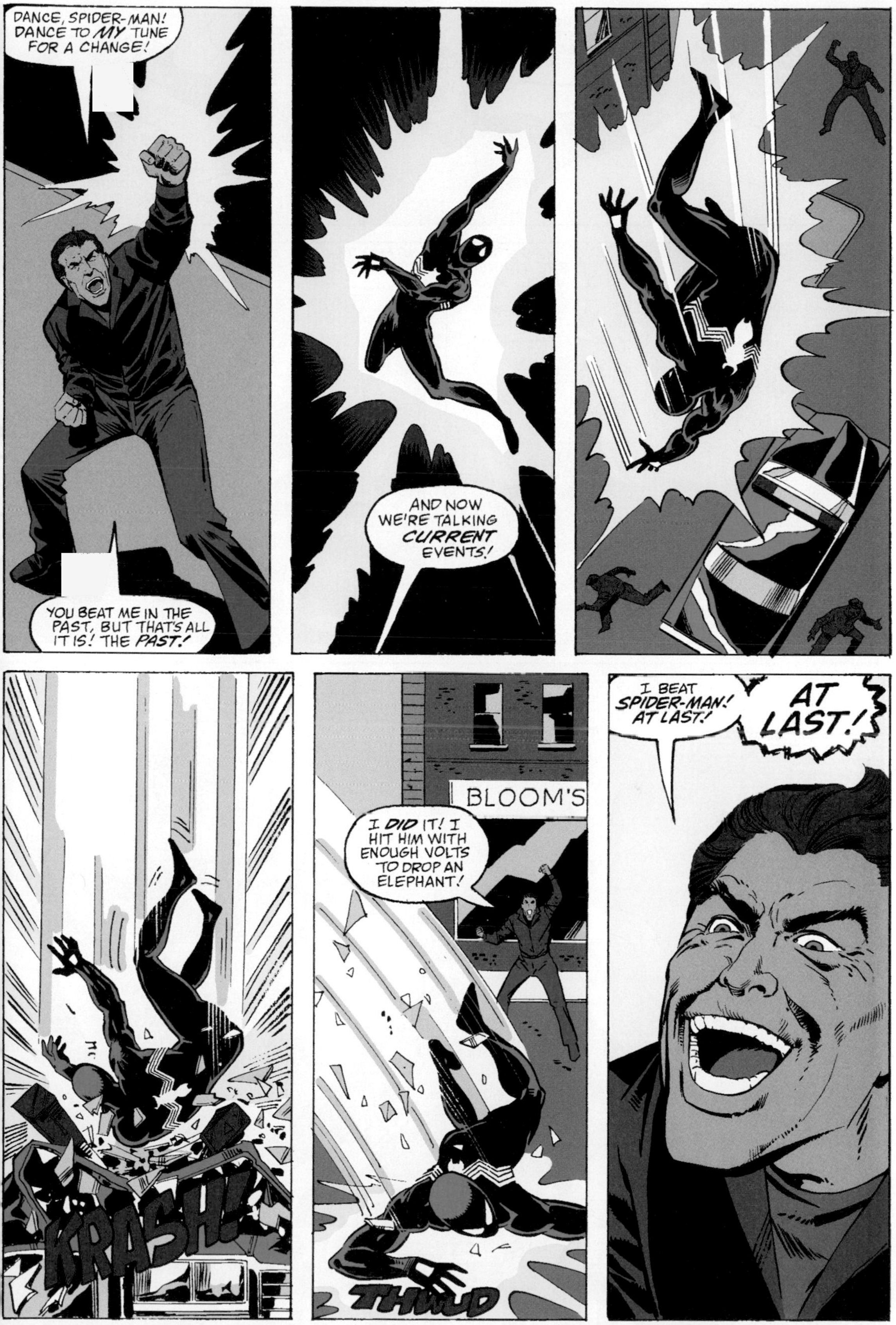
DANCE, SPIDER-MAN! DANCE TO MY TUNE FOR A CHANGE!
YOU BEAT ME IN THE PAST, BUT THAT'S ALL IT IS! THE PAST!
AND NOW WE'RE TALKING CURRENT EVENTS!
KRASH!
BLOOM'S
I DID IT! I HIT HIM WITH ENOUGH VOLTS TO DROP AN ELEPHANT!
THWUD
I BEAT SPIDER-MAN! AT LAST!
AT LAST!

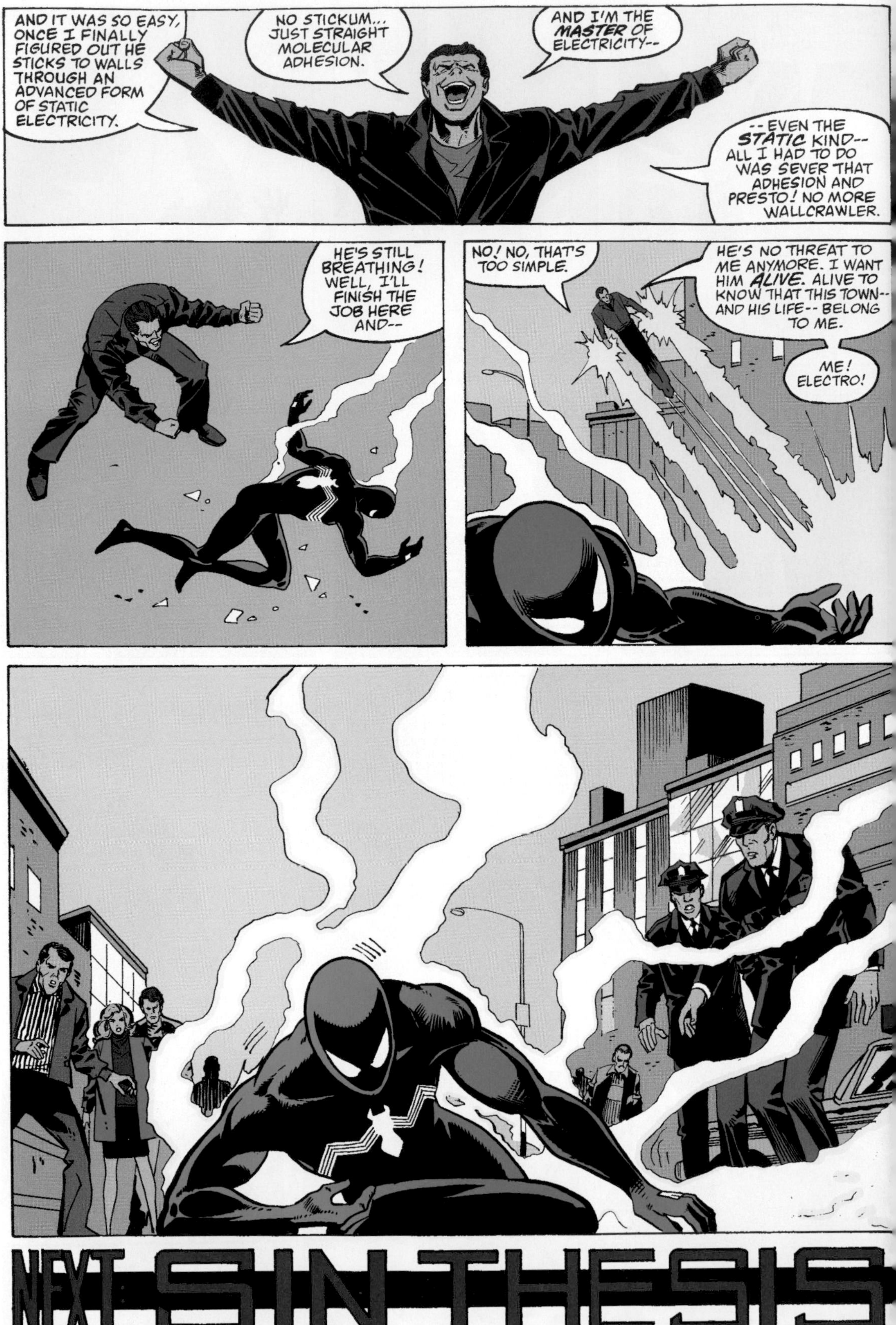
AND IT WAS SO EASY, ONCE I FINALLY FIGURED OUT HE STICKS TO WALLS THROUGH AN ADVANCED FORM OF STATIC ELECTRICITY.
NO STICKUM... JUST STRAIGHT MOLECULAR ADHESION.
AND I'M THE MASTER OF ELECTRICITY--
-- EVEN THE STATIC KIND-- ALL I HAD TO DO WAS SEVER THAT ADHESION AND PRESTO! NO MORE WALLCRAWLER.
HE'S STILL BREATHING! WELL, I'LL FINISH THE JOB HERE AND--
NO! NO, THAT'S TOO SIMPLE.
HE'S NO THREAT TO ME ANYMORE. I WANT HIM ALIVE. ALIVE TO KNOW THAT THIS TOWN-- AND HIS LIFE-- BELONG TO ME.
ME! ELECTRO!
NEXT SIN THESIS

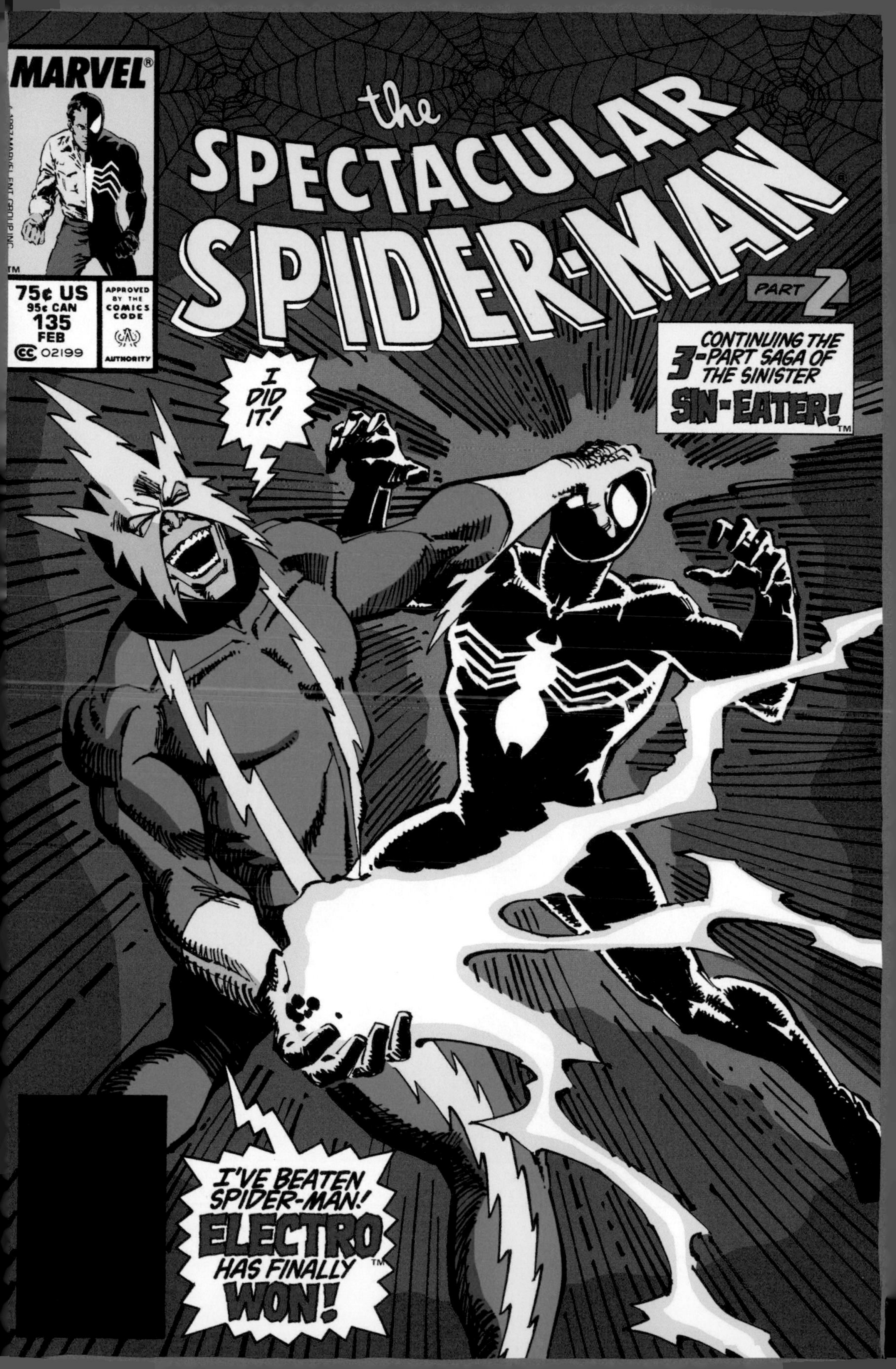

MARVEL
75¢ US
95¢ CAN
135
FEB
02199
APPROVED BY THE COMICS CODE AUTHORITY
the SPECTACULAR SPIDER-MAN
PART 2
CONTINUING THE 3-PART SAGA OF THE SINISTER SIN-EATER!
I DID IT!
I'VE BEATEN SPIDER-MAN! ELECTRO HAS FINALLY WON!

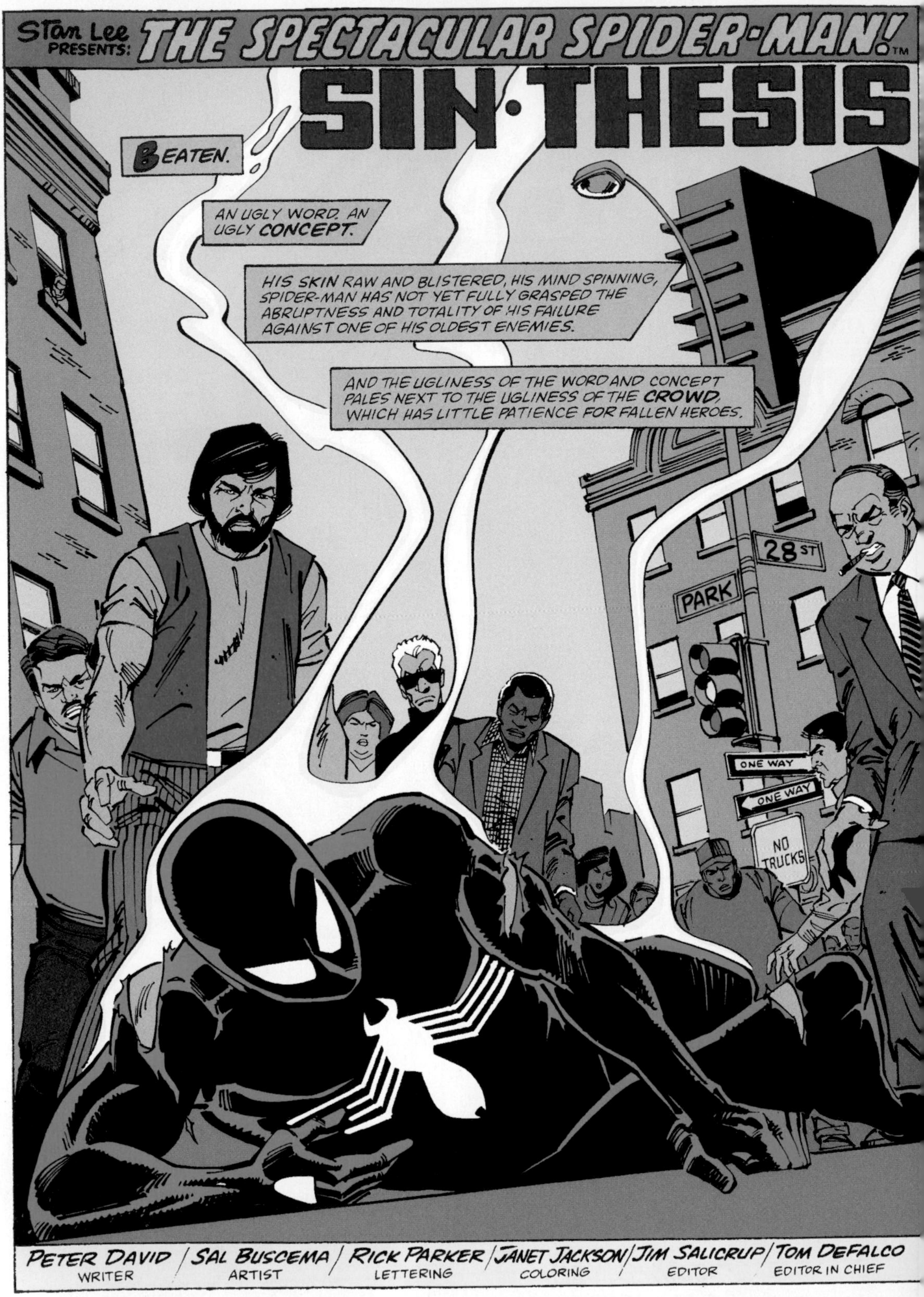
Stan Lee PRESENTS: THE SPECTACULAR SPIDER-MAN!™
SIN·THESIS
BEATEN.
AN UGLY WORD. AN UGLY CONCEPT.
HIS SKIN RAW AND BLISTERED, HIS MIND SPINNING, SPIDER-MAN HAS NOT YET FULLY GRASPED THE ABRUPTNESS AND TOTALITY OF HIS FAILURE AGAINST ONE OF HIS OLDEST ENEMIES.
AND THE UGLINESS OF THE WORD AND CONCEPT PALES NEXT TO THE UGLINESS OF THE CROWD, WHICH HAS LITTLE PATIENCE FOR FALLEN HEROES.
28 ST
PARK
ONE WAY
ONE WAY
NO TRUCKS
PETER DAVID WRITER / SAL BUSCEMA ARTIST / RICK PARKER LETTERING / JANET JACKSON COLORING / JIM SALICRUP EDITOR / TOM DEFALCO EDITOR IN CHIEF

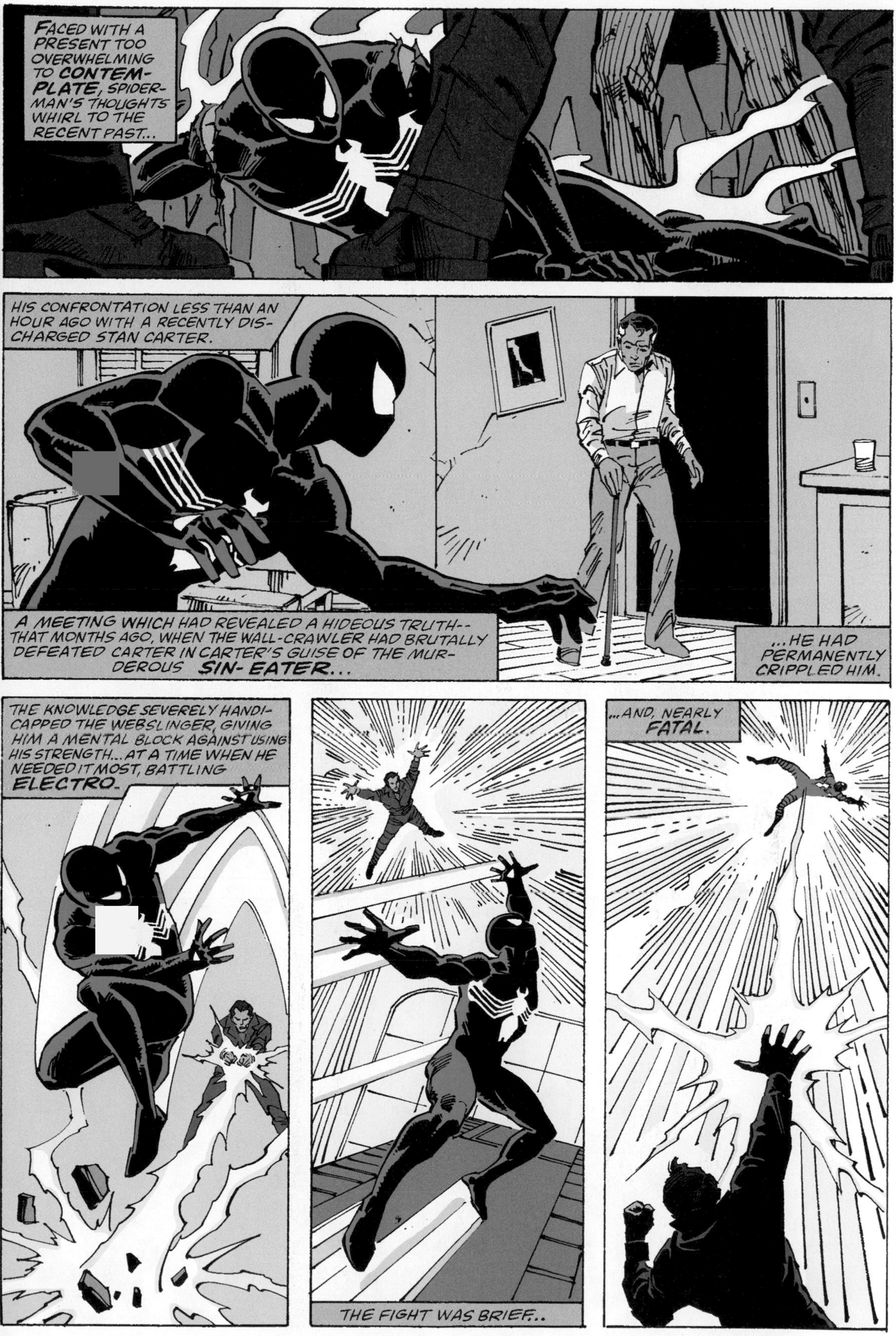

FACED WITH A PRESENT TOO OVERWHELMING TO CONTEMPLATE, SPIDER-MAN'S THOUGHTS WHIRL TO THE RECENT PAST...
HIS CONFRONTATION LESS THAN AN HOUR AGO WITH A RECENTLY DISCHARGED STAN CARTER.
A MEETING WHICH HAD REVEALED A HIDEOUS TRUTH--THAT MONTHS AGO, WHEN THE WALL-CRAWLER HAD BRUTALLY DEFEATED CARTER IN CARTER'S GUISE OF THE MURDEROUS SIN-EATER...
...HE HAD PERMANENTLY CRIPPLED HIM.
THE KNOWLEDGE SEVERELY HANDICAPPED THE WEBSLINGER, GIVING HIM A MENTAL BLOCK AGAINST USING HIS STRENGTH...AT A TIME WHEN HE NEEDED IT MOST, BATTLING ELECTRO.
THE FIGHT WAS BRIEF...
...AND, NEARLY FATAL.

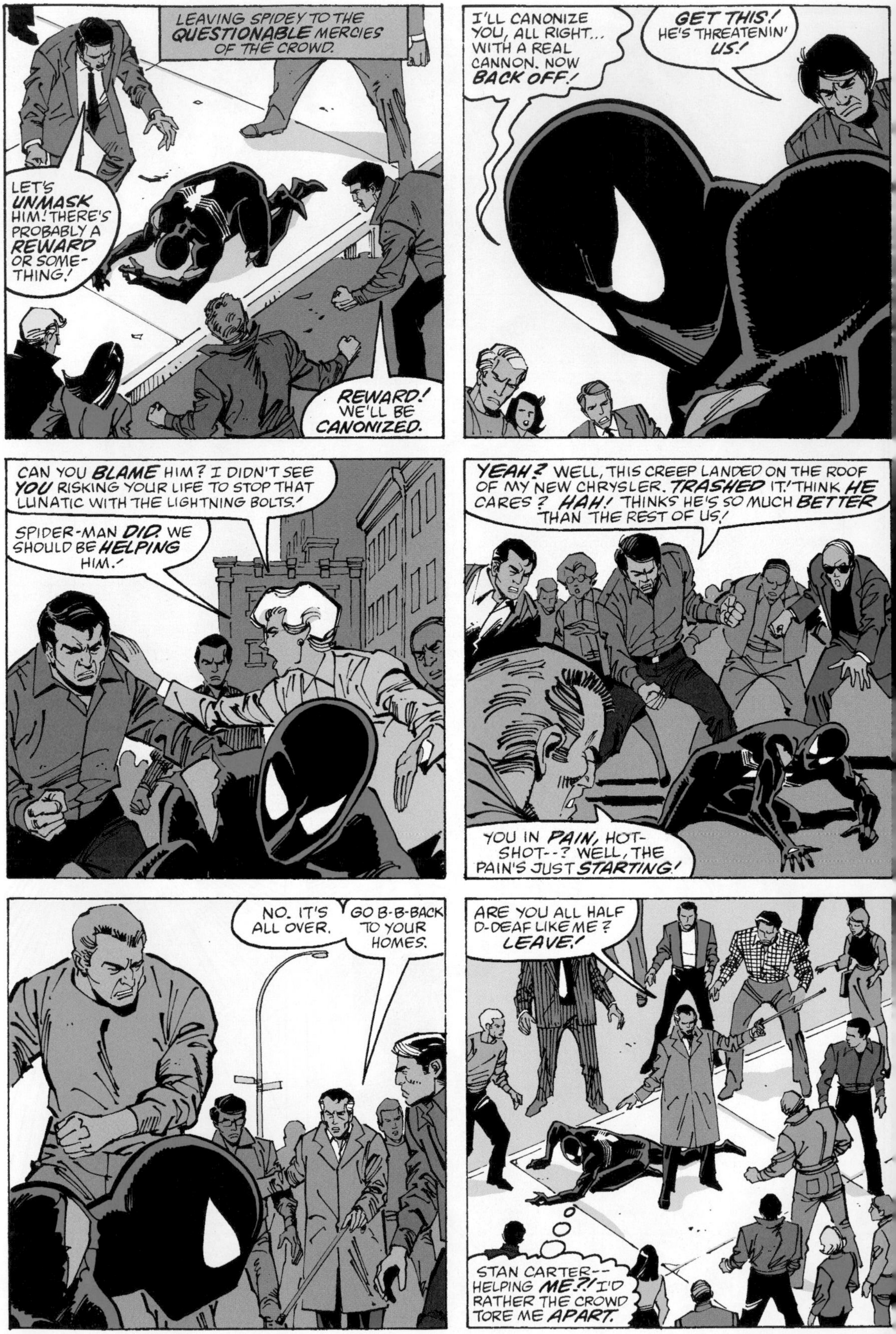
LEAVING SPIDEY TO THE QUESTIONABLE MERCIES OF THE CROWD.
LET'S UNMASK HIM! THERE'S PROBABLY A REWARD OR SOMETHING!
REWARD! WE'LL BE CANONIZED.
I'LL CANONIZE YOU, ALL RIGHT... WITH A REAL CANNON. NOW BACK OFF!
GET THIS! HE'S THREATENIN' US!
CAN YOU BLAME HIM? I DIDN'T SEE YOU RISKING YOUR LIFE TO STOP THAT LUNATIC WITH THE LIGHTNING BOLTS!
SPIDER-MAN DID. WE SHOULD BE HELPING HIM!
YEAH? WELL, THIS CREEP LANDED ON THE ROOF OF MY NEW CHRYSLER. TRASHED IT! THINK HE CARES? HAH! THINKS HE'S SO MUCH BETTER THAN THE REST OF US!
YOU IN PAIN, HOT-SHOT--? WELL, THE PAIN'S JUST STARTING!
NO. IT'S ALL OVER.
GO B-B-BACK TO YOUR HOMES.
ARE YOU ALL HALF D-DEAF LIKE ME? LEAVE!
STAN CARTER-- HELPING ME?! I'D RATHER THE CROWD TORE ME APART.

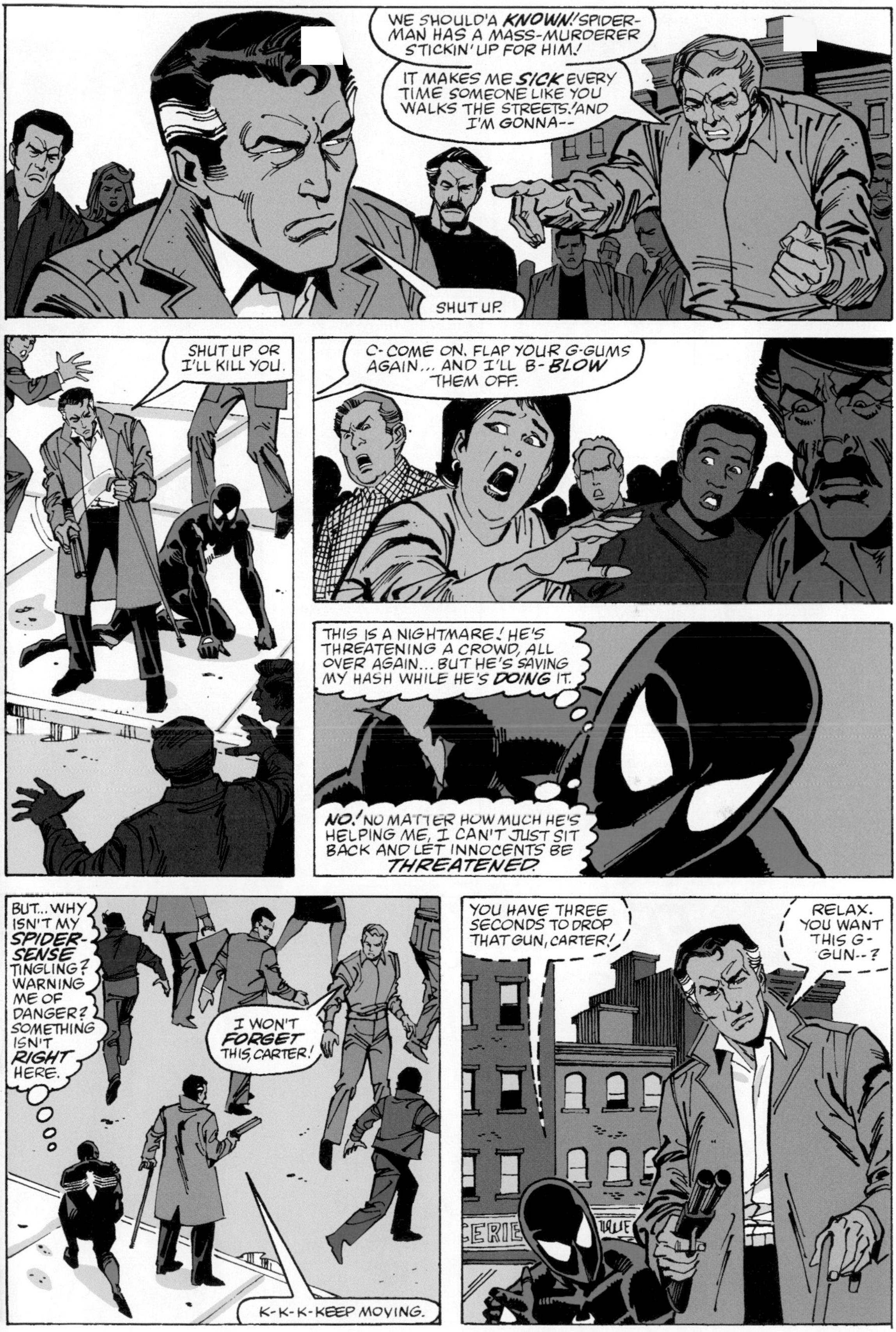
WE SHOULD'A KNOWN! SPIDER-MAN HAS A MASS-MURDERER STICKIN' UP FOR HIM!
IT MAKES ME SICK EVERY TIME SOMEONE LIKE YOU WALKS THE STREETS! AND I'M GONNA--
SHUT UP.
SHUT UP OR I'LL KILL YOU.
C-COME ON. FLAP YOUR G-GUMS AGAIN... AND I'LL B-BLOW THEM OFF.
THIS IS A NIGHTMARE! HE'S THREATENING A CROWD, ALL OVER AGAIN... BUT HE'S SAVING MY HASH WHILE HE'S DOING IT.
NO! NO MATTER HOW MUCH HE'S HELPING ME, I CAN'T JUST SIT BACK AND LET INNOCENTS BE THREATENED.
BUT... WHY ISN'T MY SPIDER-SENSE TINGLING? WARNING ME OF DANGER? SOMETHING ISN'T RIGHT HERE.
I WON'T FORGET THIS, CARTER!
K-K-K-KEEP MOVING.
YOU HAVE THREE SECONDS TO DROP THAT GUN, CARTER!
RELAX. YOU WANT THIS G-GUN--?

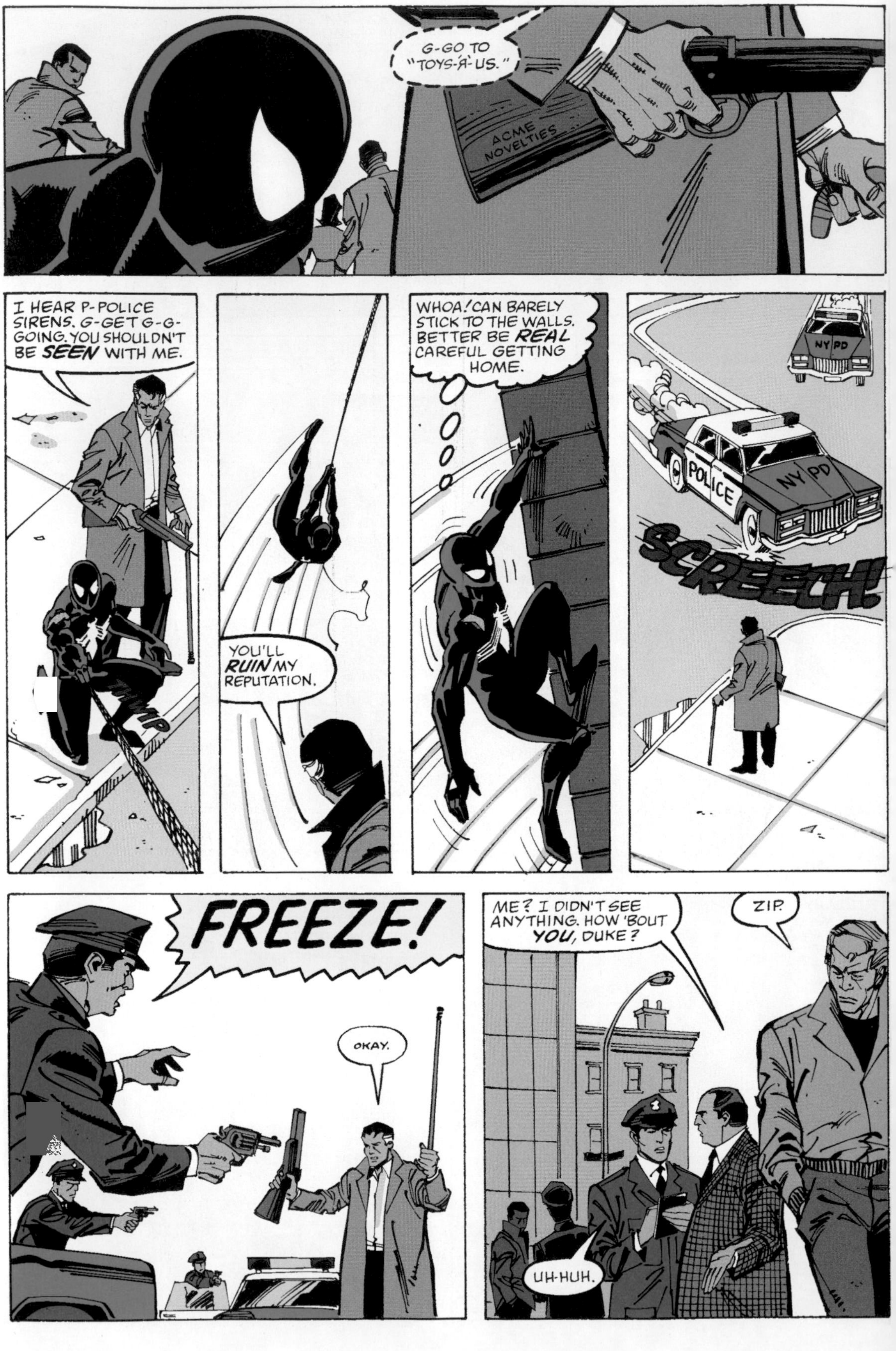
G-GO TO "TOYS-Я-US."
ACME NOVELTIES
I HEAR P-POLICE SIRENS. G-GET G-G-GOING. YOU SHOULDN'T BE SEEN WITH ME.
YOU'LL RUIN MY REPUTATION.
WHOA! CAN BARELY STICK TO THE WALLS. BETTER BE REAL CAREFUL GETTING HOME.
NYPD
POLICE
NYPD
SCREECH!
FREEZE!
OKAY.
ME? I DIDN'T SEE ANYTHING. HOW 'BOUT YOU, DUKE?
ZIP.
UH-HUH.

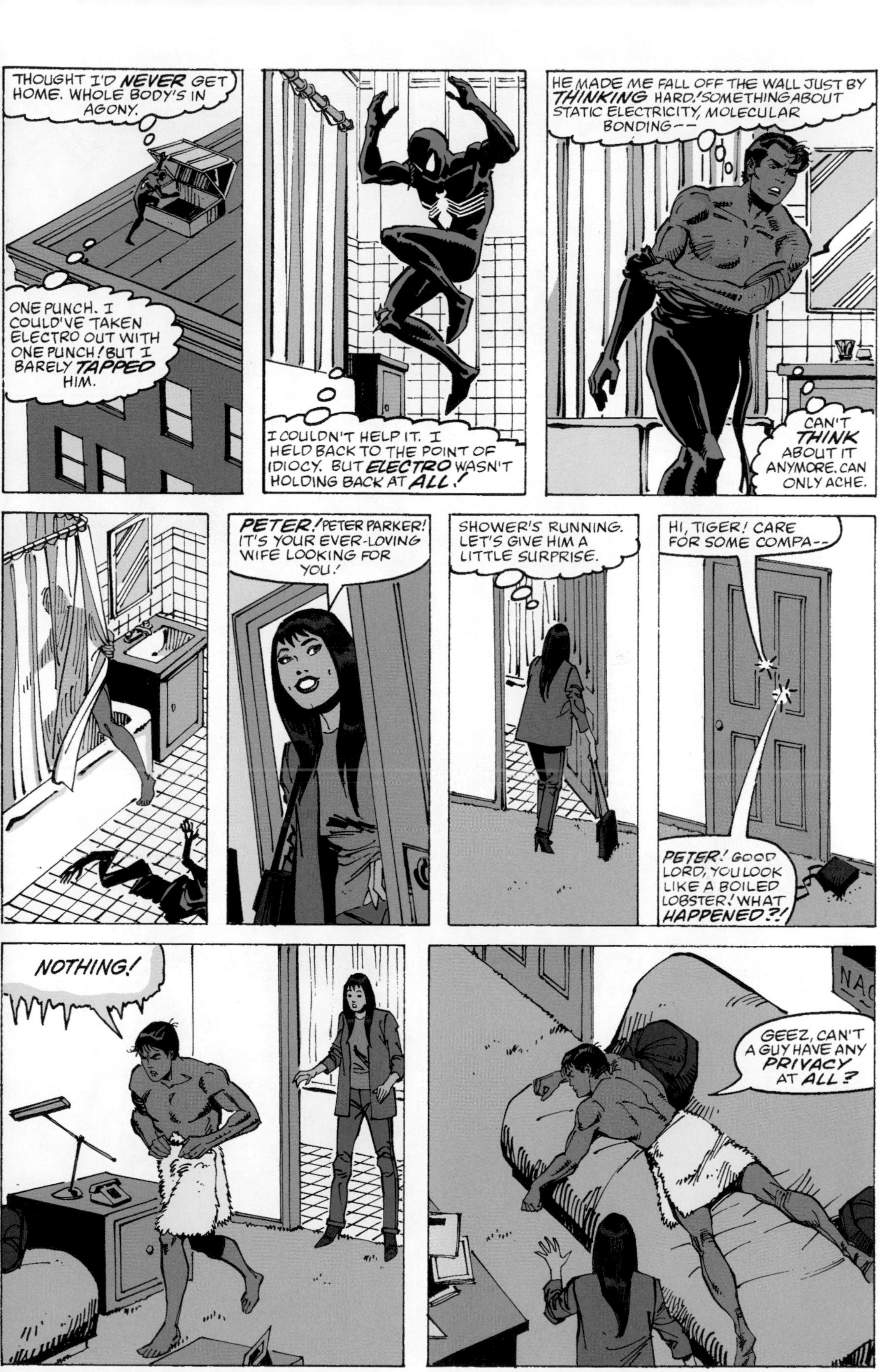
THOUGHT I'D NEVER GET HOME. WHOLE BODY'S IN AGONY.
ONE PUNCH. I COULD'VE TAKEN ELECTRO OUT WITH ONE PUNCH! BUT I BARELY TAPPED HIM.
I COULDN'T HELP IT. I HELD BACK TO THE POINT OF IDIOCY. BUT ELECTRO WASN'T HOLDING BACK AT ALL!
HE MADE ME FALL OFF THE WALL JUST BY THINKING HARD! SOMETHING ABOUT STATIC ELECTRICITY, MOLECULAR BONDING--
CAN'T THINK ABOUT IT ANYMORE. CAN ONLY ACHE.
PETER! PETER PARKER! IT'S YOUR EVER-LOVING WIFE LOOKING FOR YOU!
SHOWER'S RUNNING. LET'S GIVE HIM A LITTLE SURPRISE.
HI, TIGER! CARE FOR SOME COMPA--
PETER! GOOD LORD, YOU LOOK LIKE A BOILED LOBSTER! WHAT HAPPENED?!
NOTHING!
GEEZ, CAN'T A GUY HAVE ANY PRIVACY AT ALL?

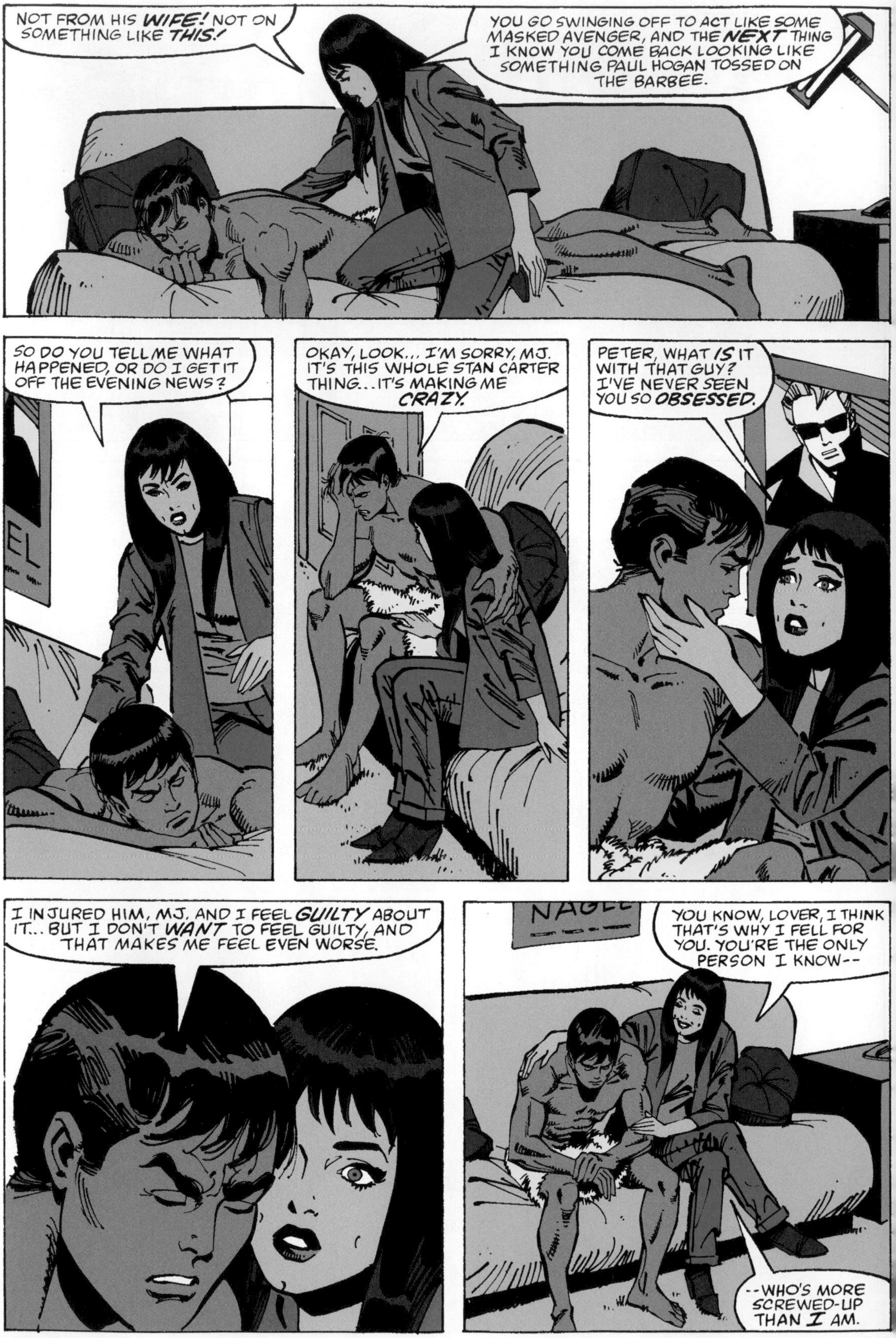
NOT FROM HIS WIFE! NOT ON SOMETHING LIKE THIS!
YOU GO SWINGING OFF TO ACT LIKE SOME MASKED AVENGER, AND THE NEXT THING I KNOW YOU COME BACK LOOKING LIKE SOMETHING PAUL HOGAN TOSSED ON THE BARBEE.
SO DO YOU TELL ME WHAT HAPPENED, OR DO I GET IT OFF THE EVENING NEWS?
OKAY, LOOK... I'M SORRY, MJ. IT'S THIS WHOLE STAN CARTER THING... IT'S MAKING ME CRAZY.
PETER, WHAT IS IT WITH THAT GUY? I'VE NEVER SEEN YOU SO OBSESSED.
I INJURED HIM, MJ. AND I FEEL GUILTY ABOUT IT... BUT I DON'T WANT TO FEEL GUILTY, AND THAT MAKES ME FEEL EVEN WORSE.
YOU KNOW, LOVER, I THINK THAT'S WHY I FELL FOR YOU. YOU'RE THE ONLY PERSON I KNOW--
--WHO'S MORE SCREWED-UP THAN I AM.

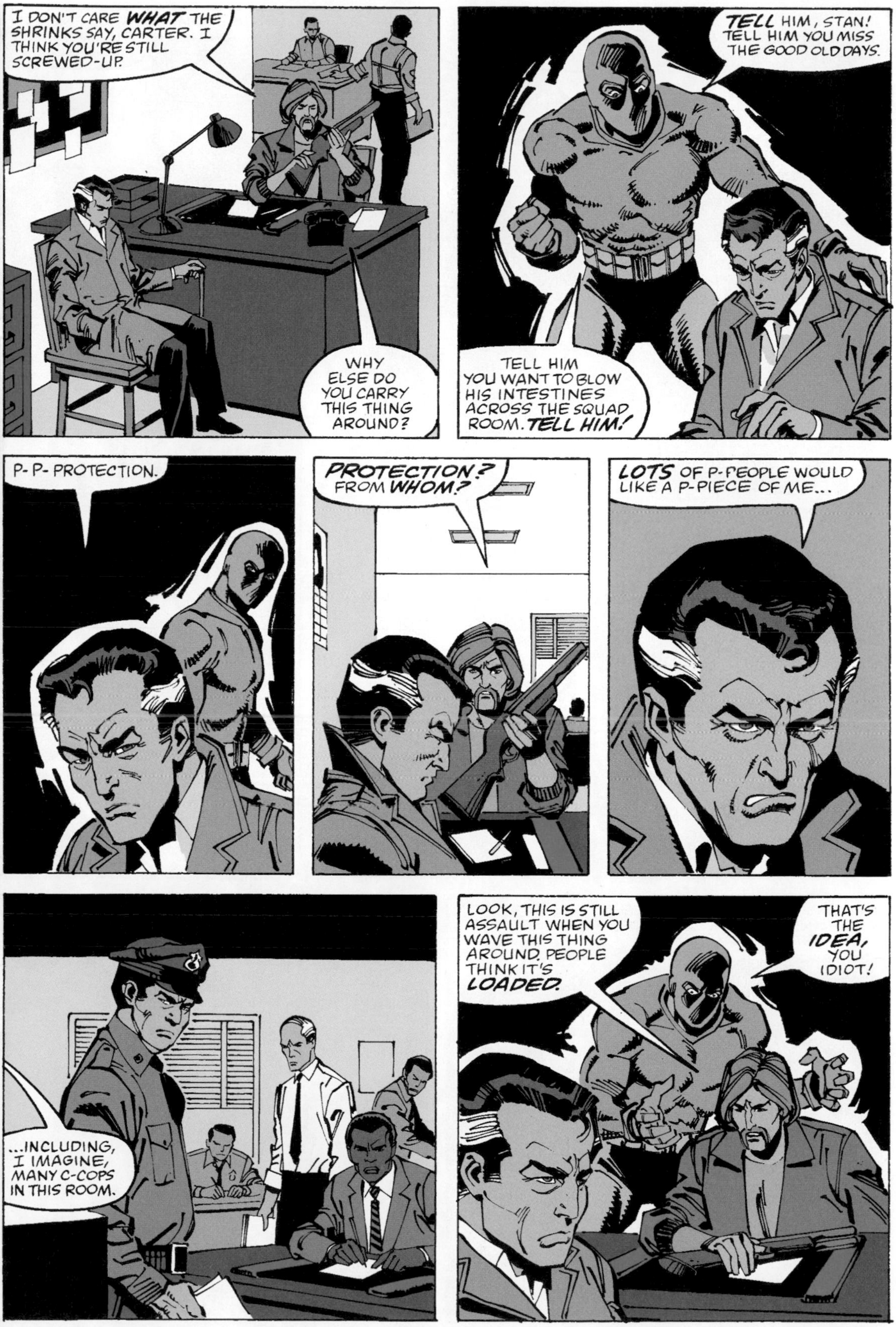
I DON'T CARE WHAT THE SHRINKS SAY, CARTER. I THINK YOU'RE STILL SCREWED-UP.
WHY ELSE DO YOU CARRY THIS THING AROUND?
TELL HIM, STAN! TELL HIM YOU MISS THE GOOD OLD DAYS.
TELL HIM YOU WANT TO BLOW HIS INTESTINES ACROSS THE SQUAD ROOM. TELL HIM!
P-P-PROTECTION.
PROTECTION? FROM WHOM?
LOTS OF P-PEOPLE WOULD LIKE A P-PIECE OF ME...
...INCLUDING, I IMAGINE, MANY C-COPS IN THIS ROOM.
LOOK, THIS IS STILL ASSAULT WHEN YOU WAVE THIS THING AROUND. PEOPLE THINK IT'S LOADED.
THAT'S THE IDEA, YOU IDIOT!

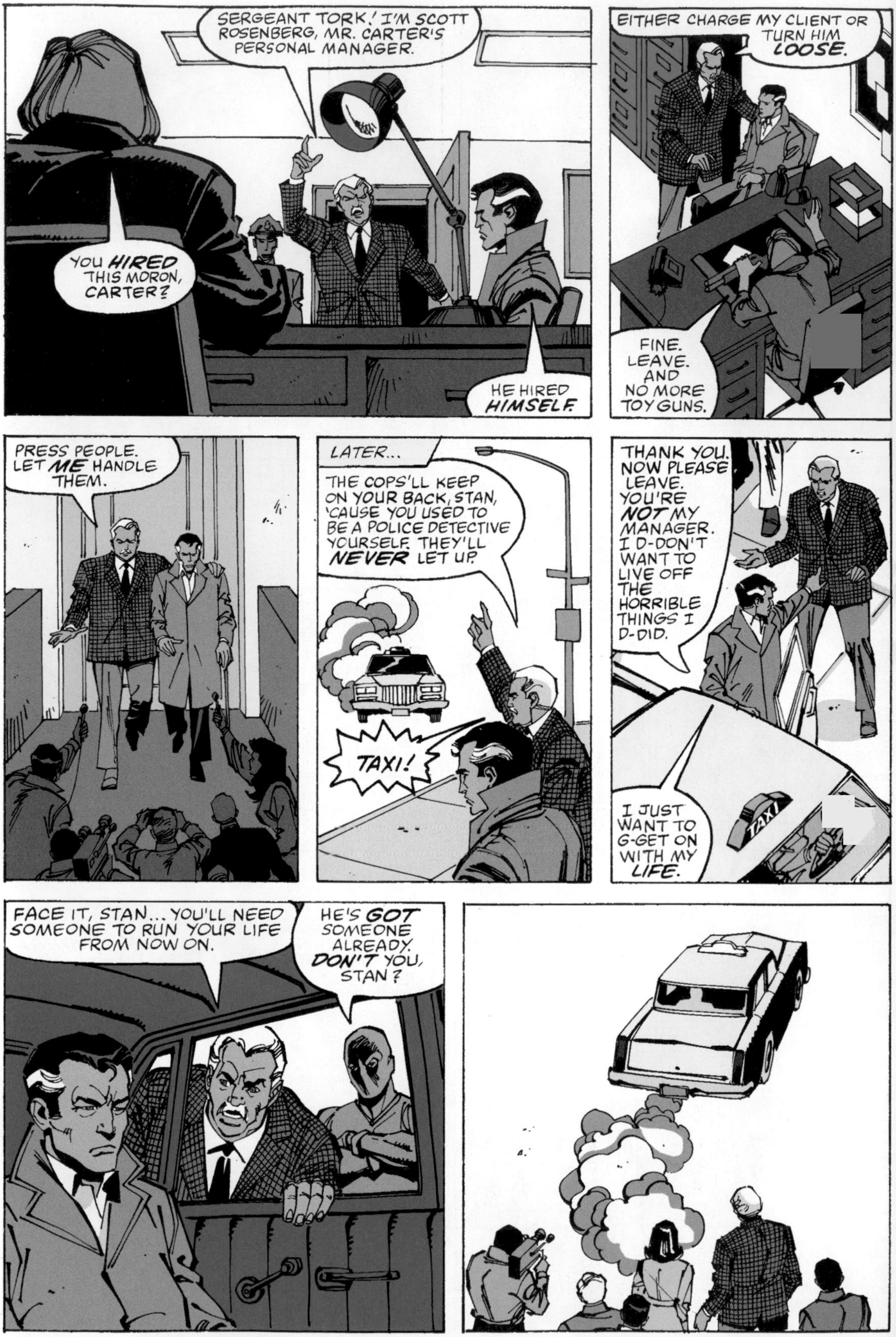
SERGEANT TORK! I'M SCOTT ROSENBERG, MR. CARTER'S PERSONAL MANAGER.
YOU HIRED THIS MORON, CARTER?
HE HIRED HIMSELF.
EITHER CHARGE MY CLIENT OR TURN HIM LOOSE.
FINE. LEAVE. AND NO MORE TOY GUNS.
PRESS PEOPLE. LET ME HANDLE THEM.
LATER...
THE COPS'LL KEEP ON YOUR BACK, STAN, 'CAUSE YOU USED TO BE A POLICE DETECTIVE YOURSELF. THEY'LL NEVER LET UP.
TAXI!
THANK YOU. NOW PLEASE LEAVE. YOU'RE NOT MY MANAGER. I D-DON'T WANT TO LIVE OFF THE HORRIBLE THINGS I D-DID.
I JUST WANT TO G-GET ON WITH MY LIFE.
FACE IT, STAN... YOU'LL NEED SOMEONE TO RUN YOUR LIFE FROM NOW ON.
HE'S GOT SOMEONE ALREADY. DON'T YOU, STAN?

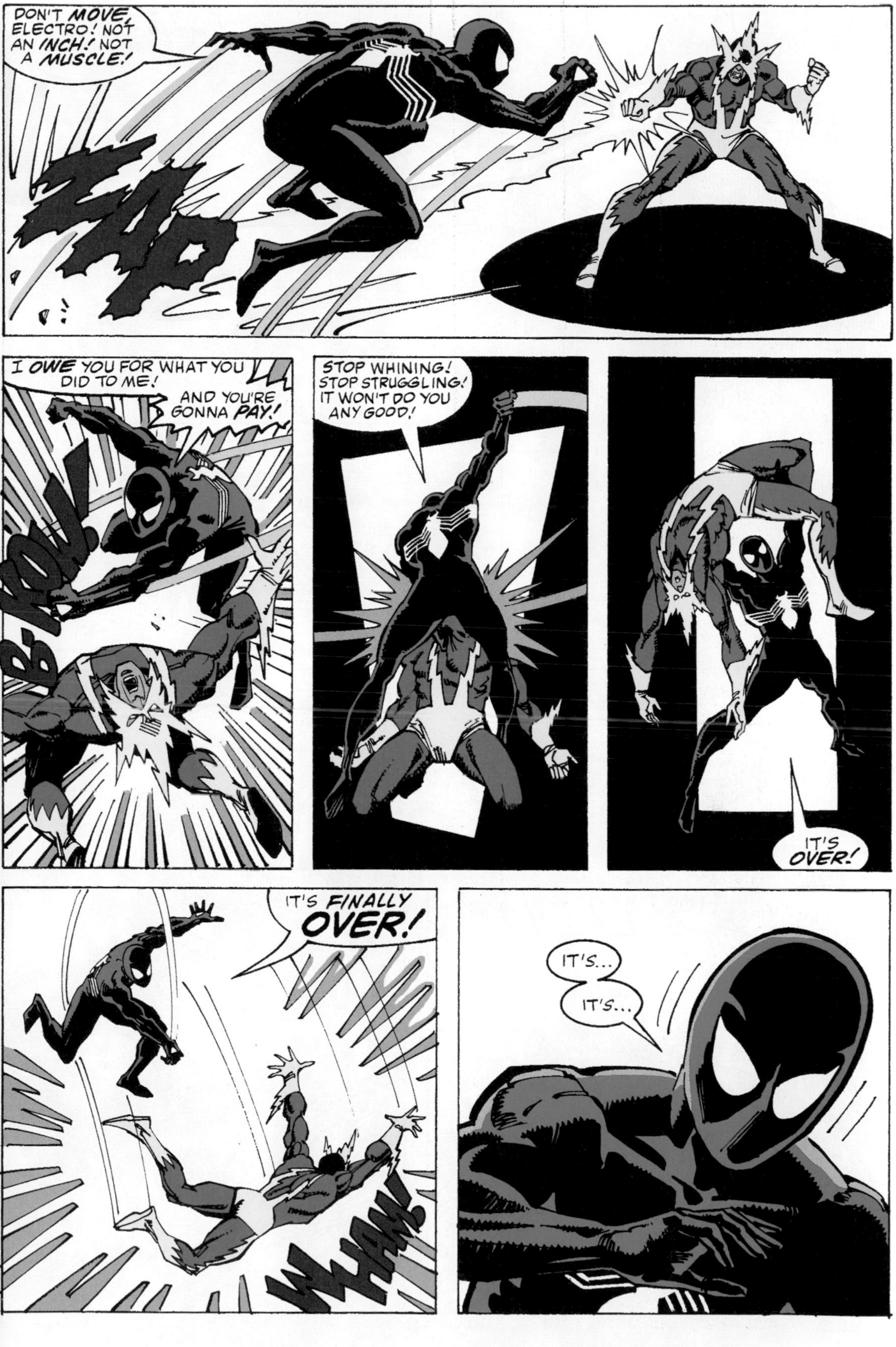
DON'T MOVE, ELECTRO! NOT AN INCH! NOT A MUSCLE!
ZAP
I OWE YOU FOR WHAT YOU DID TO ME!
AND YOU'RE GONNA PAY!
B-KOW!
STOP WHINING! STOP STRUGGLING! IT WON'T DO YOU ANY GOOD!
IT'S OVER!
IT'S FINALLY OVER!
WHAM!
IT'S...
IT'S...

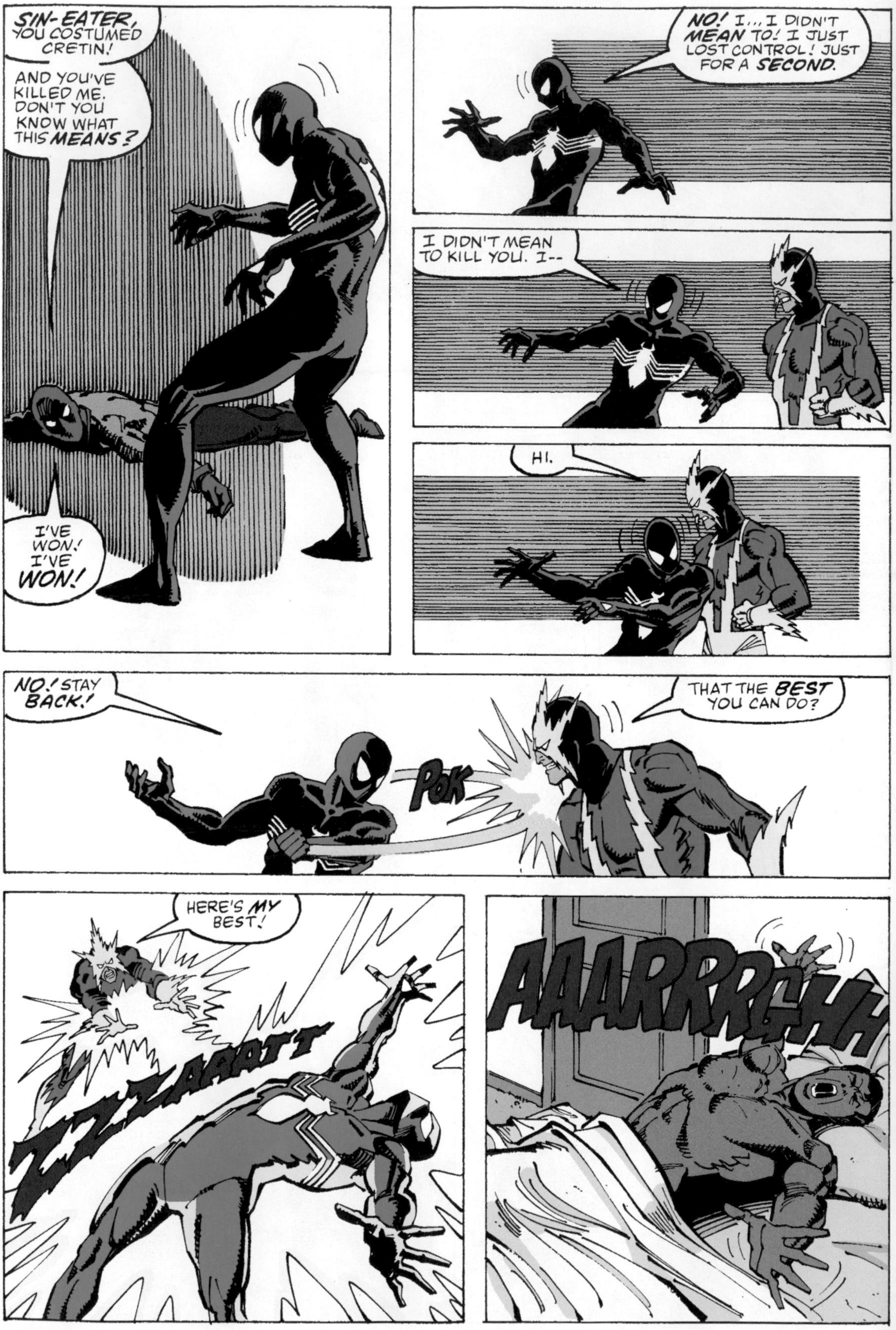
SIN-EATER, YOU COSTUMED CRETIN!
AND YOU'VE KILLED ME. DON'T YOU KNOW WHAT THIS MEANS?
I'VE WON! I'VE WON!
NO! I... I DIDN'T MEAN TO! I JUST LOST CONTROL! JUST FOR A SECOND.
I DIDN'T MEAN TO KILL YOU. I--
HI.
NO! STAY BACK!
POK
THAT THE BEST YOU CAN DO?
HERE'S MY BEST!
ZZZAAATT
AAARRRGHH

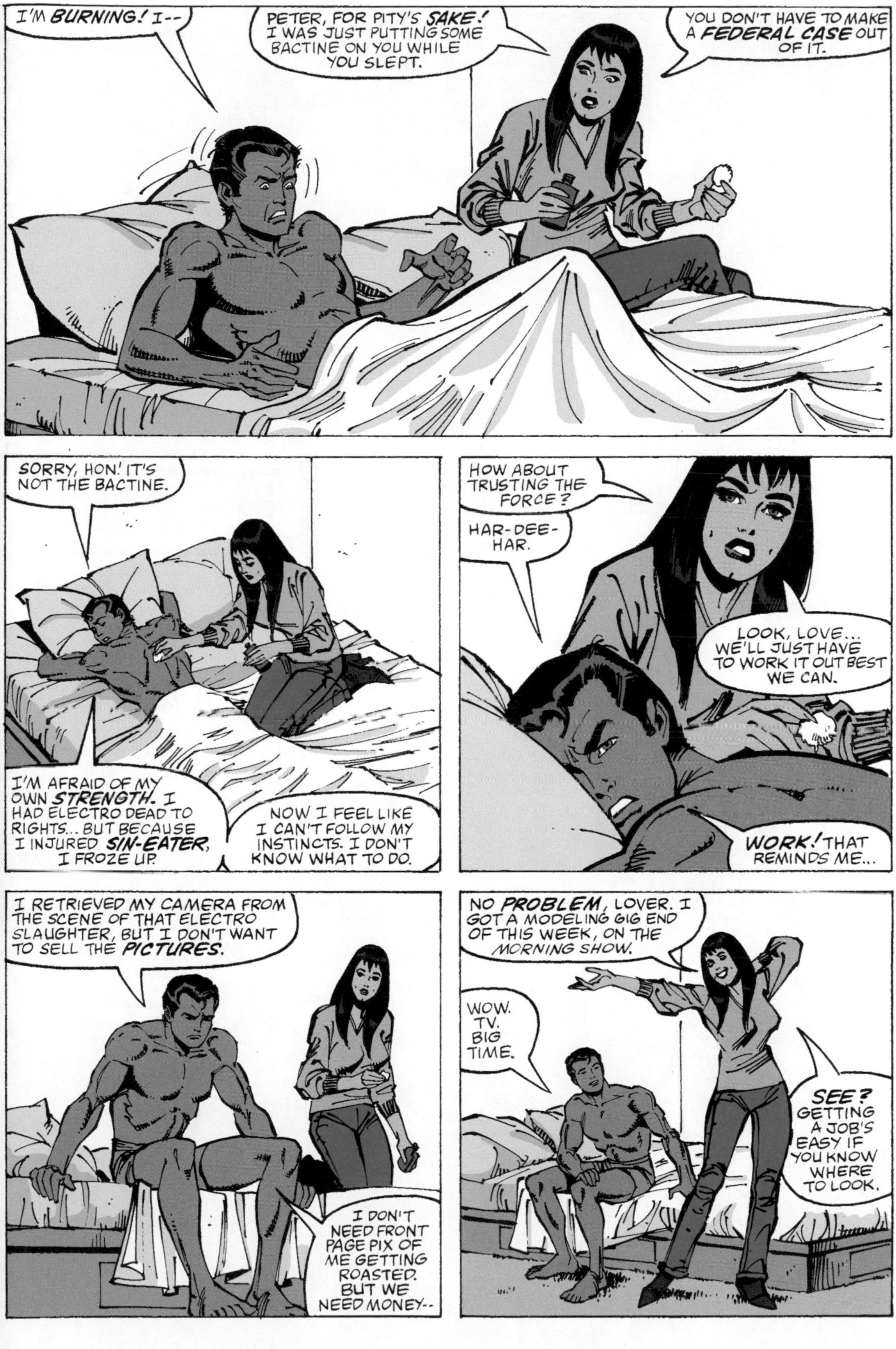
I'M BURNING! I--
PETER, FOR PITY'S SAKE! I WAS JUST PUTTING SOME BACTINE ON YOU WHILE YOU SLEPT.
YOU DON'T HAVE TO MAKE A FEDERAL CASE OUT OF IT.
SORRY, HON! IT'S NOT THE BACTINE.
I'M AFRAID OF MY OWN STRENGTH. I HAD ELECTRO DEAD TO RIGHTS... BUT BECAUSE I INJURED SIN-EATER, I FROZE UP.
NOW I FEEL LIKE I CAN'T FOLLOW MY INSTINCTS. I DON'T KNOW WHAT TO DO.
HOW ABOUT TRUSTING THE FORCE?
HAR-DEE-HAR.
LOOK, LOVE... WE'LL JUST HAVE TO WORK IT OUT BEST WE CAN.
WORK! THAT REMINDS ME...
I RETRIEVED MY CAMERA FROM THE SCENE OF THAT ELECTRO SLAUGHTER, BUT I DON'T WANT TO SELL THE PICTURES.
I DON'T NEED FRONT PAGE PIX OF ME GETTING ROASTED. BUT WE NEED MONEY--
NO PROBLEM, LOVER. I GOT A MODELING GIG END OF THIS WEEK, ON THE MORNING SHOW.
WOW. TV. BIG TIME.
SEE? GETTING A JOB'S EASY IF YOU KNOW WHERE TO LOOK.

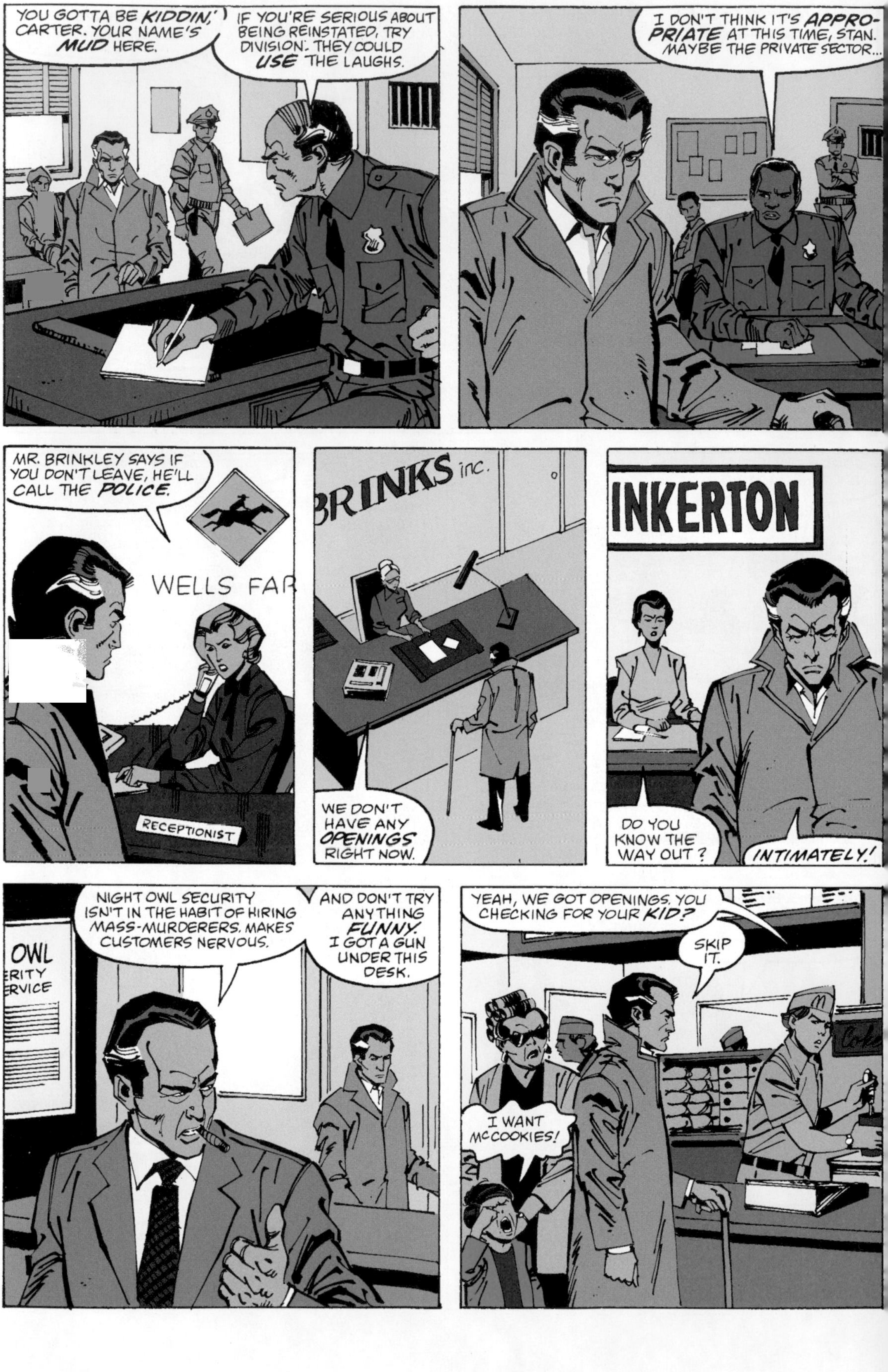
YOU GOTTA BE KIDDIN,' CARTER. YOUR NAME'S MUD HERE.
IF YOU'RE SERIOUS ABOUT BEING REINSTATED, TRY DIVISION. THEY COULD USE THE LAUGHS.
I DON'T THINK IT'S APPROPRIATE AT THIS TIME, STAN. MAYBE THE PRIVATE SECTOR...
MR. BRINKLEY SAYS IF YOU DON'T LEAVE, HE'LL CALL THE POLICE.
WELLS FAR
RECEPTIONIST
BRINKS inc.
WE DON'T HAVE ANY OPENINGS RIGHT NOW.
INKERTON
DO YOU KNOW THE WAY OUT?
INTIMATELY!
OWL
ERITY
ERVICE
NIGHT OWL SECURITY ISN'T IN THE HABIT OF HIRING MASS-MURDERERS. MAKES CUSTOMERS NERVOUS.
AND DON'T TRY ANYTHING FUNNY. I GOT A GUN UNDER THIS DESK.
YEAH, WE GOT OPENINGS. YOU CHECKING FOR YOUR KID?
SKIP IT.
I WANT McCOOKIES!

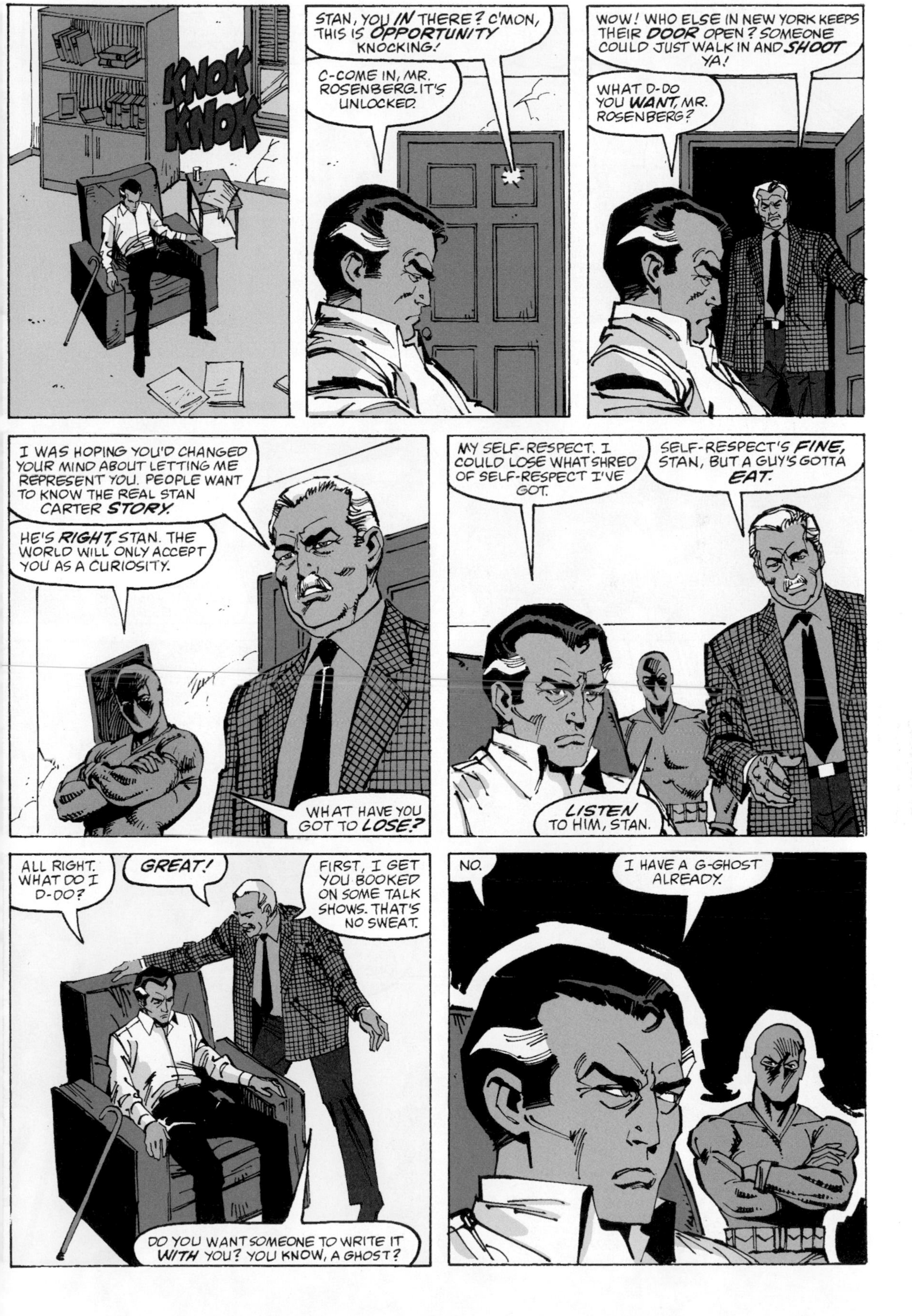
KNOK KNOK
STAN, YOU IN THERE? C'MON, THIS IS OPPORTUNITY KNOCKING!
C-COME IN, MR. ROSENBERG. IT'S UNLOCKED.
WOW! WHO ELSE IN NEW YORK KEEPS THEIR DOOR OPEN? SOMEONE COULD JUST WALK IN AND SHOOT YA!
WHAT D-DO YOU WANT, MR. ROSENBERG?
I WAS HOPING YOU'D CHANGED YOUR MIND ABOUT LETTING ME REPRESENT YOU. PEOPLE WANT TO KNOW THE REAL STAN CARTER STORY.
HE'S RIGHT, STAN. THE WORLD WILL ONLY ACCEPT YOU AS A CURIOSITY.
WHAT HAVE YOU GOT TO LOSE?
MY SELF-RESPECT. I COULD LOSE WHAT SHRED OF SELF-RESPECT I'VE GOT.
SELF-RESPECT'S FINE, STAN, BUT A GUY'S GOTTA EAT.
LISTEN TO HIM, STAN.
ALL RIGHT. WHAT DO I D-DO?
GREAT!
FIRST, I GET YOU BOOKED ON SOME TALK SHOWS. THAT'S NO SWEAT.
DO YOU WANT SOMEONE TO WRITE IT WITH YOU? YOU KNOW, A GHOST?
NO.
I HAVE A G-GHOST ALREADY.

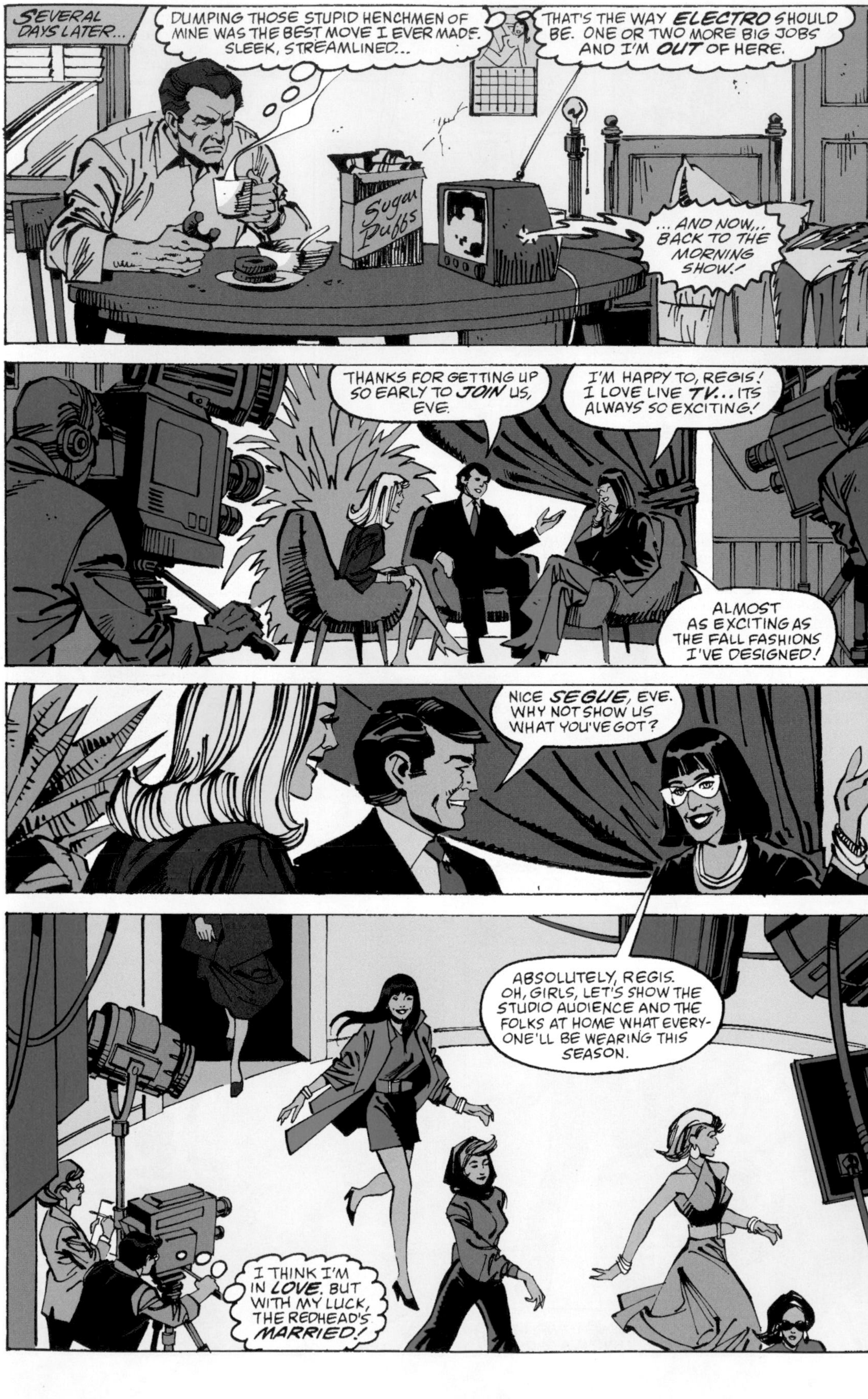
SEVERAL DAYS LATER...
DUMPING THOSE STUPID HENCHMEN OF MINE WAS THE BEST MOVE I EVER MADE. SLEEK, STREAMLINED...
THAT'S THE WAY ELECTRO SHOULD BE. ONE OR TWO MORE BIG JOBS AND I'M OUT OF HERE.
Sugar Puffs
...AND NOW... BACK TO THE MORNING SHOW!
THANKS FOR GETTING UP SO EARLY TO JOIN US, EVE.
I'M HAPPY TO, REGIS! I LOVE LIVE TV... ITS ALWAYS SO EXCITING!
ALMOST AS EXCITING AS THE FALL FASHIONS I'VE DESIGNED!
NICE SEGUE, EVE. WHY NOT SHOW US WHAT YOU'VE GOT?
ABSOLUTELY, REGIS. OH, GIRLS, LET'S SHOW THE STUDIO AUDIENCE AND THE FOLKS AT HOME WHAT EVERYONE'LL BE WEARING THIS SEASON.
I THINK I'M IN LOVE. BUT WITH MY LUCK, THE REDHEAD'S MARRIED!

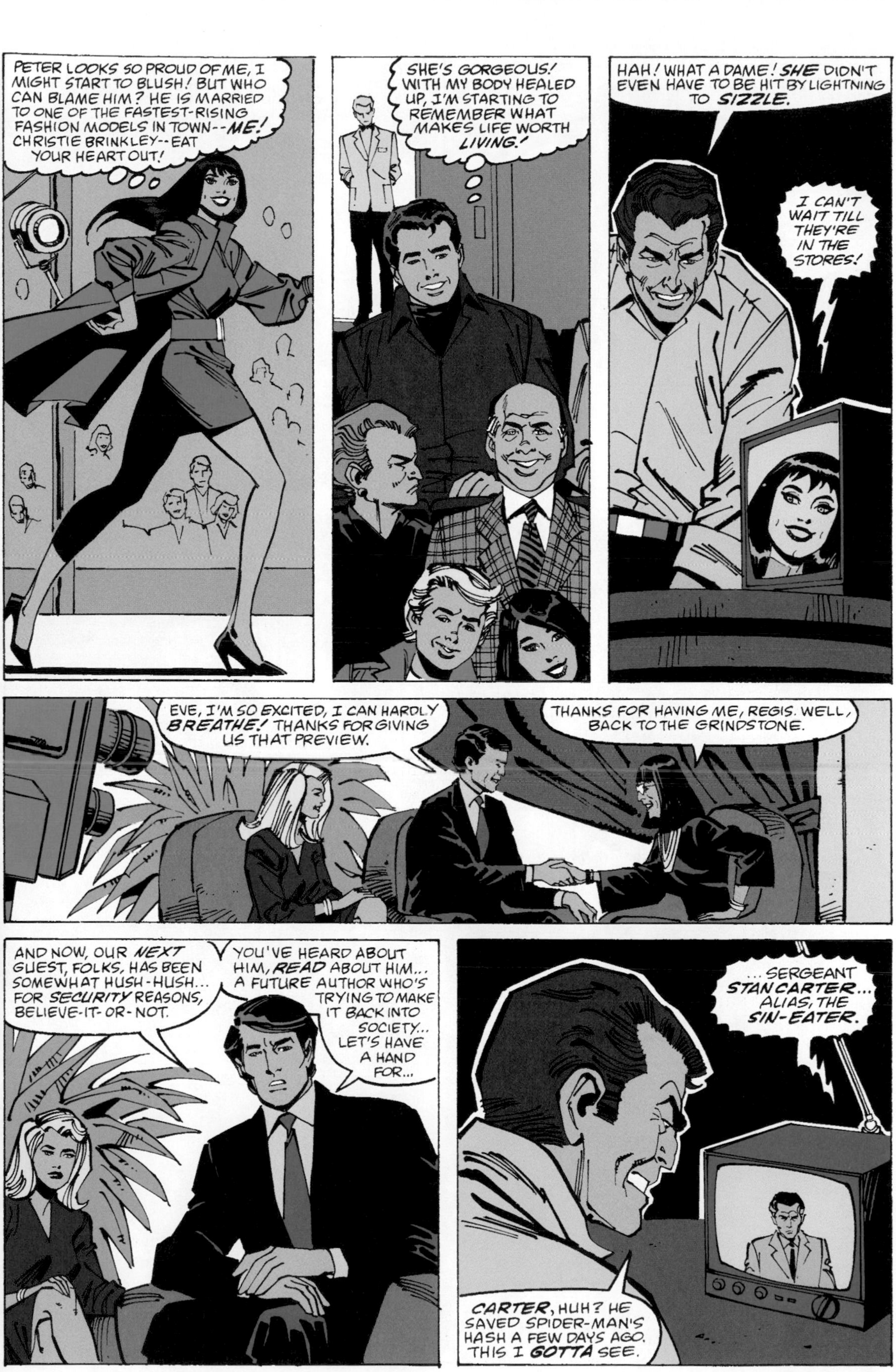
PETER LOOKS SO PROUD OF ME, I MIGHT START TO BLUSH! BUT WHO CAN BLAME HIM? HE IS MARRIED TO ONE OF THE FASTEST-RISING FASHION MODELS IN TOWN--ME! CHRISTIE BRINKLEY--EAT YOUR HEART OUT!
SHE'S GORGEOUS! WITH MY BODY HEALED UP, I'M STARTING TO REMEMBER WHAT MAKES LIFE WORTH LIVING!
HAH! WHAT A DAME! SHE DIDN'T EVEN HAVE TO BE HIT BY LIGHTNING TO SIZZLE.
I CAN'T WAIT TILL THEY'RE IN THE STORES!
EVE, I'M SO EXCITED, I CAN HARDLY BREATHE! THANKS FOR GIVING US THAT PREVIEW.
THANKS FOR HAVING ME, REGIS. WELL, BACK TO THE GRINDSTONE.
AND NOW, OUR NEXT GUEST, FOLKS, HAS BEEN SOMEWHAT HUSH-HUSH... FOR SECURITY REASONS, BELIEVE-IT-OR-NOT.
YOU'VE HEARD ABOUT HIM, READ ABOUT HIM... A FUTURE AUTHOR WHO'S TRYING TO MAKE IT BACK INTO SOCIETY... LET'S HAVE A HAND FOR...
...SERGEANT STAN CARTER... ALIAS, THE SIN-EATER.
CARTER, HUH? HE SAVED SPIDER-MAN'S HASH A FEW DAYS AGO. THIS I GOTTA SEE.

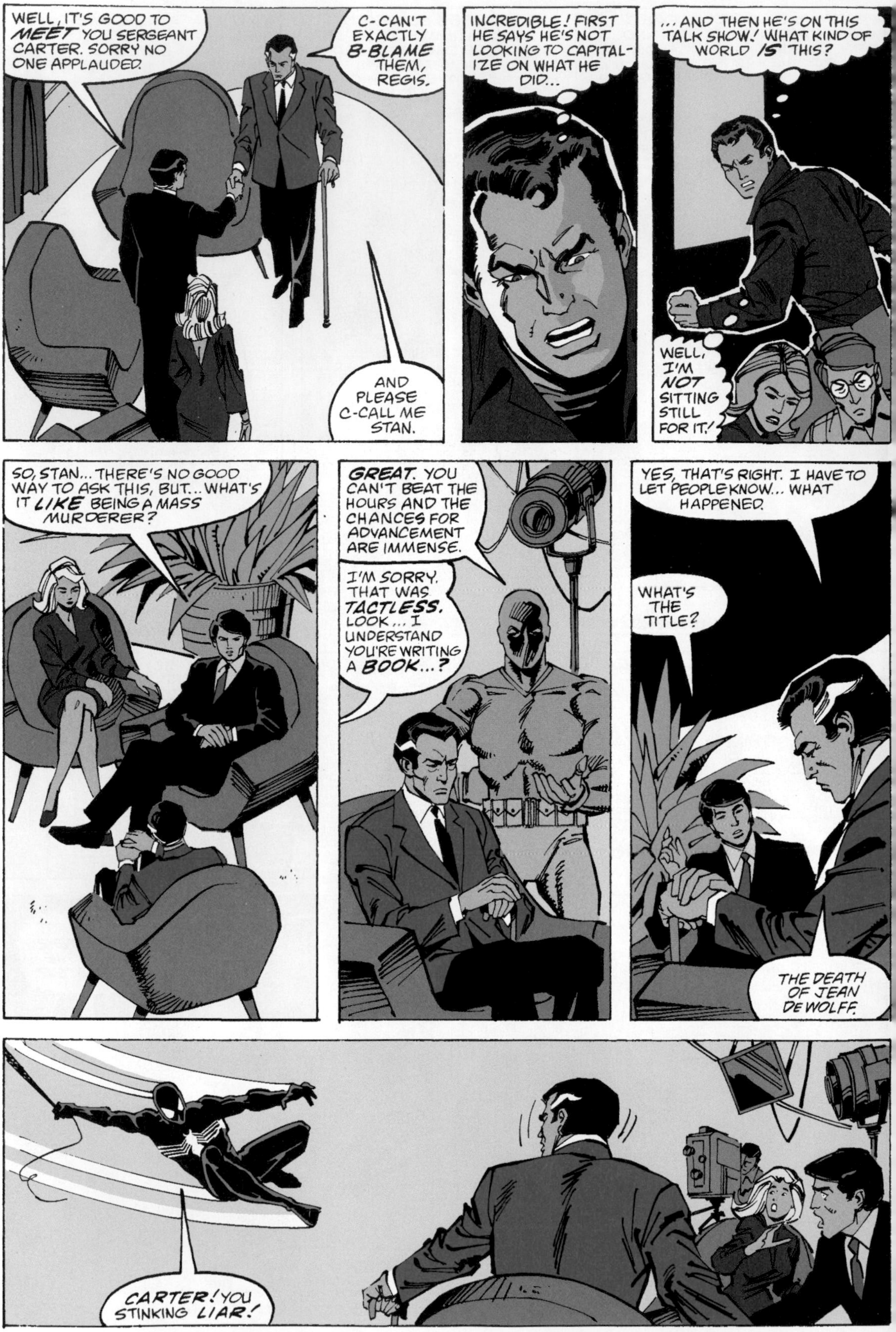
WELL, IT'S GOOD TO MEET YOU SERGEANT CARTER. SORRY NO ONE APPLAUDED.
C-CAN'T EXACTLY B-BLAME THEM, REGIS.
AND PLEASE C-CALL ME STAN.
INCREDIBLE! FIRST HE SAYS HE'S NOT LOOKING TO CAPITAL-IZE ON WHAT HE DID...
... AND THEN HE'S ON THIS TALK SHOW! WHAT KIND OF WORLD IS THIS?
WELL, I'M NOT SITTING STILL FOR IT!
SO, STAN... THERE'S NO GOOD WAY TO ASK THIS, BUT... WHAT'S IT LIKE BEING A MASS MURDERER?
GREAT. YOU CAN'T BEAT THE HOURS AND THE CHANCES FOR ADVANCEMENT ARE IMMENSE.
I'M SORRY. THAT WAS TACTLESS. LOOK... I UNDERSTAND YOU'RE WRITING A BOOK...?
YES, THAT'S RIGHT. I HAVE TO LET PEOPLE KNOW... WHAT HAPPENED.
WHAT'S THE TITLE?
THE DEATH OF JEAN DEWOLFF.
CARTER! YOU STINKING LIAR!

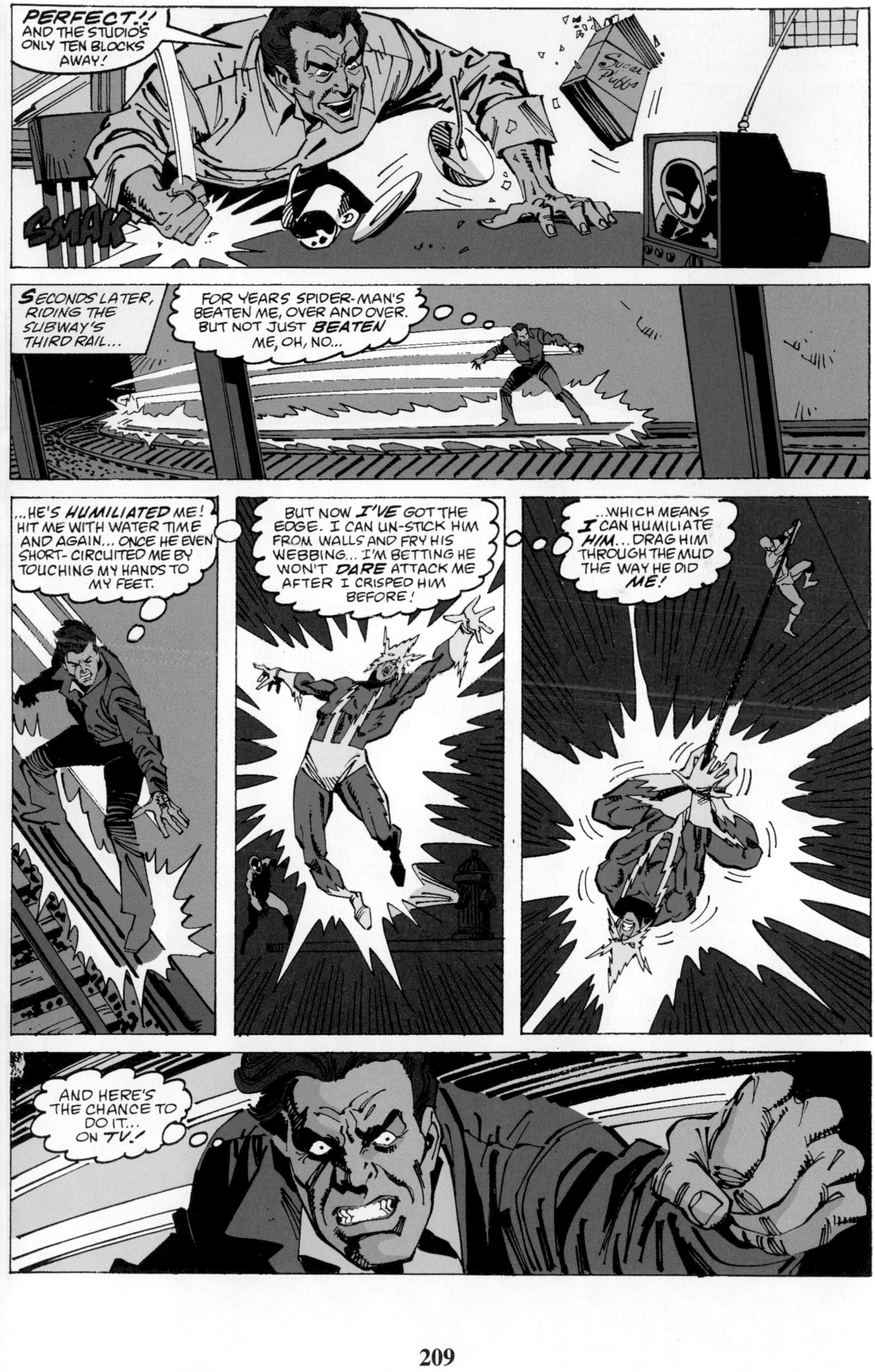
PERFECT!! AND THE STUDIO'S ONLY TEN BLOCKS AWAY!
SMAK
Sugar Puffs
SECONDS LATER, RIDING THE SUBWAY'S THIRD RAIL...
FOR YEARS SPIDER-MAN'S BEATEN ME, OVER AND OVER. BUT NOT JUST BEATEN ME, OH, NO...
...HE'S HUMILIATED ME! HIT ME WITH WATER TIME AND AGAIN... ONCE HE EVEN SHORT-CIRCUITED ME BY TOUCHING MY HANDS TO MY FEET.
BUT NOW I'VE GOT THE EDGE. I CAN UN-STICK HIM FROM WALLS AND FRY HIS WEBBING... I'M BETTING HE WON'T DARE ATTACK ME AFTER I CRISPED HIM BEFORE!
...WHICH MEANS I CAN HUMILIATE HIM... DRAG HIM THROUGH THE MUD THE WAY HE DID ME!
AND HERE'S THE CHANCE TO DO IT... ON TV!

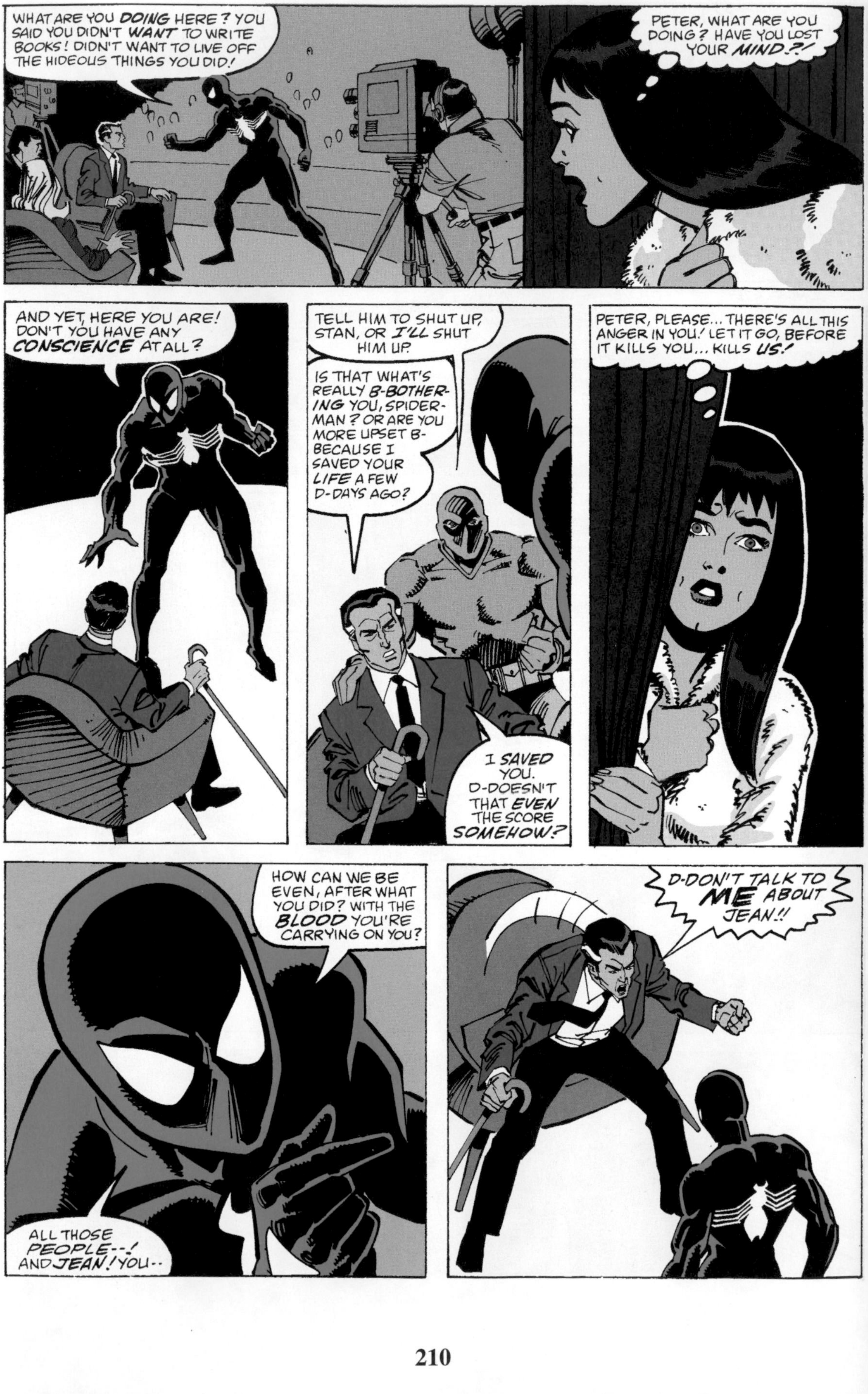

WHAT ARE YOU DOING HERE? YOU SAID YOU DIDN'T WANT TO WRITE BOOKS! DIDN'T WANT TO LIVE OFF THE HIDEOUS THINGS YOU DID!
PETER, WHAT ARE YOU DOING? HAVE YOU LOST YOUR MIND?!
AND YET, HERE YOU ARE! DON'T YOU HAVE ANY CONSCIENCE AT ALL?
TELL HIM TO SHUT UP, STAN, OR I'LL SHUT HIM UP.
IS THAT WHAT'S REALLY B-BOTHERING YOU, SPIDER-MAN? OR ARE YOU MORE UPSET B-BECAUSE I SAVED YOUR LIFE A FEW D-DAYS AGO?
I SAVED YOU. D-DOESN'T THAT EVEN THE SCORE SOMEHOW?
PETER, PLEASE... THERE'S ALL THIS ANGER IN YOU! LET IT GO, BEFORE IT KILLS YOU... KILLS US!
HOW CAN WE BE EVEN, AFTER WHAT YOU DID? WITH THE BLOOD YOU'RE CARRYING ON YOU?
ALL THOSE PEOPLE--! AND JEAN! YOU--
D-DON'T TALK TO ME ABOUT JEAN!!

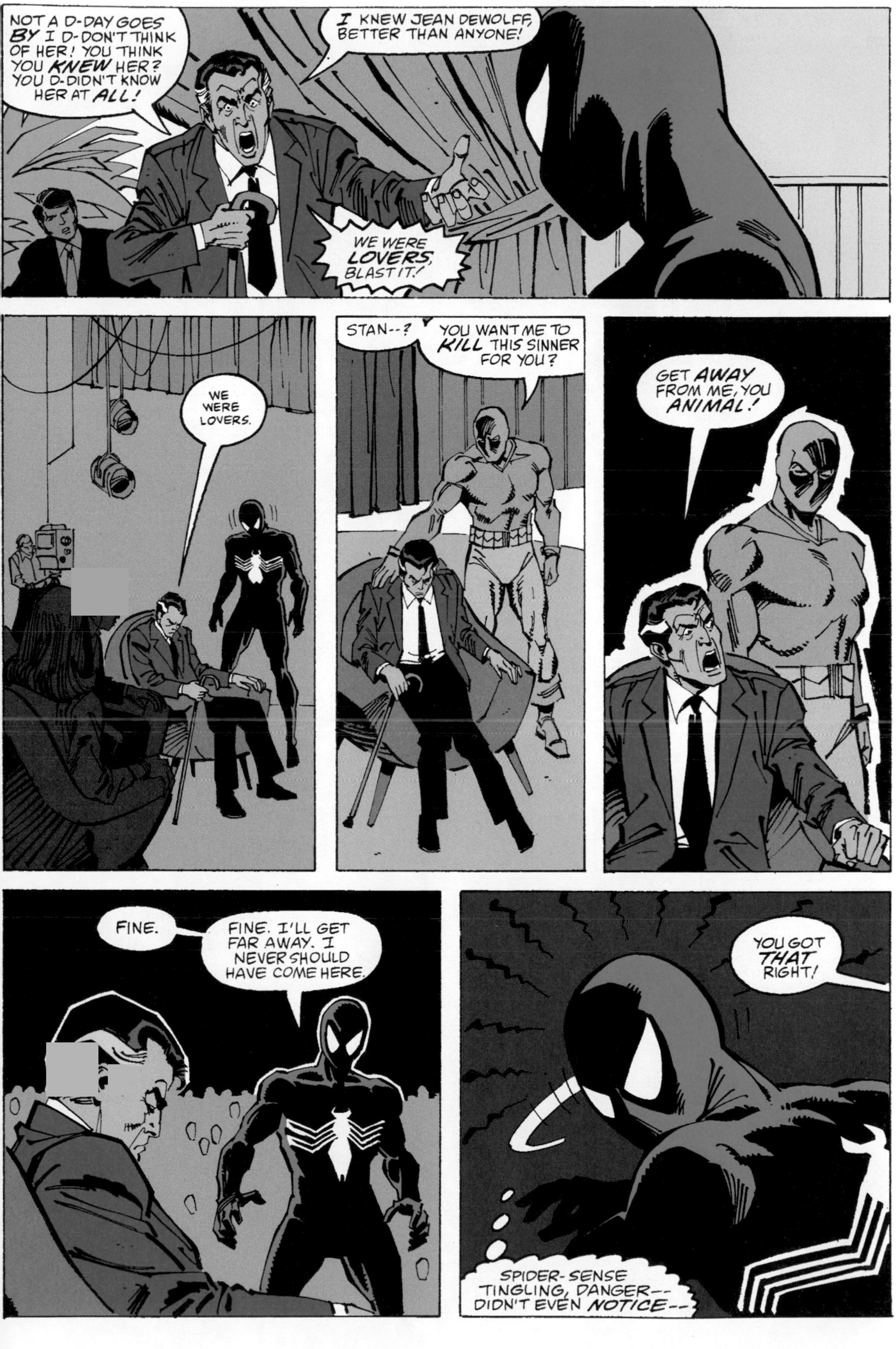
NOT A D-DAY GOES BY I D-DON'T THINK OF HER! YOU THINK YOU KNEW HER? YOU D-DIDN'T KNOW HER AT ALL!
I KNEW JEAN DEWOLFF, BETTER THAN ANYONE!
WE WERE LOVERS, BLAST IT!
WE WERE LOVERS.
STAN--?
YOU WANT ME TO KILL THIS SINNER FOR YOU?
GET AWAY FROM ME, YOU ANIMAL!
FINE.
FINE. I'LL GET FAR AWAY. I NEVER SHOULD HAVE COME HERE.
YOU GOT THAT RIGHT!
SPIDER-SENSE TINGLING, DANGER-- DIDN'T EVEN NOTICE--

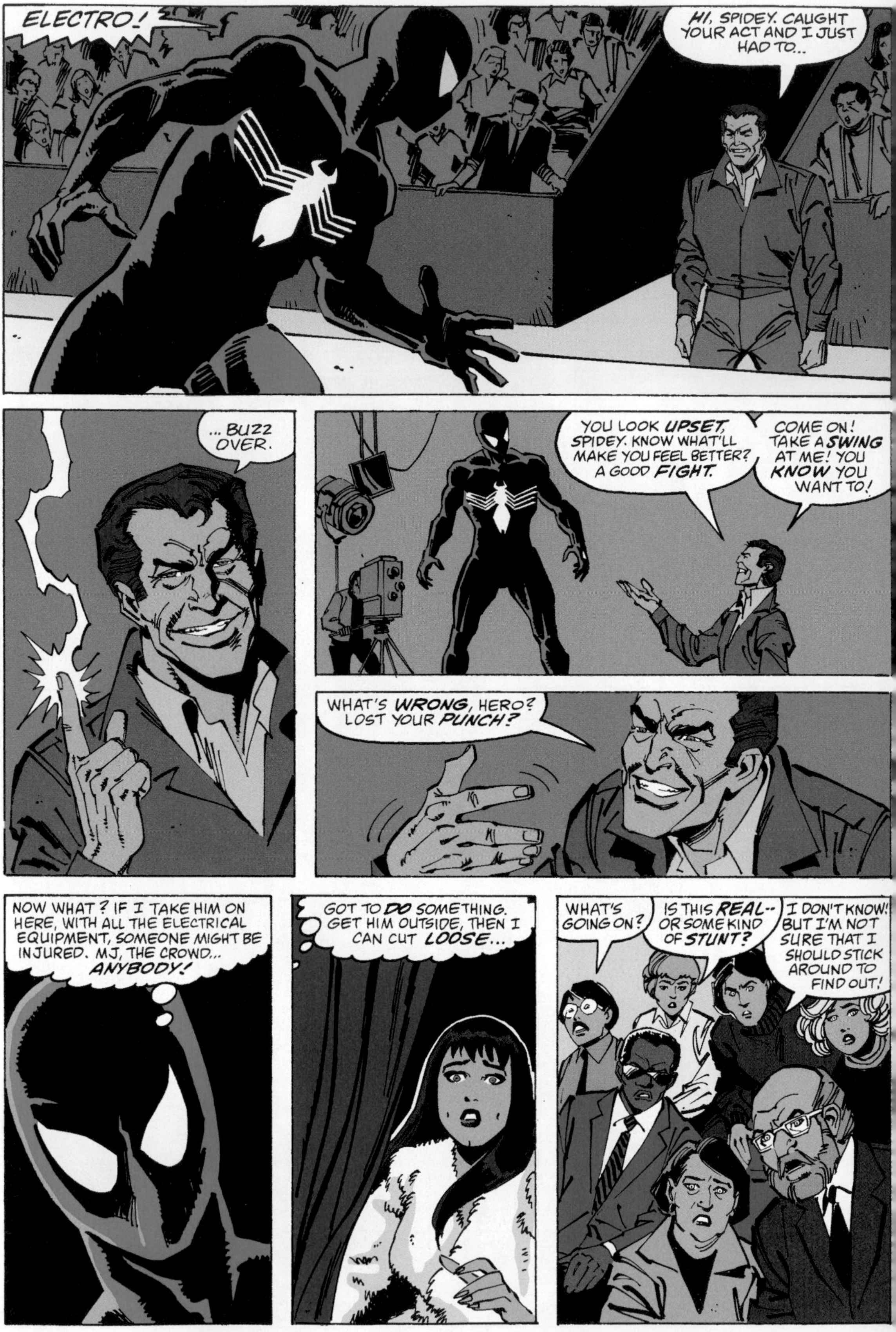
ELECTRO!
HI, SPIDEY. CAUGHT YOUR ACT AND I JUST HAD TO...
...BUZZ OVER.
YOU LOOK UPSET, SPIDEY. KNOW WHAT'LL MAKE YOU FEEL BETTER? A GOOD FIGHT.
COME ON! TAKE A SWING AT ME! YOU KNOW YOU WANT TO!
WHAT'S WRONG, HERO? LOST YOUR PUNCH?
NOW WHAT? IF I TAKE HIM ON HERE, WITH ALL THE ELECTRICAL EQUIPMENT, SOMEONE MIGHT BE INJURED. MJ, THE CROWD... ANYBODY!
GOT TO DO SOMETHING. GET HIM OUTSIDE, THEN I CAN CUT LOOSE...
WHAT'S GOING ON?
IS THIS REAL-- OR SOME KIND OF STUNT?
I DON'T KNOW! BUT I'M NOT SURE THAT I SHOULD STICK AROUND TO FIND OUT!

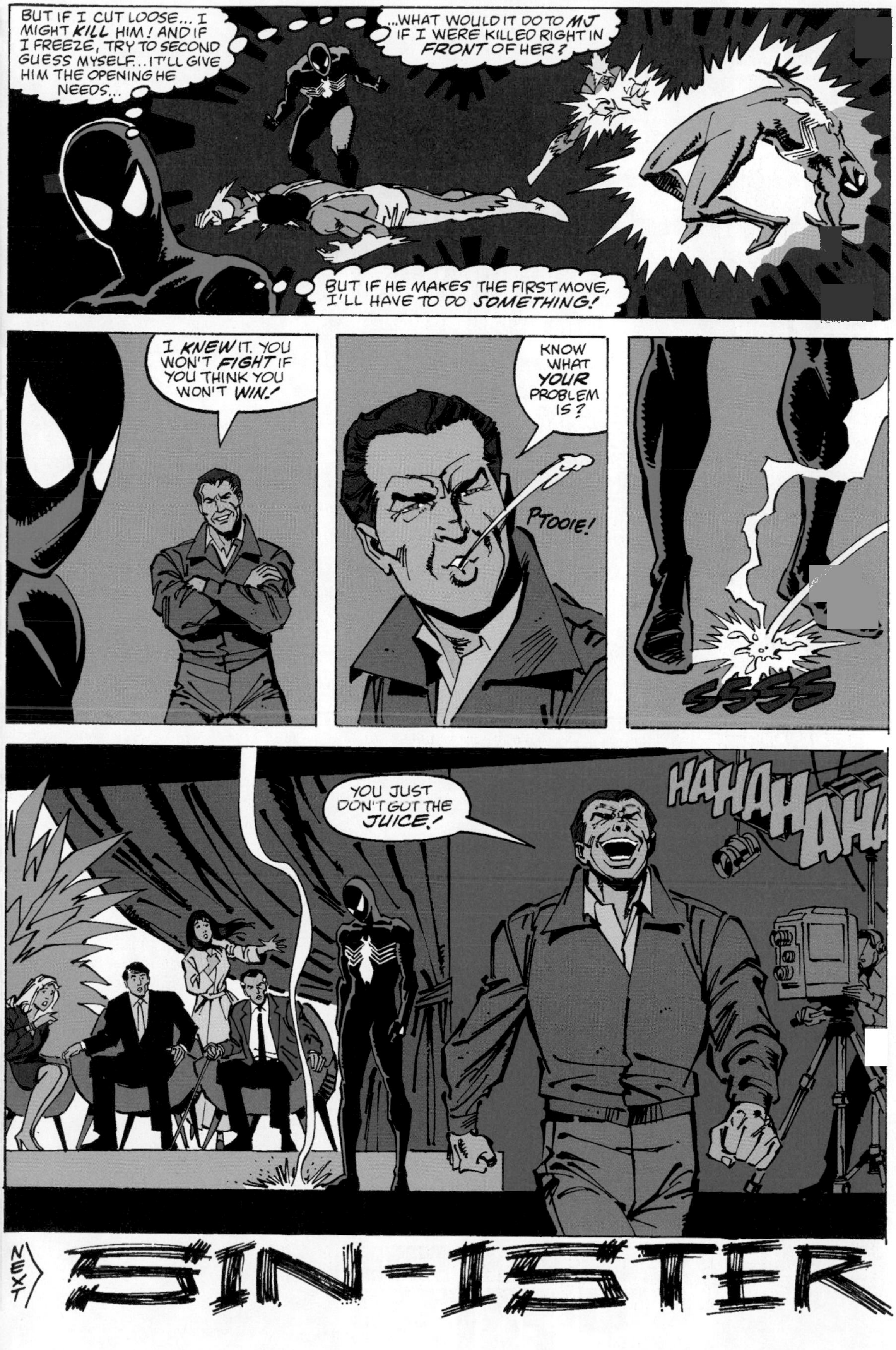

BUT IF I CUT LOOSE... I MIGHT KILL HIM! AND IF I FREEZE, TRY TO SECOND GUESS MYSELF... IT'LL GIVE HIM THE OPENING HE NEEDS...
...WHAT WOULD IT DO TO MJ IF I WERE KILLED RIGHT IN FRONT OF HER?
BUT IF HE MAKES THE FIRST MOVE, I'LL HAVE TO DO SOMETHING!
I KNEW IT. YOU WON'T FIGHT IF YOU THINK YOU WON'T WIN!
KNOW WHAT YOUR PROBLEM IS?
PTOOIE!
SSSSS
YOU JUST DON'T GOT THE JUICE!
HAHAHAHAHA
NEXT
SIN-ISTER

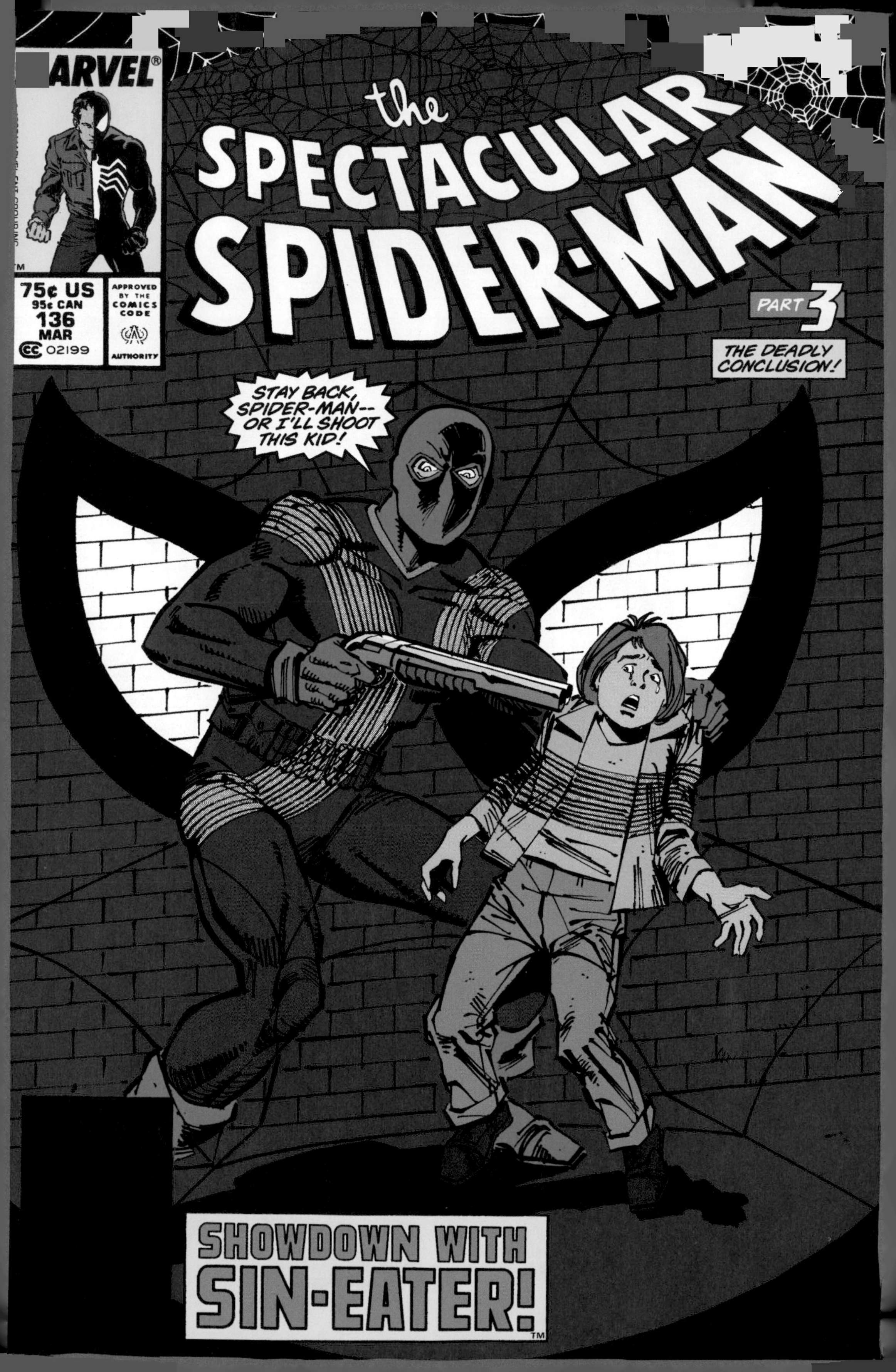

ARVEL
75¢ US
95¢ CAN
136
MAR
02199
APPROVED BY THE COMICS CODE AUTHORITY
the SPECTACULAR SPIDER-MAN
PART 3
THE DEADLY CONCLUSION!
STAY BACK, SPIDER-MAN-- OR I'LL SHOOT THIS KID!
SHOWDOWN WITH SIN-EATER!

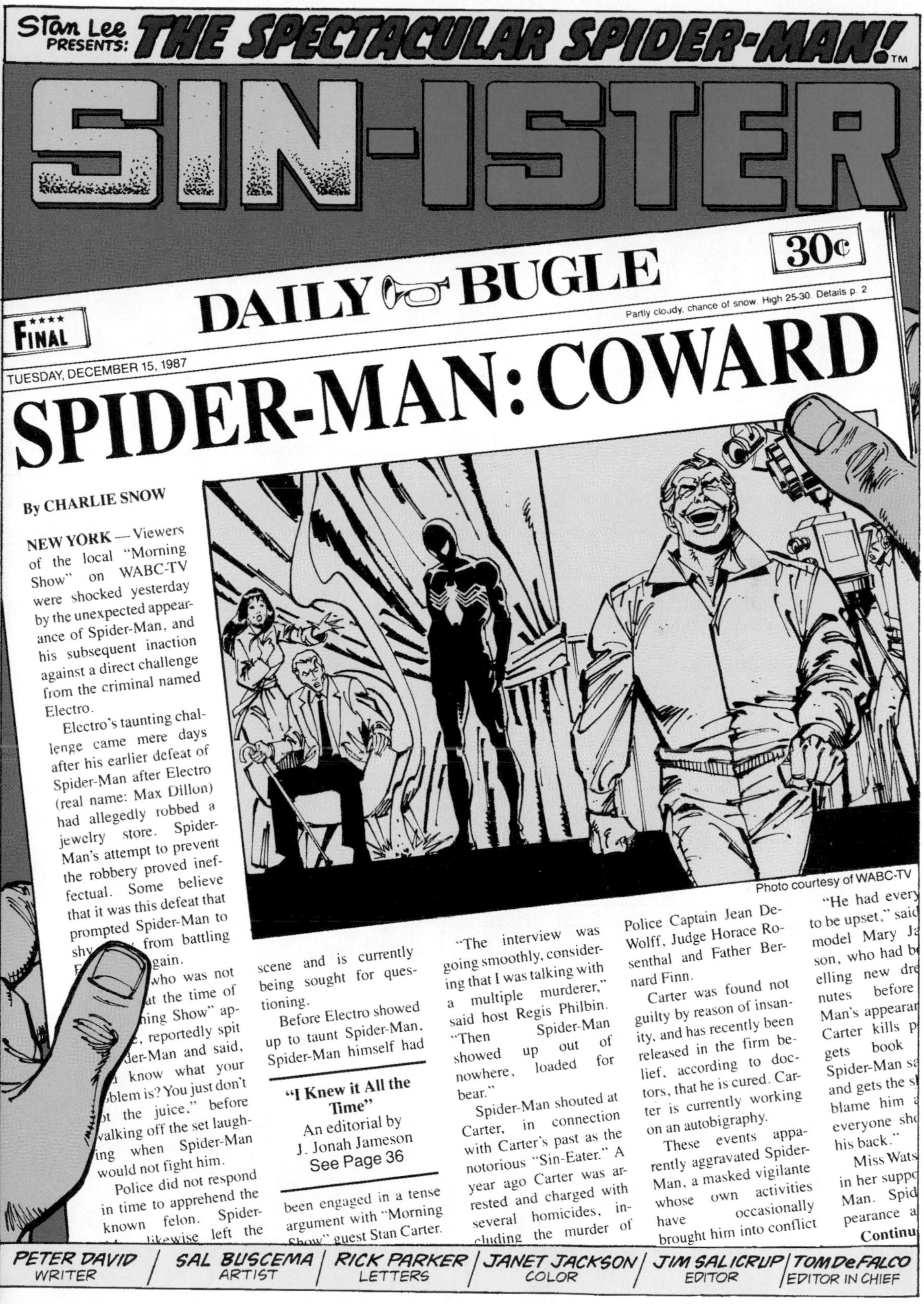

Stan Lee PRESENTS: THE SPECTACULAR SPIDER-MAN!™
SIN-ISTER
30¢
DAILY BUGLE
Partly cloudy, chance of snow. High 25-30. Details p. 2
★★★★ FINAL
TUESDAY, DECEMBER 15, 1987
SPIDER-MAN: COWARD
By CHARLIE SNOW
NEW YORK — Viewers of the local "Morning Show" on WABC-TV were shocked yesterday by the unexpected appearance of Spider-Man, and his subsequent inaction against a direct challenge from the criminal named Electro.
Electro's taunting challenge came mere days after his earlier defeat of Spider-Man after Electro (real name: Max Dillon) had allegedly robbed a jewelry store. Spider-Man's attempt to prevent the robbery proved ineffectual. Some believe that it was this defeat that prompted Spider-Man to
from battling
gain.
who was not
at the time of
ning Show" ap-
, reportedly spit
der-Man and said,
know what your
blem is? You just don't
t the juice," before
valking off the set laugh-
ing when Spider-Man would not fight him.
Police did not respond in time to apprehend the known felon. Spider-
likewise left the
scene and is currently being sought for questioning.
Before Electro showed up to taunt Spider-Man, Spider-Man himself had
"I Knew it All the Time"
An editorial by
J. Jonah Jameson
See Page 36
been engaged in a tense argument with "Morning Show" guest Stan Carter.
"The interview was going smoothly, considering that I was talking with a multiple murderer," said host Regis Philbin. "Then Spider-Man showed up out of nowhere, loaded for bear."
Spider-Man shouted at Carter, in connection with Carter's past as the notorious "Sin-Eater." A year ago Carter was arrested and charged with several homicides, including the murder of
Police Captain Jean DeWolff, Judge Horace Rosenthal and Father Bernard Finn.
Carter was found not guilty by reason of insanity, and has recently been released in the firm belief, according to doctors, that he is cured. Carter is currently working on an autobiography.
These events apparently aggravated Spider-Man, a masked vigilante whose own activities have occasionally brought him into conflict
"He had every
to be upset," said
model Mary J
son, who had b
elling new dr
nutes before
Man's appeara
Carter kills
gets book
Spider-Man s
and gets the s
blame him
everyone sh
his back."
Miss Wats
in her supp
Man. Spid
pearance a
Continu
Photo courtesy of WABC-TV
PETER DAVID WRITER
SAL BUSCEMA ARTIST
RICK PARKER LETTERS
JANET JACKSON COLOR
JIM SALICRUP EDITOR
TOM DeFALCO EDITOR IN CHIEF

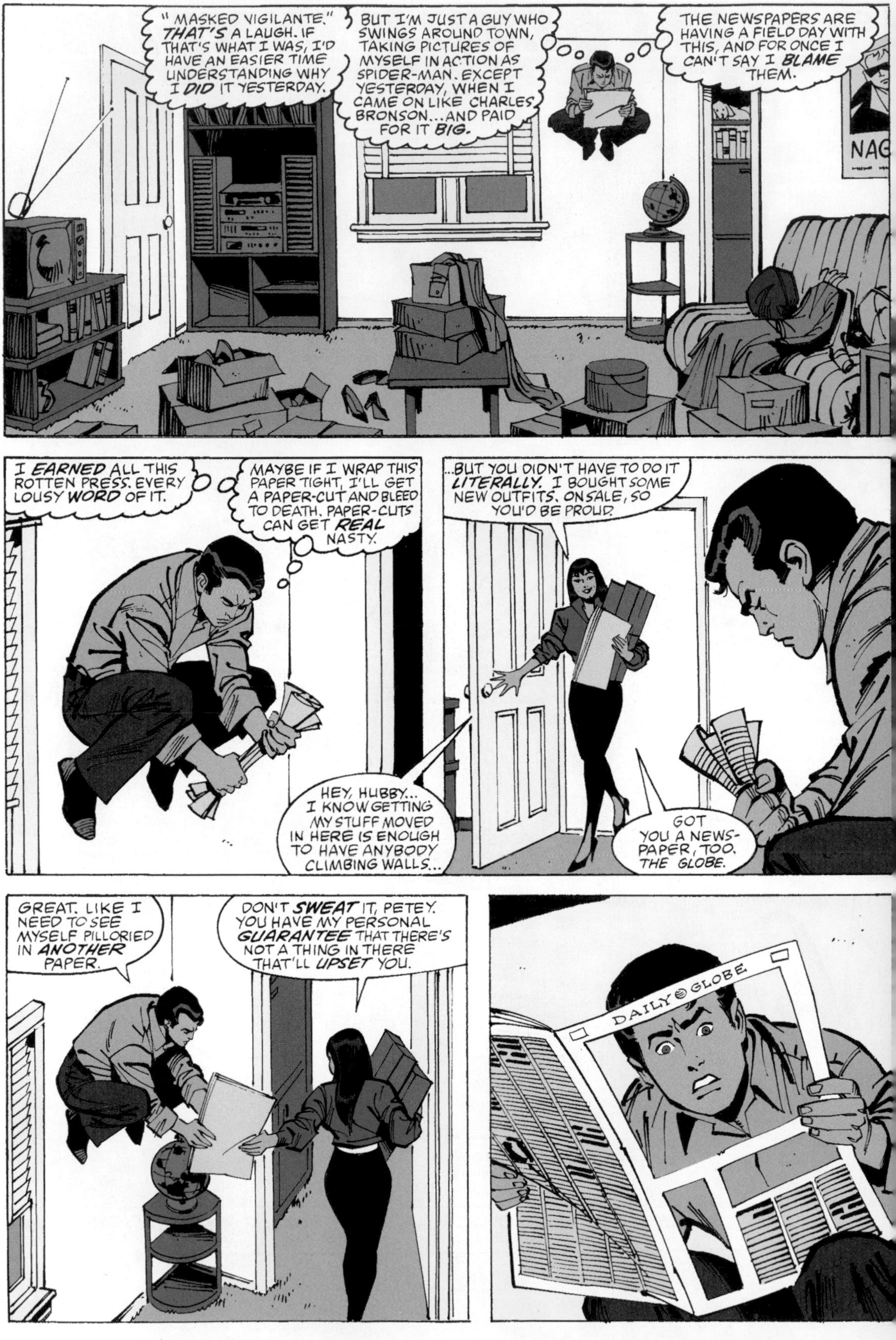
"MASKED VIGILANTE." THAT'S A LAUGH. IF THAT'S WHAT I WAS, I'D HAVE AN EASIER TIME UNDERSTANDING WHY I DID IT YESTERDAY.
BUT I'M JUST A GUY WHO SWINGS AROUND TOWN, TAKING PICTURES OF MYSELF IN ACTION AS SPIDER-MAN. EXCEPT YESTERDAY, WHEN I CAME ON LIKE CHARLES BRONSON...AND PAID FOR IT BIG.
THE NEWSPAPERS ARE HAVING A FIELD DAY WITH THIS, AND FOR ONCE I CAN'T SAY I BLAME THEM.
I EARNED ALL THIS ROTTEN PRESS. EVERY LOUSY WORD OF IT.
MAYBE IF I WRAP THIS PAPER TIGHT, I'LL GET A PAPER-CUT AND BLEED TO DEATH. PAPER-CUTS CAN GET REAL NASTY.
HEY, HUBBY... I KNOW GETTING MY STUFF MOVED IN HERE IS ENOUGH TO HAVE ANYBODY CLIMBING WALLS...
...BUT YOU DIDN'T HAVE TO DO IT LITERALLY. I BOUGHT SOME NEW OUTFITS. ON SALE, SO YOU'D BE PROUD.
GOT YOU A NEWS-PAPER, TOO. THE GLOBE.
GREAT. LIKE I NEED TO SEE MYSELF PILLORIED IN ANOTHER PAPER.
DON'T SWEAT IT, PETEY. YOU HAVE MY PERSONAL GUARANTEE THAT THERE'S NOT A THING IN THERE THAT'LL UPSET YOU.
DAILY GLOBE

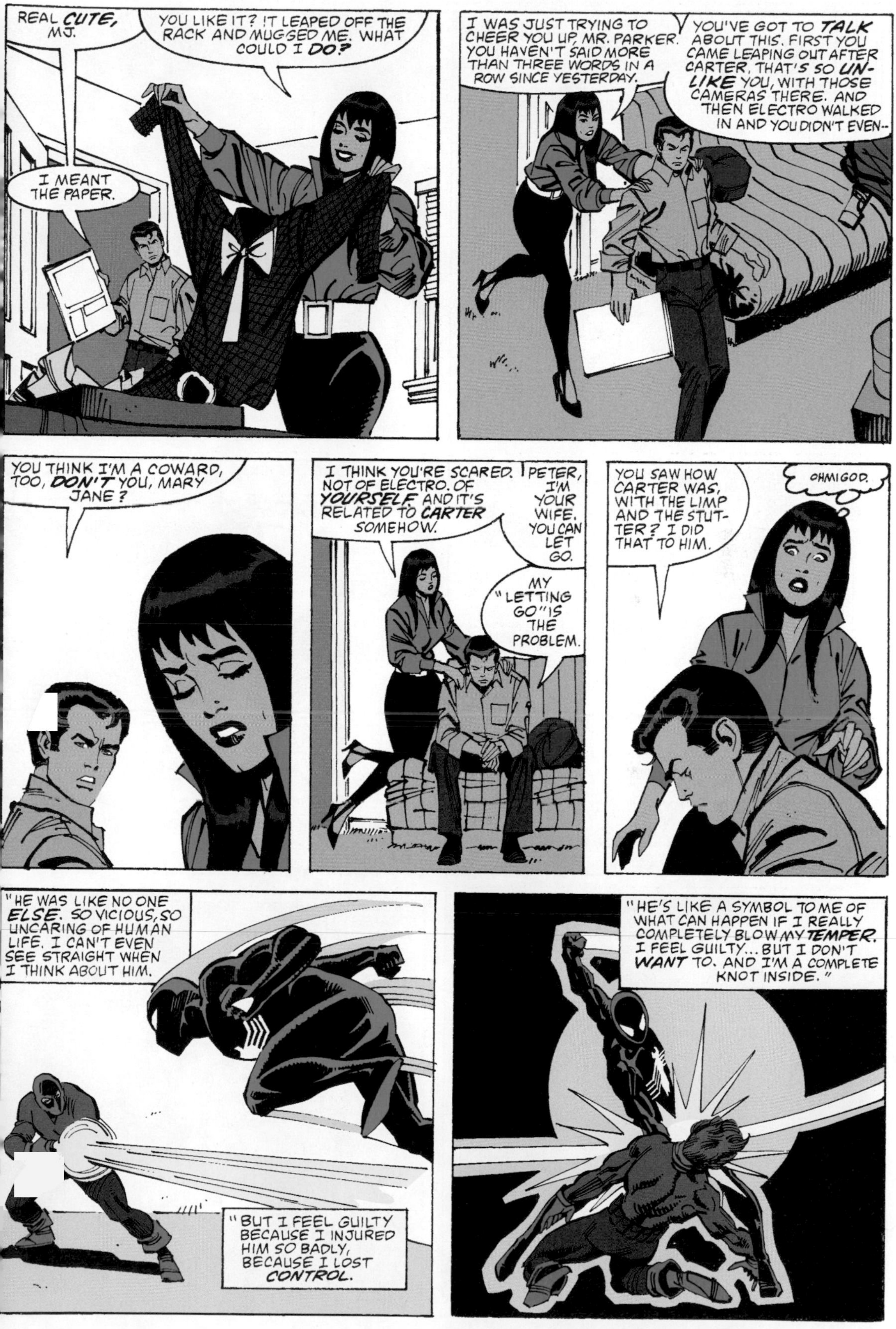
REAL CUTE, MJ.
YOU LIKE IT? !T LEAPED OFF THE RACK AND MUGGED ME. WHAT COULD I DO?
I MEANT THE PAPER.
I WAS JUST TRYING TO CHEER YOU UP, MR. PARKER. YOU HAVEN'T SAID MORE THAN THREE WORDS IN A ROW SINCE YESTERDAY.
YOU'VE GOT TO TALK ABOUT THIS. FIRST YOU CAME LEAPING OUT AFTER CARTER, THAT'S SO UNLIKE YOU, WITH THOSE CAMERAS THERE. AND THEN ELECTRO WALKED IN AND YOU DIDN'T EVEN--
YOU THINK I'M A COWARD, TOO, DON'T YOU, MARY JANE?
I THINK YOU'RE SCARED. NOT OF ELECTRO. OF YOURSELF AND IT'S RELATED TO CARTER SOMEHOW.
PETER, I'M YOUR WIFE. YOU CAN LET GO.
MY "LETTING GO" IS THE PROBLEM.
YOU SAW HOW CARTER WAS, WITH THE LIMP AND THE STUTTER? I DID THAT TO HIM.
OHMIGOD.
"HE WAS LIKE NO ONE ELSE. SO VICIOUS, SO UNCARING OF HUMAN LIFE. I CAN'T EVEN SEE STRAIGHT WHEN I THINK ABOUT HIM.
"BUT I FEEL GUILTY BECAUSE I INJURED HIM SO BADLY, BECAUSE I LOST CONTROL.
"HE'S LIKE A SYMBOL TO ME OF WHAT CAN HAPPEN IF I REALLY COMPLETELY BLOW MY TEMPER. I FEEL GUILTY... BUT I DON'T WANT TO. AND I'M A COMPLETE KNOT INSIDE."

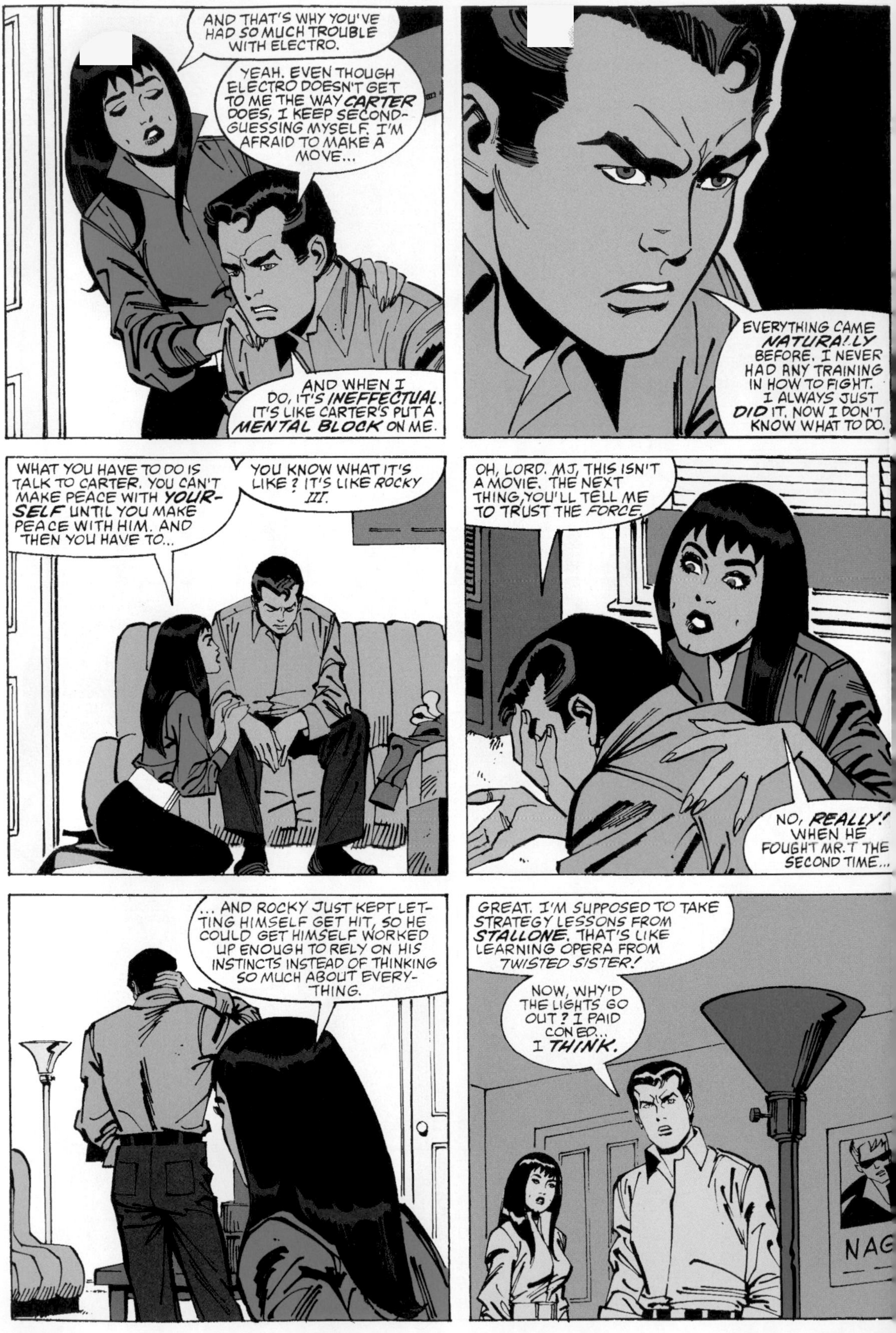
AND THAT'S WHY YOU'VE HAD SO MUCH TROUBLE WITH ELECTRO.
YEAH. EVEN THOUGH ELECTRO DOESN'T GET TO ME THE WAY CARTER DOES, I KEEP SECOND-GUESSING MYSELF. I'M AFRAID TO MAKE A MOVE...
AND WHEN I DO, IT'S INEFFECTUAL. IT'S LIKE CARTER'S PUT A MENTAL BLOCK ON ME.
EVERYTHING CAME NATURALLY BEFORE. I NEVER HAD ANY TRAINING IN HOW TO FIGHT. I ALWAYS JUST DID IT. NOW I DON'T KNOW WHAT TO DO.
WHAT YOU HAVE TO DO IS TALK TO CARTER. YOU CAN'T MAKE PEACE WITH YOURSELF UNTIL YOU MAKE PEACE WITH HIM. AND THEN YOU HAVE TO...
YOU KNOW WHAT IT'S LIKE? IT'S LIKE ROCKY III.
OH, LORD. MJ, THIS ISN'T A MOVIE. THE NEXT THING, YOU'LL TELL ME TO TRUST THE FORCE.
NO, REALLY! WHEN HE FOUGHT MR. T THE SECOND TIME...
... AND ROCKY JUST KEPT LETTING HIMSELF GET HIT, SO HE COULD GET HIMSELF WORKED UP ENOUGH TO RELY ON HIS INSTINCTS INSTEAD OF THINKING SO MUCH ABOUT EVERYTHING.
GREAT. I'M SUPPOSED TO TAKE STRATEGY LESSONS FROM STALLONE. THAT'S LIKE LEARNING OPERA FROM TWISTED SISTER!
NOW, WHY'D THE LIGHTS GO OUT? I PAID CON ED... I THINK.
NAG

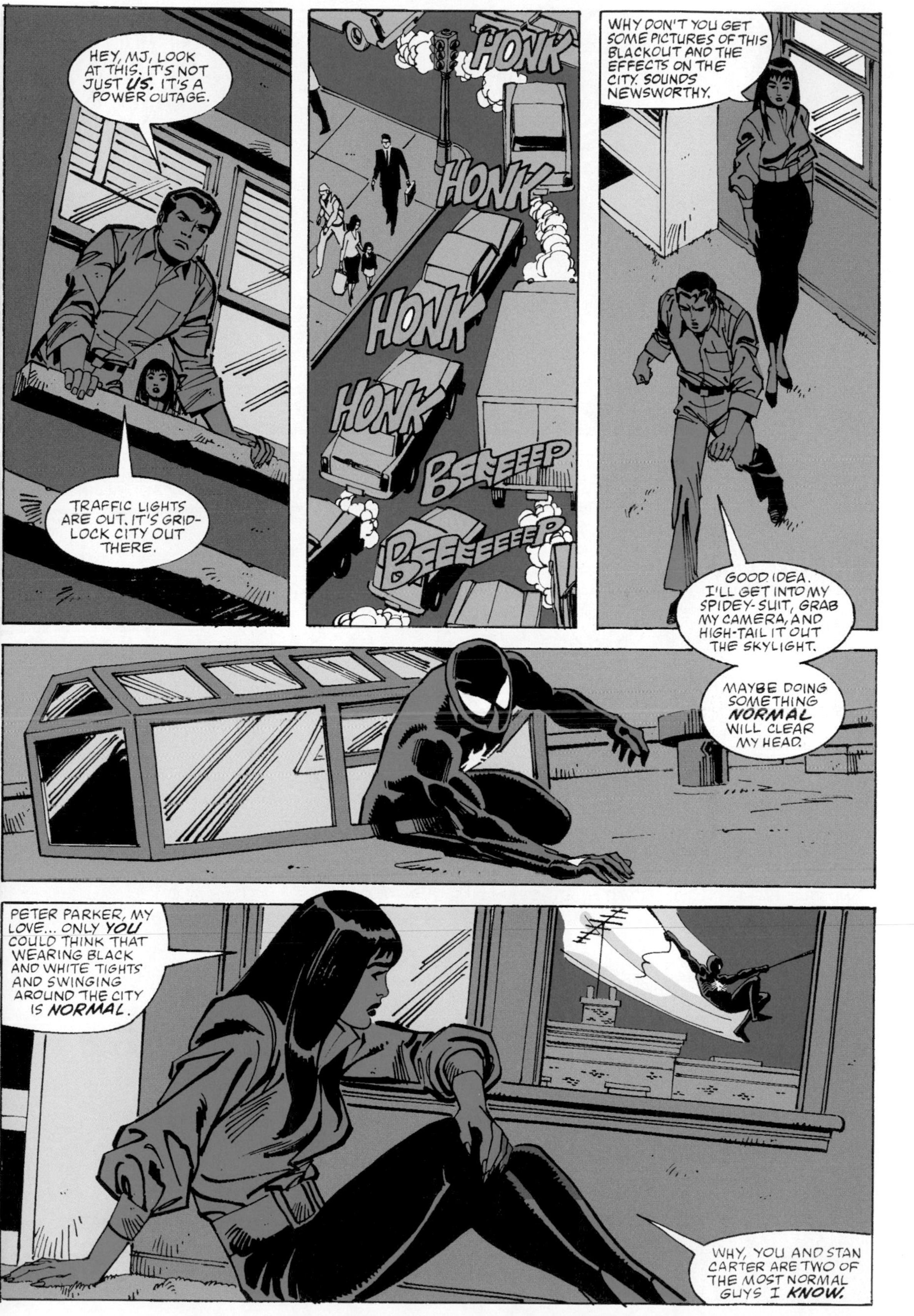
HEY, MJ, LOOK AT THIS. IT'S NOT JUST US. IT'S A POWER OUTAGE.
TRAFFIC LIGHTS ARE OUT. IT'S GRID-LOCK CITY OUT THERE.
HONK
HONK
HONK
HONK
BEEEEEP
BEEEEEEEP
WHY DON'T YOU GET SOME PICTURES OF THIS BLACKOUT AND THE EFFECTS ON THE CITY. SOUNDS NEWSWORTHY.
GOOD IDEA. I'LL GET INTO MY SPIDEY-SUIT, GRAB MY CAMERA, AND HIGH-TAIL IT OUT THE SKYLIGHT.
MAYBE DOING SOMETHING NORMAL WILL CLEAR MY HEAD.
PETER PARKER, MY LOVE... ONLY YOU COULD THINK THAT WEARING BLACK AND WHITE TIGHTS AND SWINGING AROUND THE CITY IS NORMAL.
WHY, YOU AND STAN CARTER ARE TWO OF THE MOST NORMAL GUYS I KNOW.

CHAPTER ONE. I C-COULD TELL YOU, THE READER, ALL K-KINDS OF THINGS ABOUT MY EARLY LIFE. MY FAMILY, MY FRIENDS, THE FIRST FROG I CAUGHT, THE FIRST G-G-GIRL I K-KISSED...

B-BUT THAT'S NOT WHAT YOU P-PAID MONEY TO READ ABOUT, IS IT? YOU WANT TO KNOW ABOUT... AFTER. ABOUT D-DEATH. ABOUT NOW.

OY.

I HAVEN'T SLEPT FOR MORE THAN AN HOUR AT A TIME FOR A YEAR. HOW'S THAT FOR STARTERS?

I K-KEEP THINKING ABOUT JEAN, THE LAST NIGHT I WAS WITH HER B-BEFORE I K-K-K-...B-BEFORE SHE DIED.

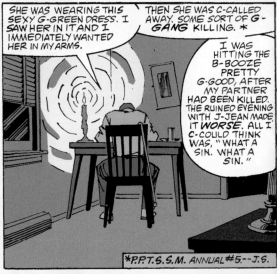

SHE WAS WEARING THIS SEXY G-GREEN DRESS. I SAW HER IN IT AND I IMMEDIATELY WANTED HER IN MY ARMS.

THEN SHE WAS C-CALLED AWAY. SOME SORT OF G-GANG KILLING. *

I WAS HITTING THE B-BOOZE PRETTY G-GOOD, AFTER MY PARTNER HAD BEEN KILLED. THE RUINED EVENING WITH J-JEAN MADE IT WORSE. ALL I C-COULD THINK WAS, "WHAT A SIN. WHAT A SIN."

*P.P.T.S.S.M. ANNUAL #5.--J.S.

AND THAT NIGHT... I HEARD HIM C-CALL ME THE FIRST TIME.

IS THAT WHAT ALL YOU VOYEURS WANTED TO KNOW?

OH, STAAAAAN......

I GOT SOMETHING FOR YOU.

ARRRRHH!

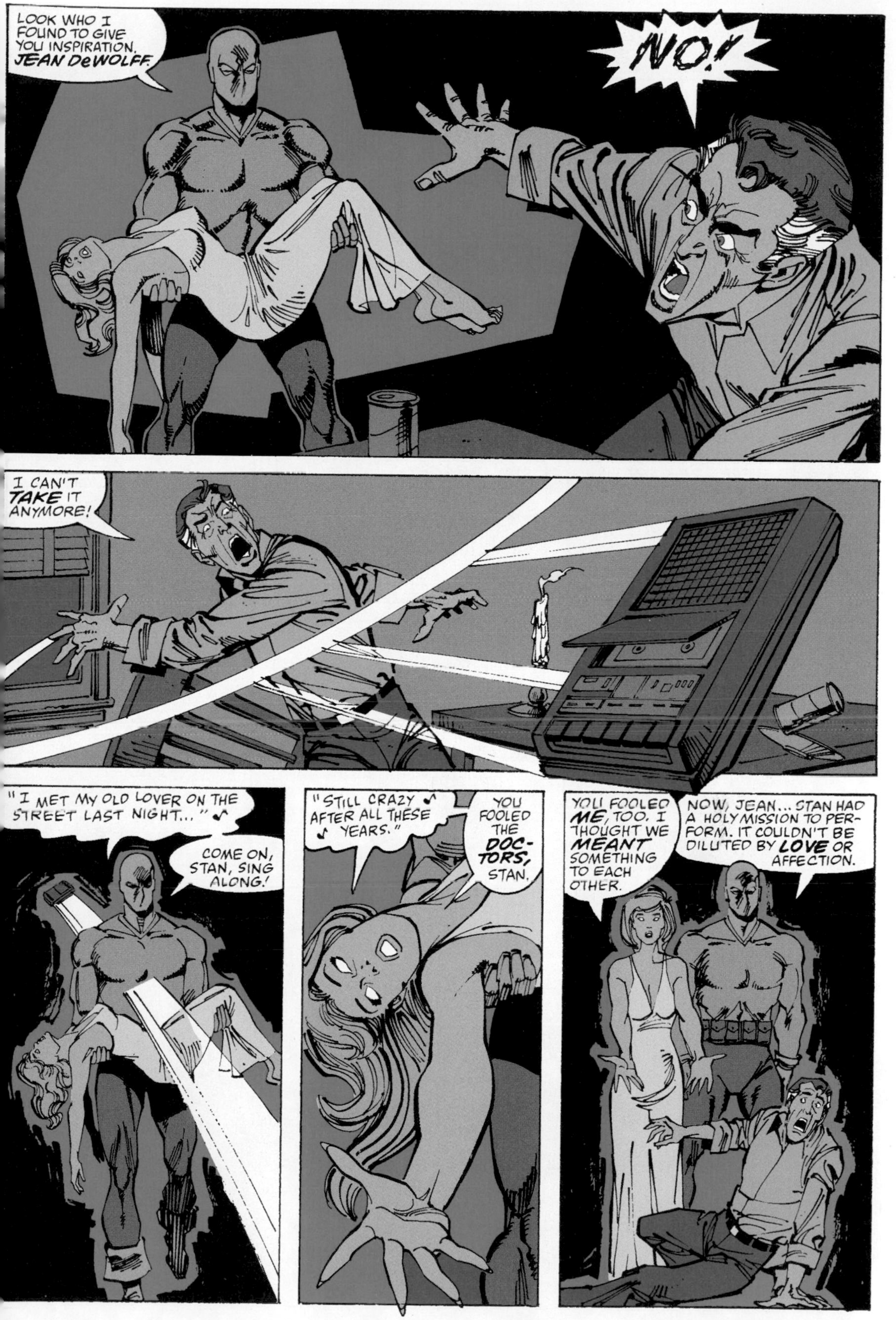
LOOK WHO I FOUND TO GIVE YOU INSPIRATION. JEAN DeWOLFF.
NO!
I CAN'T TAKE IT ANYMORE!
"I MET MY OLD LOVER ON THE STREET LAST NIGHT..."
COME ON, STAN, SING ALONG!
"STILL CRAZY AFTER ALL THESE YEARS."
YOU FOOLED THE DOCTORS, STAN.
YOU FOOLED ME, TOO. I THOUGHT WE MEANT SOMETHING TO EACH OTHER.
NOW, JEAN... STAN HAD A HOLY MISSION TO PERFORM. IT COULDN'T BE DILUTED BY LOVE OR AFFECTION.

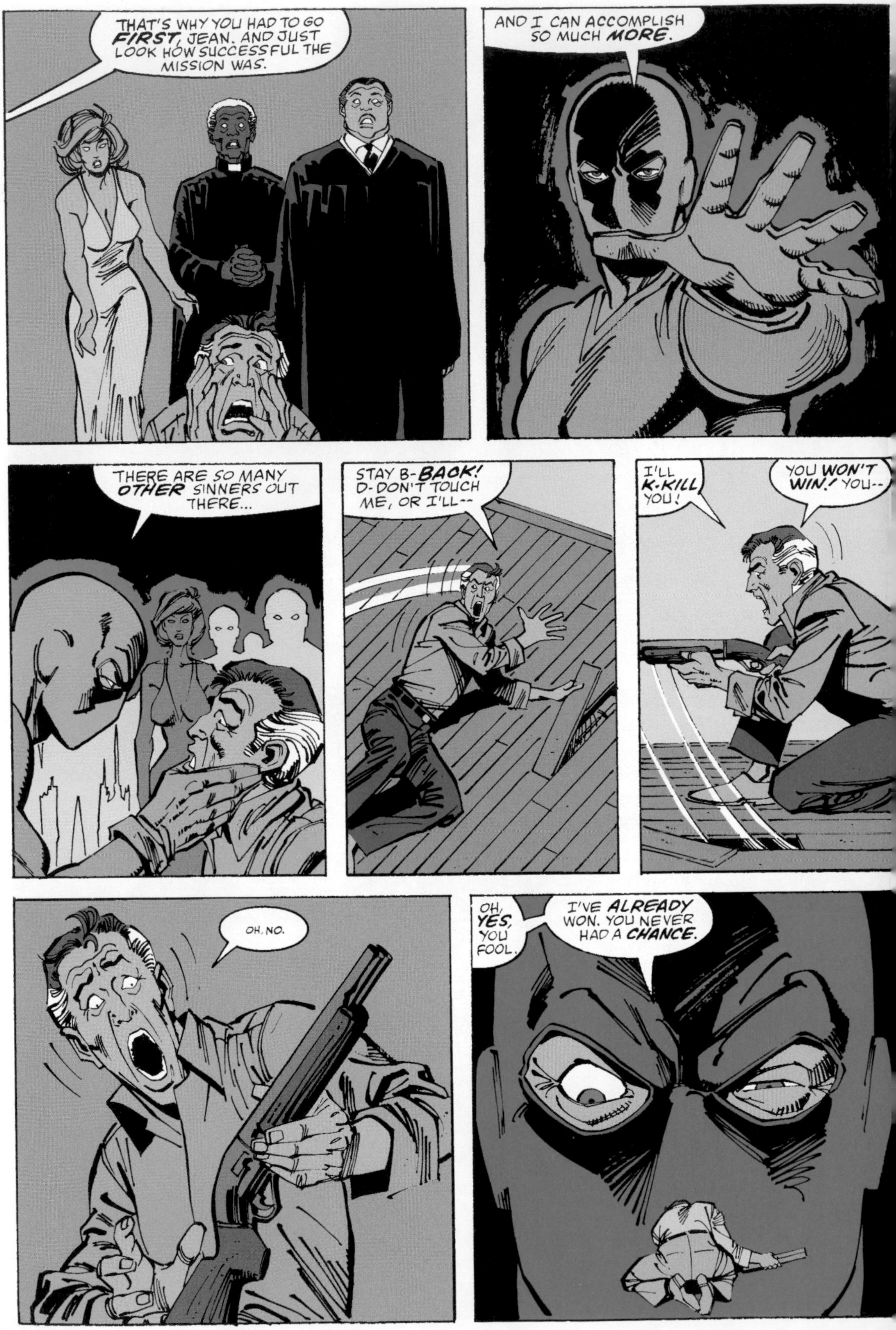
THAT'S WHY YOU HAD TO GO FIRST, JEAN. AND JUST LOOK HOW SUCCESSFUL THE MISSION WAS.
AND I CAN ACCOMPLISH SO MUCH MORE.
THERE ARE SO MANY OTHER SINNERS OUT THERE...
STAY B-BACK! D-DON'T TOUCH ME, OR I'LL--
I'LL K-KILL YOU!
YOU WON'T WIN! YOU--
OH, NO.
OH, YES, YOU FOOL.
I'VE ALREADY WON. YOU NEVER HAD A CHANCE.

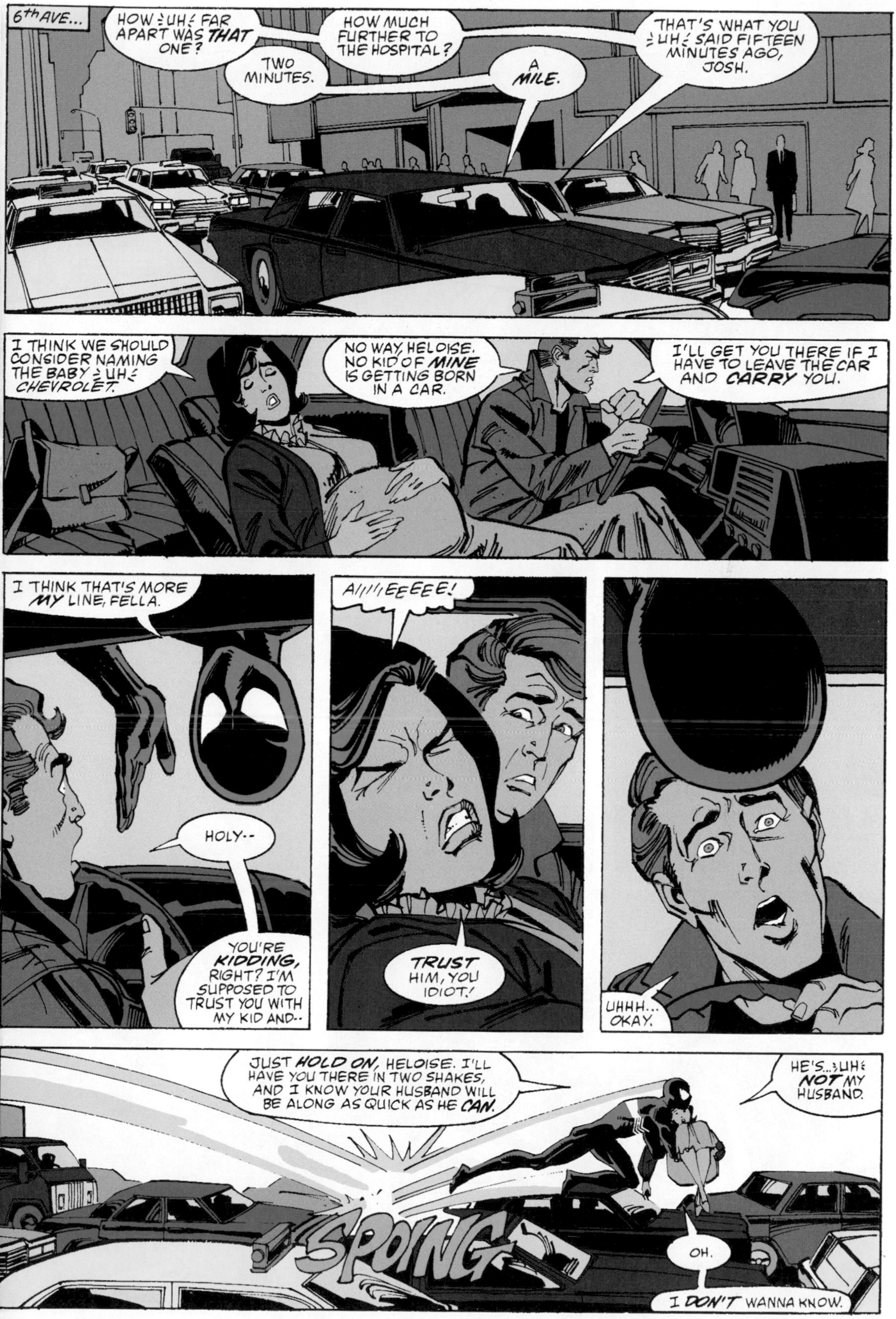
6th AVE...
HOW -UH- FAR APART WAS THAT ONE?
TWO MINUTES.
HOW MUCH FURTHER TO THE HOSPITAL?
A MILE.
THAT'S WHAT YOU -UH- SAID FIFTEEN MINUTES AGO, JOSH.
I THINK WE SHOULD CONSIDER NAMING THE BABY -UH- CHEVROLET.
NO WAY, HELOISE. NO KID OF MINE IS GETTING BORN IN A CAR.
I'LL GET YOU THERE IF I HAVE TO LEAVE THE CAR AND CARRY YOU.
I THINK THAT'S MORE MY LINE, FELLA.
HOLY--
YOU'RE KIDDING, RIGHT? I'M SUPPOSED TO TRUST YOU WITH MY KID AND--
AIIIIEEEEE!
TRUST HIM, YOU IDIOT!
UHHH... OKAY.
JUST HOLD ON, HELOISE. I'LL HAVE YOU THERE IN TWO SHAKES, AND I KNOW YOUR HUSBAND WILL BE ALONG AS QUICK AS HE CAN.
HE'S...-UH- NOT MY HUSBAND.
SPOING
OH.
I DON'T WANNA KNOW.

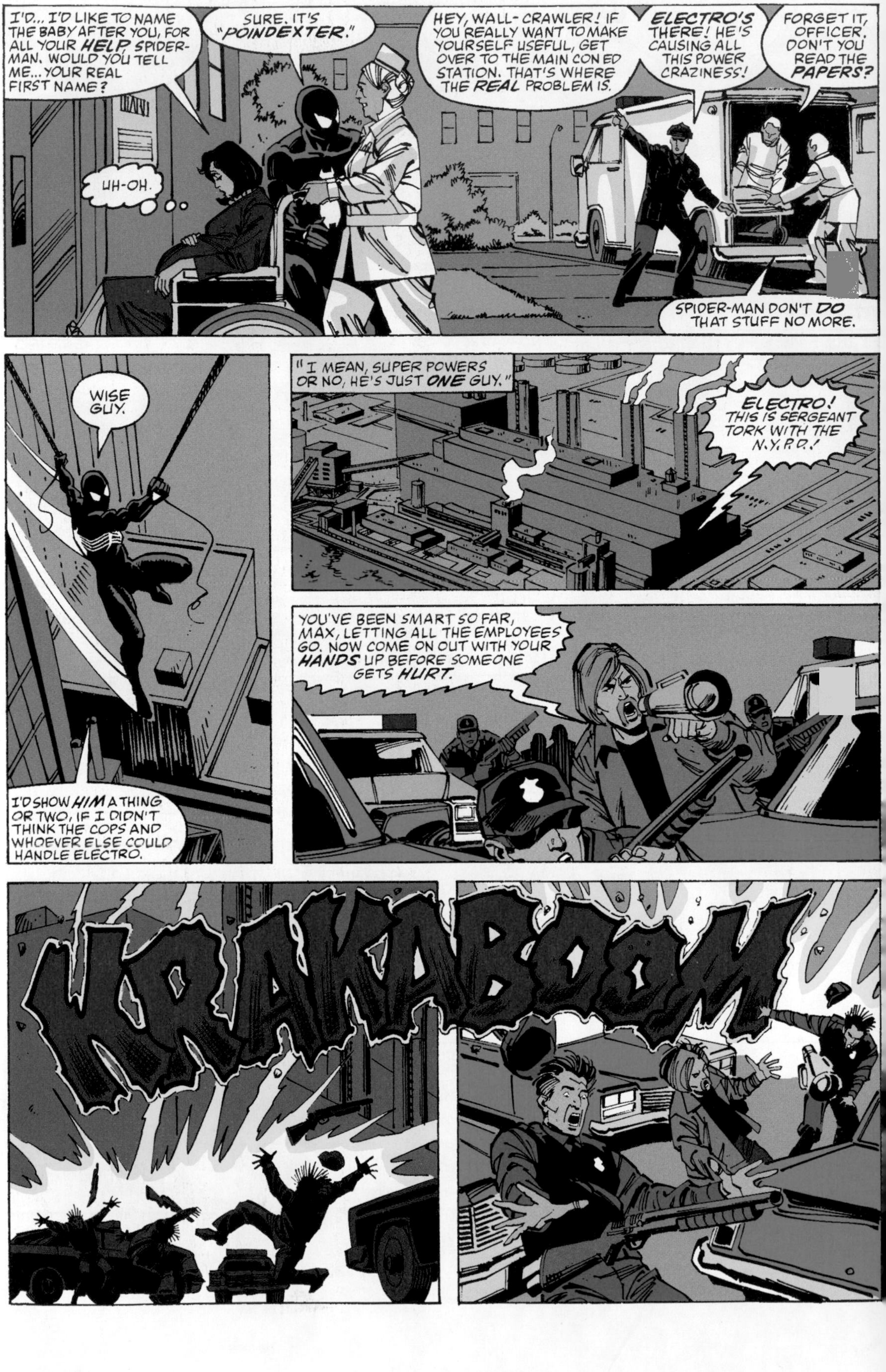
I'D... I'D LIKE TO NAME THE BABY AFTER YOU, FOR ALL YOUR HELP SPIDER-MAN. WOULD YOU TELL ME... YOUR REAL FIRST NAME?
SURE. IT'S "POINDEXTER."
UH-OH.
HEY, WALL-CRAWLER! IF YOU REALLY WANT TO MAKE YOURSELF USEFUL, GET OVER TO THE MAIN CON ED STATION. THAT'S WHERE THE REAL PROBLEM IS.
ELECTRO'S THERE! HE'S CAUSING ALL THIS POWER CRAZINESS!
FORGET IT, OFFICER. DON'T YOU READ THE PAPERS?
SPIDER-MAN DON'T DO THAT STUFF NO MORE.
WISE GUY.
I'D SHOW HIM A THING OR TWO, IF I DIDN'T THINK THE COPS AND WHOEVER ELSE COULD HANDLE ELECTRO.
"I MEAN, SUPER POWERS OR NO, HE'S JUST ONE GUY."
ELECTRO! THIS IS SERGEANT TORK WITH THE N.Y.P.D.!
YOU'VE BEEN SMART SO FAR, MAX, LETTING ALL THE EMPLOYEES GO. NOW COME ON OUT WITH YOUR HANDS UP BEFORE SOMEONE GETS HURT.
KRAKABOOM

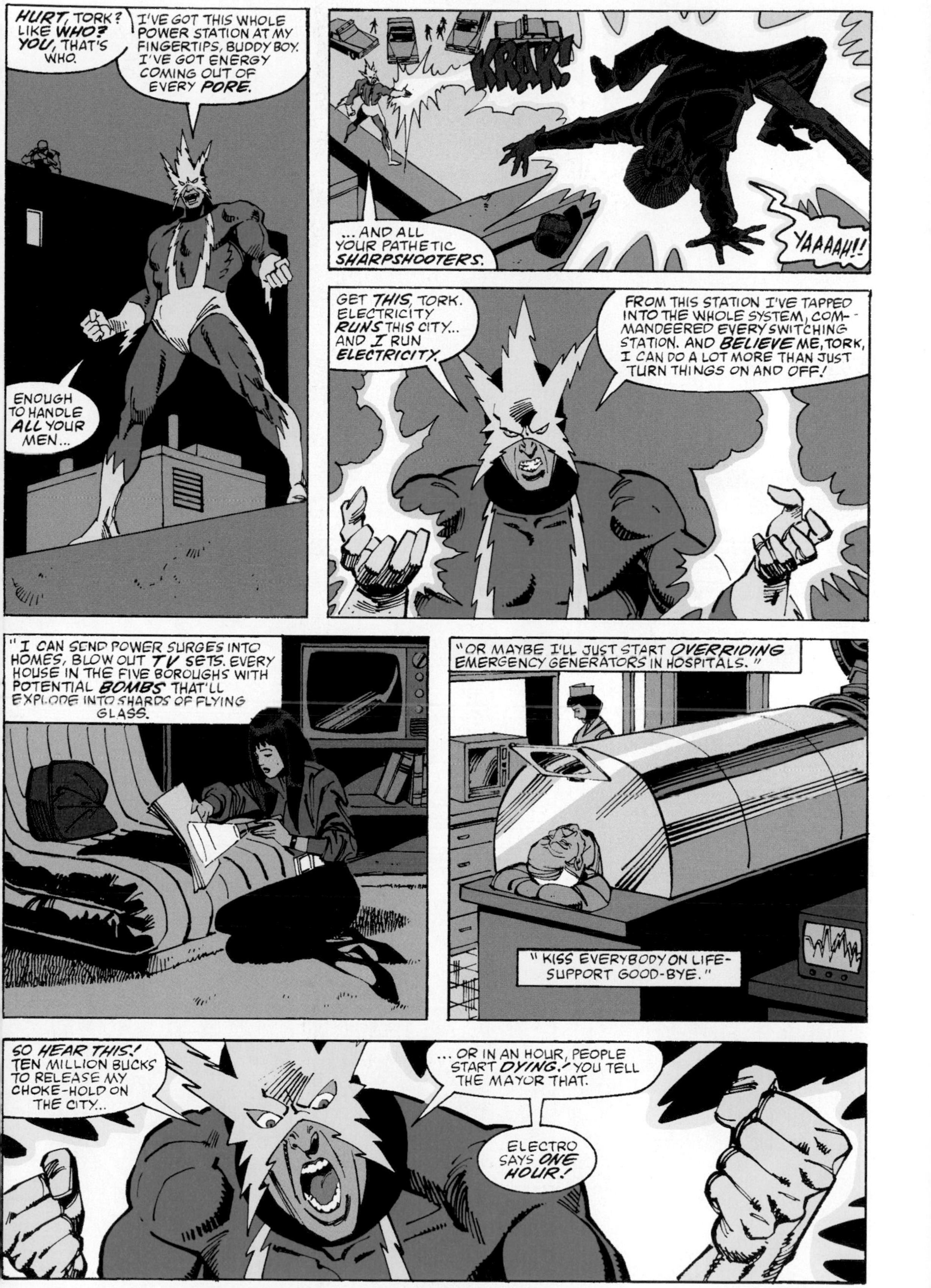
HURT, TORK? LIKE WHO? YOU, THAT'S WHO.
I'VE GOT THIS WHOLE POWER STATION AT MY FINGERTIPS, BUDDY BOY. I'VE GOT ENERGY COMING OUT OF EVERY PORE.
ENOUGH TO HANDLE ALL YOUR MEN...
KRAK!
...AND ALL YOUR PATHETIC SHARPSHOOTERS.
YAAAAH!!
GET THIS, TORK. ELECTRICITY RUNS THIS CITY... AND I RUN ELECTRICITY.
FROM THIS STATION I'VE TAPPED INTO THE WHOLE SYSTEM, COMMANDEERED EVERY SWITCHING STATION. AND BELIEVE ME, TORK, I CAN DO A LOT MORE THAN JUST TURN THINGS ON AND OFF!
"I CAN SEND POWER SURGES INTO HOMES, BLOW OUT TV SETS. EVERY HOUSE IN THE FIVE BOROUGHS WITH POTENTIAL BOMBS THAT'LL EXPLODE INTO SHARDS OF FLYING GLASS.
"OR MAYBE I'LL JUST START OVERRIDING EMERGENCY GENERATORS IN HOSPITALS."
"KISS EVERYBODY ON LIFE-SUPPORT GOOD-BYE."
SO HEAR THIS! TEN MILLION BUCKS TO RELEASE MY CHOKE-HOLD ON THE CITY...
...OR IN AN HOUR, PEOPLE START DYING! YOU TELL THE MAYOR THAT.
ELECTRO SAYS ONE HOUR!

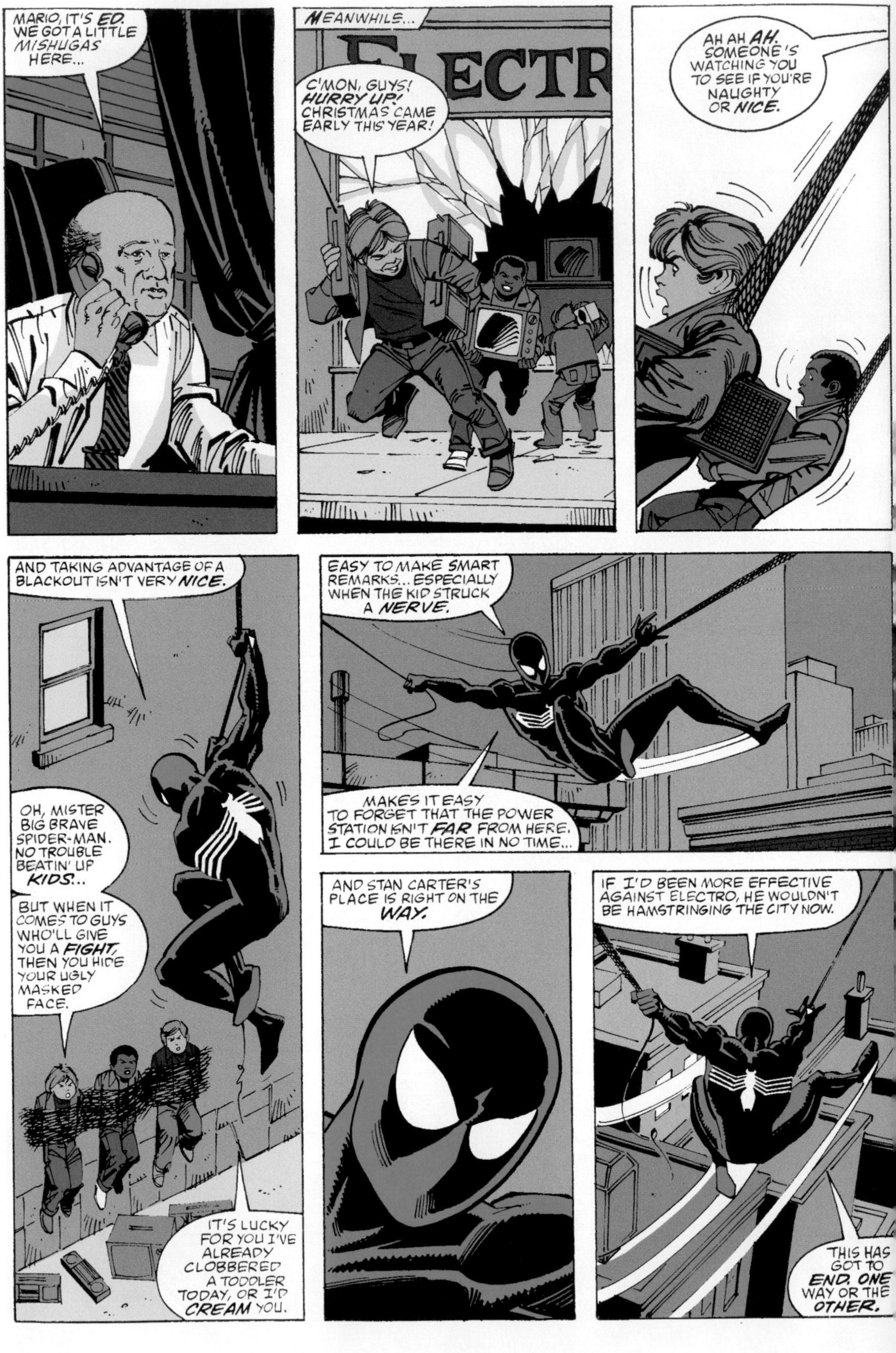

MARIO, IT'S ED. WE GOT A LITTLE MISHUGAS HERE...
MEANWHILE...
ELECTR
C'MON, GUYS! HURRY UP! CHRISTMAS CAME EARLY THIS YEAR!
AH AH AH. SOMEONE'S WATCHING YOU TO SEE IF YOU'RE NAUGHTY OR NICE.
AND TAKING ADVANTAGE OF A BLACKOUT ISN'T VERY NICE.
OH, MISTER BIG BRAVE SPIDER-MAN. NO TROUBLE BEATIN' UP KIDS...
BUT WHEN IT COMES TO GUYS WHO'LL GIVE YOU A FIGHT, THEN YOU HIDE YOUR UGLY MASKED FACE.
IT'S LUCKY FOR YOU I'VE ALREADY CLOBBERED A TODDLER TODAY, OR I'D CREAM YOU.
EASY TO MAKE SMART REMARKS... ESPECIALLY WHEN THE KID STRUCK A NERVE.
MAKES IT EASY TO FORGET THAT THE POWER STATION ISN'T FAR FROM HERE. I COULD BE THERE IN NO TIME...
AND STAN CARTER'S PLACE IS RIGHT ON THE WAY.
IF I'D BEEN MORE EFFECTIVE AGAINST ELECTRO, HE WOULDN'T BE HAMSTRINGING THE CITY NOW.
THIS HAS GOT TO END, ONE WAY OR THE OTHER.

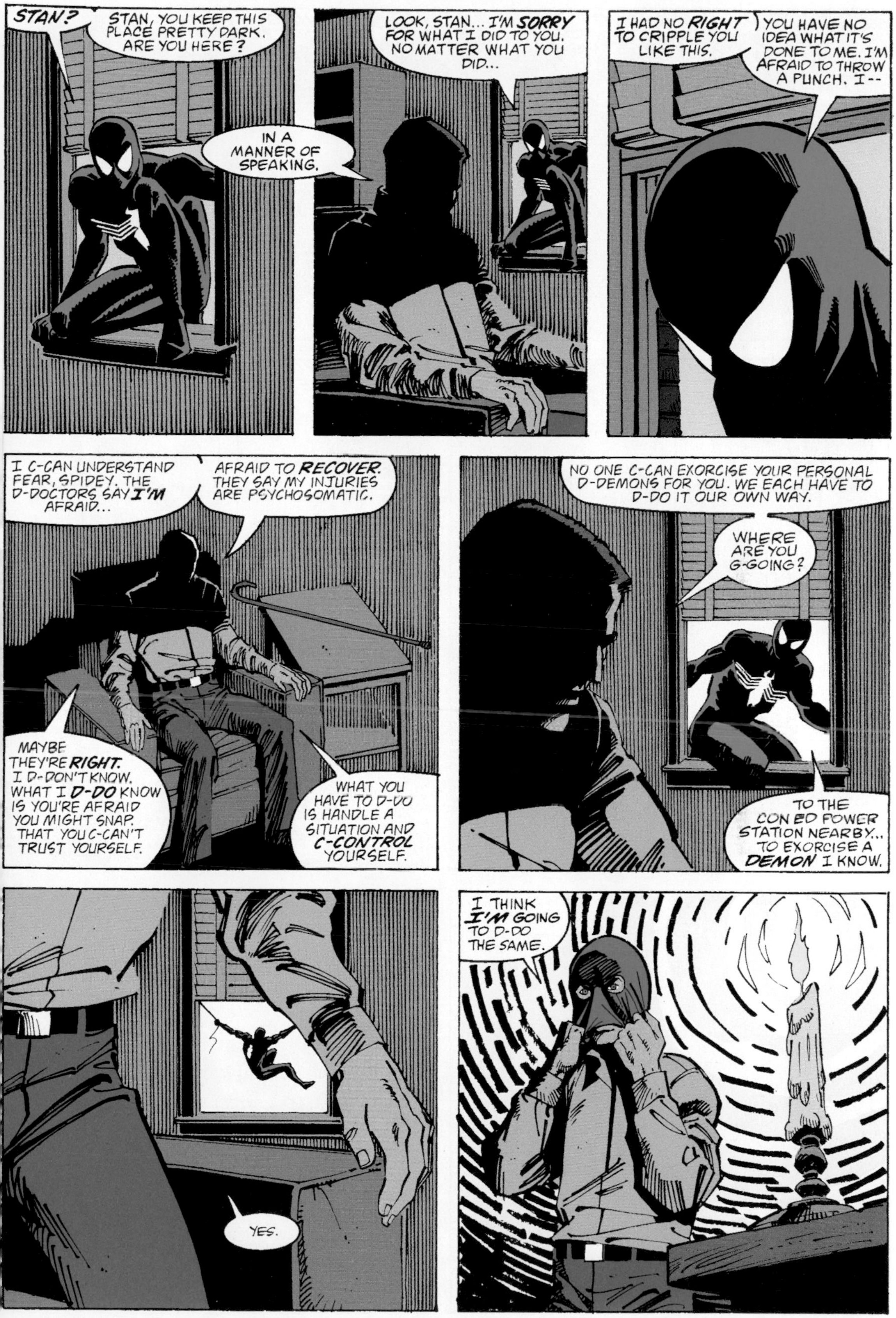
STAN?
STAN, YOU KEEP THIS PLACE PRETTY DARK. ARE YOU HERE?
IN A MANNER OF SPEAKING.
LOOK, STAN... I'M SORRY FOR WHAT I DID TO YOU. NO MATTER WHAT YOU DID...
I HAD NO RIGHT TO CRIPPLE YOU LIKE THIS.
YOU HAVE NO IDEA WHAT IT'S DONE TO ME. I'M AFRAID TO THROW A PUNCH. I --
I C-CAN UNDERSTAND FEAR, SPIDEY. THE D-DOCTORS SAY I'M AFRAID...
AFRAID TO RECOVER. THEY SAY MY INJURIES ARE PSYCHOSOMATIC.
MAYBE THEY'RE RIGHT. I D-DON'T KNOW. WHAT I D-DO KNOW IS YOU'RE AFRAID YOU MIGHT SNAP. THAT YOU C-CAN'T TRUST YOURSELF.
WHAT YOU HAVE TO D-DO IS HANDLE A SITUATION AND C-CONTROL YOURSELF.
NO ONE C-CAN EXORCISE YOUR PERSONAL D-DEMONS FOR YOU. WE EACH HAVE TO D-DO IT OUR OWN WAY.
WHERE ARE YOU G-GOING?
TO THE CON ED POWER STATION NEARBY... TO EXORCISE A DEMON I KNOW.
YES.
I THINK I'M GOING TO D-DO THE SAME.

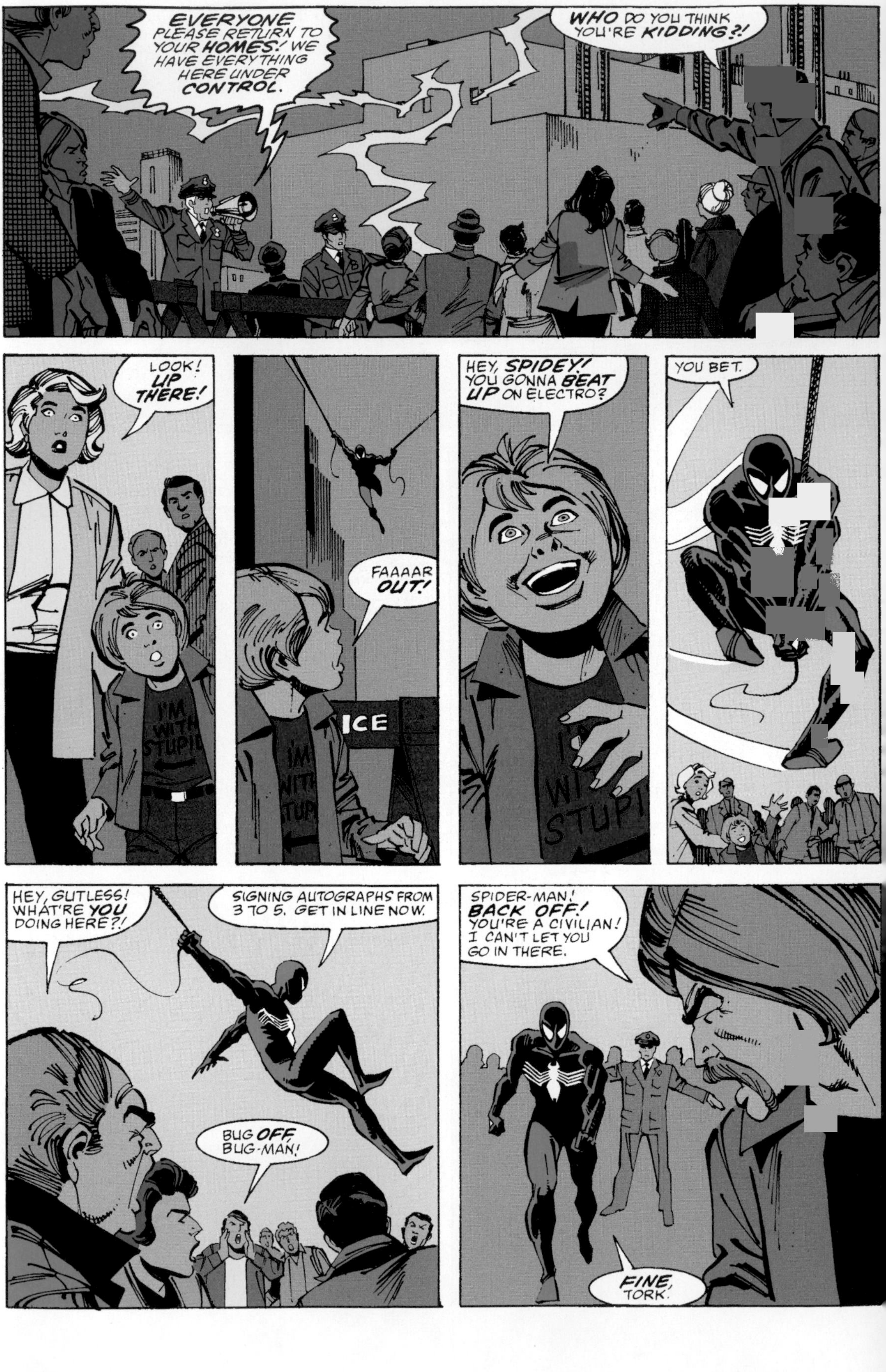
EVERYONE PLEASE RETURN TO YOUR HOMES! WE HAVE EVERYTHING HERE UNDER CONTROL.
WHO DO YOU THINK YOU'RE KIDDING?!
LOOK! UP THERE!
I'M WITH STUPID
FAAAAR OUT!
ICE
HEY, SPIDEY! YOU GONNA BEAT UP ON ELECTRO?
YOU BET.
HEY, GUTLESS! WHAT'RE YOU DOING HERE?!
SIGNING AUTOGRAPHS FROM 3 TO 5. GET IN LINE NOW.
BUG OFF, BUG-MAN!
SPIDER-MAN! BACK OFF! YOU'RE A CIVILIAN! I CAN'T LET YOU GO IN THERE.
FINE, TORK.

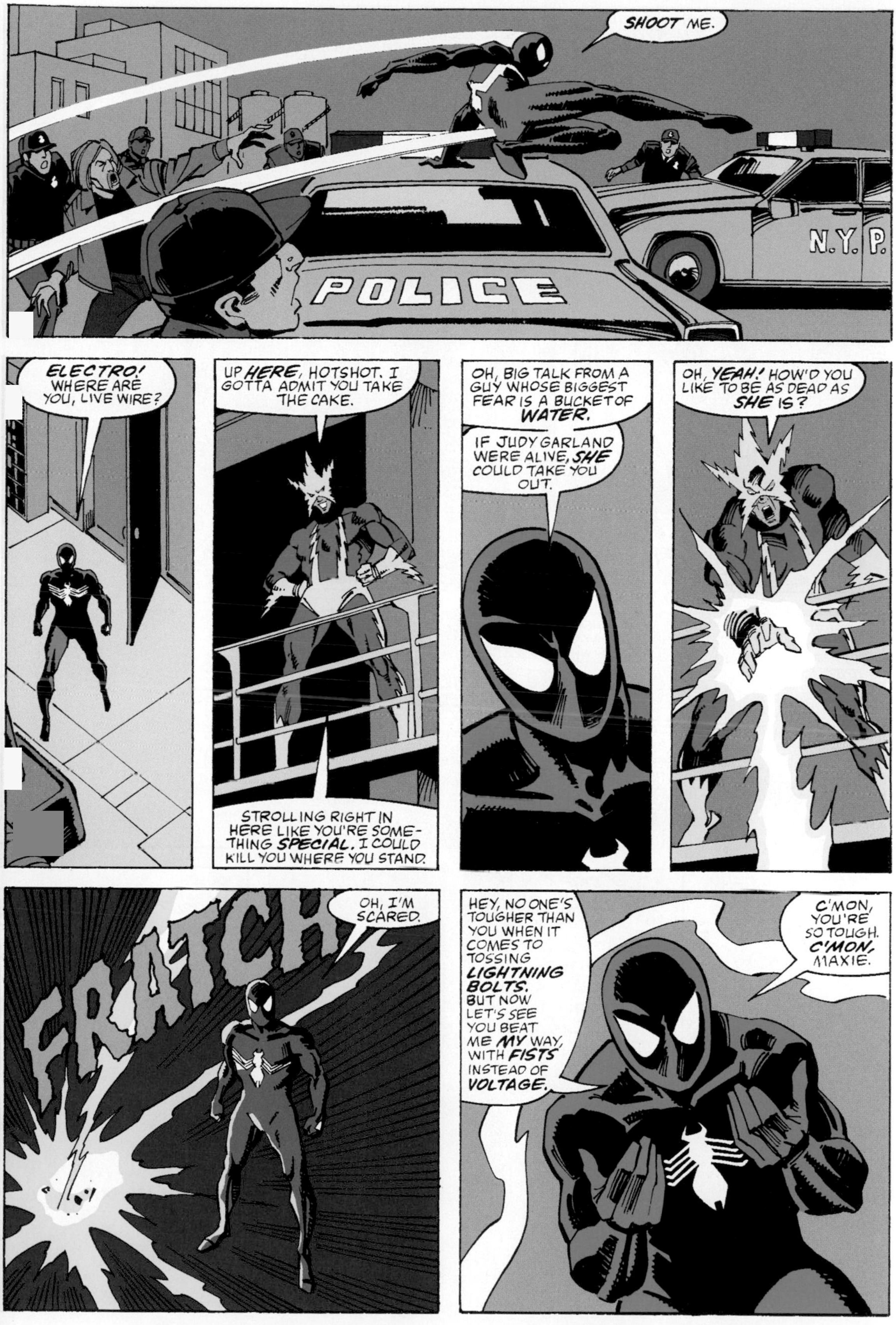
SHOOT ME.
ELECTRO! WHERE ARE YOU, LIVE WIRE?
UP HERE, HOTSHOT. I GOTTA ADMIT YOU TAKE THE CAKE.
STROLLING RIGHT IN HERE LIKE YOU'RE SOME-THING SPECIAL. I COULD KILL YOU WHERE YOU STAND.
OH, BIG TALK FROM A GUY WHOSE BIGGEST FEAR IS A BUCKET OF WATER.
IF JUDY GARLAND WERE ALIVE, SHE COULD TAKE YOU OUT.
OH, YEAH! HOW'D YOU LIKE TO BE AS DEAD AS SHE IS?
FRATCH
OH, I'M SCARED.
HEY, NO ONE'S TOUGHER THAN YOU WHEN IT COMES TO TOSSING LIGHTNING BOLTS. BUT NOW LET'S SEE YOU BEAT ME MY WAY, WITH FISTS INSTEAD OF VOLTAGE.
C'MON, YOU'RE SO TOUGH. C'MON, MAXIE.

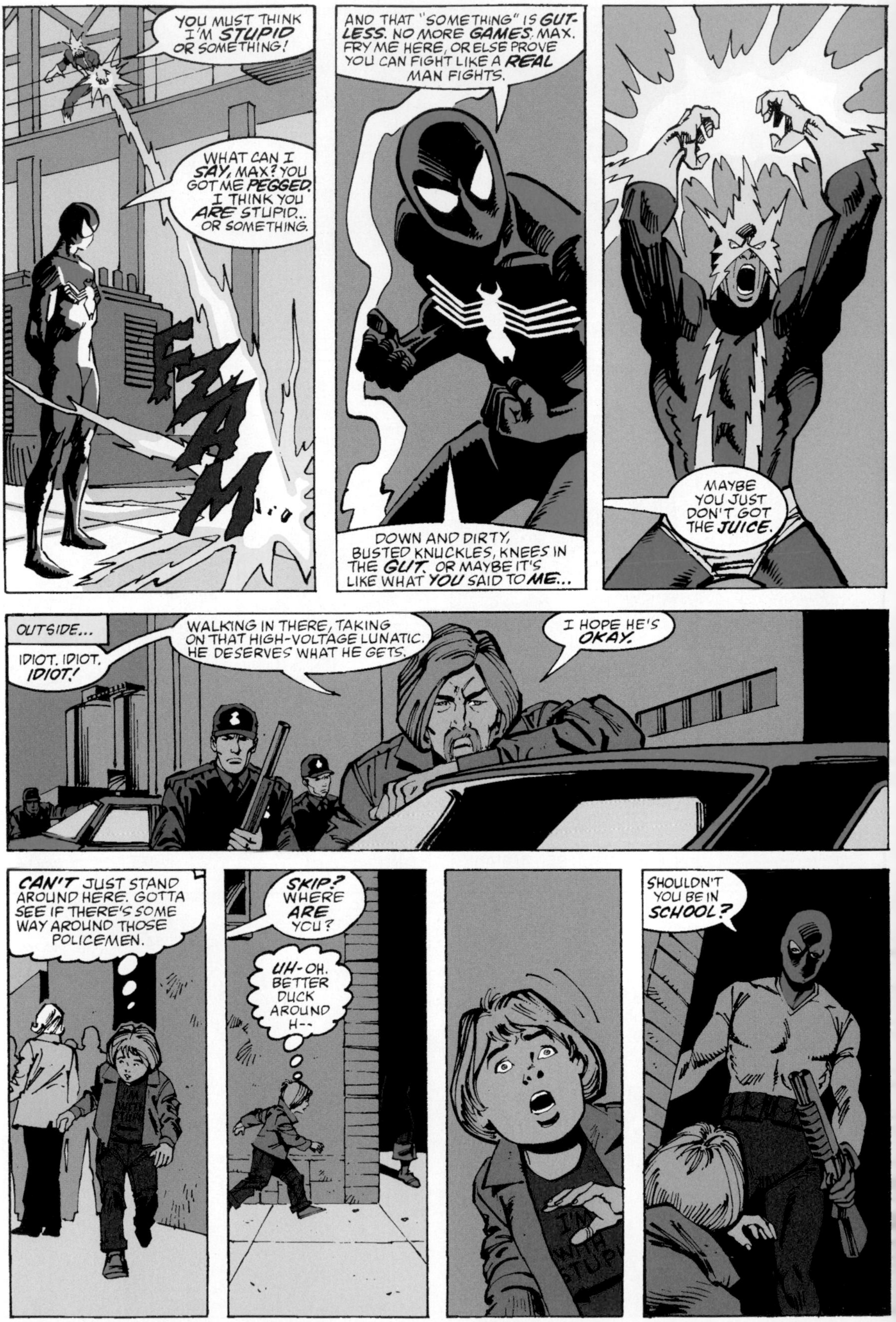
YOU MUST THINK I'M STUPID OR SOMETHING!
WHAT CAN I SAY, MAX? YOU GOT ME PEGGED. I THINK YOU ARE STUPID.. OR SOMETHING.
FWAM
AND THAT "SOMETHING" IS GUTLESS. NO MORE GAMES, MAX. FRY ME HERE, OR ELSE PROVE YOU CAN FIGHT LIKE A REAL MAN FIGHTS.
DOWN AND DIRTY, BUSTED KNUCKLES, KNEES IN THE GUT. OR MAYBE IT'S LIKE WHAT YOU SAID TO ME...
MAYBE YOU JUST DON'T GOT THE JUICE.
OUTSIDE...
IDIOT. IDIOT. IDIOT!
WALKING IN THERE, TAKING ON THAT HIGH-VOLTAGE LUNATIC. HE DESERVES WHAT HE GETS.
I HOPE HE'S OKAY.
CAN'T JUST STAND AROUND HERE. GOTTA SEE IF THERE'S SOME WAY AROUND THOSE POLICEMEN.
SKIP? WHERE ARE YOU?
UH-OH. BETTER DUCK AROUND H--
SHOULDN'T YOU BE IN SCHOOL?

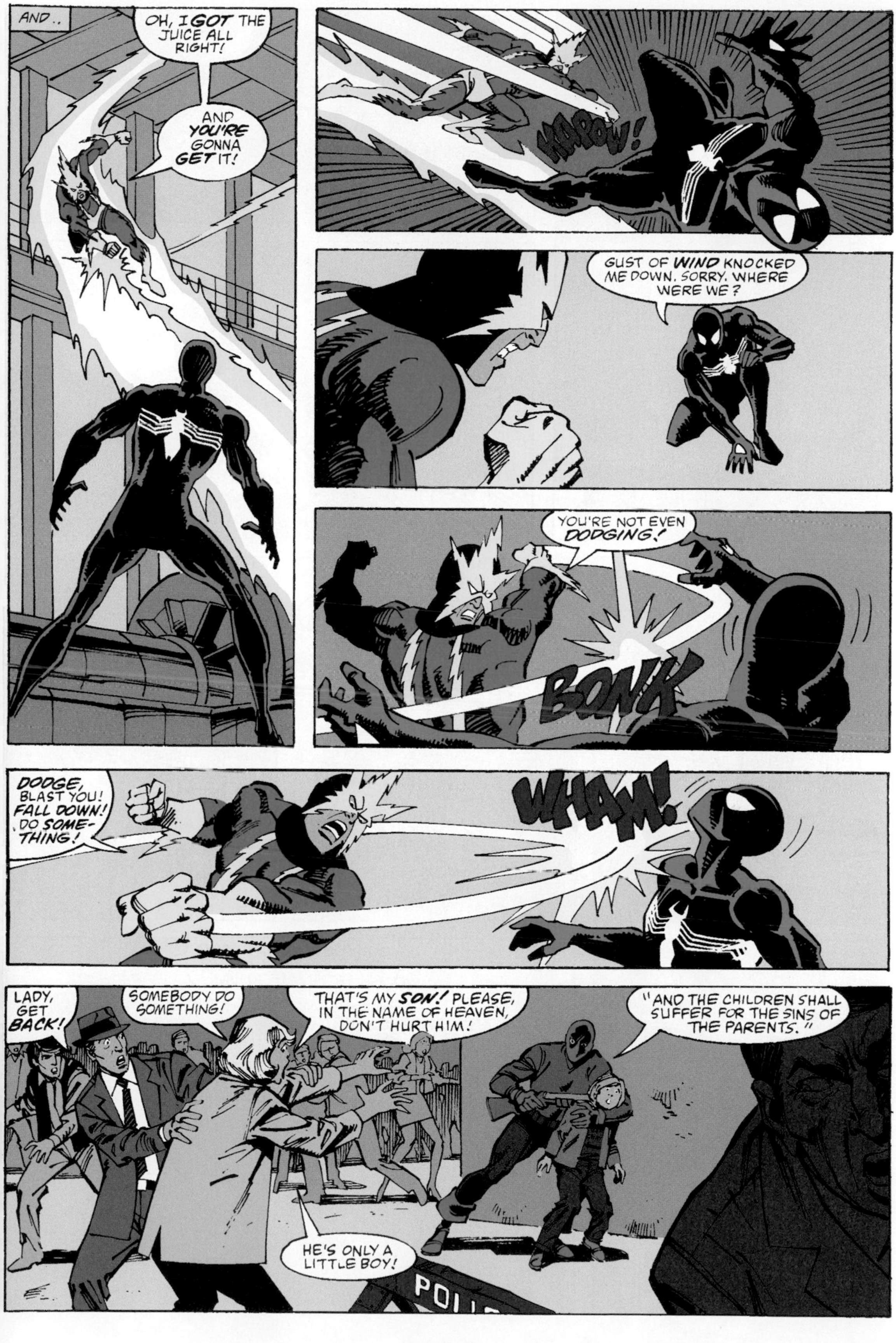
AND..
OH, I GOT THE JUICE ALL RIGHT!
AND YOU'RE GONNA GET IT!
KAPOW!
GUST OF WIND KNOCKED ME DOWN. SORRY. WHERE WERE WE?
YOU'RE NOT EVEN DODGING!
BONK
DODGE, BLAST YOU! FALL DOWN! DO SOMETHING!
WHAM!
LADY, GET BACK!
SOMEBODY DO SOMETHING!
THAT'S MY SON! PLEASE, IN THE NAME OF HEAVEN, DON'T HURT HIM!
"AND THE CHILDREN SHALL SUFFER FOR THE SINS OF THE PARENTS."
HE'S ONLY A LITTLE BOY!
POLI

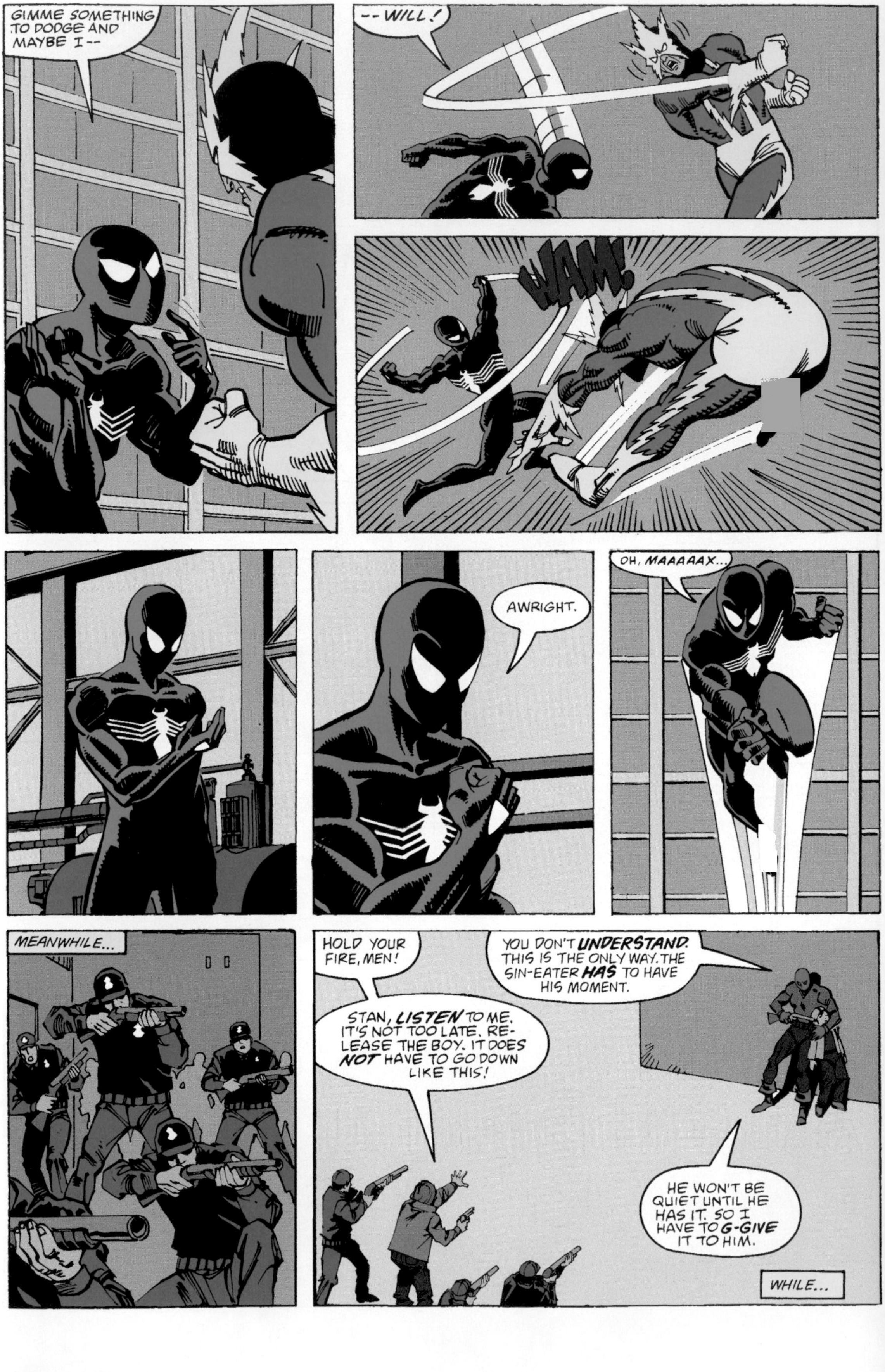
GIMME SOMETHING TO DODGE AND MAYBE I --
-- WILL!
WAM!
AWRIGHT.
OH, MAAAAAX...
MEANWHILE...
HOLD YOUR FIRE, MEN!
YOU DON'T UNDERSTAND. THIS IS THE ONLY WAY. THE SIN-EATER HAS TO HAVE HIS MOMENT.
STAN, LISTEN TO ME. IT'S NOT TOO LATE. RELEASE THE BOY. IT DOES NOT HAVE TO GO DOWN LIKE THIS!
HE WON'T BE QUIET UNTIL HE HAS IT. SO I HAVE TO G-GIVE IT TO HIM.
WHILE...

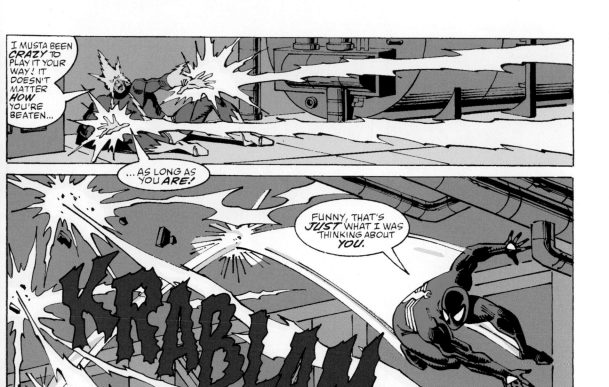

I MUSTA BEEN *CRAZY* TO PLAY IT YOUR WAY! IT DOESN'T MATTER *HOW* YOU'RE BEATEN...

...AS LONG AS YOU *ARE!*

FUNNY, THAT'S *JUST* WHAT I WAS THINKING ABOUT *YOU.*

KRABLAM

GIVE IT *UP*, SPIDER-MAN! I CAN STILL SEVER THE ELECTRICAL BONDING THAT LETS YOU CRAWL WALLS. AND NOW I'LL ELECTRIFY THE ENTIRE *BUILDING!* YOU *CAN'T* ESCAPE!

WHAT MAKES YOU THINK I *WANT* TO ESCAPE? ESPECIALLY WITH THESE INSULATED PIPES THAT *WON'T* CONDUCT YOUR WATTAGE.

AND SO *WHAT* IF YOU CAN STOP ME FROM STICKING? I'M NOT A ONE-TRICK PONY LIKE *SOME* GUYS I KNOW.

THWIP   THWIP

YOU THINK YOU CAN STOP ME WITH *THAT* PUNY MOVE?

FRAZZLE

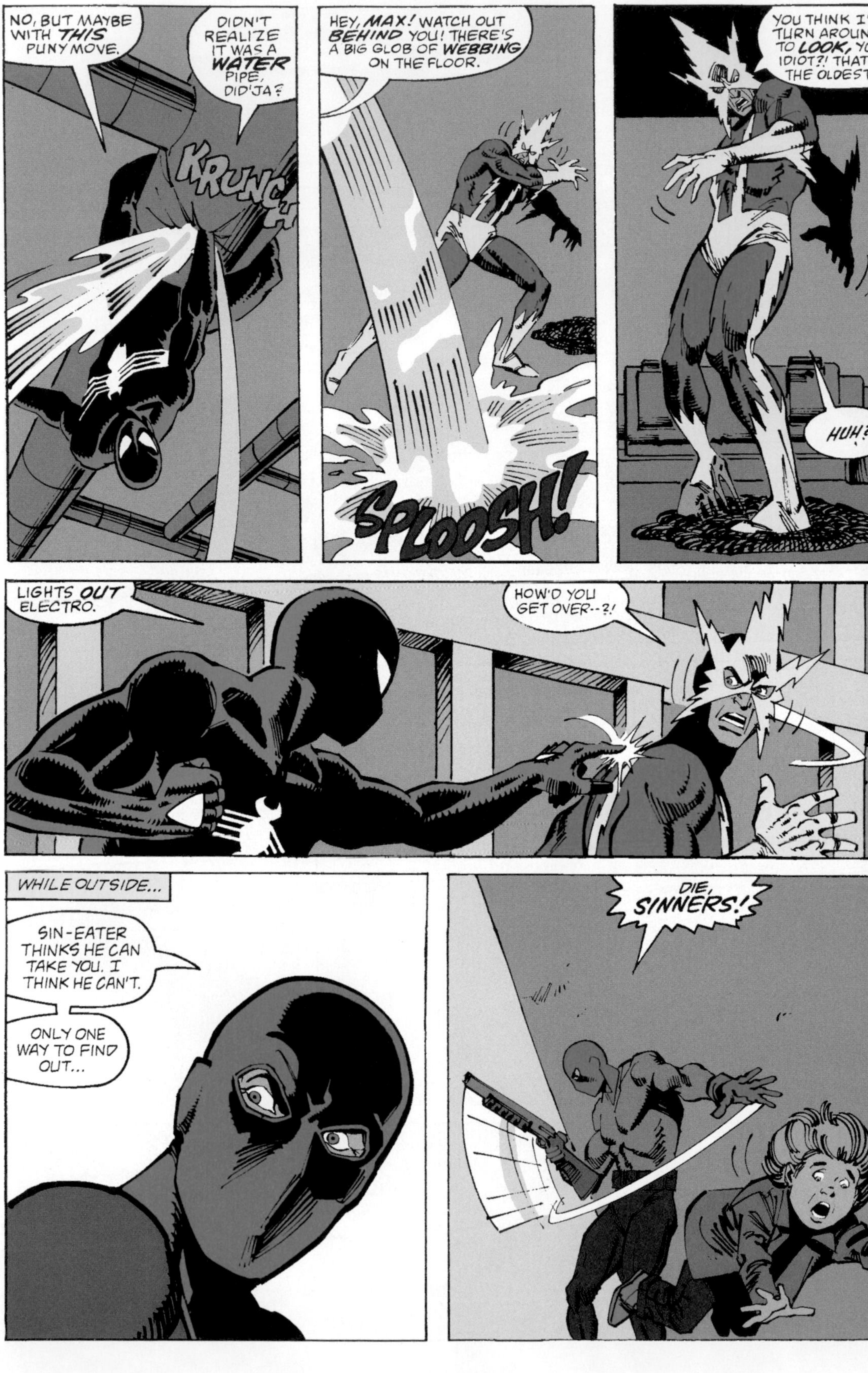
NO, BUT MAYBE WITH THIS PUNY MOVE.
DIDN'T REALIZE IT WAS A WATER PIPE, DID'JA?
KRUNCH
HEY, MAX! WATCH OUT BEHIND YOU! THERE'S A BIG GLOB OF WEBBING ON THE FLOOR.
SPLOOSH!
YOU THINK I'LL TURN AROUND TO LOOK, YOU IDIOT?! THAT'S THE OLDEST--
HUH?
LIGHTS OUT ELECTRO.
HOW'D YOU GET OVER--?!
WHILE OUTSIDE...
SIN-EATER THINKS HE CAN TAKE YOU. I THINK HE CAN'T.
ONLY ONE WAY TO FIND OUT...
DIE, SINNERS!

POW
BLAM
BLAM
BLAM
BLAM
BLAM
STOP!
FOR THE LOVE OF HEAVEN, THAT'S ENOUGH!

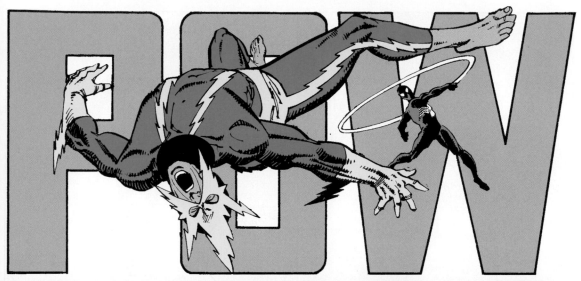

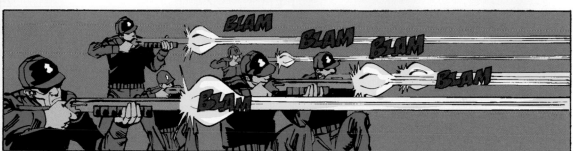

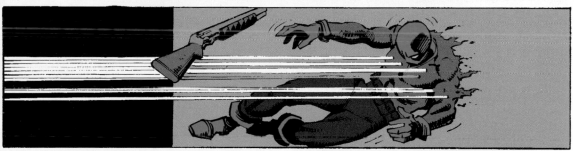

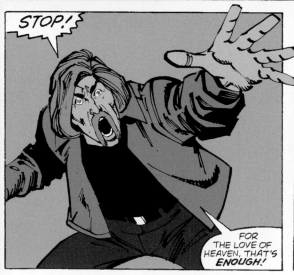

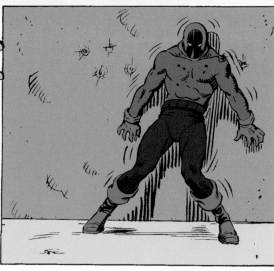

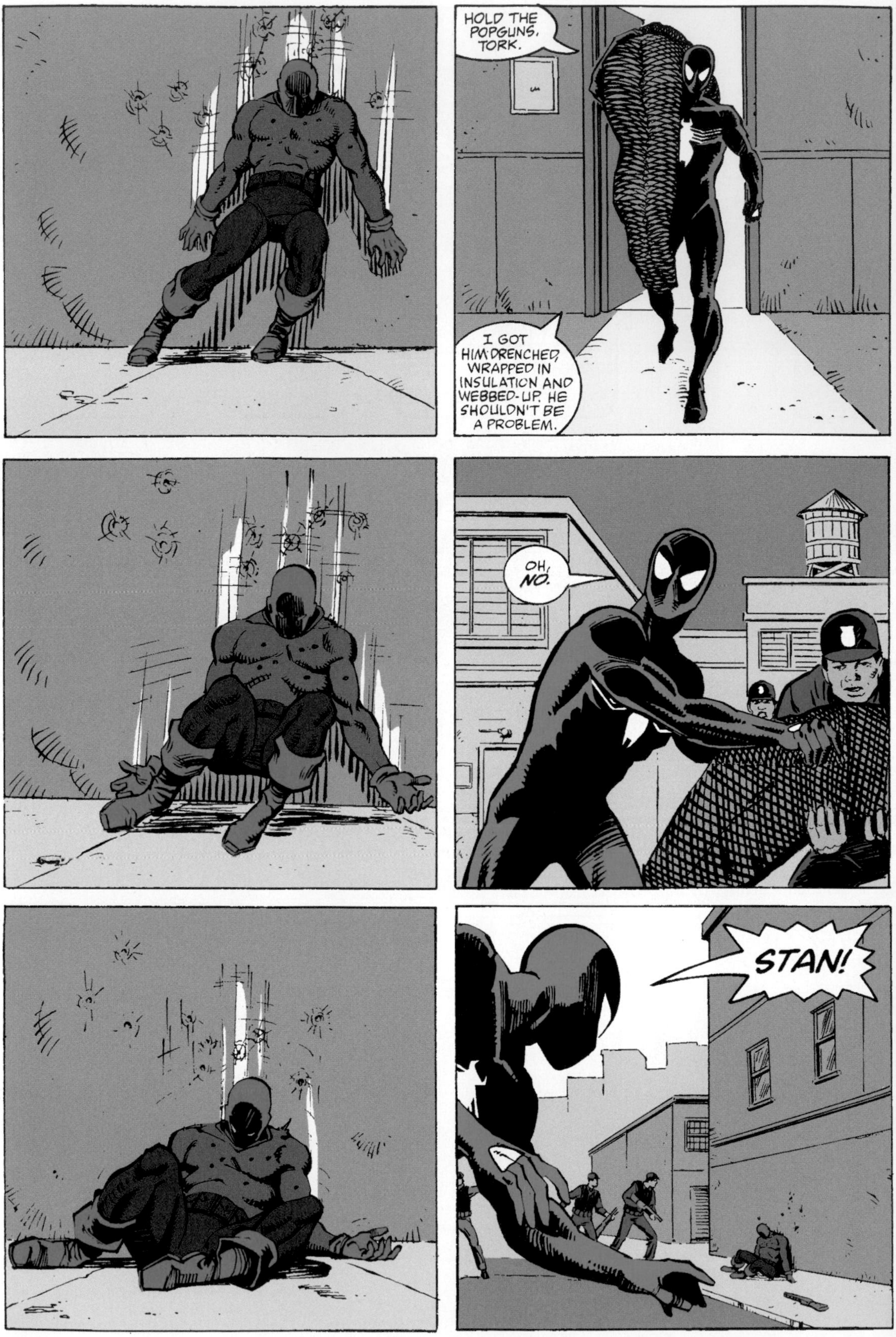
HOLD THE POPGUNS, TORK.
I GOT HIM DRENCHED, WRAPPED IN INSULATION AND WEBBED-UP. HE SHOULDN'T BE A PROBLEM.
OH, NO.
STAN!

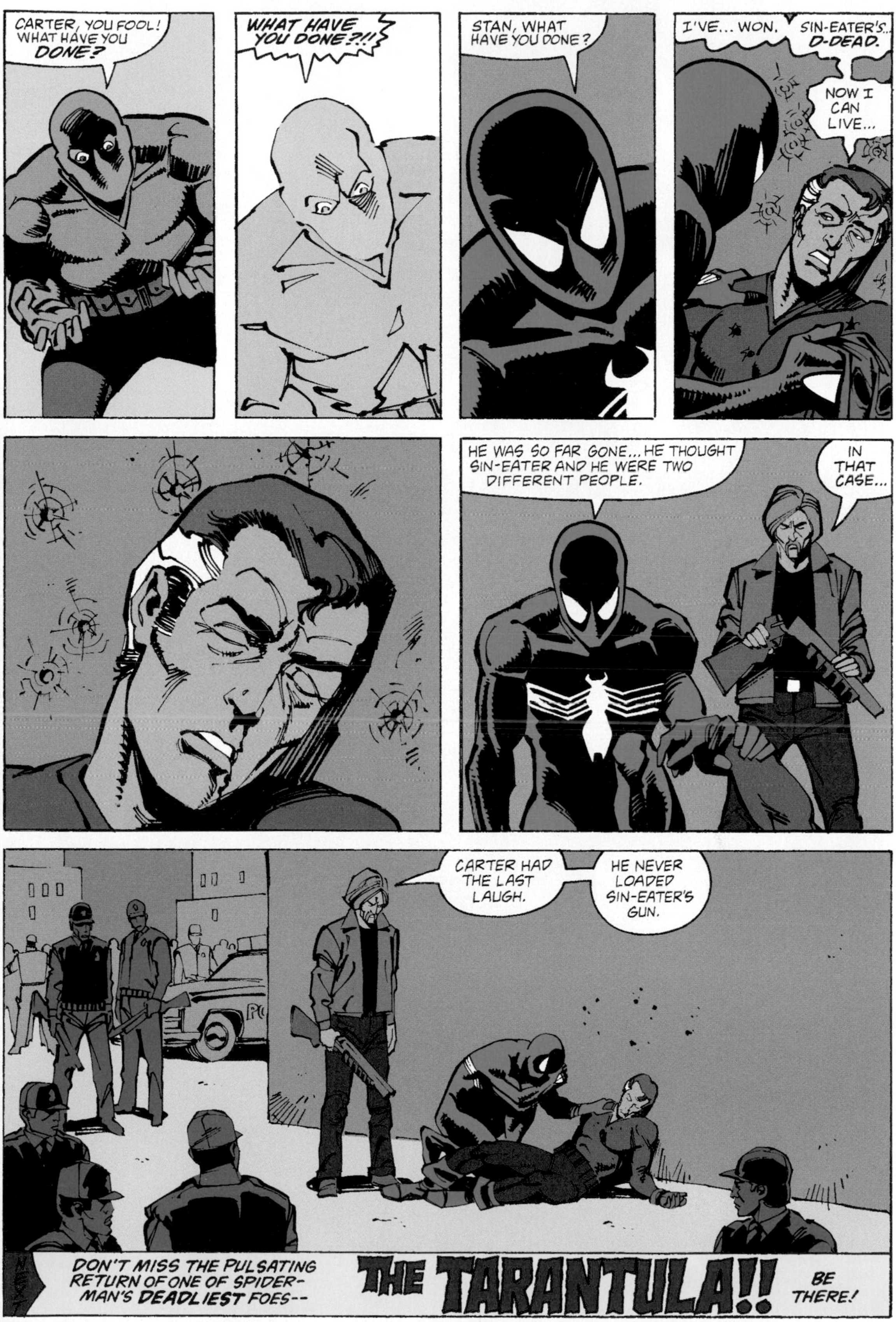
CARTER, YOU FOOL! WHAT HAVE YOU DONE?
WHAT HAVE YOU DONE?!!
STAN, WHAT HAVE YOU DONE?
I'VE... WON.
SIN-EATER'S... D-DEAD.
NOW I CAN LIVE...
HE WAS SO FAR GONE... HE THOUGHT SIN-EATER AND HE WERE TWO DIFFERENT PEOPLE.
IN THAT CASE...
CARTER HAD THE LAST LAUGH.
HE NEVER LOADED SIN-EATER'S GUN.
DON'T MISS THE PULSATING RETURN OF ONE OF SPIDER-MAN'S DEADLIEST FOES--
THE TARANTULA!!
BE THERE!

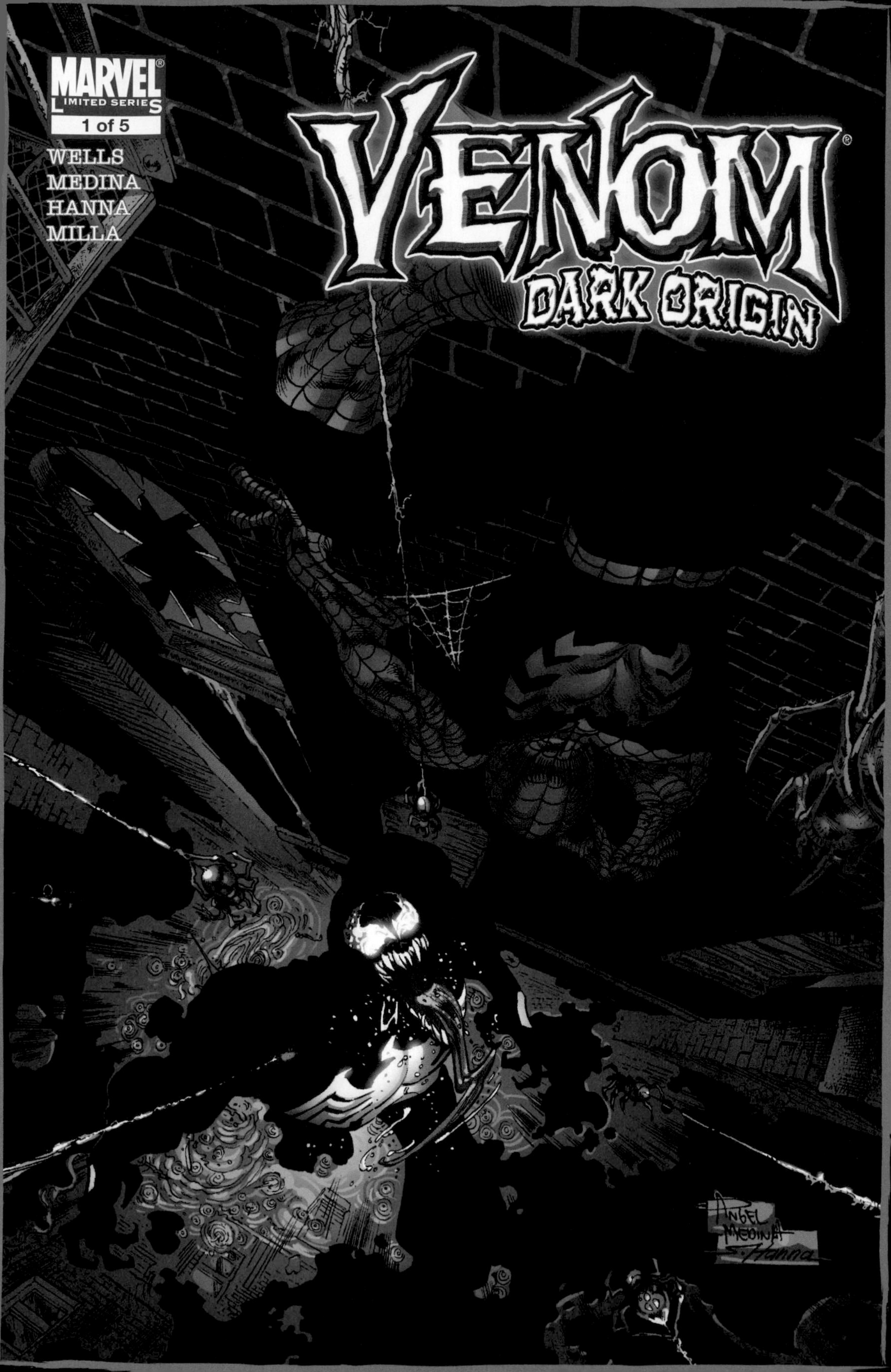
MARVEL
LIMITED SERIES
1 of 5
WELLS
MEDINA
HANNA
MILLA
VENOM
DARK ORIGIN
ANGEL MEDINA
S. Hanna

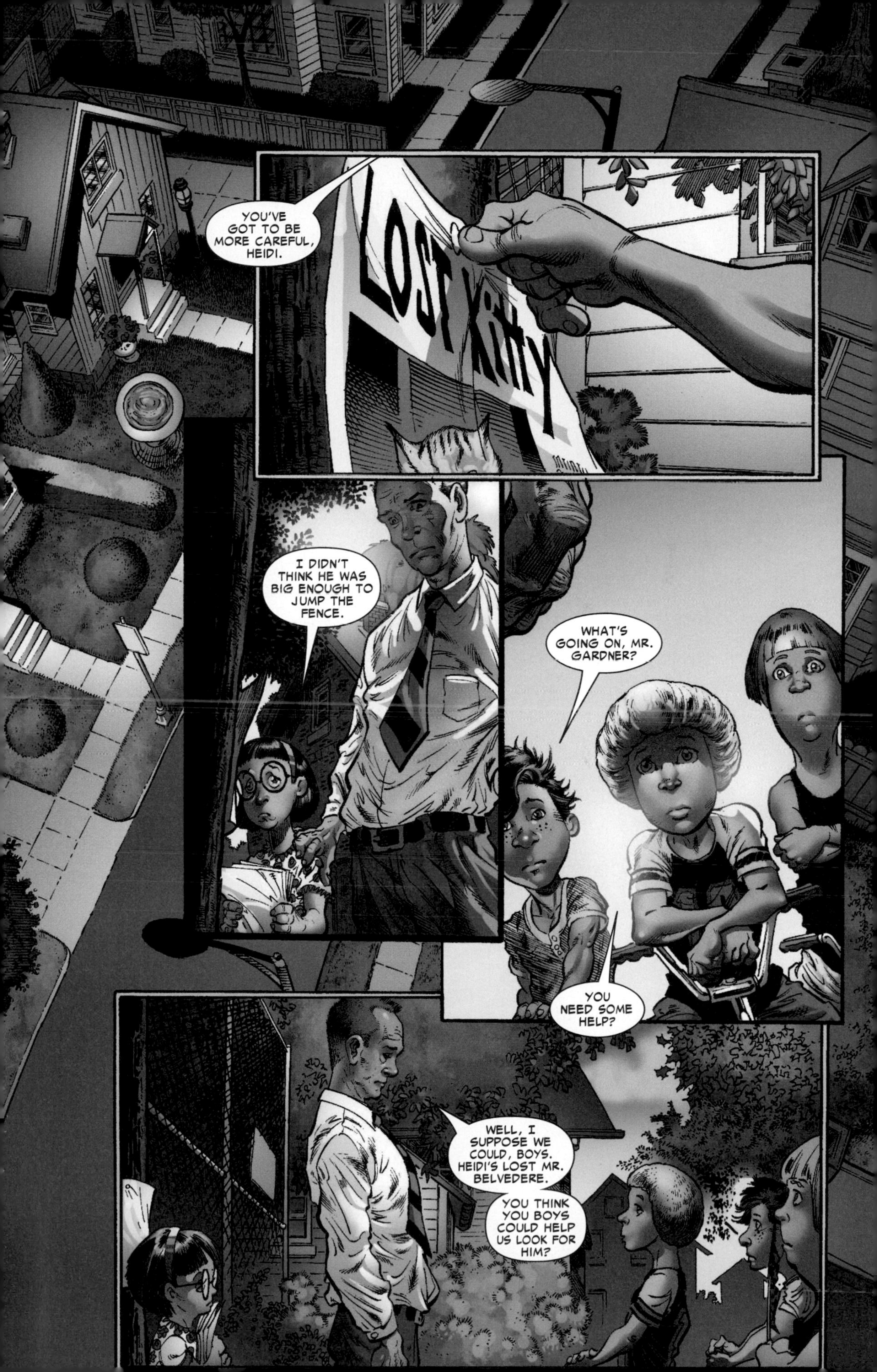

YOU'VE GOT TO BE MORE CAREFUL, HEIDI.
LOST Kitty
I DIDN'T THINK HE WAS BIG ENOUGH TO JUMP THE FENCE.
WHAT'S GOING ON, MR. GARDNER?
YOU NEED SOME HELP?
WELL, I SUPPOSE WE COULD, BOYS. HEIDI'S LOST MR. BELVEDERE.
YOU THINK YOU BOYS COULD HELP US LOOK FOR HIM?

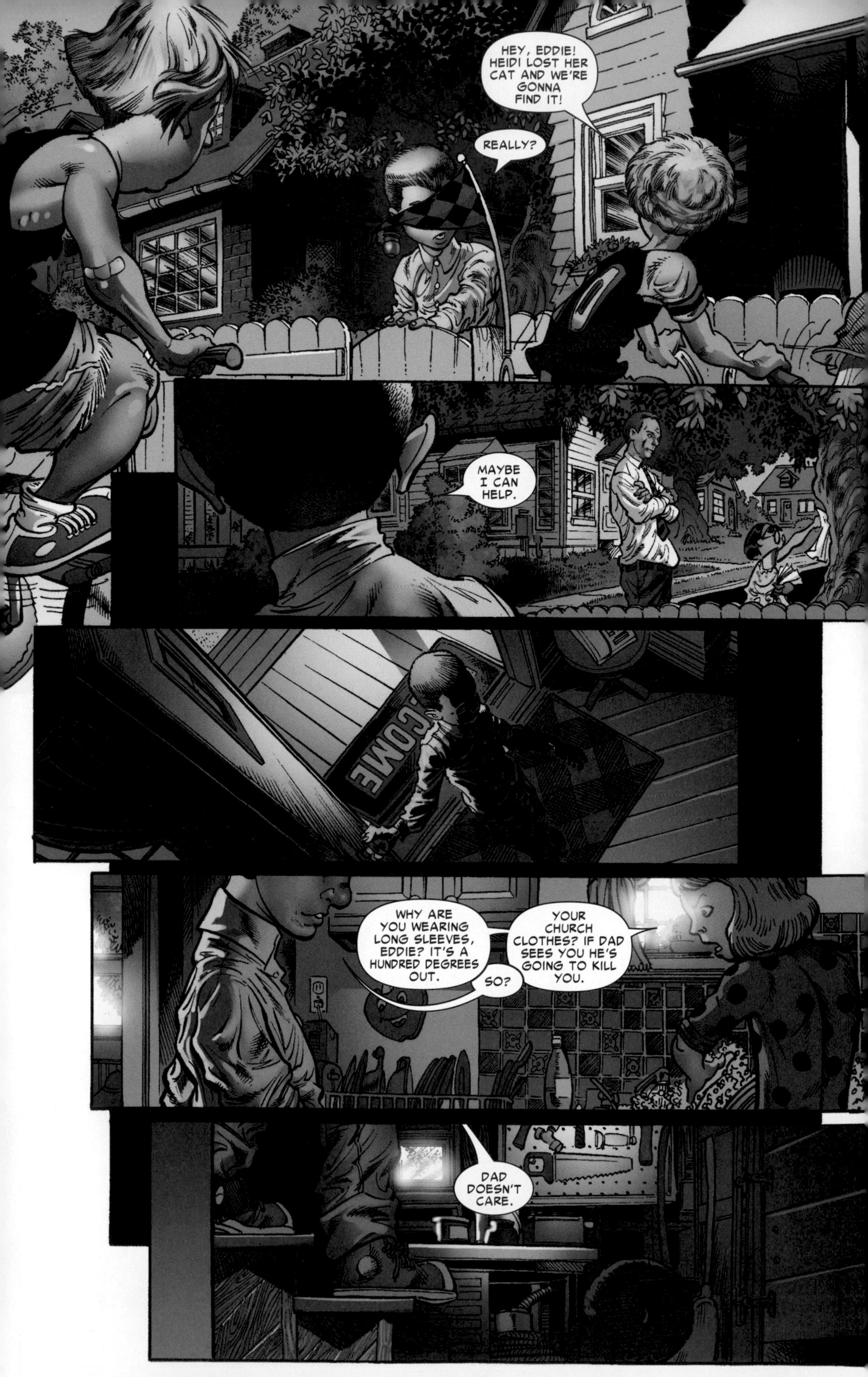
HEY, EDDIE! HEIDI LOST HER CAT AND WE'RE GONNA FIND IT!
REALLY?
MAYBE I CAN HELP.
COME
WHY ARE YOU WEARING LONG SLEEVES, EDDIE? IT'S A HUNDRED DEGREES OUT.
YOUR CHURCH CLOTHES? IF DAD SEES YOU HE'S GOING TO KILL YOU.
SO?
DAD DOESN'T CARE.

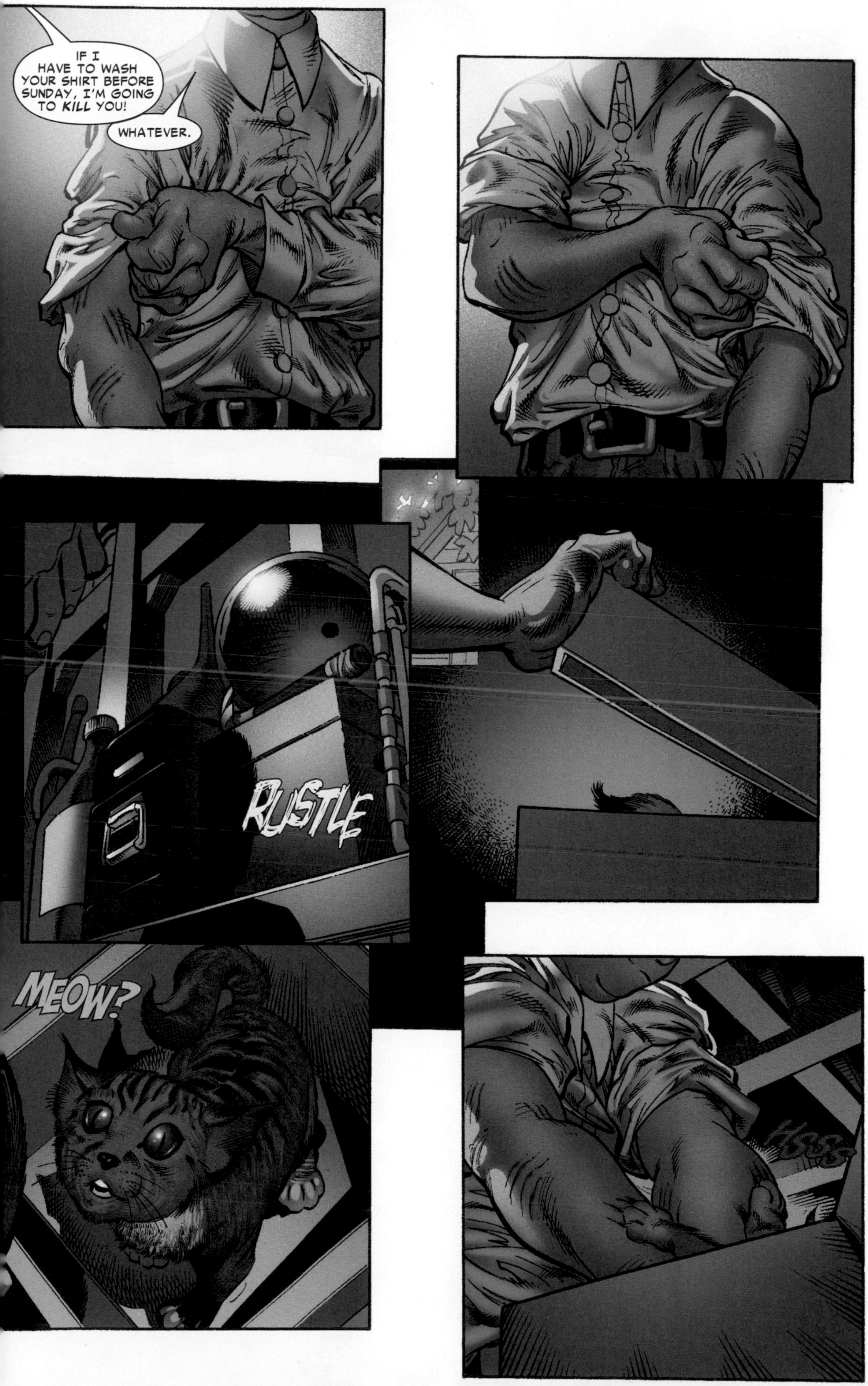
IF I HAVE TO WASH YOUR SHIRT BEFORE SUNDAY, I'M GOING TO **KILL** YOU!
WHATEVER.
RUSTLE
MEOW?

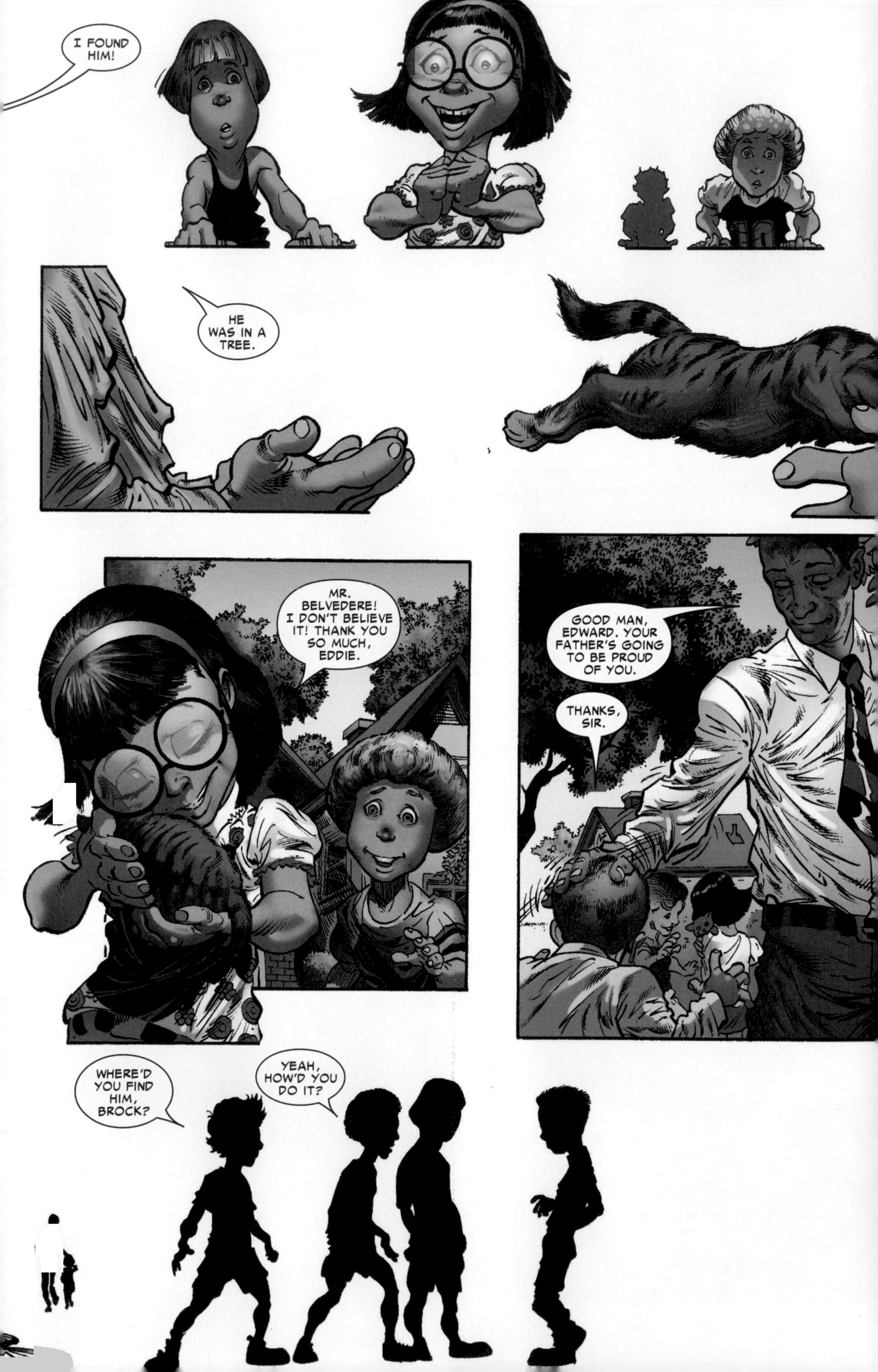
I FOUND HIM!
HE WAS IN A TREE.
MR. BELVEDERE! I DON'T BELIEVE IT! THANK YOU SO MUCH, EDDIE.
GOOD MAN, EDWARD. YOUR FATHER'S GOING TO BE PROUD OF YOU.
THANKS, SIR.
WHERE'D YOU FIND HIM, BROCK?
YEAH, HOW'D YOU DO IT?

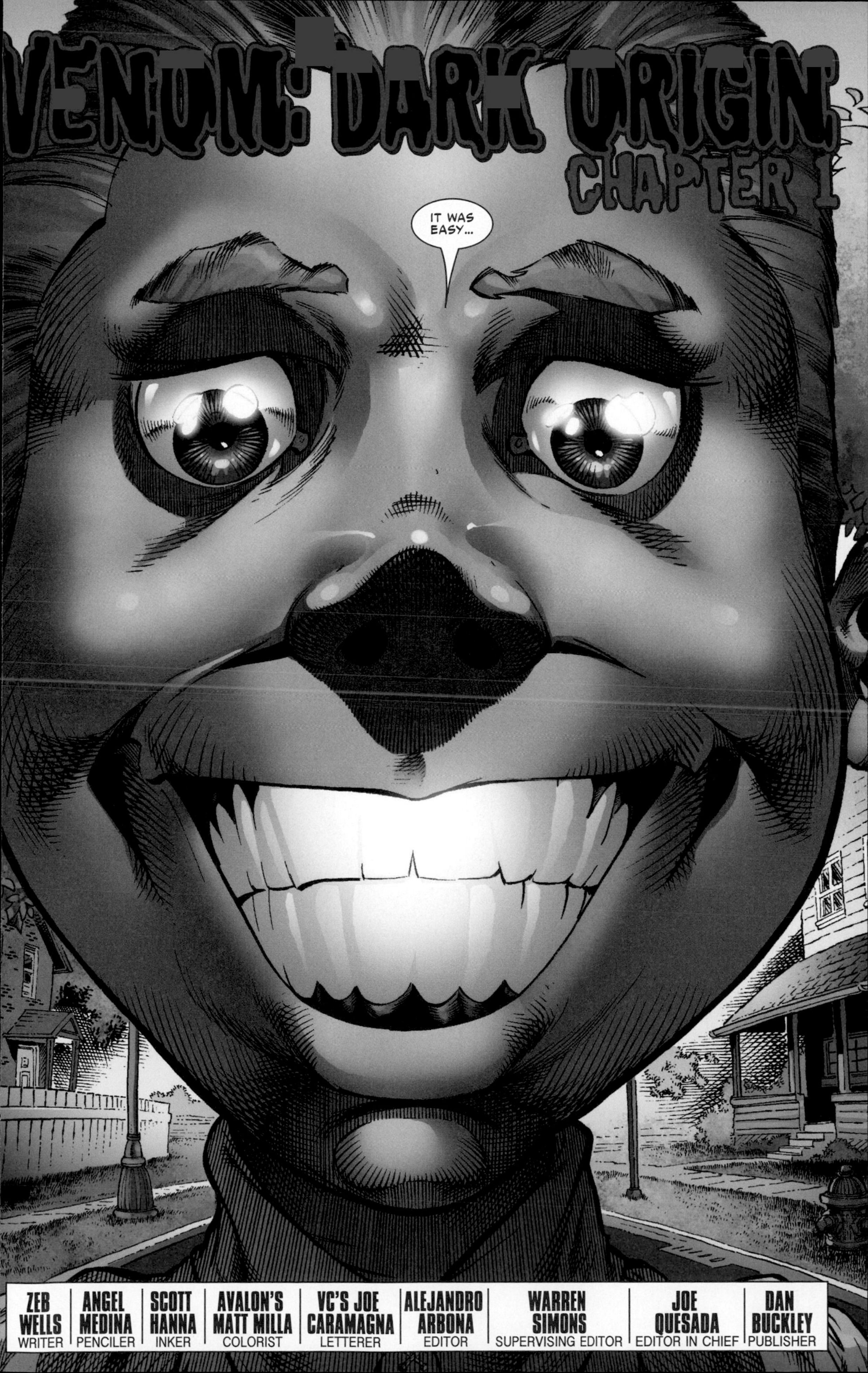
VENOM: DARK ORIGIN
CHAPTER 1
IT WAS EASY...
ZEB WELLS WRITER
ANGEL MEDINA PENCILER
SCOTT HANNA INKER
AVALON'S MATT MILLA COLORIST
VC'S JOE CARAMAGNA LETTERER
ALEJANDRO ARBONA EDITOR
WARREN SIMONS SUPERVISING EDITOR
JOE QUESADA EDITOR IN CHIEF
DAN BUCKLEY PUBLISHER

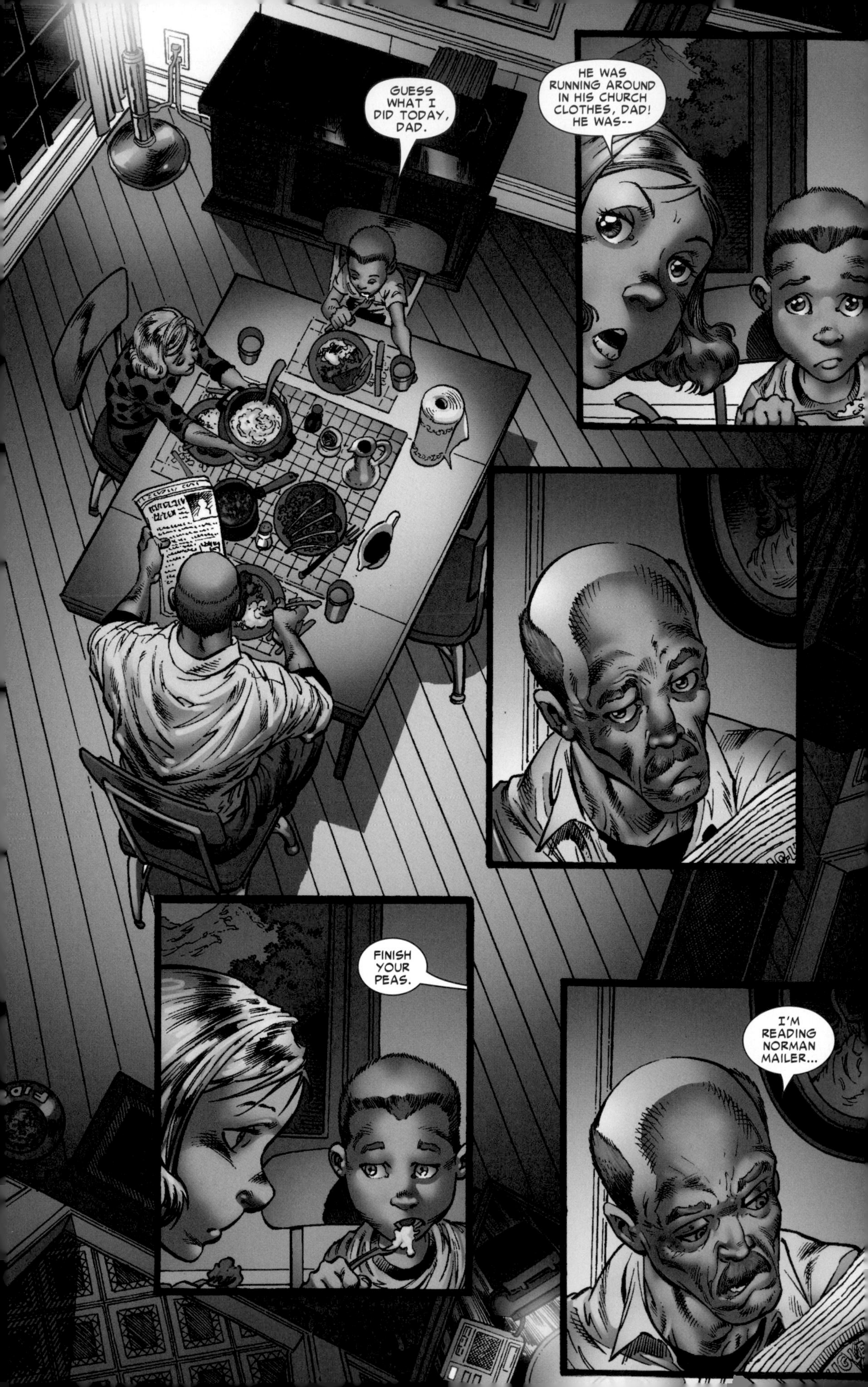

GUESS WHAT I DID TODAY, DAD.
HE WAS RUNNING AROUND IN HIS CHURCH CLOTHES, DAD! HE WAS--
FINISH YOUR PEAS.
I'M READING NORMAN MAILER...

I CAN ASSURE THE MEMBERS OF CONGRESS THAT I CAME HERE TO TELL THE TRUTH...

THE GOOD, THE BAD, AND THE UGLY.

AND THE TRUTH IS THAT I HAVE NOT, IN THE TWENTY-ODD YEARS I HAVE BEEN IN THE UNIFORMED SERVICES OF THE UNITED STATES OF AMERICA, EVER VIOLATED AN ORDER.

HE'S LYING.

WHAT WAS THAT?

HE'S LYING. CAN'T YOU TELL?

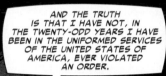

I DON'T THINK THERE'S ANOTHER PERSON IN AMERICA WHO WANTS TO TELL THIS STORY AS MUCH AS I DO.

I CAN ALWAYS TELL.

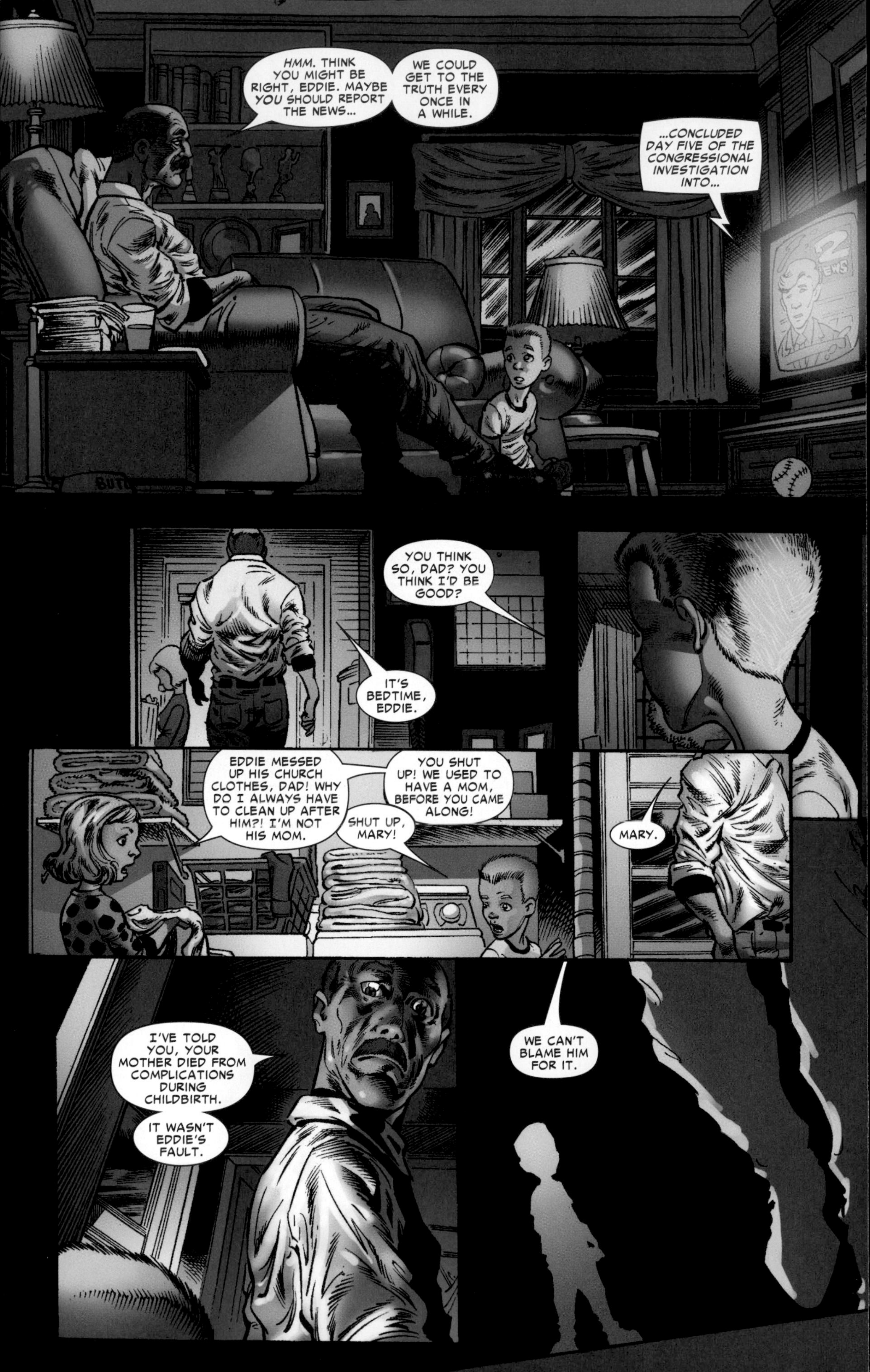
HMM. THINK YOU MIGHT BE RIGHT, EDDIE. MAYBE YOU SHOULD REPORT THE NEWS...
WE COULD GET TO THE TRUTH EVERY ONCE IN A WHILE.
...CONCLUDED DAY FIVE OF THE CONGRESSIONAL INVESTIGATION INTO...
YOU THINK SO, DAD? YOU THINK I'D BE GOOD?
IT'S BEDTIME, EDDIE.
EDDIE MESSED UP HIS CHURCH CLOTHES, DAD! WHY DO I ALWAYS HAVE TO CLEAN UP AFTER HIM?! I'M NOT HIS MOM.
YOU SHUT UP! WE USED TO HAVE A MOM, BEFORE YOU CAME ALONG!
SHUT UP, MARY!
MARY.
I'VE TOLD YOU, YOUR MOTHER DIED FROM COMPLICATIONS DURING CHILDBIRTH.
IT WASN'T EDDIE'S FAULT.
WE CAN'T BLAME HIM FOR IT.

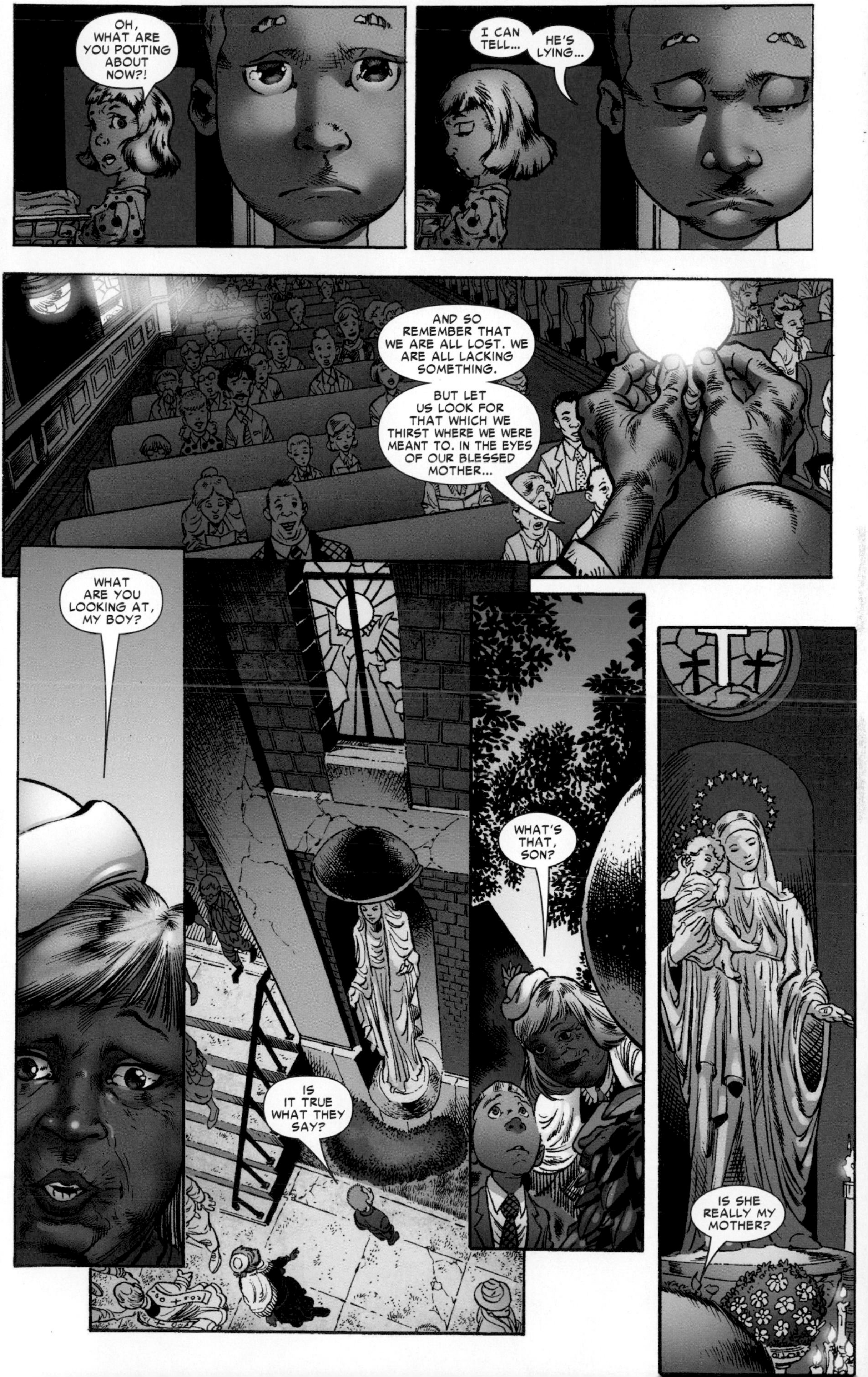

OH, WHAT ARE YOU POUTING ABOUT NOW?!
I CAN TELL...
HE'S LYING...
AND SO REMEMBER THAT WE ARE ALL LOST. WE ARE ALL LACKING SOMETHING.
BUT LET US LOOK FOR THAT WHICH WE THIRST WHERE WE WERE MEANT TO. IN THE EYES OF OUR BLESSED MOTHER...
WHAT ARE YOU LOOKING AT, MY BOY?
IS IT TRUE WHAT THEY SAY?
WHAT'S THAT, SON?
IS SHE REALLY MY MOTHER?

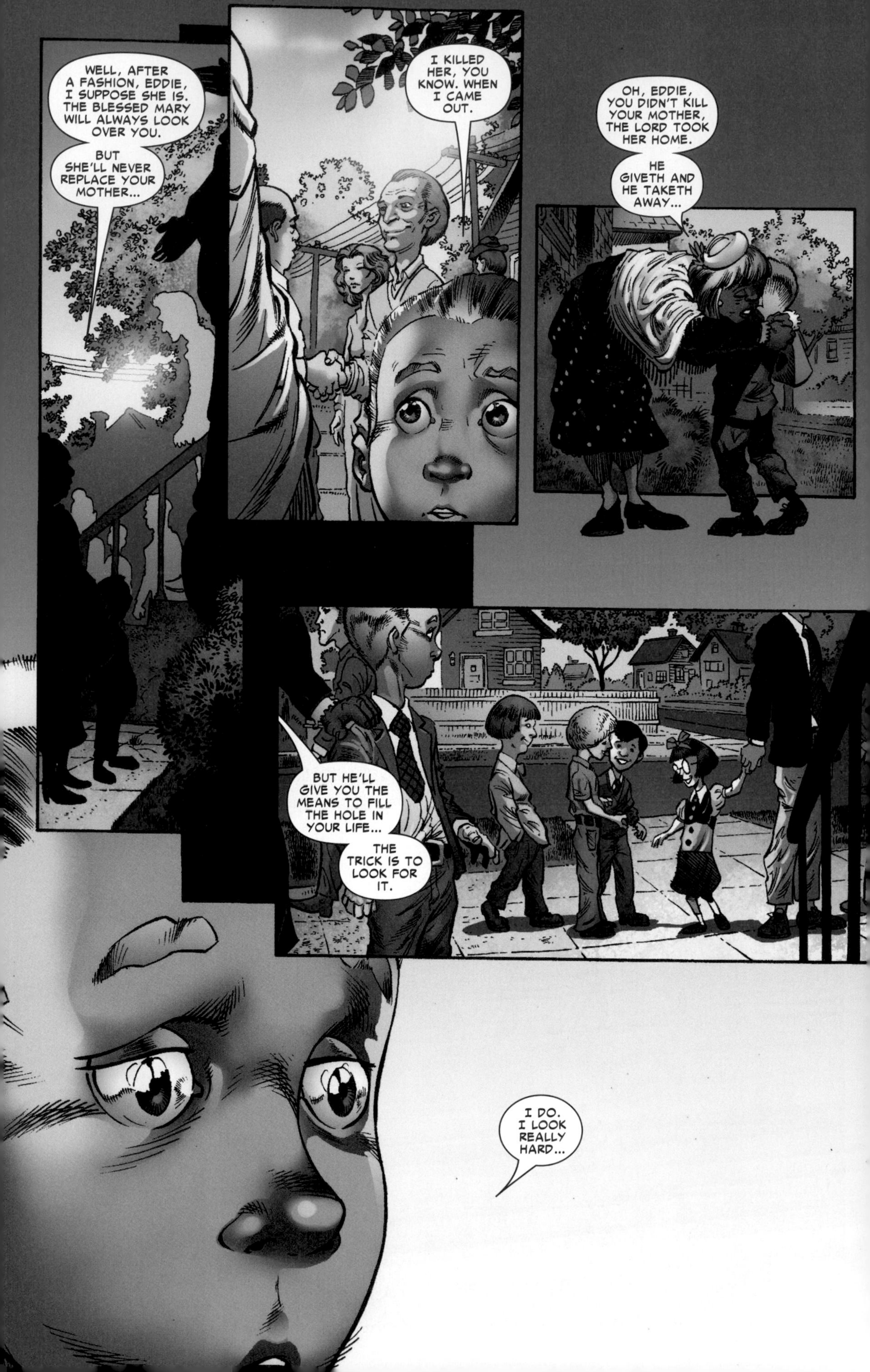
WELL, AFTER A FASHION, EDDIE, I SUPPOSE SHE IS. THE BLESSED MARY WILL ALWAYS LOOK OVER YOU.
BUT SHE'LL NEVER REPLACE YOUR MOTHER...
I KILLED HER, YOU KNOW. WHEN I CAME OUT.
OH, EDDIE, YOU DIDN'T KILL YOUR MOTHER, THE LORD TOOK HER HOME.
HE GIVETH AND HE TAKETH AWAY...
BUT HE'LL GIVE YOU THE MEANS TO FILL THE HOLE IN YOUR LIFE...
THE TRICK IS TO LOOK FOR IT.
I DO. I LOOK REALLY HARD...

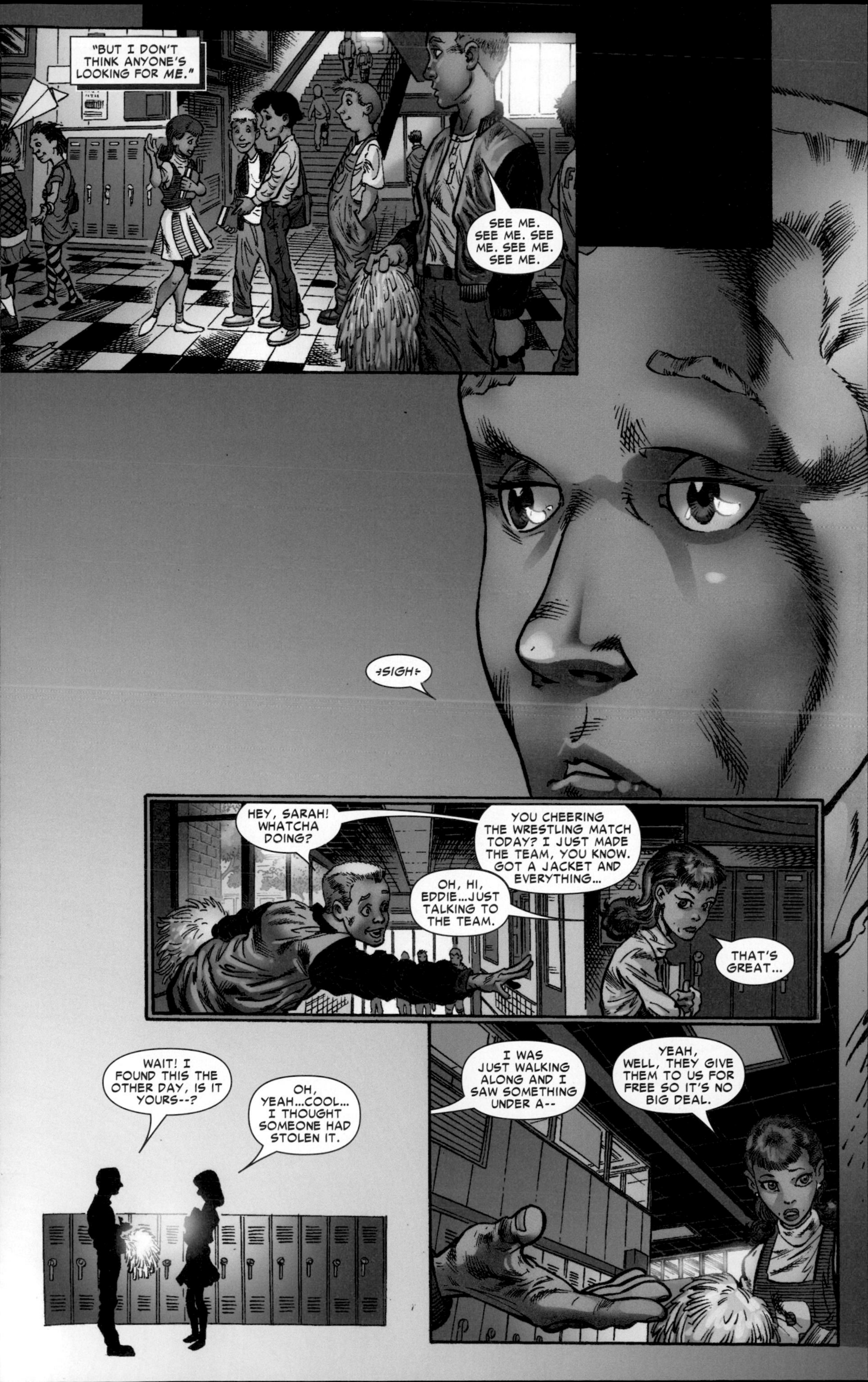
"BUT I DON'T THINK ANYONE'S LOOKING FOR ME."
SEE ME. SEE ME. SEE ME. SEE ME. SEE ME.
⊰SIGH⊱
HEY, SARAH! WHATCHA DOING?
YOU CHEERING THE WRESTLING MATCH TODAY? I JUST MADE THE TEAM, YOU KNOW. GOT A JACKET AND EVERYTHING...
OH, HI, EDDIE...JUST TALKING TO THE TEAM.
THAT'S GREAT...
WAIT! I FOUND THIS THE OTHER DAY, IS IT YOURS--?
OH, YEAH...COOL... I THOUGHT SOMEONE HAD STOLEN IT.
I WAS JUST WALKING ALONG AND I SAW SOMETHING UNDER A--
YEAH, WELL, THEY GIVE THEM TO US FOR FREE SO IT'S NO BIG DEAL.

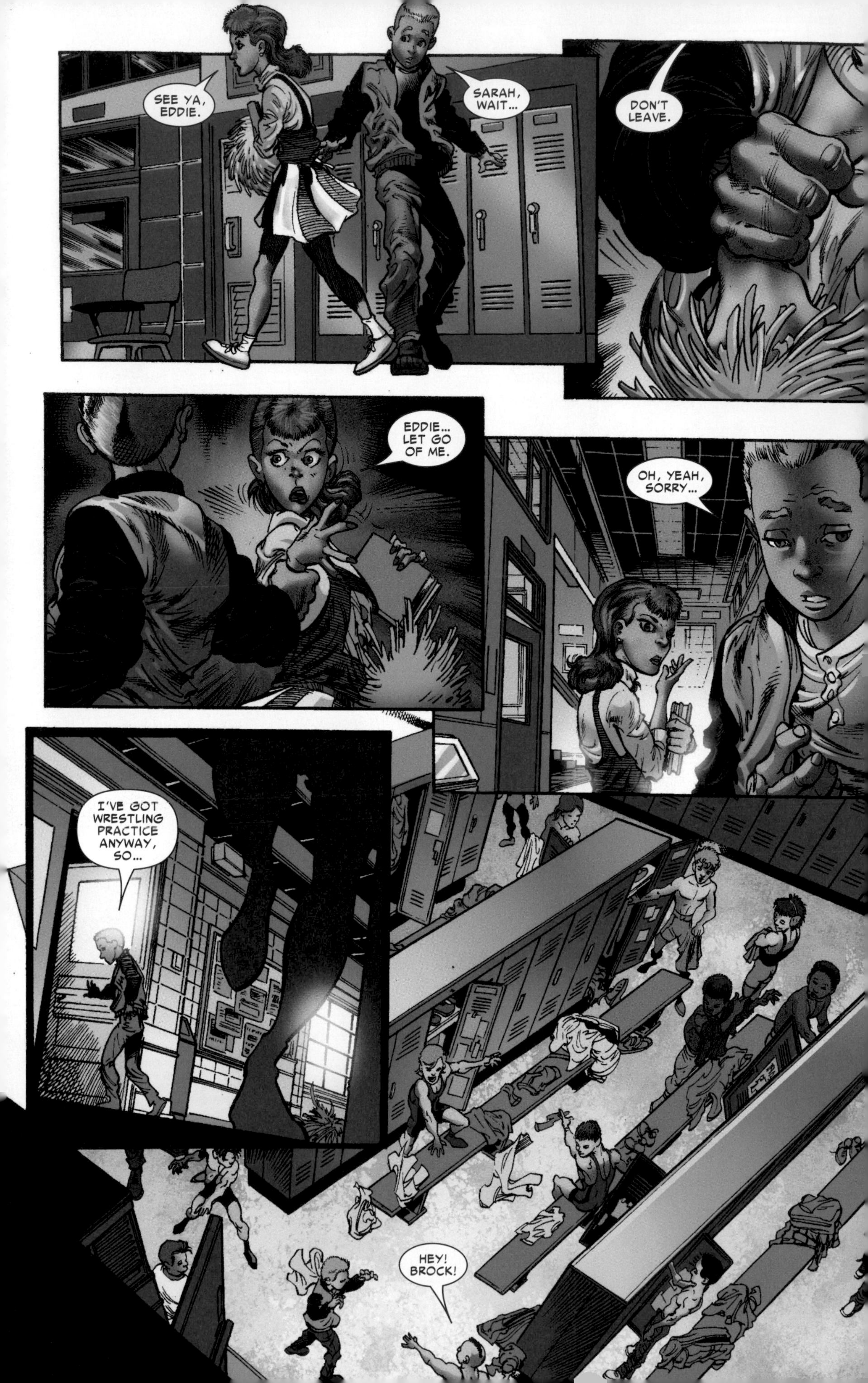
SEE YA, EDDIE.
SARAH, WAIT...
DON'T LEAVE.
EDDIE... LET GO OF ME.
OH, YEAH, SORRY...
I'VE GOT WRESTLING PRACTICE ANYWAY, SO...
HEY! BROCK!

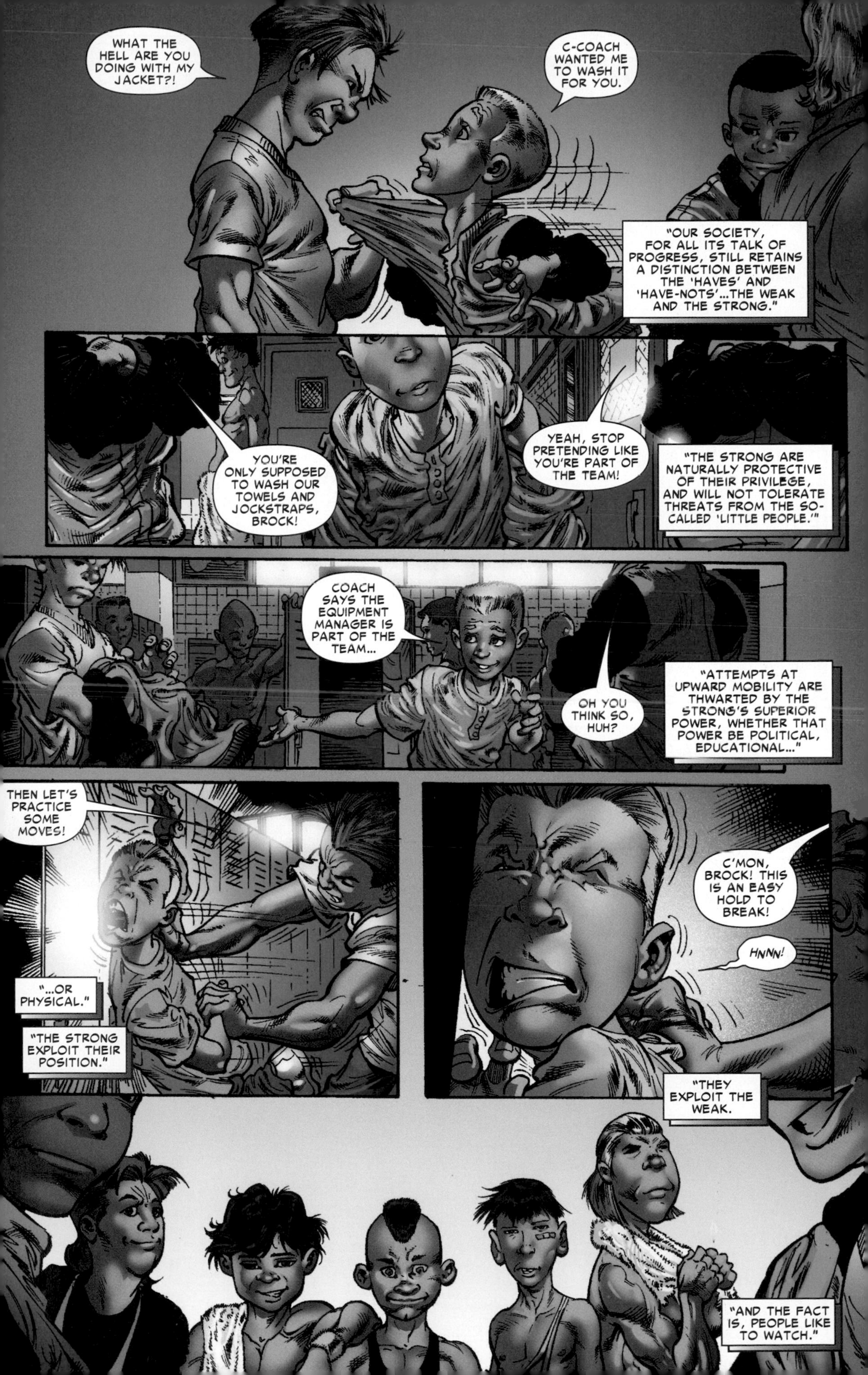
WHAT THE HELL ARE YOU DOING WITH MY JACKET?!
C-COACH WANTED ME TO WASH IT FOR YOU.
"OUR SOCIETY, FOR ALL ITS TALK OF PROGRESS, STILL RETAINS A DISTINCTION BETWEEN THE 'HAVES' AND 'HAVE-NOTS'...THE WEAK AND THE STRONG."
YOU'RE ONLY SUPPOSED TO WASH OUR TOWELS AND JOCKSTRAPS, BROCK!
YEAH, STOP PRETENDING LIKE YOU'RE PART OF THE TEAM!
"THE STRONG ARE NATURALLY PROTECTIVE OF THEIR PRIVILEGE, AND WILL NOT TOLERATE THREATS FROM THE SO-CALLED 'LITTLE PEOPLE.'"
COACH SAYS THE EQUIPMENT MANAGER IS PART OF THE TEAM...
OH YOU THINK SO, HUH?
"ATTEMPTS AT UPWARD MOBILITY ARE THWARTED BY THE STRONG'S SUPERIOR POWER, WHETHER THAT POWER BE POLITICAL, EDUCATIONAL..."
THEN LET'S PRACTICE SOME MOVES!
"...OR PHYSICAL."
"THE STRONG EXPLOIT THEIR POSITION."
C'MON, BROCK! THIS IS AN EASY HOLD TO BREAK!
HNNN!
"THEY EXPLOIT THE WEAK.
"AND THE FACT IS, PEOPLE LIKE TO WATCH."

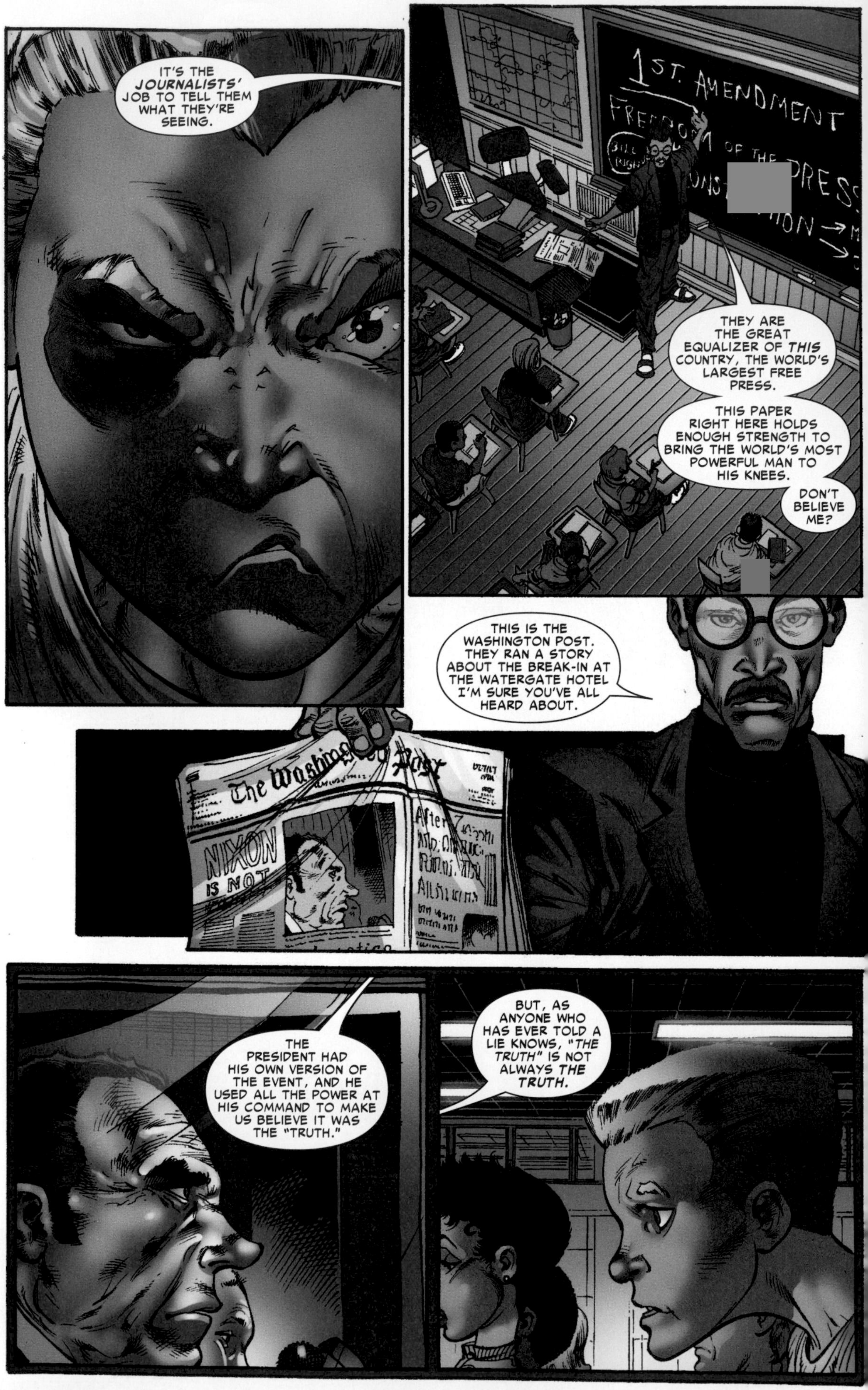
IT'S THE *JOURNALISTS'* JOB TO TELL THEM WHAT THEY'RE SEEING.
1ST. AMENDMENT
THEY ARE THE GREAT EQUALIZER OF *THIS* COUNTRY, THE WORLD'S LARGEST FREE PRESS.
THIS PAPER RIGHT HERE HOLDS ENOUGH STRENGTH TO BRING THE WORLD'S MOST POWERFUL MAN TO HIS KNEES.
DON'T BELIEVE ME?
THIS IS THE WASHINGTON POST. THEY RAN A STORY ABOUT THE BREAK-IN AT THE WATERGATE HOTEL I'M SURE YOU'VE ALL HEARD ABOUT.
NIXON IS NOT
THE PRESIDENT HAD HIS OWN VERSION OF THE EVENT, AND HE USED ALL THE POWER AT HIS COMMAND TO MAKE US BELIEVE IT WAS THE "TRUTH."
BUT, AS ANYONE WHO HAS EVER TOLD A LIE KNOWS, *"THE TRUTH"* IS NOT ALWAYS *THE TRUTH*.

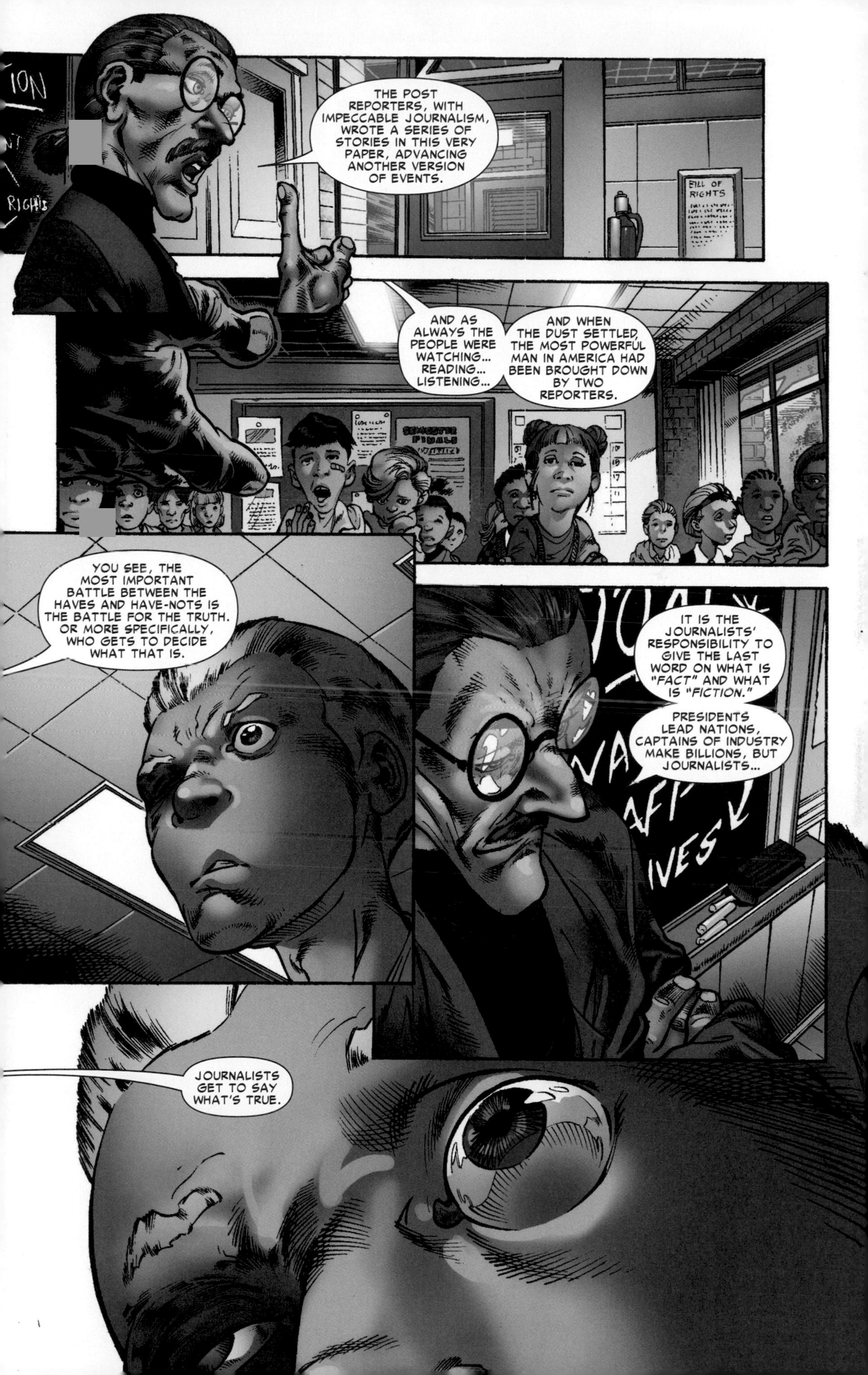

THE POST REPORTERS, WITH IMPECCABLE JOURNALISM, WROTE A SERIES OF STORIES IN THIS VERY PAPER, ADVANCING ANOTHER VERSION OF EVENTS.
BILL OF RIGHTS
AND AS ALWAYS THE PEOPLE WERE WATCHING... READING... LISTENING...
AND WHEN THE DUST SETTLED, THE MOST POWERFUL MAN IN AMERICA HAD BEEN BROUGHT DOWN BY TWO REPORTERS.
YOU SEE, THE MOST IMPORTANT BATTLE BETWEEN THE HAVES AND HAVE-NOTS IS THE BATTLE FOR THE TRUTH. OR MORE SPECIFICALLY, WHO GETS TO DECIDE WHAT THAT IS.
IT IS THE JOURNALISTS' RESPONSIBILITY TO GIVE THE LAST WORD ON WHAT IS "FACT" AND WHAT IS "FICTION."
PRESIDENTS LEAD NATIONS, CAPTAINS OF INDUSTRY MAKE BILLIONS, BUT JOURNALISTS...
JOURNALISTS GET TO SAY WHAT'S TRUE.

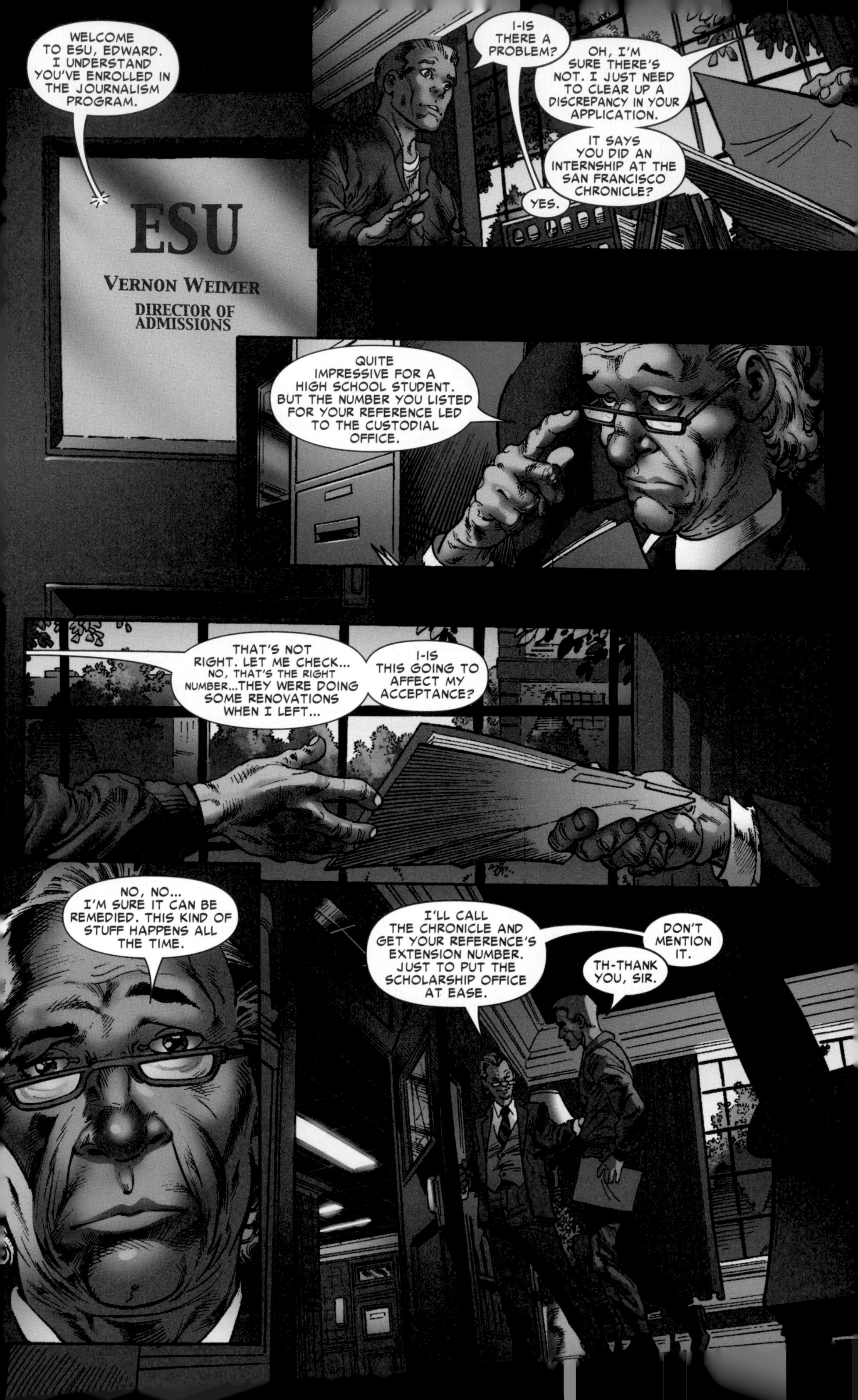
WELCOME TO ESU, EDWARD. I UNDERSTAND YOU'VE ENROLLED IN THE JOURNALISM PROGRAM.
I-IS THERE A PROBLEM?
OH, I'M SURE THERE'S NOT. I JUST NEED TO CLEAR UP A DISCREPANCY IN YOUR APPLICATION.
IT SAYS YOU DID AN INTERNSHIP AT THE SAN FRANCISCO CHRONICLE?
YES.
ESU
VERNON WEIMER
DIRECTOR OF ADMISSIONS
QUITE IMPRESSIVE FOR A HIGH SCHOOL STUDENT. BUT THE NUMBER YOU LISTED FOR YOUR REFERENCE LED TO THE CUSTODIAL OFFICE.
THAT'S NOT RIGHT. LET ME CHECK... NO, THAT'S THE RIGHT NUMBER...THEY WERE DOING SOME RENOVATIONS WHEN I LEFT...
I-IS THIS GOING TO AFFECT MY ACCEPTANCE?
NO, NO... I'M SURE IT CAN BE REMEDIED. THIS KIND OF STUFF HAPPENS ALL THE TIME.
I'LL CALL THE CHRONICLE AND GET YOUR REFERENCE'S EXTENSION NUMBER. JUST TO PUT THE SCHOLARSHIP OFFICE AT EASE.
TH-THANK YOU, SIR.
DON'T MENTION IT.

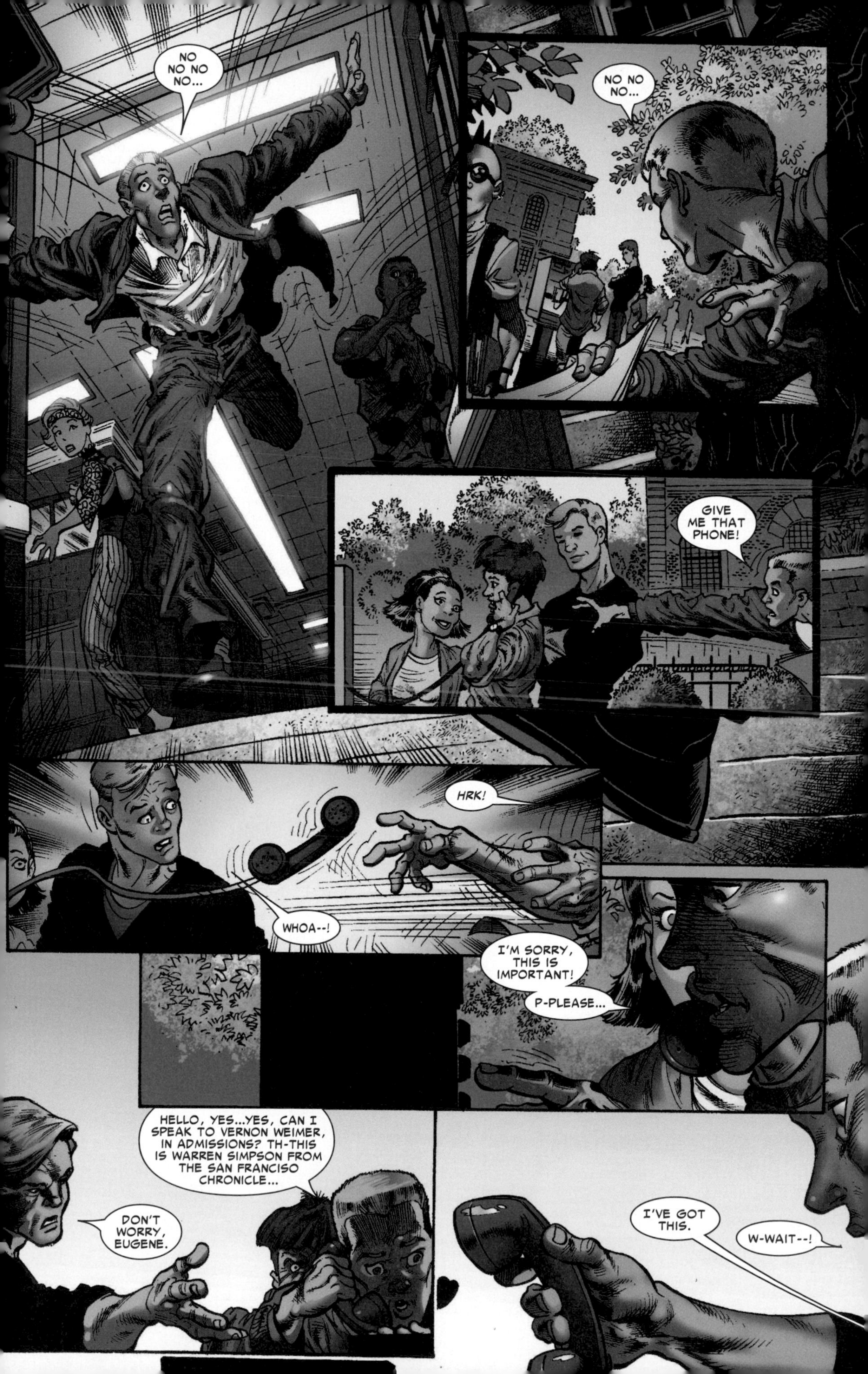
NO NO NO NO...
NO NO NO...
GIVE ME THAT PHONE!
HRK!
WHOA--!
I'M SORRY, THIS IS IMPORTANT!
P-PLEASE...
HELLO, YES...YES, CAN I SPEAK TO VERNON WEIMER, IN ADMISSIONS? TH-THIS IS WARREN SIMPSON FROM THE SAN FRANCISO CHRONICLE...
DON'T WORRY, EUGENE.
I'VE GOT THIS.
W-WAIT--!

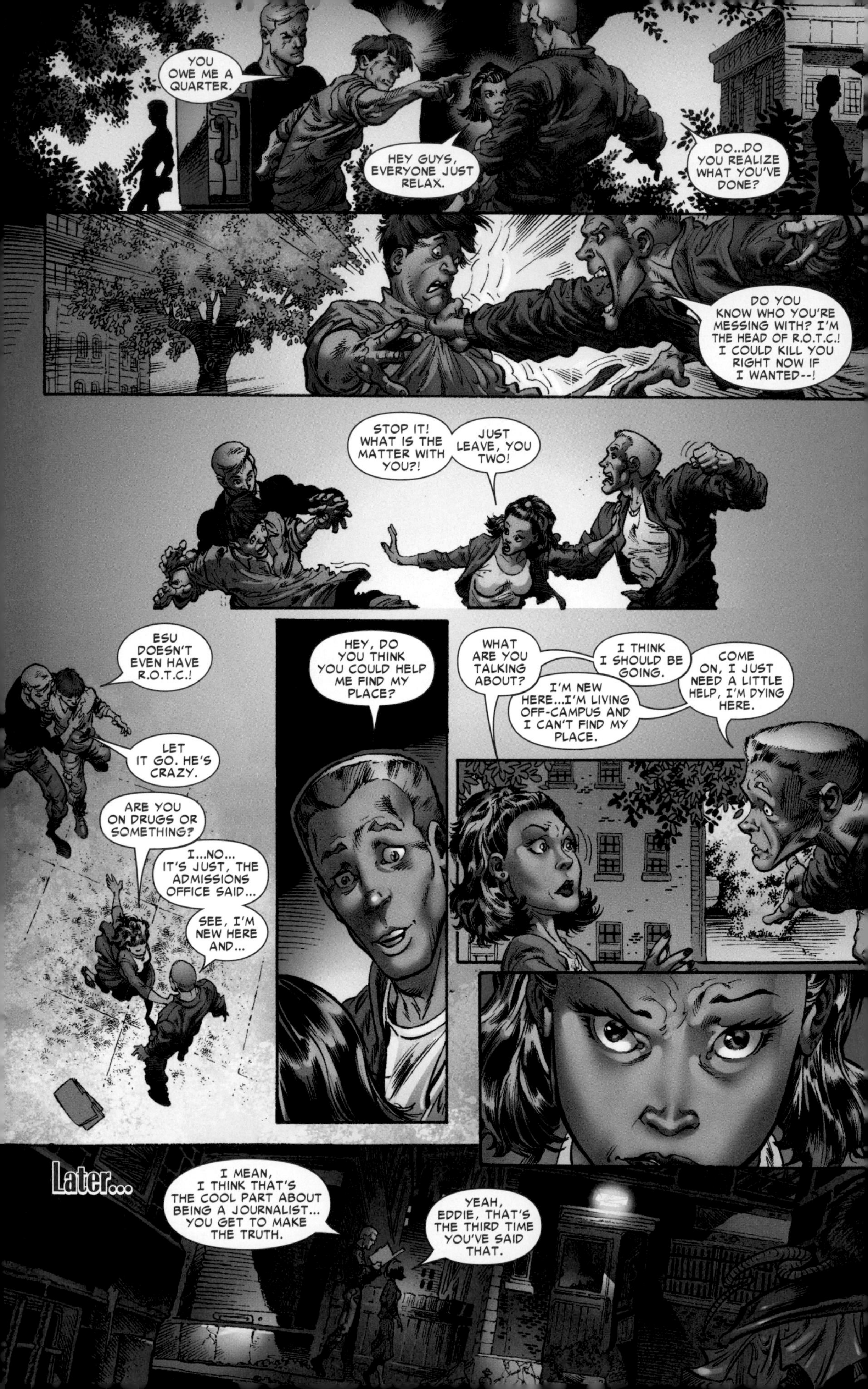
YOU OWE ME A QUARTER.
HEY GUYS, EVERYONE JUST RELAX.
DO...DO YOU REALIZE WHAT YOU'VE DONE?
DO YOU KNOW WHO YOU'RE MESSING WITH? I'M THE HEAD OF R.O.T.C.! I COULD KILL YOU RIGHT NOW IF I WANTED--!
STOP IT! WHAT IS THE MATTER WITH YOU?!
JUST LEAVE, YOU TWO!
ESU DOESN'T EVEN HAVE R.O.T.C.!
LET IT GO. HE'S CRAZY.
ARE YOU ON DRUGS OR SOMETHING?
I...NO... IT'S JUST, THE ADMISSIONS OFFICE SAID...
SEE, I'M NEW HERE AND...
HEY, DO YOU THINK YOU COULD HELP ME FIND MY PLACE?
WHAT ARE YOU TALKING ABOUT?
I'M NEW HERE...I'M LIVING OFF-CAMPUS AND I CAN'T FIND MY PLACE.
I THINK I SHOULD BE GOING.
COME ON, I JUST NEED A LITTLE HELP, I'M DYING HERE.
Later...
I MEAN, I THINK THAT'S THE COOL PART ABOUT BEING A JOURNALIST... YOU GET TO MAKE THE TRUTH.
YEAH, EDDIE, THAT'S THE THIRD TIME YOU'VE SAID THAT.

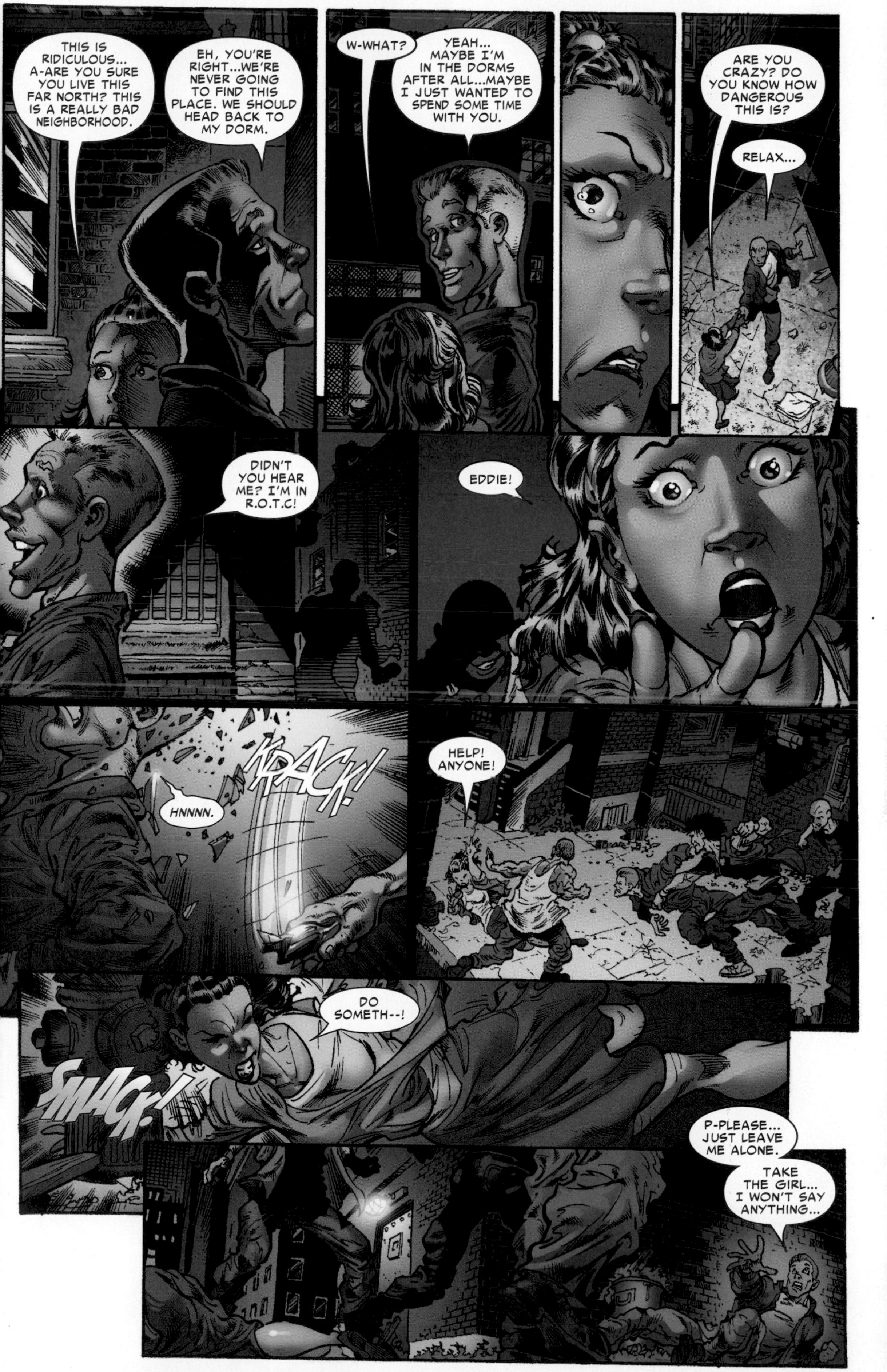
THIS IS RIDICULOUS... A-ARE YOU SURE YOU LIVE THIS FAR NORTH? THIS IS A REALLY BAD NEIGHBORHOOD.
EH, YOU'RE RIGHT...WE'RE NEVER GOING TO FIND THIS PLACE. WE SHOULD HEAD BACK TO MY DORM.
W-WHAT?
YEAH... MAYBE I'M IN THE DORMS AFTER ALL...MAYBE I JUST WANTED TO SPEND SOME TIME WITH YOU.
ARE YOU CRAZY? DO YOU KNOW HOW DANGEROUS THIS IS?
RELAX...
DIDN'T YOU HEAR ME? I'M IN R.O.T.C!
EDDIE!
HNNNN.
KRACK!
HELP! ANYONE!
DO SOMETH--!
SMACK!
P-PLEASE... JUST LEAVE ME ALONE.
TAKE THE GIRL... I WON'T SAY ANYTHING...

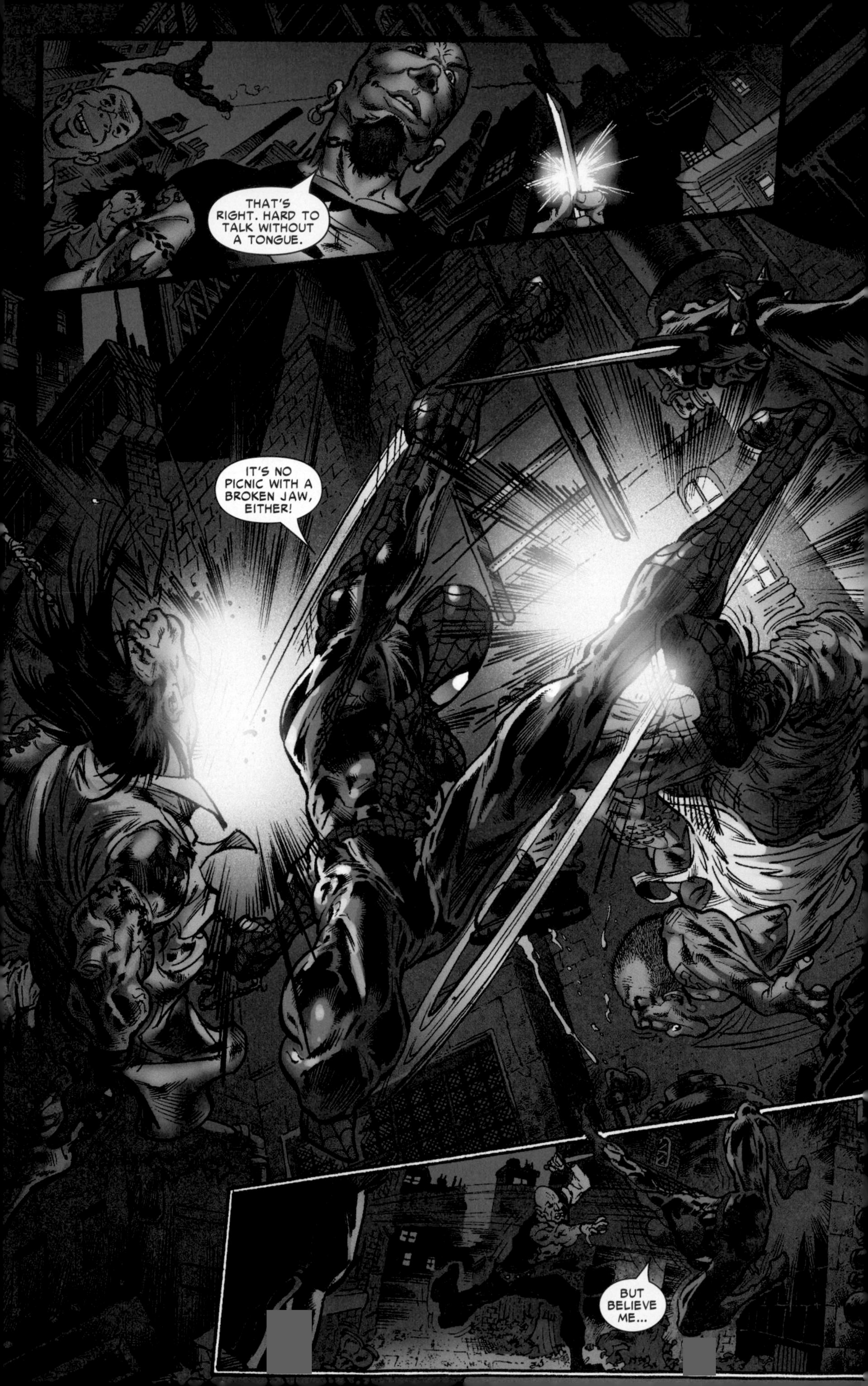
THAT'S RIGHT. HARD TO TALK WITHOUT A TONGUE.
IT'S NO PICNIC WITH A BROKEN JAW, EITHER!
BUT BELIEVE ME...

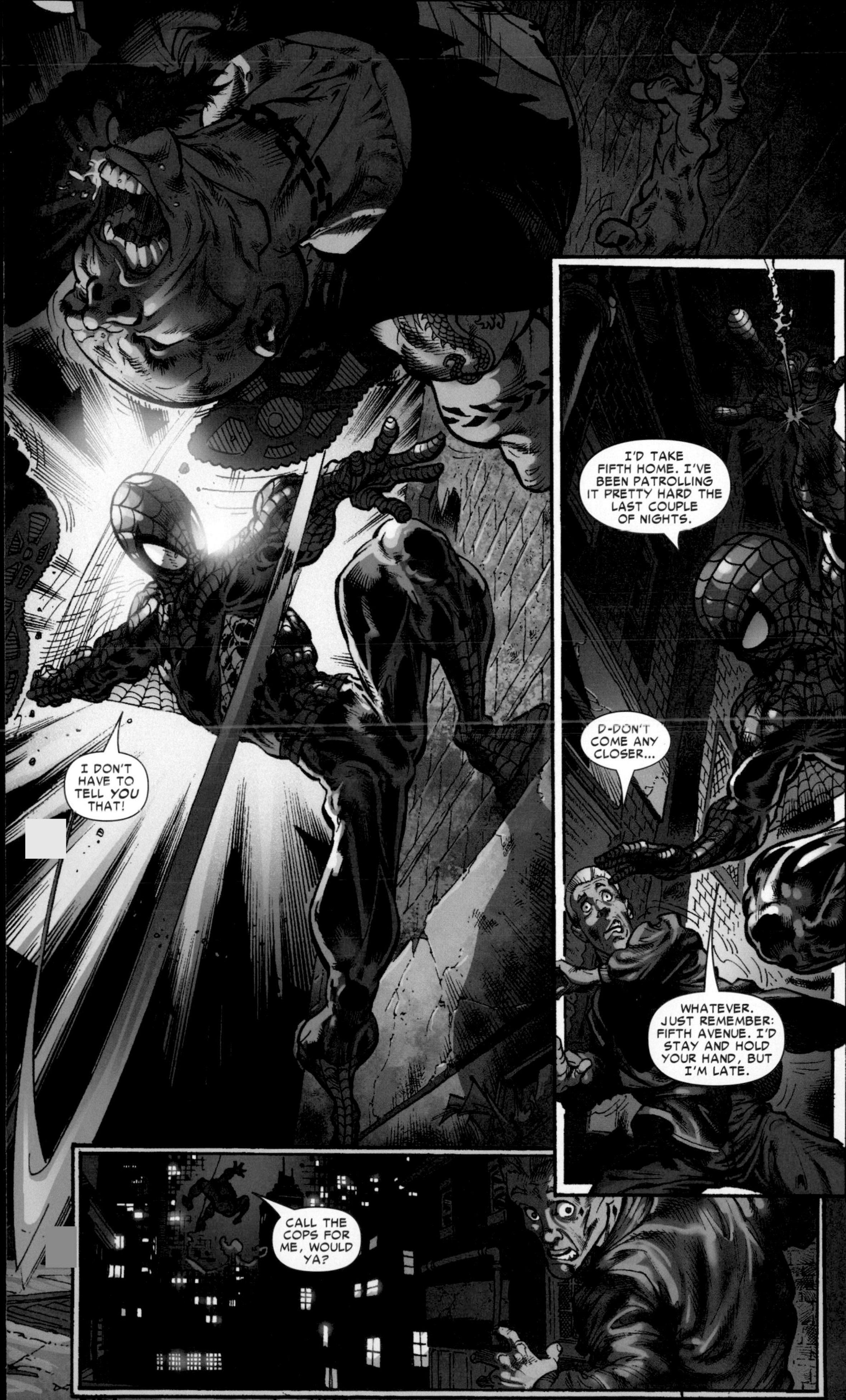
I DON'T HAVE TO TELL YOU THAT!
I'D TAKE FIFTH HOME. I'VE BEEN PATROLLING IT PRETTY HARD THE LAST COUPLE OF NIGHTS.
D-DON'T COME ANY CLOSER...
WHATEVER. JUST REMEMBER: FIFTH AVENUE. I'D STAY AND HOLD YOUR HAND, BUT I'M LATE.
CALL THE COPS FOR ME, WOULD YA?

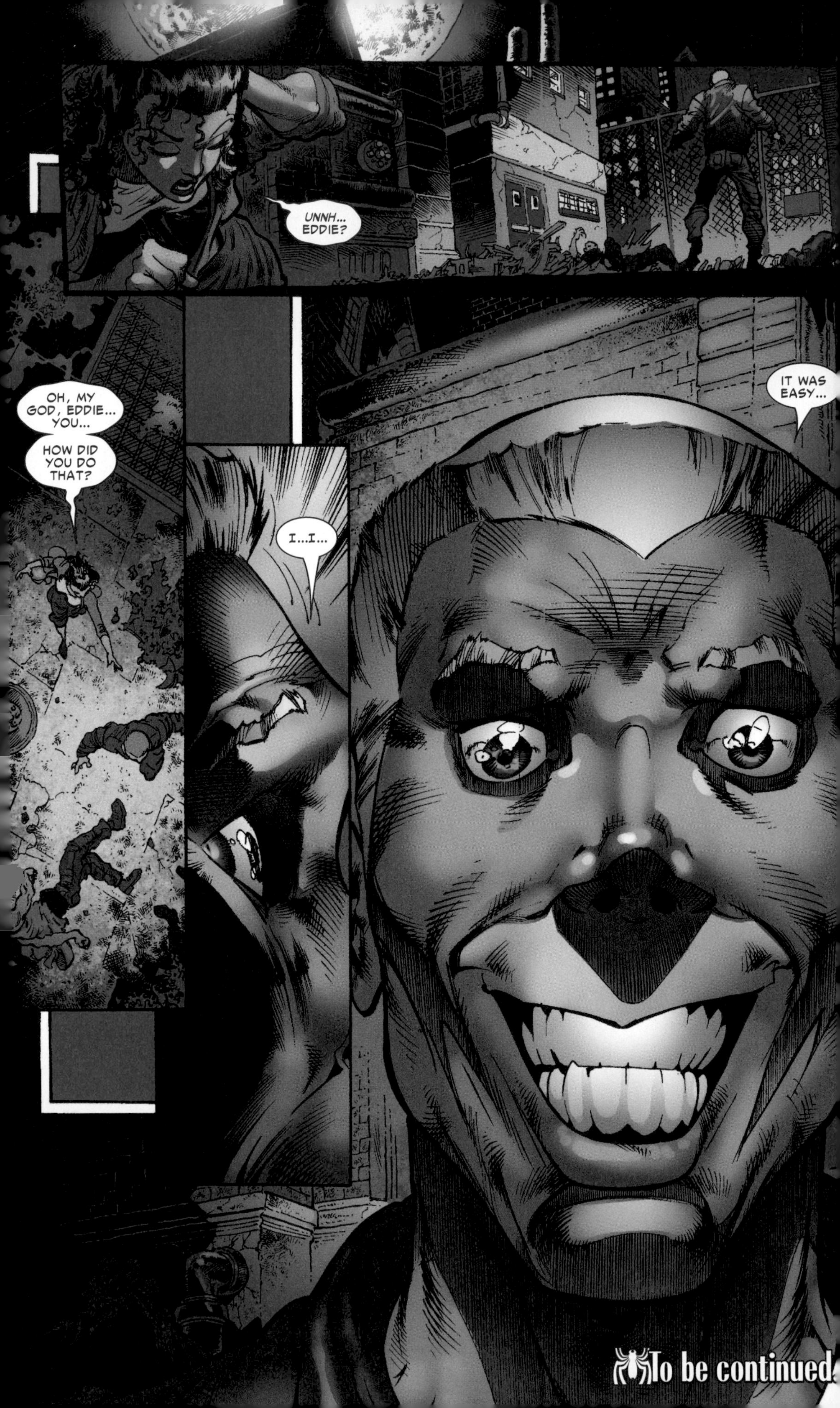
UNNH... EDDIE?
OH, MY GOD, EDDIE... YOU...
HOW DID YOU DO THAT?
I...I...
IT WAS EASY...
To be continued.

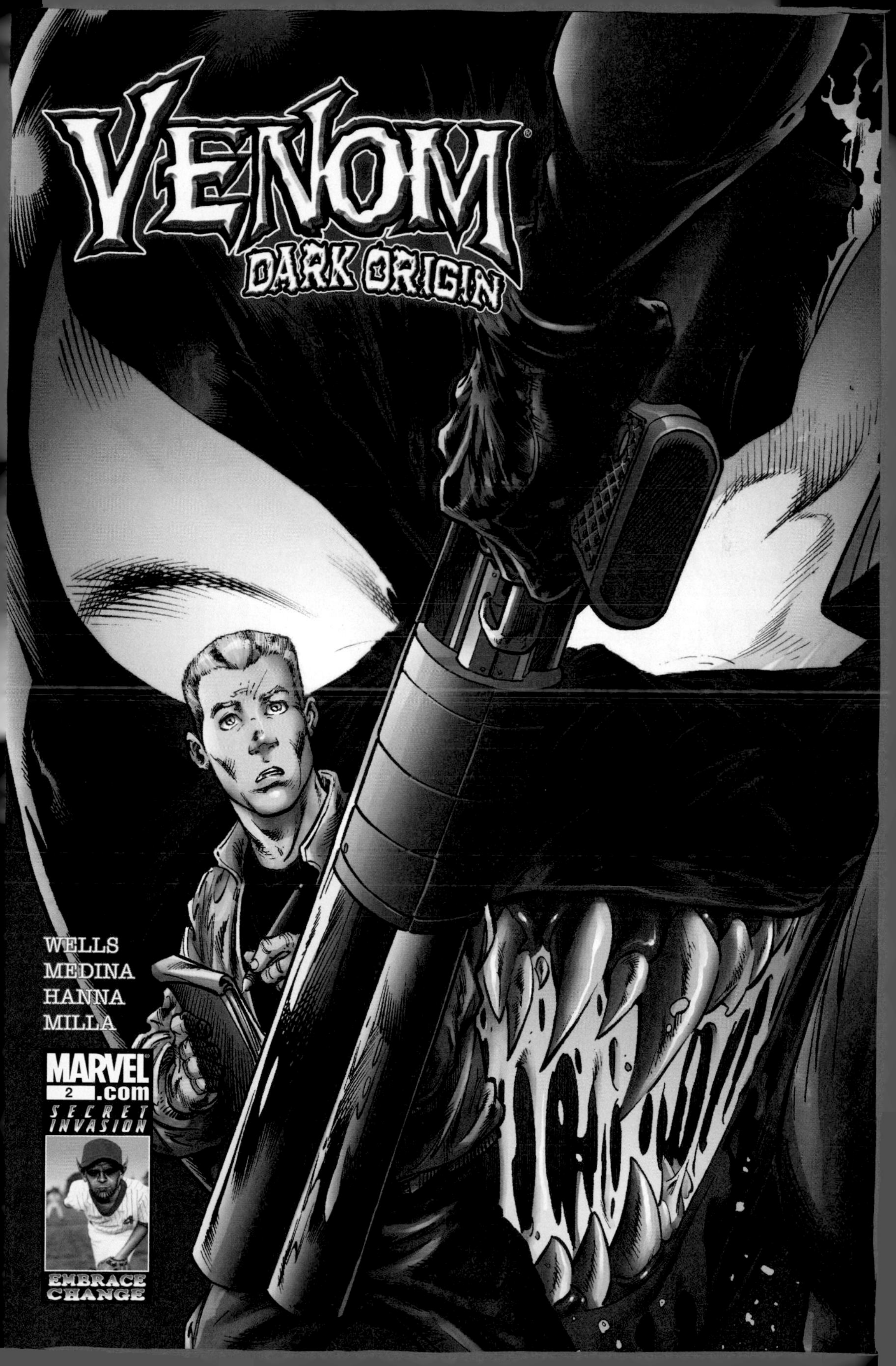
VENOM
DARK ORIGIN
WELLS
MEDINA
HANNA
MILLA
MARVEL
2 .com
SECRET INVASION
EMBRACE CHANGE

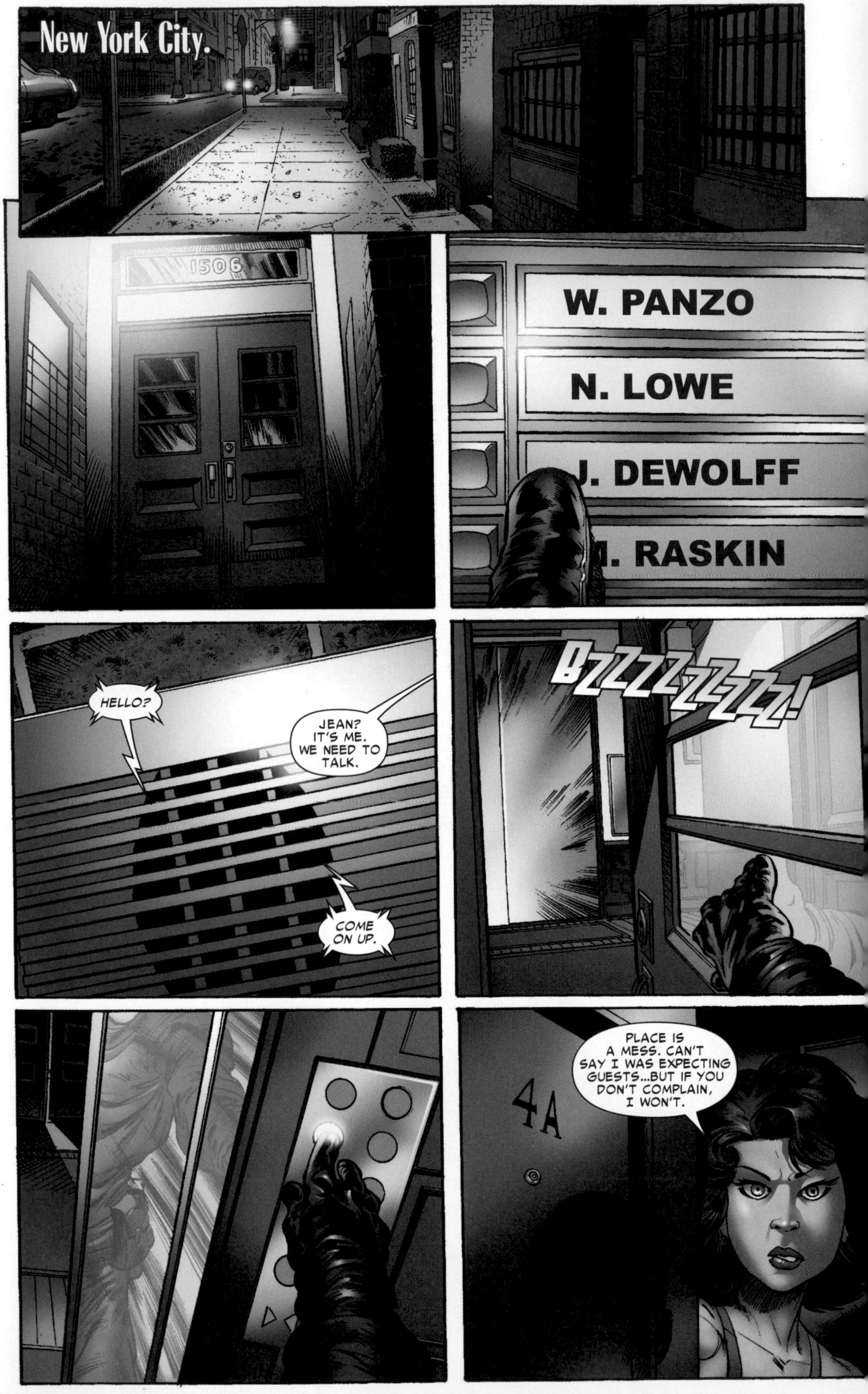
New York City.
1506
W. PANZO
N. LOWE
J. DEWOLFF
M. RASKIN
HELLO?
JEAN? IT'S ME. WE NEED TO TALK.
COME ON UP.
BZZZZZZZZZ!
4A
PLACE IS A MESS. CAN'T SAY I WAS EXPECTING GUESTS...BUT IF YOU DON'T COMPLAIN, I WON'T.

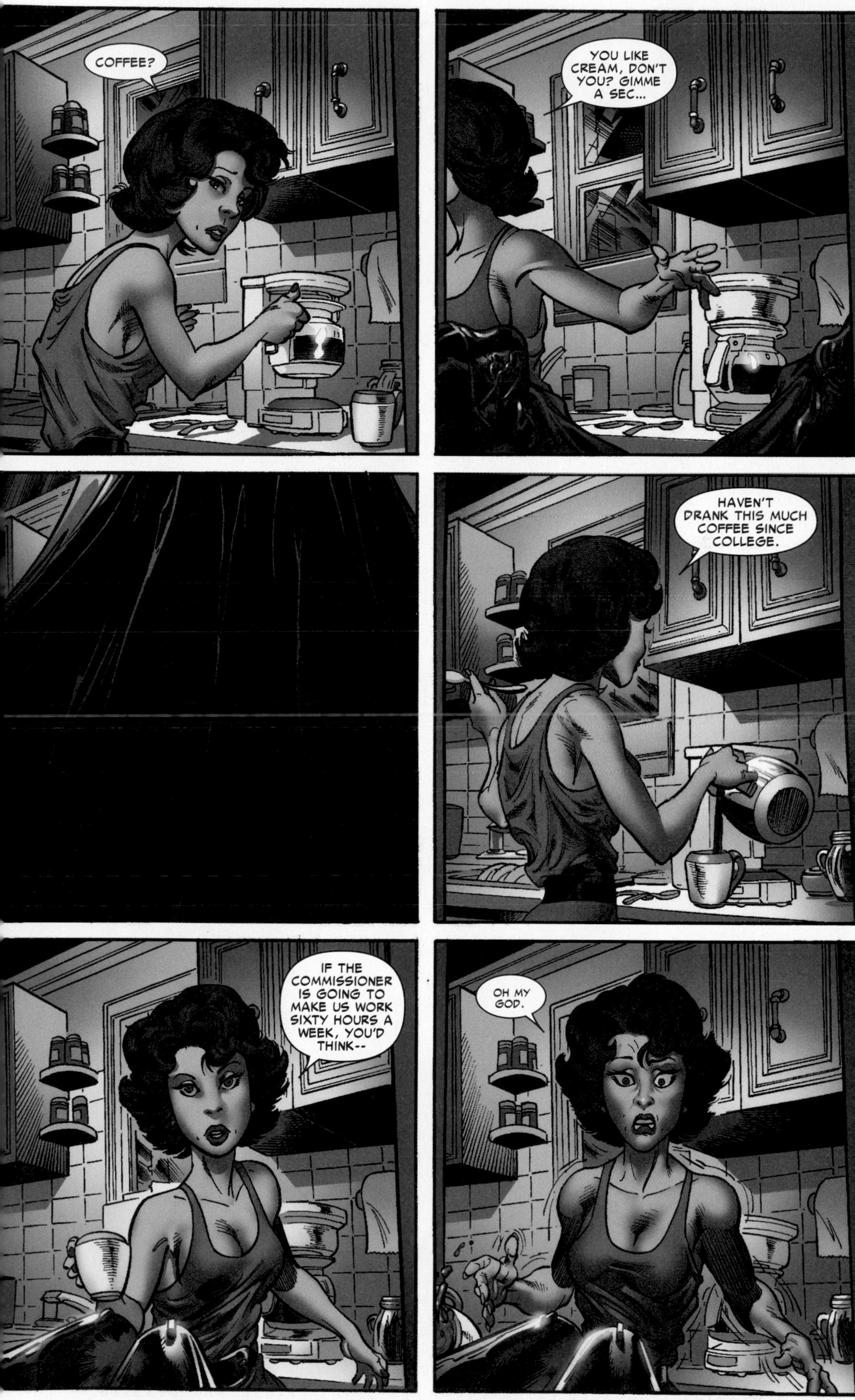
COFFEE?
YOU LIKE CREAM, DON'T YOU? GIMME A SEC...
HAVEN'T DRANK THIS MUCH COFFEE SINCE COLLEGE.
IF THE COMMISSIONER IS GOING TO MAKE US WORK SIXTY HOURS A WEEK, YOU'D THINK--
OH MY GOD.

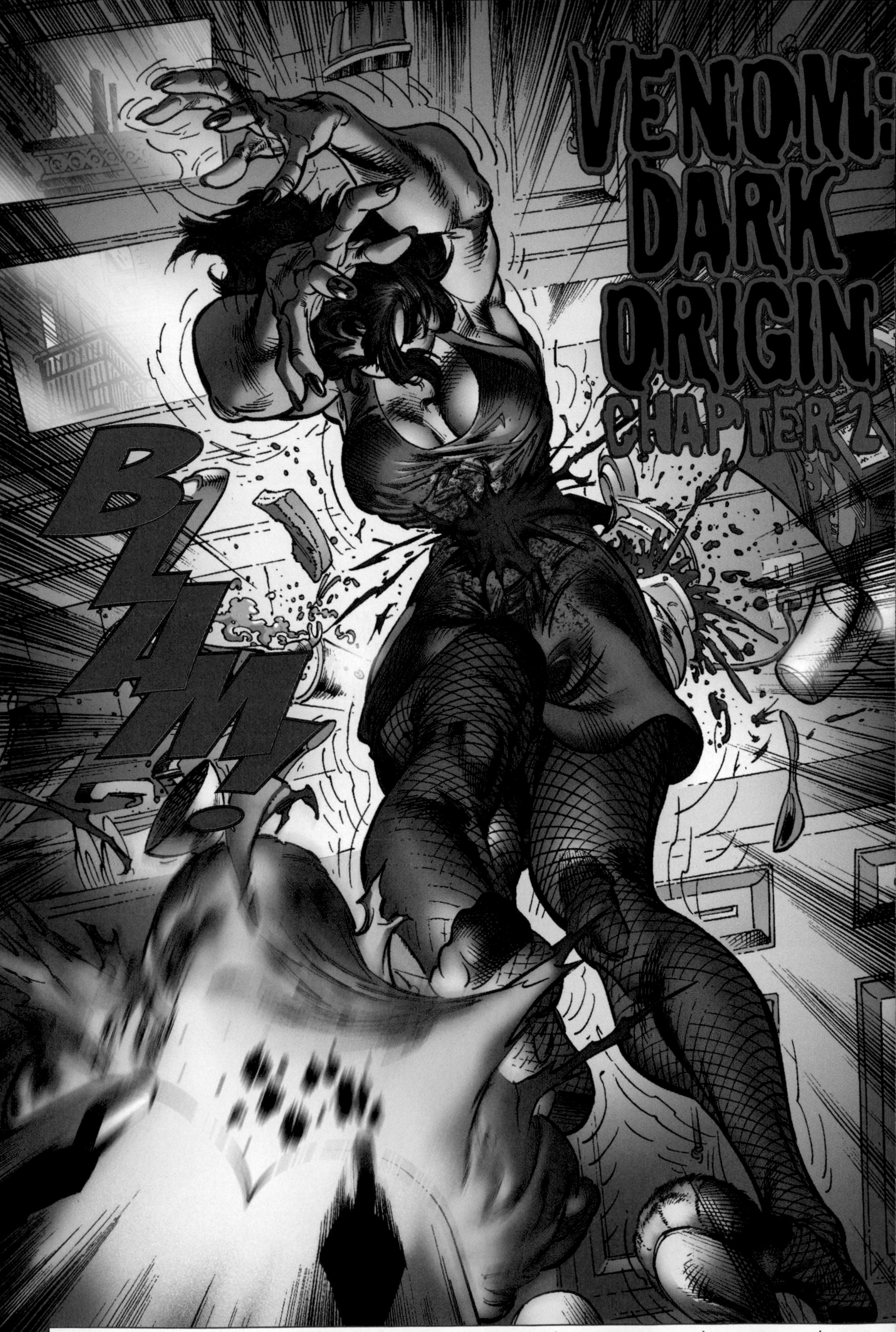
VENOM: DARK ORIGIN
CHAPTER 2
BLAM!

ZEB WELLS WRITER | ANGEL MEDINA PENCILER | SCOTT HANNA INKER | AVALON'S MATT MILLA COLORIST | VC'S JOE CARAMAGNA LETTERER | ALEJANDRO ARBONA EDITOR | WARREN SIMONS SUPERVISING EDITOR | JOE QUESADA EDITOR IN CHIEF | DAN BUCKLEY PUBLISHER

SPECIAL THANKS TO PETER DAVID FOR GREAT SPIDER-MAN STORIES

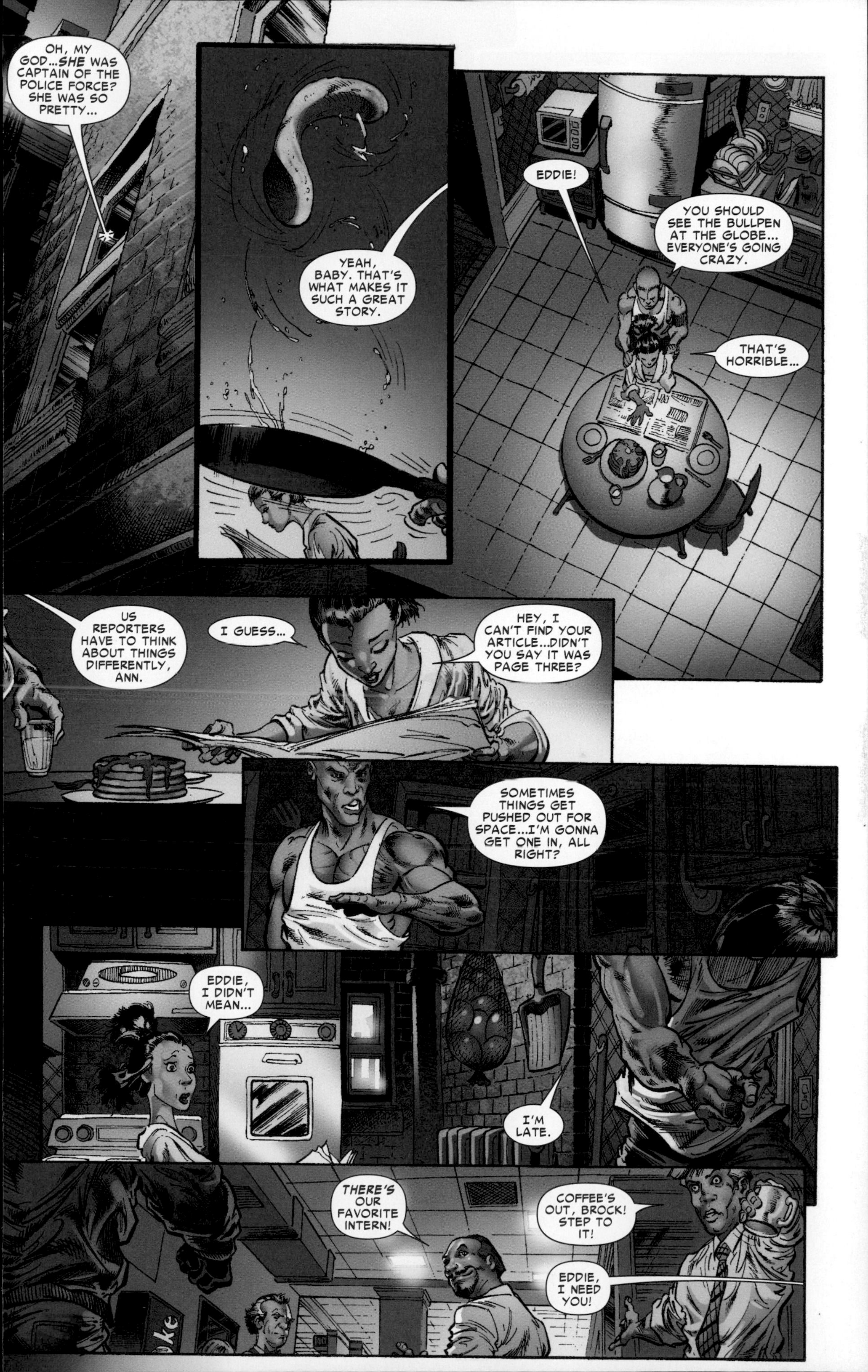
OH, MY GOD...SHE WAS CAPTAIN OF THE POLICE FORCE? SHE WAS SO PRETTY...
YEAH, BABY. THAT'S WHAT MAKES IT SUCH A GREAT STORY.
EDDIE!
YOU SHOULD SEE THE BULLPEN AT THE GLOBE... EVERYONE'S GOING CRAZY.
THAT'S HORRIBLE...
US REPORTERS HAVE TO THINK ABOUT THINGS DIFFERENTLY, ANN.
I GUESS...
HEY, I CAN'T FIND YOUR ARTICLE...DIDN'T YOU SAY IT WAS PAGE THREE?
SOMETIMES THINGS GET PUSHED OUT FOR SPACE...I'M GONNA GET ONE IN, ALL RIGHT?
EDDIE, I DIDN'T MEAN...
I'M LATE.
THERE'S OUR FAVORITE INTERN!
COFFEE'S OUT, BROCK! STEP TO IT!
EDDIE, I NEED YOU!

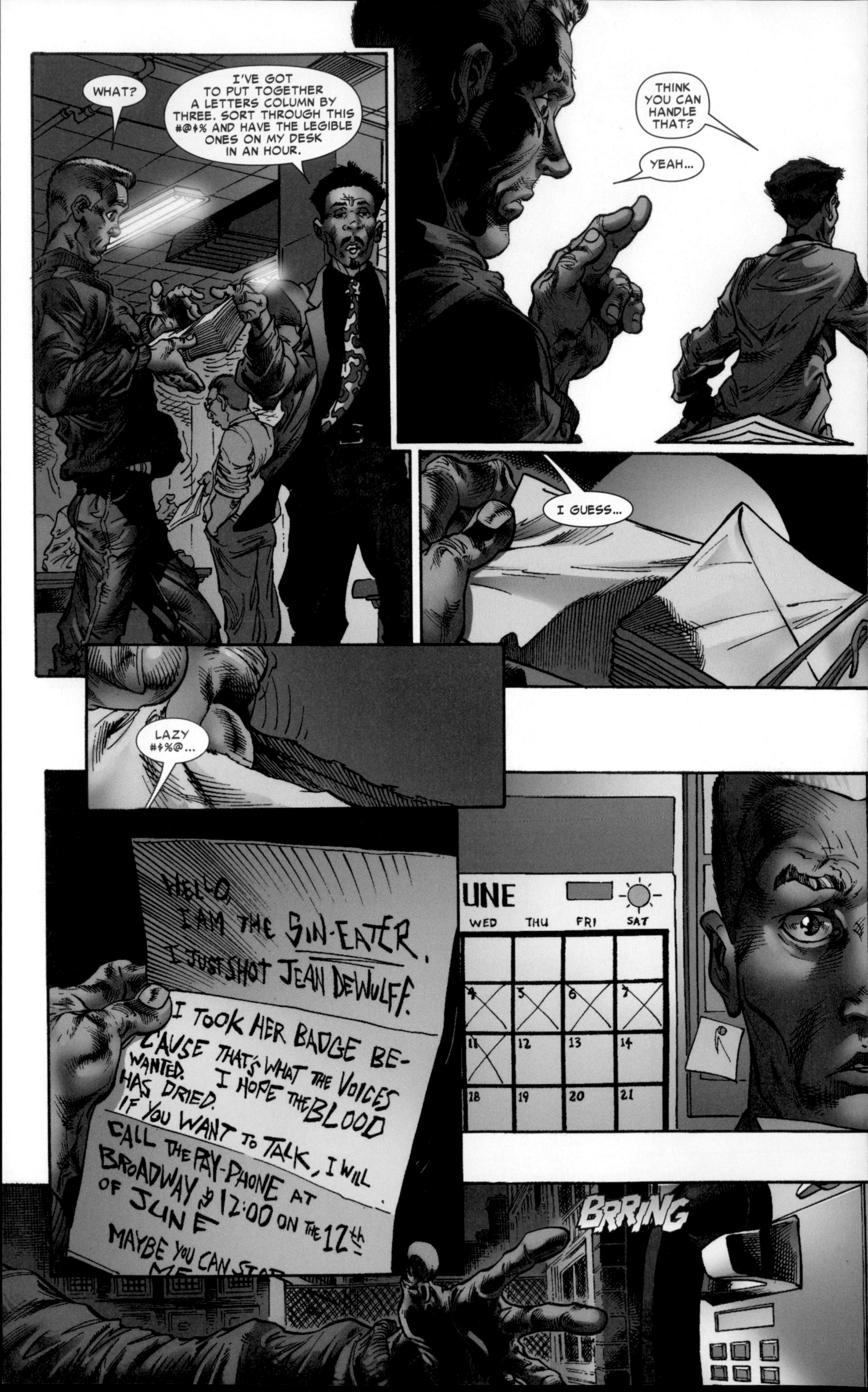
WHAT?
I'VE GOT TO PUT TOGETHER A LETTERS COLUMN BY THREE. SORT THROUGH THIS #@$% AND HAVE THE LEGIBLE ONES ON MY DESK IN AN HOUR.
THINK YOU CAN HANDLE THAT?
YEAH...
I GUESS...
LAZY #$%@...
HELLO, I AM THE SIN-EATER. I JUST SHOT JEAN DEWULFF.
I TOOK HER BADGE BE-CAUSE THAT'S WHAT THE VOICES WANTED. I HOPE THE BLOOD HAS DRIED.
IF YOU WANT TO TALK, I WILL CALL THE PAY-PHONE AT BROADWAY & 12:00 ON THE 12th OF JUNE
MAYBE YOU CAN STOP ME
UNE
WED
THU
FRI
SAT
BRRING

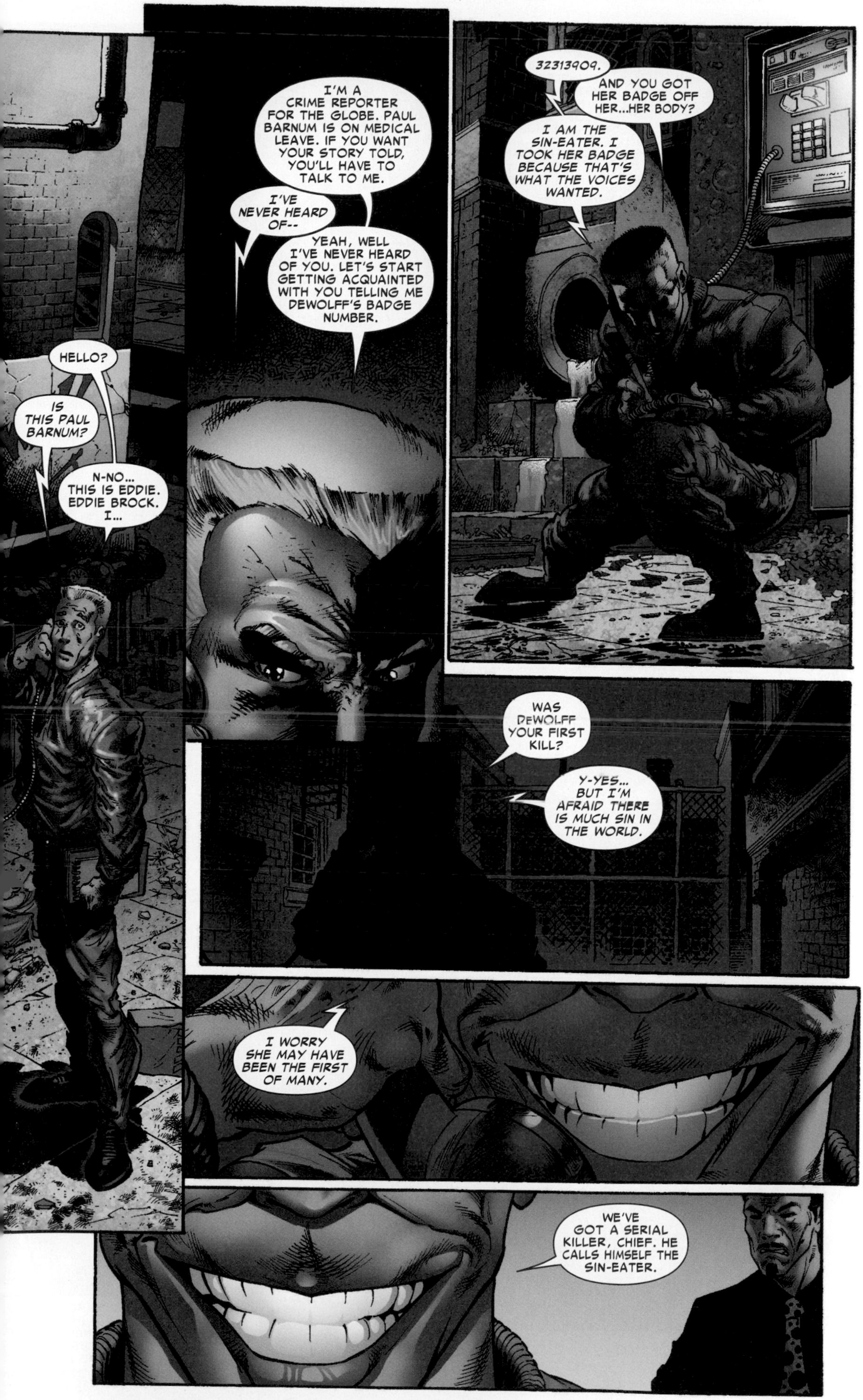
HELLO?
IS THIS PAUL BARNUM?
N-NO... THIS IS EDDIE. EDDIE BROCK. I...
I'M A CRIME REPORTER FOR THE GLOBE. PAUL BARNUM IS ON MEDICAL LEAVE. IF YOU WANT YOUR STORY TOLD, YOU'LL HAVE TO TALK TO ME.
I'VE NEVER HEARD OF--
YEAH, WELL I'VE NEVER HEARD OF YOU. LET'S START GETTING ACQUAINTED WITH YOU TELLING ME DEWOLFF'S BADGE NUMBER.
32313909.
AND YOU GOT HER BADGE OFF HER...HER BODY?
I AM THE SIN-EATER. I TOOK HER BADGE BECAUSE THAT'S WHAT THE VOICES WANTED.
WAS DEWOLFF YOUR FIRST KILL?
Y-YES... BUT I'M AFRAID THERE IS MUCH SIN IN THE WORLD.
I WORRY SHE MAY HAVE BEEN THE FIRST OF MANY.
WE'VE GOT A SERIAL KILLER, CHIEF. HE CALLS HIMSELF THE SIN-EATER.

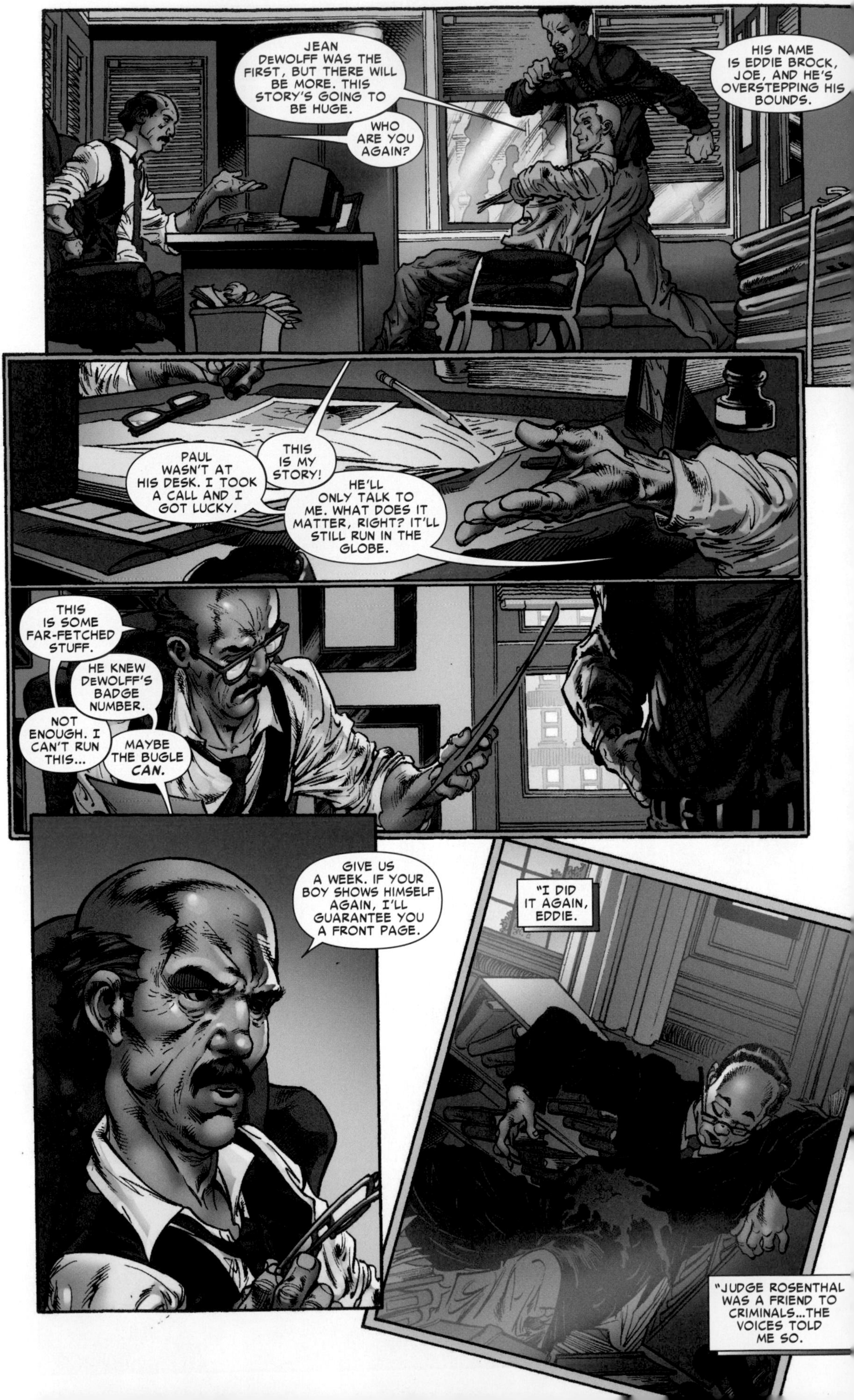
JEAN DeWOLFF WAS THE FIRST, BUT THERE WILL BE MORE. THIS STORY'S GOING TO BE HUGE.
WHO ARE YOU AGAIN?
HIS NAME IS EDDIE BROCK, JOE, AND HE'S OVERSTEPPING HIS BOUNDS.
PAUL WASN'T AT HIS DESK. I TOOK A CALL AND I GOT LUCKY.
THIS IS MY STORY!
HE'LL ONLY TALK TO ME. WHAT DOES IT MATTER, RIGHT? IT'LL STILL RUN IN THE GLOBE.
THIS IS SOME FAR-FETCHED STUFF.
HE KNEW DeWOLFF'S BADGE NUMBER.
NOT ENOUGH. I CAN'T RUN THIS...
MAYBE THE BUGLE *CAN.*
GIVE US A WEEK. IF YOUR BOY SHOWS HIMSELF AGAIN, I'LL GUARANTEE YOU A FRONT PAGE.
"I DID IT AGAIN, EDDIE.
"JUDGE ROSENTHAL WAS A FRIEND TO CRIMINALS...THE VOICES TOLD ME SO.

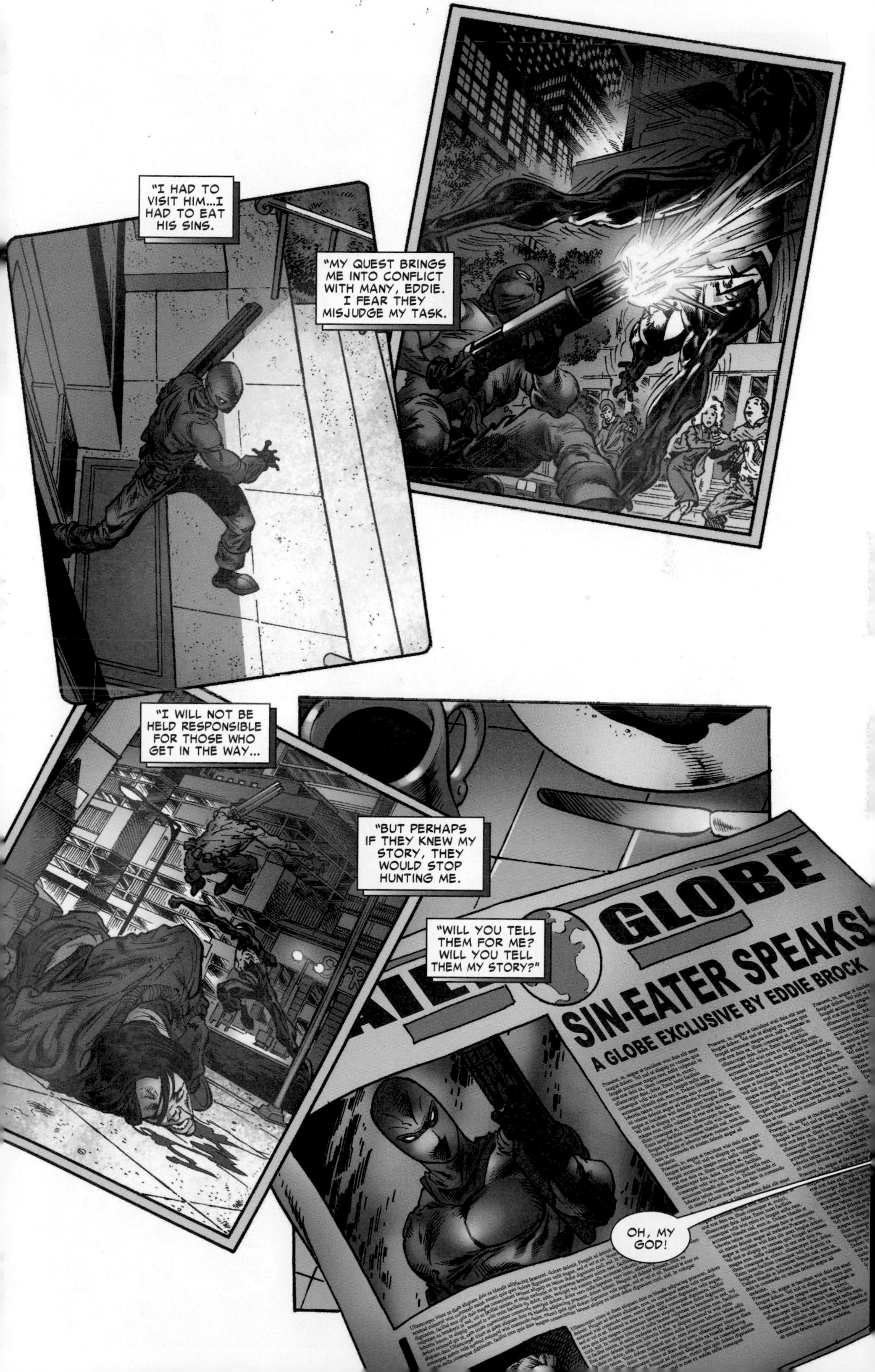
"I HAD TO VISIT HIM...I HAD TO EAT HIS SINS.
"MY QUEST BRINGS ME INTO CONFLICT WITH MANY, EDDIE. I FEAR THEY MISJUDGE MY TASK.
"I WILL NOT BE HELD RESPONSIBLE FOR THOSE WHO GET IN THE WAY...
"BUT PERHAPS IF THEY KNEW MY STORY, THEY WOULD STOP HUNTING ME.
"WILL YOU TELL THEM FOR ME? WILL YOU TELL THEM MY STORY?"
GLOBE
SIN-EATER SPEAKS!
A GLOBE EXCLUSIVE BY EDDIE BROCK
OH, MY GOD!

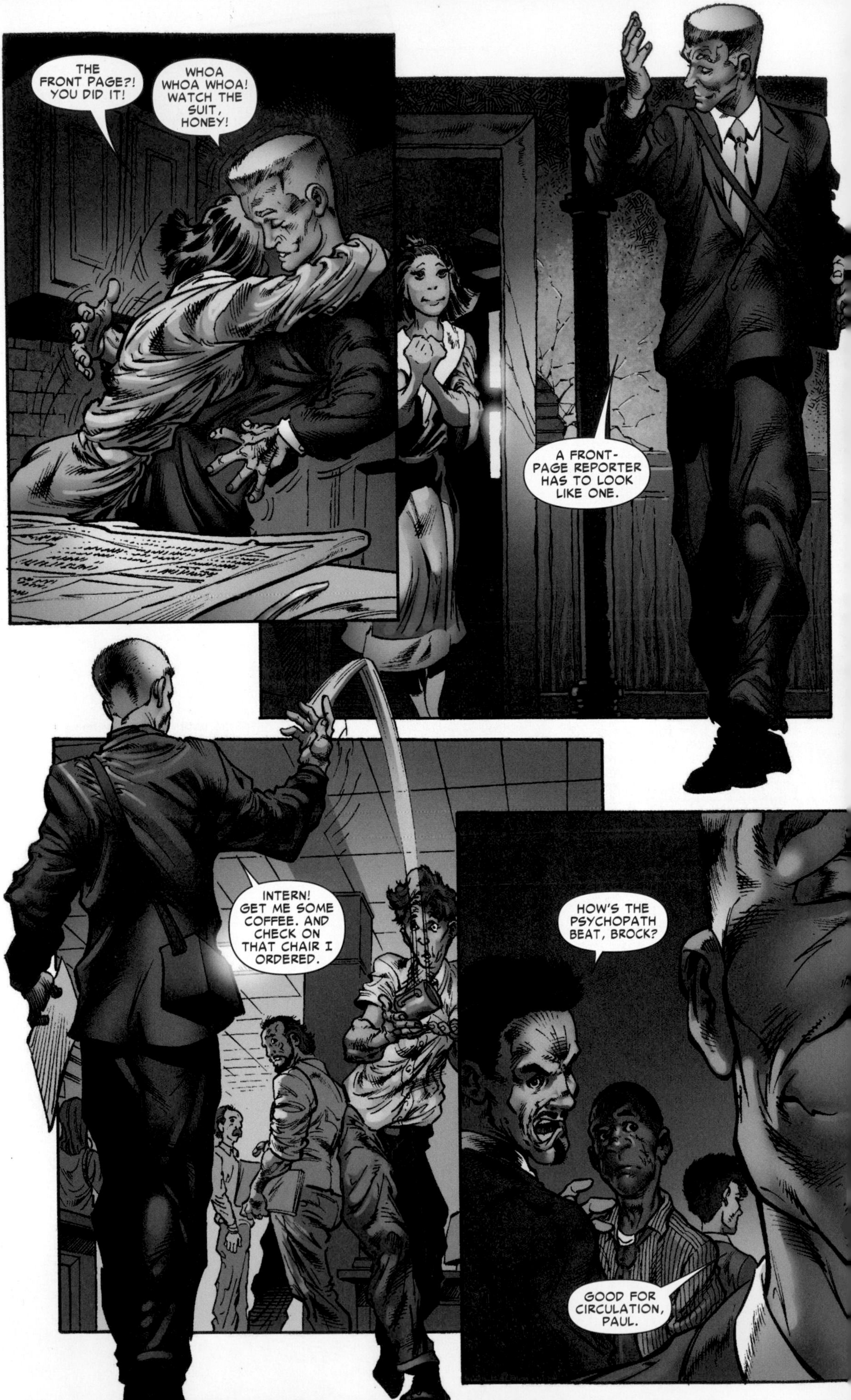
THE FRONT PAGE?! YOU DID IT!
WHOA WHOA WHOA! WATCH THE SUIT, HONEY!
A FRONT-PAGE REPORTER HAS TO LOOK LIKE ONE.
INTERN! GET ME SOME COFFEE. AND CHECK ON THAT CHAIR I ORDERED.
HOW'S THE PSYCHOPATH BEAT, BROCK?
GOOD FOR CIRCULATION, PAUL.

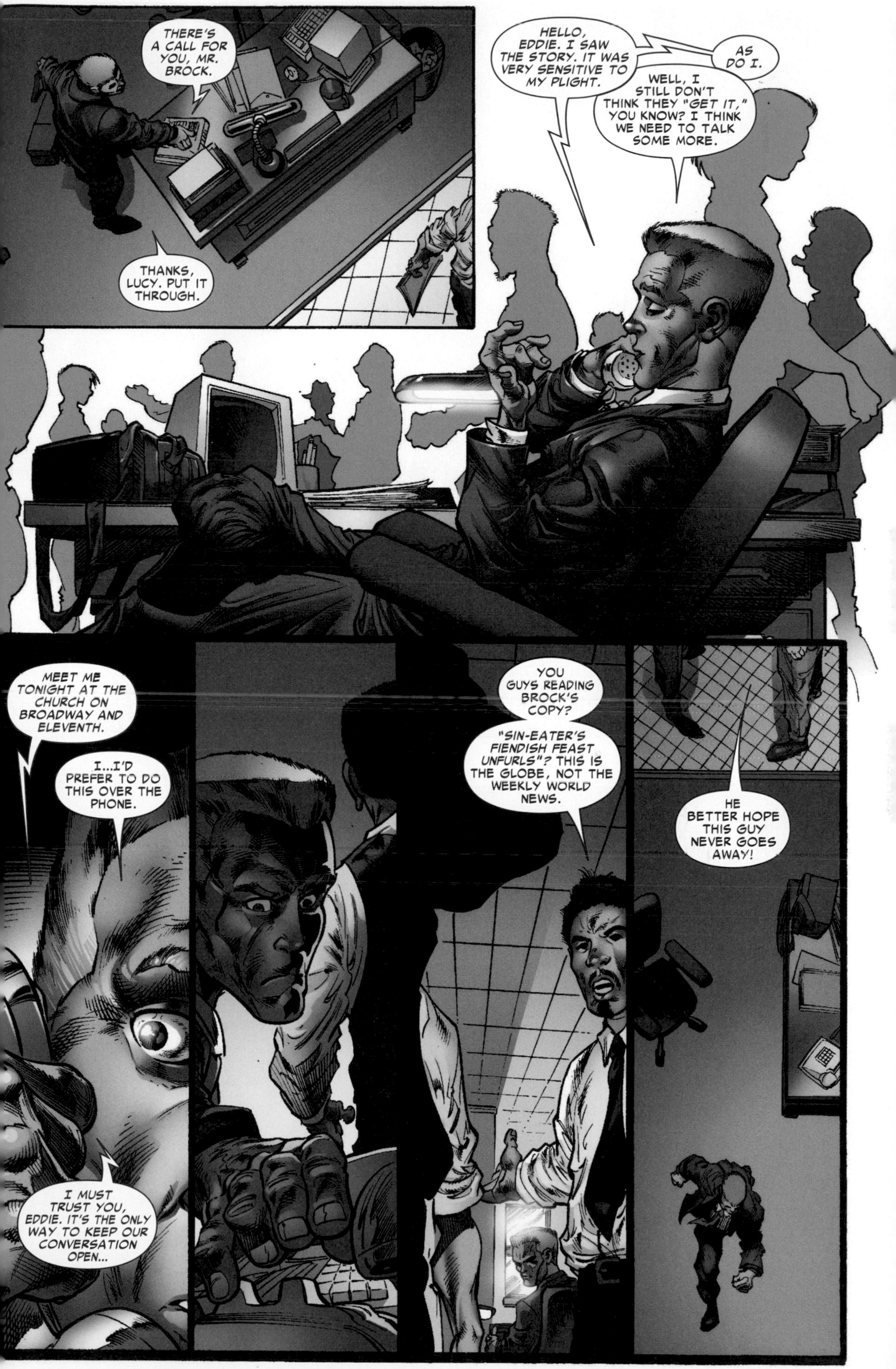
THERE'S A CALL FOR YOU, MR. BROCK.
THANKS, LUCY. PUT IT THROUGH.
HELLO, EDDIE. I SAW THE STORY. IT WAS VERY SENSITIVE TO MY PLIGHT.
AS DO I.
WELL, I STILL DON'T THINK THEY "GET IT," YOU KNOW? I THINK WE NEED TO TALK SOME MORE.
MEET ME TONIGHT AT THE CHURCH ON BROADWAY AND ELEVENTH.
I...I'D PREFER TO DO THIS OVER THE PHONE.
I MUST TRUST YOU, EDDIE. IT'S THE ONLY WAY TO KEEP OUR CONVERSATION OPEN...
YOU GUYS READING BROCK'S COPY?
"SIN-EATER'S FIENDISH FEAST UNFURLS"? THIS IS THE GLOBE, NOT THE WEEKLY WORLD NEWS.
HE BETTER HOPE THIS GUY NEVER GOES AWAY!

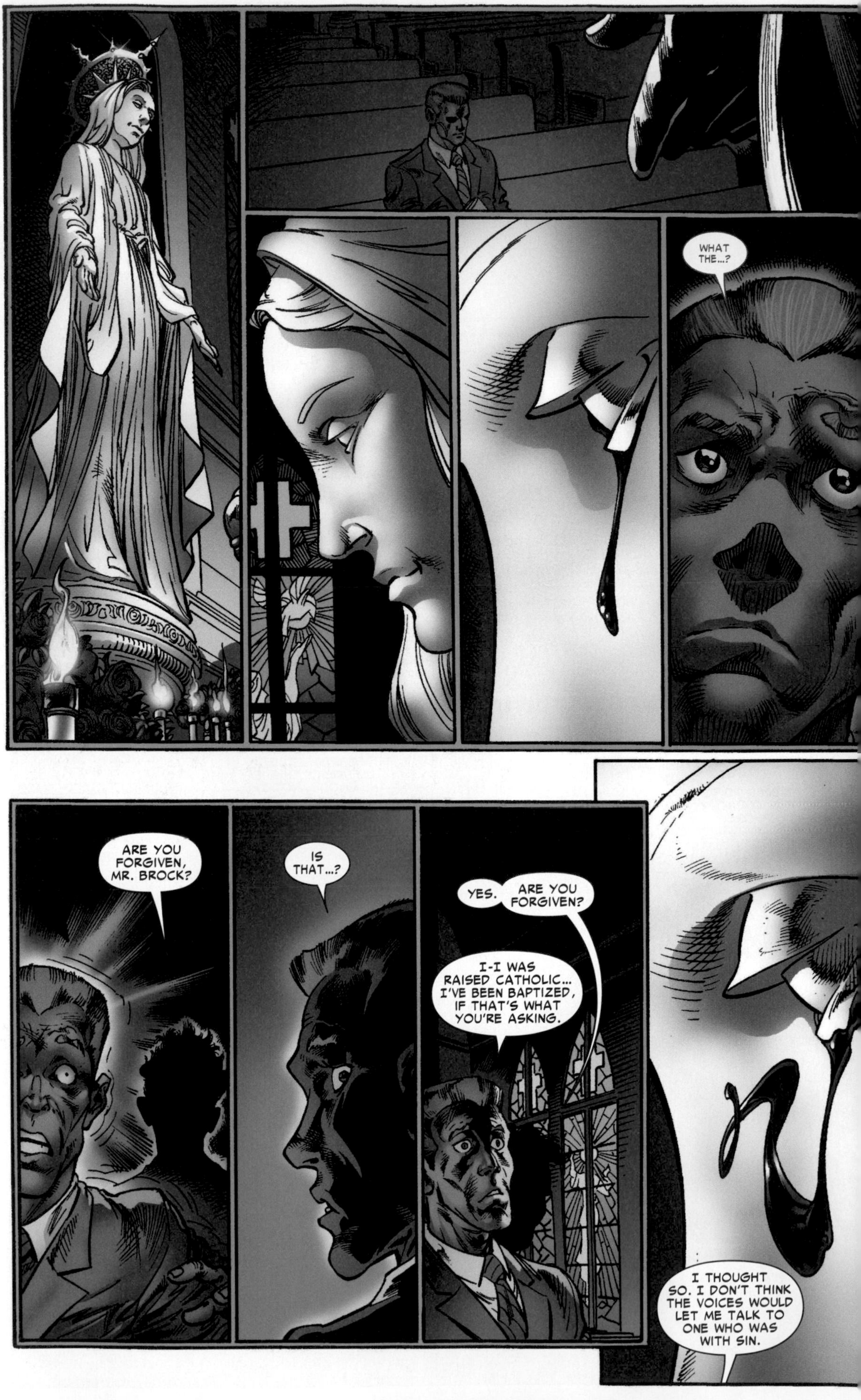
WHAT THE...?
ARE YOU FORGIVEN, MR. BROCK?
IS THAT...?
YES.
ARE YOU FORGIVEN?
I-I WAS RAISED CATHOLIC... I'VE BEEN BAPTIZED, IF THAT'S WHAT YOU'RE ASKING.
I THOUGHT SO. I DON'T THINK THE VOICES WOULD LET ME TALK TO ONE WHO WAS WITH SIN.

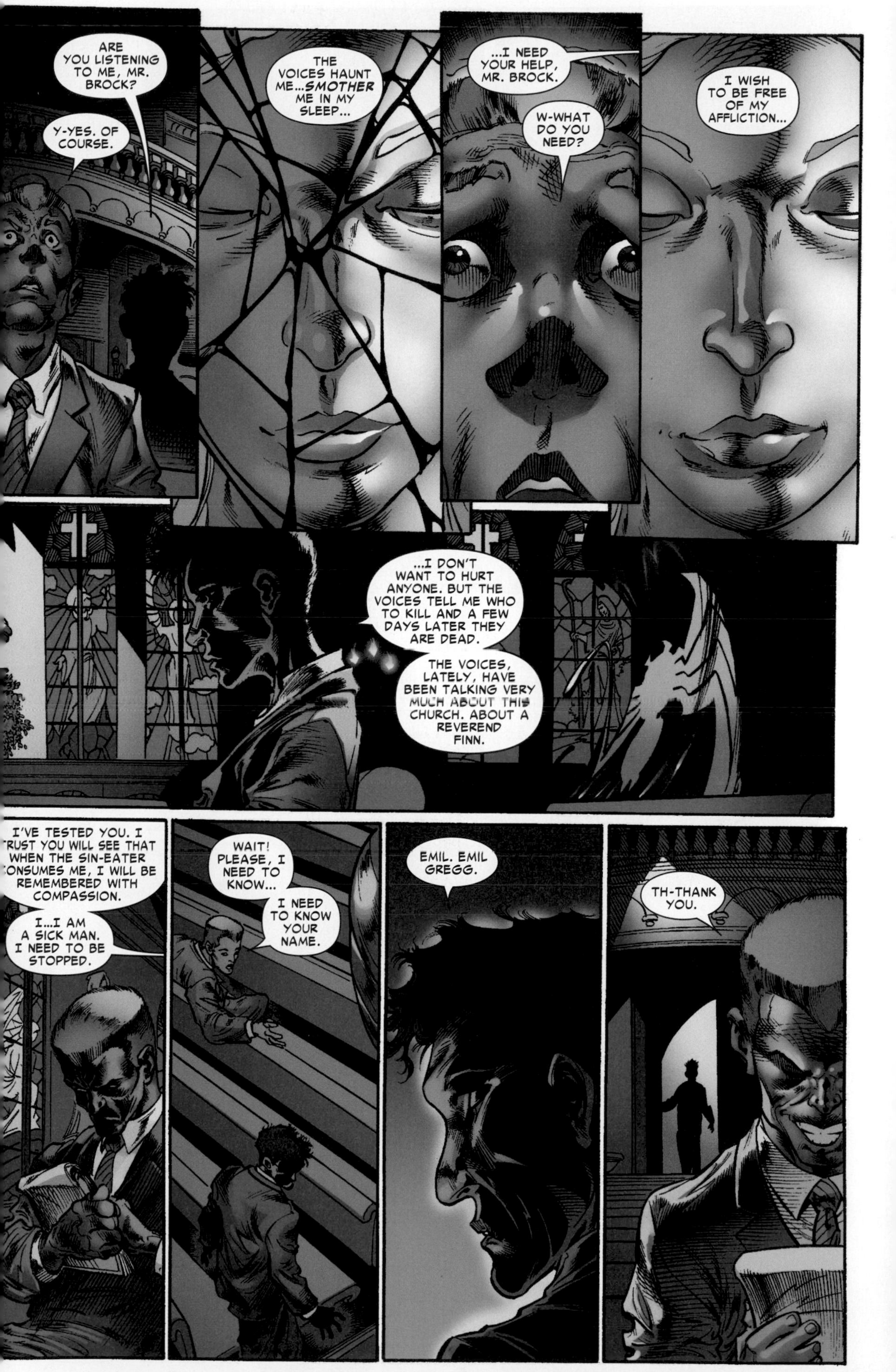

ARE YOU LISTENING TO ME, MR. BROCK?
Y-YES. OF COURSE.
THE VOICES HAUNT ME...SMOTHER ME IN MY SLEEP...
...I NEED YOUR HELP, MR. BROCK.
W-WHAT DO YOU NEED?
I WISH TO BE FREE OF MY AFFLICTION...
...I DON'T WANT TO HURT ANYONE. BUT THE VOICES TELL ME WHO TO KILL AND A FEW DAYS LATER THEY ARE DEAD.
THE VOICES, LATELY, HAVE BEEN TALKING VERY MUCH ABOUT THIS CHURCH. ABOUT A REVEREND FINN.
I'VE TESTED YOU. I TRUST YOU WILL SEE THAT WHEN THE SIN-EATER CONSUMES ME, I WILL BE REMEMBERED WITH COMPASSION.
I...I AM A SICK MAN. I NEED TO BE STOPPED.
WAIT! PLEASE, I NEED TO KNOW...
I NEED TO KNOW YOUR NAME.
EMIL. EMIL GREGG.
TH-THANK YOU.

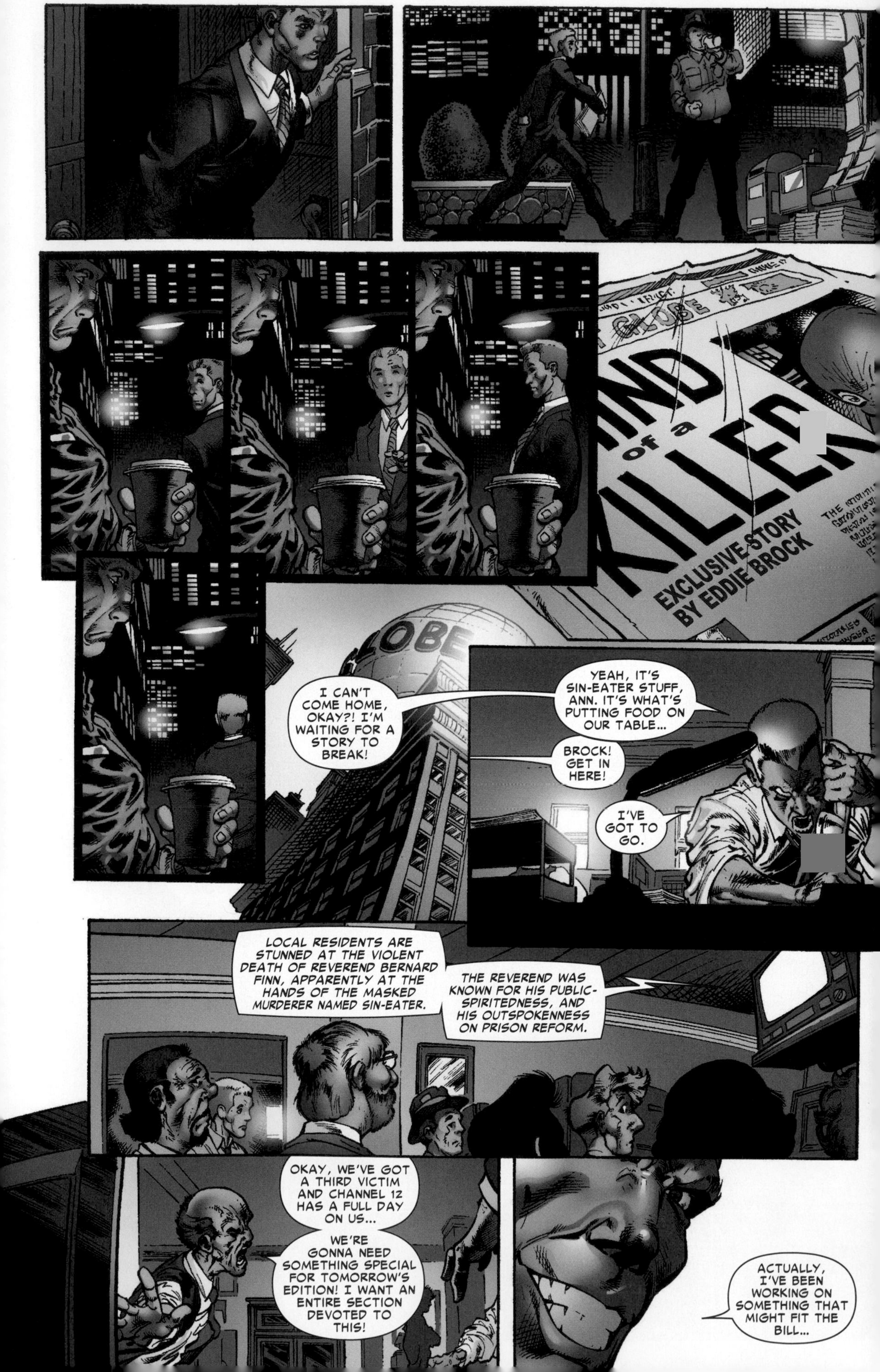
THE GLOBE
MIND of a KILLER
EXCLUSIVE STORY BY EDDIE BROCK
GLOBE
I CAN'T COME HOME, OKAY?! I'M WAITING FOR A STORY TO BREAK!
YEAH, IT'S SIN-EATER STUFF, ANN. IT'S WHAT'S PUTTING FOOD ON OUR TABLE...
BROCK! GET IN HERE!
I'VE GOT TO GO.
LOCAL RESIDENTS ARE STUNNED AT THE VIOLENT DEATH OF REVEREND BERNARD FINN, APPARENTLY AT THE HANDS OF THE MASKED MURDERER NAMED SIN-EATER.
THE REVEREND WAS KNOWN FOR HIS PUBLIC-SPIRITEDNESS, AND HIS OUTSPOKENNESS ON PRISON REFORM.
OKAY, WE'VE GOT A THIRD VICTIM AND CHANNEL 12 HAS A FULL DAY ON US...
WE'RE GONNA NEED SOMETHING SPECIAL FOR TOMORROW'S EDITION! I WANT AN ENTIRE SECTION DEVOTED TO THIS!
ACTUALLY, I'VE BEEN WORKING ON SOMETHING THAT MIGHT FIT THE BILL...

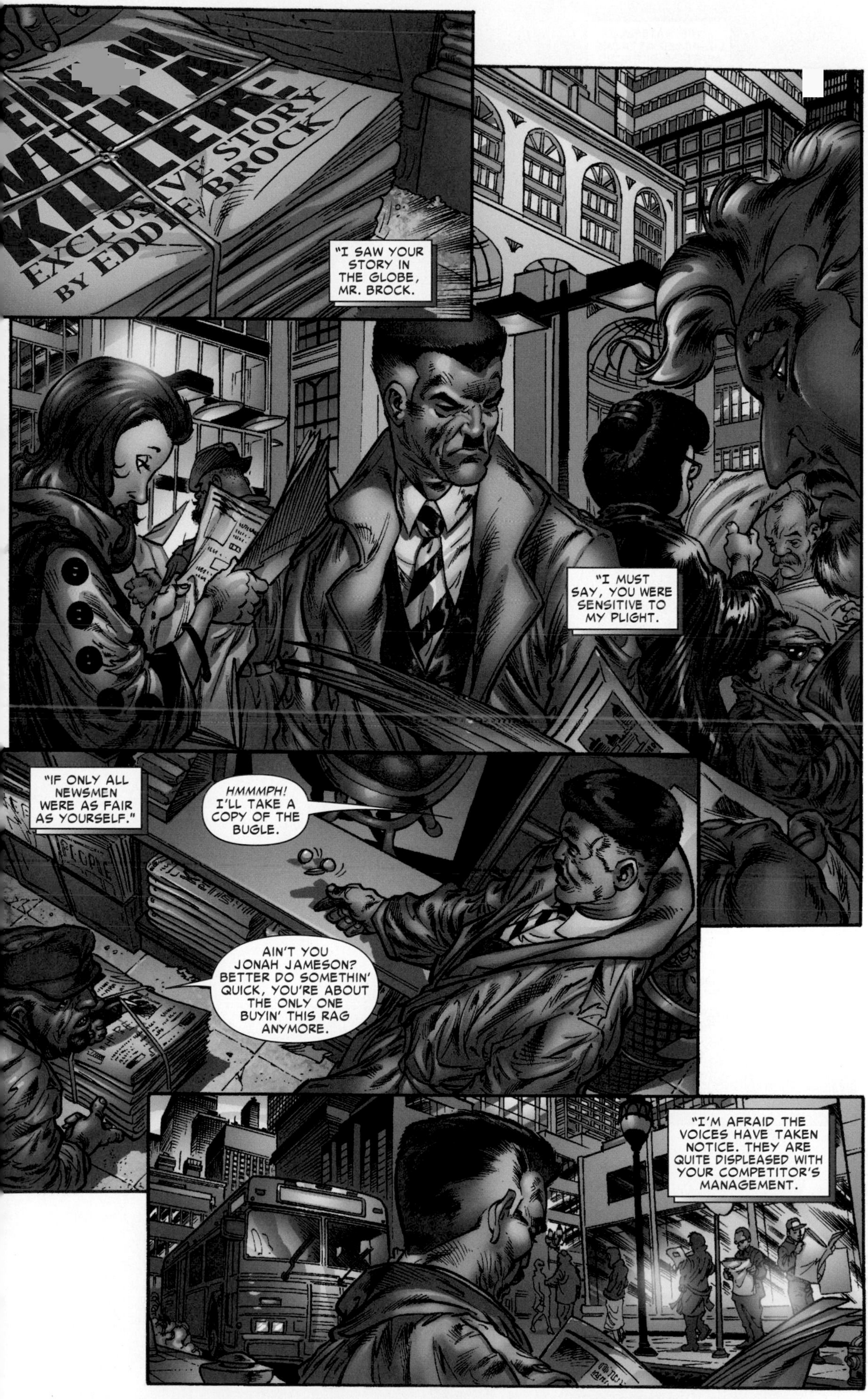
EXCLUSIVE STORY
BY EDDIE BROCK
"I SAW YOUR STORY IN THE GLOBE, MR. BROCK.
"I MUST SAY, YOU WERE SENSITIVE TO MY PLIGHT.
"IF ONLY ALL NEWSMEN WERE AS FAIR AS YOURSELF."
HMMMPH! I'LL TAKE A COPY OF THE BUGLE.
AIN'T YOU JONAH JAMESON? BETTER DO SOMETHIN' QUICK, YOU'RE ABOUT THE ONLY ONE BUYIN' THIS RAG ANYMORE.
"I'M AFRAID THE VOICES HAVE TAKEN NOTICE. THEY ARE QUITE DISPLEASED WITH YOUR COMPETITOR'S MANAGEMENT.

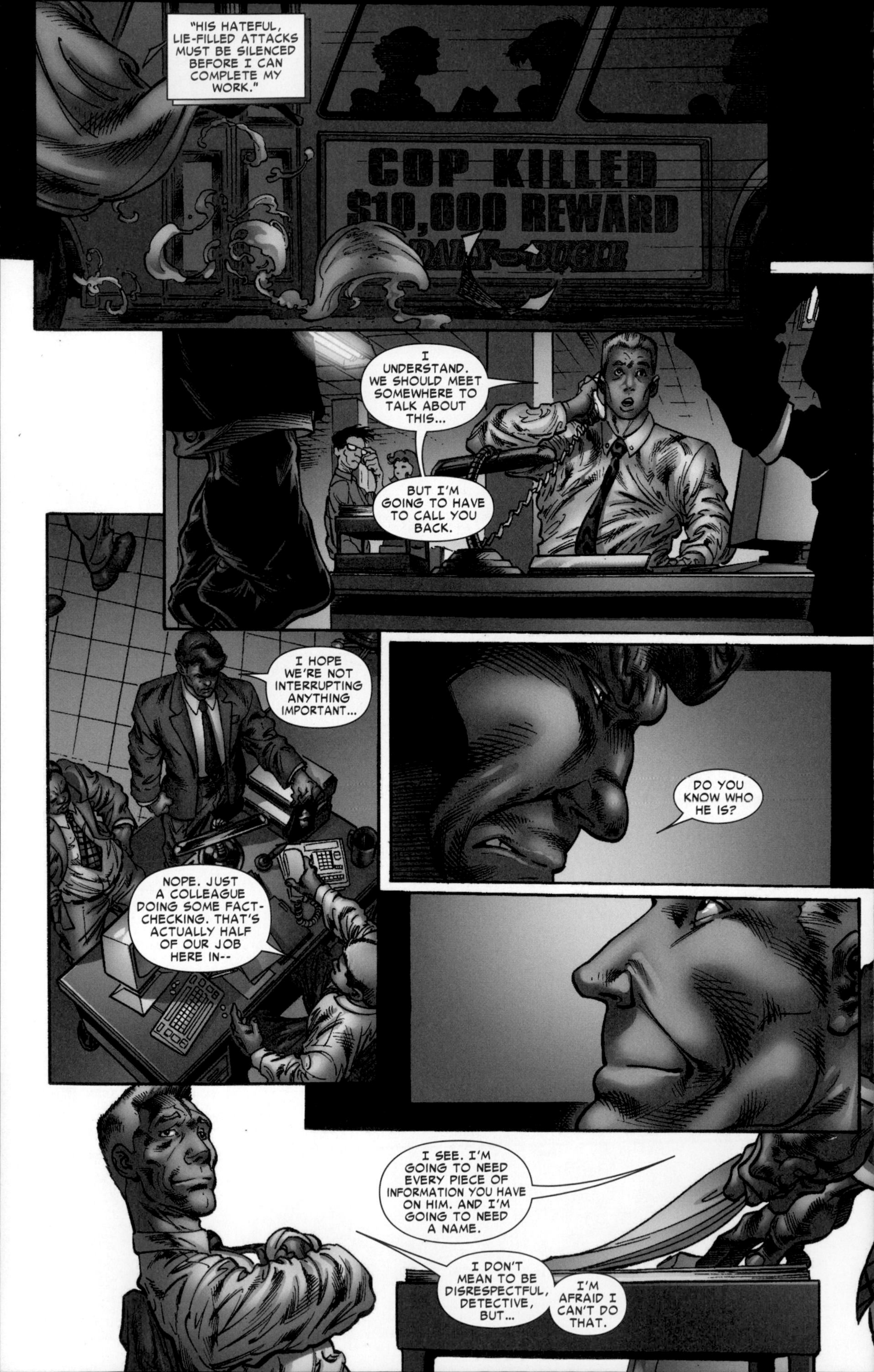
"HIS HATEFUL, LIE-FILLED ATTACKS MUST BE SILENCED BEFORE I CAN COMPLETE MY WORK."
COP KILLED $10,000 REWARD
DAILY BUGLE
I UNDERSTAND. WE SHOULD MEET SOMEWHERE TO TALK ABOUT THIS...
BUT I'M GOING TO HAVE TO CALL YOU BACK.
I HOPE WE'RE NOT INTERRUPTING ANYTHING IMPORTANT...
NOPE. JUST A COLLEAGUE DOING SOME FACT-CHECKING. THAT'S ACTUALLY HALF OF OUR JOB HERE IN--
DO YOU KNOW WHO HE IS?
I SEE. I'M GOING TO NEED EVERY PIECE OF INFORMATION YOU HAVE ON HIM. AND I'M GOING TO NEED A NAME.
I DON'T MEAN TO BE DISRESPECTFUL, DETECTIVE, BUT...
I'M AFRAID I CAN'T DO THAT.

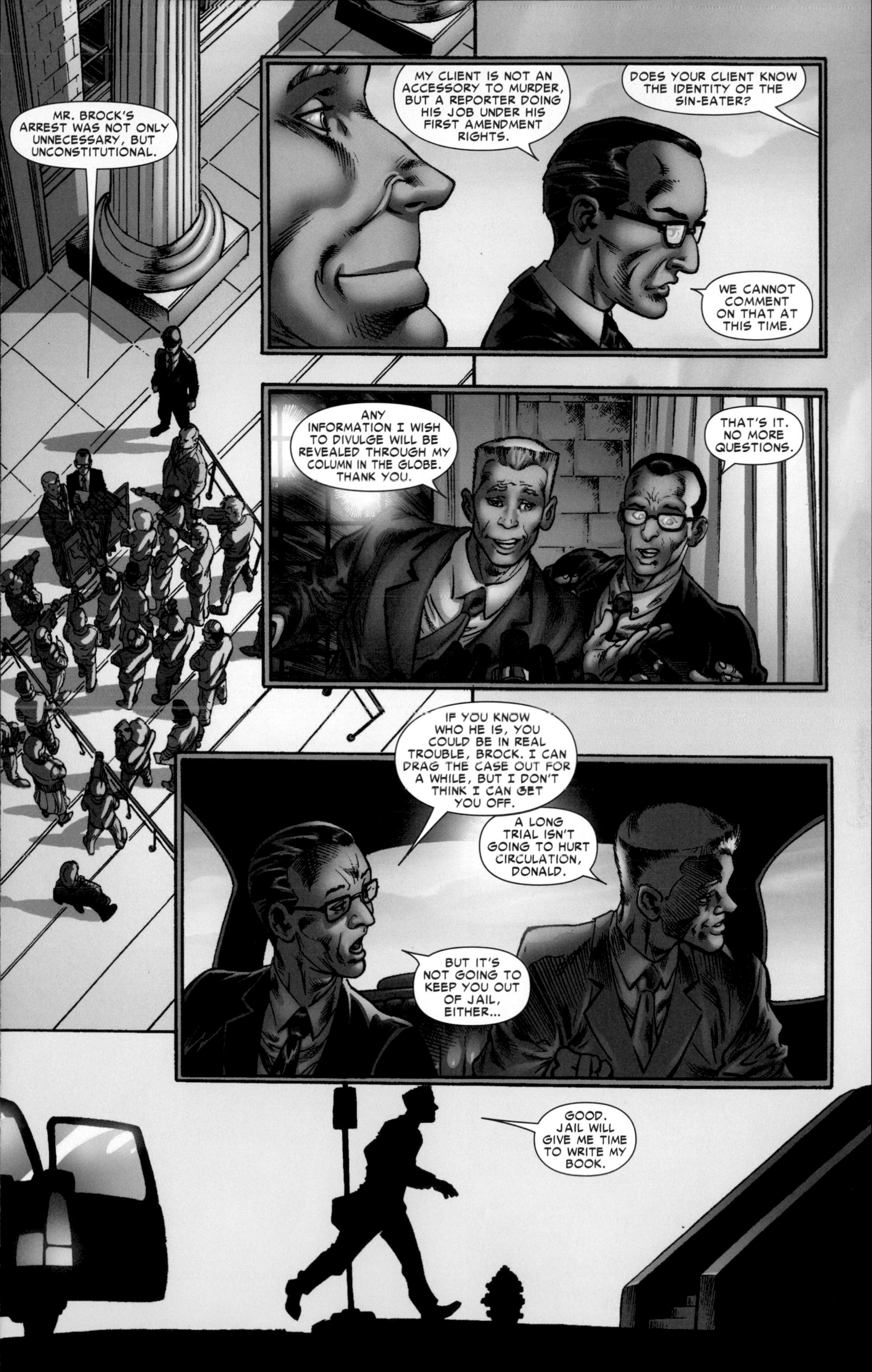
MR. BROCK'S ARREST WAS NOT ONLY UNNECESSARY, BUT UNCONSTITUTIONAL.
MY CLIENT IS NOT AN ACCESSORY TO MURDER, BUT A REPORTER DOING HIS JOB UNDER HIS FIRST AMENDMENT RIGHTS.
DOES YOUR CLIENT KNOW THE IDENTITY OF THE SIN-EATER?
WE CANNOT COMMENT ON THAT AT THIS TIME.
ANY INFORMATION I WISH TO DIVULGE WILL BE REVEALED THROUGH MY COLUMN IN THE GLOBE. THANK YOU.
THAT'S IT. NO MORE QUESTIONS.
IF YOU KNOW WHO HE IS, YOU COULD BE IN REAL TROUBLE, BROCK. I CAN DRAG THE CASE OUT FOR A WHILE, BUT I DON'T THINK I CAN GET YOU OFF.
A LONG TRIAL ISN'T GOING TO HURT CIRCULATION, DONALD.
BUT IT'S NOT GOING TO KEEP YOU OUT OF JAIL, EITHER...
GOOD. JAIL WILL GIVE ME TIME TO WRITE MY BOOK.

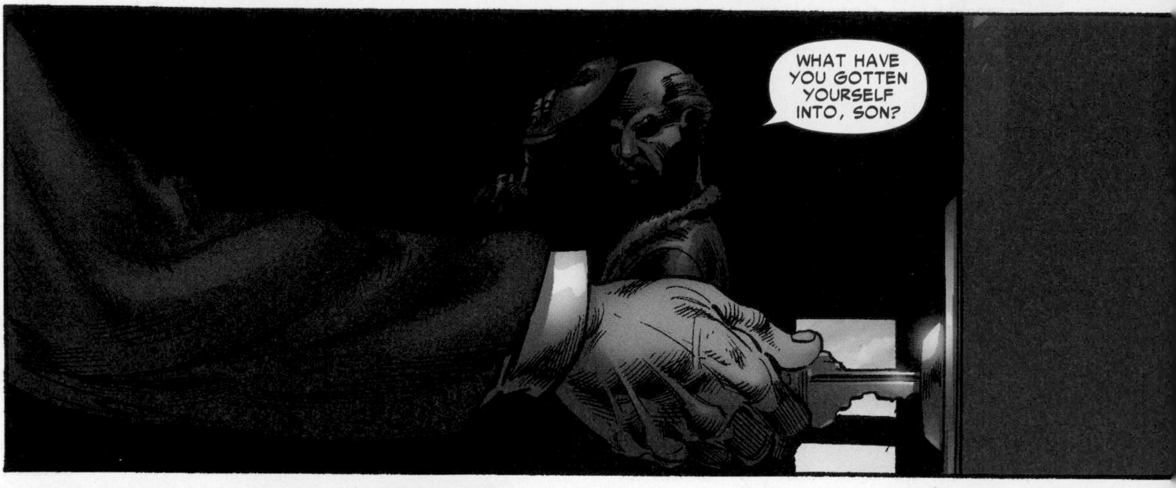
WHAT HAVE YOU GOTTEN YOURSELF INTO, SON?

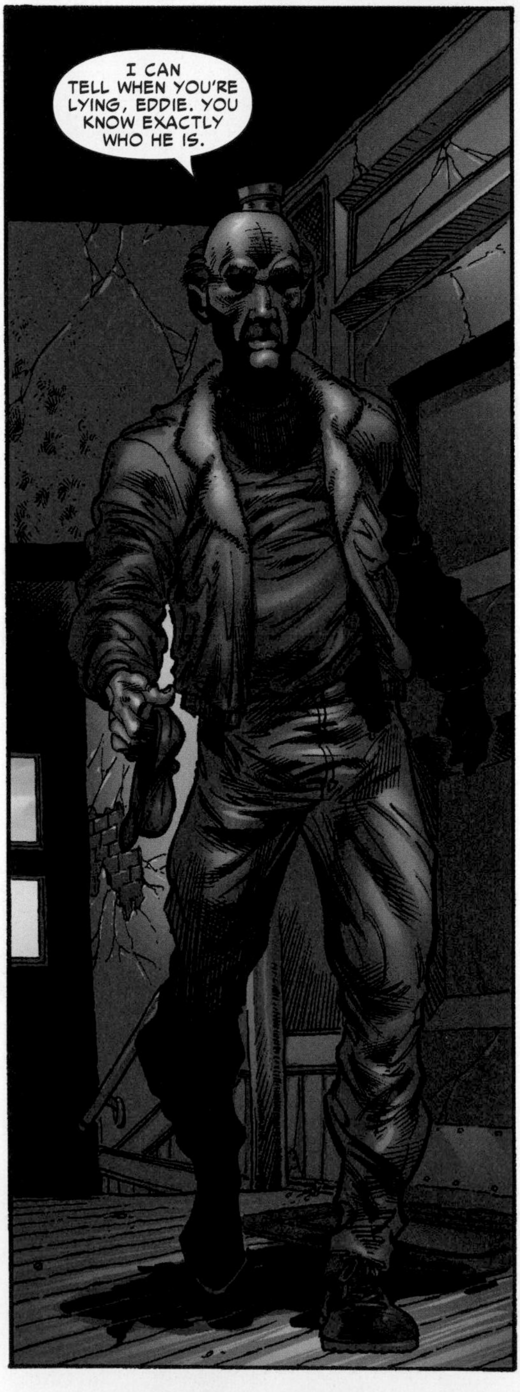
I CAN TELL WHEN YOU'RE LYING, EDDIE. YOU KNOW EXACTLY WHO HE IS.

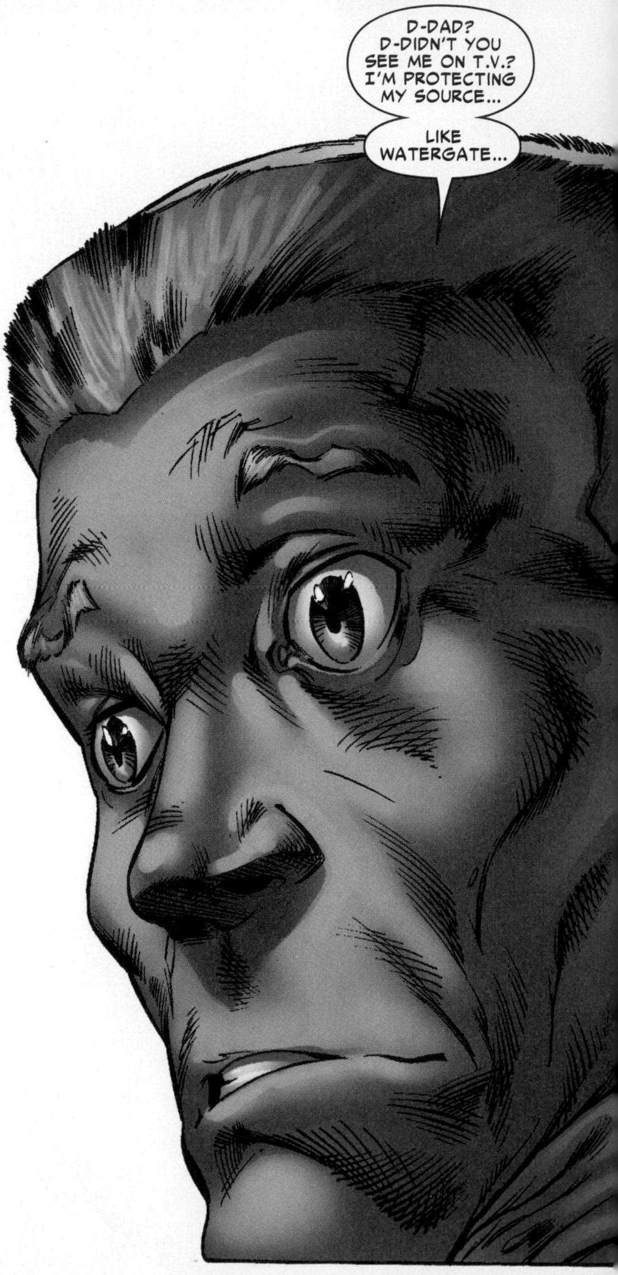
D-DAD? D-DIDN'T YOU SEE ME ON T.V.? I'M PROTECTING MY SOURCE...
LIKE WATERGATE...

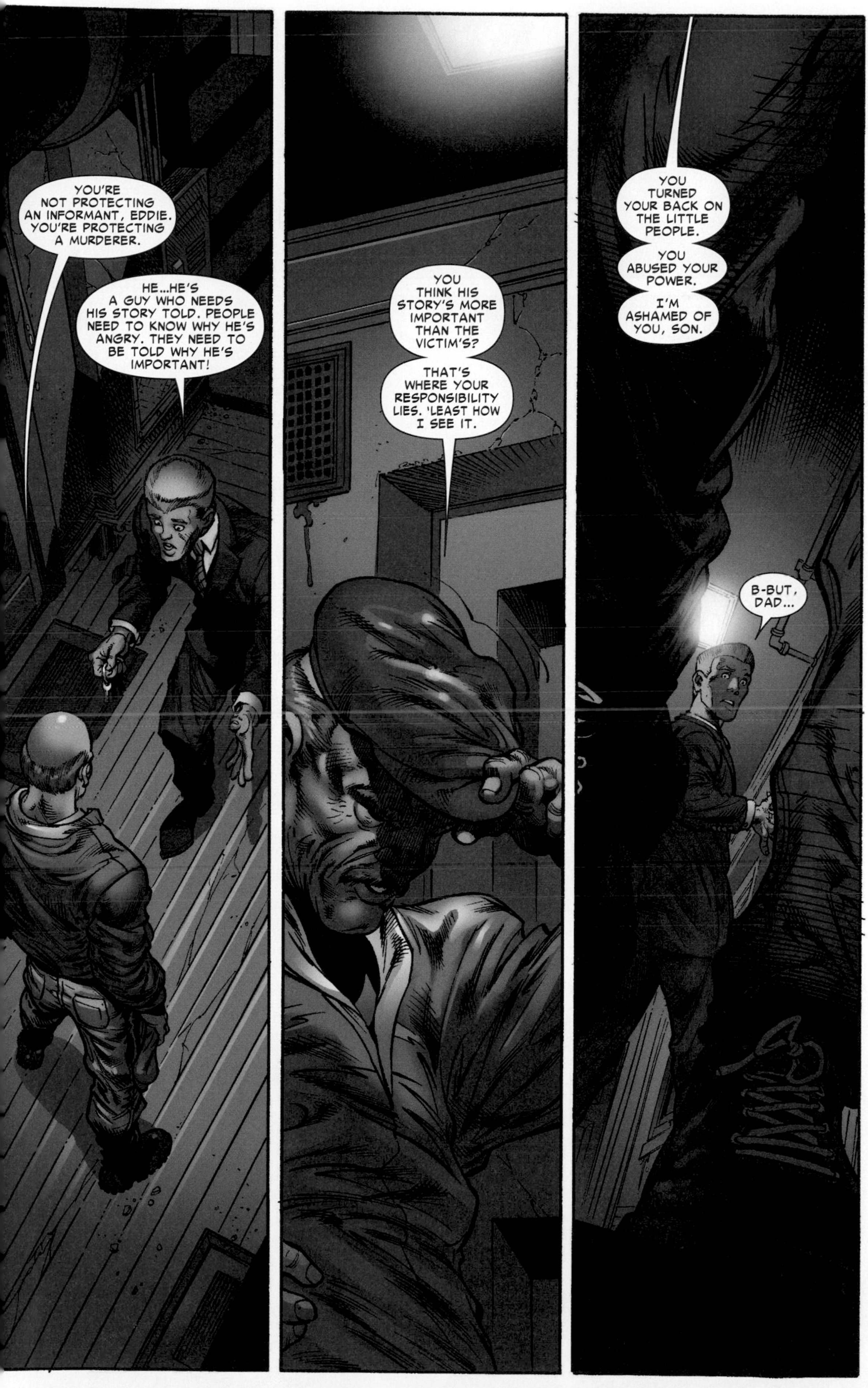
YOU'RE NOT PROTECTING AN INFORMANT, EDDIE. YOU'RE PROTECTING A MURDERER.
HE...HE'S A GUY WHO NEEDS HIS STORY TOLD. PEOPLE NEED TO KNOW WHY HE'S ANGRY. THEY NEED TO BE TOLD WHY HE'S IMPORTANT!
YOU THINK HIS STORY'S MORE IMPORTANT THAN THE VICTIM'S?
THAT'S WHERE YOUR RESPONSIBILITY LIES. 'LEAST HOW I SEE IT.
YOU TURNED YOUR BACK ON THE LITTLE PEOPLE.
YOU ABUSED YOUR POWER.
I'M ASHAMED OF YOU, SON.
B-BUT, DAD...

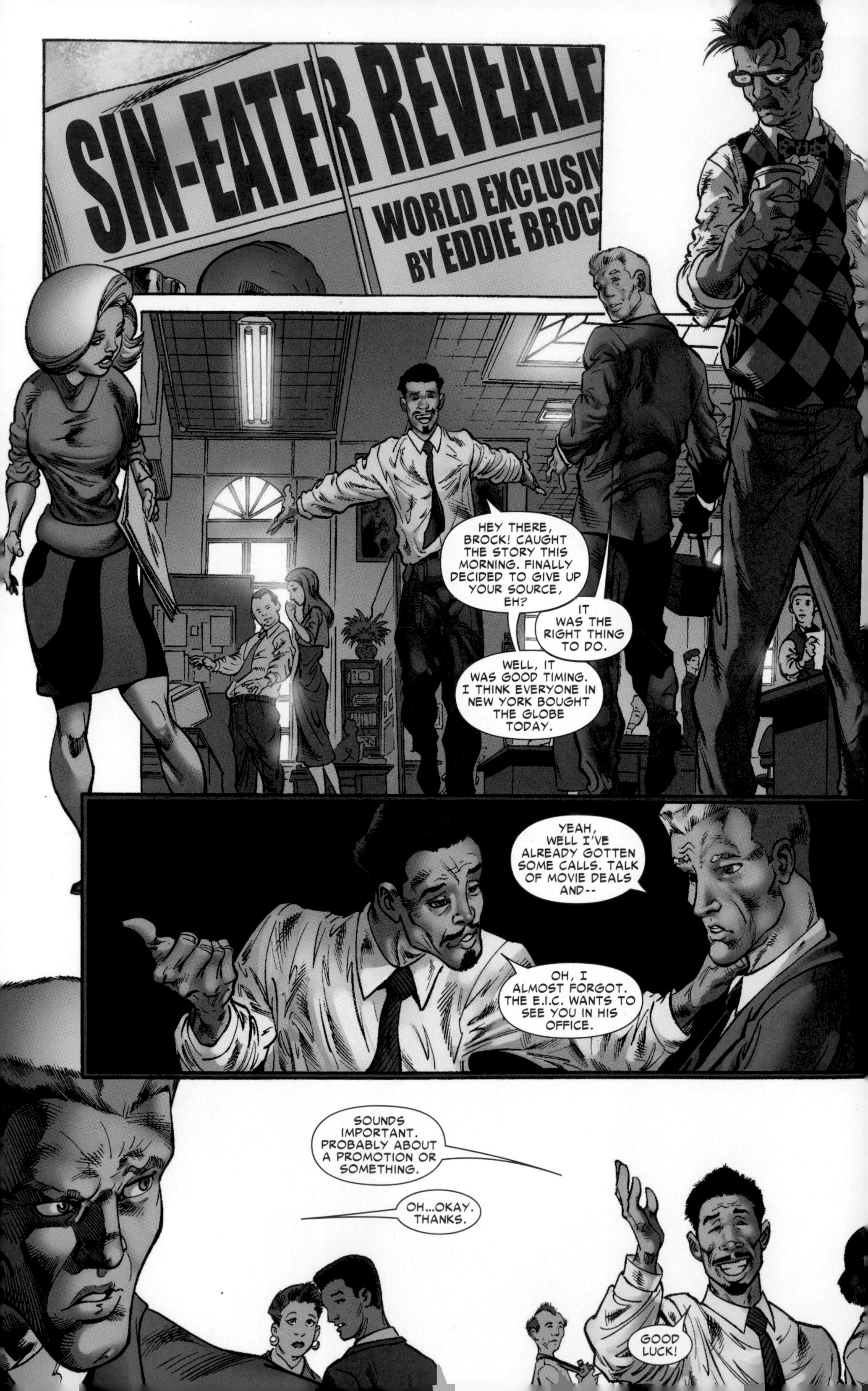
SIN-EATER REVEALE
WORLD EXCLUSIV
BY EDDIE BROC
HEY THERE, BROCK! CAUGHT THE STORY THIS MORNING. FINALLY DECIDED TO GIVE UP YOUR SOURCE, EH?
IT WAS THE RIGHT THING TO DO.
WELL, IT WAS GOOD TIMING. I THINK EVERYONE IN NEW YORK BOUGHT THE GLOBE TODAY.
YEAH, WELL I'VE ALREADY GOTTEN SOME CALLS. TALK OF MOVIE DEALS AND--
OH, I ALMOST FORGOT. THE E.I.C. WANTS TO SEE YOU IN HIS OFFICE.
SOUNDS IMPORTANT. PROBABLY ABOUT A PROMOTION OR SOMETHING.
OH...OKAY. THANKS.
GOOD LUCK!

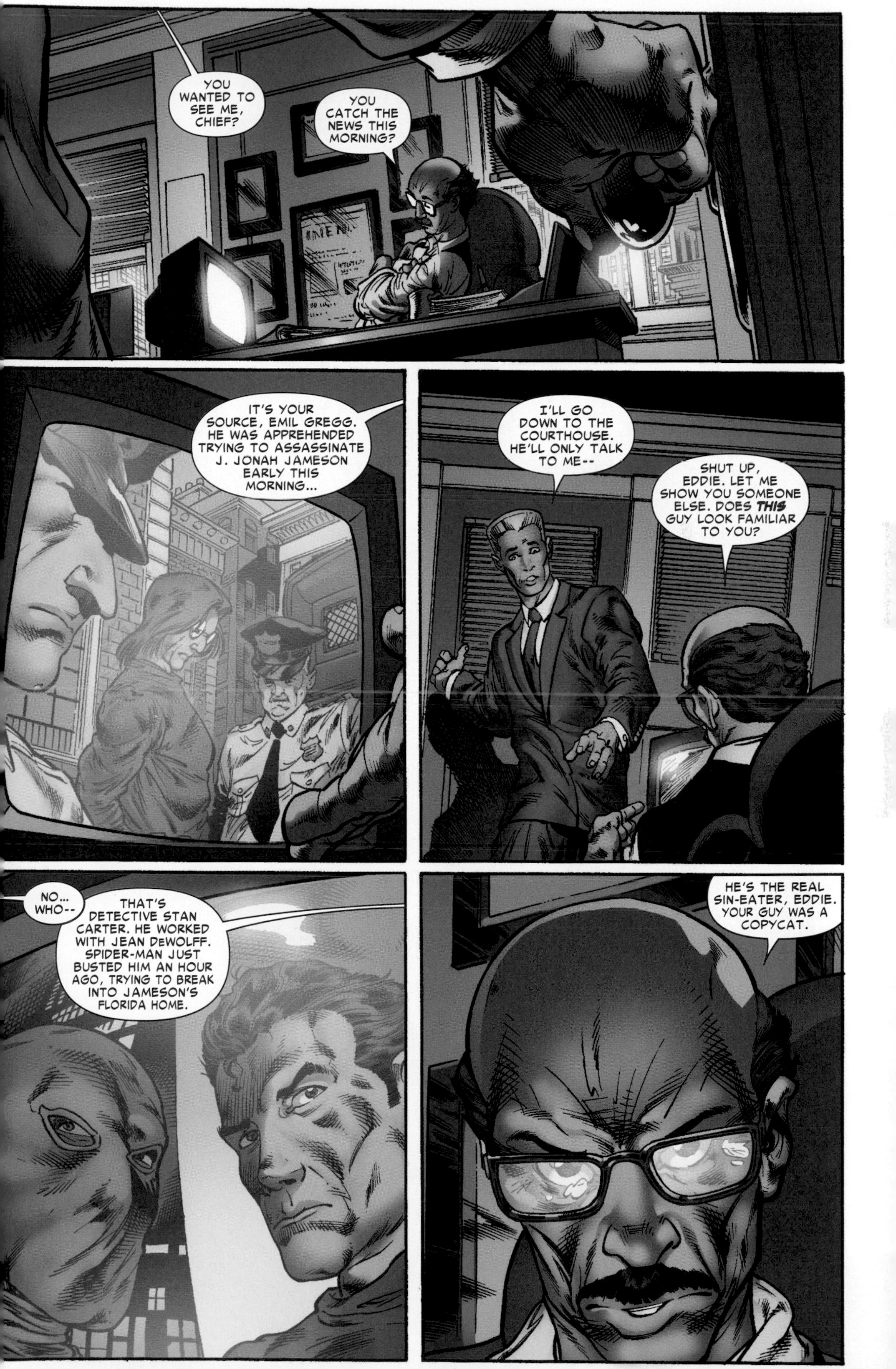
YOU WANTED TO SEE ME, CHIEF?
YOU CATCH THE NEWS THIS MORNING?
IT'S YOUR SOURCE, EMIL GREGG. HE WAS APPREHENDED TRYING TO ASSASSINATE J. JONAH JAMESON EARLY THIS MORNING...
I'LL GO DOWN TO THE COURTHOUSE. HE'LL ONLY TALK TO ME--
SHUT UP, EDDIE. LET ME SHOW YOU SOMEONE ELSE. DOES THIS GUY LOOK FAMILIAR TO YOU?
NO... WHO--
THAT'S DETECTIVE STAN CARTER. HE WORKED WITH JEAN DEWOLFF. SPIDER-MAN JUST BUSTED HIM AN HOUR AGO, TRYING TO BREAK INTO JAMESON'S FLORIDA HOME.
HE'S THE REAL SIN-EATER, EDDIE. YOUR GUY WAS A COPYCAT.

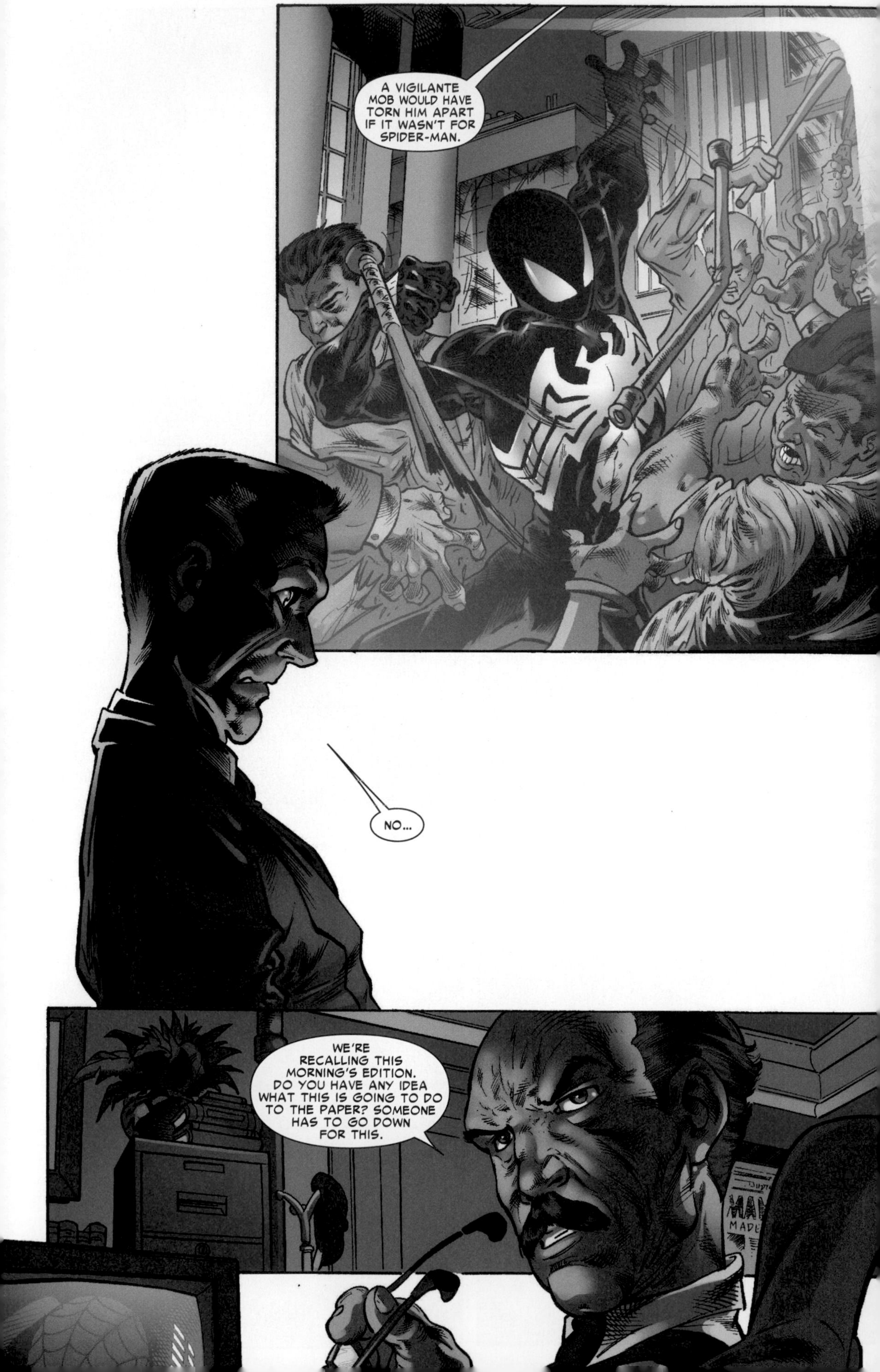
A VIGILANTE MOB WOULD HAVE TORN HIM APART IF IT WASN'T FOR SPIDER-MAN.
NO...
WE'RE RECALLING THIS MORNING'S EDITION. DO YOU HAVE ANY IDEA WHAT THIS IS GOING TO DO TO THE PAPER? SOMEONE HAS TO GO DOWN FOR THIS.

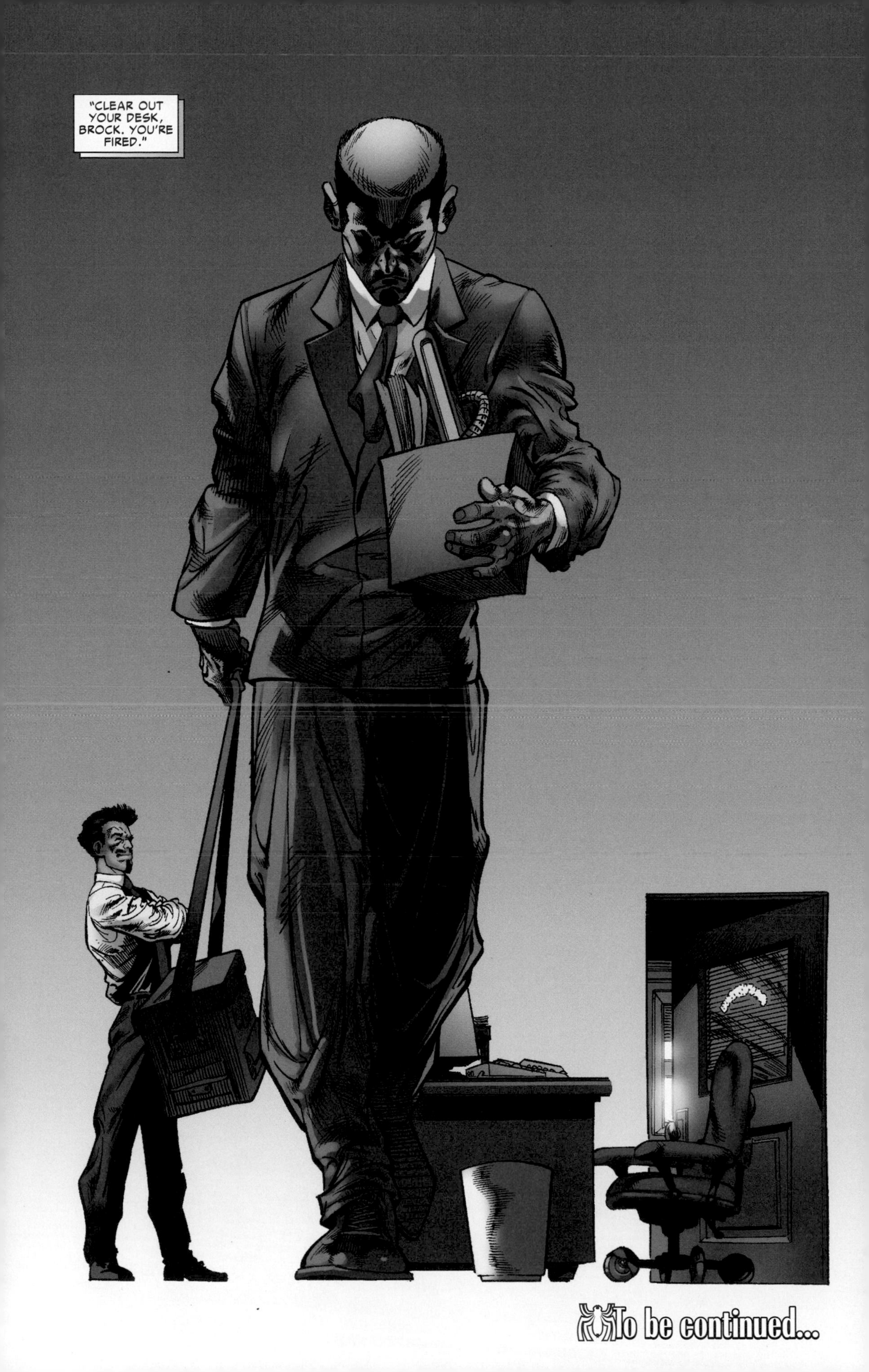
"CLEAR OUT YOUR DESK, BROCK. YOU'RE FIRED."
To be continued...

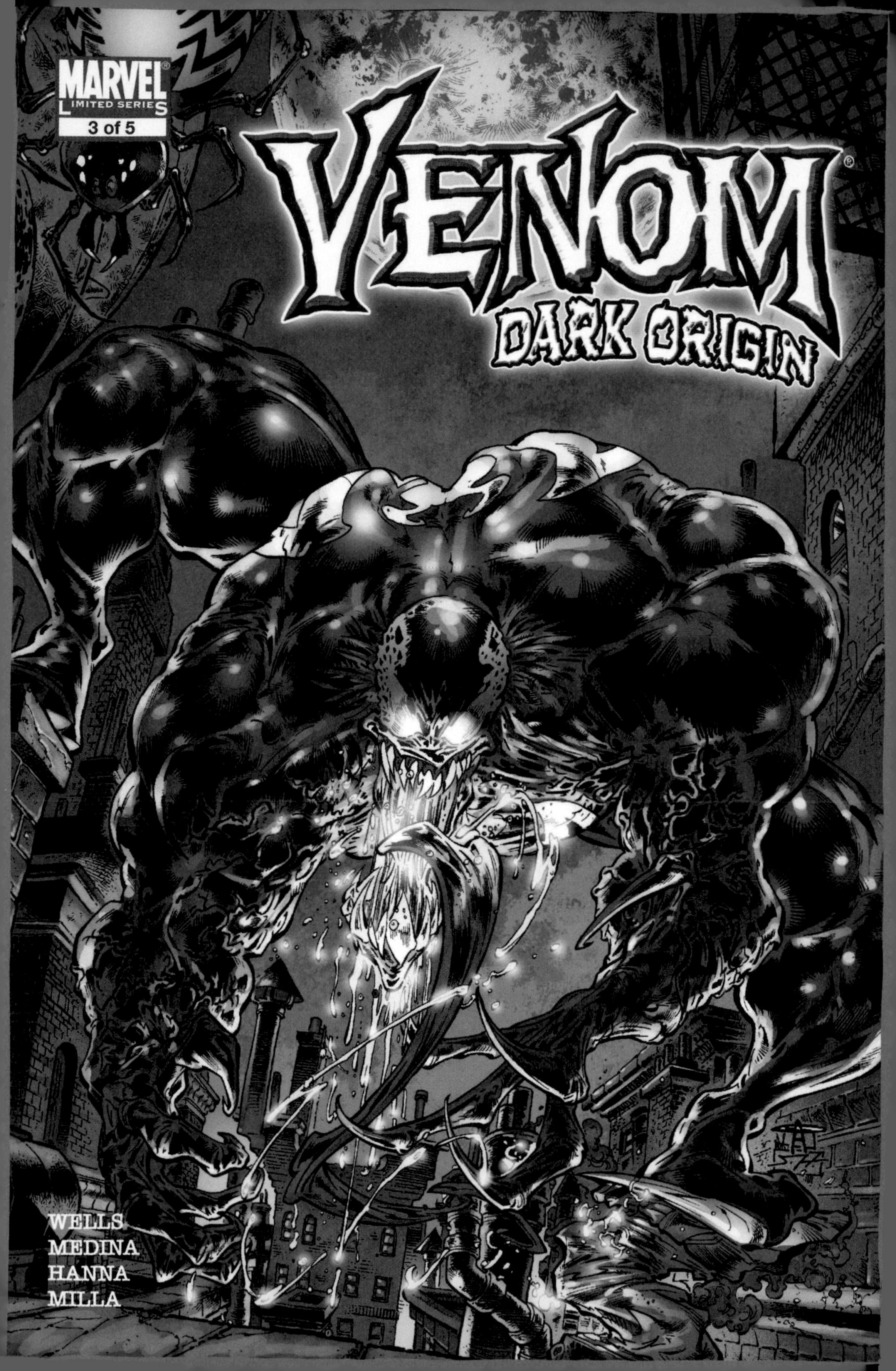
MARVEL®
LIMITED SERIES
3 of 5
VENOM®
DARK ORIGIN
WELLS
MEDINA
HANNA
MILLA

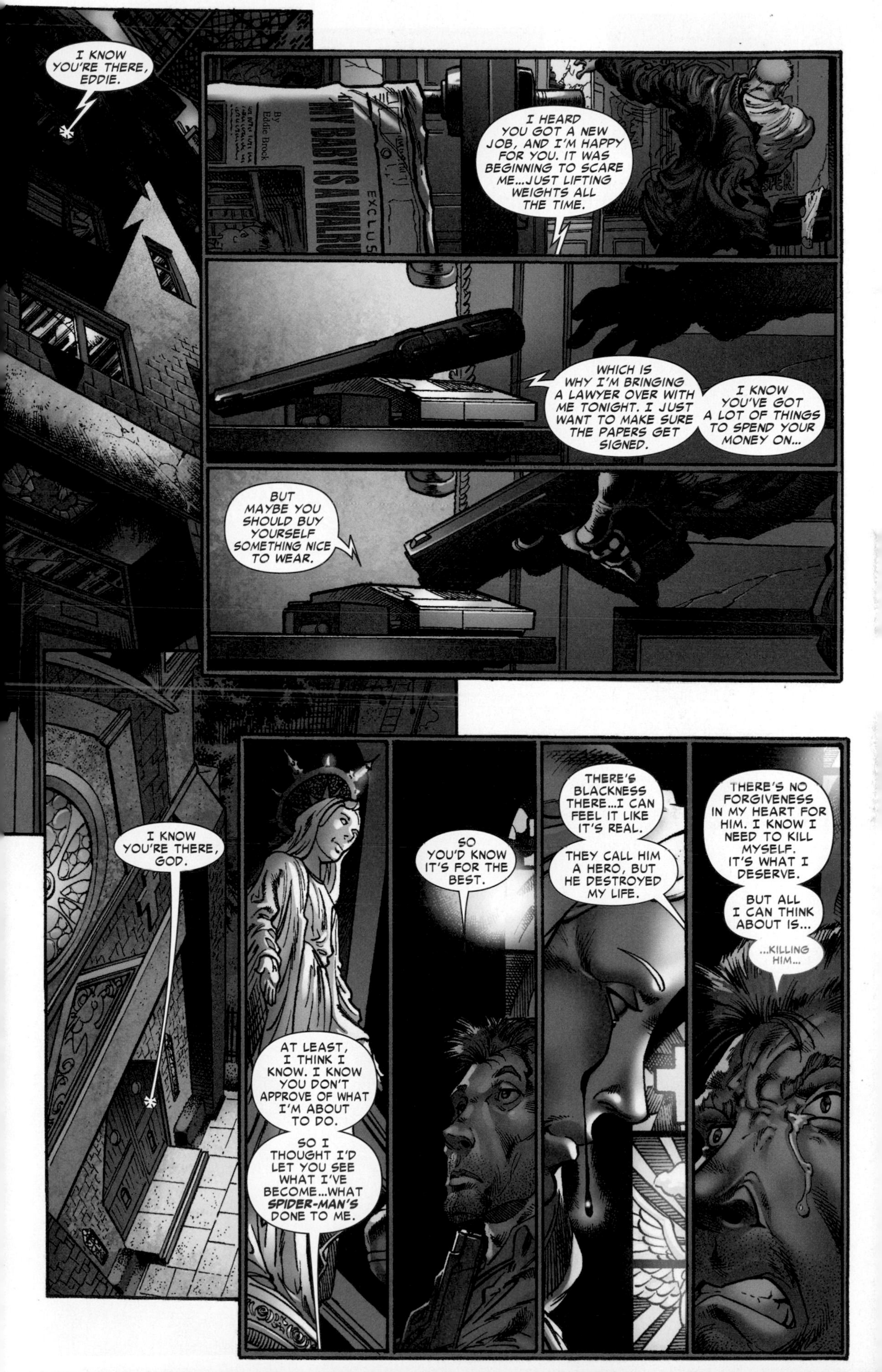
MY BABY IS A WALRU
By Eddie Brock
EXCLUS
I KNOW YOU'RE THERE, EDDIE.
I HEARD YOU GOT A NEW JOB, AND I'M HAPPY FOR YOU. IT WAS BEGINNING TO SCARE ME...JUST LIFTING WEIGHTS ALL THE TIME.
WHICH IS WHY I'M BRINGING A LAWYER OVER WITH ME TONIGHT. I JUST WANT TO MAKE SURE THE PAPERS GET SIGNED.
I KNOW YOU'VE GOT A LOT OF THINGS TO SPEND YOUR MONEY ON...
BUT MAYBE YOU SHOULD BUY YOURSELF SOMETHING NICE TO WEAR.
I KNOW YOU'RE THERE, GOD.
AT LEAST, I THINK I KNOW. I KNOW YOU DON'T APPROVE OF WHAT I'M ABOUT TO DO.
SO I THOUGHT I'D LET YOU SEE WHAT I'VE BECOME...WHAT SPIDER-MAN'S DONE TO ME.
SO YOU'D KNOW IT'S FOR THE BEST.
THERE'S BLACKNESS THERE...I CAN FEEL IT LIKE IT'S REAL.
THEY CALL HIM A HERO, BUT HE DESTROYED MY LIFE.
THERE'S NO FORGIVENESS IN MY HEART FOR HIM. I KNOW I NEED TO KILL MYSELF. IT'S WHAT I DESERVE.
BUT ALL I CAN THINK ABOUT IS...
...KILLING HIM...

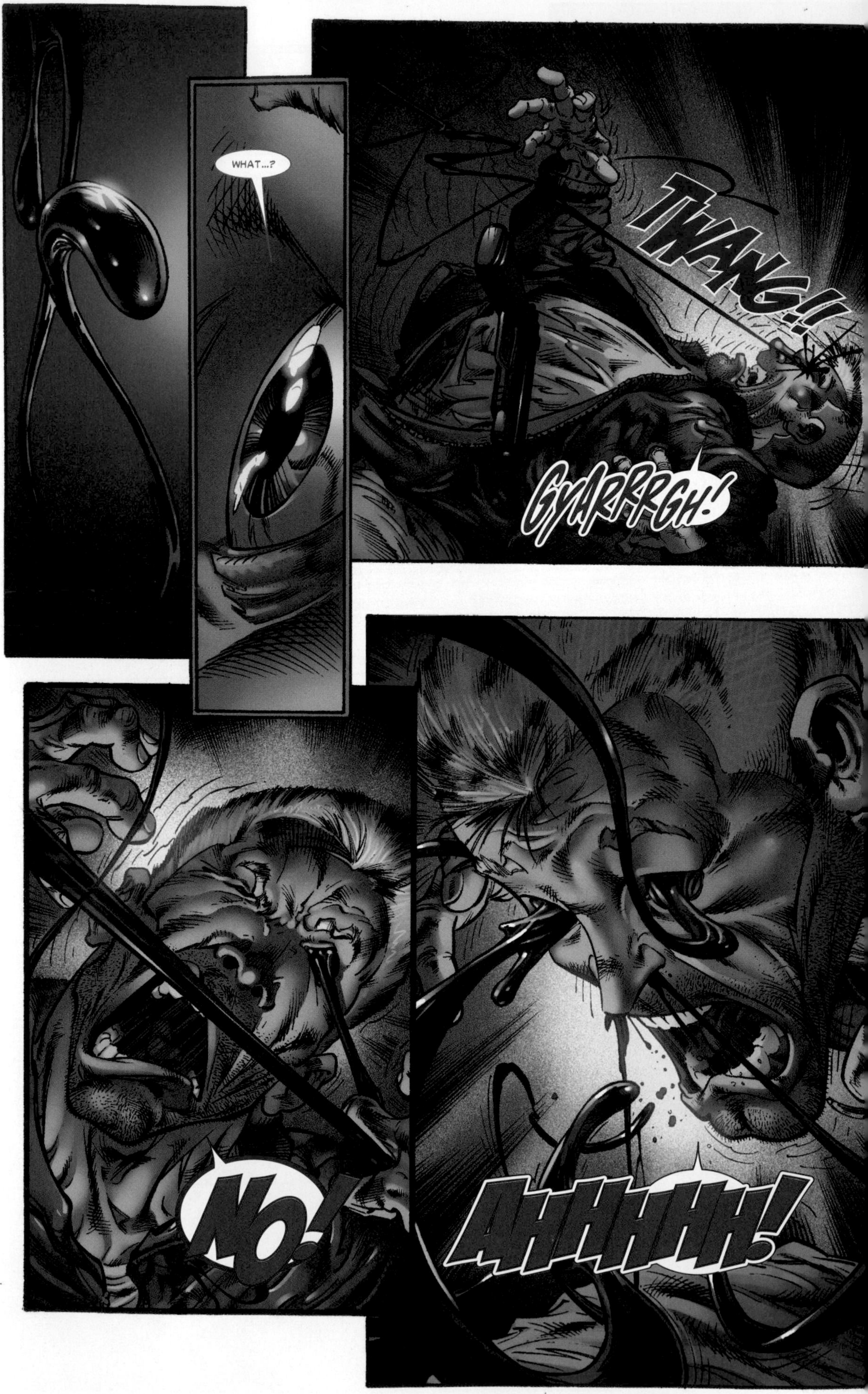
WHAT...?
TWANG!!
GYARRRGH!
NO!
AHHHHH!

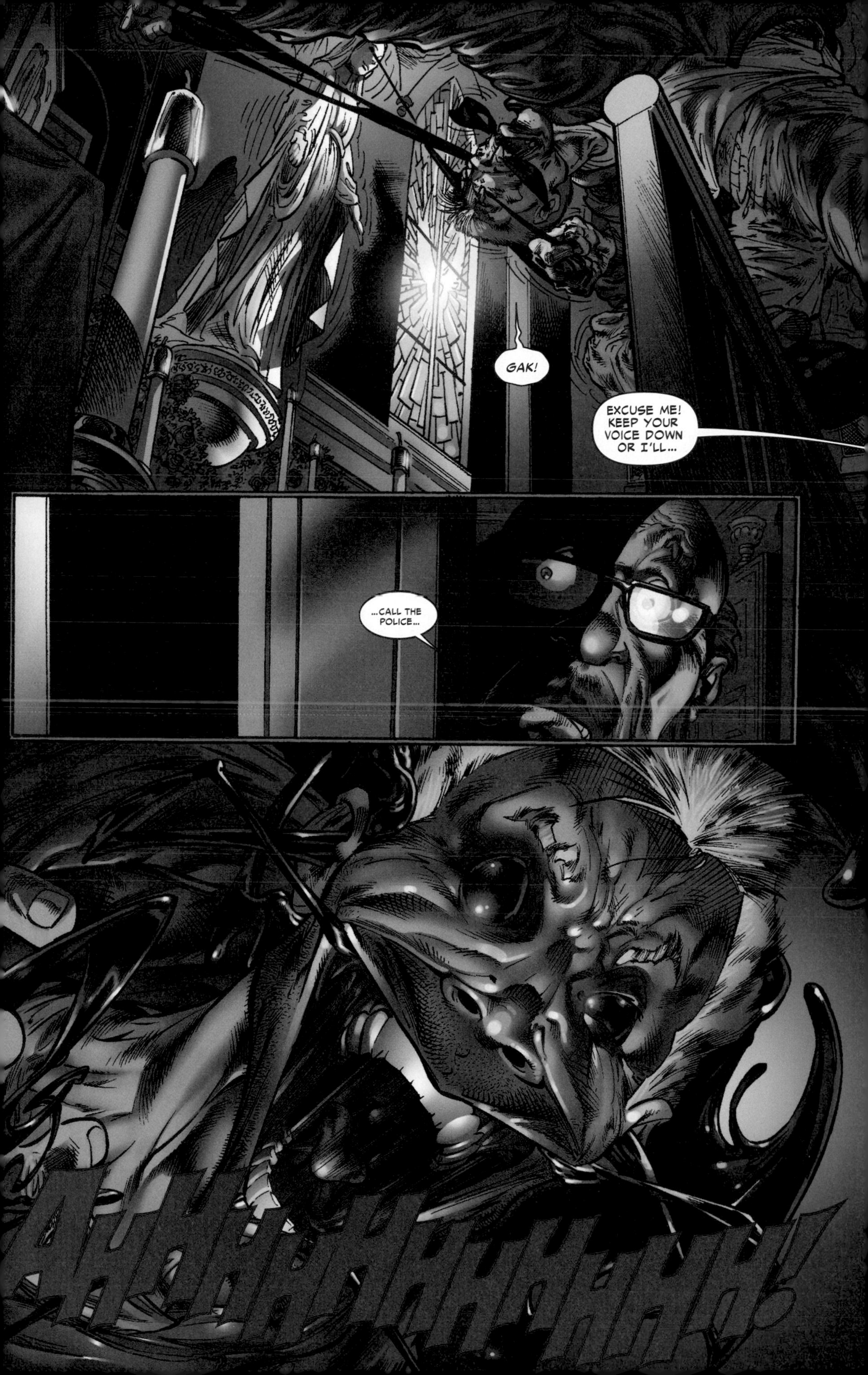
GAK!
EXCUSE ME! KEEP YOUR VOICE DOWN OR I'LL...
...CALL THE POLICE...
AHHHAAAAHHHHHH!

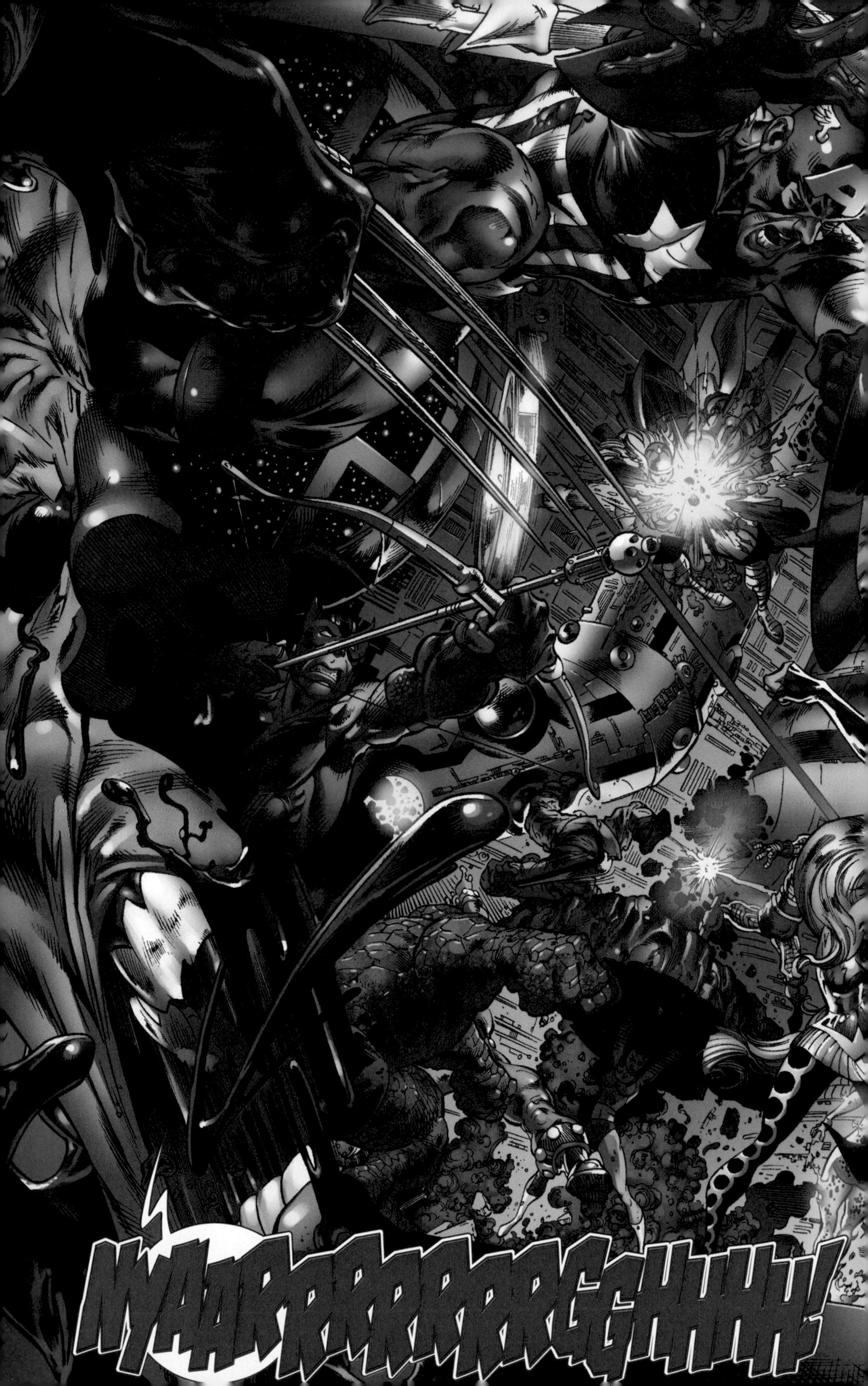
NYAARRRRRRRGHHHH!

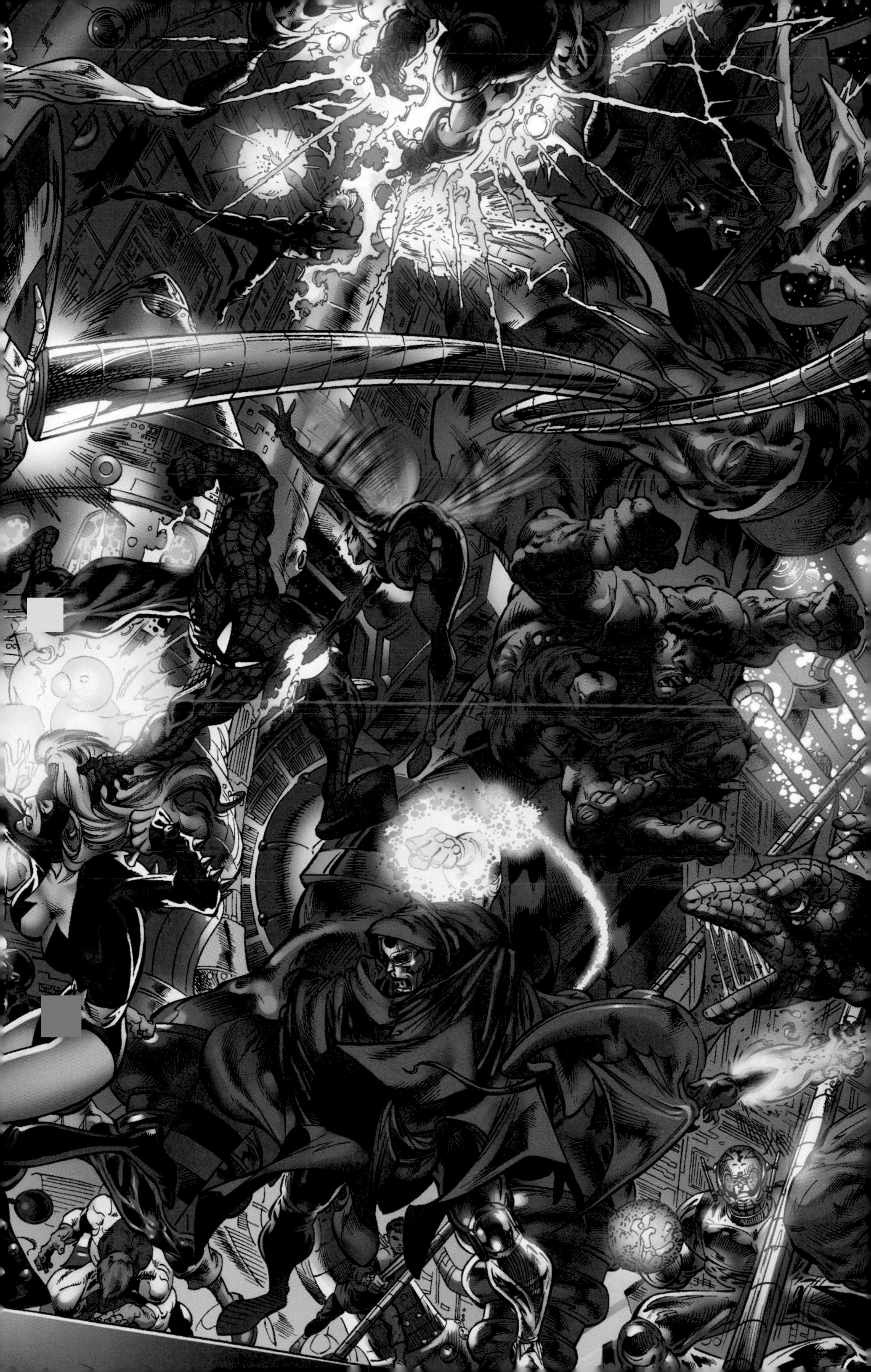

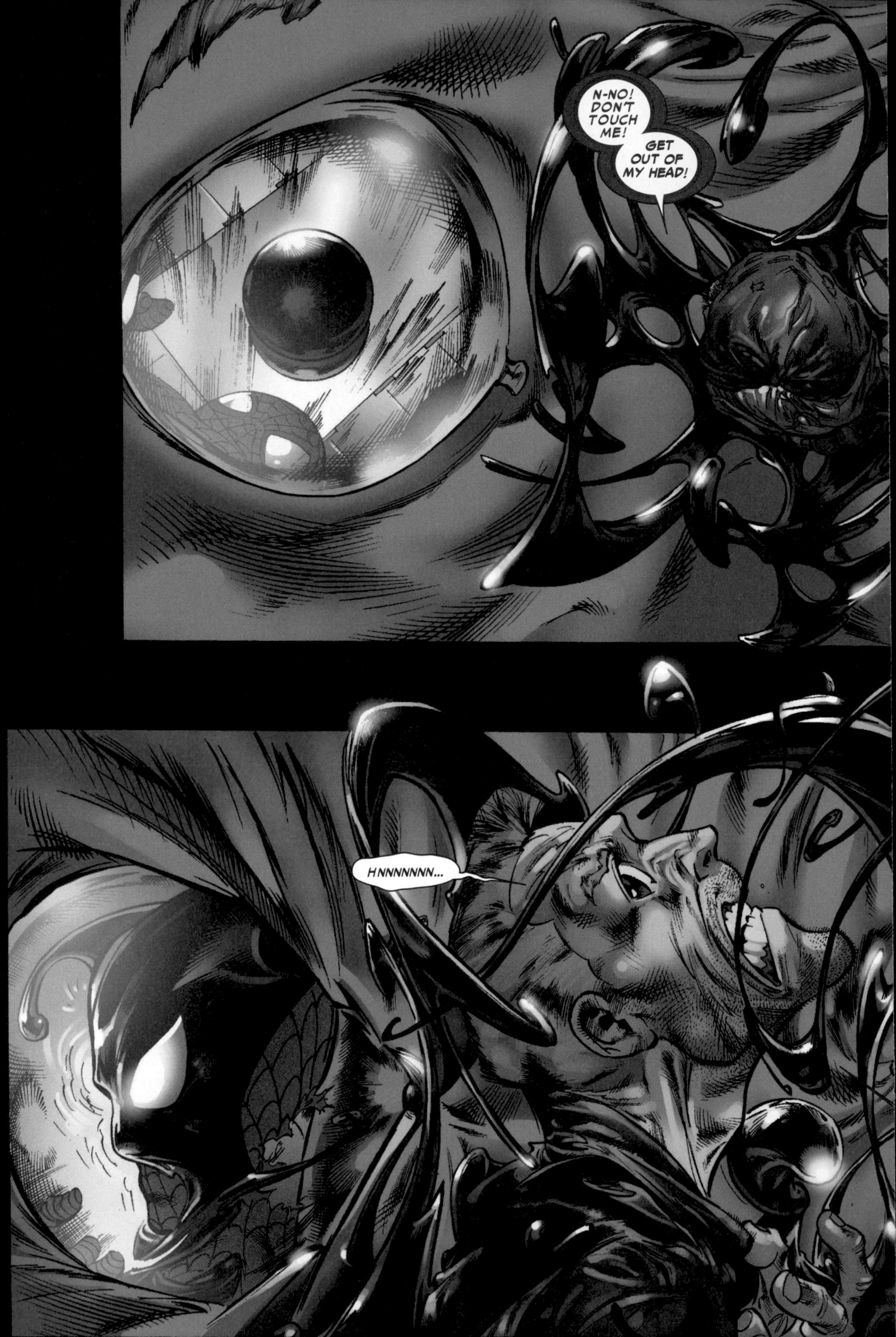

N-NO! DON'T TOUCH ME!
GET OUT OF MY HEAD!
HNNNNNNN...

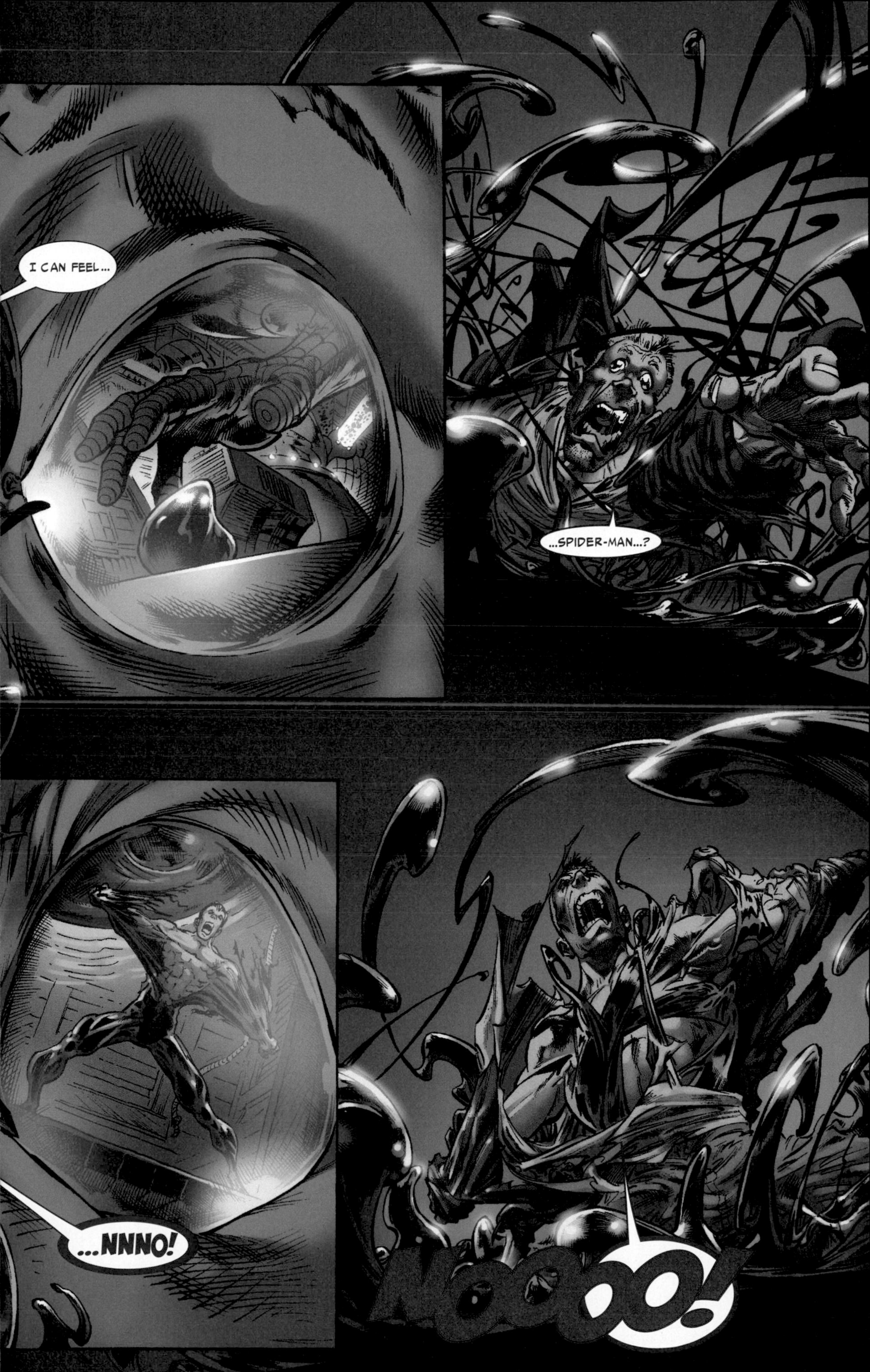
I CAN FEEL...
...SPIDER-MAN...?
...NNNO!
NOOOOO!

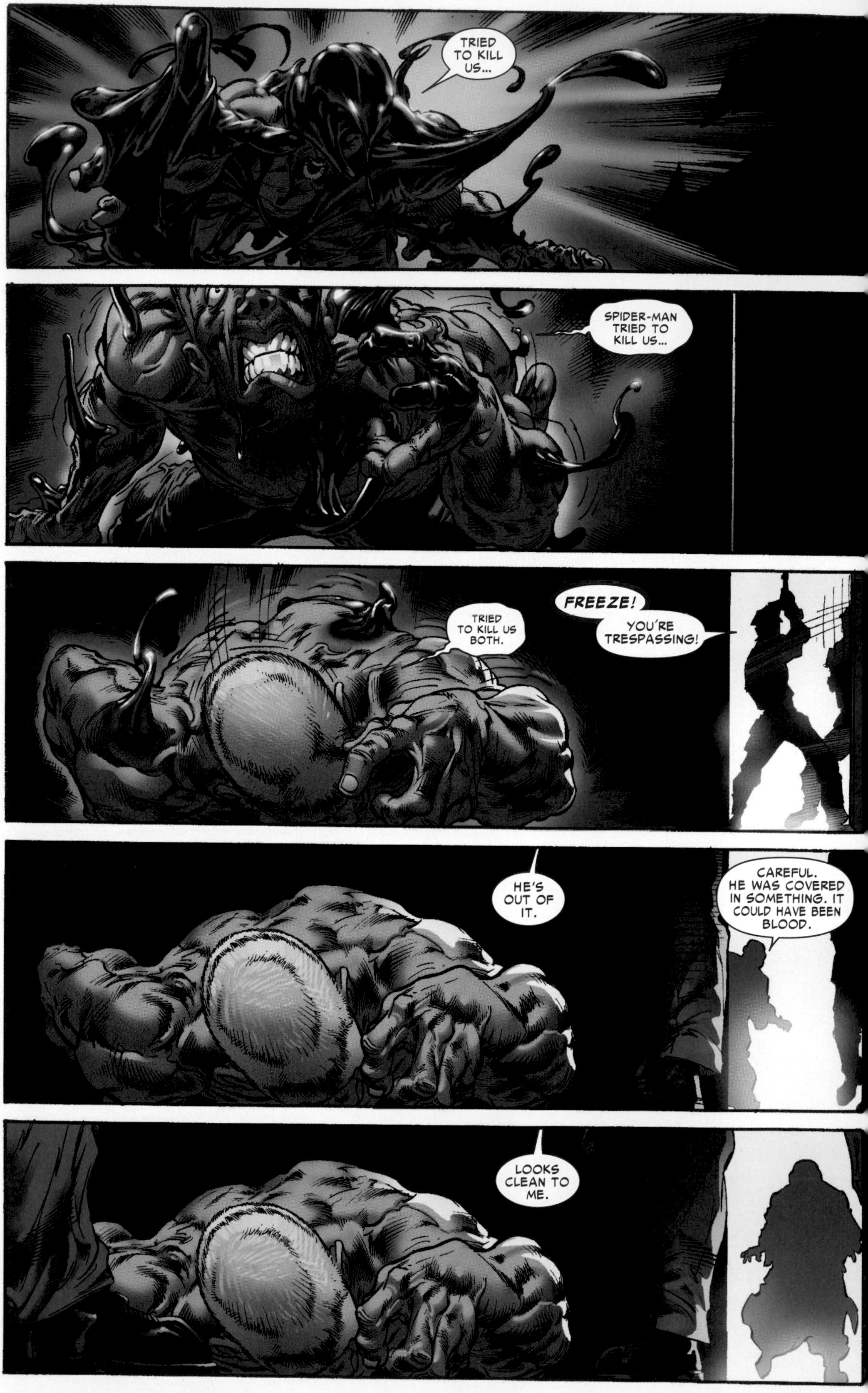
TRIED TO KILL US...
SPIDER-MAN TRIED TO KILL US...
TRIED TO KILL US BOTH.
FREEZE!
YOU'RE TRESPASSING!
HE'S OUT OF IT.
CAREFUL. HE WAS COVERED IN SOMETHING. IT COULD HAVE BEEN BLOOD.
LOOKS CLEAN TO ME.

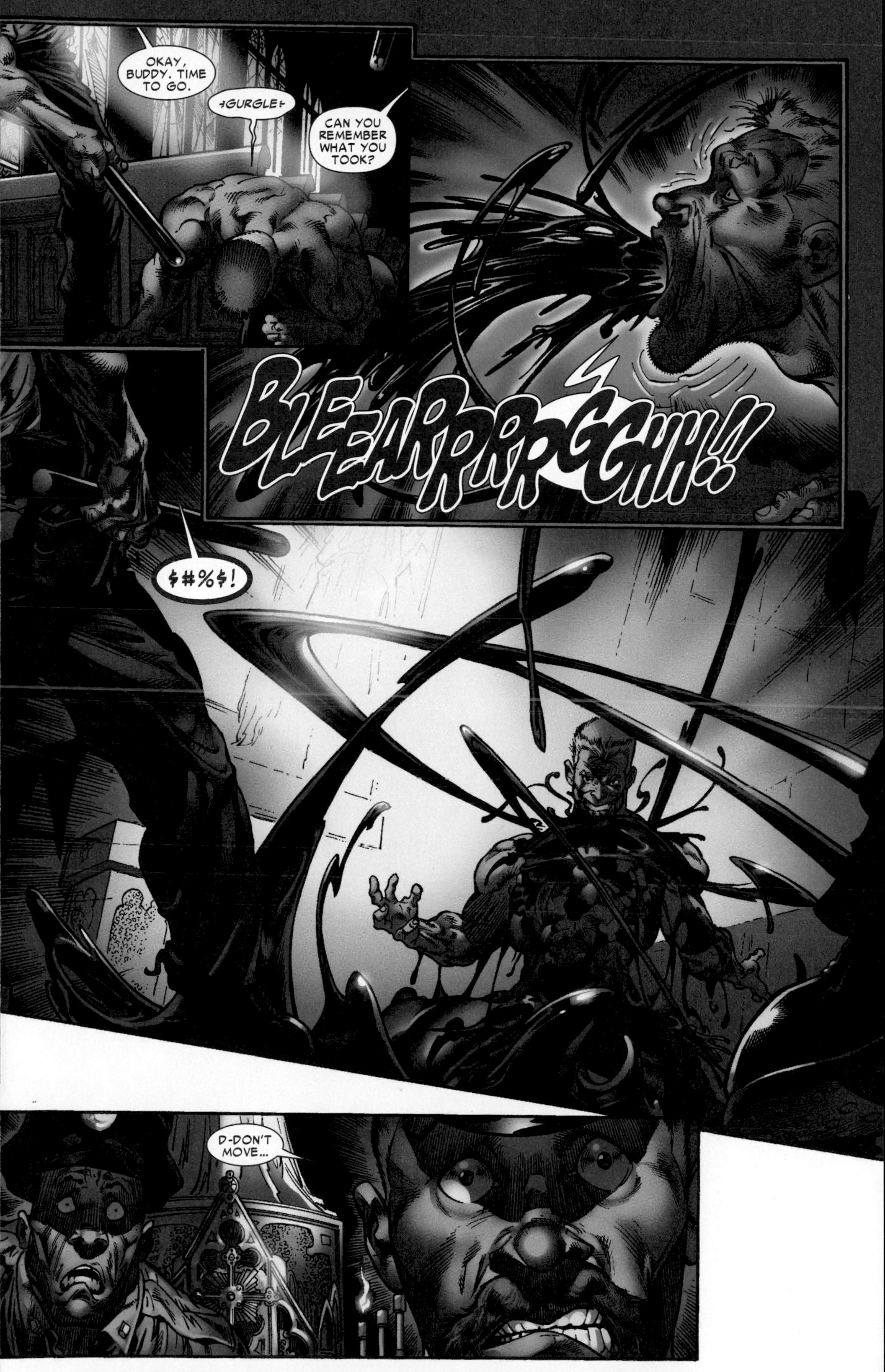
OKAY, BUDDY. TIME TO GO.
=GURGLE=
CAN YOU REMEMBER WHAT YOU TOOK?
BLEEARRRRGGHH!!
$#%$!
D-DON'T MOVE...

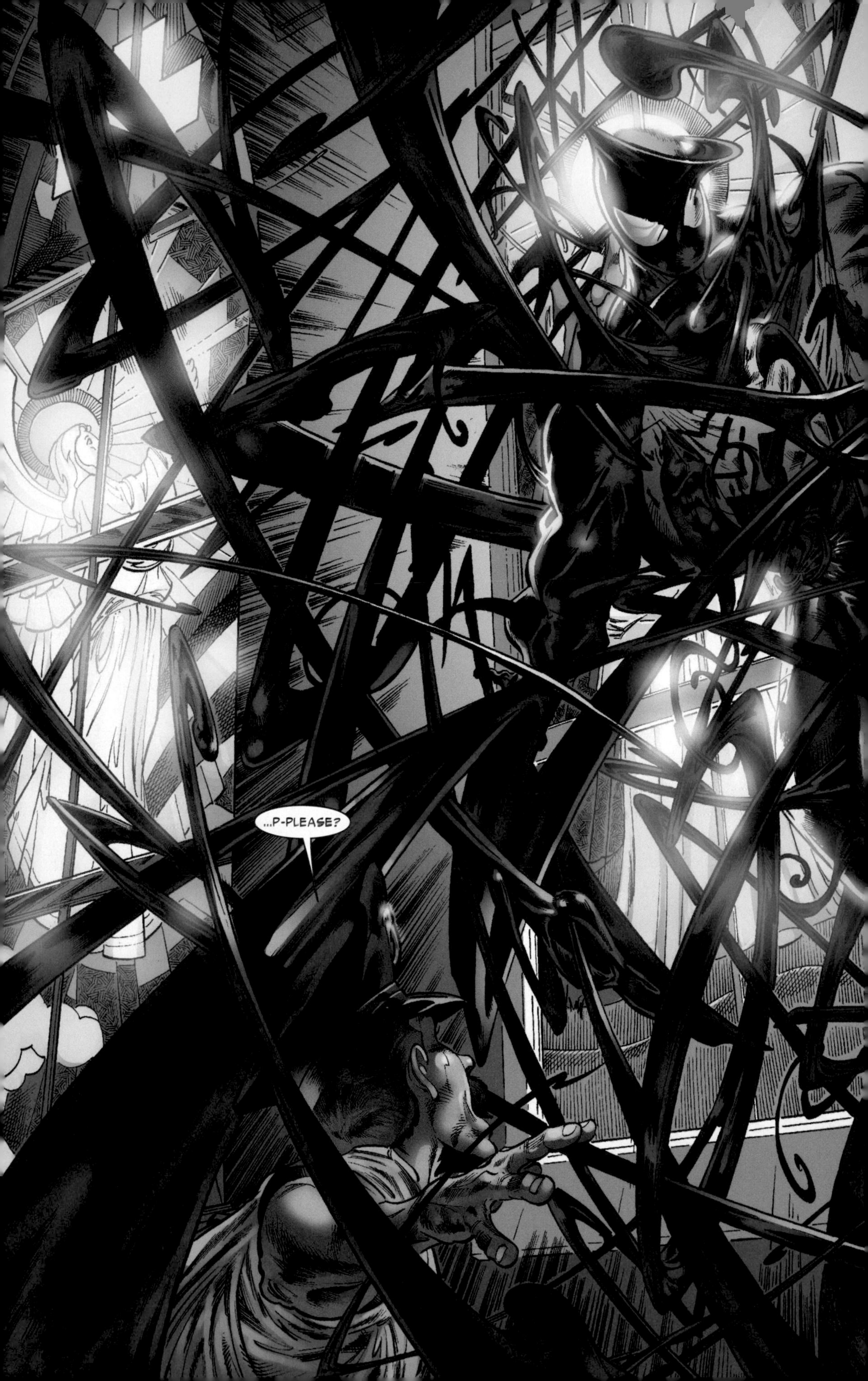
...P-PLEASE?

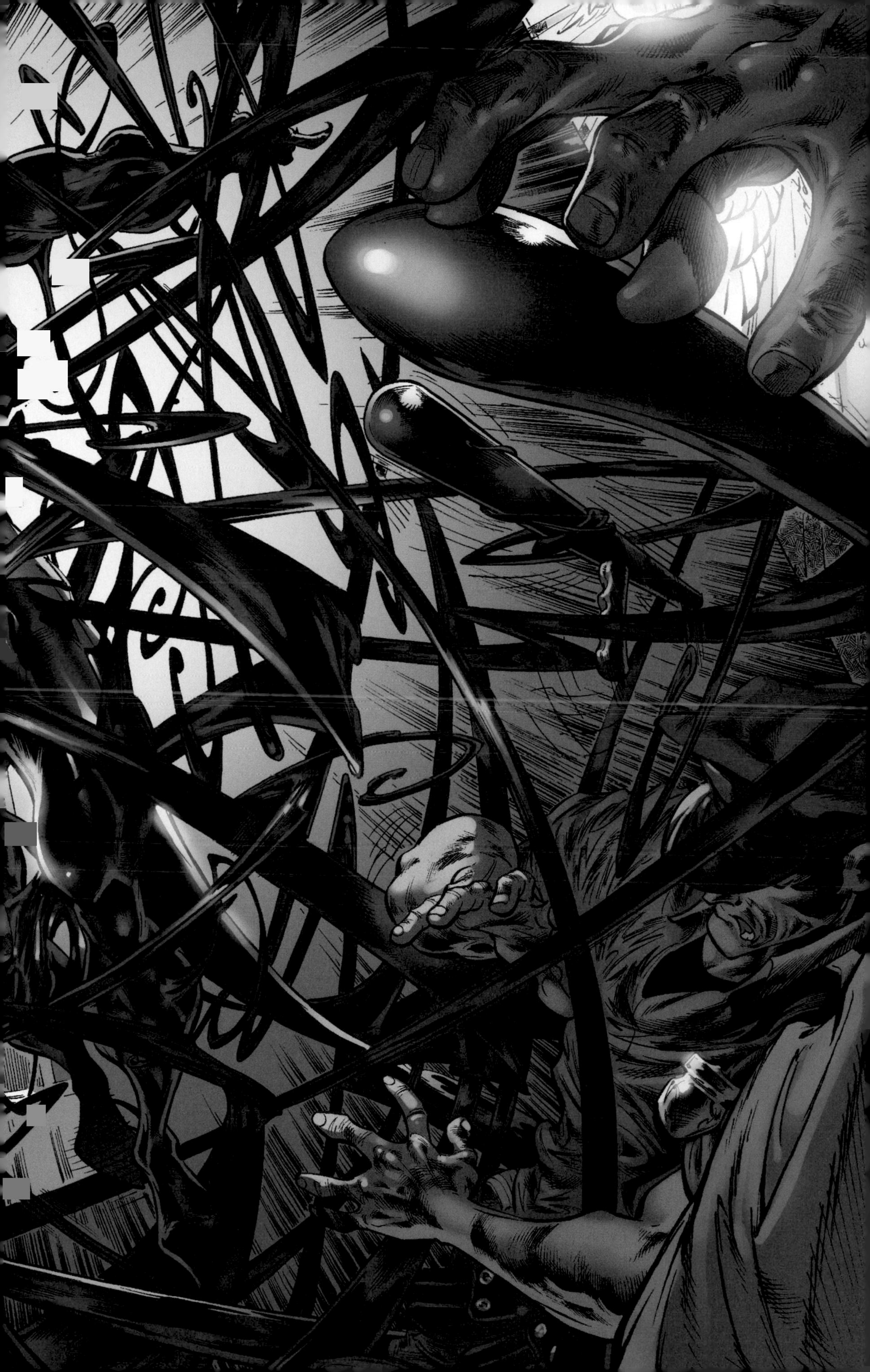

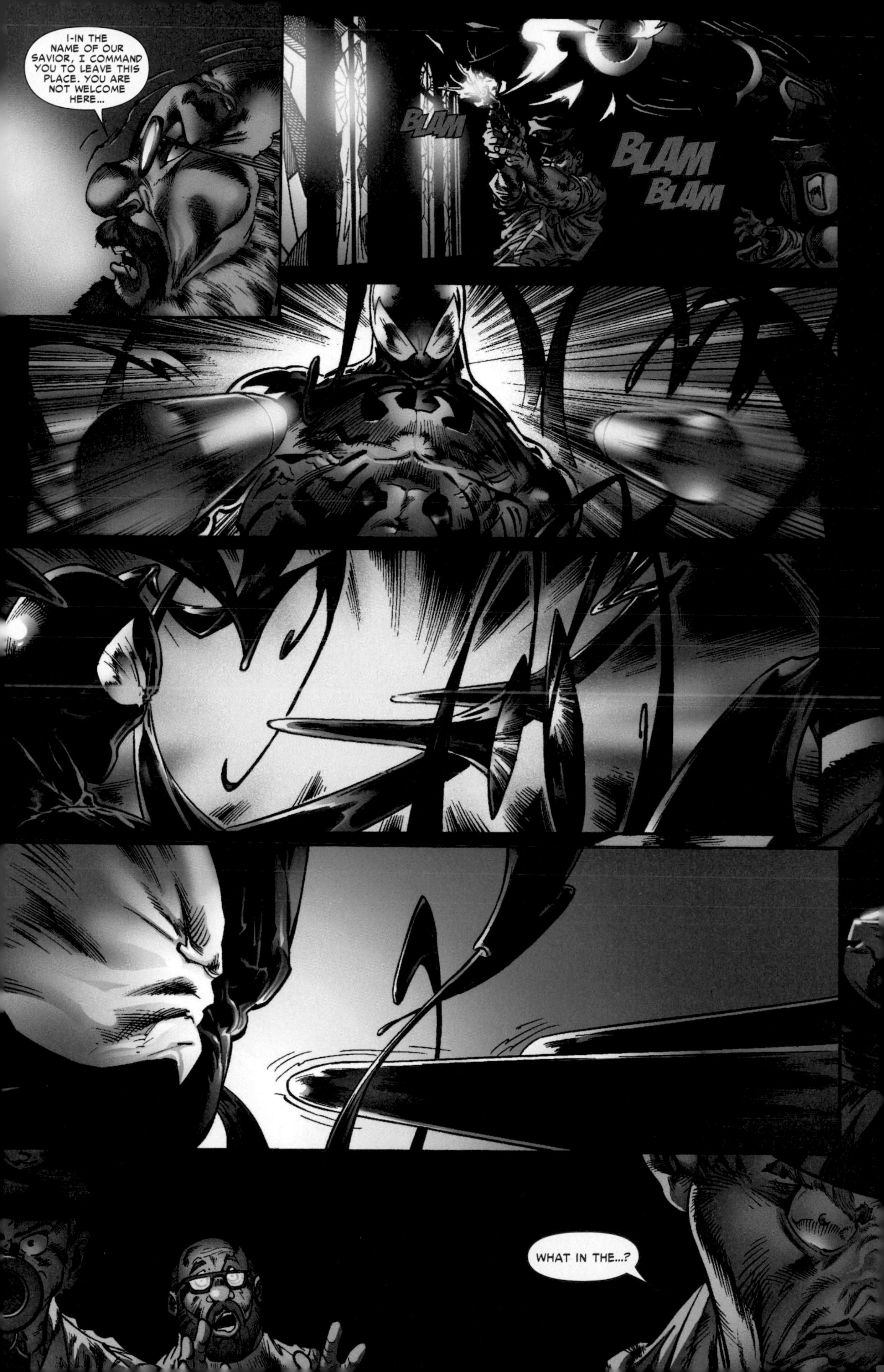
I-IN THE NAME OF OUR SAVIOR, I COMMAND YOU TO LEAVE THIS PLACE. YOU ARE NOT WELCOME HERE...
BLAM
BLAM
BLAM
WHAT IN THE...?

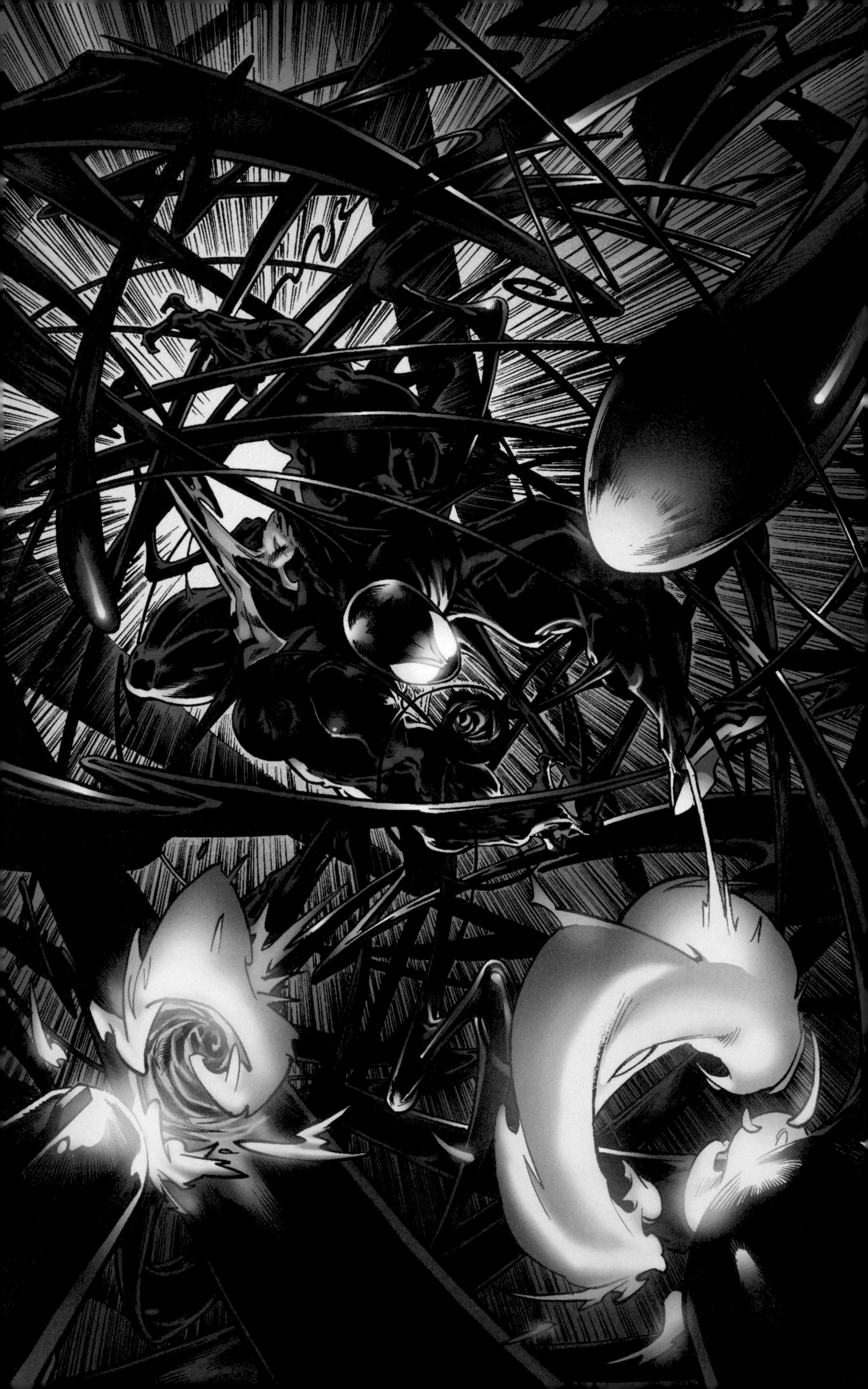

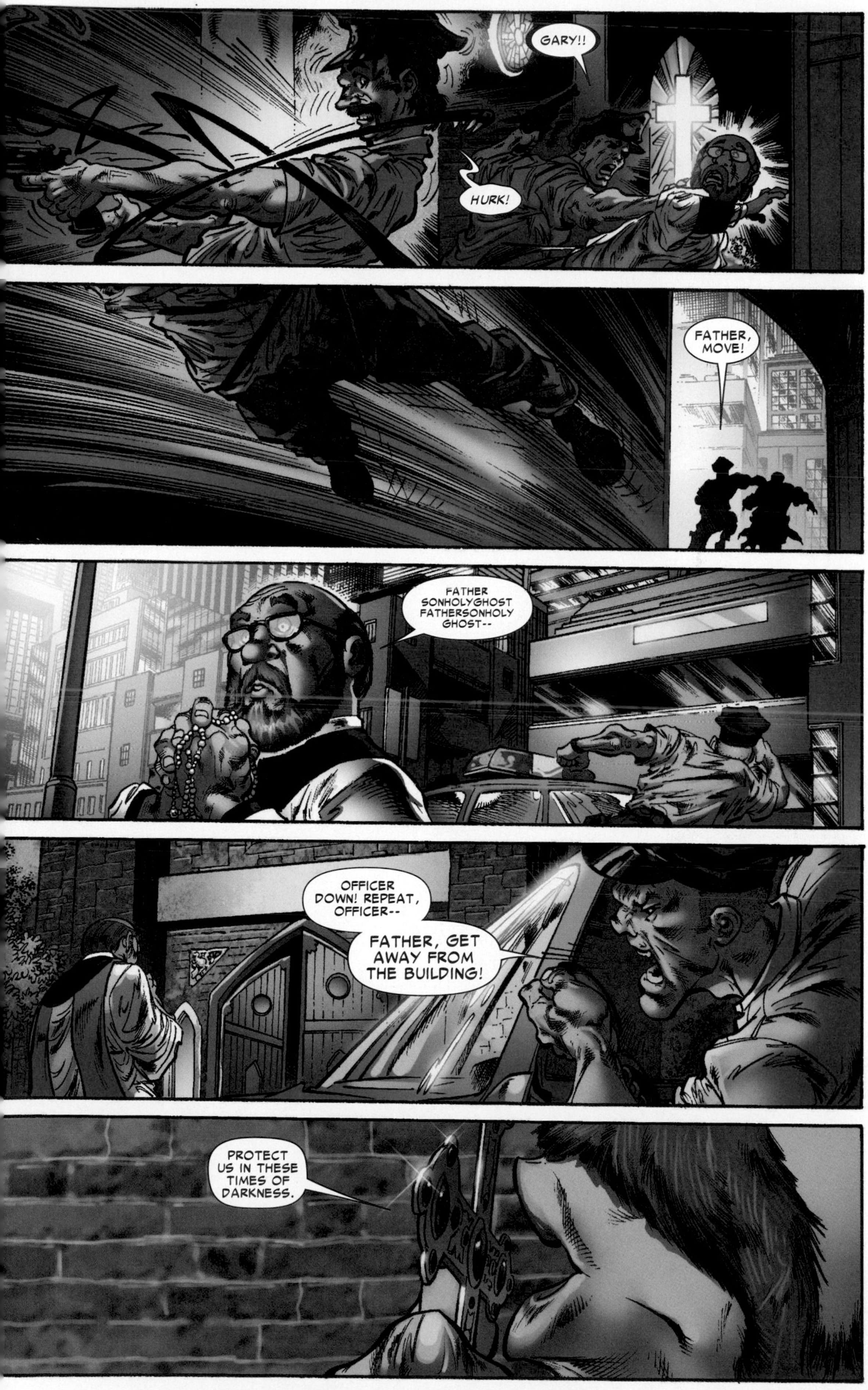
GARY!!
HURK!
FATHER, MOVE!
FATHER SONHOLYGHOST FATHERSONHOLY GHOST--
OFFICER DOWN! REPEAT, OFFICER--
FATHER, GET AWAY FROM THE BUILDING!
PROTECT US IN THESE TIMES OF DARKNESS.

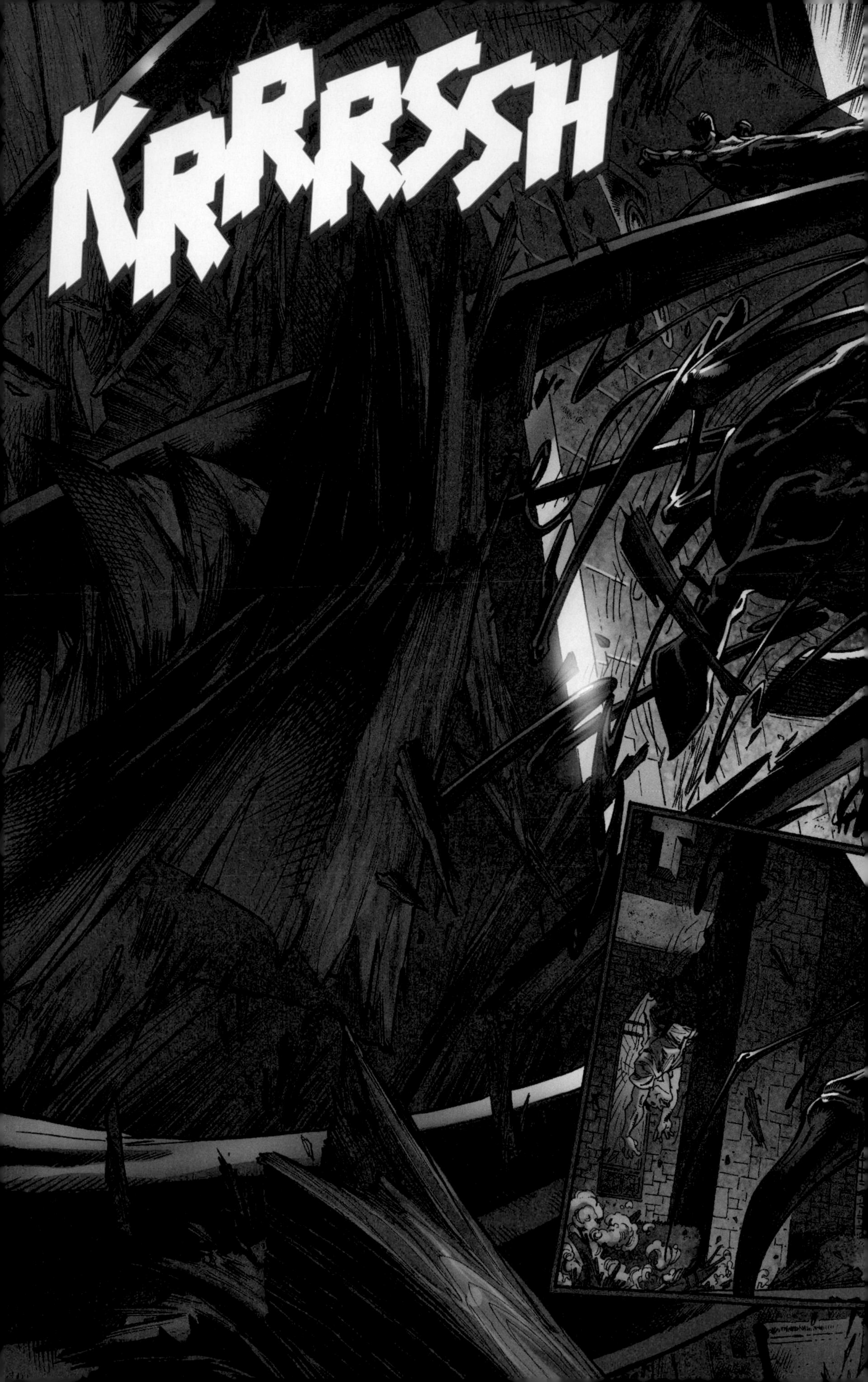
KRRRSSH

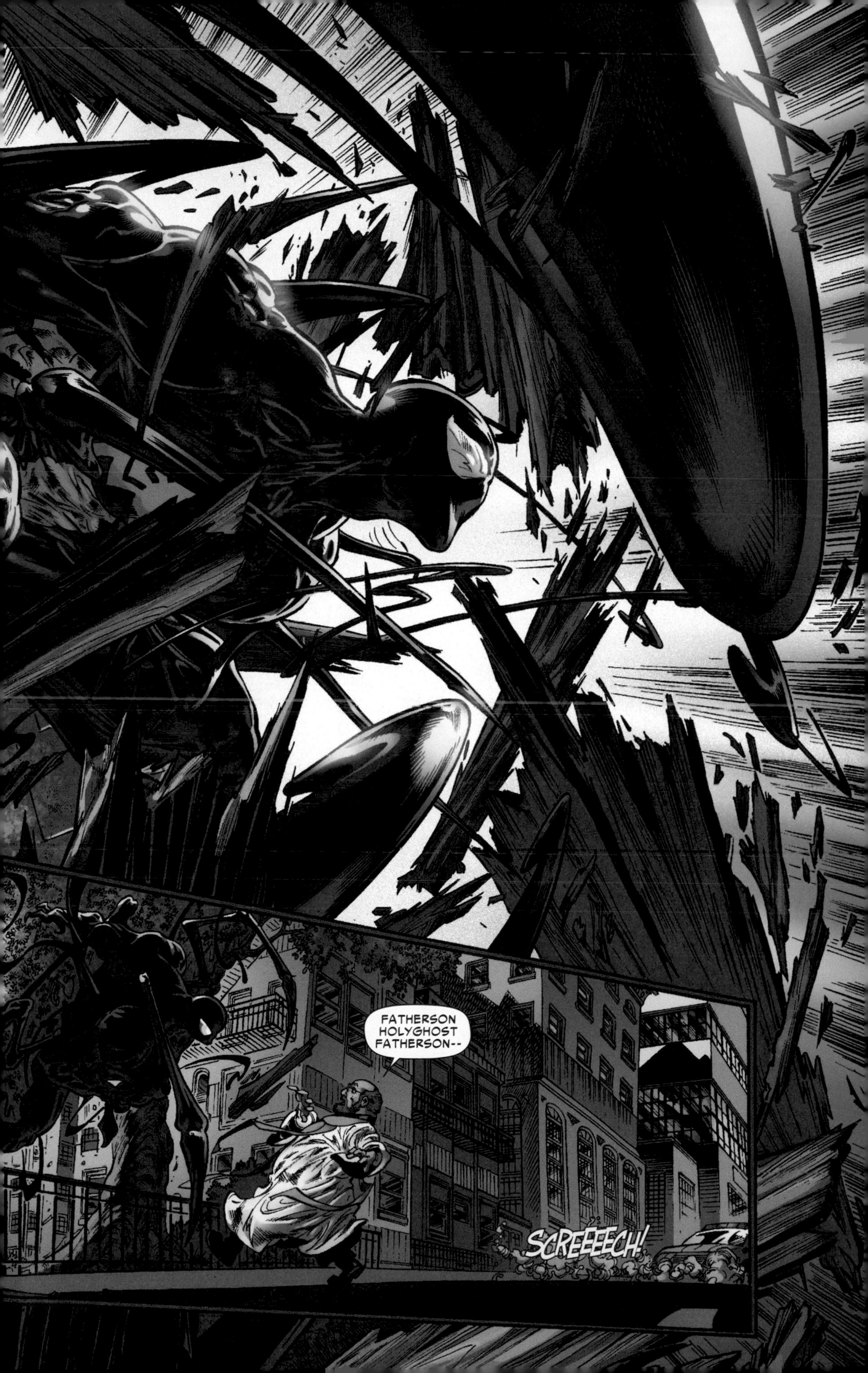
FATHERSON HOLYGHOST FATHERSON--
SCREEEECH!

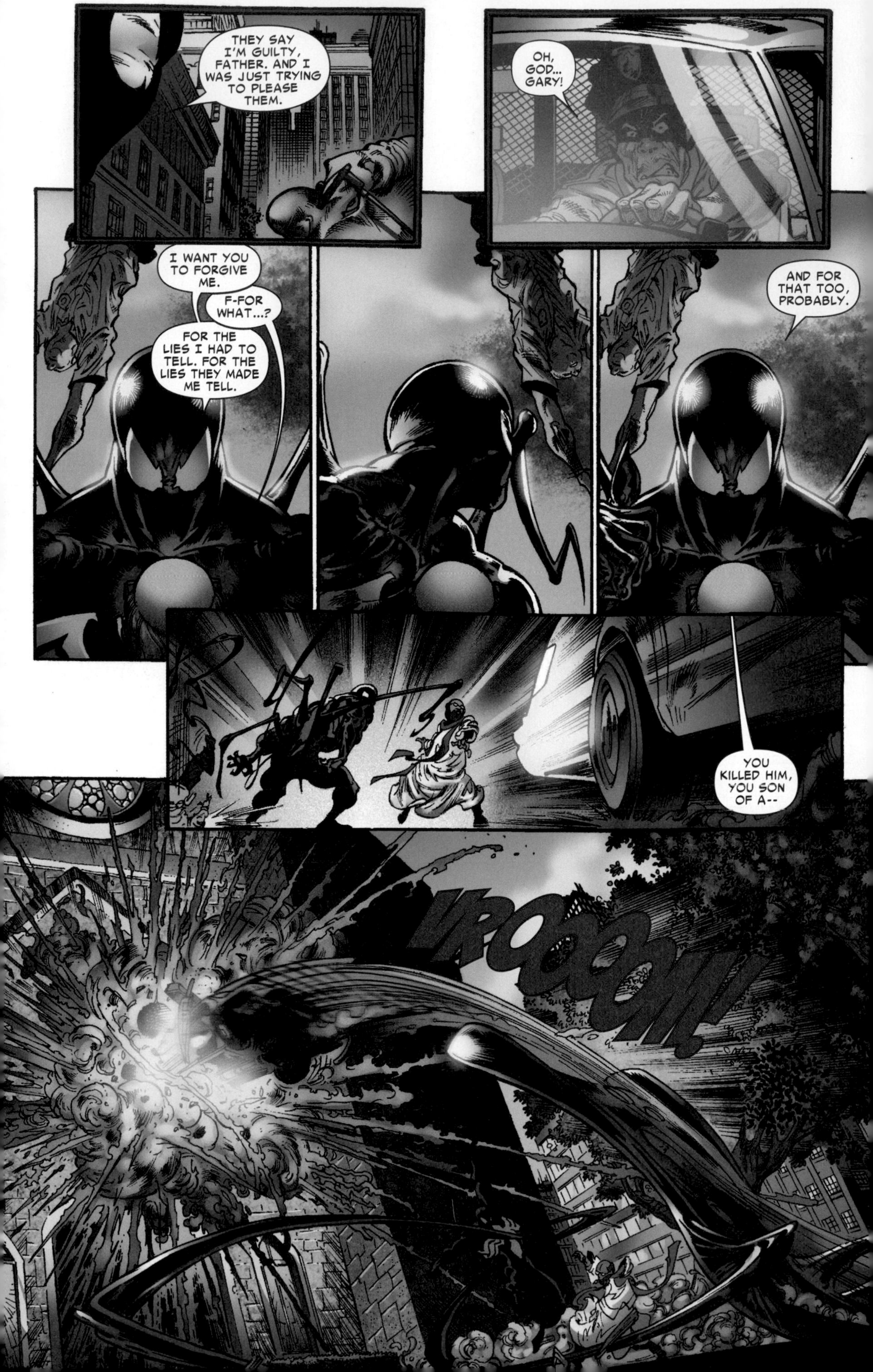
THEY SAY I'M GUILTY, FATHER. AND I WAS JUST TRYING TO PLEASE THEM.
OH, GOD... GARY!
I WANT YOU TO FORGIVE ME.
F-FOR WHAT...?
FOR THE LIES I HAD TO TELL. FOR THE LIES THEY MADE ME TELL.
AND FOR THAT TOO, PROBABLY.
YOU KILLED HIM, YOU SON OF A--
VROOOM!

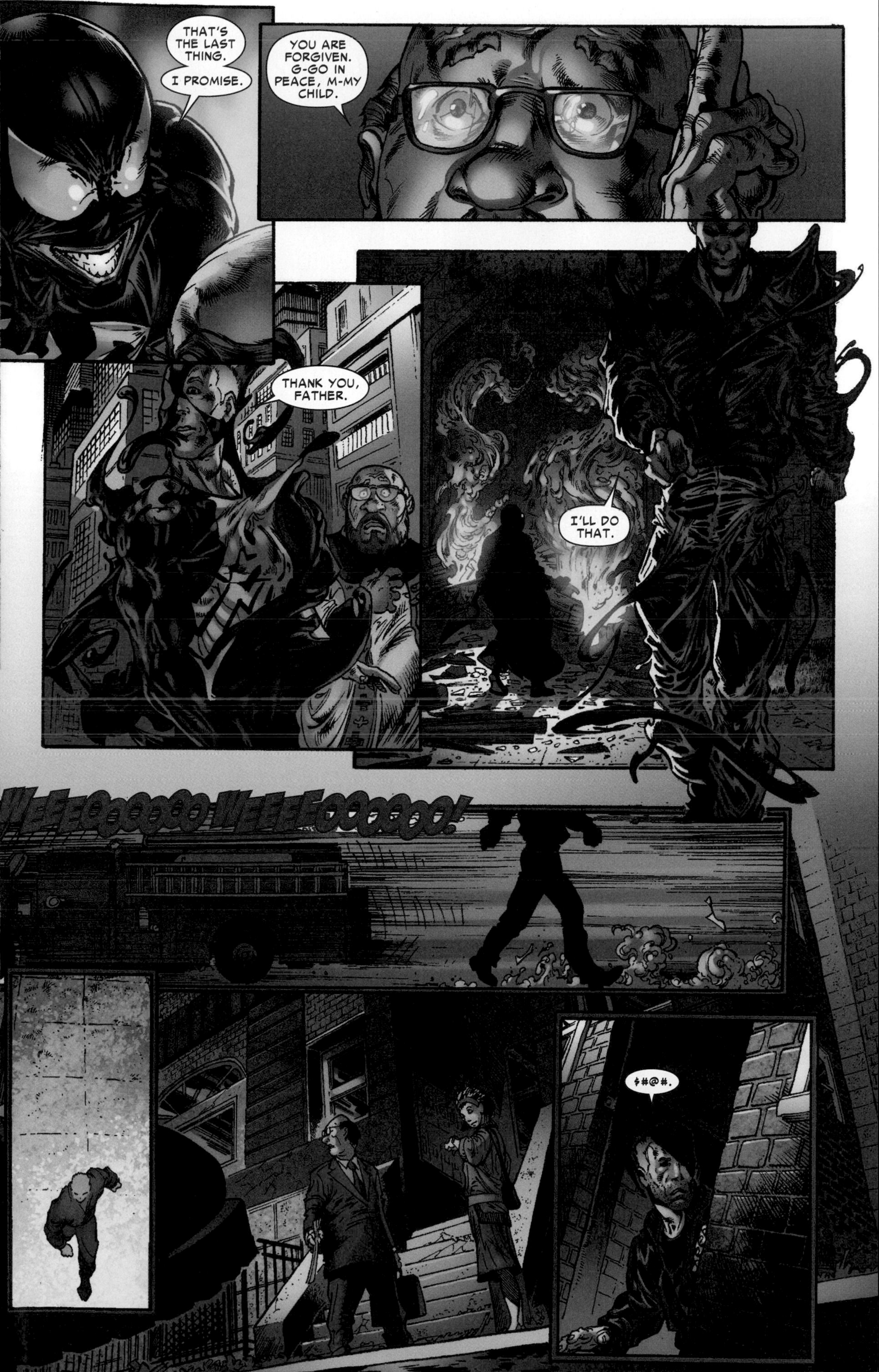
THAT'S THE LAST THING.
I PROMISE.
YOU ARE FORGIVEN. G-GO IN PEACE, M-MY CHILD.
THANK YOU, FATHER.
I'LL DO THAT.
WEEEOOOOOO WEEEEOOOOOO!
$#@#.

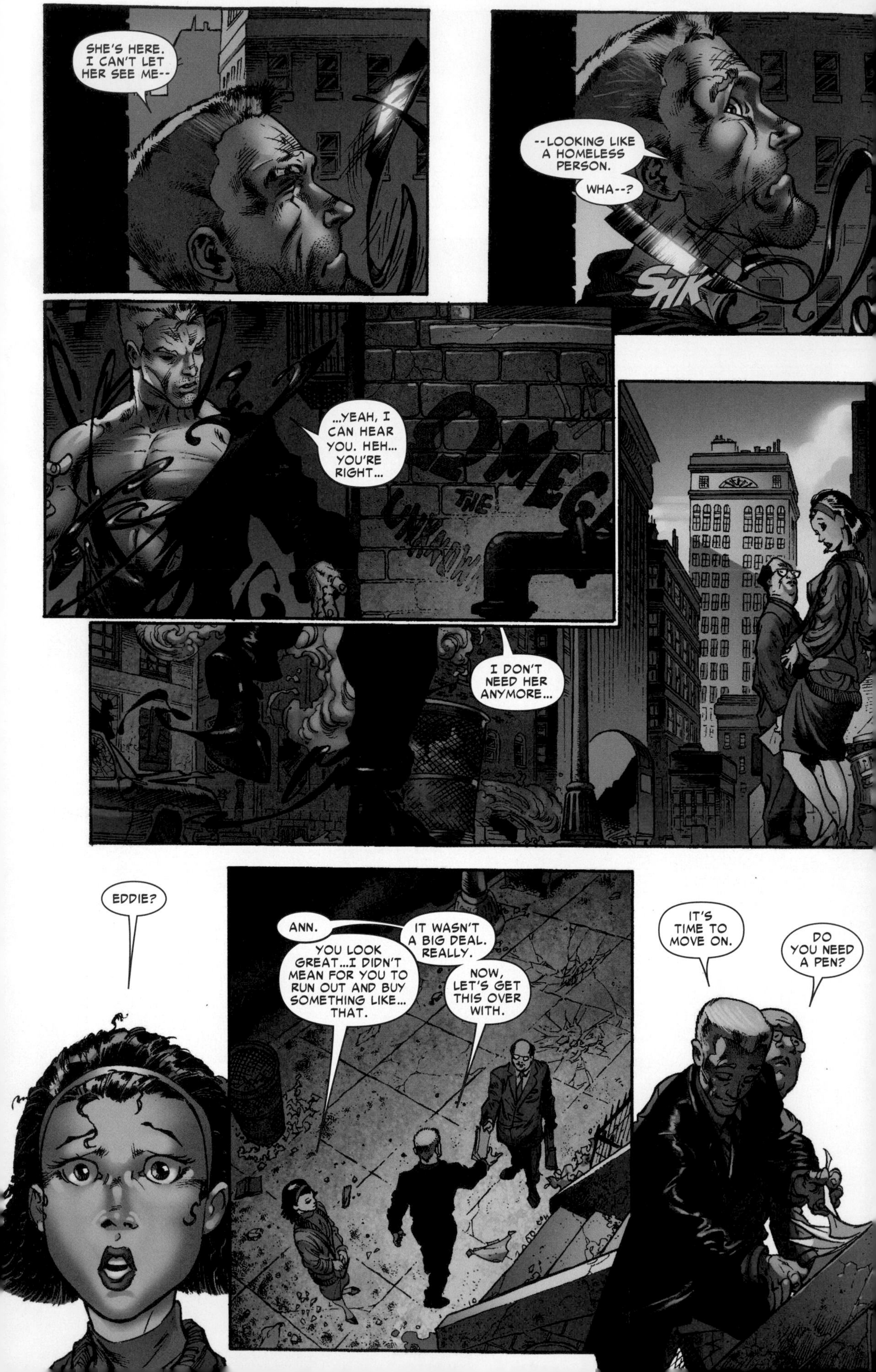
SHE'S HERE. I CAN'T LET HER SEE ME--
--LOOKING LIKE A HOMELESS PERSON.
WHA--?
SHK
...YEAH, I CAN HEAR YOU. HEH... YOU'RE RIGHT...
OMEGA THE UNKNOWN
I DON'T NEED HER ANYMORE...
EDDIE?
ANN.
YOU LOOK GREAT...I DIDN'T MEAN FOR YOU TO RUN OUT AND BUY SOMETHING LIKE... THAT.
IT WASN'T A BIG DEAL. REALLY.
NOW, LET'S GET THIS OVER WITH.
IT'S TIME TO MOVE ON.
DO YOU NEED A PEN?

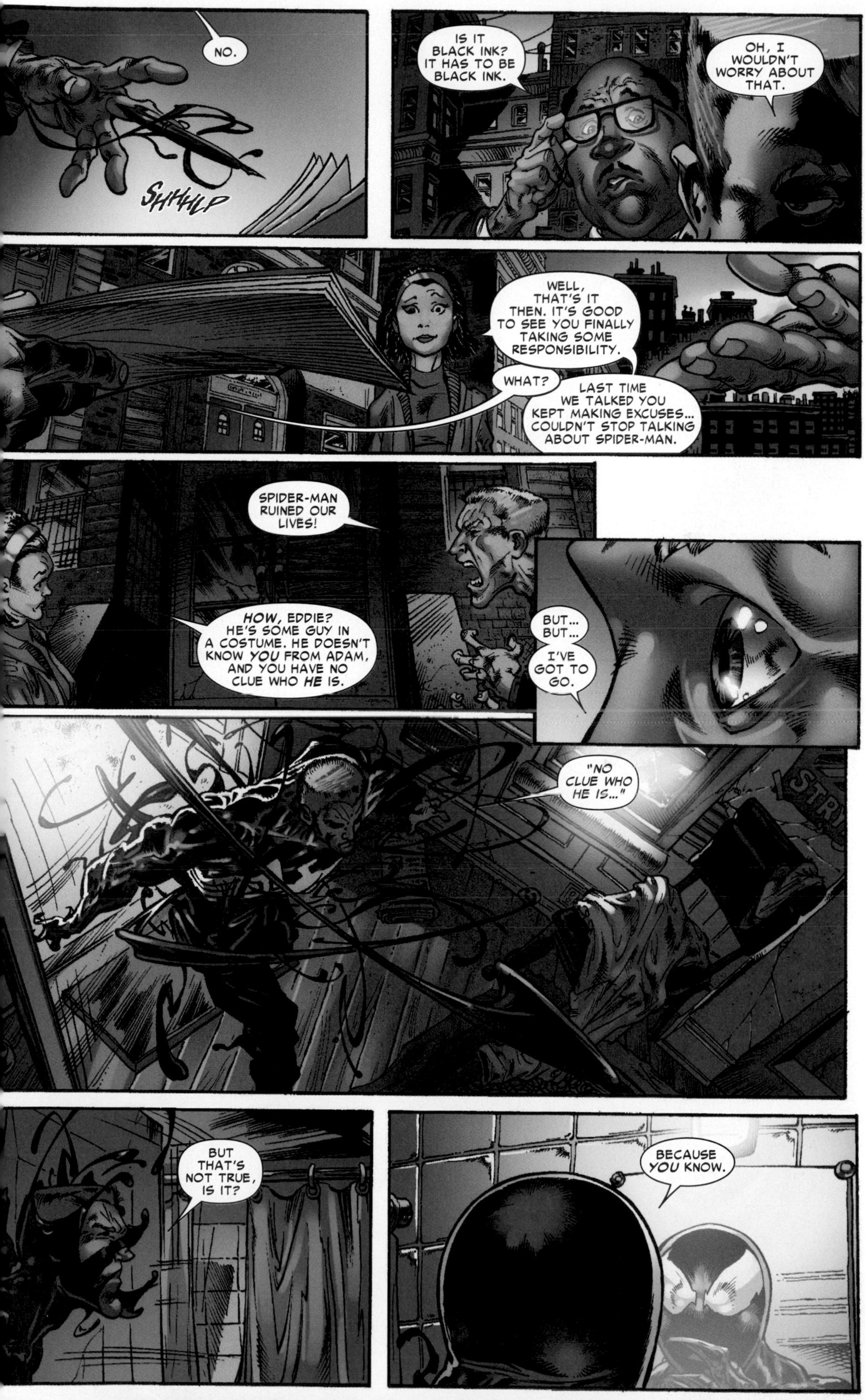
NO.
SHHHLP
IS IT BLACK INK? IT HAS TO BE BLACK INK.
OH, I WOULDN'T WORRY ABOUT THAT.
WELL, THAT'S IT THEN. IT'S GOOD TO SEE YOU FINALLY TAKING SOME RESPONSIBILITY.
WHAT?
LAST TIME WE TALKED YOU KEPT MAKING EXCUSES... COULDN'T STOP TALKING ABOUT SPIDER-MAN.
SPIDER-MAN RUINED OUR LIVES!
HOW, EDDIE? HE'S SOME GUY IN A COSTUME. HE DOESN'T KNOW YOU FROM ADAM, AND YOU HAVE NO CLUE WHO HE IS.
BUT... BUT...
I'VE GOT TO GO.
"NO CLUE WHO HE IS..."
BUT THAT'S NOT TRUE, IS IT?
BECAUSE YOU KNOW.

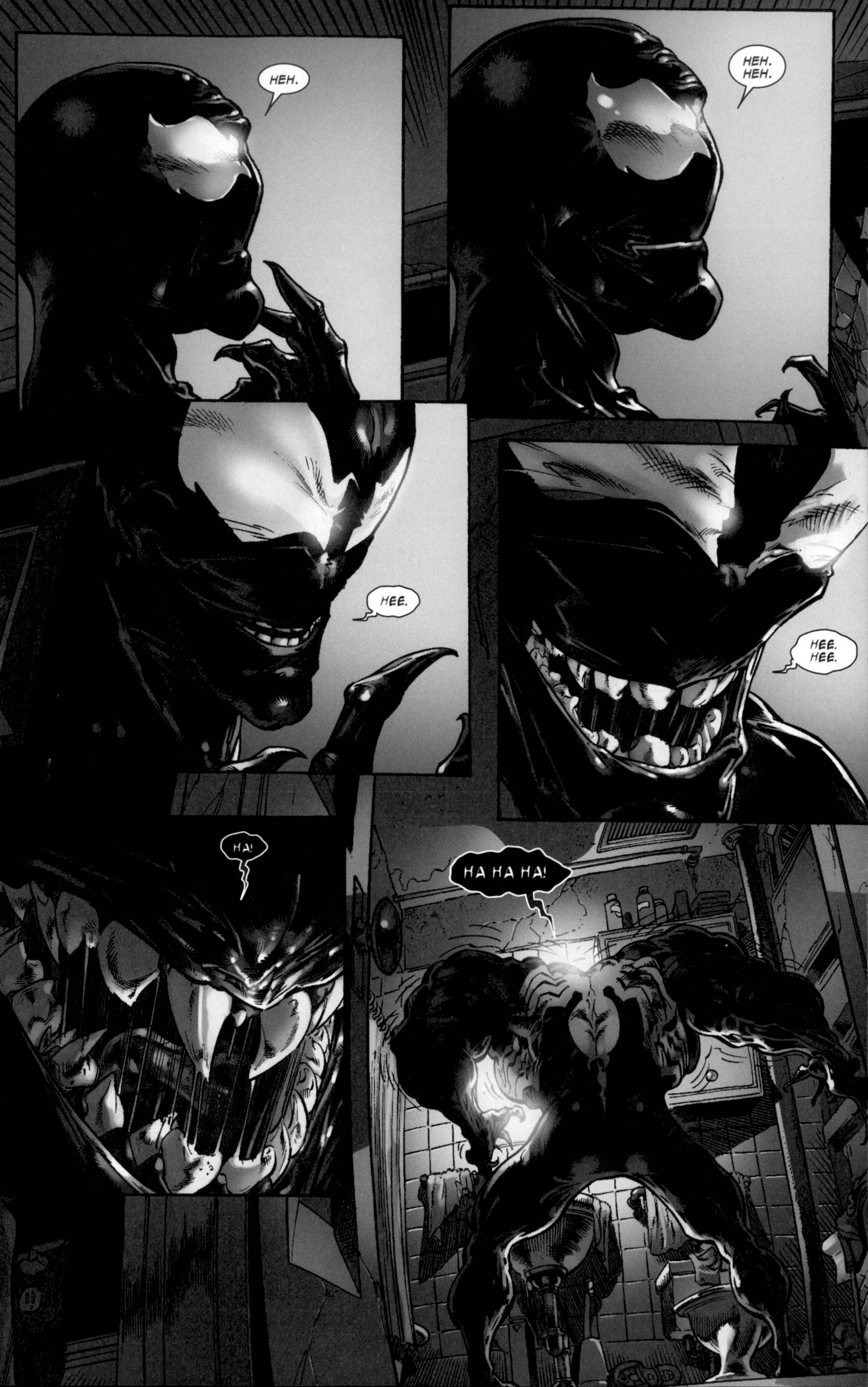
HEH.
HEH. HEH.
HEE.
HEE. HEE.
HA!
HA HA HA!

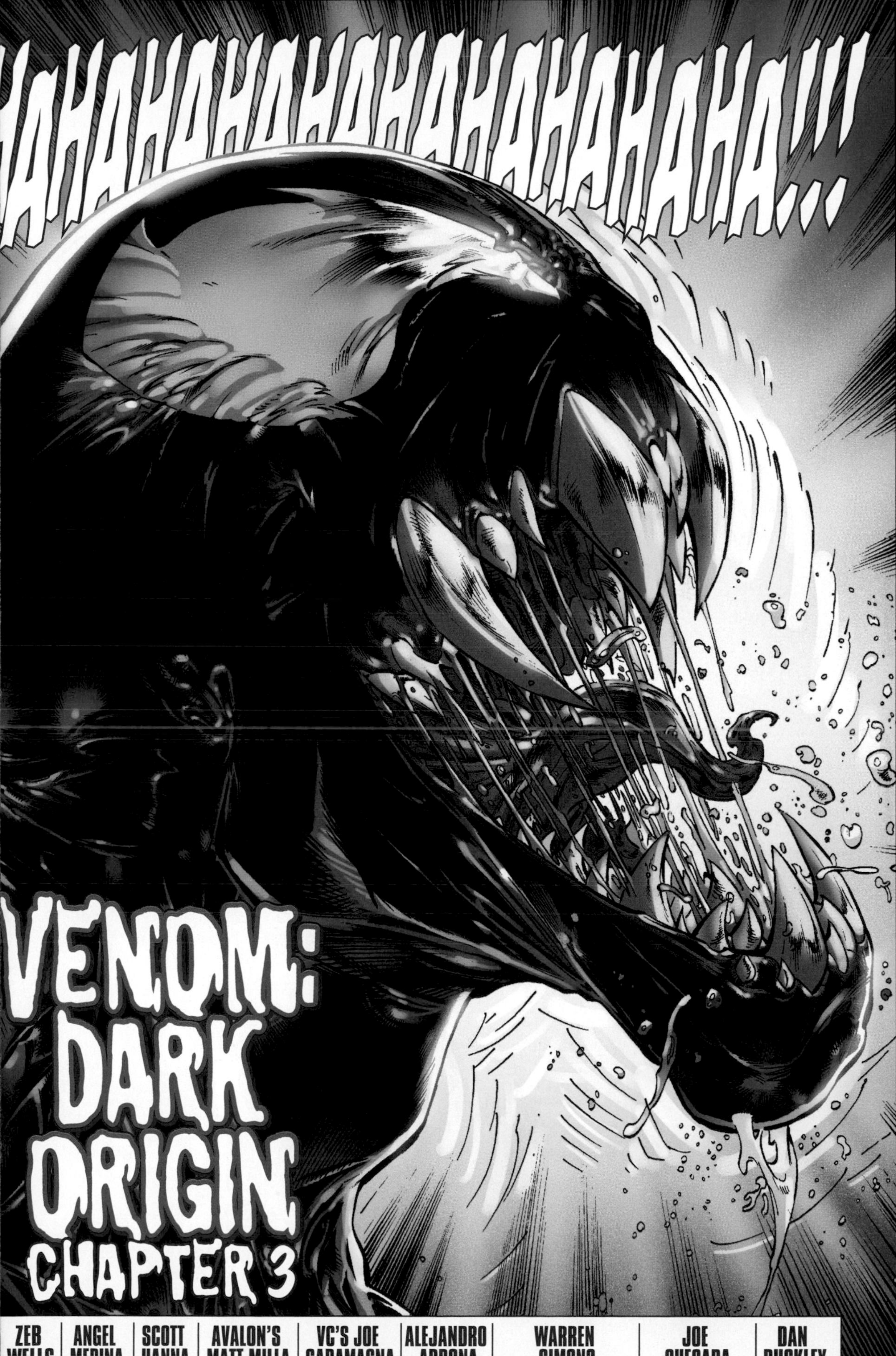
HAHAHAHAHAHAHAHAHAHAHA!!!
VENOM: DARK ORIGIN
CHAPTER 3

ZEB WELLS	ANGEL MEDINA	SCOTT HANNA	AVALON'S MATT MILLA	VC'S JOE CARAMAGNA	ALEJANDRO ARBONA	WARREN SIMONS	JOE QUESADA	DAN BUCKLEY
WRITER	PENCILER	INKER	COLORIST	LETTERER	EDITOR	SUPERVISING EDITOR	EDITOR IN CHIEF	PUBLISHER

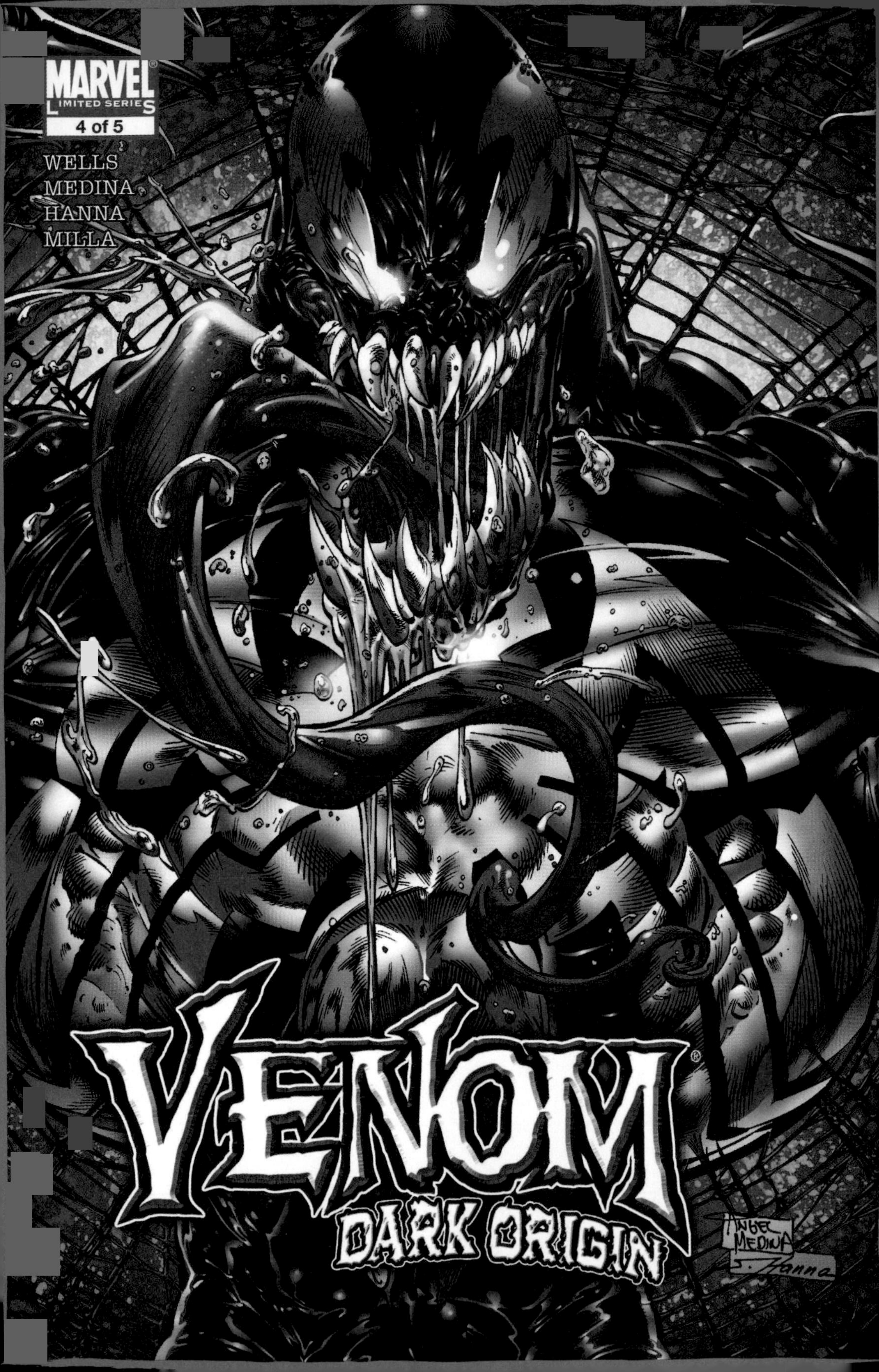
MARVEL
LIMITED SERIES
4 of 5
WELLS
MEDINA
HANNA
MILLA
VENOM
DARK ORIGIN

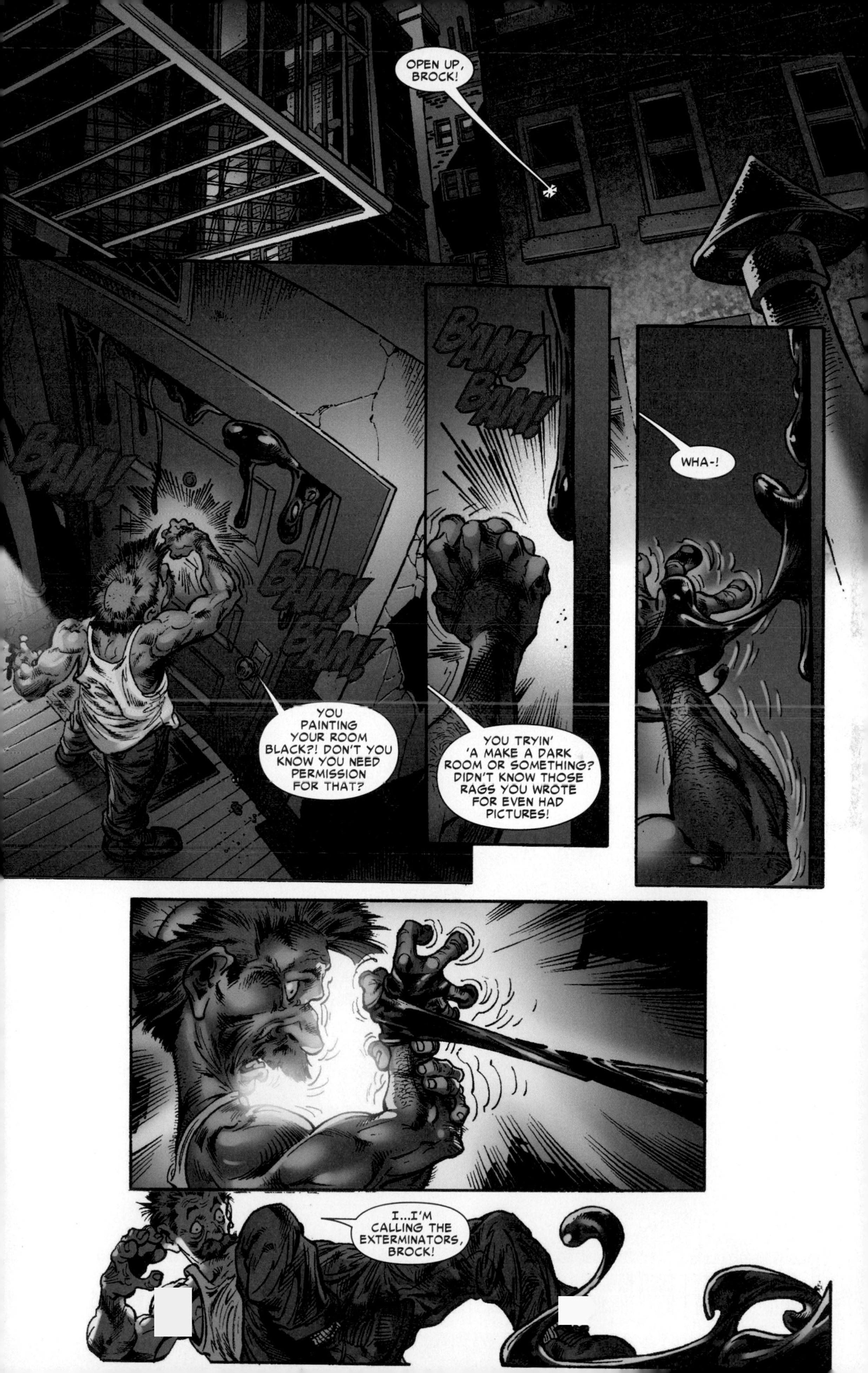

OPEN UP, BROCK!
BAM! BAM!
BAM! BAM!
YOU PAINTING YOUR ROOM BLACK?! DON'T YOU KNOW YOU NEED PERMISSION FOR THAT?
BAM! BAM!
YOU TRYIN' 'A MAKE A DARK ROOM OR SOMETHING? DIDN'T KNOW THOSE RAGS YOU WROTE FOR EVEN HAD PICTURES!
WHA-!
I...I'M CALLING THE EXTERMINATORS, BROCK!

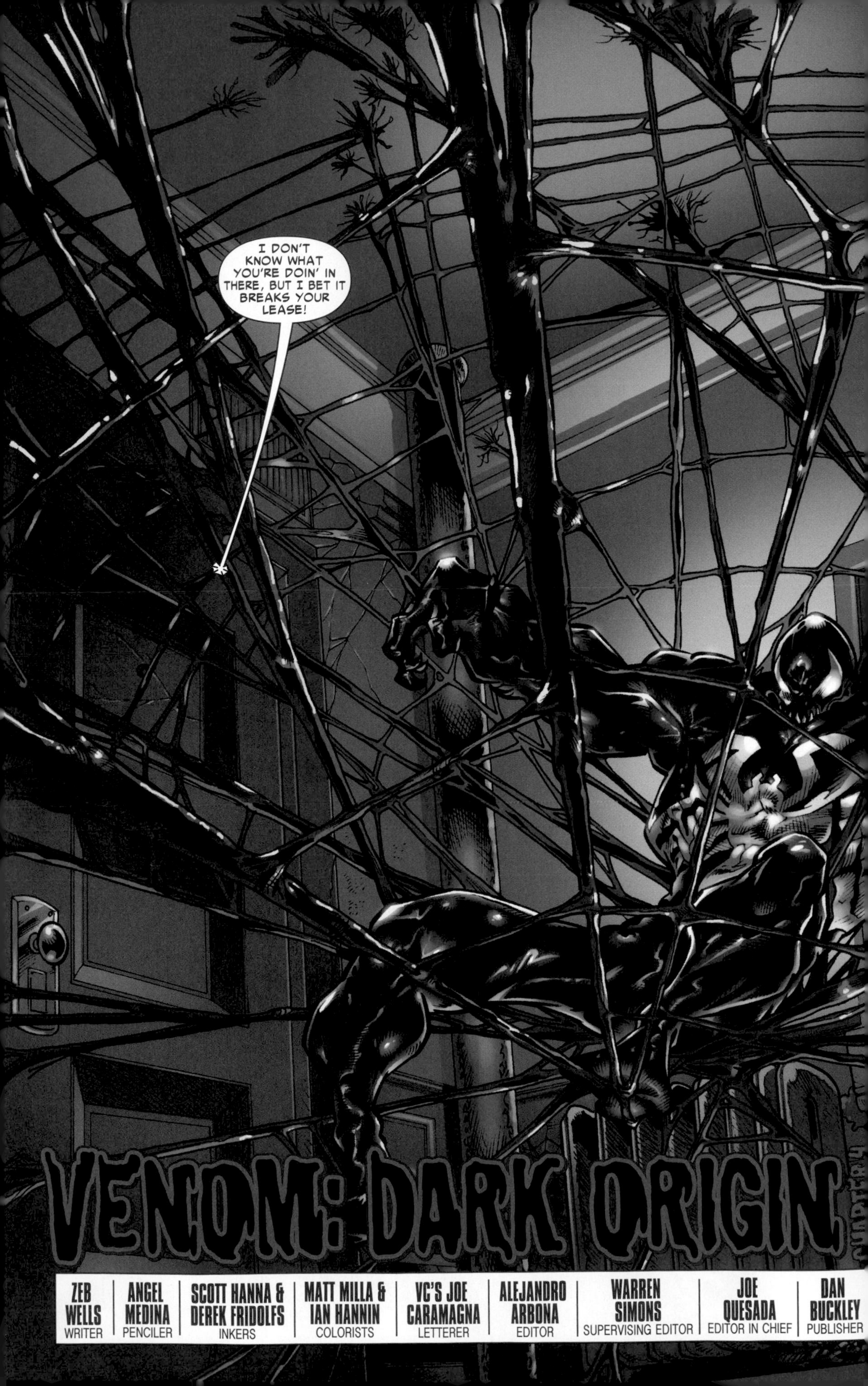

I DON'T KNOW WHAT YOU'RE DOIN' IN THERE, BUT I BET IT BREAKS YOUR LEASE!
VENOM: DARK ORIGIN
CHAPTER 4
ZEB WELLS WRITER
ANGEL MEDINA PENCILER
SCOTT HANNA & DEREK FRIDOLFS INKERS
MATT MILLA & IAN HANNIN COLORISTS
VC'S JOE CARAMAGNA LETTERER
ALEJANDRO ARBONA EDITOR
WARREN SIMONS SUPERVISING EDITOR
JOE QUESADA EDITOR IN CHIEF
DAN BUCKLEY PUBLISHER

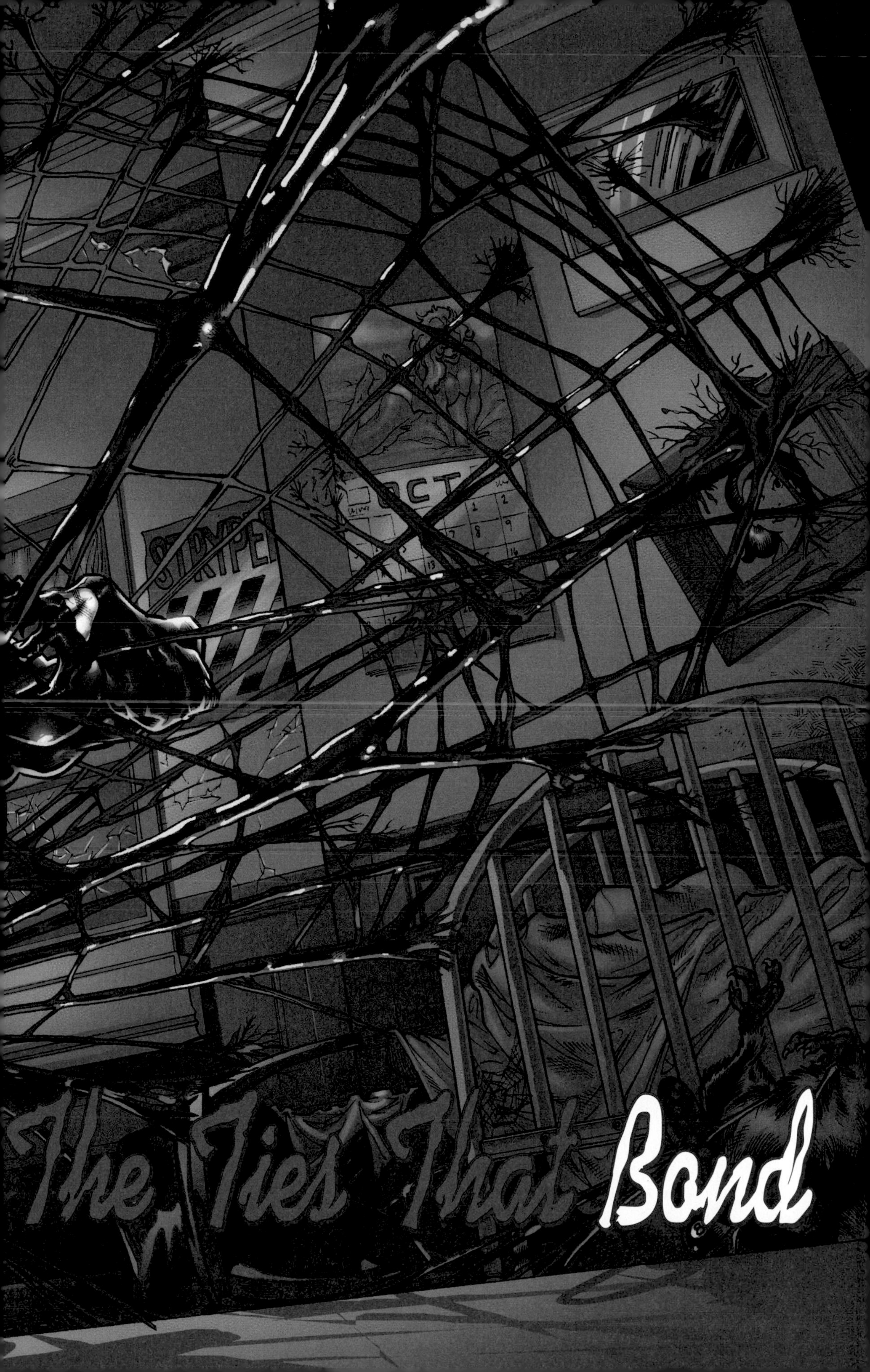

STRYPE
OCT
The Ties That Bond

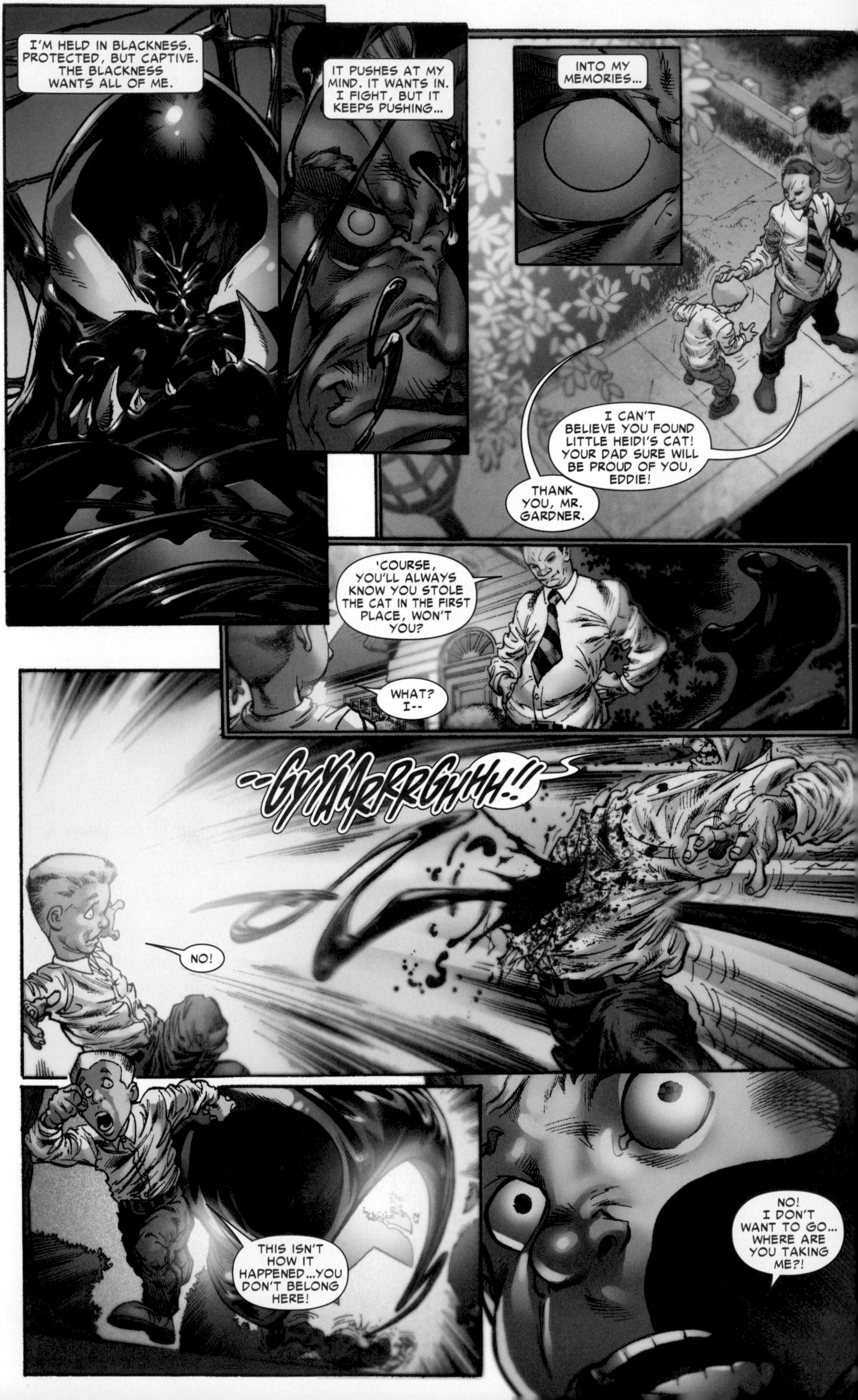
I'M HELD IN BLACKNESS. PROTECTED, BUT CAPTIVE. THE BLACKNESS WANTS ALL OF ME.
IT PUSHES AT MY MIND. IT WANTS IN. I FIGHT, BUT IT KEEPS PUSHING...
INTO MY MEMORIES...
I CAN'T BELIEVE YOU FOUND LITTLE HEIDI'S CAT! YOUR DAD SURE WILL BE PROUD OF YOU, EDDIE!
THANK YOU, MR. GARDNER.
'COURSE, YOU'LL ALWAYS KNOW YOU STOLE THE CAT IN THE FIRST PLACE, WON'T YOU?
WHAT? I--
--GYAARRRGHHH!!
NO!
THIS ISN'T HOW IT HAPPENED...YOU DON'T BELONG HERE!
NO! I DON'T WANT TO GO... WHERE ARE YOU TAKING ME?!

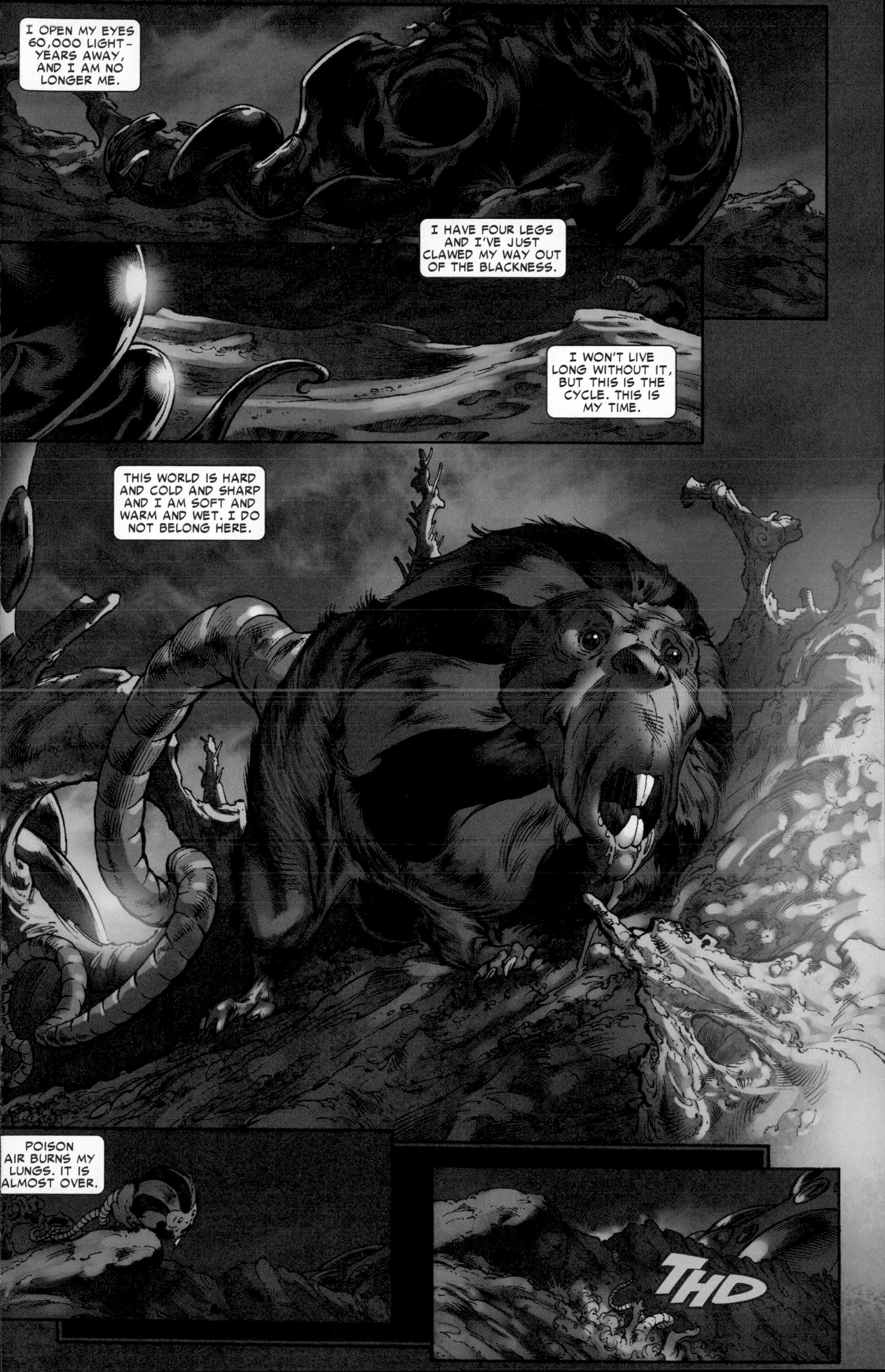
I OPEN MY EYES 60,000 LIGHT-YEARS AWAY, AND I AM NO LONGER ME.
I HAVE FOUR LEGS AND I'VE JUST CLAWED MY WAY OUT OF THE BLACKNESS.
I WON'T LIVE LONG WITHOUT IT, BUT THIS IS THE CYCLE. THIS IS MY TIME.
THIS WORLD IS HARD AND COLD AND SHARP AND I AM SOFT AND WARM AND WET. I DO NOT BELONG HERE.
POISON AIR BURNS MY LUNGS. IT IS ALMOST OVER.
THD

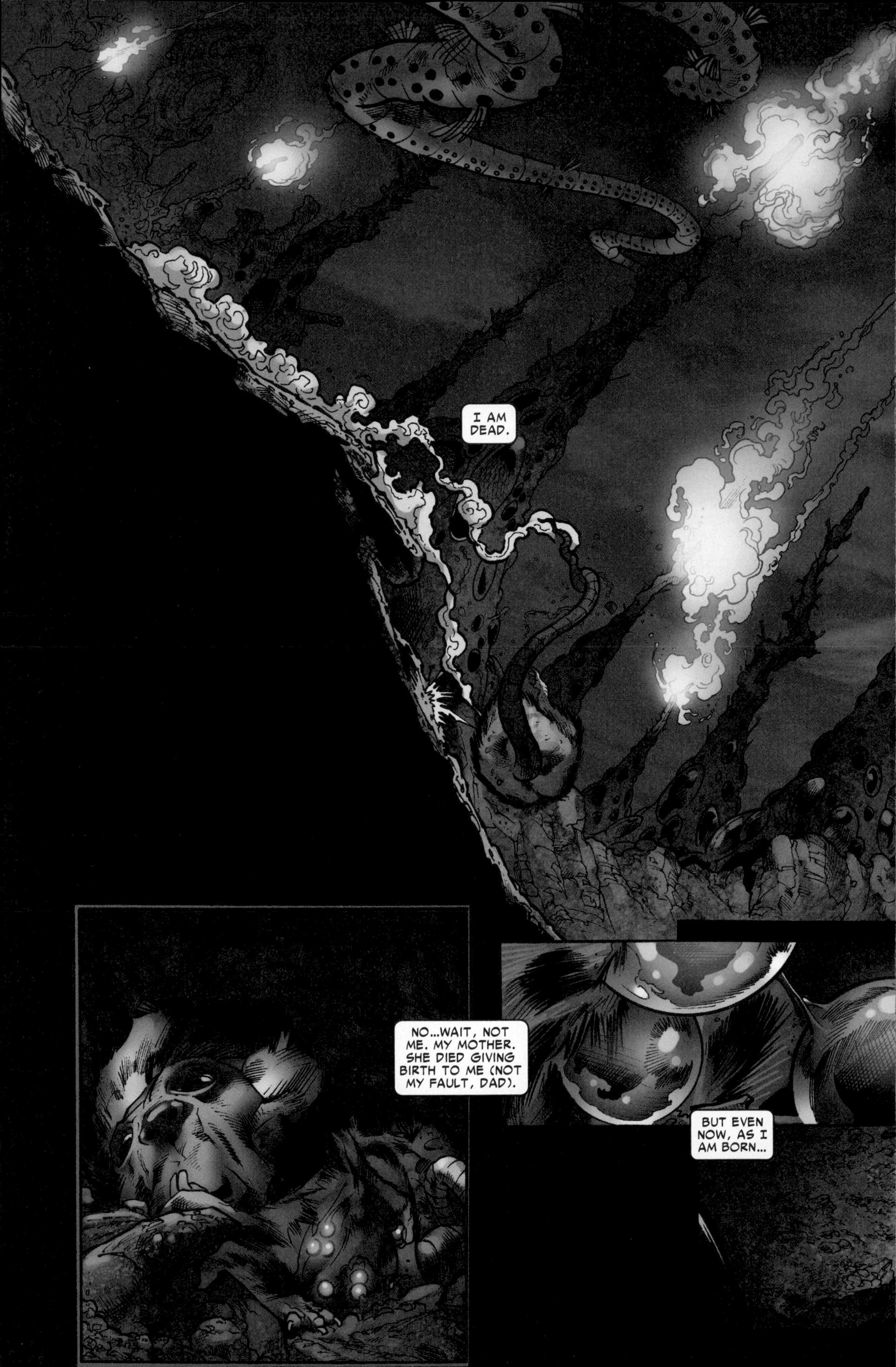
I AM DEAD.
NO...WAIT, NOT ME. MY MOTHER. SHE DIED GIVING BIRTH TO ME (NOT MY FAULT, DAD).
BUT EVEN NOW, AS I AM BORN...

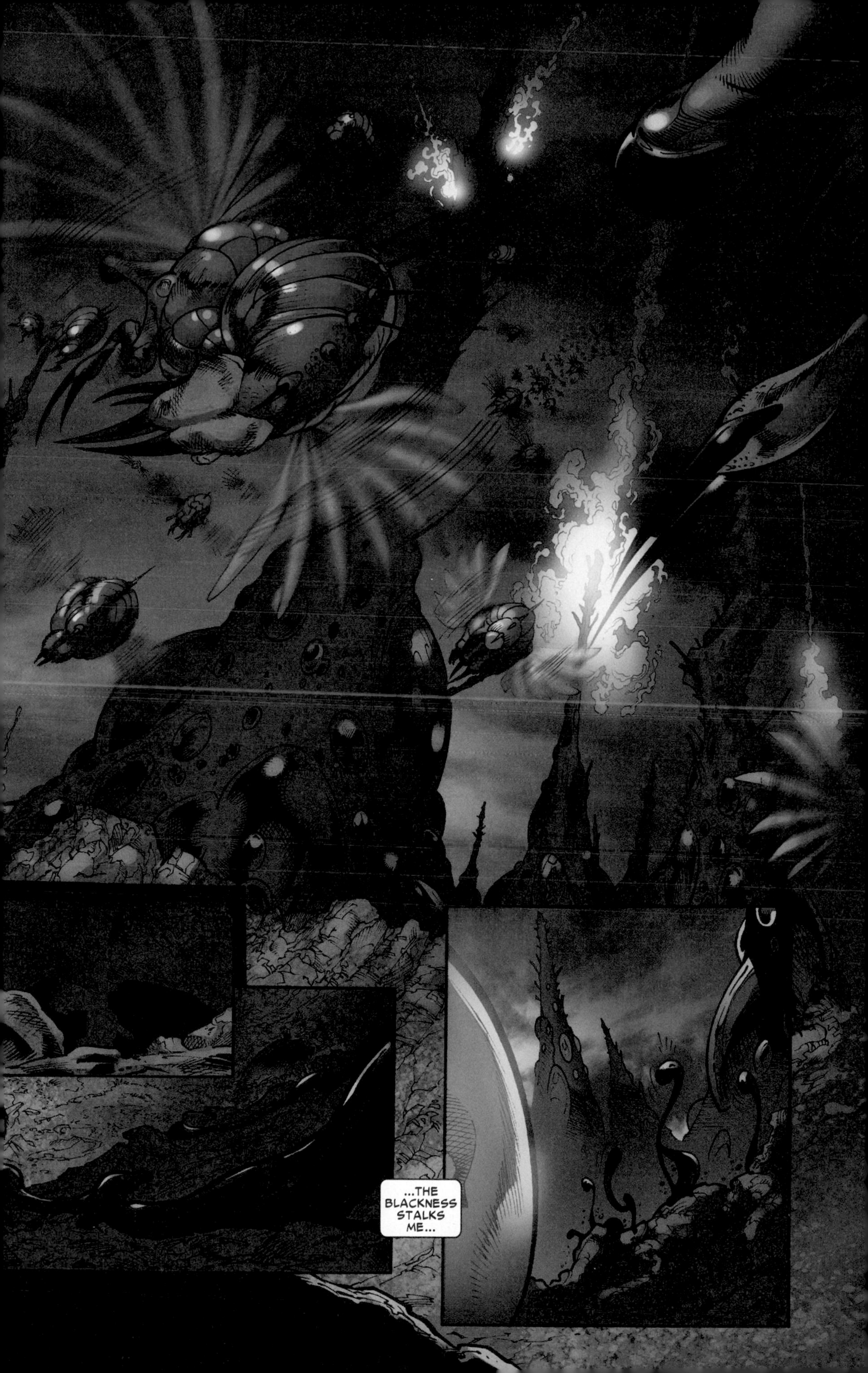
...THE BLACKNESS STALKS ME...

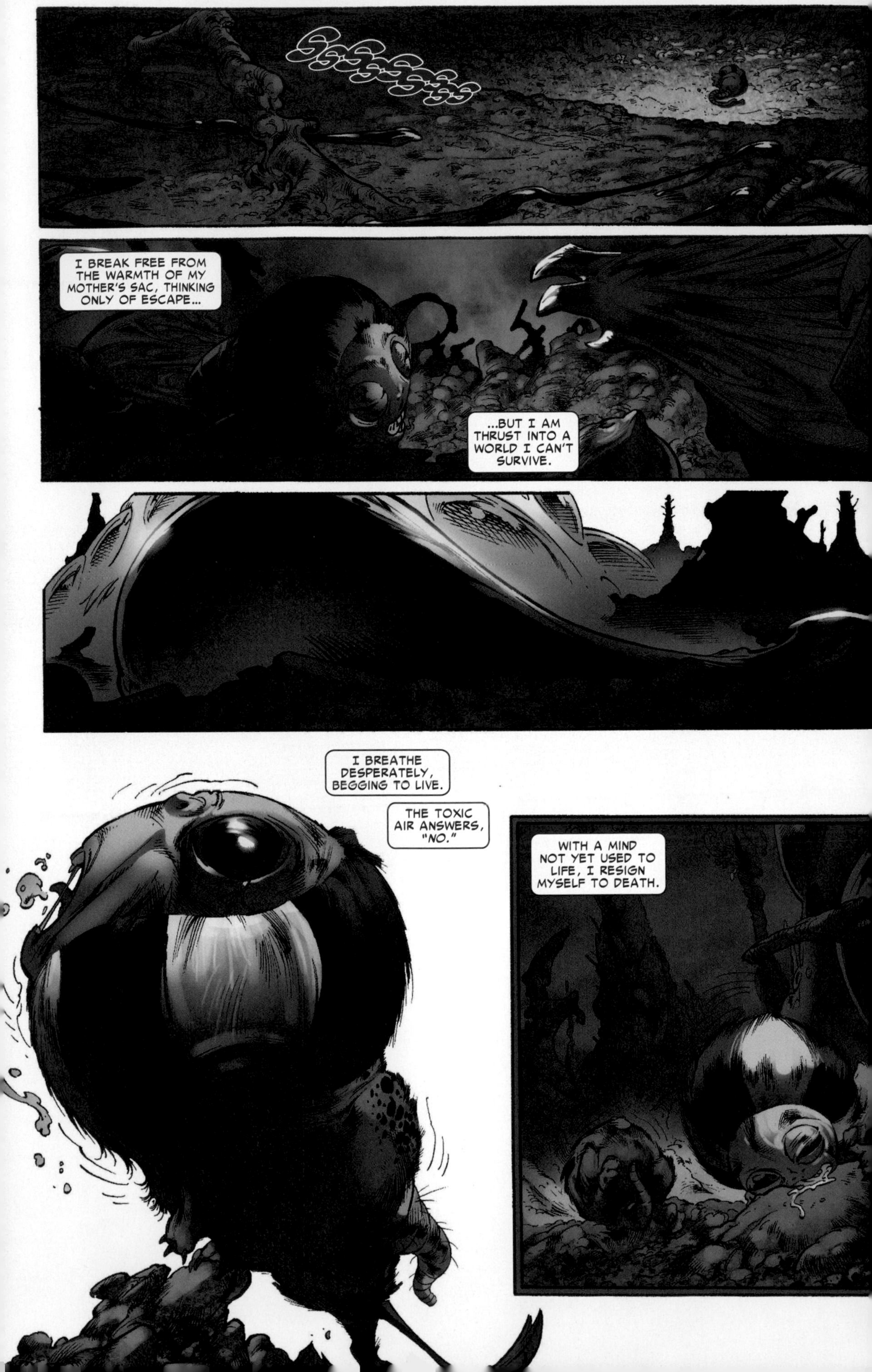
SSSSSSSSS
I BREAK FREE FROM THE WARMTH OF MY MOTHER'S SAC, THINKING ONLY OF ESCAPE...
...BUT I AM THRUST INTO A WORLD I CAN'T SURVIVE.
I BREATHE DESPERATELY, BEGGING TO LIVE.
THE TOXIC AIR ANSWERS, "NO."
WITH A MIND NOT YET USED TO LIFE, I RESIGN MYSELF TO DEATH.

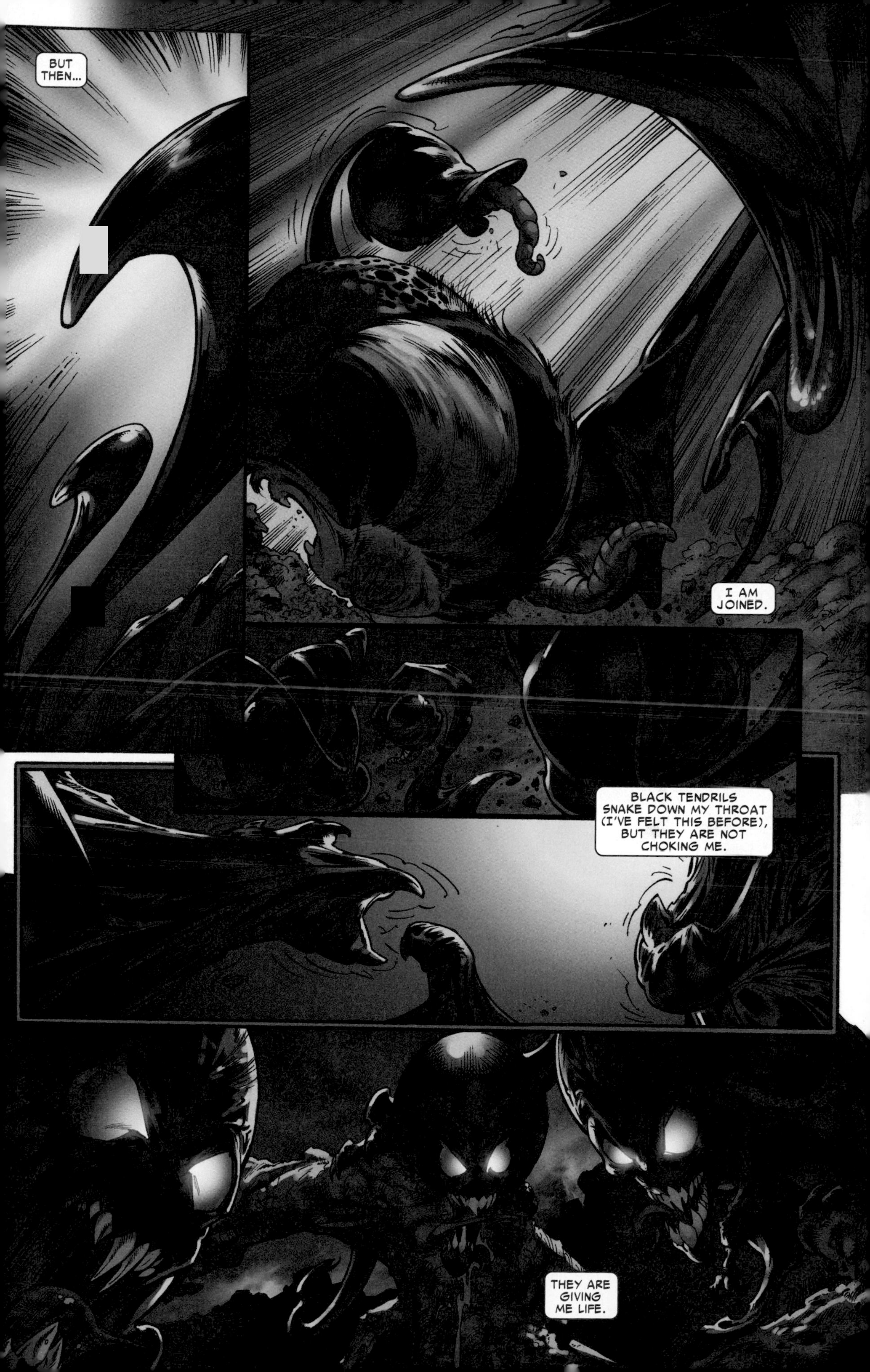
BUT THEN...
I AM JOINED.
BLACK TENDRILS SNAKE DOWN MY THROAT (I'VE FELT THIS BEFORE), BUT THEY ARE NOT CHOKING ME.
THEY ARE GIVING ME LIFE.

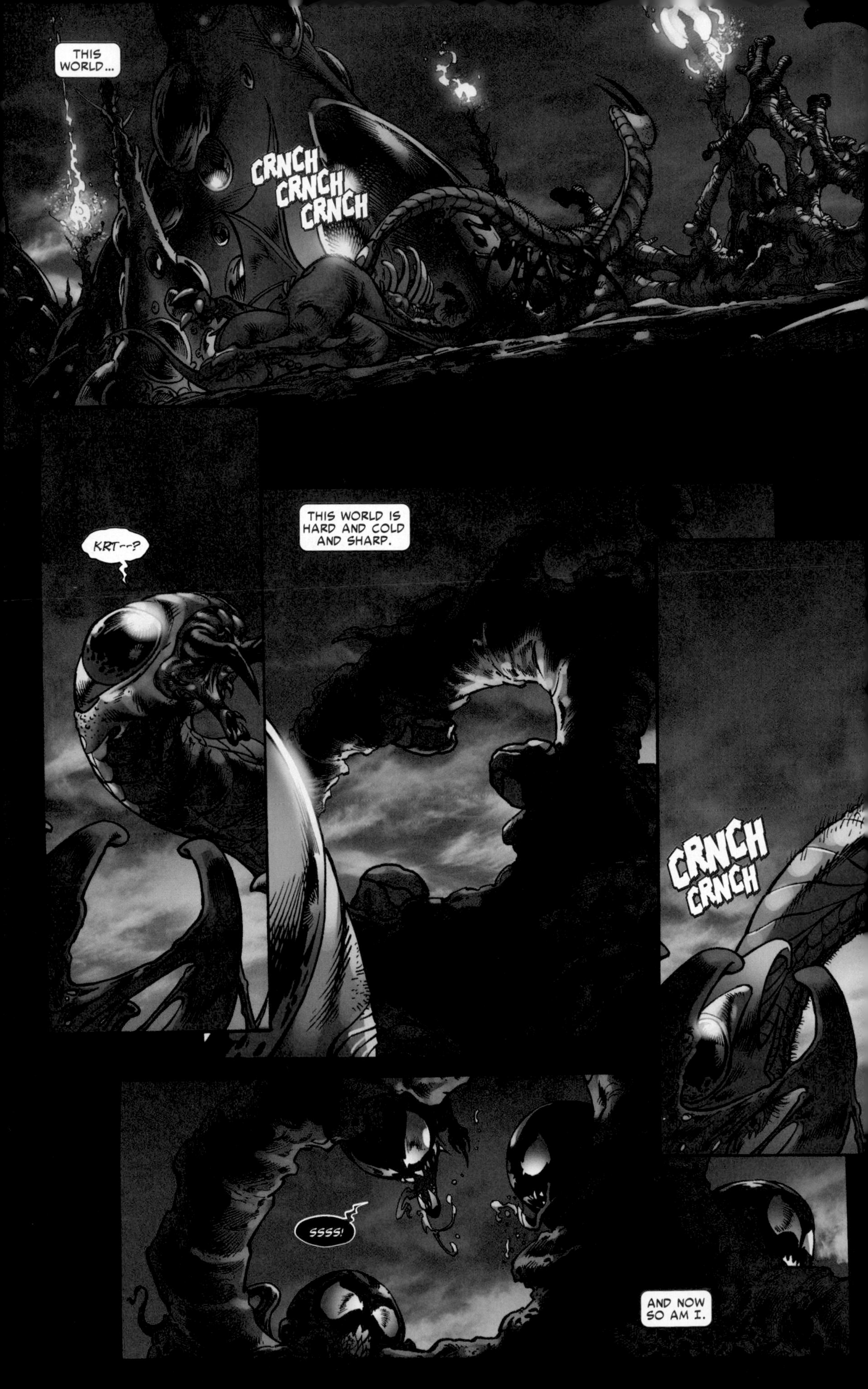
THIS WORLD...
CRNCH CRNCH CRNCH
KRT--?
THIS WORLD IS HARD AND COLD AND SHARP.
CRNCH CRNCH
SSSS!
AND NOW SO AM I.

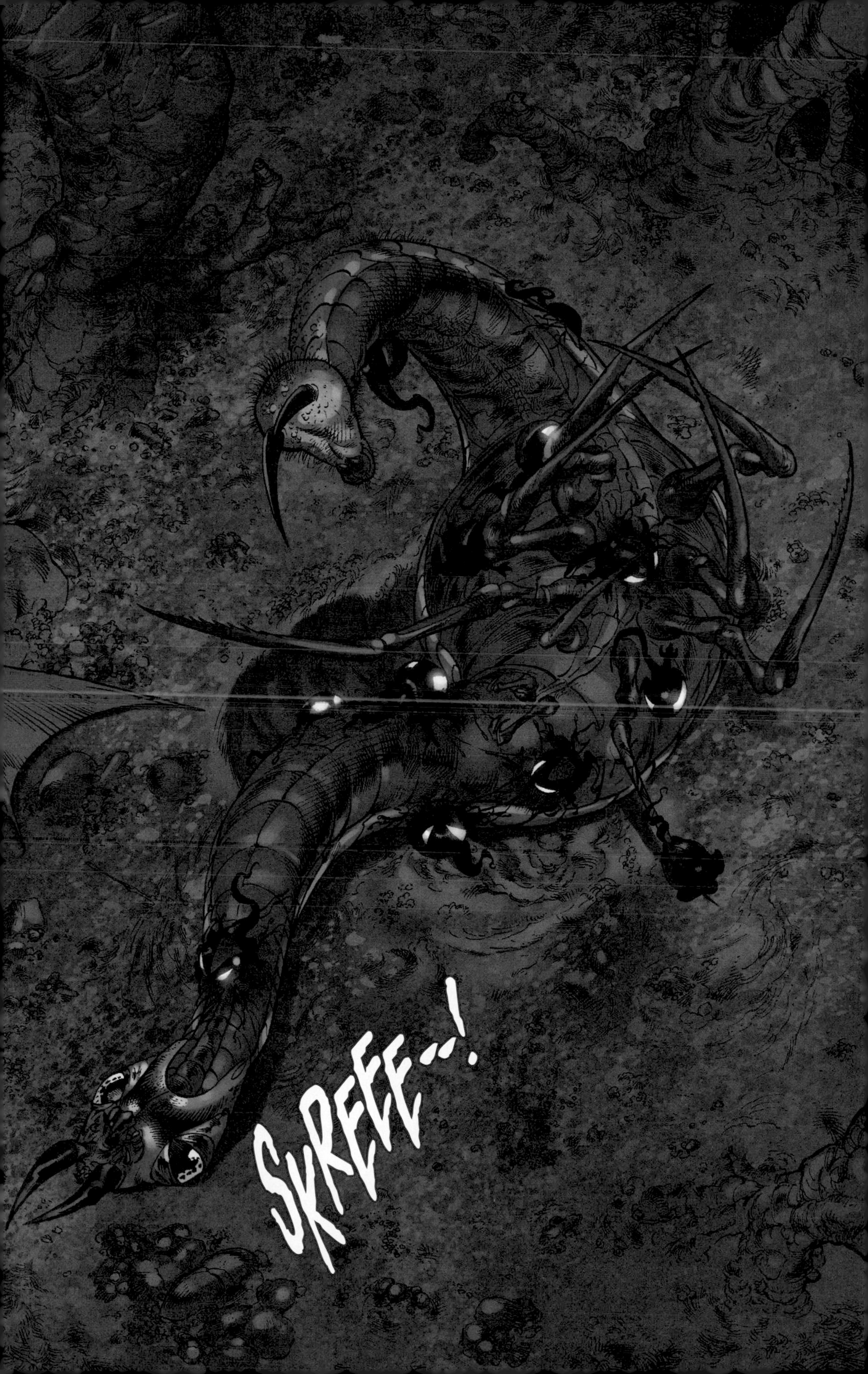
SKREEE--!

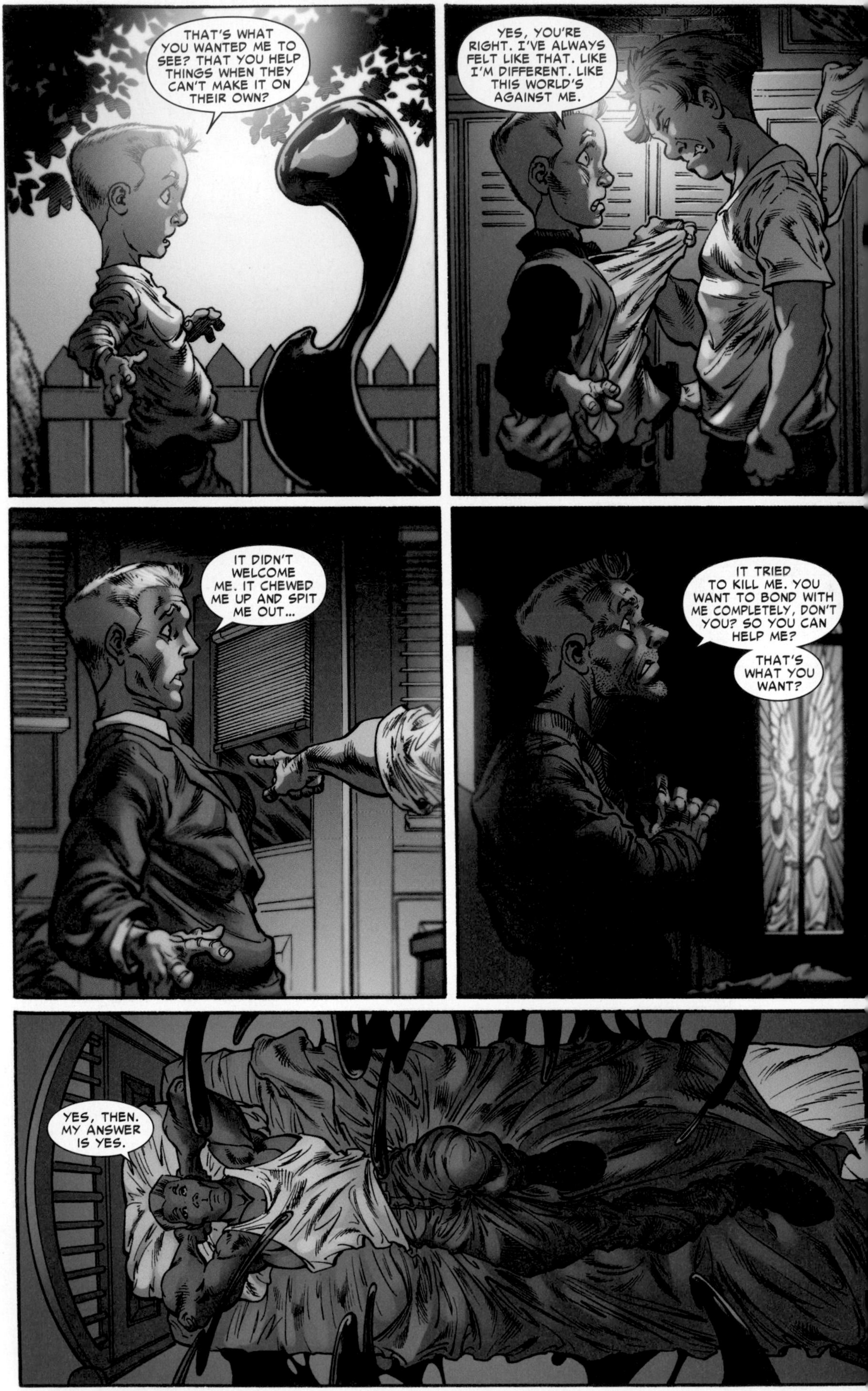
THAT'S WHAT YOU WANTED ME TO SEE? THAT YOU HELP THINGS WHEN THEY CAN'T MAKE IT ON THEIR OWN?
YES, YOU'RE RIGHT. I'VE ALWAYS FELT LIKE THAT. LIKE I'M DIFFERENT. LIKE THIS WORLD'S AGAINST ME.
IT DIDN'T WELCOME ME. IT CHEWED ME UP AND SPIT ME OUT...
IT TRIED TO KILL ME. YOU WANT TO BOND WITH ME COMPLETELY, DON'T YOU? SO YOU CAN HELP ME?
THAT'S WHAT YOU WANT?
YES, THEN. MY ANSWER IS YES.

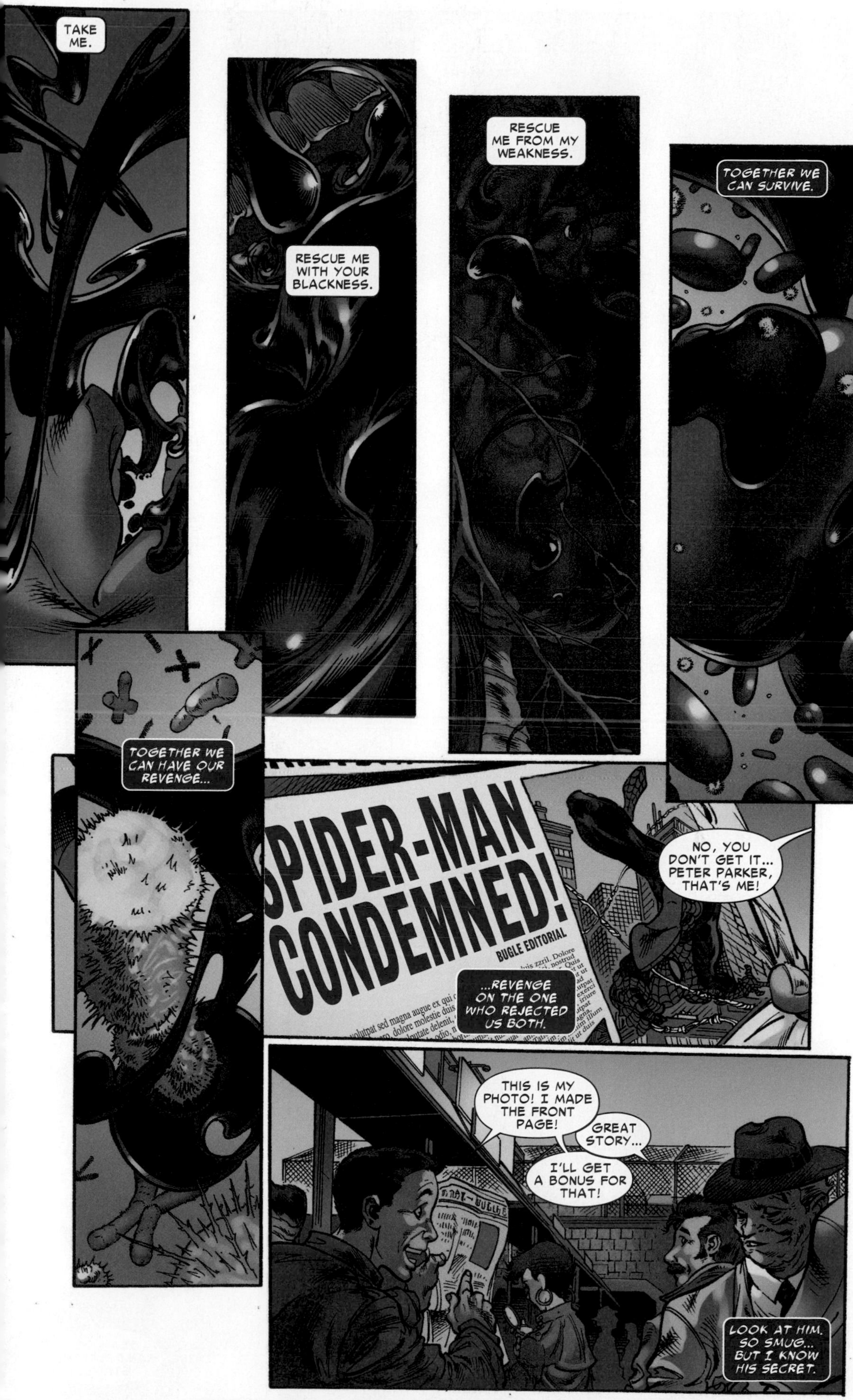
TAKE ME.
RESCUE ME WITH YOUR BLACKNESS.
RESCUE ME FROM MY WEAKNESS.
TOGETHER WE CAN SURVIVE.
TOGETHER WE CAN HAVE OUR REVENGE...
SPIDER-MAN CONDEMNED!
BUGLE EDITORIAL
...REVENGE ON THE ONE WHO REJECTED US BOTH.
NO, YOU DON'T GET IT... PETER PARKER, THAT'S ME!
THIS IS MY PHOTO! I MADE THE FRONT PAGE!
GREAT STORY...
I'LL GET A BONUS FOR THAT!
LOOK AT HIM. SO SMUG... BUT I KNOW HIS SECRET.

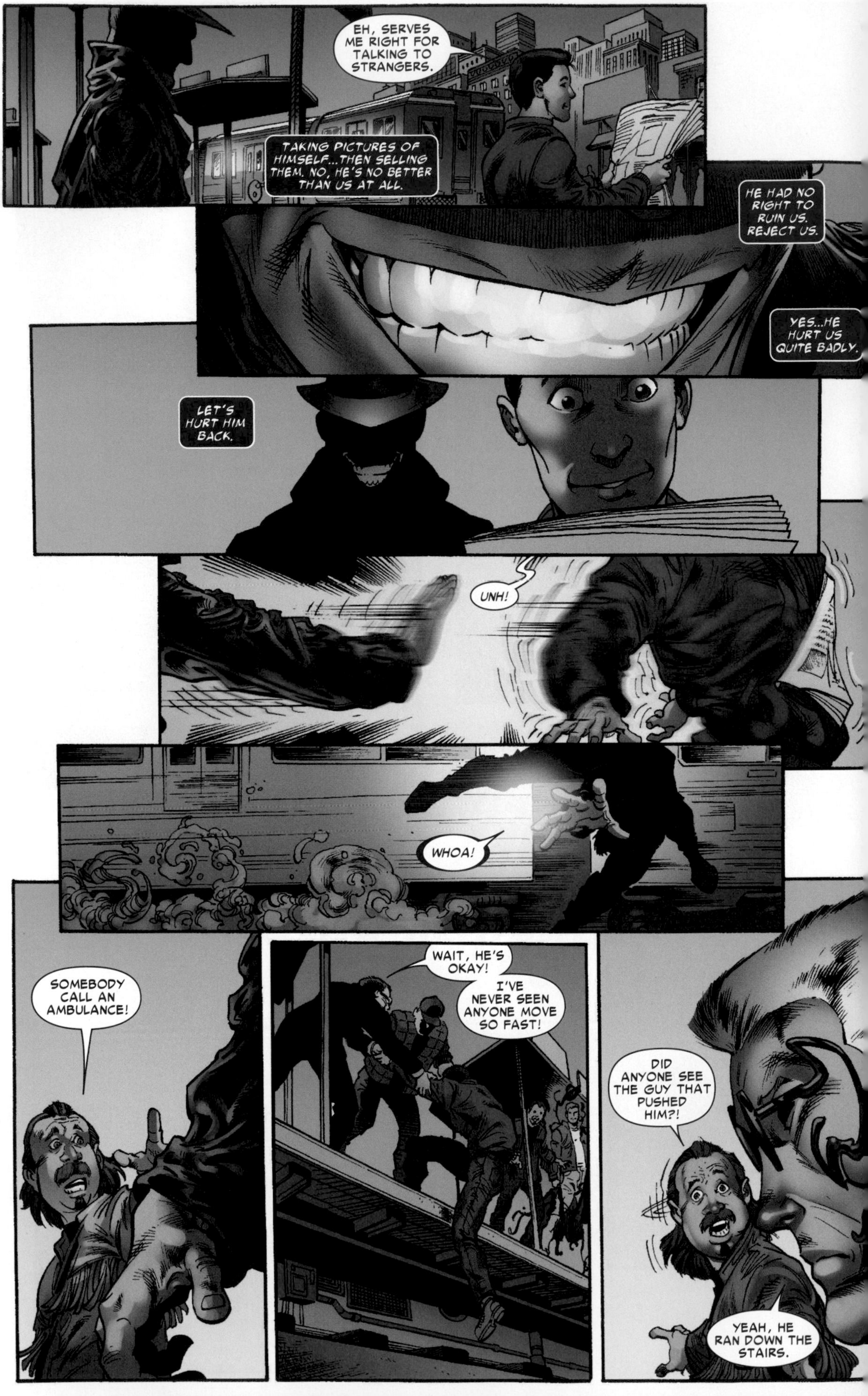
EH, SERVES ME RIGHT FOR TALKING TO STRANGERS.
TAKING PICTURES OF HIMSELF...THEN SELLING THEM. NO, HE'S NO BETTER THAN US AT ALL.
HE HAD NO RIGHT TO RUIN US. REJECT US.
YES...HE HURT US QUITE BADLY.
LET'S HURT HIM BACK.
UNH!
WHOA!
SOMEBODY CALL AN AMBULANCE!
WAIT, HE'S OKAY!
I'VE NEVER SEEN ANYONE MOVE SO FAST!
DID ANYONE SEE THE GUY THAT PUSHED HIM?!
YEAH, HE RAN DOWN THE STAIRS.

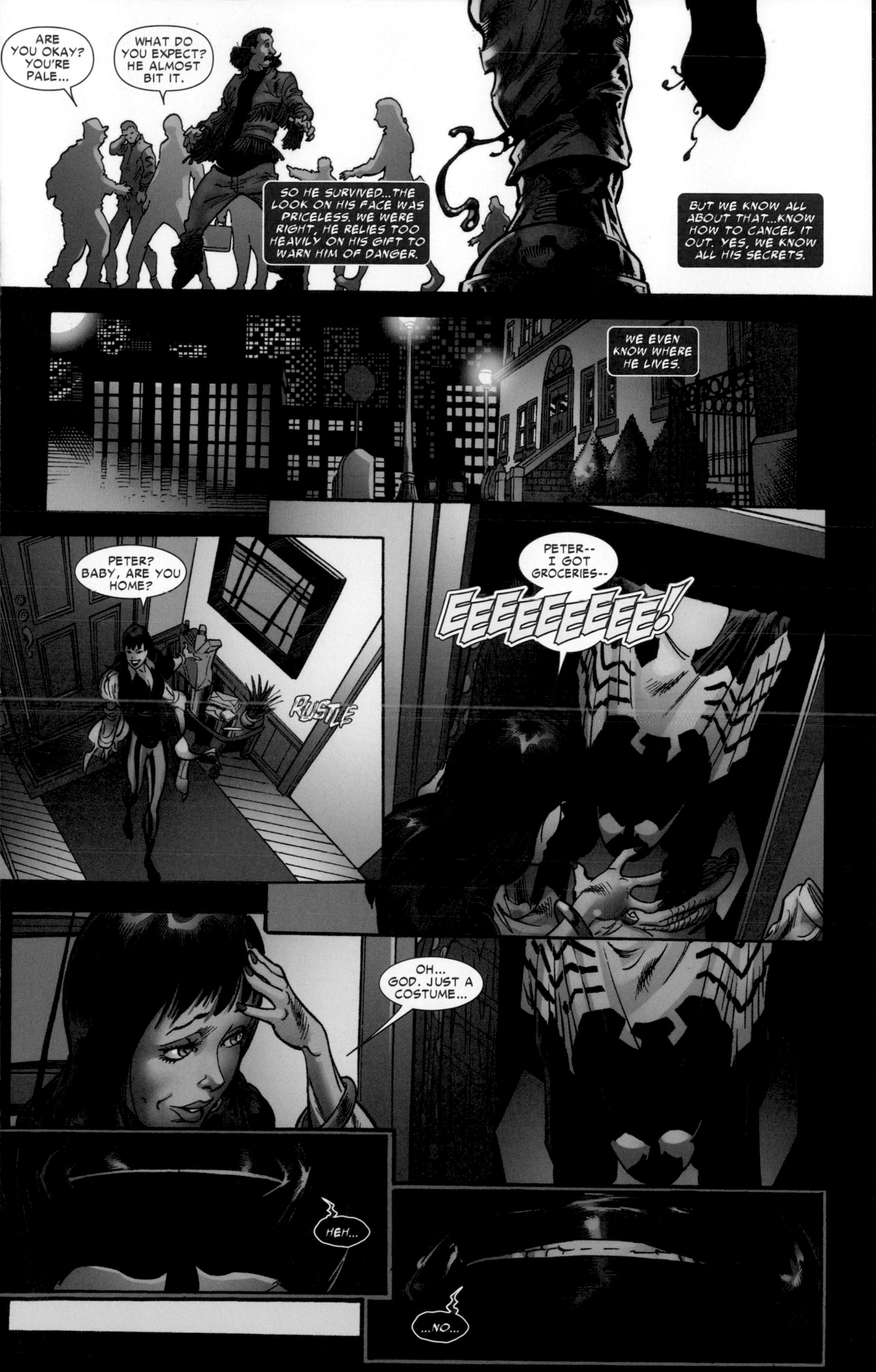
ARE YOU OKAY? YOU'RE PALE...
WHAT DO YOU EXPECT? HE ALMOST BIT IT.
SO HE SURVIVED...THE LOOK ON HIS FACE WAS PRICELESS. WE WERE RIGHT, HE RELIES TOO HEAVILY ON HIS GIFT TO WARN HIM OF DANGER.
BUT WE KNOW ALL ABOUT THAT...KNOW HOW TO CANCEL IT OUT. YES, WE KNOW ALL HIS SECRETS.
WE EVEN KNOW WHERE HE LIVES.
PETER? BABY, ARE YOU HOME?
RUSTLE
PETER-- I GOT GROCERIES--
EEEEEEEEEE!
OH... GOD. JUST A COSTUME...
HEH...
...NO...

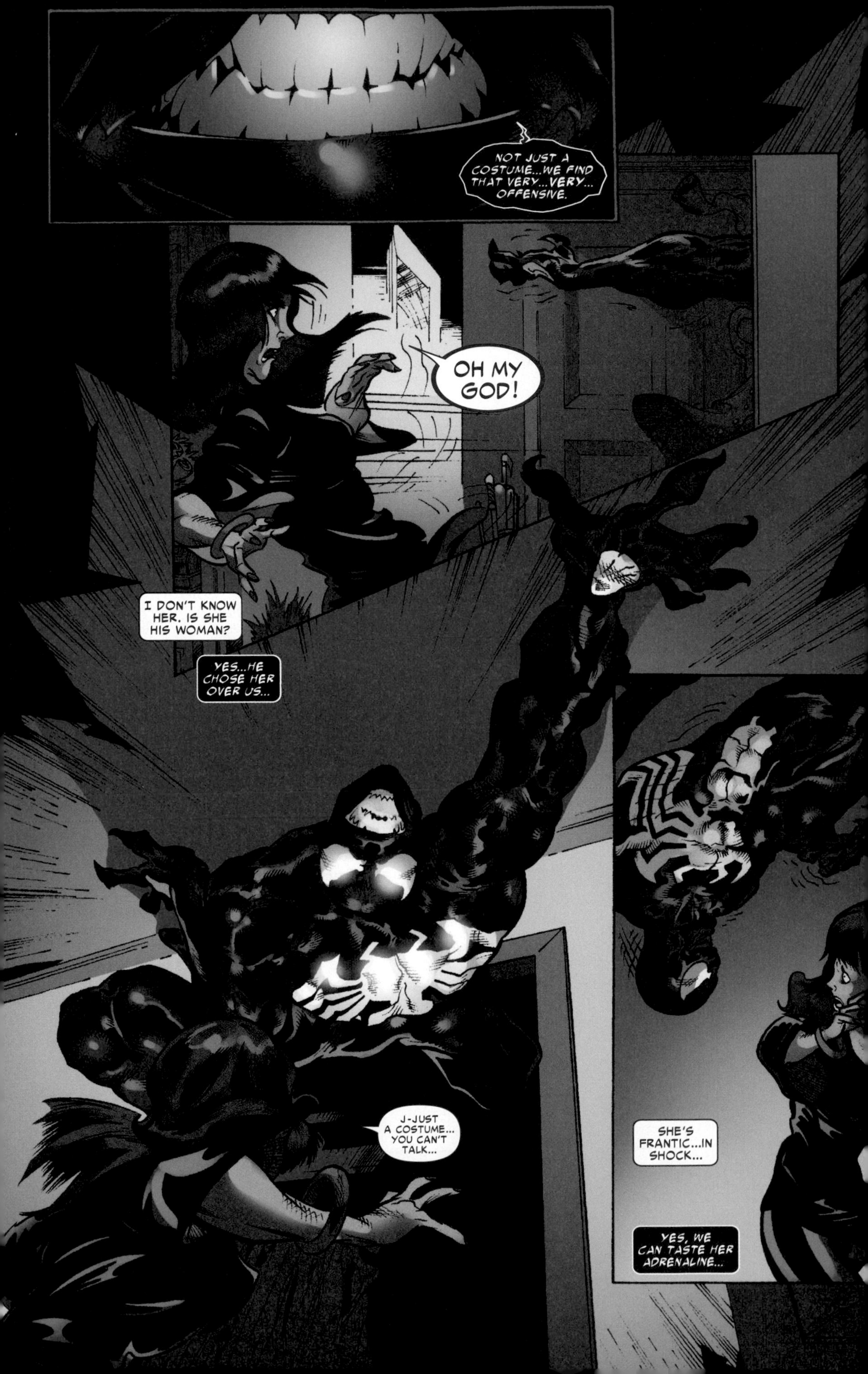

NOT JUST A COSTUME...WE FIND THAT VERY...VERY... OFFENSIVE.
OH MY GOD!
I DON'T KNOW HER. IS SHE HIS WOMAN?
YES...HE CHOSE HER OVER US...
J-JUST A COSTUME... YOU CAN'T TALK...
SHE'S FRANTIC...IN SHOCK...
YES, WE CAN TASTE HER ADRENALINE...

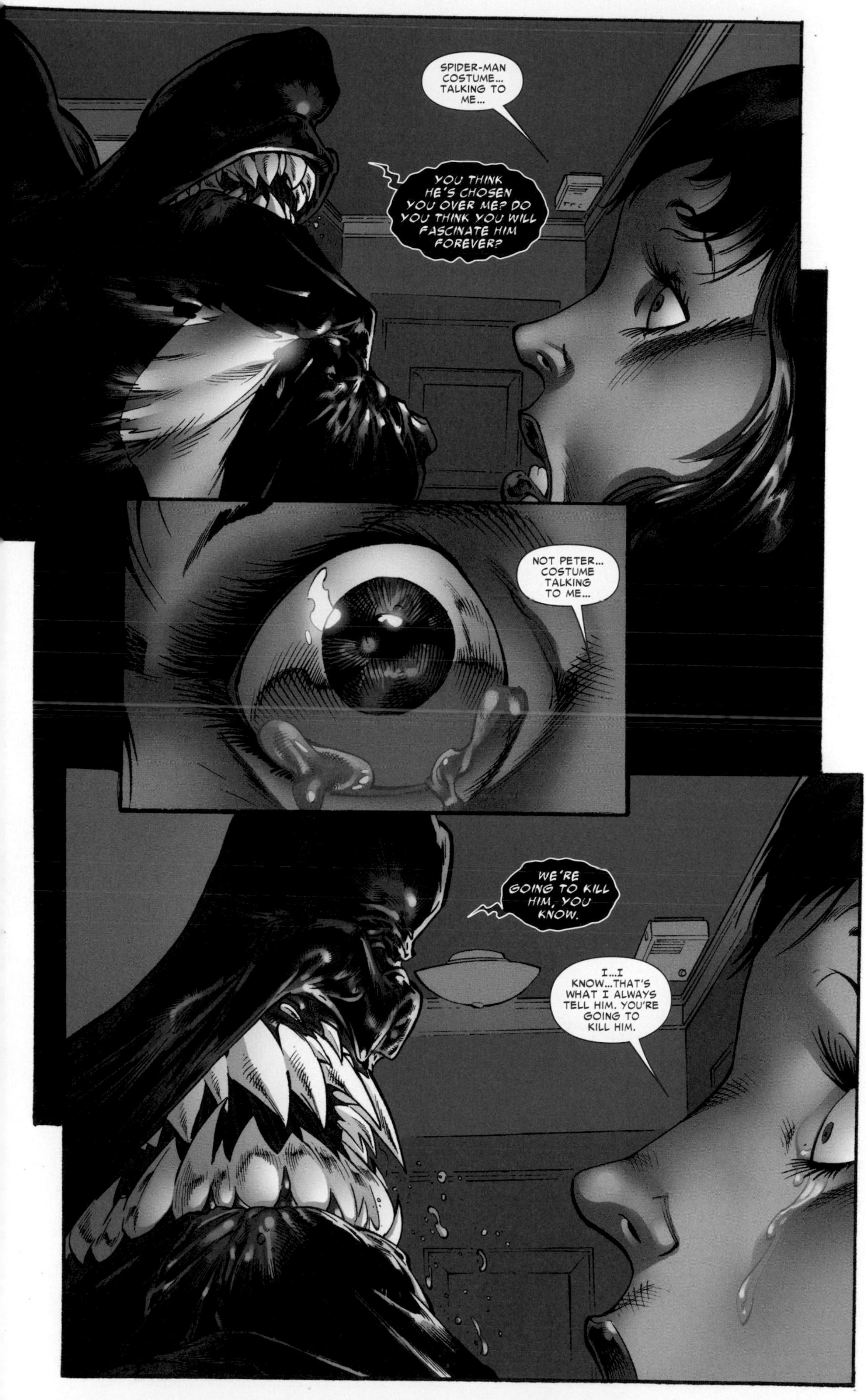
SPIDER-MAN COSTUME... TALKING TO ME...
YOU THINK HE'S CHOSEN YOU OVER ME? DO YOU THINK YOU WILL FASCINATE HIM FOREVER?
NOT PETER... COSTUME TALKING TO ME...
WE'RE GOING TO KILL HIM, YOU KNOW.
I...I KNOW...THAT'S WHAT I ALWAYS TELL HIM. YOU'RE GOING TO KILL HIM.

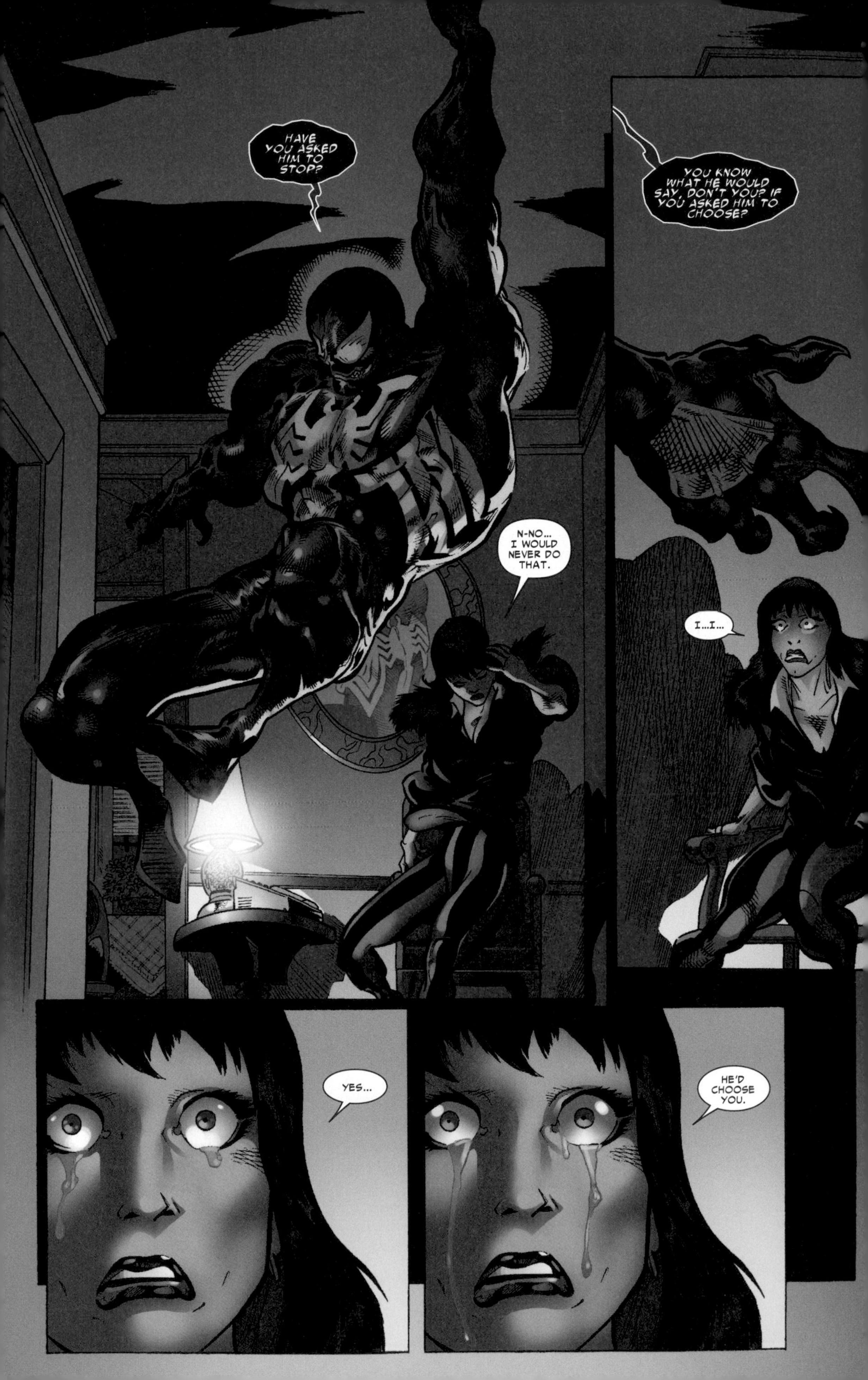
HAVE YOU ASKED HIM TO STOP?
YOU KNOW WHAT HE WOULD SAY, DON'T YOU? IF YOU ASKED HIM TO CHOOSE?
N-NO... I WOULD NEVER DO THAT.
I...I...
YES...
HE'D CHOOSE YOU.

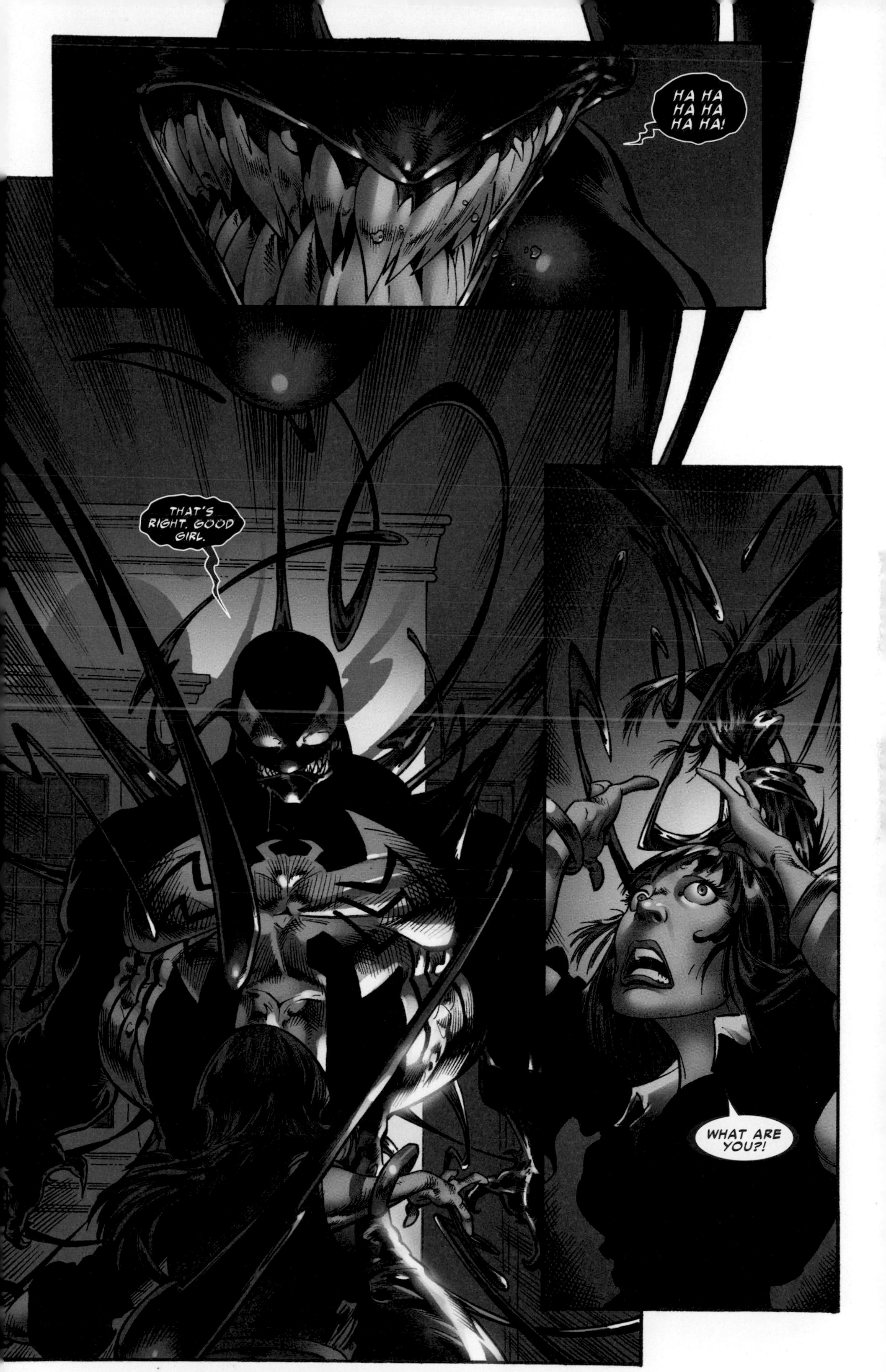
HA HA
HA HA
HA HA!
THAT'S RIGHT. GOOD GIRL.
WHAT ARE YOU?!

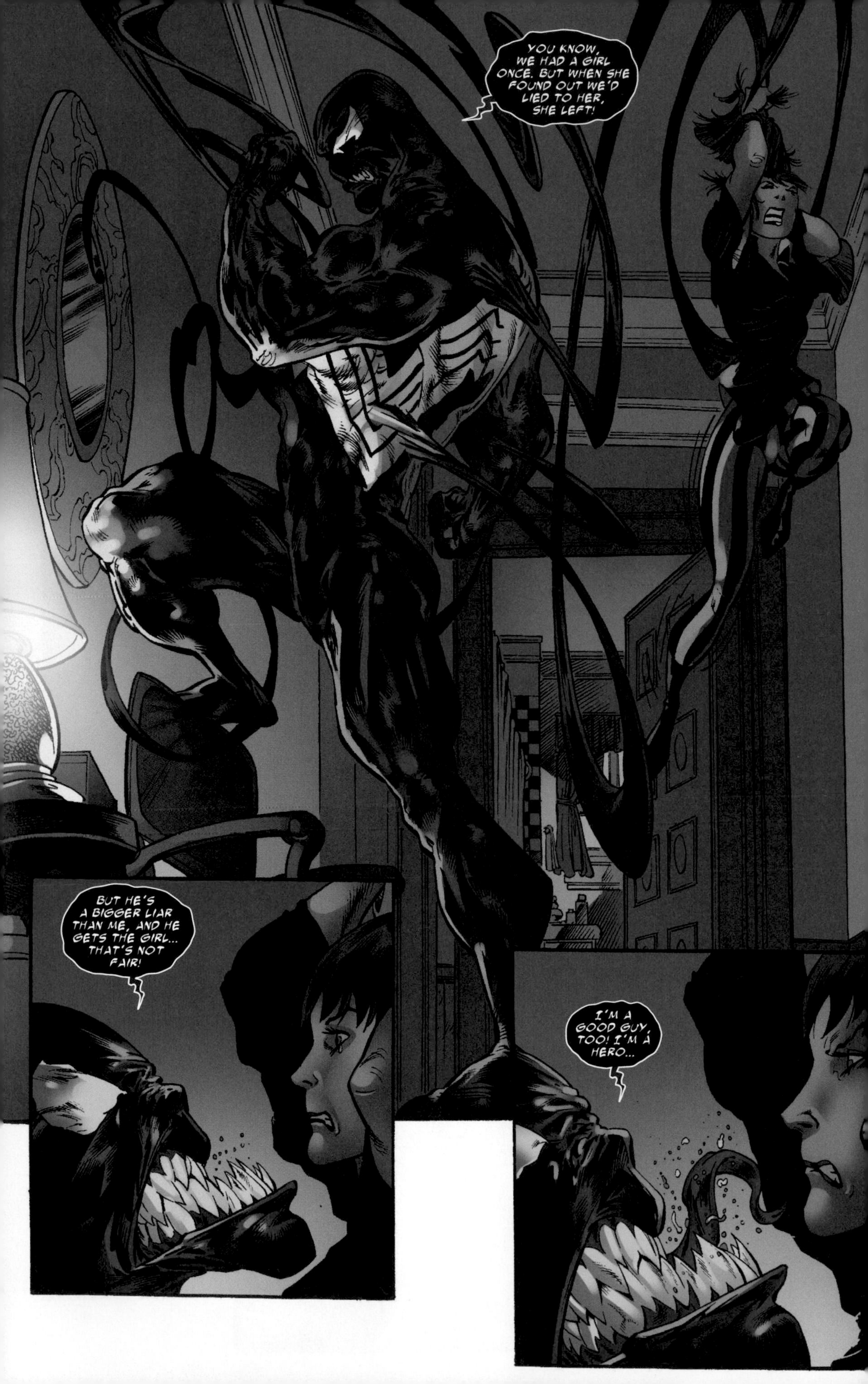
YOU KNOW, WE HAD A GIRL ONCE. BUT WHEN SHE FOUND OUT WE'D LIED TO HER, SHE LEFT!
BUT HE'S A BIGGER LIAR THAN ME, AND HE GETS THE GIRL... THAT'S NOT FAIR!
I'M A GOOD GUY, TOO! I'M A HERO...

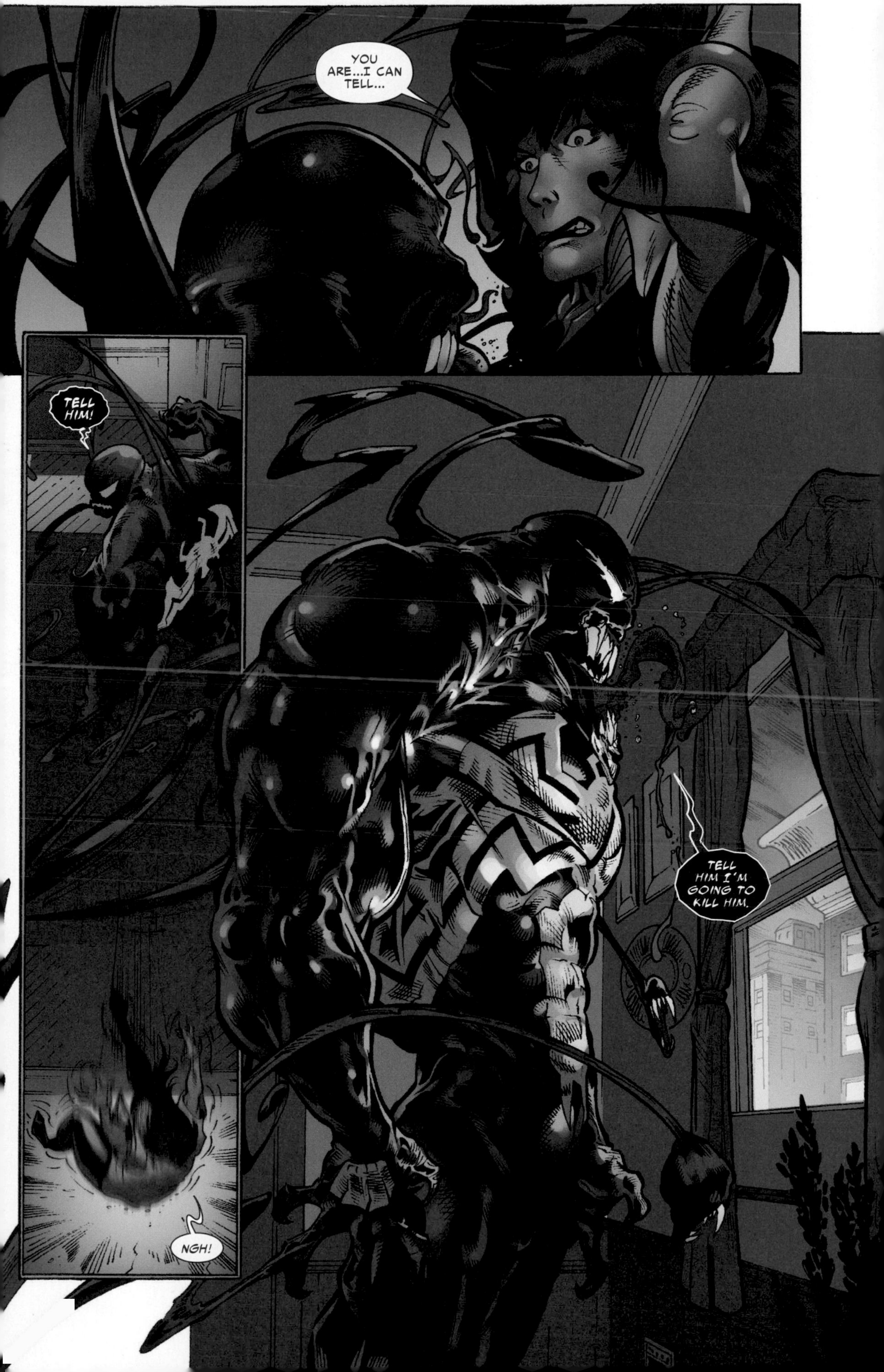
YOU ARE...I CAN TELL...
TELL HIM!
NGH!
TELL HIM I'M GOING TO KILL HIM.

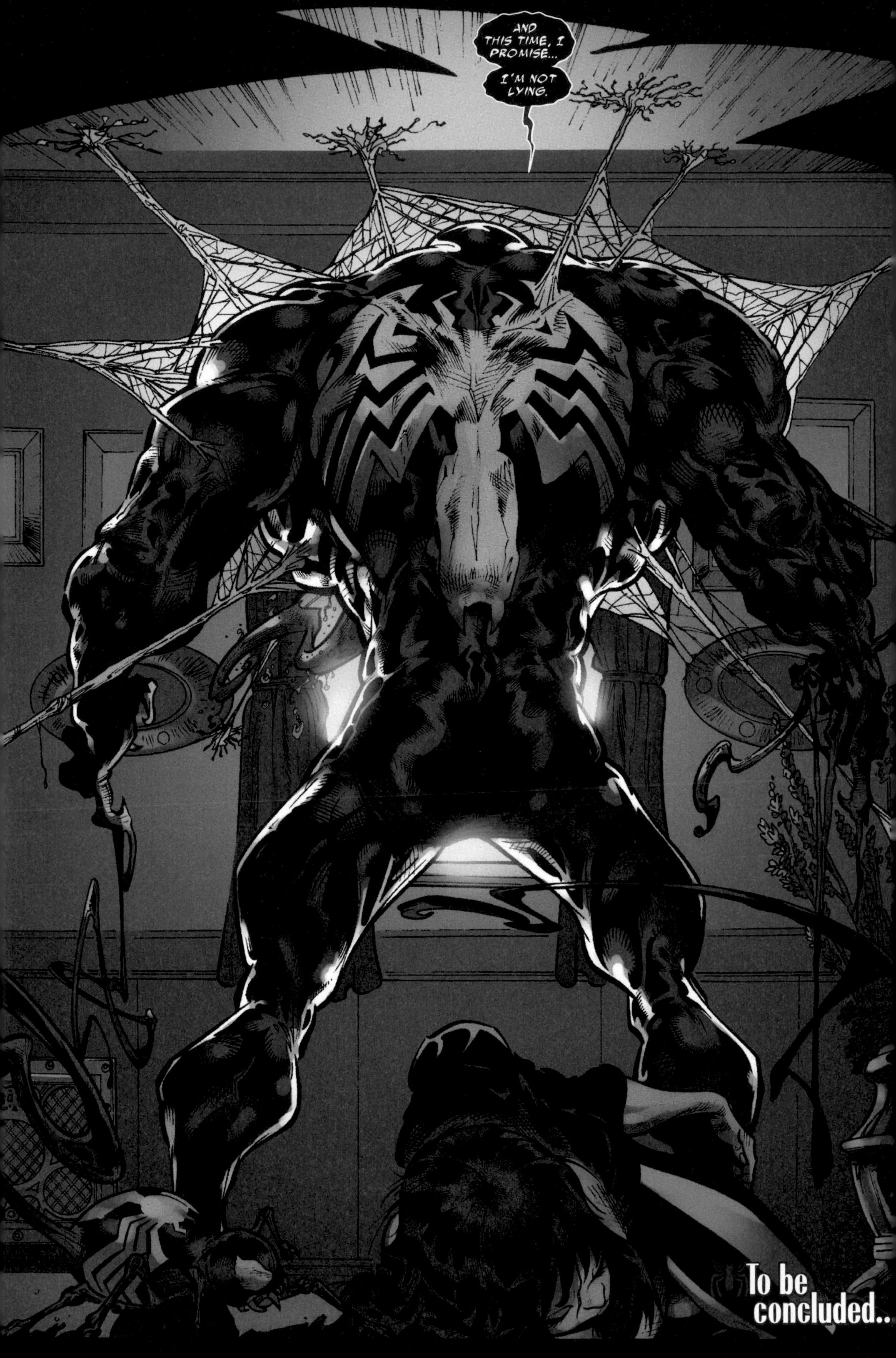
AND THIS TIME, I PROMISE...
I'M NOT LYING.
To be concluded...

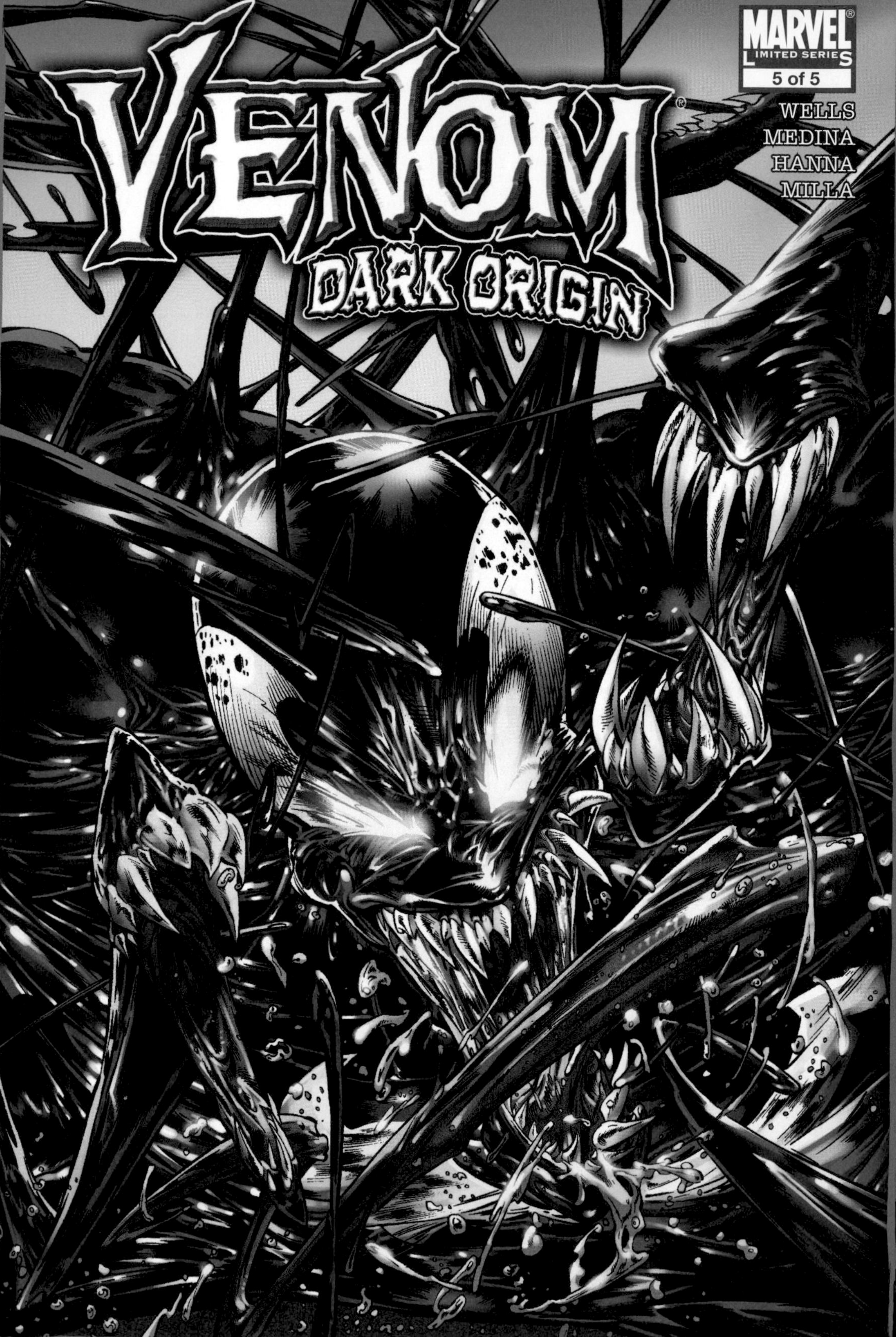

MARVEL®
LIMITED SERIES
5 of 5
VENOM®
DARK ORIGIN
WELLS
MEDINA
HANNA
MILLA

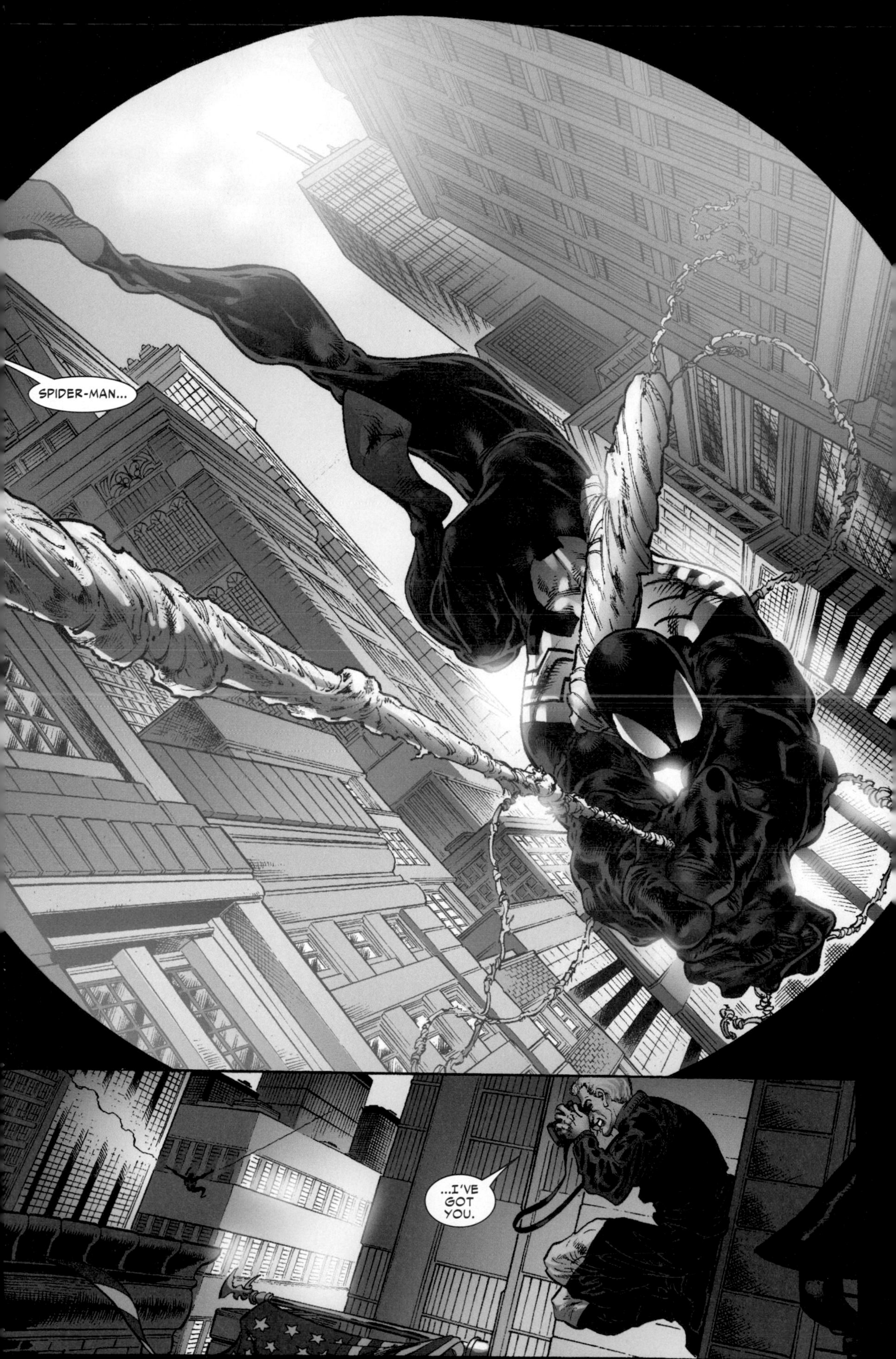
SPIDER-MAN...
...I'VE GOT YOU.

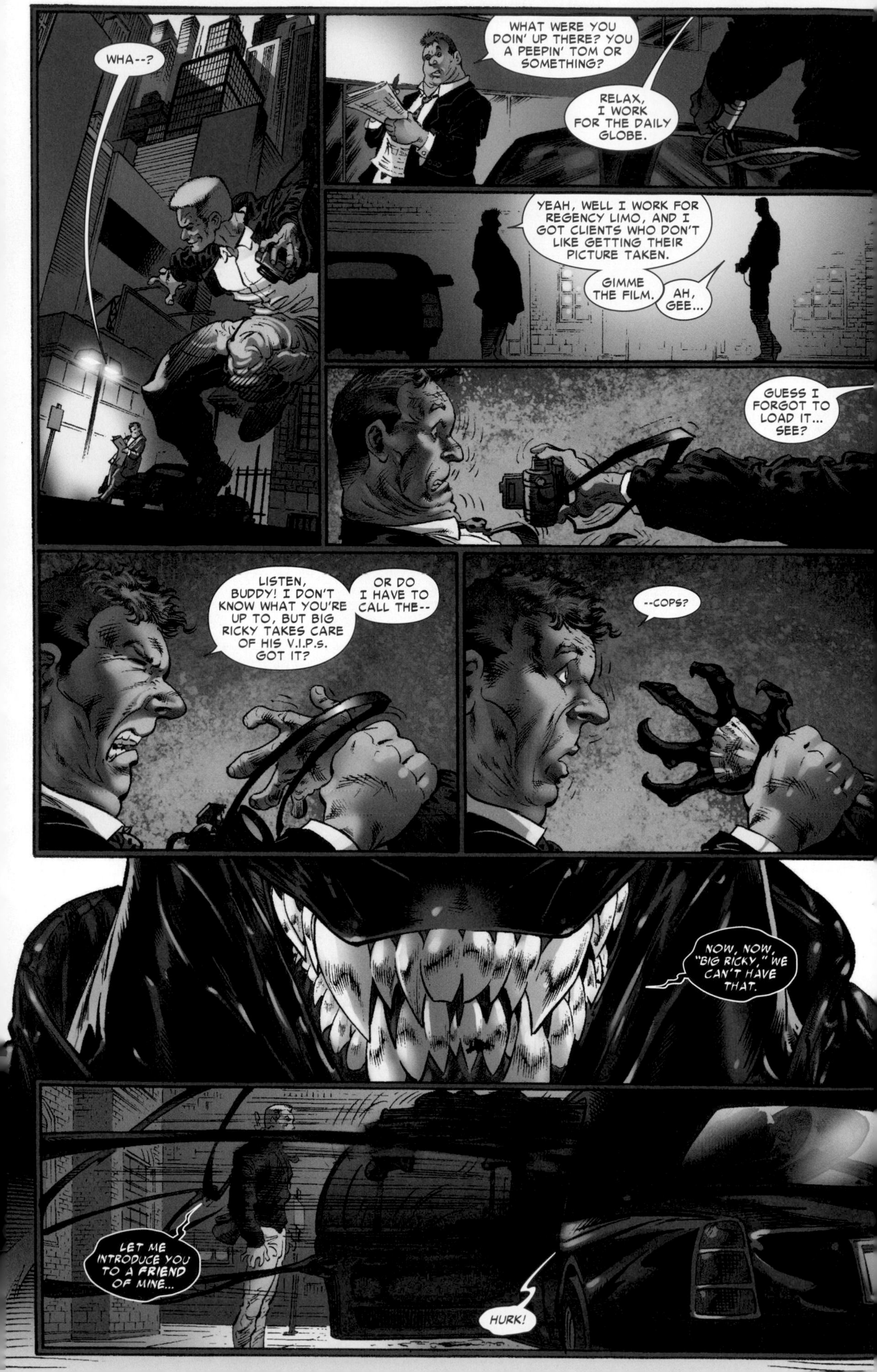
WHA--?
WHAT WERE YOU DOIN' UP THERE? YOU A PEEPIN' TOM OR SOMETHING?
RELAX, I WORK FOR THE DAILY GLOBE.
YEAH, WELL I WORK FOR REGENCY LIMO, AND I GOT CLIENTS WHO DON'T LIKE GETTING THEIR PICTURE TAKEN.
GIMME THE FILM.
AH, GEE...
GUESS I FORGOT TO LOAD IT... SEE?
LISTEN, BUDDY! I DON'T KNOW WHAT YOU'RE UP TO, BUT BIG RICKY TAKES CARE OF HIS V.I.P.s. GOT IT?
OR DO I HAVE TO CALL THE--
--COPS?
NOW, NOW, "BIG RICKY," WE CAN'T HAVE THAT.
LET ME INTRODUCE YOU TO A FRIEND OF MINE...
HURK!

I AGREE. INNOCENT DEATH IS ALWAYS UNPLEASANT... BUT HE WOULD HAVE BETRAYED US.

PARKER CAN'T KNOW WE FOUND HIM, OR HE MIGHT MOVE AGAIN...LIKE HE DID AFTER OUR VISIT TO HIS *WOMAN.*

HELLO, MA'AM.

WE SHOULD QUIET THIS MAN *PERMANENTLY.* IT'S EASIER THAT WAY.

Eddie Brock's Apartment.

NO...NO... THIS IS NECESSARY. MORE MUSCLE IS MORE FOR YOU TO WORK WITH.

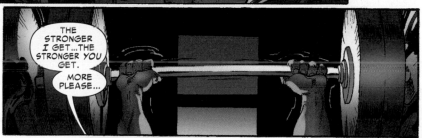

THE STRONGER *I* GET...THE STRONGER *YOU* GET.

MORE PLEASE...

BUT YOU'RE RIGHT... WE'VE HAD OUR FUN.

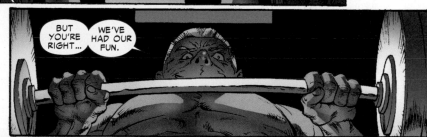

HHHNNNNNNNARRGH!

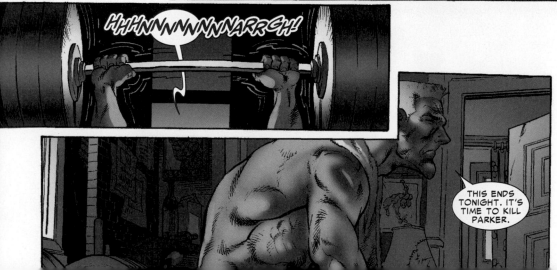

THIS ENDS TONIGHT. IT'S TIME TO KILL PARKER.

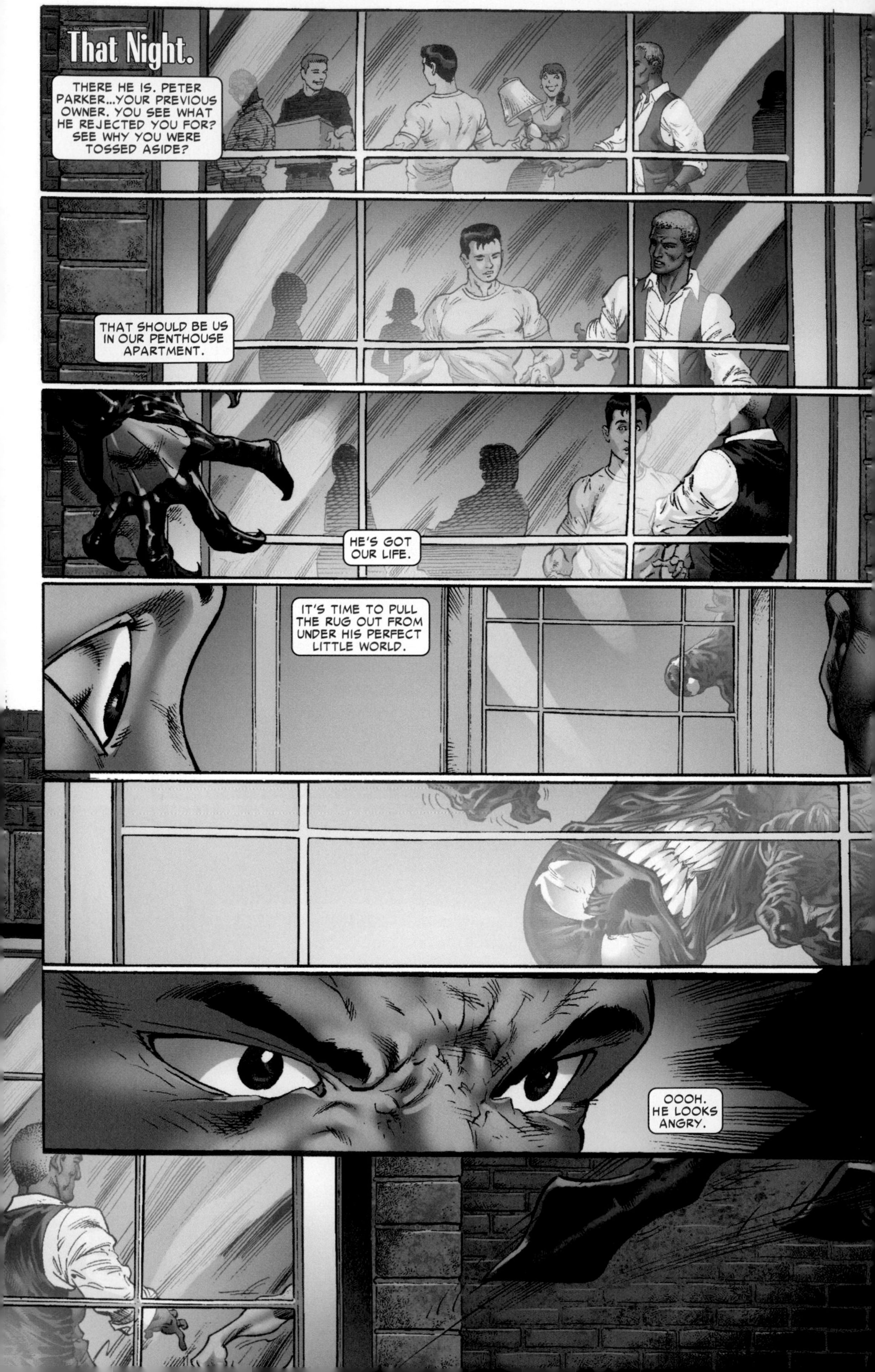
That Night.
THERE HE IS. PETER PARKER...YOUR PREVIOUS OWNER. YOU SEE WHAT HE REJECTED YOU FOR? SEE WHY YOU WERE TOSSED ASIDE?
THAT SHOULD BE US IN OUR PENTHOUSE APARTMENT.
HE'S GOT OUR LIFE.
IT'S TIME TO PULL THE RUG OUT FROM UNDER HIS PERFECT LITTLE WORLD.
OOOH. HE LOOKS ANGRY.

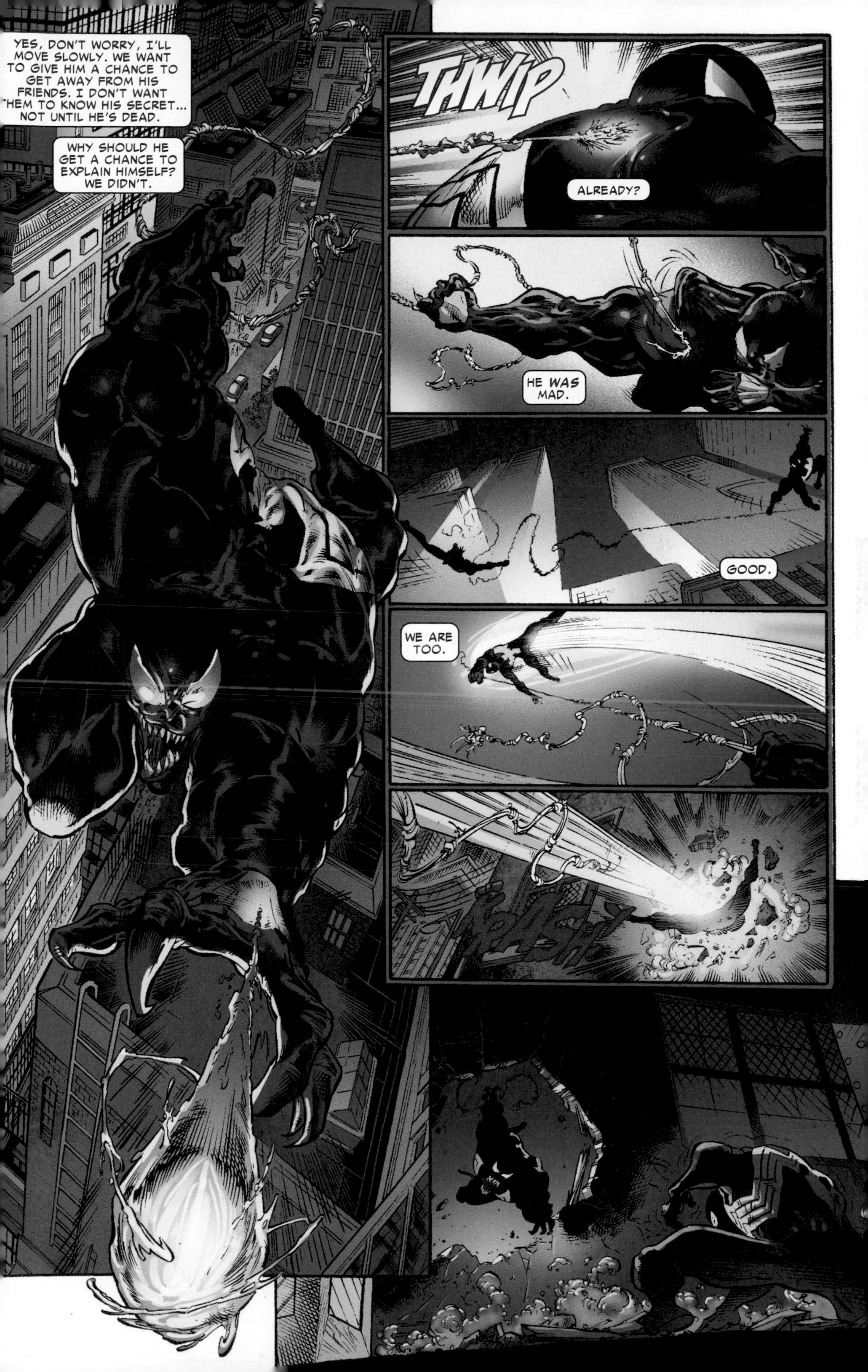
YES, DON'T WORRY, I'LL MOVE SLOWLY. WE WANT TO GIVE HIM A CHANCE TO GET AWAY FROM HIS FRIENDS. I DON'T WANT THEM TO KNOW HIS SECRET... NOT UNTIL HE'S DEAD.
WHY SHOULD HE GET A CHANCE TO EXPLAIN HIMSELF? WE DIDN'T.
THWIP
ALREADY?
HE WAS MAD.
GOOD.
WE ARE TOO.

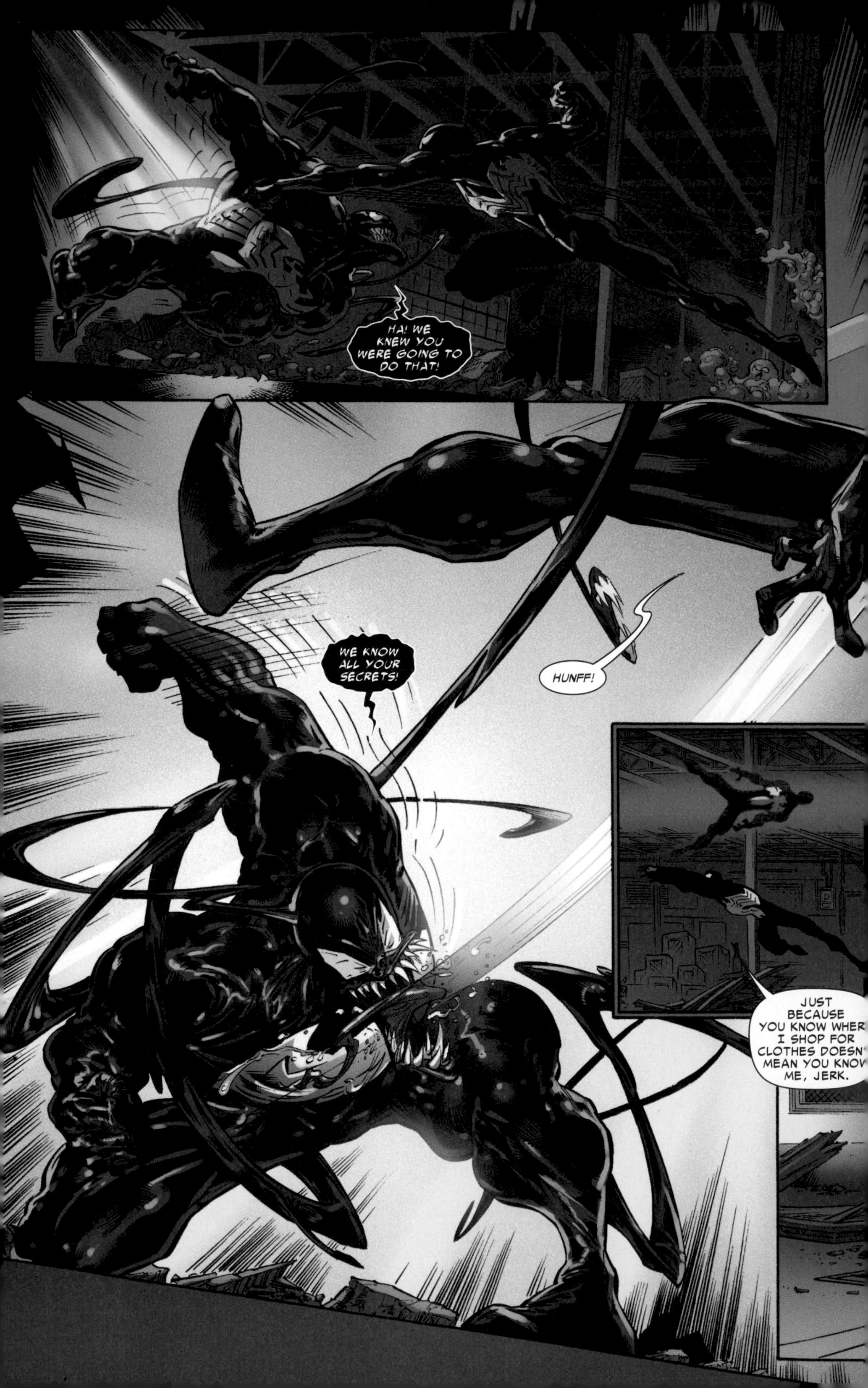
HA! WE KNEW YOU WERE GOING TO DO THAT!
WE KNOW ALL YOUR SECRETS!
HUNFF!
JUST BECAUSE YOU KNOW WHER I SHOP FOR CLOTHES DOESN' MEAN YOU KNOW ME, JERK.

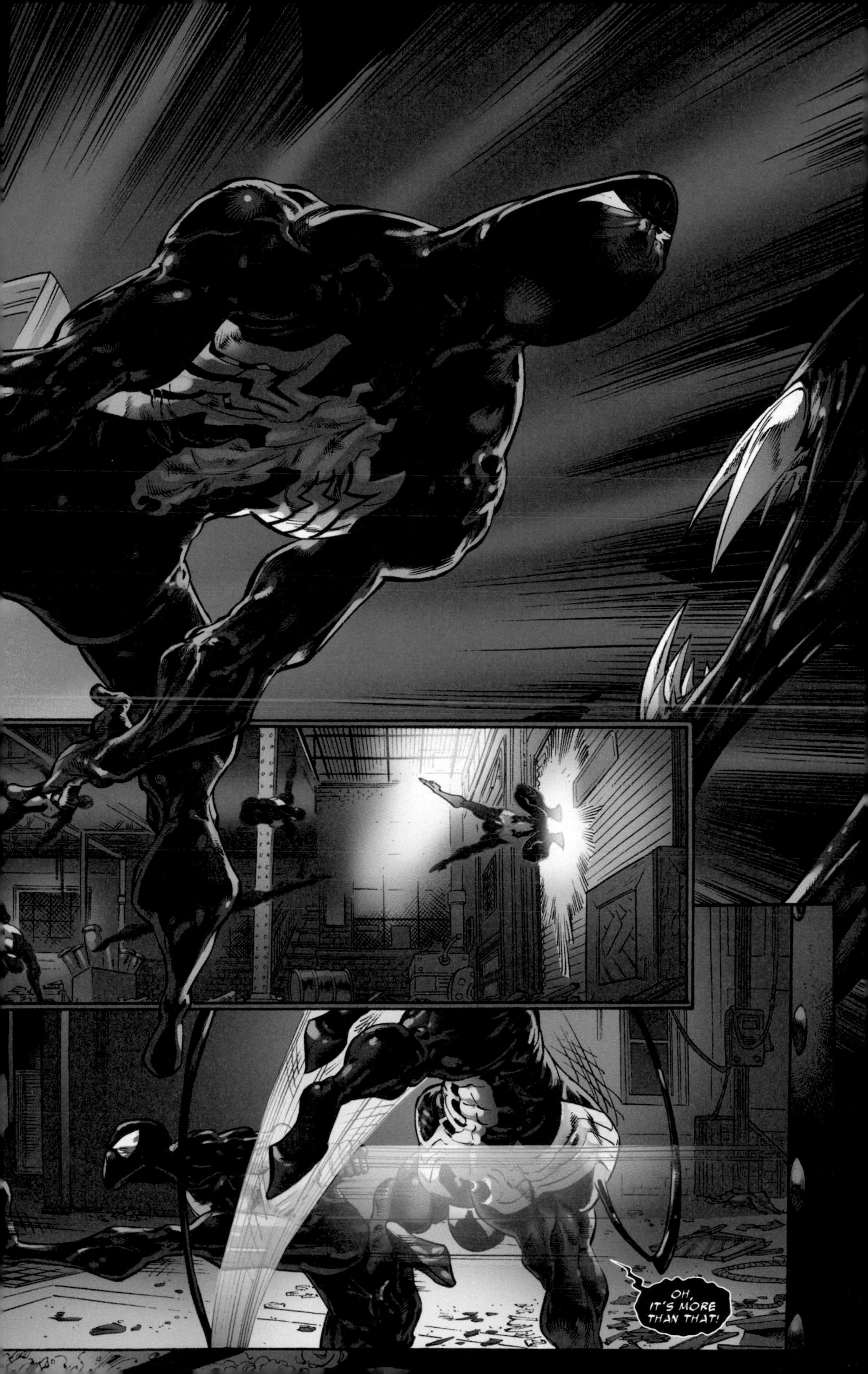
OH, IT'S MORE THAN THAT!

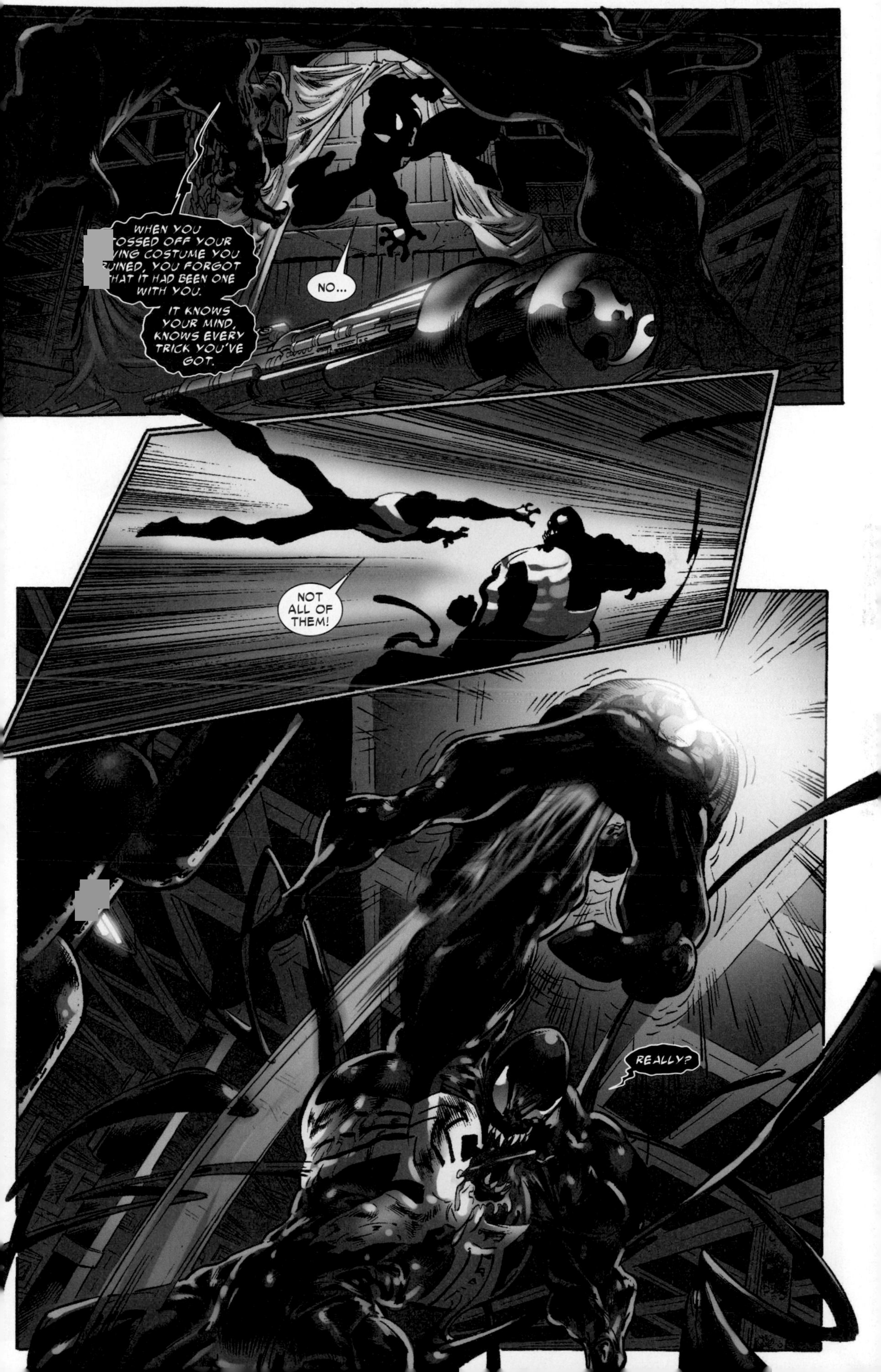
WHEN YOU TOSSED OFF YOUR VING COSTUME YOU UINED, YOU FORGOT THAT IT HAD BEEN ONE WITH YOU.
NO...
IT KNOWS YOUR MIND, KNOWS EVERY TRICK YOU'VE GOT.
NOT ALL OF THEM!
REALLY?

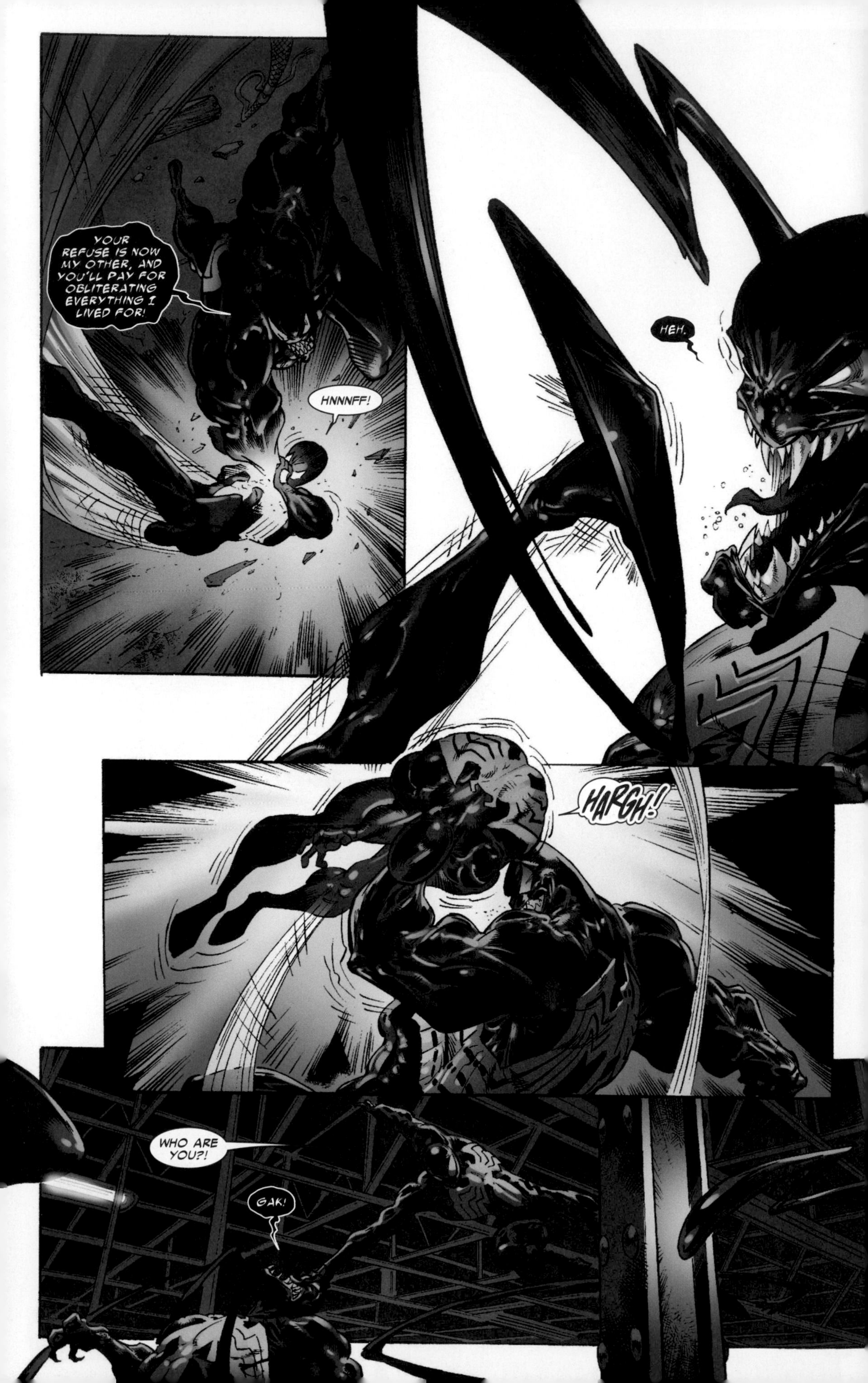

YOUR REFUSE IS NOW MY OTHER, AND YOU'LL PAY FOR OBLITERATING EVERYTHING I LIVED FOR!
HNNNFF!
HEH.
HARGH!
WHO ARE YOU?!
GAK!

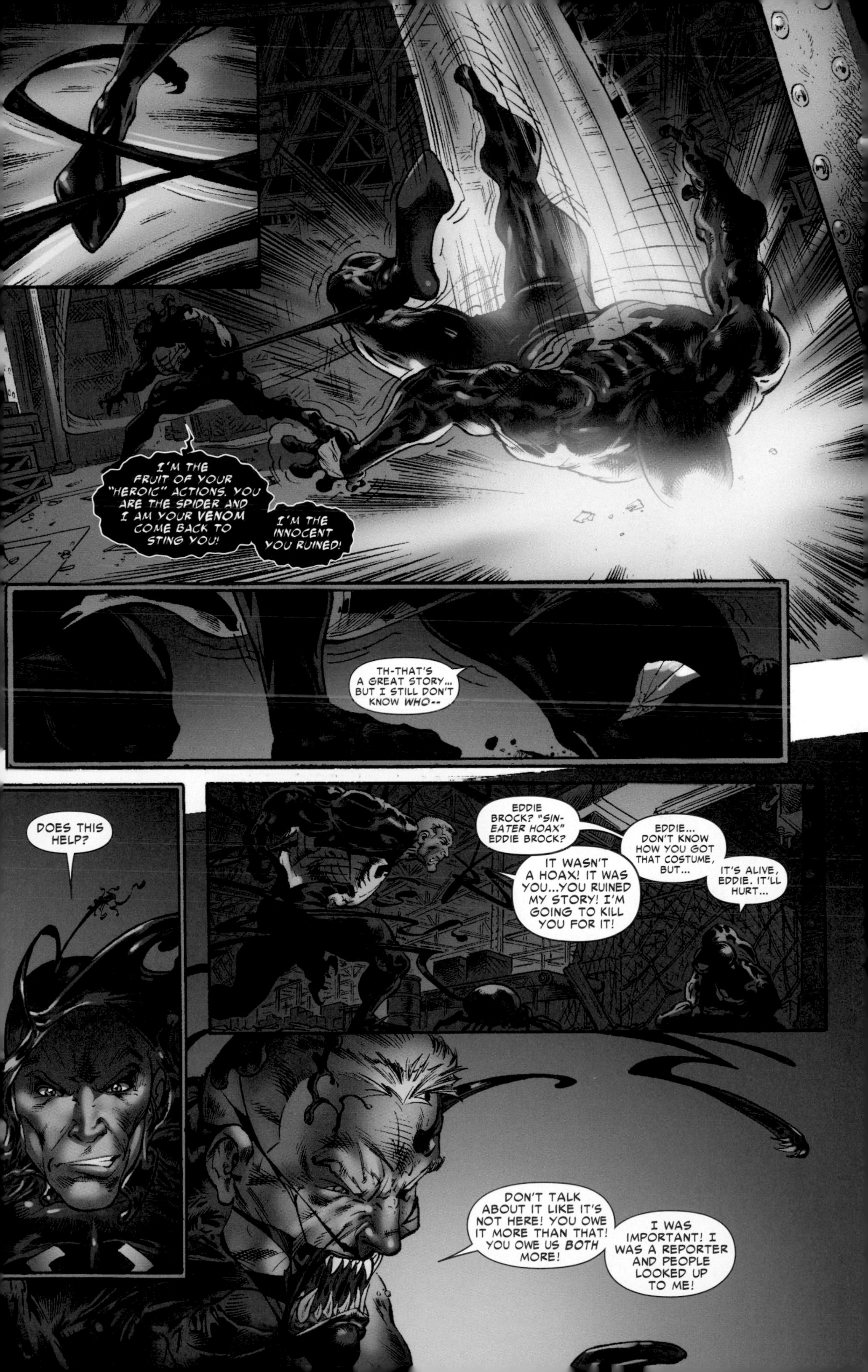
I'M THE FRUIT OF YOUR "HEROIC" ACTIONS. YOU ARE THE SPIDER AND I AM YOUR VENOM COME BACK TO STING YOU!
I'M THE INNOCENT YOU RUINED!
TH-THAT'S A GREAT STORY... BUT I STILL DON'T KNOW WHO--
DOES THIS HELP?
EDDIE BROCK? "SIN-EATER HOAX" EDDIE BROCK?
IT WASN'T A HOAX! IT WAS YOU...YOU RUINED MY STORY! I'M GOING TO KILL YOU FOR IT!
EDDIE... DON'T KNOW HOW YOU GOT THAT COSTUME, BUT...
IT'S ALIVE, EDDIE. IT'LL HURT...
DON'T TALK ABOUT IT LIKE IT'S NOT HERE! YOU OWE IT MORE THAN THAT! YOU OWE US BOTH MORE!
I WAS IMPORTANT! I WAS A REPORTER AND PEOPLE LOOKED UP TO ME!

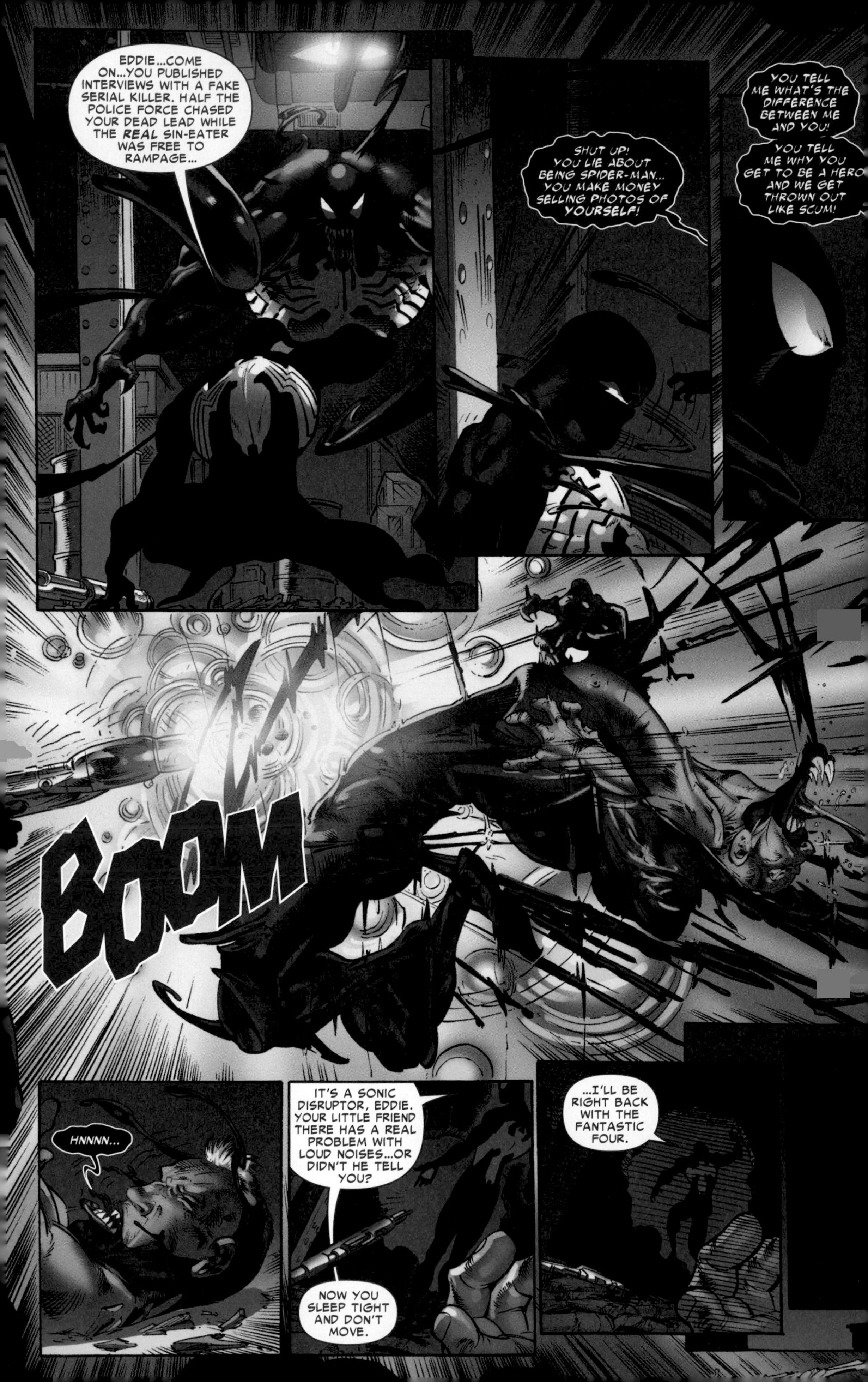
EDDIE...COME ON...YOU PUBLISHED INTERVIEWS WITH A FAKE SERIAL KILLER. HALF THE POLICE FORCE CHASED YOUR DEAD LEAD WHILE THE REAL SIN-EATER WAS FREE TO RAMPAGE...
SHUT UP! YOU LIE ABOUT BEING SPIDER-MAN... YOU MAKE MONEY SELLING PHOTOS OF YOURSELF!
YOU TELL ME WHAT'S THE DIFFERENCE BETWEEN ME AND YOU!
YOU TELL ME WHY YOU GET TO BE A HERO AND WE GET THROWN OUT LIKE SCUM!
BOOM
HNNNN...
IT'S A SONIC DISRUPTOR, EDDIE. YOUR LITTLE FRIEND THERE HAS A REAL PROBLEM WITH LOUD NOISES...OR DIDN'T HE TELL YOU?
NOW YOU SLEEP TIGHT AND DON'T MOVE.
...I'LL BE RIGHT BACK WITH THE FANTASTIC FOUR.

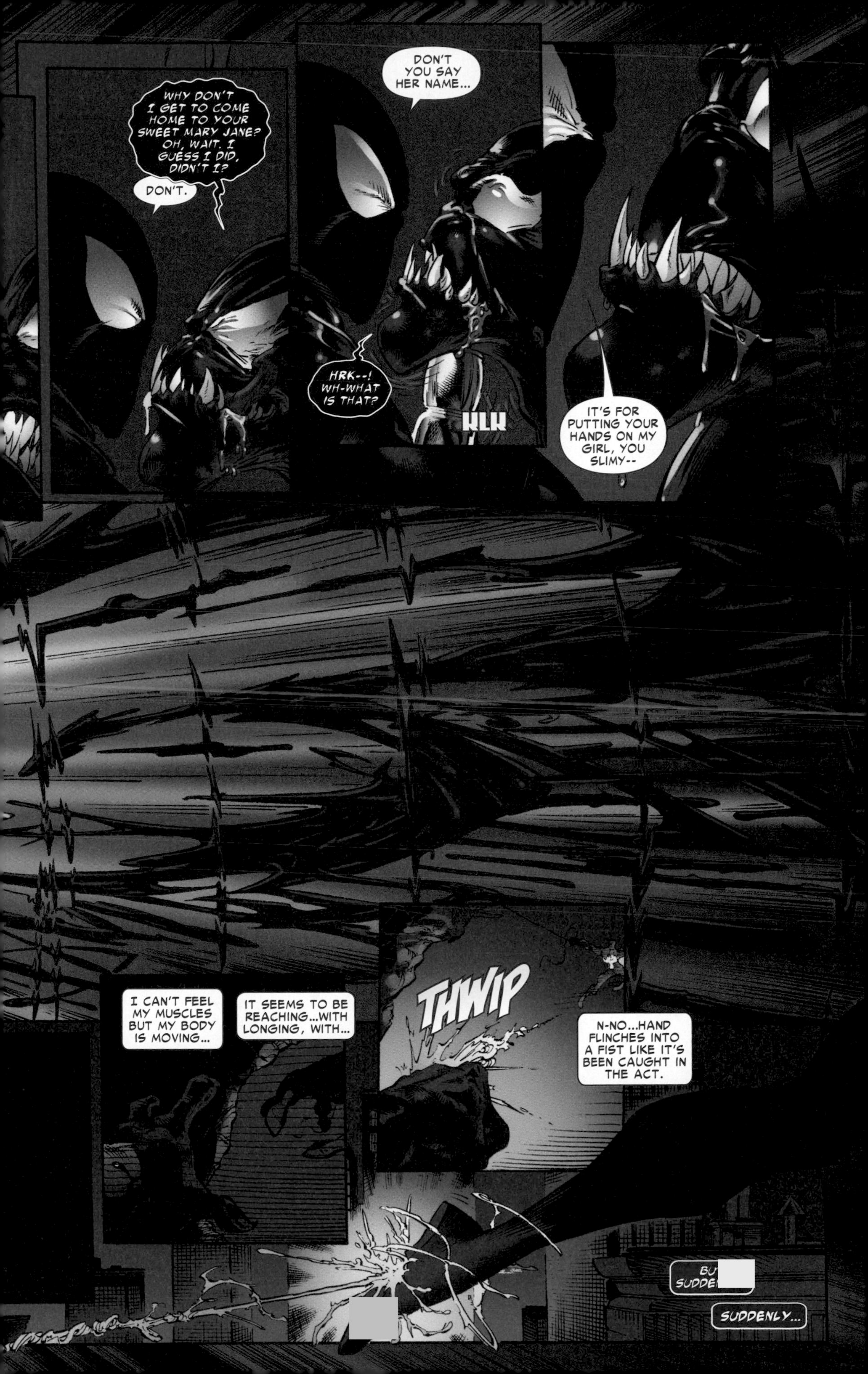
WHY DON'T I GET TO COME HOME TO YOUR SWEET MARY JANE? OH, WAIT. I GUESS I DID, DIDN'T I?
DON'T.
DON'T YOU SAY HER NAME...
HRK--! WH-WHAT IS THAT?
KLK
IT'S FOR PUTTING YOUR HANDS ON MY GIRL, YOU SLIMY--
I CAN'T FEEL MY MUSCLES BUT MY BODY IS MOVING...
IT SEEMS TO BE REACHING...WITH LONGING, WITH...
THWIP
N-NO...HAND FLINCHES INTO A FIST LIKE IT'S BEEN CAUGHT IN THE ACT.
SUDDENLY...

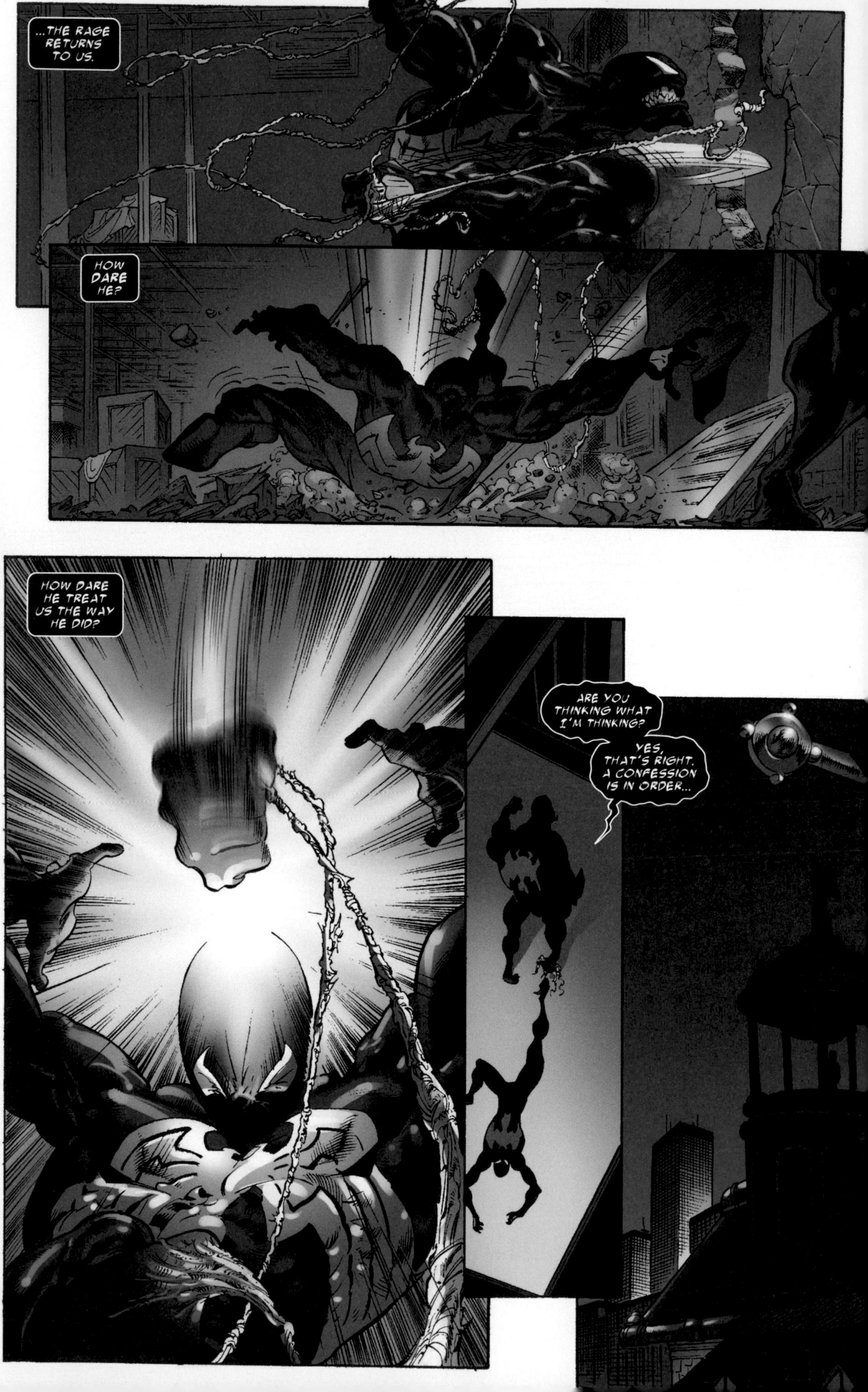
...THE RAGE RETURNS TO US.
HOW DARE HE?
HOW DARE HE TREAT US THE WAY HE DID?
ARE YOU THINKING WHAT I'M THINKING?
YES, THAT'S RIGHT. A CONFESSION IS IN ORDER...

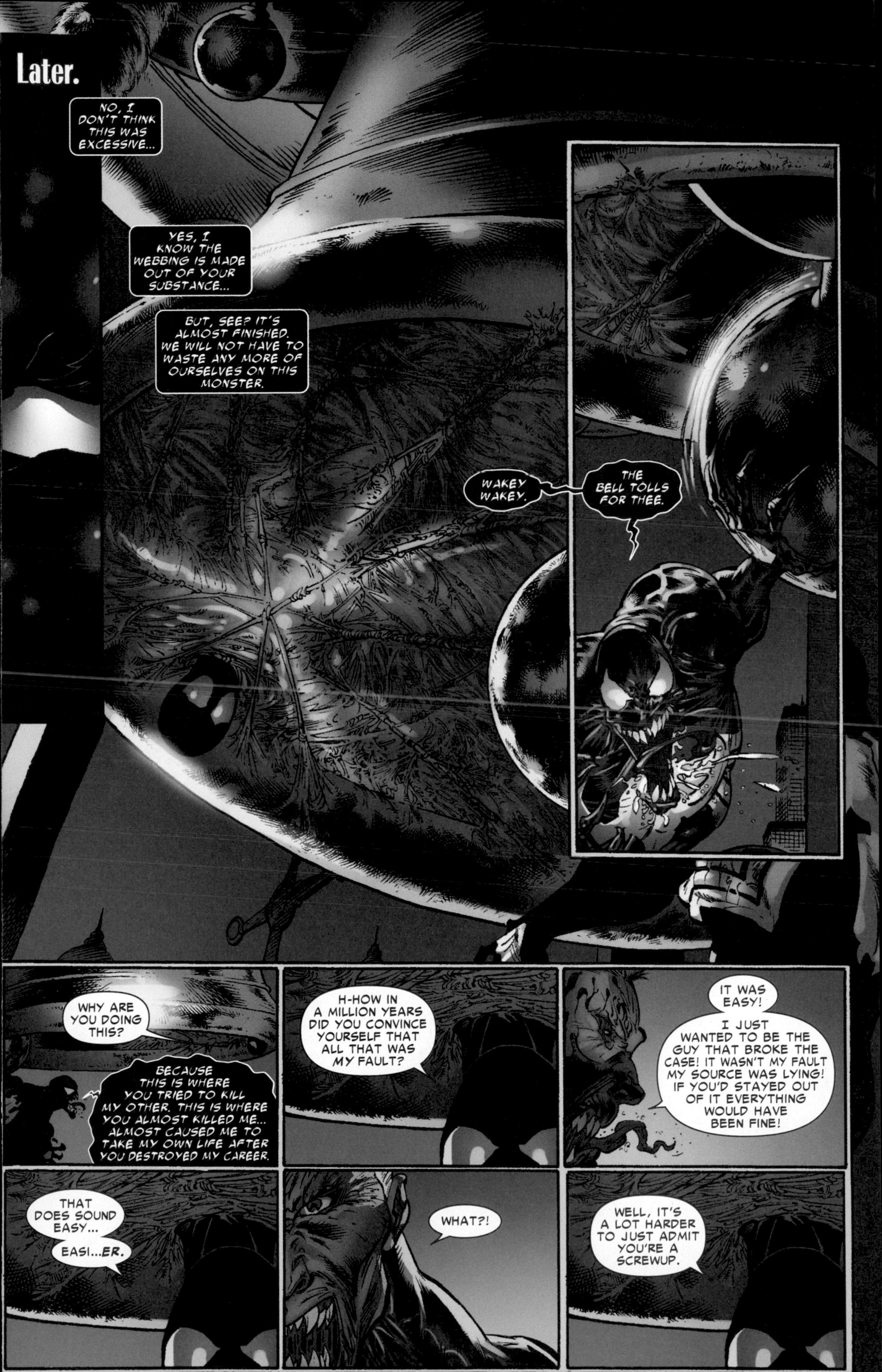

Later.
NO, I DON'T THINK THIS WAS EXCESSIVE...
YES, I KNOW THE WEBBING IS MADE OUT OF YOUR SUBSTANCE...
BUT, SEE? IT'S ALMOST FINISHED. WE WILL NOT HAVE TO WASTE ANY MORE OF OURSELVES ON THIS MONSTER.
WAKEY WAKEY.
THE BELL TOLLS FOR THEE.
WHY ARE YOU DOING THIS?
BECAUSE THIS IS WHERE YOU TRIED TO KILL MY OTHER. THIS IS WHERE YOU ALMOST KILLED ME... ALMOST CAUSED ME TO TAKE MY OWN LIFE AFTER YOU DESTROYED MY CAREER.
H-HOW IN A MILLION YEARS DID YOU CONVINCE YOURSELF THAT ALL THAT WAS MY FAULT?
IT WAS EASY!
I JUST WANTED TO BE THE GUY THAT BROKE THE CASE! IT WASN'T MY FAULT MY SOURCE WAS LYING! IF YOU'D STAYED OUT OF IT EVERYTHING WOULD HAVE BEEN FINE!
THAT DOES SOUND EASY...
EASI...ER.
WHAT?!
WELL, IT'S A LOT HARDER TO JUST ADMIT YOU'RE A SCREWUP.

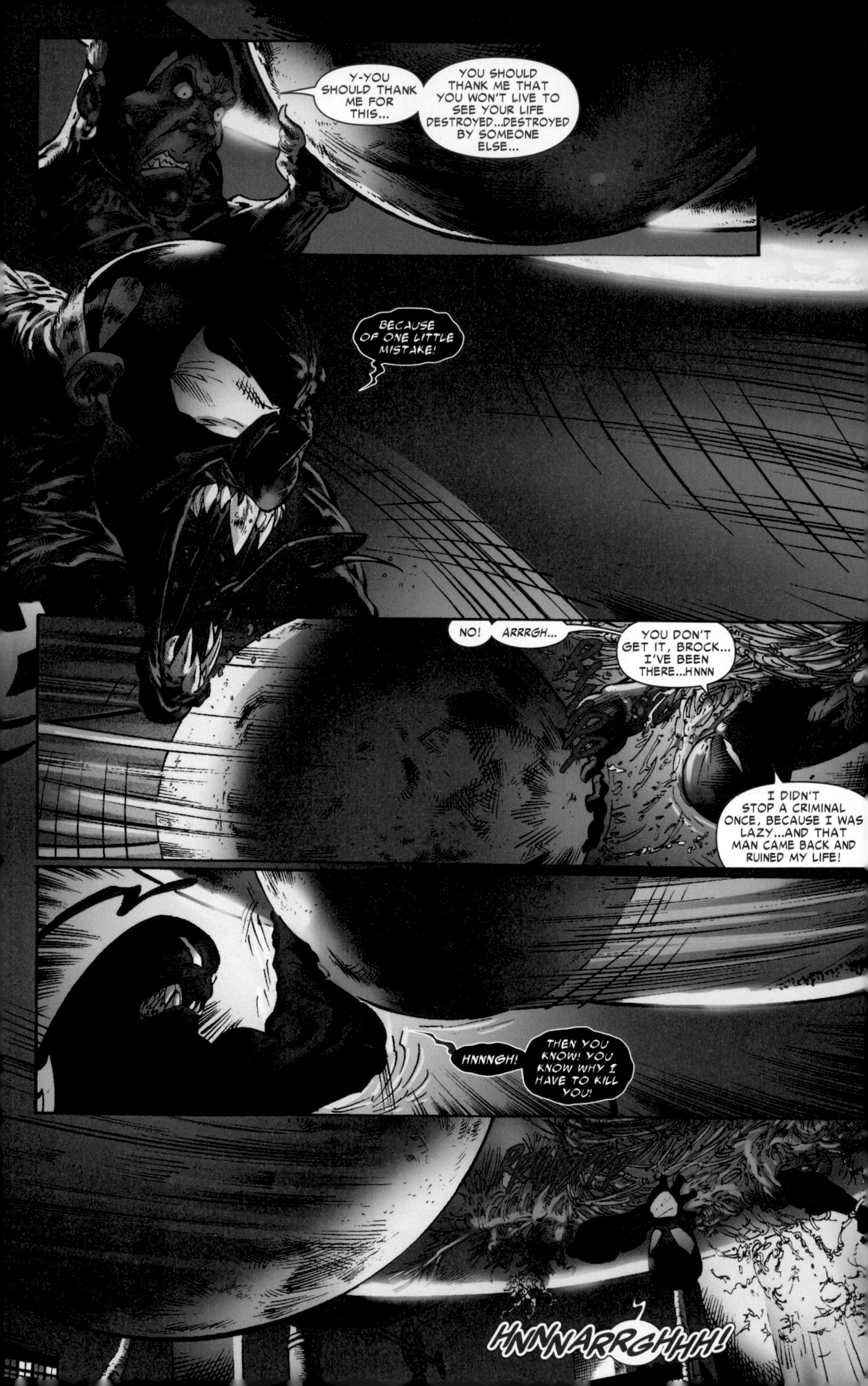
Y-YOU SHOULD THANK ME FOR THIS...
YOU SHOULD THANK ME THAT YOU WON'T LIVE TO SEE YOUR LIFE DESTROYED...DESTROYED BY SOMEONE ELSE...
BECAUSE OF ONE LITTLE MISTAKE!
NO!
ARRRGH...
YOU DON'T GET IT, BROCK... I'VE BEEN THERE...HNNN
I DIDN'T STOP A CRIMINAL ONCE, BECAUSE I WAS LAZY...AND THAT MAN CAME BACK AND RUINED MY LIFE!
HNNNGH!
THEN YOU KNOW! YOU KNOW WHY I HAVE TO KILL YOU!
HNNNARRGHHH!

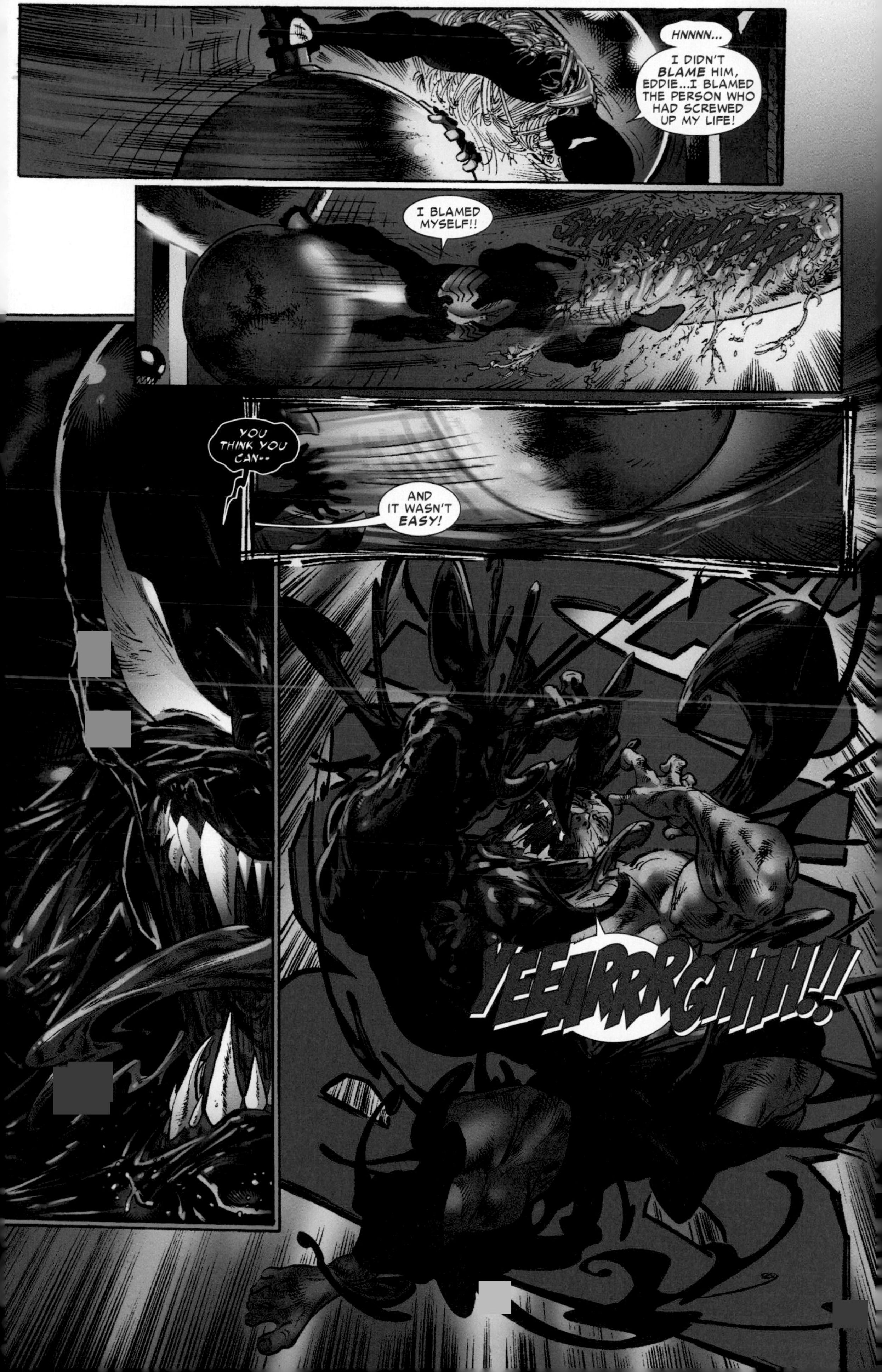
HNNNN...
I DIDN'T BLAME HIM, EDDIE...I BLAMED THE PERSON WHO HAD SCREWED UP MY LIFE!
I BLAMED MYSELF!!
SHHRIPPPP
YOU THINK YOU CAN--
AND IT WASN'T EASY!
YEEARRRGHHH!!

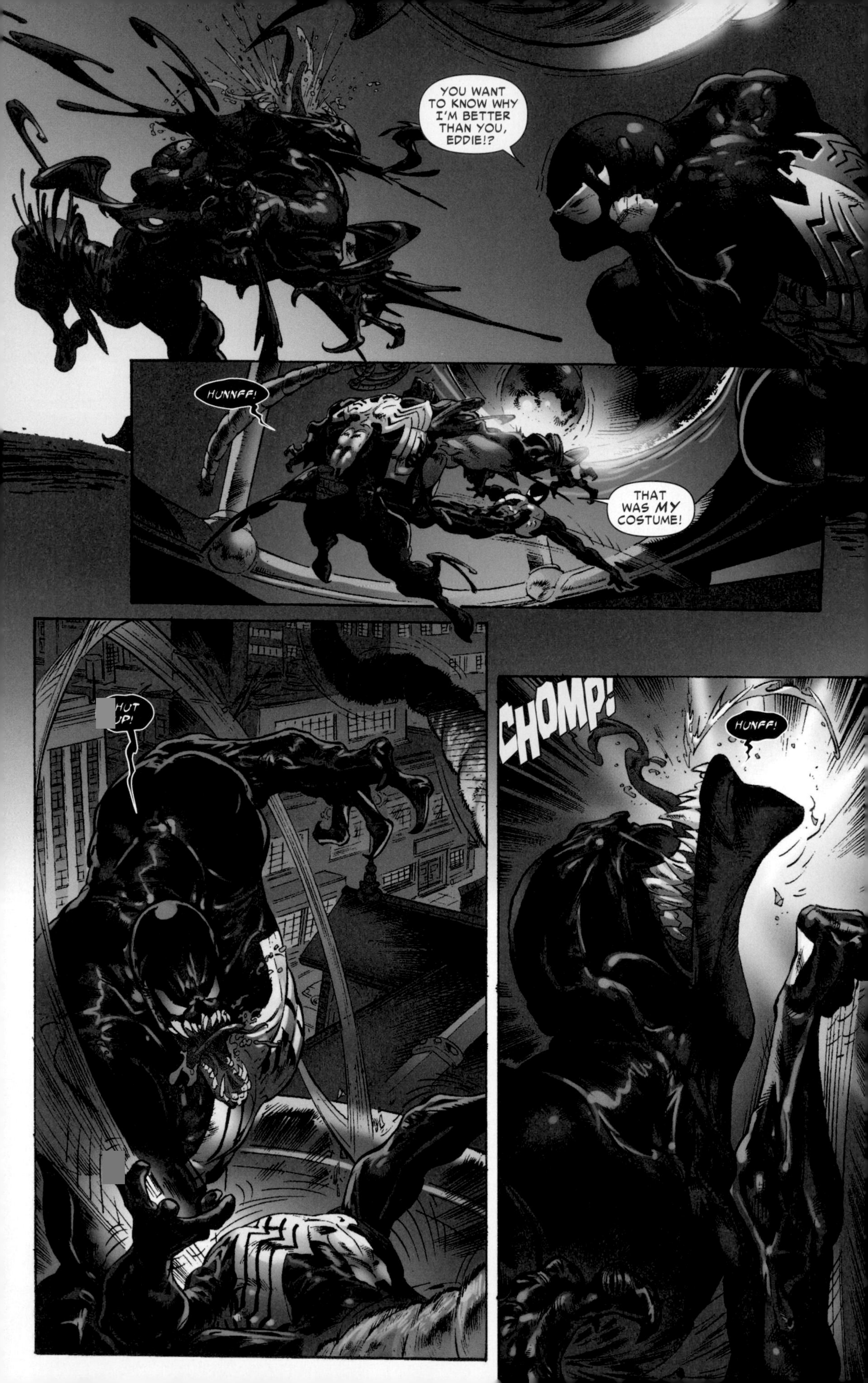
YOU WANT TO KNOW WHY I'M BETTER THAN YOU, EDDIE!?
HUNNFF!
THAT WAS MY COSTUME!
CHOMP!
HUNFF!

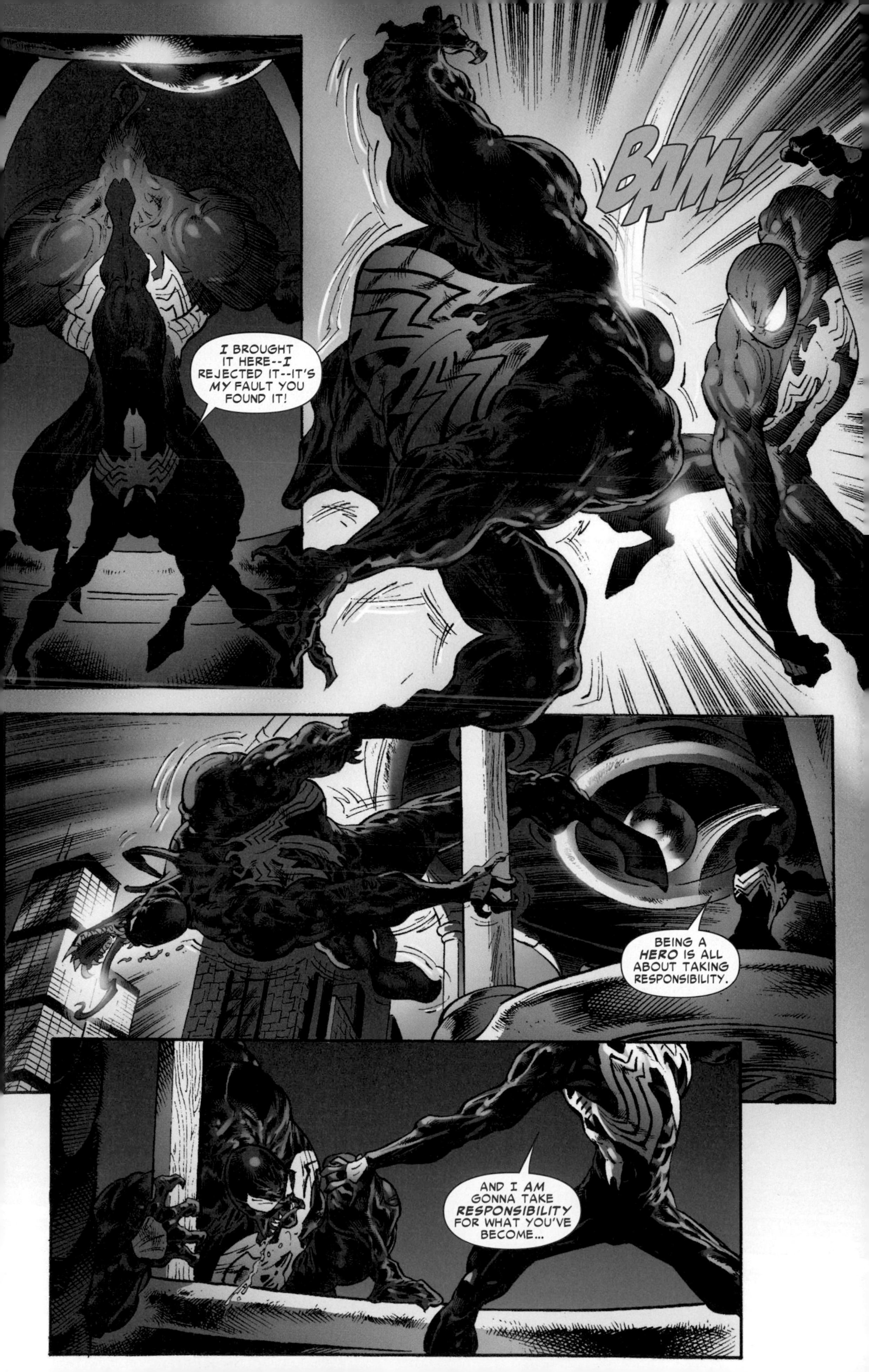
BAM!!
I BROUGHT IT HERE--I REJECTED IT--IT'S MY FAULT YOU FOUND IT!
BEING A HERO IS ALL ABOUT TAKING RESPONSIBILITY.
AND I AM GONNA TAKE RESPONSIBILITY FOR WHAT YOU'VE BECOME...

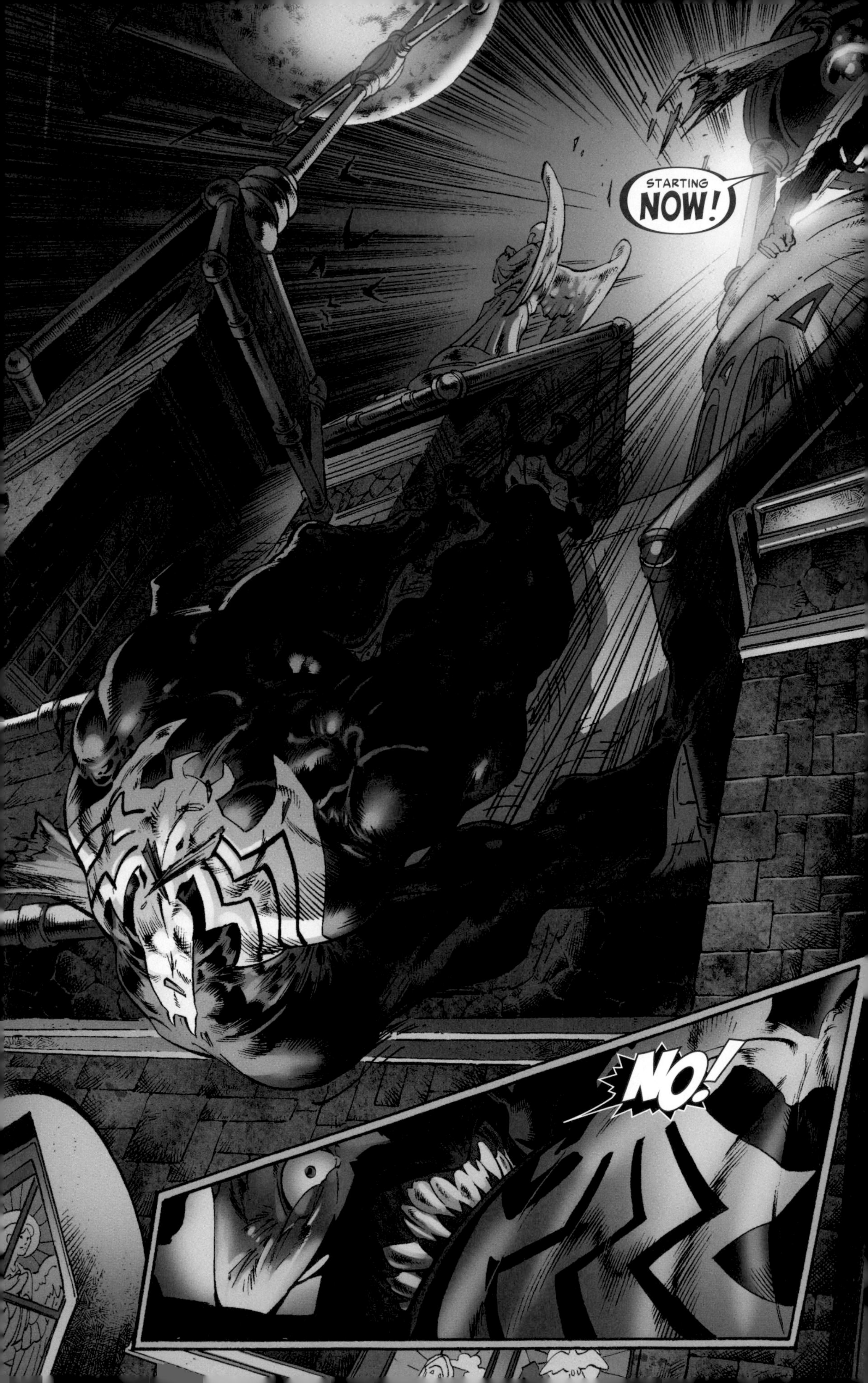
STARTING NOW!
NO!

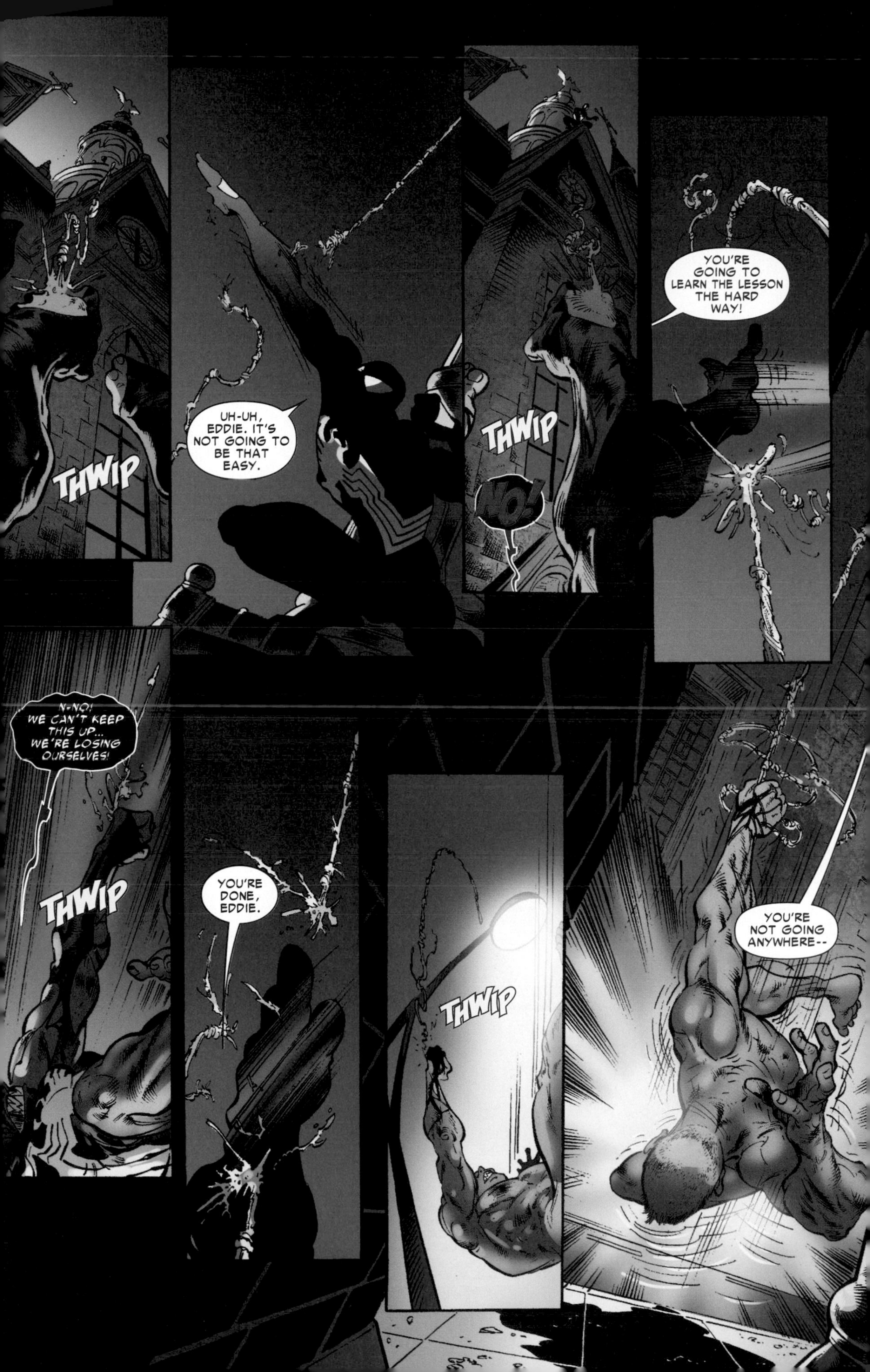
THWIP
UH-UH, EDDIE. IT'S NOT GOING TO BE THAT EASY.
THWIP
NO!
YOU'RE GOING TO LEARN THE LESSON THE HARD WAY!
N-NO! WE CAN'T KEEP THIS UP... WE'RE LOSING OURSELVES!
THWIP
YOU'RE DONE, EDDIE.
THWIP
YOU'RE NOT GOING ANYWHERE--

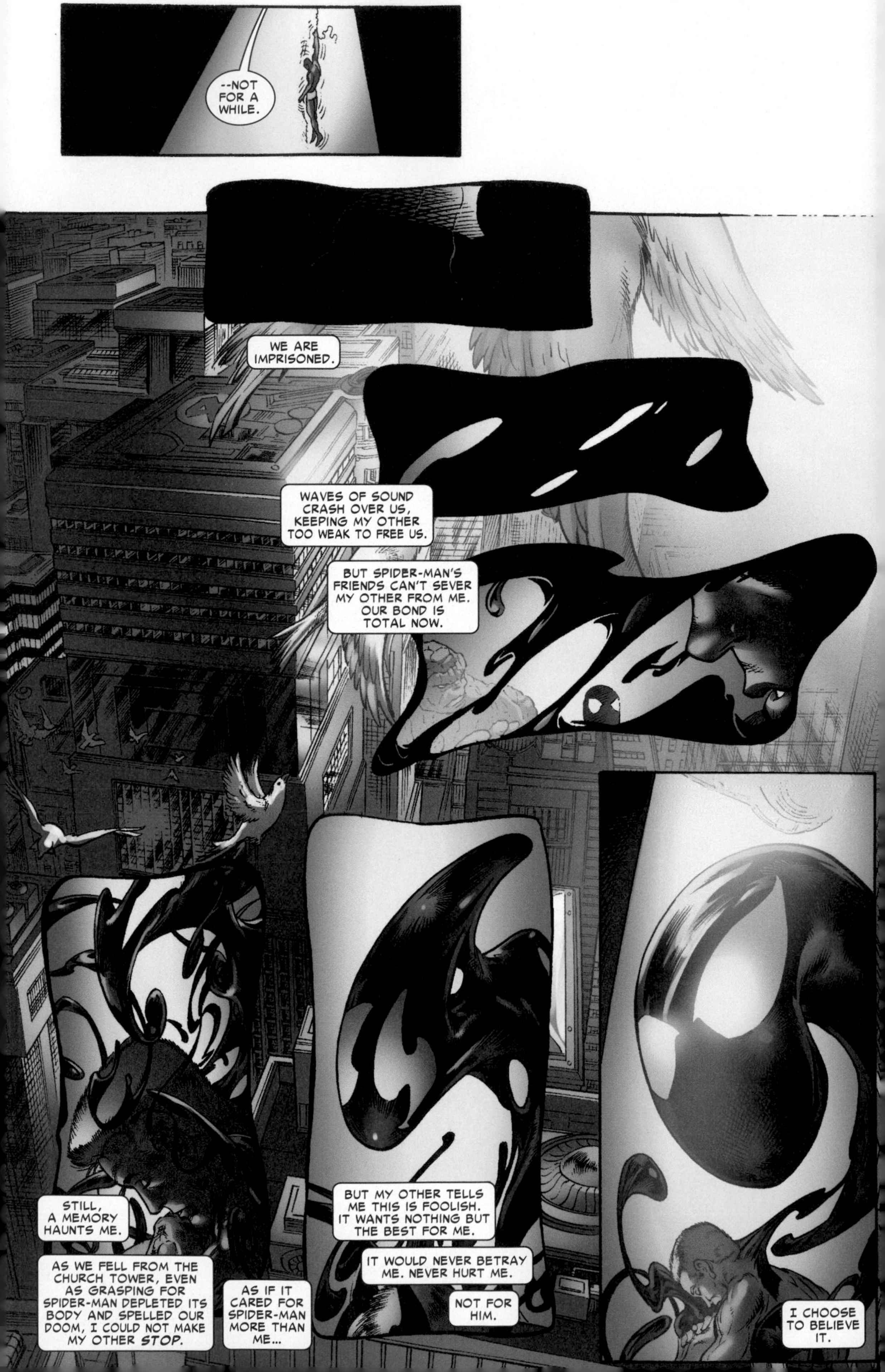

--NOT FOR A WHILE.
WE ARE IMPRISONED.
WAVES OF SOUND CRASH OVER US, KEEPING MY OTHER TOO WEAK TO FREE US.
BUT SPIDER-MAN'S FRIENDS CAN'T SEVER MY OTHER FROM ME. OUR BOND IS TOTAL NOW.
STILL, A MEMORY HAUNTS ME.
AS WE FELL FROM THE CHURCH TOWER, EVEN AS GRASPING FOR SPIDER-MAN DEPLETED ITS BODY AND SPELLED OUR DOOM, I COULD NOT MAKE MY OTHER *STOP*.
AS IF IT CARED FOR SPIDER-MAN MORE THAN ME...
BUT MY OTHER TELLS ME THIS IS FOOLISH. IT WANTS NOTHING BUT THE BEST FOR ME.
IT WOULD NEVER BETRAY ME. NEVER HURT ME.
NOT FOR HIM.
I CHOOSE TO BELIEVE IT.

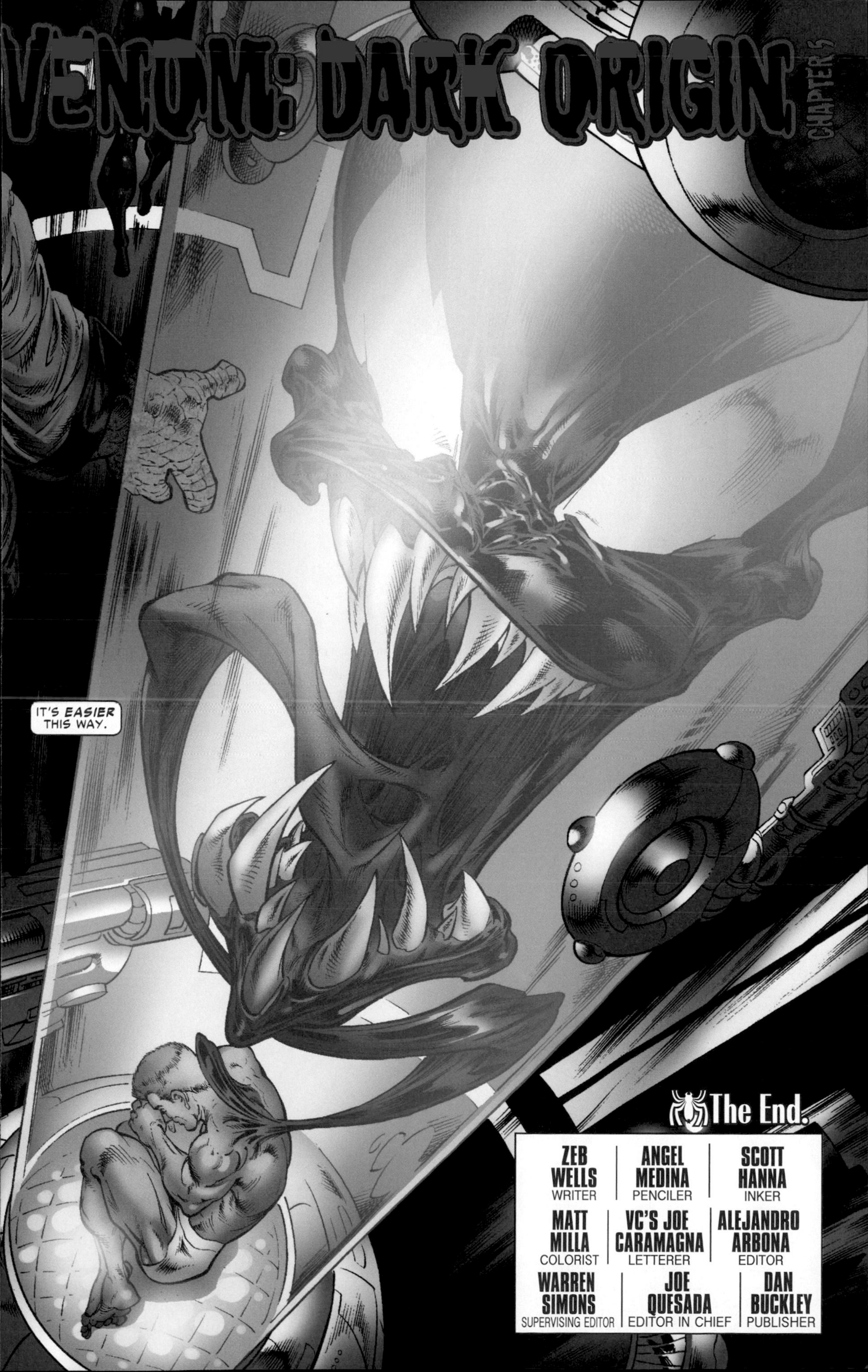
VENOM: DARK ORIGIN
CHAPTER 5
IT'S EASIER THIS WAY.
The End.
ZEB WELLS WRITER
ANGEL MEDINA PENCILER
SCOTT HANNA INKER
MATT MILLA COLORIST
VC'S JOE CARAMAGNA LETTERER
ALEJANDRO ARBONA EDITOR
WARREN SIMONS SUPERVISING EDITOR
JOE QUESADA EDITOR IN CHIEF
DAN BUCKLEY PUBLISHER

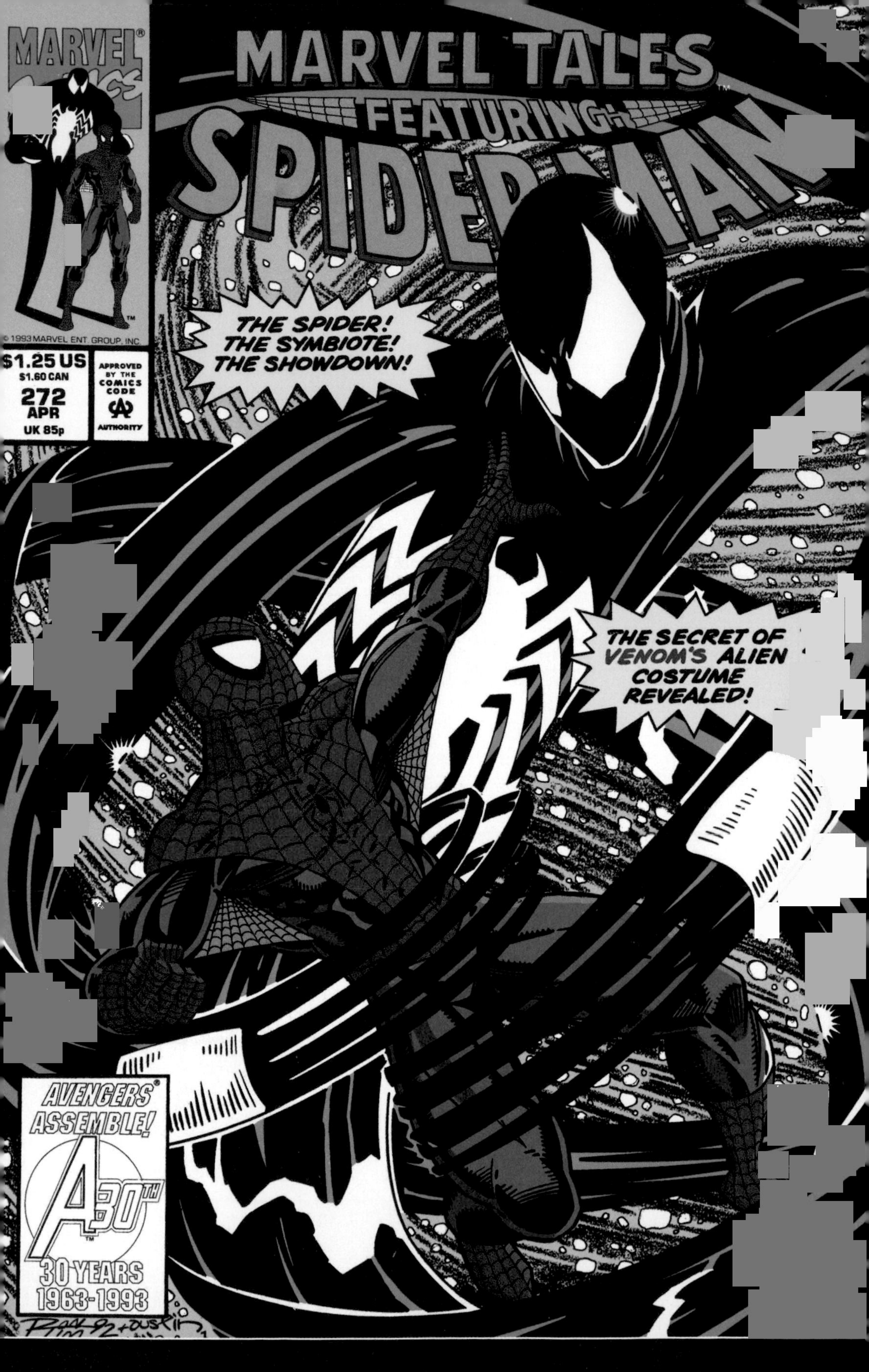
MARVEL COMICS
MARVEL TALES
FEATURING:
SPIDER-MAN
© 1993 MARVEL ENT. GROUP, INC.
$1.25 US
$1.60 CAN
272
APR
UK 85p
APPROVED BY THE COMICS CODE AUTHORITY
THE SPIDER! THE SYMBIOTE! THE SHOWDOWN!
THE SECRET OF VENOM'S ALIEN COSTUME REVEALED!
AVENGERS ASSEMBLE!
30TH
30 YEARS 1963-1993

Marvel Tales #272 reprinted *Amazing Spider-Man* #258. Cover art by Ron Lim & Terry Austin

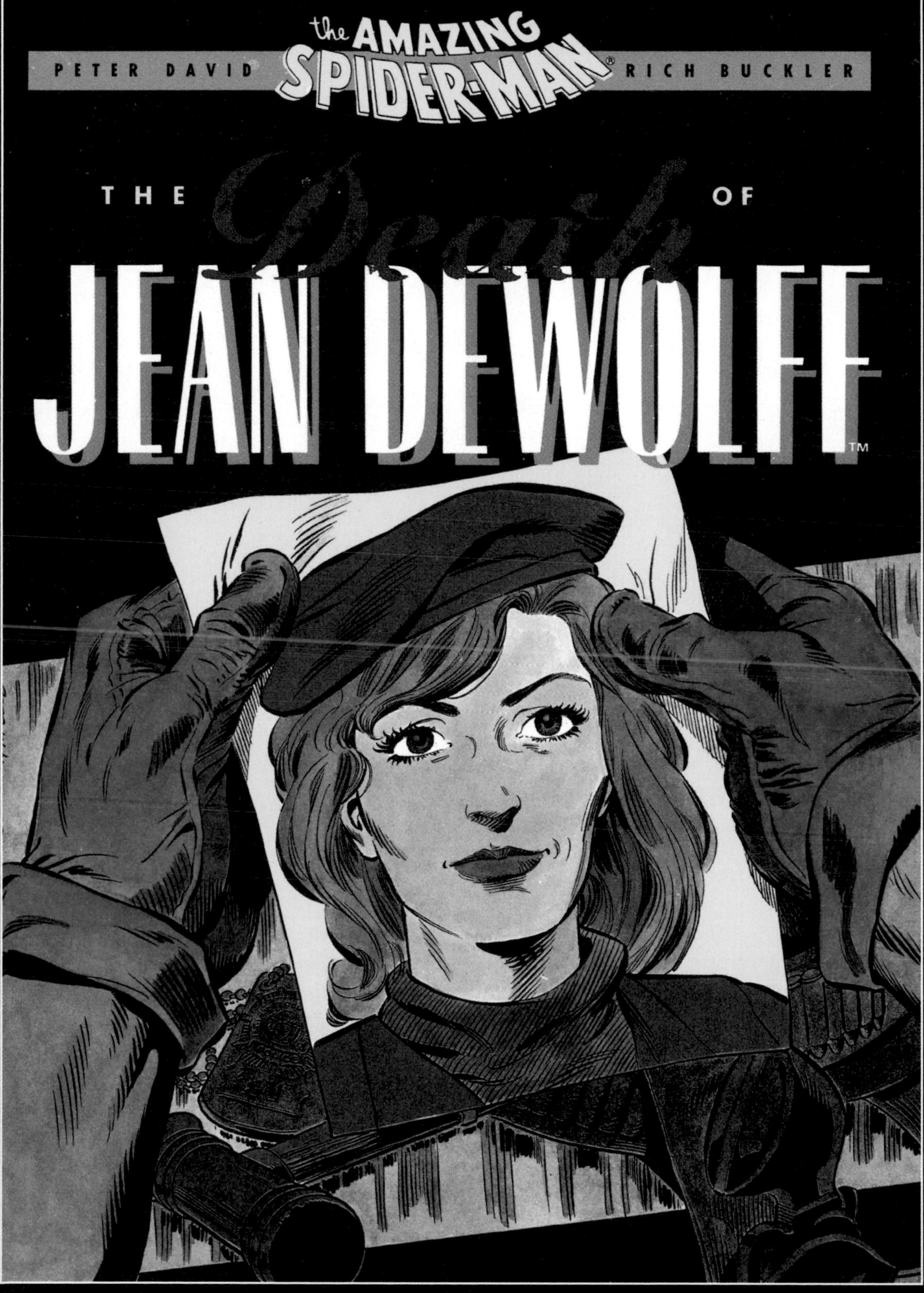
PETER DAVID
the AMAZING SPIDER-MAN®
RICH BUCKLER
THE Death OF
JEAN DEWOLFF™

Amazing Spider-Man: The Death of Jean DeWolff TPB (1990) cover art by Rich Buckler & Bob McLeod

INTRODUCTION

When I was around 17 or so, I was at a picnic/get-together with a bunch of friends in Philadelphia. We assembled intermittently as part of a Star Trek/SF club we belonged to called "Space Time Continuum" (long since defunct, although back issues of the club fanzine contain my earliest published fiction. Awful stuff, although I was proud of it back then).

At the time, I was no longer reading comic books. I had gone cold turkey when I was about thirteen, self-conscious since my local news dealer thought I was mentally defective for reading comics while over the age of seven (this was before direct sales comic shops, such as the one you probably bought this volume in). At the picnic, I ran into a comics fan named Neil Harris, who mentioned that he was still reading comics in general and *Spider-Man* in particular.

"Did Spider-Man ever marry Gwen?" I asked.

"No, Gwen's dead," Neil told me. "The Green Goblin killed her by dropping her off a bridge."

I'm told by my friends that I was positively ashen upon learning of the untimely demise of Peter Parker's great love. And I made a vow that very day: That if I ever went on to become a writer, I would never — ever — kill off a character. I would never put a reader through the living hell that I went through because of Gwen Stacy's death.

So much for that. Beware of the vows of 17-year-old boys. Especially if you're (a) a 17-year-old girl or (b) a female supporting character in a *Spider-Man* book.

—Peter David

CONTRADICTION

A.A. Milne, in *Winnie-the-Pooh*, stated that the opposite of an Introduction was a Contradiction.

"The Death of Jean DeWolff" was a contradiction in many ways, all deliberately so. First, we flew in the face of standard comic book tradition by giving a character, not a noble death in battle at the climax of a story, but an inglorious death, in her sleep, at the beginning. To kill off Jean by page four of a 90 page story was considered bizarre, to say the least.

Second, we killed off a character who had a lot of potential. Readers couldn't fathom why we did that. "Why kill off a character with whom you could have done so much?" we were asked over and over again. Ah, but where is the dramatic impact in killing off someone with no potential? Someone who the readers are sick of? There's no drama in that, no sense of "it might have been." Death should be a tragedy, not a relief. Perhaps in a world where moviegoers laugh at innocent teens being slaughtered by masked madmen, that's been forgotten.

Third, Jean was really dead. This was difficult for comics fans to understand. "Maybe it was a clone," "maybe it was an LMD," "maybe she's on life support somewhere." Sure, right next to JFK, Elvis and Walt Disney. Gimme a break, guys. She was autopsied and planted. She was dead. I'm certain that readers finished the last page of the last issue and were still convinced that somehow, some way, Jean would be brought back.

Why Jean? Why Daredevil? Years later, I still get these questions. As with most things in comics, it was a combination of events.

I was going to be starting on *Spectacular Spider-Man* and editor Jim Owsley wanted to shake up Spider-Man and the fans. He wanted to see a story in which Jean DeWolff was killed and there were all sorts of cover-ups in the police department. So in answer to the second most-asked question I get at conventions, the answer is — Owsley wanted to kill her. Not me. I actually had storylines planned with her alive.

(The most asked question, for the record, is why did I turn the Hulk gray? The answer is, I didn't. Al Milgrom did. Al turned Hulk gray, Jim chose Jean. I just came in and took credit for everything.)

As for me, there were two storylines I wanted to pursue. First, I wanted to do a story in which Spider-

Man was confronted by a villain who committed crimes so heinous, so appalling, that Spidey was pushed to the edge and over. It always struck me as unrealistic how super heroes could turn fights on and off. When you're in a fistfight, adrenaline flows, your heart is thumping. If you knock the guy down and he's not getting up, most times you kick him because you're so pumped and angry. You don't back off and say "had enough?" Usually someone has to pull you off the guy. I wanted to do that to Spider-Man because I felt it would bring some hard-edged reality to him.

I also wanted to do a story underscoring the philosophical differences between Daredevil and Spider-Man (although DD's views have gotten somewhat weirder since then), which I won't detail here since, hopefully, you've discerned them from what you just read.

As you can see, "The Death of Jean DeWolff" incorporated all three stories to varying degrees. This was accomplished when Owsley came over to my house early one evening and stayed until after midnight as we hammered out all the kinks in the story in a marathon, four-issues'-worth head-banging session.

The Sin-Eater came from a TV-movie entitled The Incredible Journey of Doctor Meg Laurel, in which Lindsay Wagner played a woman doctor around the turn of the century, who was bringing (then) modern medicine to uneducated people in the Ozarks. There was a character in the film, tall, gangling and ghastly, called the Sin-Eater, who ate fruit placed on or near the bodies of recently deceased. This fruit represented the sins of the dear departed. I was intrigued by this and filed it away for use in a story, should I ever need a costumed lunatic to kill off a female detective.

Virtually no readers, judging by the letters, tumbled to Stan Carter being the Sin-Eater, even though much of his dialogue fairly screamed it. I knew they wouldn't. First off, I named him Stan. Stan is a friendly name to readers after years of association with Stan Lee. Second, I made him Jewish. Isaac Asimov said if you want to have someone whose evil intent must be hidden, make him Jewish and have him speak in semi-Yiddish inverted sentence order. You know. Like Yoda. ("So a murderer that makes me?") Readers will mentally categorize this as someone who is friendly and even comic relief. Works it does.

A couple of dangling threads. First off, Santa Claus does a couple of walk-ons in the course of this story. This has *nothing* to do with Jean DeWolff. I was doing then what I still do, namely set up story threads for future issues in the course of other stories. The Santa thief story was brought to fruition and wrapped in issue #112. It's got a great Kyle Baker cover with Santa Claus as the Terminator.

Second, the story of the tragic Stan Carter was concluded a couple of years later in *Spectacular Spider-Man #134-136*. In it, we saw the long-term effects of the brutal beating that Spidey gave Stan at the climax of this story. Stan was a wreck afterwards, unable to walk or talk properly. He was also mentally a mess, his mind splitting in my first experimentation with multiple personalities that I would later explore more fully in *The Incredible Hulk*. He was ultimately blown away by the police in what was a dramatic, tragic and, perhaps, merciful ending. We also revealed why he really did kill Jean DeWolff — namely that Stan was in love with her, and that made the Sin-Eater jealous.

A mention must be made of Rich Buckler, whose dynamic and energetic storytelling and gritty texture brought the story to pulsing life. He gave it the kind of down-and-dirty feeling that we were looking for. Kind of Spidey meets *Hill Street Blues*.

To this day, people still tell me that "The Death of Jean DeWolff" is their favorite of my work. Time has passed, and I think I've done better since then. And, like those early fanzine stories, I look at "Jean" now and see mostly the flaws and things I'd do differently. Still, if I never wrote another word, and readers still felt this story was the best I'd ever done, I suppose I could live with that.

Kind of a pity Jean DeWolff couldn't.

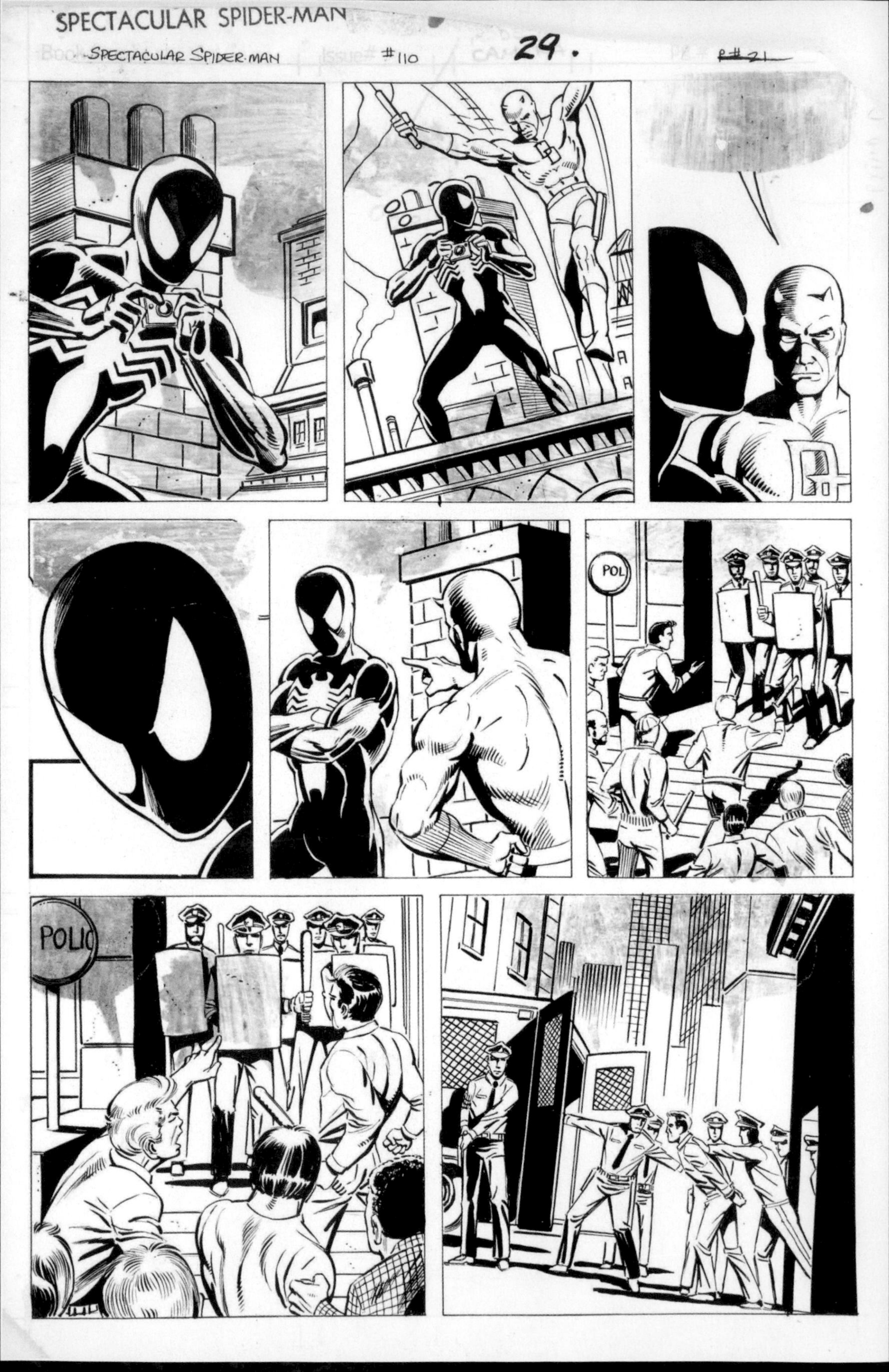
SPECTACULAR SPIDER-MAN
SPECTACULAR SPIDER-MAN
#110
29.
POL
POLIC

Peter Parker, the Spectacular Spider-Man #110, page 22 art by Rich Buckler

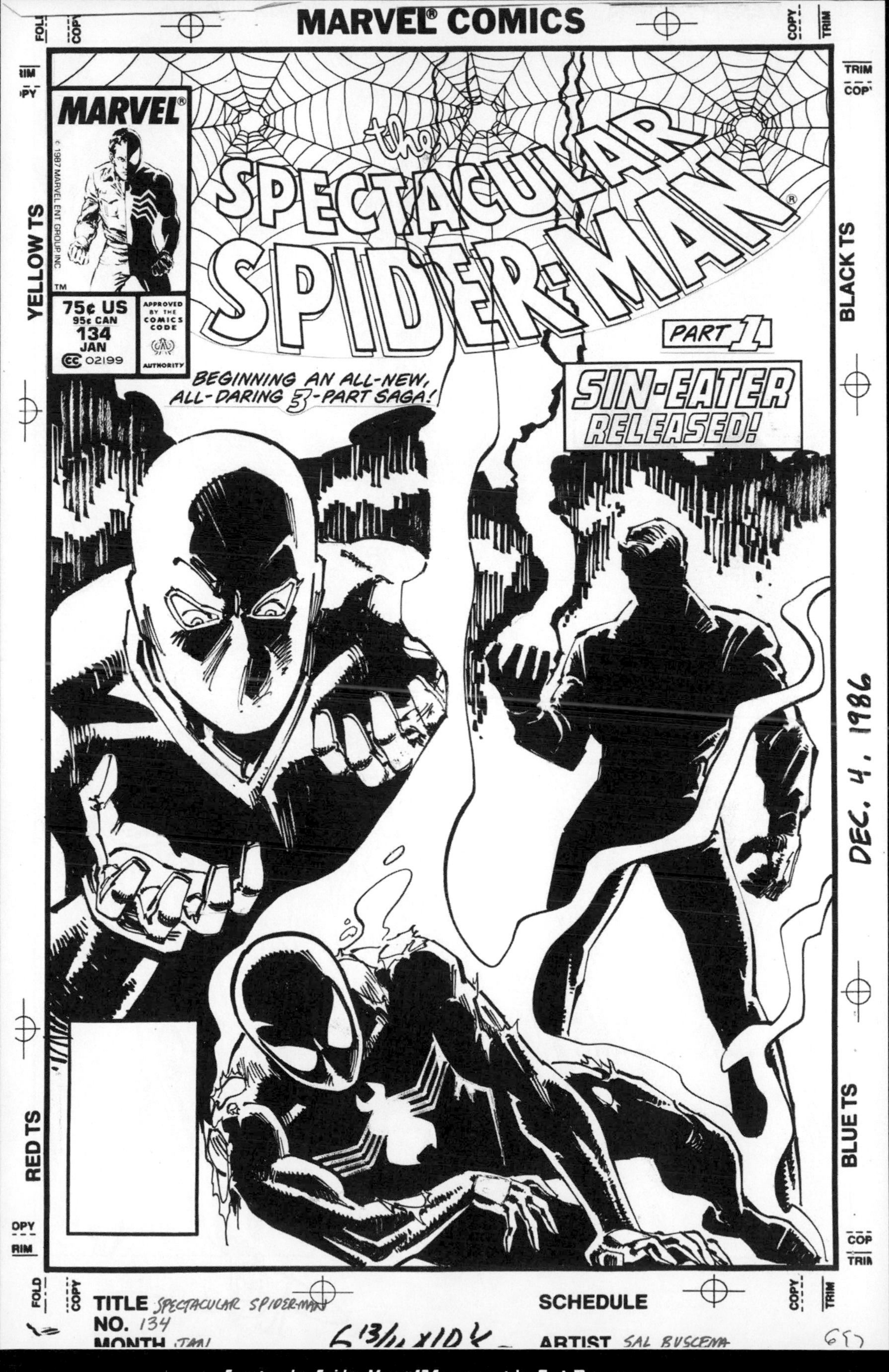
MARVEL® COMICS
MARVEL®
© 1987 MARVEL ENT GROUP INC
the SPECTACULAR SPIDER-MAN®
75¢ US
95¢ CAN
134
JAN
APPROVED BY THE COMICS CODE AUTHORITY
PART 1
BEGINNING AN ALL-NEW, ALL-DARING 3-PART SAGA!
SIN-EATER RELEASED!
DEC. 4. 1986
YELLOW TS
BLACK TS
RED TS
BLUE TS
TITLE SPECTACULAR SPIDER-MAN
NO. 134
SCHEDULE
ARTIST SAL BUSCEMA

Spectacular Spider-Man #134 cover art by Sal Buscema

Courtesy of HeritageAuctions.com

VENOM COVER #2 MEDINA-HANNA

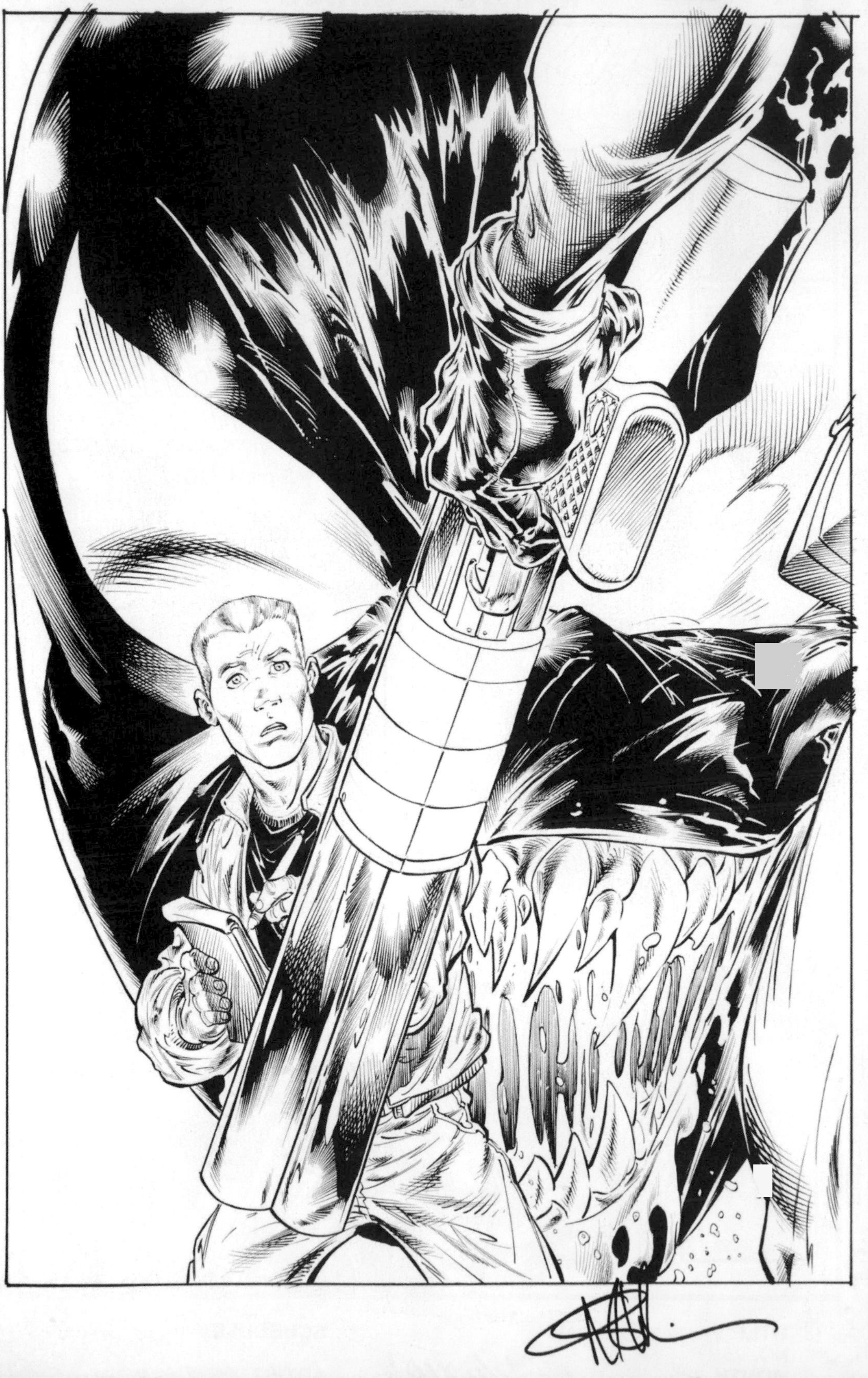

Venom: Dark Origin #2 cover art by Angel Medina & Scott Hanna

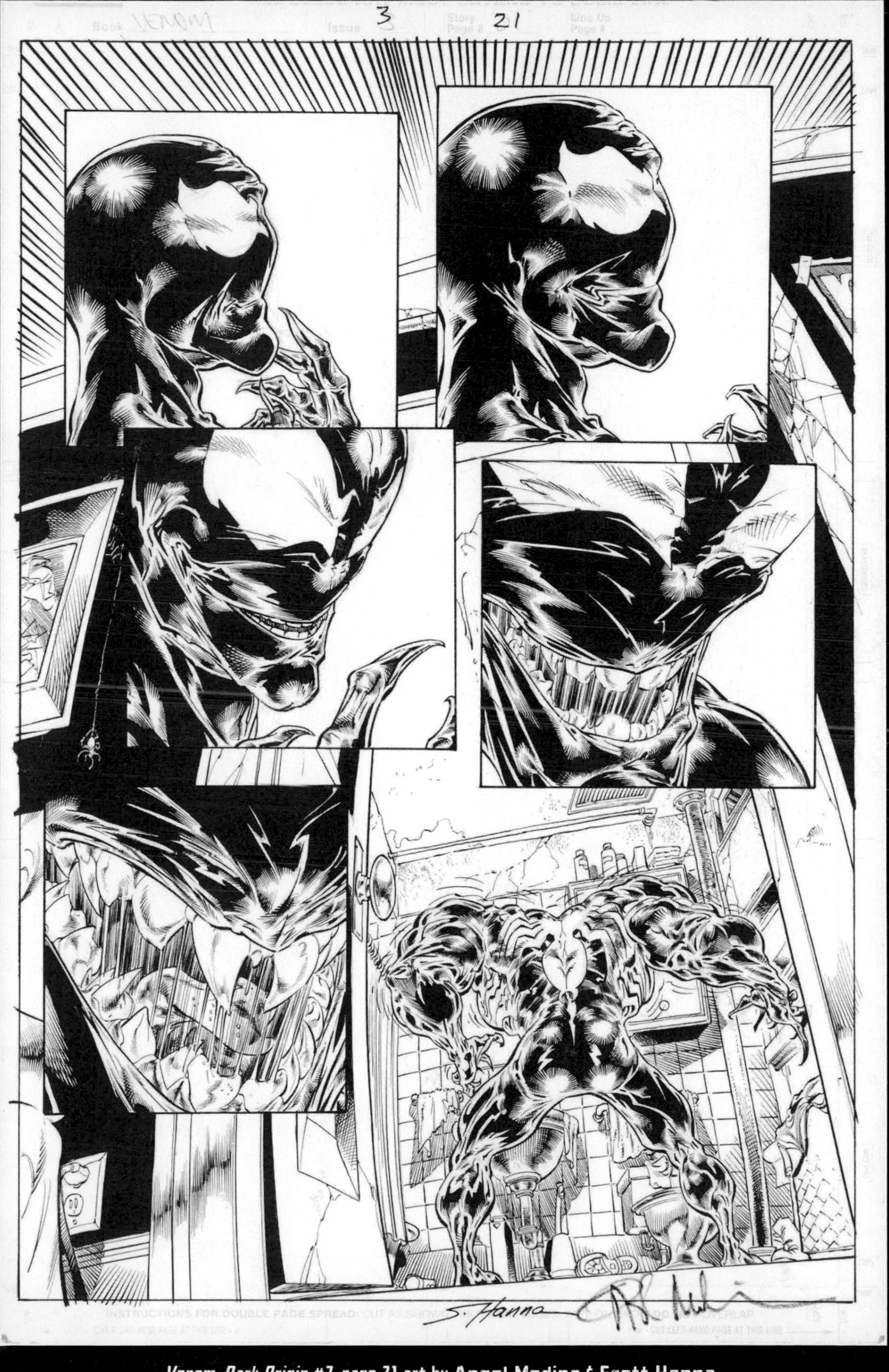
Book VENOM
Issue 3
Story Page # 21
Line Up Page #
S. Hanna

Venom: Dark Origin #3, page 21 art by Angel Medina & Scott Hanna

Courtesy of HeritageAuctions.com

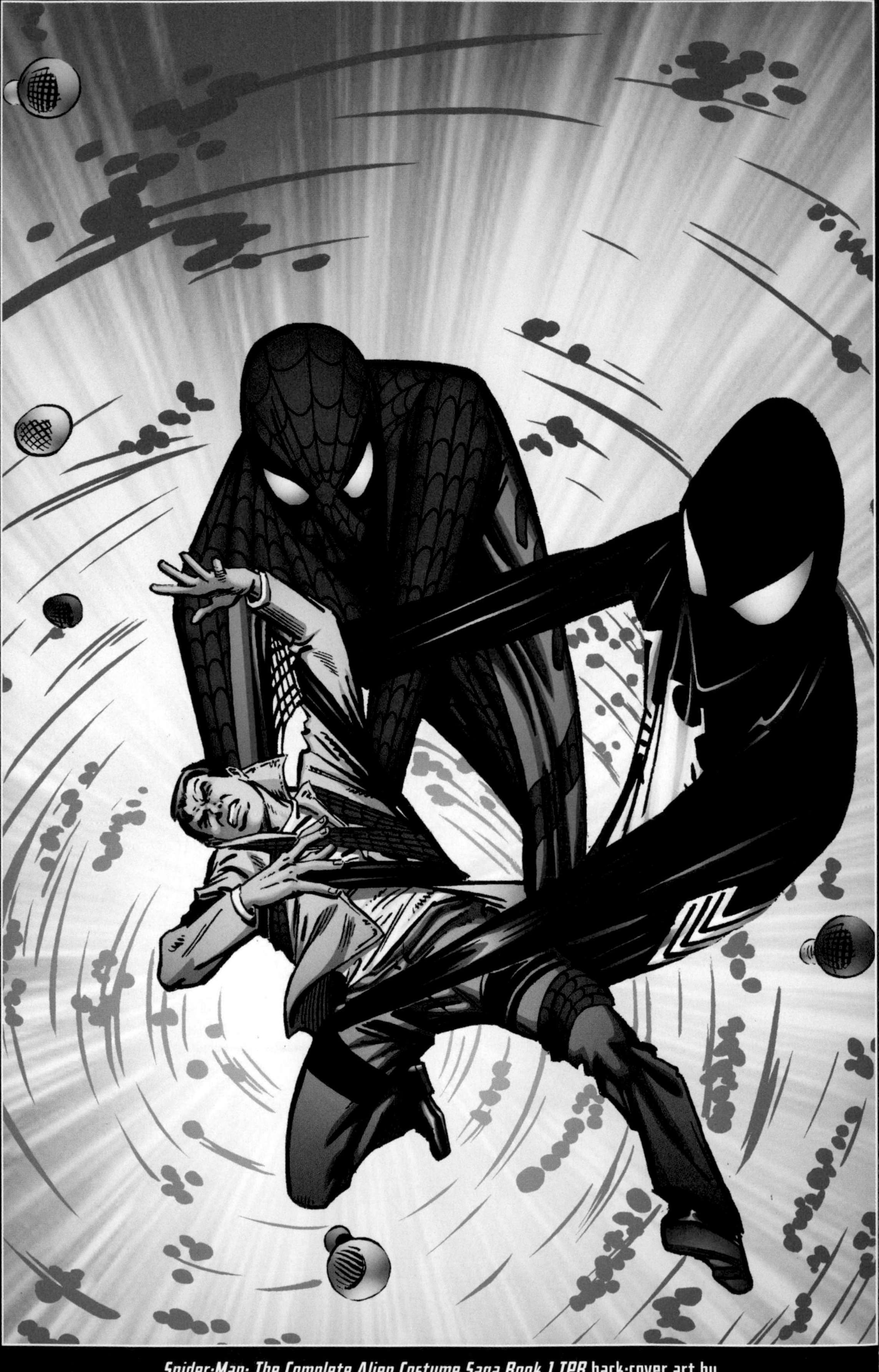

Spider-Man: The Complete Alien Costume Saga Book 1 TPB back-cover art by
Ron Frenz, Josef Rubinstein & Thomas Mason

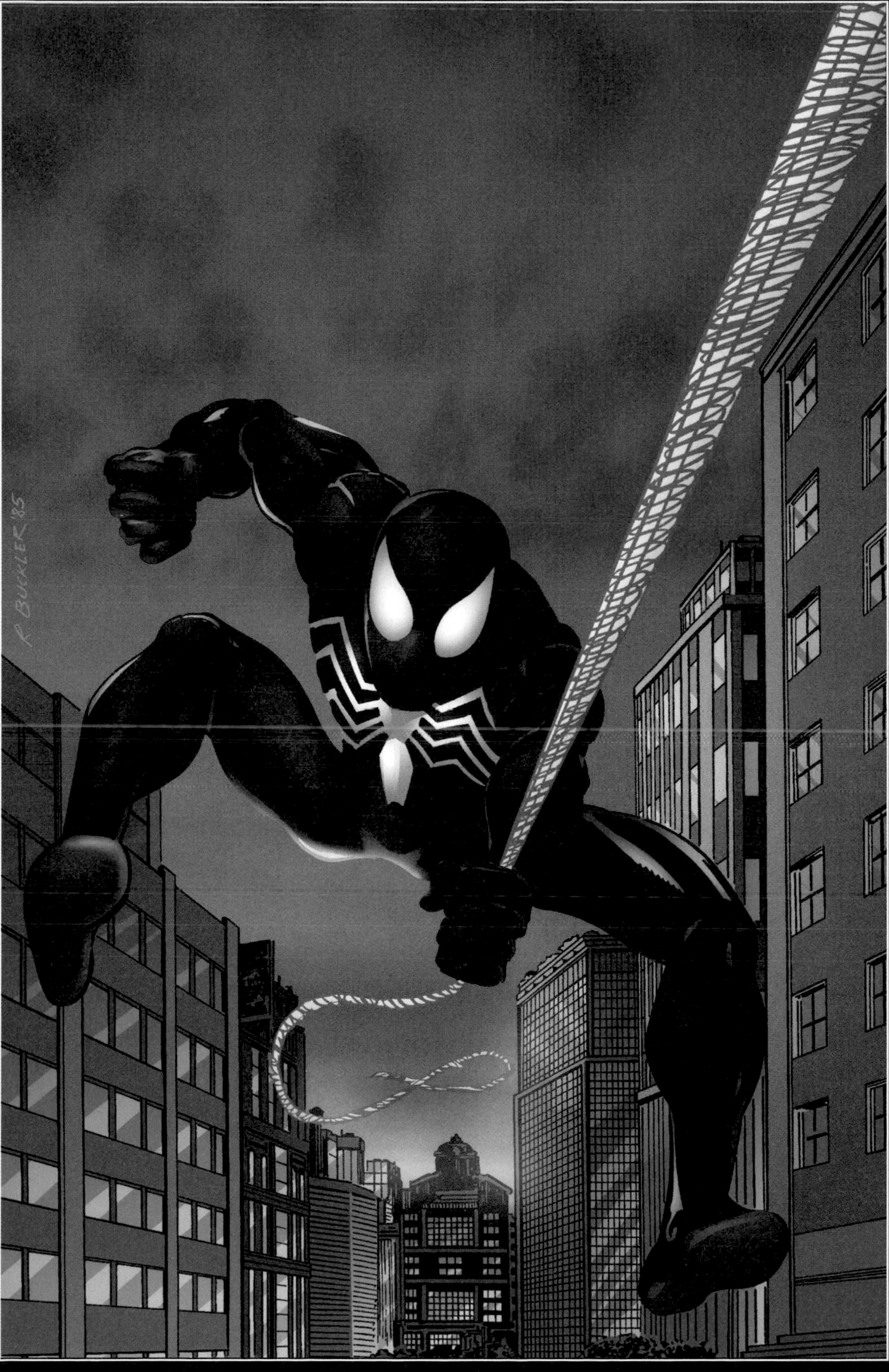
R BUCKLER '85

Essential Peter Parker, the Spectacular Spider-Man Vol. 5 TPB cover art by **Rich Buckler & Tom Chu**

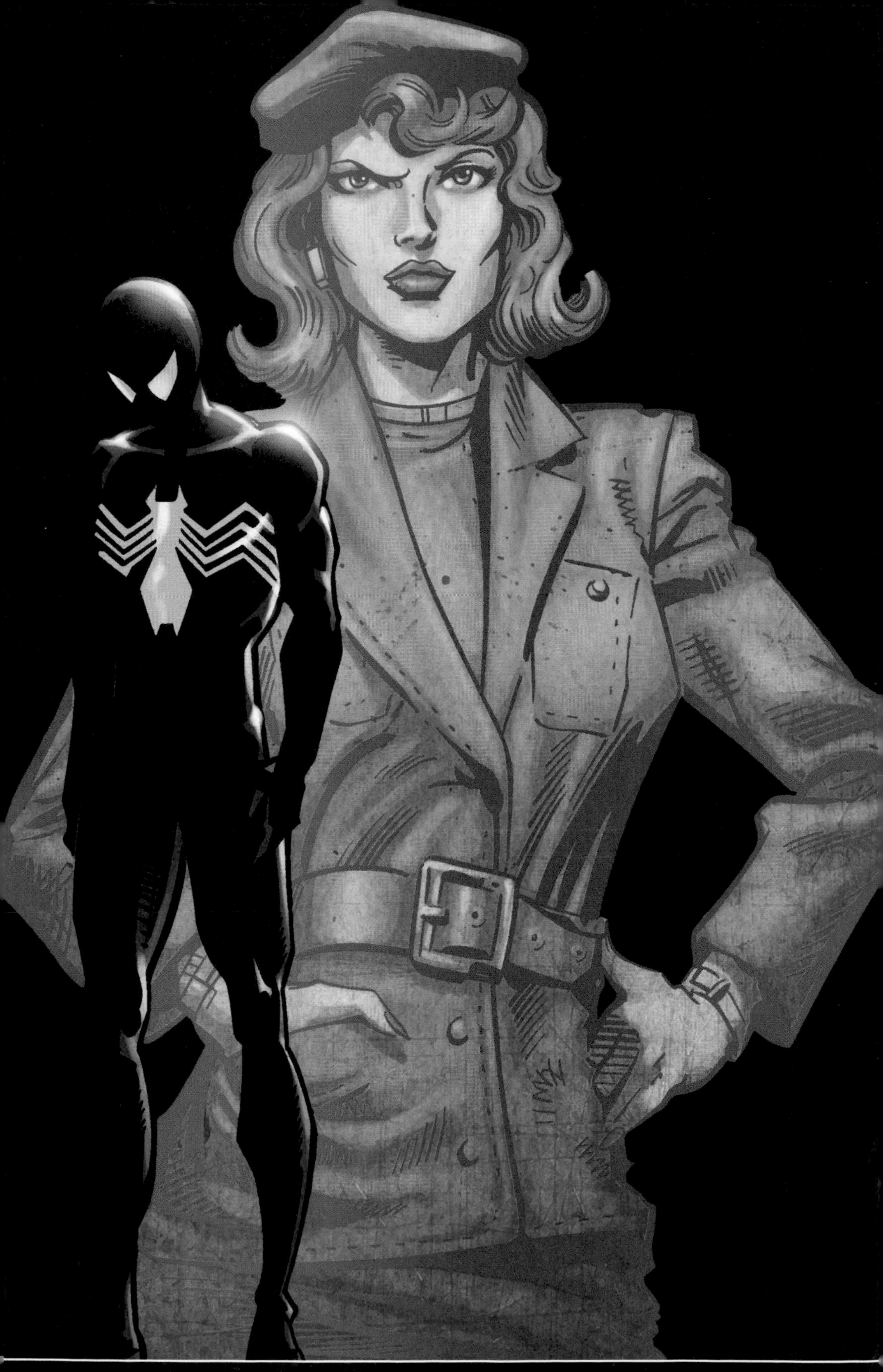

Spider-Man: The Death of Jean DeWolff Premiere HC cover art by
Sal Buscema, Mark Texeira, Josef Rubinstein & Fabio D'Auria

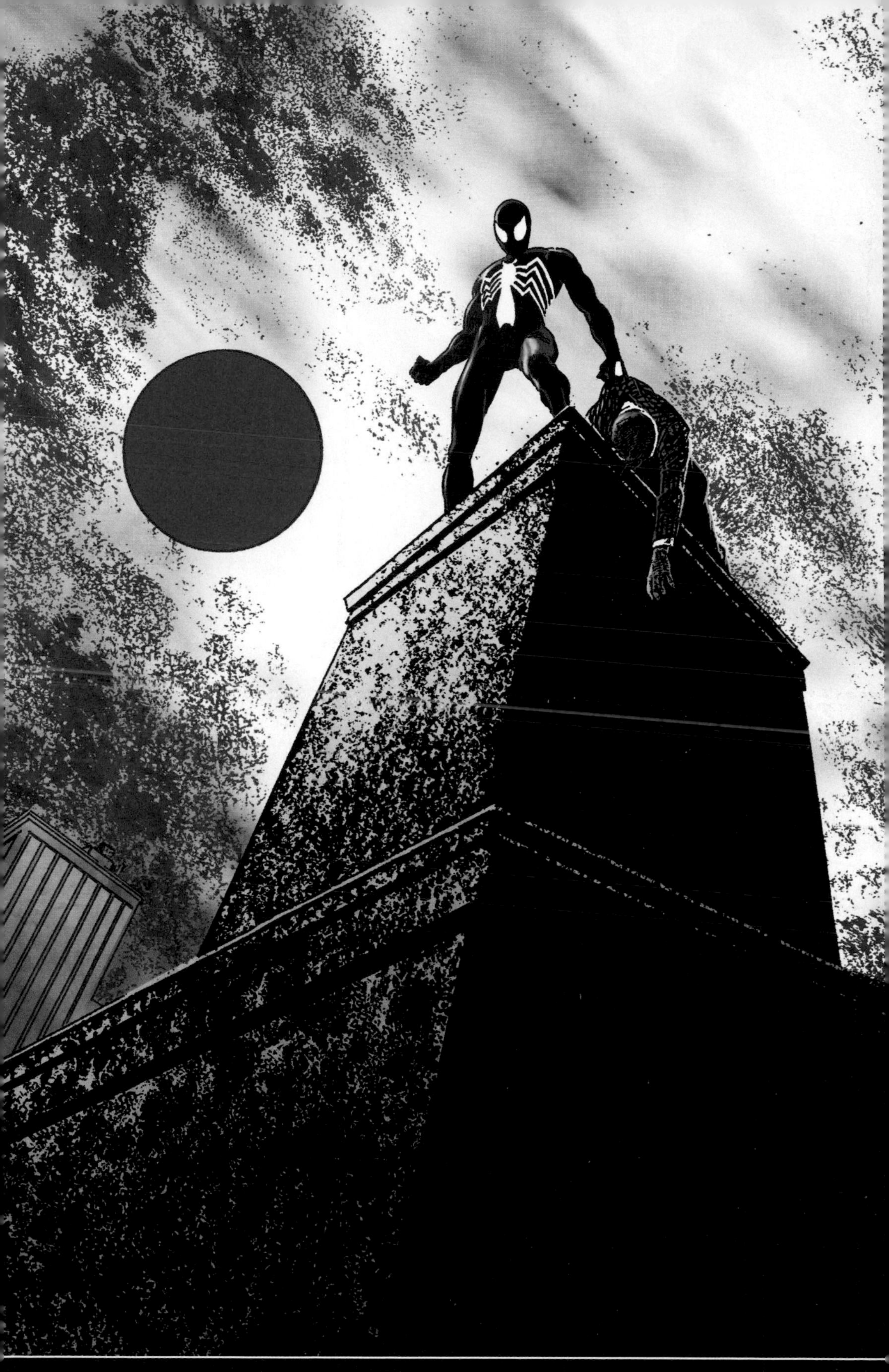

Spider-Man: The Death of Jean DeWolff Premiere HC back-cover art by Rich Buckler & Fabio D'Auria